Principles of Radical CV Phonology

Edinburgh Studies in Theoretical Linguistics

Series Editors: Nikolas Gisborne, University of Edinburgh and Andrew Hippisley, Wichita State University

Books in the series address the core sub-disciplines of linguistics – phonology, morphology, syntax, semantics and pragmatics – and their interfaces, with a particular focus on novel data from various sources and their challenges to linguistic theorising.

Series Editors
Nikolas Gisborne is Professor of Linguistics at the University of Edinburgh.

Andrew Hippisley is Dean of Arts and Sciences at Wichita State University.

Editorial Board
Umberto Ansaldo, University of Sydney
Balthasar Bickel, Universität Zürich
Olivier Bonami, Université Paris Diderot
Heinz Giegerich, University of Edinburgh
Jen Hay, University of Canterbury
Stefan Müller, Humboldt-Universität zu Berlin
Mitsuhiko Ota, University of Edinburgh
Robert Truswell, University of Edinburgh
David Willis, University of Cambridge
Alan Yu, University of Chicago

Titles available in the series:
1 *Lexical Structures: Compounding and the Modules of Grammar*
   Heinz J. Giegerich

2 *A Substance-free Framework for Phonology: An Analysis of the Breton Dialect of Bothoa*
   Pavel Iosad

3 *Principles of Radical CV Phonology: A Theory of Segmental and Syllabic Structure*
   Harry van der Hulst

Visit the Edinburgh Studies in Theoretical Linguistics website at www.edinburghuniversitypress.com/series-edinburgh-studies-in-theoretical-linguistics.html

Principles of Radical CV Phonology
A Theory of Segmental and Syllabic Structure

Harry van der Hulst

With the editorial assistance of Jeroen van de Weijer

EDINBURGH
University Press

To Nancy

Edinburgh University Press is one of the leading university presses in the UK. We publish academic books and journals in our selected subject areas across the humanities and social sciences, combining cutting-edge scholarship with high editorial and production values to produce academic works of lasting importance. For more information visit our website: edinburghuniversitypress.com

© Harry van der Hulst, 2020, 2022

Edinburgh University Press Ltd
The Tun – Holyrood Road, 12(2f) Jackson's Entry, Edinburgh EH8 8PJ

First published in hardback by Edinburgh University Press 2020

Typeset in Sabon
by Servis Filmsetting Ltd, Stockport, Cheshire

A CIP record for this book is available from the British Library

ISBN 978 1 4744 5466 7 (hardback)
ISBN 978 1 4744 5467 4 (paperback)
ISBN 978 1 4744 5468 1 (webready PDF)
ISBN 978 1 4744 5469 8 (epub)

The right of Harry van der Hulst to be identified as the author of this work has been asserted in accordance with the Copyright, Designs and Patents Act 1988, and the Copyright and Related Rights Regulations 2003 (SI No. 2498).

Contents

Preface		xi
List of abbreviations		xiv
Introduction: contents of this book		1
1	Basic assumptions about phonology	2
2	Background: Dependency and Government Phonology	3
3	Radical CV Phonology	3
4	Manner	3
5	Place	3
6	Laryngeal: phonation and tone	4
7	Special structures	4
8	Predictability and preference	4
9	Minimal specification	5
10	Radical CV Phonology applied to sign phonology	5
11	Comparison to other models	5
12	Conclusions	6
Chapter 1 Basic assumptions about phonology		7
1.1	Introduction	7
1.2	What is phonology?	7
1.3	Six theses concerning phonological primes	17
	1.3.1 Are features based on perception or articulation?	18
	1.3.2 Are features innate?	18
	1.3.3 Are features, or is phonology in general, substance-free?	19
	1.3.4 Are phonological representations fully specified?	20
	1.3.5 Is there such a thing as a segment inventory?	21
	1.3.6 Are there still phonemes?	22
1.4	Is phonology different?	26
1.5	Alternations and processes	28
1.6	Summary and concluding remarks	34

Contents

Chapter 2	Background: Dependency and Government Phonology	35
2.1	Introduction	35
2.2	Monovalency, grouping, dependency and contrastivity	35
	2.2.1 Monovalency	36
	2.2.2 The triangular set	40
	2.2.3 Grouping and elements in Dependency Phonology	45
	2.2.4 Developments in Dependency Phonology	56
	2.2.5 Minimal specification and polysystematicity	58
2.3	Government Phonology	60
2.4	Towards Radical CV Phonology	69
2.5	Summary and concluding remarks	71
Chapter 3	Radical CV Phonology	73
3.1	Introduction	73
3.2	An outline of Radical CV Phonology	73
	3.2.1 The segmental model	73
	3.2.2 Syllable structure	89
	3.2.3 Empirical issues	96
	3.2.4 The segment–syllable connection	98
	3.2.5 Recursivity in syllables or foot structure in Radical CV Phonology	100
3.3	Summary and concluding remarks	105
Chapter 4	Manner	107
4.1	Introduction	107
4.2	Onset	109
	4.2.1 Edge (onset head): obstruents	110
	4.2.1.1 Edge (onset head): head class	110
	4.2.1.2 Edge (onset head): dependent class	120
	4.2.2 Bridge (onset dependent): sonorants	131
	4.2.3 Sonorant consonants as onset heads (including taps/flaps)	138
	4.2.4 Laryngeal consonants	147
4.3	Rhyme	150
	4.3.1 Nucleus (rhyme head): vowels	150
	4.3.1.1 Nucleus (rhyme head): head class	150
	4.3.1.2 Nucleus (rhyme head): dependent class	154
	4.3.2 Coda (rhyme dependent): sonorants	164
	4.3.3 Coda conditions	165
4.4	Syllabic consonants (sonorants)	173
4.5	Long vowels, diphthongs and geminates	174
4.6	Summary and concluding remarks	176

		Contents	vii

Chapter 5	Place		179
5.1	Introduction		179
5.2	Edge (onset head): obstruents		179
	5.2.1	Edge (onset head): head class	180
	5.2.2	Edge (onset head): dependent class	187
	5.2.3	Post-velar consonants: pharyngeals and laryngeals	192
	5.2.4	Place distinctions for sonorant consonants in the edge	197
5.3	Nucleus (rhyme head): vowels		198
	5.3.1	Nucleus (rhyme head): head class	199
	5.3.2	Nucleus (rhyme head): dependent class	201
	5.3.3	Syllabic consonants (sonorants)	202
5.4	Bridge and coda		204
5.5	Summary and concluding remarks		204
Chapter 6	Laryngeal: phonation and tone		207
6.1	Introduction		207
6.2	Edge (onset head): consonants (phonation)		207
6.3	Nucleus (rhyme head): vowels (tone)		217
6.4	Four issues		224
	6.4.1	Phonation oppositions in obstruents and sonorants	225
	6.4.2	Laryngeal realism	230
	6.4.3	Phonation in the nucleus	235
	6.4.4	The correlation between tone and phonation	238
6.5	Bridge and coda		240
6.6	Summary and concluding remarks		240
Chapter 7	Special structures		242
7.1	Introduction		242
7.2	Incomplete structures		243
	7.2.1	No content at all	243
		7.2.1.1 Vowel/zero alternations	244
		7.2.1.2 Consonant clusters	249
		7.2.1.3 Initial geminates	257
		7.2.1.4 Schwa	258
		7.2.1.5 Consonant/zero alternations	258
		7.2.1.6 Ghost consonants	259
		7.2.1.7 Morphological templates	260
	7.2.2	Partial content	261
		7.2.2.1 No 'no manner'	261
		7.2.2.2 Manner only	261

7.3	Overcomplete structures			263
	7.3.1	Complex consonants		263
		7.3.1.1	Affricates	264
		7.3.1.2	Consonants with secondary manner	265
		7.3.1.3	Consonants with secondary place	265
	7.3.2	Consonants with two major places (clicks and multiply-articulated consonants)		266
	7.3.3	Complex vowels		279
		7.3.3.1	Short diphthongs	279
		7.3.3.2	Vowels with contour tones	279
		7.3.3.3	Vowels with special phonation	280
		7.3.3.4	Vowels with special manner	280
	7.3.4	Branching syllabic constituents or 'two-root structures'		281
7.4	Summary and concluding remarks			282

Chapter 8 Predictability and preference — 283

8.1	Introduction			283
8.2	Harmony			284
	8.2.1	Paradigmatic and cross-class harmony		284
	8.2.2	Disharmony		300
8.3	Preference rankings of segments per syllabic position			300
	8.3.1	Two determining principles: harmony and dispersion		301
		8.3.1.1	Manner preferences	303
			8.3.1.1.1 Manner preferences: edge	303
			8.3.1.1.2 Manner preferences: nucleus	305
			8.3.1.1.3 Manner preferences: bridge and coda	306
		8.3.1.2	Place preferences	313
			8.3.1.2.1 Place preferences: edge	313
			8.3.1.2.2 Place preferences: nucleus	314
		8.3.1.3	Laryngeal preferences	315
			8.3.1.3.1 Laryngeal preferences: edge (phonation)	315
			8.3.1.3.2 Laryngeal preferences: nucleus (tone)	315
		8.3.1.4	Concluding remarks	316
8.4	Preferred segmental systems			318
	8.4.1	The overall structure of segmental systems		318
	8.4.2	Polysystematicity		322
	8.4.3	Conclusions		323
8.5	Summary and concluding remarks			323

Contents ix

Chapter 9	Minimal specification	324
9.1	Introduction	324
9.2	A typology of redundant properties	325
9.3	Radical underspecification	328
9.4	Contrastive and radical underspecification in a unary framework	331
9.5	Markedness, complexity and salience	339
9.6	Examples of minimal specification	340
9.7	Can redundant elements become active?	346
9.8	Constraints and learnability	346
9.9	Summary and concluding remarks	352
Chapter 10	Radical CV Phonology applied to sign phonology	353
10.1	Introduction	353
10.2	The macrostructure of signs	357
10.3	The microstructure of signs	363
	10.3.1 The articulator	363
	10.3.1.1 FingerSelection	364
	10.3.1.2 FingerConfiguration	366
	10.3.2 Orientation	366
	10.3.3 Place	368
	10.3.4 Manner ('movement')	370
10.4	Two-handed signs	372
10.5	What about syllable structure?	374
10.6	Summary and concluding remarks	377
Chapter 11	Comparison to other models	378
11.1	Introduction	378
11.2	Feature Geometry models	378
11.3	Other models	389
	11.3.1 Dependency models	389
	11.3.2 The nested subregister model	391
	11.3.3 The Toronto model	392
	11.3.4 The parallel structure model	393
	11.3.5 The channel-neutral model	398
	11.3.6 The Duanmu model	403
	11.3.7 Government Phonology 2.0	404
	11.3.8 Q-theory	407
11.4	Summary and concluding remarks	409
Chapter 12	Conclusions	411
12.1	Introduction	411
12.2	Goals and basic principles	411
12.3	X-bar structure everywhere	414

12.4	Strengths and weaknesses	415
12.5	Some unresolved issues	419
12.6	What's next?	424

Appendix   425
References   431
Subject index   479
Language index   494

Preface

This book has been a long time in the making. My work on features and segmental structure started in the early 1980s when I began exploring the new wave of autosegmental and metrical theories, applying the former to vowel harmony cases (leading to another book that was long in the making: van der Hulst (2018)) and the latter to my analysis of syllable structure and stress in Dutch (van der Hulst (1984)). Around that same time, learning about Dependency Phonology from my colleague Colin Ewen, I started considering the use of single-valued features and dependency. In 1990, I finished a manuscript that was entitled 'The book of segments', which I distributed on a small scale. This manuscript (essentially a forerunner of the present book), which contained an ambitiously 'complete' account of segmental representation in terms of unary features and dependency, has been the backbone of a lot of my work in this area since then. For each paper or talk on this subject, I would update the theory, which, in my view at least, each time made it better, giving it wider empirical scope and greater theoretical simplicity and elegance. In this endeavour, I collaborated with various colleagues such as Colin Ewen, Marcel den Dikken, Helga Humbert, Maarten Mous and Norval Smith. The model underwent many changes, slowly moving to an approach that uses a minimal number of phonological primes. Along the way, it became clearer to me what I was trying to achieve with my attempt to develop a structure that would account for all phonological 'features' and their interrelationships. In the early days of phonology, the basic units that form the perceptual side of language were thought to be 'speech sounds', or more technically *phonemes*, meaningless mental units of sound that in linear sequences would form meaningful units like morphemes and words. Phonemes were taken to be the 'atoms' of language. A new development introduced units that are smaller than phonemes, called (distinctive) features, which stand for properties of speech sounds, or could be seen as building blocks of phonemes. Early proposals for feature sets (such as Jakobson, Fant & Halle (1952)) presented a list of features arranged in certain groups, but these groups did not find a formal acknowledgement in theories of phonological structure (such as Chomsky & Halle (1968)). Later, formal grouping structures were proposed (such as in Anderson & Ewen (1980); Clements (1985)). My dissatisfaction with these proposals was due to the fact that the sets of features being proposed essentially formed a list, or a group of lists (which could have been longer or shorter and structured in different ways). The lists and structures were inductively derived from observed processes and mechanism of articulation. In my proposal, the set of primes is no longer an arbitrary list, organised into an arbitrary geometry, but instead a set to which no prime could simply be added and from which no prime could be removed without implications elsewhere in the structure. Essentially, I was developing a *metatheory* of phonological 'features', which provides a principled, explanatory account of the structure of the set of 'features', based on cognitive principles of categorisation. Of course, the phonetic substance and processes have a say in the matter, but the emphasis in Radical CV Phonology is on cognitive principles that structure the phonetic substance into categories that then correlate with bits and pieces of this substance.

To appreciate this theory, one has to share the idea that it makes sense to derive the set of primes that is necessary to express all possible phonemic contrasts from a few general principles which determine the categorisation of acoustic percepts and their articulatory correlates. In my view, it is much more interesting to derive primes from general principles than to enumerate an essentially random list on a need-to-be basis. Phonological primes are basic mental concepts that as such (like most or perhaps all mental concepts) are *created* through mental categorisation processes, based on percepts of a pre-given substance. In the case of phonology, basic concepts are created from acoustic percepts and proprioceptive percepts of articulation for the specific purpose of being effective contrastive units whose function is to optimally differentiate meaningful entities (like morphemes and words). We thus expect the resulting categorisation to reflect properties of the perception of phonetic acoustic and articulatory substance, as well as properties that follow from whatever principles guide categorisation. My assumption is that these principles lead to the creation of discrete unary primes that are organised in a hierarchical dependency structure. This hierarchical structure, firstly, accommodates the set of primes and the paradigmatic relationships (i.e. affinities) that hold between them. Secondly, the structure also provides a basis for how the primes relate to the syntagmatic (that is, syllabic) structure. Thirdly, the structure accounts for the behaviour of primes in phonological alternations, that is phonological (as opposed to suppletive) allomorphy. Given that my proposal adopts the principles of Dependency Phonology, we will see that the head–dependent relationship pervades all phonological constructions. Crucially, in a dependency approach constructions are *not* constituents as understood in constituent formalisms.

The basic tenet of my approach was much inspired by John Anderson's Dependency Phonology model. The developments of my own version of Dependency Phonology turned out to converge with certain aspects of Jonathan Kaye's Government Phonology model, which undoubtedly had its own influence on my thinking processes. Having published bits and pieces of the model during the 1990s and early 2000s, I formulated a complete proposal in van der Hulst (2005a) in a Festschrift for John Anderson. After this, another period followed of fine tuning and modifying which has led to the present monograph, which, no doubt, does not contain the final version of the theory. At some point, after I had proposed that the minimal set of elements could just contain two elements, |C| and |V|, someone (I forget who, sorry), suggested that I call my theory Radical CV Phonology (RCVP).

I am first and foremost indebted to John Anderson and Jonathan Kaye, leading thinkers in the field of modern phonology. Over the years, I have collaborated with many other phonologists and I owe them for the development of RCVP: Norval Smith, Colin Ewen, Jeroen van de Weijer, Marcel den Dikken, Rob Goedemans, Helga Humbert, Nancy Ritter, Maarten Mous and Chris Golston. I am also grateful to several people who have commented on a synopsis of the RCVP model that I made for the specific purpose of getting feedback without burdening them with the entire book manuscript or who have answered specific queries: John Anderson, Ksenia Bogomolets, Cor van Bree, Marcel den Dikken, Matthew Gordon, Alex Vaxman, Song Zhenjun and Jeroen van de Weijer. Of course my thinking about features has also been inspired by the work of numerous other phonologists, through their work or during personal conversations. I single out Nick Clements, whose original ideas, enthusiasm and encouragement have always been an inspiration. Finally, I would like to thank Fiona Sewell for her careful editing of the final manuscript.

List of abbreviations

AC	arytenoid cartilages
AE	Anderson & Ewen (1987)
ASL	American Sign Language
ATR	Advanced Tongue Root
C, V	the two basic elements of Radical CV Phonology
CG	consonant–glide
CL	consonant–liquid
CN	consonant–nasal
DP	Dependency Phonology
FG	Feature Geometry
GP	Government Phonology
h, l	high, low (tonal register)
H, L, M	high, low, mid (tone)
IPA	International Phonetic Alphabet
KLV85	Kaye, Lowenstamm & Vergnaud (1985)
KLV90	Kaye, Lowenstamm & Vergnaud (1990)
LM	Ladefoged & Maddieson (1996)
MAC	multiply-articulated consonant
MD	Maddieson (1984)
OT	Optimality Theory
PP	Particle Phonology
RcvP	Radical CV Phonology
RTR	Retracted Tongue Root
SAA	Structural Analogy Assumption
SCL	Syllable Contact Law
SDA	Successive Division Algorithm
SPE	*The Sound Pattern of English*
S	Strong
TR	Tongue Root
UHR	Universal Harmony Rule
VOT	Voice Onset Time
W	Weak

Introduction: contents of this book

This book presents a theory of phonological structures with roots in the framework of Dependency Phonology (henceforth DP), but proposes a rather different 'geometry', which reduces the set of unary elements to just two: |C| and |V| (which explains the name of the theory). The structure that is proposed accommodates all and only phonological distinctions that have been found to function contrastively in (at least one of) the world's languages. As such, the theory *explains* the set of contrastive distinctions, rather than (as is common) presenting it as a 'random' list (with or without a 'random' geometrical organisation). The book also provides an account of the relationship between syllable structure and segmental structure, but not in detail of phonological alternations (allomorphy). Although the theory mainly deals with spoken language phonology, it is also shown how it provides an account of segmental and syllabic structure in sign languages.

The proposal made here concurs with the view that the building blocks of segmental structures are unary elements, a view shared with models such as DP and Government Phonology (henceforth GP) as well as several other models. In agreement with DP and the approach called 'Feature Geometry' (henceforth FG), my proposal organises the elements into a segment-internal structure. Both this structure and the 'syntax' of element combinations are fundamentally based on the notion of dependency, with a striking recurrence of an 'X-bar'-like structure (that is, a head with two levels of dependents). My proposal can be regarded as a *metatheory* of phonological features. It will be shown that many prior proposals for feature systems (for manner, place or laryngeal distinctions) find a 'home' in this model. The detailed analysis of phonological contrast provides a typological window on segmental and syllabic inventories in the world's languages, as well as on the relationship between these two levels.

The book introduces the reader to the central role of dependency relations in phonological structure, while advocating the idea that this structure can be derived from a small set of basic principles. Through comparison to other models, this work also provides a window on current theories of segmental structure, commonly used feature systems and recurrent controversies.

My approach is to first outline the background to my proposal in DP and GP (although mainly the former), followed by a systematic presentation of my model of segmental and syllabic structure (Chapters 1–3). I then develop this model in subsequent chapters for the element classes *manner*, *place* and *laryngeal*, motivating the details of the proposal on the basis of typological findings regarding segment inventories and contrast (and with reference to phonological rules, e.g. vowel harmony) (Chapters 4–6). Chapter 7 deals with 'special structures' which are either incomplete (missing, for example, place or manner) or overcomplete (such as different kinds of 'complex segments'). Subsequently, I show how the model accounts for a number of central claims in phonology involving predictability (Chapter 8) and 'minimal specification' (Chapter 9). In Chapter 10, I show how the Radical CV Phonology (henceforth RCVP) model can be applied to *sign language* structure (based on my own work in this area), while Chapter 11 offers a comparison between my model and a selection of other, prevalent models. Finally, Chapter 12 reviews my goals and the basic principles of RCVP and mentions strengths, weaknesses and possible further developments.

The RCVP model has been developed in a series of earlier articles over the last two decades. However, this work is not simply a collection of articles; far from this, it is a new, completely (re)written text, with many new proposals and coverage of content that was never addressed in earlier articles.

Following, I offer a chapter-by-chapter summary so that the reader can decide whether to read the book in sequence or skip to certain preferred chapters. If the reader wants to tackle the RCVP model head-on, the first two chapters can be skipped at first to focus on Chapters 3–7.

1 Basic assumptions about phonology

In this chapter, I outline my basic assumptions about the enterprise called phonology, starting with my understanding of the scope of phonology, which I break down into three assumptions: the need for a separation of *grammatical phonology* and *phonetic implementation*, the idea that 'phoneme'-sized segments are pivotal units in phonological representations, and the idea that there is a syllabic organisation. I then situate RCVP within the field of current phonological approaches. Subsequently, I discuss six theses regarding phonological primes and representations. I conclude with addressing the question of structural analogy, that is, whether phonology is different in a fundamental way from syntax, answering this question in the negative.

2 Background: Dependency and Government Phonology

In this chapter, I briefly discuss the background of the theory that is proposed in this book, which I see as a development of DP, with which it thus necessarily shares a number of design properties which are presented in some detail, both with respect to the DP proposal for elements, and with respect to its basic principles. My model also has certain properties in common with varieties of GP, which I also review in this chapter. Comparison to other phonological models is covered in Chapter 11.

3 Radical CV Phonology

In this chapter, I present an introduction to the RCVP model, focusing on the 'syntax' of C/V combinations but without providing details of the segmental structure or empirical underpinning. In the chapters that follow, I go into the details for each class of phonological elements (manner, place, laryngeal) and provide typological empirical support. In this chapter, I also provide the RCVP model of the syllable (which accommodates four core positions) and discuss how segmental structure and syllable structure are connected. This chapter also discusses the question of whether major class distinctions can be expressed structurally, as opposed to adopting a separate major category class. I show how the two RCVP 'C' and 'V' elements are phonetically interpreted by providing a set of interpretation functions that form part of the phonetic implementation system.

4 Manner

In this chapter, I focus on the *manner class*. I take manner to be the head class of the segmental structure because manner elements determine the distribution of segments in the phonotactic organisation of words. Also, manner elements are the most stable elements, often resisting assimilation. Following the notion of *polysystematicity* (the idea that sets of contrastive segments differ for different phonotactic positions) I discuss manner distinctions for each of the four core syllabic positions and, where relevant, for the head (primary) and dependent (secondary) class separately.

5 Place

Place elements are mostly relevant for the syllabic head position (that is, the onset head and the rhyme head position), because dependent units (onset dependent and rhyme dependent or coda), as proposed in Chapter 3, have limited distinctive location properties. In this chapter, I adopt the same structure as for the chapter on manner (which is also used for the laryngeal class in the next chapter).

6 Laryngeal: phonation and tone

In this chapter, I discuss the laryngeal class as needed for phonation types in consonants. For vowels, laryngeal distinctions cover tone proper and register. I discuss at length the position of *laryngeal realism* as it plays out in analyses of phonation types in different Germanic languages. I then turn to a number of specific issues in typologies of phonation types and phonation on vowels. Finally, I review correlations between tone and phonation.

7 Special structures

In this chapter, I propose both incomplete and overcomplete structures for segment types that call for one or the other. Incomplete structures are structures that miss one of the element classes. In previous chapters, we have seen examples of this, in the sense that a non-tonal language does not use the laryngeal node for vowels. We have also seen that the place class can be missing, as in central vowels and pharyngeal and laryngeal consonants. What cannot be missing is the manner class because this, being the head class, is obligatory. I discuss one possible exception to this. I consider whether the manner class, being obligatory, can be 'empty', then provide a different approach that may not require this kind of 'abstractness'. Subsequently, I turn to overcomplete structures which are necessary for various classes of so-called complex segments, such as clicks, multiply-articulated consonants (henceforth MACs), short diphthongs and some others.

8 Predictability and preference

In this chapter I discuss how RCVP relates to some recurrent concepts in phonological theory. This discussion is framed by the following issues and questions:

- Predictability of elements: can some C/V choices be predicted from the syllable structure specification of segments or other elements within the segmental structure?
- Preference of occurrence (lexical or token frequency): how does RCVP predict preference of occurrence of segment types, with reference to position in the syllable (or larger units)?
- Preferred segmental systems (system typology, type frequency): how does RCVP predict the shape of preferred phoneme systems?

Throughout the preceding chapters, I have occasionally indicated how RCVP addresses these questions, but in this chapter I offer a systematic account.

9 Minimal specification

In this chapter I address the following issues:

- Redundancy and default: are predictable (i.e. redundant) elements underspecified, and what about elements that are contrastive? In other words, is there a role for (contrastive and radical) underspecification in RCVP?
- Markedness: how does RCVP express markedness? What is 'markedness' in RCVP?
- Minimal specification: given that underspecification plays a role in RCVP, how are minimal (i.e. maximally underspecified) representations determined?
- Phonological activity: can redundant or default properties be phonologically active?
- Constraints: which types of constraints can be formulated to restrict the set of possible segments to precisely those that occur in a given language?

10 Radical CV Phonology applied to sign phonology

As explained in Chapter 1, a central aspect of RCVP is that 'features' (elements) are not as such innate. Elements emerge from successive splitting during language acquisition, based on the occurrence of contrast. However, the RCVP splitting model is not specific to the phonetic modality. This implies that the model can also be applied to sign language phonology, for which I have developed an explicit model in previous work over the last two decades. In this previous work, I have not emphasised how an appropriate structure for signs can be derived from the principles of RCVP, instead using more 'descriptive' labels for contrastive specifications. In this chapter I show how such a structure can be represented in terms of a binary 'C/V' choice within the relevant classes.

11 Comparison to other models

In this chapter, I offer a comparison between my model and a selection of other models. While it is of course important to highlight how the RCVP model differs from other models, primarily in its radical proposal to reduce all distinctions to two elements which occur in multiple roles (head, dependent) in different element classes, I am more interested in showing how the RCVP model is compatible with feature sets and FGs that have been proposed, and motivated, in other proposals. To the extent that these proposals have been made on solid empirical grounds, they also support the RCVP choices. What RCVP adds to these specific proposals is that it is shown how they can be *derived* from the basic RCVP principles, adding an element of *explanatory adequacy* to these proposals. I point out striking analogies between RCVP and other proposals which have often been developed independently of DP and RCVP, with no apparent knowledge of such historically earlier models, which only adds to their value as independent confirmation of the model proposed here.

12 Conclusions

This chapter summarises the contribution of RCVP to our understanding of segmental and syllabic representations. I outline strengths as well as weaknesses, and point to future research which will contribute to the advancement of models in this domain. I also briefly consider the extension of RCVP to higher levels of phonological/prosodic structure.

In the Appendix, I provide a summary of all relevant structures and their interpretations.

1

Basic assumptions about phonology

1.1 Introduction

In this chapter, in § 1.2, I outline my basic assumptions about the enterprise called phonology, starting with my understanding of the scope of phonology, which I break down into three assumptions: the need for a separation of grammatical phonology and utterance phonology (which I equate with phonetic implementation), the idea that 'phoneme'-sized segments are pivotal units in phonological representations, and the idea that there *is* a syllabic organisation. I then situate RcvP within the broader context of phonology as a whole. Subsequently, in § 1.3, I discuss six theses regarding phonological primes and representations. In § 1.4 I raise the question of structural analogy, that is, whether phonology is different in a fundamental way from syntax, answering this question in the negative. Finally, in § 1.5, I motivate why this book does not deal with allomorphic alternation and phonological processes, the so-called dynamic aspects of phonology.

1.2 What is phonology?

In a broad sense, phonology can be defined as the study of the *perceptible form* of language, granted that this perceptible form is a mind-internal representation.[1] As such, phonology studies the observable (indeed perceived) form of languages with full consideration not only of the articulatory and psycho-acoustic properties –often referred to as 'phonetics' – but also of the mind-internal representations that encode those properties of the signal that are 'linguistically relevant', in particular those that are contrastive, and thus 'phonemic'.[2] I assume here that the perceived signal

---

[1] This book will largely focus on the perceptible side of *spoken* languages, although in Chapter 10 I will also show in some detail how the proposed model can be applied to sign language phonology.
[2] It is an open question what the precise nature is of this shallowest internal representation, which, traditionally, is often called the '(systematic) phonetic representation'.

and the shallowest internal representation are related by a system of *phonetic implementation*, which I take to be part of phonology in the broad sense.

A narrower use of the term 'phonology' limits this field to 'phonemics', although in practice this approach includes the formulation of 'automatic' rules that account for allophonic variation, which immediately blurs any intended distinction between phonology-as-phonemics and phonology-as-phonetics, that is, phonetic implementation. Usually allophonic rules are provided when they account for properties of the signal that *could* be contrastive, but are not in the language at hand, leaving 'low-level' properties that are claimed to never be contrastive in any language to the 'phonetics'. However, this limitation is (or can) not always be observed, because whether or not a property *could* be contrastive in some yet undescribed language cannot be known without knowing what is contrastive in all languages, which is impossible in principle. Many languages have not been properly studied, while many languages that once existed are now extinct without leaving a trace. Moreover, conceivably, extant languages that are not likely to go extinct any time soon may undergo diachronic changes which introduce new possibilities for phonemic contrast. More to the point, apart from the fact that there is thus no independent criterion for identifying a process as being allophonic, as opposed to 'low-level', there is no justification for treating these two alleged process types differently. My position is that all properties of an utterance that are due to *automatic processes* belong to the implementation system, leaving to the phonology an account of allomorphic alternations for which I adopt a non-rule-based approach (see § 1.5.).[3] In accordance with this division of labour, I will refer to phonetic implementation as 'utterance phonology' and to the treatment of allomorphy as 'grammatical phonology'. A caveat must be made for allophonic processes that are neutralising. The system of phonological representation that I will develop in this book must be able to account for allomorphy as just defined, because allomorphy involves an alternation between segments that are contrastive in the language, that is, between phonemes. However, neutralising processes that can be regarded as allophonic on account of their automatic character *can* also be analysed in terms of the phonological system developed here, precisely because their output is formed by units that can also be inputs. Both input and output are phonemes in the language; this is what it means to be neutralising. Due to this ambiguity, neutralising allophonic processes can be the gateway from

---

In van der Hulst (2018) I refer to this level as 'word' level. Some discussion of this issue occurs in § 12.5.

[3] See van der Hulst (2011a, 2018) and Liberman (2017) for a similar view; also see Flemming (2001).

what I regard as utterance phonology to what I regard as grammatical phonology. I will briefly discuss this point in § 1.5.

Secondly, I mention what I will call the Segmentation Assumption. The idea that the perceptible form of a *monomorphemic* word[4] is not holistic – like, let us say, a scream that is uttered after a painful experience – has been unequivocally assumed by grammarians and linguists throughout the ages. In the study of spoken language, there is, I believe, no record, in descriptive grammars or theoretical treatises, that states the belief that words as lexical items are formally holistic or non-compositional (see Sproat (to appear) and other chapters in Dresher & van der Hulst (to appear)). Rather, it would seem that from the earliest written records onwards, there has been an assumption that 'words' (more specifically morphemes) can be segmented into *meaningless units* such as 'speech sounds' (and, depending on the writer, also into larger units such as syllables and smaller units such as 'features').[5] This awareness has usually come with the explicit or implicit recognition that the relevant submorphemic units abstract away from lots of phonetic details. That morphemes (and larger units) thus consist of segments, as well as having a level of analysis of these segments that encodes only contrastive properties, is of course a hypothesis. There are non-segmental phonological theories that deny the 'reality' of segment-sized units (whether called phonemes or morphophonemes) such as Griffen (1976, 1985) and Browman & Goldstein (1986). In a recent introductory textbook, Silverman (2017) also argues against the segment. In cognitive phonology approaches, however, the phoneme is taken to be a 'basic level category', although in this case the idea of an analysis of the phoneme in terms of features is called into question; see Taylor (2006) and Nathan (2009). Given that segments/phonemes have played a crucial and seemingly indispensable instrumental role in over a century of phonology analysis, and the fact that 'phonemes' fall into classes with different distributional and combinatorial behaviours, it seems reasonable to me to give this unit, as well as the features that compose it, a fighting chance as a genuine cognitive unit in (grammatical) phonology, despite the fact that its discreteness is rendered opaque in the output of the phonetic implementation,

---

[4] The limitation to monomorphemic words is necessary because, by definition, words consisting of more than one morpheme have a formal compositional structure, albeit that the composing formal units/components, by definition, are endowed with a meaning, or with a morphological or syntactic function.

[5] I do not find the idea that phonemes are an artefact of alphabetic writing plausible, although phonemic awareness might be, but for reasons of space I will not go into this issue here; see Sproat (to appear). Here I also put aside the fact that the alleged meaningless segments may be endowed with 'meaning aspects', as in ideophones and other similar phenomena; see Perniss, Thompson & Vigliocco (2007) and Dingemanse (2012).

that is, in utterances. Without features, and the co-occurrence constraints that they facilitate, there also cannot be an explanatory account of the systematic structure of segmental inventories, beyond merely listing the members of such inventories. 'Phonetic explanations', such as Dispersion Theory (Liljencrants & Lindblom (1972); Flemming (2017)), cannot be the only answer (Vaux & Samuels (2015); Gordon (2016: 62)).

Thirdly, I will assume that segments are organised into syllables, which are further organised into larger units such as feet and (phonological or prosodic) words. For each language, there is thus a set of constraints that determines what is and what is not a possible phonological syntagmatic structure in terms of syllables (and possible bigger units). A property of the model proposed here it that syllable structure is not simply built 'on top of' segments. Rather, as I will argue, segmental structure and syllable structure are closely connected in the sense that syllable structure can be seen as a projection of segment-internal structure. Of course, the syllable has also been questioned as the appropriate unit for phonotactics, most notably in Steriade (1999, 2003).[6] My point is once more that the explanatory success of postulating syllable structure is not affected much by the possibility of relating the distributional behaviour of segments to their 'phonetic properties' in certain cases. Attempts to shift the burden of (all) explanation to 'phonetics' reflects an aversion to theoretical constructs that finds little analogue in the studies of other levels of linguistic structure, although even among proponents of Generative Grammar, there is a pervasive view that phonology is different from syntax. A main point of this book is that such a view is not warranted and not productive.

Both the syntagmatic dimension (i.e. the syllabic organisation of segments) and the paradigmatic dimension (i.e. the feature composition of segments) define the space of phonological representations, or *the representational aspect of phonology*. There is also a derivational aspect to most phonological theories, and the present theory is not an exception. However, the notion of phonological derivation is very limited in my account. Given that I make a distinction between grammatical phonology and phonetic implementation (see above), this in itself creates the idea of a derivation. However, beyond that I am hesitant to adopt derivational, extrinsically ordered steps within these two levels.[7]

---

[6] GP (see below) also claims to reject the syllable as a unit, even though at least earlier versions of it recognise the units onset and rhyme.

[7] That said, within the grammatical part of the theory, van der Hulst (2018) motivated a distinction between a 'cyclic' level and a non-cyclic (or word) level, the former being strictly phonemic (in the sense of being structure preserving) and dealing in contrastive primes only, while the latter allows the participation of non-contrastive primes. For discussion of this proposal, see § 1.5.

Phonology is a particularly lively field of inquiry within linguistics, less popular perhaps than other areas such as syntax; yet insiders and attentive bystanders would presumably agree that this subfield of linguistics has played a leading role in the development of structuralist and generative theories of language. In the generative era, phonology has developed in spectacular ways over the last four decades, both producing entirely new perspectives and reconnecting with some of the earliest insights in this field. A pivotal moment was Chomsky & Halle (1968), which proposed a formal theory of phonology, compatible with the principles of the generative approach.[8] Since then, several complementary and rival theories of phonological structure (representation) and variability (derivation) have been developed, leading to what one might call 'mainstream' and 'non-mainstream' schools of thought.[9] While several of these developments are reflected in or compatible with the current proposal, the present work is mostly influenced by two non-mainstream theories: DP and GP, which nevertheless remain within the generative approach to phonology, at least to some extent.

The theory of DP was conceived by John Anderson in the early 1970s and has been developed by him and others to the present day.[10] This approach has influenced my own phonological thinking rather fundamentally, which will be evident throughout this book. The central idea of adopting the notion of dependency is that in complex entities (linguistic entities in this case) coherence results from the fact that the units that make up the complex entity enter into a set of dependency relations. Thus, for example, in a string ABCD, A could be dependent on B, B on C and C on D, which would make D the element that is dependent on nothing. This unit is then called the *head* of the string.[11] Dependency approaches (differing in formal details) have existed for quite some time in the study of sentence structure (e.g. Tesnière (1959), Hays (1964) and Robinson (1970)). Anderson showed how the same ideas could also be fruitfully applied to phonology (and morphology). With dependency relations being the central organisational notion, many linguistic phenomena can be explained as manifestations of the dependency organisation. For example, the most 'sonorous' part of the syllable is the head of the syllable (typically a vowel), while the most prominent syllable in the word (the

---

[8] I do not wish to suggest that phonology was invented in 1968. See Dresher and van der Hulst (to appear) for chapters that discuss essential prior work, going back almost a century, if not much longer.
[9] Roughly, mainstream developments stemmed from American phonologists from or closely linked to MIT trends, condoned by Morris Halle.
[10] Milestone publications are Anderson & Ewen (1987) (henceforth AE) and Anderson (2011c, in prep.); see Chapter 2 for more details of this development.
[11] The idea that a head can have at most one dependent follows from a separate constraint, which I adopt here.

one that carries primary word accent) is the head syllable in the dependency structure that comprises the whole word, with the foot likely to be an intermediate unit.[12] Almost all linguists subscribe to the view that relations of this sort play a role in theories of linguistic structure, but the dependency approach has made dependency the foundation of everything, arguing specifically that dependency relations are not augmentations of constituent structure, but rather *replace* constituent structure.[13] With reference to the alphabets for each 'plane' (the phonological plane and the syntactic plane), Anderson has advocated a strong substantive, or grounded, position. Phonological units and structures are firmly grounded in *perceptual acoustics*, while the basic units and structures of morphosyntax are grounded in meaning/conceptual structure. Groundedness also extends to structure, that is, the formation of constructions, in both planes. Headedness in both planes correlates with a substantive notion of *cognitive salience*. I refer to Anderson & Ewen (1980), Anderson & Durand (1987), van der Hulst (2006a) and of course AE for general overviews of the dependency approach to phonology, but see also § 2.2.

During the early 1990s another theory, called GP (originally formulated in two seminal articles by Jonathan Kaye, Jean Lowenstamm and Jean-Roger Vergnaud (1985), (1990)) (henceforth KLV85, KLV90), embraced concepts that are very similar to the cornerstone ideas of DP, while adding important additional proposals. This theory too has further developed up to the present day, currently showing an array of clearly related but divergent approaches (see Scheer (2004), Scheer & Kula (2018), Scheer & Cyran (2018a, 2018b), Ritter (to appear) and § 2.3).[14]

Both DP and GP arose from the desire to abandon or replace aspects of the *Sound Pattern of English* (henceforth SPE) model of phonology (developed by Noam Chomsky and Morris Halle in the late 1960s; Chomsky & Halle (1968)) by alternatives that were claimed to be more

---

[12] Here I am not making a commitment to a specific view on the head-dependency structure of the prosodic organisation of sentences or utterances, the latter two being different levels in my account.

[13] The notion of dependency can also be fruitfully applied to other units than those that make up linguistic expressions (phonemes, syllables, etc.). In general terms, wherever entities of whatever sort enter into a combination or collaboration, the issue of dependency can be raised. For example, different components of the grammar (phonology and syntax, or phonology and morphology) can enter into dependency relations. Subcomponents can enter into dependency relations. Finally, constraints that are relevant in the same domain and thus interfere may enter into dependency relations (for example, primary accent and rhythm constraints). However, it is not my goal here to show how dependency relations may obtain in these various other domains.

[14] There are, to be sure, fundamental differences between DP and GP, especially regarding the latter's adoption of so-called empty nuclei, which John Anderson rejects as not being 'substance-based'; see § 2.2.4 for further discussion.

restrictive and more explanatory. At the same time, these approaches maintained the original cognitive, mentalistic bias of the generative approach to knowledge of language, namely, trying to characterise the interplay between the assumed innate apparatus that children bring to bear on the acquisition of phonology and the linguistic stimuli that are present in their environment.[15]

Key characteristics of DP are (a) the use of a small set of monovalent 'primes'[16] to replace binary features, (b) an approach which accounts for representational structures that relies of a variety of head-dependency relations, and (c) the idea of an intra-segmental structure, similar to what is called 'FG'. GP shares the idea of unary primes (called *elements*, the term that I will adopt here) and the use of dependency relations (although different names, such as government or licensing, are also used for such relations). A hallmark of GP is a very restrictive view of 'syllabic' structure,[17] the systematic use of phonetically silent syllabic positions[18] (among others to account for vowel-zero alternations). Both approaches reject an underlying–surface structure mapping that involves extrinsically ordered rules that would account for allomorphic relations between related words. In fact, both Anderson and Kaye regard such alternations as falling, for the most part, outside the purview of synchronic phonology.[19] The focus on representational issues and the rejection of extrinsic ordering makes these approaches largely 'non-derivational'.

There is now a considerable and steadily growing number of articles and books coming from various GP centres, mostly in Europe, and a number of varieties of this approach have emerged. Meanwhile DP has diversified less, with a smaller number of active proponents, again mostly in Europe.

---

[15] John Anderson, however, does not currently accept the notion of an innate language-specific module, appealing to general cognitive principles. I refer to Anderson (2011c), a trilogy that details his approach to all aspects of grammar, and Anderson (in prep.); see van der Hulst & van de Weijer (2018b) for a recent review of this theory as it applies to phonology.

[16] Here and elsewhere I use the term 'prime' to refer to the basic, ultimate units that cannot be analysed into smaller units. Of course, as in physics/chemistry, we can never be sure when the level of primes has been reached. What are primes at one point (like phonemes in early phonology) may turn out to be composed of smaller units later on (such as features).

[17] The unit of 'syllable' is actually rejected for the syntagmatic relationship between onset and rhyme, which, however, are still tied together in terms of a licensing relation (which is essentially a head-dependency relation). In more recent approaches, the onset and rhyme constituents are eliminated in favour of a 'strict CV' (or 'strict CVCV') organisation (Lowenstamm 1996; Scheer 2004). All coherence in the string of CV units is due to 'lateral relations' that do not as such encode or represent constituency. The replacement of constituency by dependency relations is then shared with the orthodoxy of DP.

[18] Such units are rejected in DP, given its substance-based stance.

[19] I will discuss this matter in some depth in § 5.1.

The most far-reaching revision of DP proposals for intra-segmental structure is embodied in my own variant, developed since the early 1990s and presented here, which is called Radical CV Phonology (RCVP). Anderson (2011b) also provides an update of his own thinking which reflects some influence of RCVP, although Anderson also criticises RCVP for taking the structural analogy between the various intra-segmental 'class nodes' perhaps too far. Both DP and GP will be discussed, and compared, in detail in subsequent chapters, especially Chapters 2 and 11.

While my approach owes a great debt to Anderson's DP, converging with certain developments in Kaye's GP, this book presents a distinct theory of segmental and syllabic structure, hallmarked by the reduction of the inventory of phonological primes to precisely two units, notated as |C| and |V|. This is an extreme (indeed radical) idea, which calls for the adoption of a considerable amount of 'structure', agreeing with proposals that have been advanced in mainstream models of phonological features, including FGs. The background of RCVP in DP and GP is discussed in detail in Chapter 2, which is followed in Chapter 3 with an outline of the RCVP model.

The present author has perhaps been among only a small group of researchers who early on recognised the importance and explanatory potential of both DP and GP, which were and remained largely unnoticed or unreferenced in the US and other parts of the world. In part, the relative lack of attention paid to DP and GP may be due to the fact that these approaches were not conceived at those quarters (particularly the Massachusetts Institute of Technology, MIT) that have dominated the field of generative linguistics to a large extent.[20] I am sure, but of course cannot prove, that if DP and GP had emanated from MIT or other sympathising US-based quarters, their acceptance and spread would have been practically guaranteed. The changes vis-à-vis SPE that these approaches advanced are certainly no more dramatic than the changes that Chomsky has consistently been making in his approach to syntax over the same time period (arguably reflecting similar tendencies), and these changes were diligently followed within the generative community.[21] Moreover, post-SPE developments in Generative Phonology regarding representations essentially recapitulate what were the fundamental properties of DP to begin with; see van der Hulst (2011b).

I will here add a few further remarks about the 'sociology' of Dependency Grammar. While an appeal to dependency as the organisational relation

---

[20] No doubt this has also been the fate of other phonology theories that have been developed in other parts of the world; see various chapters in Dresher & van der Hulst (to appear).

[21] In fact, some of the most recent developments in syntax are conceptually related to the dependency approaches; see Boston, Hale & Kuhlmann (2010).

that binds words together into sentences has deep roots in ancient approaches to language (Percival 1990), it is due to the work of a few scholars that this approach has developed into a branch of linguistics in modern times. In particular, Tesnière (1959) is a foundational work, but other relevant references are Hays (1964), Gaifman (1965), Heringer (1967) and Marcus (1967). As far as I can tell, Anderson was the first linguist who has applied this approach to phonology. While, as mentioned, various ingredients of his proposal (developed in the early 1970s, in collaboration with others) bear strong resemblances to versions of Generative Phonology that were developed in the 1970s and 1980s, these later developments took place independently, mostly in the United States. Indeed, Anderson, working in Edinburgh (Scotland), did not 'found a school' which could exercise influence in other countries, let alone continents. I am aware of only one dissertation in this framework written in the US (Kang (1991)). Among the works of his own students only Ewen (1980a) is a dissertation on phonology and Heijkoop (1998) about phonological acquisition. DP's major resource remains *Principles of Dependency Phonology* (AE). Various other phonologists have also contributed to DP, mostly with publications in European journals and in some edited volumes (see den Dikken & van der Hulst (1988), van der Hulst (2006a) and § 2.2).[22]

An argument for believing that DP and GP could easily have made more headway is, as mentioned, that several mainstream innovations during the 1970s are extremely close to the main thrust of these approaches. Here one could think of the essentially dependency-based theory of Metrical Phonology and, with reference to segmental structure, the adoption of unary features (albeit, in most works, only 'here and there') and of the idea of assigning hierarchical structure ('FG') internal to segments, sometimes with the notion of dependency added (as in the work by McCarthy (1988) and Mester (1988)).[23] All three properties are fundamental to DP.

As for GP, it is clear that this approach mirrored in several ways the developments that had taken place in generative syntax, firstly, in rejecting the notion of rules and derivation (analogous to the simplification and eventual voiding of the transformational machinery in syntax) and, secondly, in making use of empty categories and principles that control

---

[22] Progress in segmental phonological theory in general has been halting, I believe, as a result of the rise of Optimality Theory (henceforth OT). I hope that renewed interest in this field, e.g. based on advances in cognitive science, will pay special attention to the dependency relation.
[23] Strikingly, the introduction of unary primes, dependency and segment-internal grouping in mainstream Generative Phonology would characteristically come with no reference to DP. This was not due, I am convinced, to malicious omission of references, but simply because phonologists were not aware of work in DP.

their distribution. Where mainstream phonology came to be characterised as being 'different from syntax' (see Bromberger & Halle (1989)), GP restored the parallelism between phonology and syntax that characterised early generative theory. Of course, establishing parallelisms between these two components lies at the centre of Anderson's notion of structural analogy.

The present author is reasonably well informed about mainstream representational theories. In the late 1980s and early 1990s, I was among the first European phonologists to draw attention to the emergence of new ideas that were put forth in an impressive series of MIT dissertations, including Kahn (1976) on recognising the syllable as a hierarchical object; Leben (1973), Goldsmith (1976a) and McCarthy (1979) on developing a multitiered 'autosegmental' approach to phonology; and Prince (1975), Liberman (1975) and Hayes (1980) on the metrical theory of word stress and sentence-level prosodic organisation (see Selkirk (1980)). I helped to promote these ideas with several edited volumes (van der Hulst & Smith (1982b), with a lengthy introduction that was widely read, van der Hulst & Smith (1982a); van der Hulst & Smith (1988a, 1988b)). Recognising the resemblances between these theories and DP or GP, I tried, from the beginning, to draw attention to dependency and government models and to contribute to integrating proposals from both areas. These attempts had little impact. Unfortunately, the neglect of DP and GP, especially outside Europe, is still very much ongoing. This neglect has only increased with a decrease in attention for representational questions which followed the rise of OT in the early 1990s.[24]

There have been other contemporary and highly relevant alternatives to mainstream Generative Phonology, such as Declarative Phonology (Scobbie 1991, 1992), which focuses especially on the formal-computational side, and, like DP and GP, rejects extrinsic ordering and other formal means that pose a threat to a restrictive theory of phonology. Interestingly, Declarative Phonology, as do DP and GP, with their emphasis on developing a constraint-based phonology and rejecting extrinsically ordered transformations, echoes early criticism of standard Generative Phonology, especially with regard to its use of extrinsic rule ordering and its 'one rule format treatment' of all forms of phonological variability (collapsing allophonic and allomorphic variation); see Koutsoudas, Sanders & Noll (1974). Declarative Phonology, in particular, acknowledges its debt to Natural Generative Phonology,

---

[24] One reviewer of the proposal for the present book: 'it is true to say that the representational kind of phonology that [van der Hulst] does is not the mainstream, especially not in the USA, so certain phonologists may not understand its value'.

which grew out of work by Theo Vennemann, Catherine Ringen and Joan Hooper (now Bybee).[25] See Vennemann (1971, 1974), Ringen (1975) and Hooper (1976).

Within mainstream Generative Phonology, the notion of constraints has also gradually risen to prominence, due in particular to Kisseberth's (1970) notion of conspiracies (see LaCharité & Paradis (1993); van der Hulst (2004, 2011a) for historical reviews). Early on, several phonologists proposed using 'surface constraints' (thus shifting the attention from underlying input to surface output), often combined with rules that were now seen as 'repair strategies'. Calabrese (to appear) offers a comprehensive defence of this constraint-and-repair approach.

The pivotal role of constraints culminated in OT, which accounts for the whole of phonology in terms of parochially ranked universal constraints. OT promoted a non-derivational approach, which, in this case, means that the mapping from 'underlying', lexical representations to surface outputs takes place in a one-step derivation, through simultaneous ranking of a candidate set of possible outputs. Ironically, while several of the theories mentioned here converge on the rejection of extrinsically ordered rules, often relegating the opacity effects that seemed to require such ordering to other modes of explanations (involving a denial of the lexical relatedness that called for deriving a variety of surface form from a unique underlying representation), OT practitioners have not been able to abandon their 'SPE past' in this respect, transforming their theory into a multi-step derivational theory that effectively mimics extrinsic rule ordering (see McCarthy (2010)).[26]

Having placed DP within the broader landscape of phonological theories, the next section will discuss some issues that specifically regard the phonological primes.[27]

1.3 Six theses concerning phonological primes

In this section I will briefly discuss my position (following, for the most part, the views of John Anderson, or at least, how I understand them)

---

[25] Interestingly, my very first official article (published in (1977)) was a favourable and lengthy review of Hooper's (1976) persuasive statement of this theory.

[26] It is worth pointing out that, while the DP and GP approaches are very much constraint-based, most proponents of these approaches do not appeal to the idea of constraint *ranking*. However, ranking is by no means incompatible with these theories. Polgárdi (1998), coming from the corner of GP, adopts constraint ranking as part of her analyses.

[27] Chapter 11 will compare RCVP to some other theories of phonological structure, specifically those that have proposed a segmental internal hierarchical organisation.

with respect to six fundamental questions concerning the nature and specification of phonological features and segments.[28]

1.3.1 Are features based on perception or articulation?

John Anderson's thesis is firmly that phonological primitives are acoustic and perception-based (Anderson 2011c). This view is shared with proponents of GP (KLV85); Scheer (2004); Backley (2011)). Anderson argues that both syntax and phonology are grounded in cognitive substance: conceptual (meaning) substance and perceptual (phonetic) substance, respectively. The exclusion of articulation is presumably based on the idea that motor movement, while it has to be driven by an articulatory plan that as such is cognitive, does not count as a 'cognitive substance'. It is assumed that articulation is secondary to perception. One of the arguments for this view point is that children form accurate representations of the speech signal that allow them to recognise words before they themselves can articulate speech 'correctly'; see Harris & Lindsey (1995) and Backley (2011) for additional arguments.

I suggest a compromise view that there is no need to exclude articulation from the grammar, but rather that both acoustics and articulation deliver cognitive substances that provide the 'raw material' that phonological elements categorise. To include articulation as a cognitive substance, we do not have to rely on the motor theory of speech perception (Liberman & Mattingly (1985)). Arguably, alongside percepts of the acoustic speech signal, speakers also have *proprioceptions*, which refer to the sense of the relative position of one's own parts of the body and strength of effort being employed in movemen' (Glanze, Anderson & Anderson 1990).[29] While one might argue that there are two sets of features, one perceptual and one articulatory (cf. Boersma (1998) for extensive discussion), I will assume that there is just one set, which is dual-sided or 'hybrid' (Boersma (1998: 24ff.)).

1.3.2 Are features innate?

I do not assume that features are innate. Here we broach a large and important topic on which several researchers have recently weighed in (see e.g. Mielke (2008), and recently Duanmu (2016); Nazarov (2014);

---

[28] This section is adapted from a similar section in van der Hulst & van de Weijer (2018a).

[29] Van der Hulst (2015b) suggests that the relative importance of articulation and perception might be different for consonants and vowels (showing a kind of head/dependency difference). In the former, articulatory properties may be more salient than acoustic properties, while this may be the reverse for vowels.

Cowper & Hall (2015)). I will only mention one argument against innate features, which is related to sign language phonology. Several phonologists (see e.g. van der Hulst (1993a), Morén (2003), Krämer (2012)) have argued that attempts to postulate a single set of features that applies to both modalities (spoken and visual) must fail, because there is no reasonable relationship between a unified set of features and phonetic implementation in both modalities (see also van der Hulst (2000b)). Adopting the view that features are responsible for allowing the expression of contrast, I suggest that features for spoken languages and for sign languages (or for any other modality that might lend itself to the expression of a human language) result from a categorisation principle that splits phonetic substances into two opposing categories. Van der Hulst (2015b) calls this the Opponent Principle. This principle (which is rooted in categorical perception; see e.g. Kuhl (1991) and Harnad (1990) among many others) directs a specific categorisation of phonetic substances that 'produces' feature systems for spoken and signed languages in the course of ontogenetic development.[30] The splitting is a recursive process, which means that categories resulting from a split can themselves be subject to further division. Given an inventory of segments for any language, this procedure delivers a minimal specification for each element class.[31] The idea that phonological categories result from a modality-neutral categorisation system in which the Opponent Principle plays a key role is at the core of the RCVP theory that is developed in this book. As I show in Chapter 10, it is simply not the case that a single set of features applies to both spoken and signed languages.

The conclusion is that while features as such do not need to be innate, and plausibly are not, the categorisation system that delivers features is innate, albeit probably not specific to language.

1.3.3 Are features, or is phonology in general, substance-free?

Sometimes it is argued that phonology should be 'substance-free', that is, not refer to the phonetic content it describes (see e.g. Hale & Reiss (2000), Blaho (2008), Iosad (2013), Reiss (2018), and references cited there). In one sense, this thesis is self-evident. Phonological generalisations should *never* refer to the substance that the categories and structures phonologise; they should only make reference to the symbolic units that have phonetic substances as their 'meaning'. This point was already

---

[30] See van der Hulst (1993b, 2000b) and Chapter 10 for an application to sign language.
[31] In this sense, RCVP's basic assumption is very similar to Dresher's (2009) *Successive Division Algorithm*; see § 10.4.

made very explicitly in the Glossematics theory of Louis Hjelmslev (Hjelmslev 1943 [1953]).[32] However, what the substance-free thesis does not imply, at least not for me, is that these categories and structures are in some sense 'unrelated' to phonetic substance. As mentioned above, I assume with John Anderson that features are substance-based, arising during the process of language acquisition, based on perceptions (and proprioceptions) and guided by the recursive splitting process. I therefore would accept neither features that are 'purely abstract' (that are phonetically 'meaningless', as proposed in Foley (1977)), nor that structures can arise that are 'phonological unicorns', that is, constellations that are well-formed, but that are not phonologisations of actual phonetic events that occur in human languages.[33] It is not clear to me that the substance-based approach that I adopt stands in stark contrast to so-called substance-free theories proposed in Hale & Reiss (2000) and Blaho (2008). We all agree that phonology only deals with phonological units, but we also agree that these units must be correlated with phonetic substance; see Clements & Hertz (1991) and Volenec & Reiss (2017) for perspectives of phonetic implementation as a cognitive system. Since I make a difference between grammatical phonology and utterance phonology, the latter being phonetic implementation, it stands to reason that utterance phonology, unlike grammatical phonology, does refer directly to substance, namely in assigning substance to the symbolic phonological units and structures.

1.3.4 Are phonological representations fully specified?

I adopt Anderson's view that phonological representations are *minimally* specified and that the criterion for specification is contrast.[34] Using unary elements dramatically reduces the need for underspecification, but this notion is still relevant if only contrastive element specifications are postulated in lexical representations (see van der Hulst (2016a), (2018)), which means that we need a system that recognises only contrastive elements. However, minimal specification does not entail a system of rules that *fill in* redundant information. I assume that minimally specified representations are directly phonetically implementable and implemented, possibly with the intervention of enhancement rules that supply

---

[32] This view is not undisputed. For a recent example, see Flemming (1995 [2002], 2001) or the approach called Articulatory Phonology (Browman & Goldstein (1986)).

[33] For Anderson, this stance also entails that there cannot be phonological units that are phonetically 'empty', such as the empty nuclei that are proposed in GP; see § 1.5.

[34] See Dresher (2009) for a perspective on minimal specification using binary features. His approach is discussed in § 9.4.

redundant elements which enhance contrast (see van der Hulst (2015b), (2018)). That said, in van der Hulst (2018) I consider the possibility that redundant elements can become active at 'the word level', which precedes phonetic implementation.

Adherence to minimal specification bears directly on the issue of phonological complexity. If only contrastive specifications are adopted, we do not evaluate fully specified representations when computing complexity (which would be the only option in Articulatory Phonology or exemplar-based approaches; see Browman & Goldstein (1986) and Johnson (2007), respectively).

1.3.5 Is there such a thing as a segment inventory?

Anderson assumes that contrast (and ultimately the notion of segmental inventory) is relative to phonological positions (in the syllable or larger domains) and refers to this as the idea of *polysystematicity*, a view (originating in Firth's prosodic phonology; Firth (1948)) that rejects the notion of a phoneme as a unit that generalises over sets of segments that occur in different positions (or even in different classes of words, like nouns and verbs). Related to this distinction, Twaddell (1935) distinguished the notion 'microphoneme' from the notion 'macrophoneme'. Each position or context allows the identification of microphonemes, that is, segments that are contrastive in that position or context. Microphonemes in different positions/contexts can be collapsed into a macrophoneme if each context allows for the exact same set of oppositions. For example, [p] in *pill* enters into a set of contrasts (with *kill, till, bill*, etc.) which is exactly the same as the contrast that [p] in *lip* enters into. Hence initial [p] and final [p], both microphonemes, can be grouped into one macrophoneme, even though the latter may be phonetically unreleased [p˺]. However, the [p] in *spill* cannot be grouped into the same macrophoneme because it does not contrast with [b] in that position. In Firth's conception of polysystemacity, then, initial and final position in the syllable would not *necessarily* constitute different systems, due to the sharing of the same set of oppositions.[35] Compared to English, syllable-initial and syllable-final position in Dutch does not define the same system because there is no voicing contrast syllable-finally in Dutch.

---

[35] Attributing initial and final [p] to the same system can be problematic because due to accidental gaps it may not be the case that both segments are preceded by the same set of vowels, which, technically, can lead to attributing these sounds to different systems. Also, as is well known, initial position lacks [ŋ] and final position lacks [h]. That said, Firth's conception of polysystematicity can be applied more 'pragmatically' and simply depend on which 'fragment' of the language the linguist is analysing.

I am doubtful that there is no 'reality' to a unifying notion of a phoneme /p/ which includes initial, final and post-s [p], even though the latter does not contrast with [b], or, in Dutch, in the absence of a voicing contrast syllable-finally. Such unification would be justified due to the *phonetic similarity* of the [p]'s in all three environments. While it is undoubtedly true that familiarity with an alphabetic writing system influences this unification (see Anderson (2014)), it strikes me as plausible that this unification (which is an instance of categorisation) was and is the psychological basis for the invention and use of alphabetic writing. But even if we grant a cognitive status to phonemes (independent of their distribution), this does not imply that phonemes will be specified with the same degree of complexity in all positions *in lexical entries*, because minimal specification will indeed require that in positions in which there is neutralisation of contrast fewer specifications are necessary. For example, in *blink*, /l/ only contrasts with /r/, whereas in initial and final position it contrasts with a much larger set of segments, at least in English. It has been claimed that for speakers of languages that do not have an alphabetic writing system, recognition, at some cognitive level, either conscious or subconscious, of the unified phoneme may be absent. Indeed, Jeroen van de Weijer (p.c.) reports that speakers of Chinese, which has a logographic writing system, are not likely to identify initial and final [n] (the only segments that can occur in both positions) as the same, and neither are Japanese speakers (in Japanese, initial and final [n] have a different spelling). In § 2.2.5 I will briefly return to the notion of polysystematicity.

1.3.6 Are there still phonemes?

Whether or not one adopts the polysystematic approach is independent from assuming a distinction between phonemes and allophones. A well-known distinction is that allophonic rules can create allophones that are unique to a specific phoneme (aspiration in English; see 5a) *or* create allophones that fall in the intersection of the allophone sets of two phonemes (flapping in English; see 5b). The latter rules are called neutralising rules.[36] Neutralisation occurs when in a given context the contrast between two phonemes of language L is neutralised. In the case of flapping the *product of neutralising* the contrast between /t/ and /d/ is a shared phone that is unique to that context. In other cases, the phone can be identical to another allophone of one of the phonemes. A famous example of this occurs in Dutch where in syllable-final position there is no contrast between voiced and voiceless obstruents. The product of

---

[36] See Silverman (2012) for a broad overview of the concept of neutralisation.

neutralisation is a voiceless obstruent. Consider the following pairs of words:

(1) [hɔnt] 'dog' SG   [hɔnd -ən] 'dog' PL
    [wɑnt] 'wall' SG [wɑnd -ən] 'wall' PL

The suffix -*ən* indicates plurality. Observe that the final [t]'s correspond to [d] when the plural suffix is present. This means that [t] *alternates with* [d]. We can analyse this by postulating that the morphemes in question end in the phoneme /d/ (as witnessed by the plural) and that this /d/ gets 'realised as' [t] when it occurs word-finally (actually: syllable-finally). The observed alternation thus provides evidence for the allophonic rule of final devoicing:

(2) /d/ → [t]   / _)σ

The net effect of this rule is that it causes *phonemic overlap*:

(3)   /t/   /d/
        /   \   /   \
       [t]   [t] ← [d]

The same situation obtains for the flapping process:

(4)   /t/   /d/
        /   \   /   \
       [t] →   [ɾ] ← [d]

Thus, flapping and final devoicing neutralise a phonemic contrast that exists in the language under analysis. I take both rules to be allophonic rules because they are fully automatic, which means that there are no lexical exceptions to either rule or morphological restrictions.

We should note that final devoicing, just like flapping and aspiration, creates what I will call *phonetic allomorphy*, that is, allomorphy due to an allophonic rule.

(5) a. Aspiration: for 'invite ~ invit-ee': [ɪnvaɪt] ~ [ɪnvaɪtʰ]
    b. Flapping: for 'write ~ writ-er': [raɪt] ~ [raɪɾ]; for 'ride' ~ 'rid-er'; [raɪd] ~ [raɪɾ]
    c. Final devoicing: for 'hond ~ hond-en': [hɔnt] ~ [hɔnd]

(As I have already stated, and discuss in more detail in § 1.5, in my view this rules belong to the phonetic implementation module.)

What concerns us here is that the analysis of flapping and final devoicing departs from the American structuralist school, which adopted a principle (called *biuniqueness* in Chomsky (1964)) stating that each phone could only be an allophone of one phoneme. In the Dutch devoicing case this implies that since [t] is clearly an allophone of /t/ (in all non-final positions as well as in final position where there is no 'd~t' alternation), it must be an allophone of /t/ in *all* final positions, even where it alternates with [d].

Anderson & Lightfoot (2002: 78–9) mention three reasons for adopting biuniqueness, which, they claim, all derive from the fact that the American structuralists were focused on studying E-language (external language) as opposed to I-language (internal language). The first motivation for this principle was that a child (or linguist) being confronted with language utterances must reduce phones to phonemes before even knowing how words are morphologically structured or related to other words, thus purely based on the perceptual input. The second reason, not totally independent from the first, was that these linguists promoted the use of purely procedural steps for linguistic analysis, which had to start with the objectively perceptible phonetic level and which was to make no assumptions on what one is likely to find in languages with respect to morphological or syntactic, let alone semantic, structure. Thirdly, given that phonemes encode contrast, only contrast that can be established at the phonetic level will count as such. In short, it was claimed that the analysis of a language had to be strictly from the signal to the more abstract levels, with phonology coming before morphology and morphology before syntax. This implied that for Dutch it could not be known that some [t]'s alternate with [d]'s, because to know that, one has to analyse plural forms in terms of stem and affix, which implies morphological analysis. In other words, the identification of allomorphy presupposes morphological analysis. Hence, the only criterion available for phonemic analysis would be that of complementary distribution.[37]

The biuniqueness principle disallowed an analysis of the facts of final devoicing at the phonemic level. Still, the American structuralists wanted to analyse the alternation. To this end they postulated a second phonemic level, called the *morphophonemic level* (where the units, called *morphophonemes*, are placed between double slant lines) and a rule like final devoicing (now called a *morphophonemic rule*) would relate these two levels:

---

[37] Ladd (to appear) remarks that the strict separation of levels of analysis that leads to the biuniqueness principle is closely connected with, if not resulting from, the acceptance of the notion of dual patterning (Hockett (1960); Martinet (1949)), which places phonology and morphosyntax in different planes.

(6) //b//   //d//   //g//   //v//   //z//   //ɣ//   morphophonemic level
      ↓   ↓   ↓   ↓   ↓   ↓   morphophonemic rules
     /p/   /t/   /d/   /f/   /s/   /x/   phonemic level
      | | | | | | (allophonic rules)
     [p]   [t]   [d]   [f]   [s]   [x]   phonetic level

The morphophonemic level represents morphemes in an invariant form (e.g. //hɔnd// for the two allomorphs), but structuralists did not attribute a specific (psychologically realistic) value to this level. They merely saw it as a convenient way to capture allomorphic alternations.

Generative phonologists rejected the distinction between the morphophonemic and the phonemic level, following Halle (1959), who argued that this approach leads to undesirable consequences because sometimes what looks like a single process can have non-neutralising effects in some cases and neutralising effects in others.[38] Consider the following case in Dutch. Voiceless stops become voiced before voiced stops:

(7) o[p] + doen   >   o[b]doen   'up put'   (to put up)
     ui[t] + brengen   >   ui[d]brengen   'out bring'   (to bring out)
     za[k] + doek   >   za[g]doek   'pocket cloth' (handkerchief)

In the first two cases we get neutralisation because /b/ and /d/ are independent phonemes, distinct from /p/ and /t/. Hence changing /p/ into [b] and /t/ into [d] is neutralising. Therefore, in the approach described here the process changes //p// and //t// into /b/ and /d/; the rule is changing morphophonemes into phonemes. However, in the third case the rule is non-neutralising because Dutch does not have a phoneme /g/. So, now we have to describe this as an allophonic rule which spells out /k/ as [g]. It follows that we have to state what seems to be the same process twice, once as a morphophonemic rule and once as an allophonic rule:

(8) //p//   //t//   //k//   morphophonemic level
      ↓   ↓ | phonemic rule
     /b/   /d/   /k/   phonemic level
      | | ↓   allophonic rule
     [b]   [d]   [g]   phonetic level

Clearly, this is not a desirable approach. If one has to state the same process twice, it feels as though one is missing a generalisation. Halle

---

[38] Anderson (2000) shows how this argument was, in fact, not new and had been mentioned by others before Halle's book. However, in Anderson's view, to appreciate the argument, it was necessary that phonologists had experienced the Chomskyan turn from E-language to I-language.

(1959) argued that therefore we need to abandon the phonemic level, and this claim went into history as implying that the phoneme was no longer needed. This, of course, is not the correct conclusion. Rather, what cases of this sort show is that we must allow the allophonic process to be neutralising, so that we can state all three changes as an allophonic rule:

(9) /p/   /t/   /k/
      ↓   ↓   ↓   allophonic rule
     [b]   [d]   [g]

This implies a rejection of biuniqueness. Now the phonemic and morphophonemic level can be collapsed into one level, which we should call the phonemic level (whether impoverished or fully specified) because it represents the distinctive units that are stripped of their allophonic properties and this is what the phoneme essentially is: a minimal contrastive unit.[39]

In § 1.5 I will elaborate on the point that allophonic rules can be placed in the phonetic implementation module. We will see, in fact, that all rules considered in this section display properties of gradience and variability, which puts into question their alleged neutralising effect.[40]

In this book I do not use the traditional slant lines for phonemes, which are simply put between square brackets. Given that allophones are produced outside the grammatical phonology, there is no need for a notational difference between slant lines and square brackets.

1.4 Is phonology different?

DP adopts the basic premise of Dependency Grammar, which is that linguistic units enter into *constructions* that are characterised by a relation of dependency between heads and dependents. The relation of dependency is applied both in the *plane* that combines meaningful (conceptually based) basic units into larger constructs (i.e. syntax; the *content plane*) and in the phonological plane (whose constructs involve meaningless, perceptually based basic units: the *expression plane*).[41] Fundamental to Anderson's work is the *Structural Analogy Assumption* (henceforth SAA) (see also Anderson (1971, 1987b, 2004), Bauer (1994)

---

[39] A defence of the notion 'phoneme' is also offered in Schane (1971), Hutchinson (1972) and Stephenson (1978).
[40] In fact, some native speakers that have flapping actually deny the phonetic identity of flapped /t/ and /d/. I do not know of any experimental confirmation of this judgement. Given the claim that flapping is accounted for in the phonetic implementation, it is by no means necessary that the flaps are identical phonetically.
[41] Anderson places morphology in the lexicon. In this component the units are combinations of basic phonological and basic syntactic units; see Anderson (2011c, in prep.).

and Staun (1996a) for discussion), which holds that structural relations and principles are the same in both planes of grammar. The planes therefore primarily differ in terms of the sets of their basic units, that is, their alphabets, which are determined by the interface with phonetic substance (for the expression plane) and conceptual meaning (for the content plane).[42] The assumption of structural analogy has roots in Louis Hjelmslev's theory of Glossematics (e.g. Hjelmslev (1943 [1953])). It might seem that this assumption runs counter to the modularity assumption that is prevalent in Generative Grammar (and cognitive science in general), but this is only true if we assume that recognising different modules (within grammar, or of the mind in general) somehow entails that these modules must have radically different internal organisations. Anderson, as do I, adopts the more plausible assumption that different modules follow the *same* principles of organisation to the extent that this is possible. Indeed, there is no reason to believe that the notion of dependency, or any of the other basic principles that we will discuss, is even limited to grammatical modules; they most likely are also reflected in other cognitive modules.[43] By assuming that the analogies between the two planes are not accidental but instead reflect the relevance of general principles in both domains, Anderson's Dependency Grammar takes a position that has obvious implications for the debate about an alleged Universal Grammar that in recent views merely comprises a syntactic system, relegating phonology to a separate 'expression system' (e.g. Hauser, Chomsky & Fitch (2002)). I follow Anderson in claiming that the existence of profound analogies between the expression plane and the content plane strongly argues against separating the cognitive systems that permit humans to construct a mental grammar for their language(s) in this radical fashion. At the same time, I agree with Anderson that there is little reason to believe that these analogies reflect principles that are confined to an alleged innate Universal Grammar, especially if this Universal Grammar is construed as an exclusive syntactic system, placing phonology 'somewhere else'.[44]

---

[42] Differences between the planes can also be due to how the primitive elements combine, as well as to how these planes interface. With respect to the former point, we observe that while recursion is possible in both syntax and phonology (see van der Hulst (2010)), it is much more widespread in syntax; see § 3.2.5.

[43] Our visual system gets input from only two types of photoreceptors (cones and rods), with three types of cones. It strikes me as plausible that the input from these receptors enter into combinations, with, I surmise, dependencies, to allow for a multitude of colour experiences.

[44] We may speculate about the question of whether the head-dependency relation is a purely linguistic characteristic, or whether it belongs to a more general cognitive domain. Humans surely possess strong systems of perception and association, which help them to make sense of the world, which typically involves many parts

Dependency structures form an alternative to constituency-based approaches: there is a principled distinction between the two. In a dependency approach, all nodes are associated with units from the (phonological) alphabet. This means that there are no phrasal nodes that dominate nonterminal nodes. This fundamental difference may be obscured by several factors, however. Firstly, constituent structure in Generative Grammar has been *augmented* with the notion of headedness ever since Chomsky (1970) and fully developed in Jackendoff (1977); see also Kornai & Pullum (1990). Constituents are said to be headed, with the head being a basic, that is, lexical, unit that determines the characteristic properties of the phrase it heads. The resulting hybrid approach (constituency-cum-headedness) has also found its way into Generative Phonology (specifically in metrical theories of suprasegmental structure). Secondly, depending on how dependency graphs are interpreted, it is often very easy to map a dependency graph onto a more familiar-looking constituent structure, especially when, in dependency graphs, the relationship of subjunction is used. While such a mapping may be deemed to serve no purpose, it is nonetheless the case that the resemblance may obscure the principled difference. Despite these factors that might blur the distinction to the casual observer, the rejection of constituent structure is fundamental to Dependency Grammar (see Böhm (2018) for a cogent discussion).

If, then, both phonology and syntax are organised in analogous ways, with headedness playing a pivotal role in both (whether augmenting constituency or replacing it), it would seem that these two sides of language are not that different (see van der Hulst (2005b, 2006c)). A particular instance of parallelism between syntax and phonology is the recurrence of 'X-bar'-like structure, that is, complex structures in which the head is accompanied by two dependents at different levels.[45]

1.5 Alternations and processes

It is customary to think of phonology as a function that relates an input to an output:

and in which relations between parts are important. From birth onwards, infants will learn that in any environment some parts are vital, and some merely 'background noise'. Infants quickly learn (or perhaps know innately) that some parts are worth focusing attention on, and some parts may be discarded.

[45] The term 'X-bar' of course originates from the constituency-based approach. While I adopt a strict dependency approach, I invoke the X-bar claim with reference to the idea that dependents come in two different types, corresponding to complements and specifiers in the phrase structure approach, allowing for adjuncts as a possible third type. See den Dikken & van der Hulst (2020) for illustrations of non-trivial differences between the syntax of sentence structure and the syntax of phonology.

(10) F (I) = O

'F' is the derivational (or dynamic) aspect of the theory while I and O are the representational (or static) aspect. In Chomsky and Halle's SPE (1968), I and O are stated in the same formal language: both consist of a linear sequence of phonological segments, with each segment being an unordered and unstructured set of specified phonological features (ignoring here the issue of underspecification or m/u marking, as proposed in their chapter 9.) The string of segments is hierarchically organised in terms of morphosyntactic structure, and #-boundaries are either part of specific morphemes (like 'heavy' suffixes) or added in accordance with a particular set of conventions, due to which the number of such boundaries increases with morphosyntactic 'distance'. F consists of a single set of phonological transformations (P-rules), with a partial extrinsic ordering imposed on their application. Due to extrinsic ordering, a phonological derivation involves *intermediate levels*. Rules that apply at a point in the derivation can be rendered opaque by later rules that counterfeed or counterbleed them. While the morphemes that enter in the initial (underlying) representation are well-formed in accordance with a set of segment and morpheme structure constraints, the well-formedness of the output ('surface') representation is accounted for by the P-rules. Input representations of morphemes, other than meeting the said constraints, could differ considerably from their surface appearance because P-rules can alter their form in unlimited ways. Any set of surface forms that the analyst might regard as related, that is, as involving realisations of the same morpheme, would then require the selection of an underlying shape for that morpheme from which all surface forms (i.e. the allomorphs) can be derived. With no constraints on what could legitimately count as related, underlying forms could become wildly abstract, even permitting segments or sequences of segments that are never attested in any of the surface forms. Kiparsky (1968) called attention to the need for restricting the excessive abstractness of underlying forms. In response, various proposals were made to change the richness of the SPE system, either by head-on reducing the abstractness of underlying representations (and thus explicitly or implicitly imposing restrictions of relatedness) or by trying to relate input and output with rule sets that had no extrinsic ordering. Part of the latter idea was to divide the set of P-rules into separate subsets that, while being ordered as sets, would have no extrinsic ordering internal to the set. Effectively, such proposals entailed the adoption of more than one phonological function:

(11) $F_1 (I_1) = O_1 \quad \gg F_2 (I_2) = O_2 \quad$ (where $O_1 = I_2$)

An explicit version of such a proposal was made in Siegel (1974) and Allen (1978), and eventually developed in the model of lexical phonology in Kiparsky (1982b).[46]

(12) $F_1(I_1) = O_1 \gg F_2(I_2) = O_2 \gg F_3(I_3) = O_3$ (where $O_1 = I_2$ and $O_2 = I_3$)

In Kiparsky's model, F1 and F2 constituted the *lexical phonology*, with F1 and F2 taking different levels of morphological organisation into account, while F3 operated *post-lexically*, after words had been organised into a syntactic structure. Different variants of this approach were discussed, although eventually the validity of morphological levels was called into question (Fabb (1988); Halle & Vergnaud (1987)). Kiparsky attributed different properties to lexical and post-lexical rules, the former being categorical, obligatory and 'structure preserving' (i.e. neutralising) while the latter were, or could be, gradient, optional and introducing new segments (allophones) or sequences. As we will see below, so-called neutralising rules can fall into both categories: lexical rules *must* be neutralising (meaning that their outputs are phonemes or phoneme structure that exist in underlying forms), while post-lexical *can* (happen to) be neutralising.

Chomsky & Halle (1968) referred to their surface level as 'systematic phonetic' and they distinguished this level (which had discrete structures and binary feature specifications) from a 'gradient phonetic level', thus envisaging a module that would convert the discrete, binary systematic phonetic representations into something even closer to the 'actual realisation' of linguistic expressions.

The work of Pierrehumbert (1980) refers to a module of this kind as *phonetic implementation*, to which she attributed a significant role and which in her view goes beyond a universal phonetic system, which would 'merely' account for (co-)articulatory properties of speech that are in some sense inevitable and as such present in all languages, given that the appropriate inputs occur in a language. The phonetic implementation module that she proposed (and put to work in her analysis of English intonation) contains processes that can be language-specific. Such processes, as one would expect, would be 'automatic', making no reference to lexical and morphosyntactic information, and be exceptionless.[47]

It was then suggested in Liberman & Pierrehumbert (1984) that the processes that Kiparsky had placed in the post-lexical phonology could

---

[46] The level approach did not embody an inherent restriction on how many levels there could be. Here I assume a simplified version with only three levels.

[47] If this component contains processes that may be innovations in a language, it is possible that its application is related to the frequency of words. This was the point of the lexical diffusion theory (Wang (1969)); see also Bybee (2001).

be part of the phonetic implementation component. The question is then whether even alleged lexical, structure-preserving rules that would appear to be automatic could not also be placed into the implementation component, making this component responsible for *all* automatic processes, irrespective of their domain. This view is the position taken in Natural Generative Phonology (Vennemann (1979); Hooper (1976)), even though the automatic processes were not identified as 'phonetic implementation'. The idea of locating all automatic processes in the phonetic implementation is developed in van der Hulst (2000a, 2005a, 2011b), while Liberman (2017) advanced it more firmly.[48] A proposal to conflate phonological 'rules' and phonetic 'processes' is also developed in Flemming (2001), albeit that his conflation constitutes the 'phonology', rather than the 'phonetic implementation', but that may just be a terminological matter. In support of the idea of including automatic 'phonological rules' in the phonetic implementation is the fact that several phonologists and phoneticians have shown that alleged neutralisation (i.e. structure-preserving) rules are actually gradient and allophonic.[49]

The logical endpoint of this development is to restrict phonology proper (i.e. phonology that is not implementation) to an account of alternations that are *not* only truly categorical and structure-preserving, but also prone to lexical exceptions and obvious morphological conditioning. It would then be an independent issue whether such alternations would be handled with rules that derive allomorphs from a shared underlying input, operating with reference to the morphological structure (possibly by applying cyclically), or non-derivationally in terms of a system of lexical selection of competing allomorphs. Hooper (1976) adopted a non-derivational proposal for treating allomorphy in terms of allomorph selection (due to Hudson (1974)), which is essentially the one that is adopted in van der Hulst (2018) for the representation of vowel harmony alternations.

As already mentioned, I have made a distinction between grammatical phonology and utterance phonology, the latter being the phonetic

---

[48] Volenec & Reiss (2017) introduce the notion 'cognitive phonetics' to indicate that phonetic implementation is part of linguistic knowledge. The authors describe the nature of their proposal as follows: 'This paper aims to elucidate the nature of a cognitive system that takes as its input a representation consisting of distinctive features (i.e., the output of the phonological module) and generates a representation directly interpretable by the neuromuscular system associated with speech production. This system we will call "Cognitive Phonetics" and the representations it generates "True Phonetic Representations"' (p. 251).

[49] In a related way, the bifurcation discussed here also reconstructs older ideas of separating 'word phonology' from 'sentence phonology', which can be found in Trubetzkoy (1939 [1960]) and other works in the pre-generative, structuralist approach.

implementation system. What is contained in the grammatical phonology? As mentioned in § 1.3.6, phonetic implementation processes can lead to 'phonetic allomorphy'. We can distinguish such phonetic ('accidental') allomorphy from cases of allomorphy that are non-automatic, dependent on morphological structure and identity of morphemes and subject to lexical idiosyncrasies. My overall account of such non-automatic allomorphy appeals to the occurrence of so-called variable elements, that is, elements that will only be visible to implementation if they are locally licensed. I would adopt a similar approach to cases of allomorphy that seem to require rather 'brute-force' 'substitution rules' that are part and parcel of morphological processes. In the latter, I would include the *k~s* alternation in English (*electric ~ electricity*), many other similar alternation in English-derived words and learned backing in French (*fleur ~ floral*; Dell & Selkirk (1978)). However, I do not assume that *all* cases of non-automatic allomorphy call for such an account. Some cases of alleged allomorphy are simply examples of formally unrelated morphemes that do not call for a synchronic account in terms of a unified lexical representation. This would also be the position in DP and GP, but it remains not fully clear where to draw the line between the licensing of lexical alternatives that are specified in the form of morphemes, on the one hand, and complete synchronic separation of forms that some might see as lexically related, on the other.[50]

From early on, the approach taken by Chomsky and Halle (1968), which lumped together all cases of allomorphy (automatic, non-automatic or 'alleged'), has been criticised.[51] The typology that strikes me as the right one was described as early as Anderson (1975), who distinguished three categories of 'rules': those that are heavily dependent on morphology, those that seem 'truly phonological' and finally, lower-level rules that are 'phonetic'. The last type is here placed in the phonetic implementation, while the first type, namely rules that are dependent on specific morphological constructions, could invoke lexical listing of allomorphs which are indexed for specific morphological contexts. This would allow alternants that are fully suppletive (*go ~ wen(t)*) as well as alternants that share a part of their phonological form, with another part being variable (*electri[k] ~ electri[s]ity*). In the middle, we find rules that are regular, not tied to specific affixes, and I here mention rules of vowel harmony as a prototypical example; see van der Hulst (2018).

---

[50] Vennemann (1972) introduced a class of 'via-rules' for such unclear cases. Via-rules would state bidirectional reference to different lexical entries that 'could' be seen as related by a language user.

[51] This overall perspective on the treatment of allomorphy follows in spirit or detail early criticism of the approach taken in standard Generative Phonology such as Vennemann (1974), Skousen (1975), Hooper (1976) and Linnell (1979).

In this case too, I have employed a mechanism of lexical listing where allomorphs differ only in terms of the 'feature content' of certain segments, vowels in this case.[52]

A question that remains is whether within the middle class, cases that involve alternations that are general in not being tied to specific morphological constructions or affixes (although some affixes could be exceptions), a distinction has to be made that corresponds to the SPE distinction between cyclic rules and a class of post-cyclic or 'word-level' rules. In several publications, a particular characterisation is given to the word-level class. Borowsky (1993) and Harris (1987) discuss rules that have no apparent relevance beyond the word domain.[53] Yet they are fully regular and in some cases even allophonic. The notion of 'word' here is sensitive to morphological structure in that it is a subdomain of certain morphologically complex words, excluding certain derivational affixes and, apparently, also inflectional affixes. In van der Hulst (2018) I locate certain kinds of harmony processes at this 'post-cyclic' word level, here including harmony processes that have been called dominant/recessive, as well as clearly allophonic types of harmony such as those involving raising. I argue that such processes can not only introduce non-distinctive properties, but can also be triggered by non-distinctive, redundant properties. I assume then that at the word level, (certain) redundant properties, notably those that play an 'enhancing' role, can be specified and become phonologically active.

It could be argued that grammatical phonological rules are by their nature cyclic in that they are relevant with respect to *morphological* domains. In contrast, perhaps word-level rules make reference to *phonological* (often called *prosodic*[54]) domains which, as such, would be simultaneously available to the grammatical phonology, with morphological structure and phonological structure being represented on different planes. The 'cyclic' phonology is the phonology that operates with reference to the plane that displays morphological structure, making dependency possible on morpheme identity, word-class labels and diacritic features, while the word-level phonology refers to the phonological plane which not only can have different domains, but also allows featural properties that are not lexically distinctive. A further elaboration of these points goes beyond the scope of this chapter and book.

---

[52] The difference here echoes the difference between minor rules and major rules that was made in Lightner (1968). See Zonneveld (1978: 154ff.).
[53] See also Bermúdez-Otero (2018).
[54] Van der Hulst (2009) discusses relevant distinctions and makes the point that there are two kinds of phonological/prosodic structure, one belonging to the grammatical phonology and one belonging to the utterance phonology.

1.6 Summary and concluding remarks

In this chapter I have laid the groundwork for what will follow, namely a specific proposal for a model of phonological representations at the segmental and syllabic levels. I have taken a position on a number of recurrent issues regarding the nature of phonological primes and representations, and I have explained why I think that there is no fundamental difference between phonology and syntax, which, in my view, are two related planes that belong squarely to the grammar of every language.

2

Background: Dependency and Government Phonology

2.1 Introduction

In this chapter, I briefly discuss the background of the theory that is proposed in this book, which I see as a development of DP, with which it thus necessarily shares a number of properties which will be presented in some detail, both with respect to the DP proposals for elements, and with respect to its basic principles. My model also has certain properties in common with varieties of GP, which I will also discuss in this chapter.[1]

2.2 Monovalency, grouping, dependency and contrastivity

In the segmental domain, DP introduced at least six important innovations, several of which date back to early publications by John Anderson and Charles Jones (Anderson & Jones 1972, 1974):[2]

(1) Segmental structure:

- Phonological primes (here called 'elements') are monovalent.
- Phonological primes are organised into intra-segmental classes (called 'gestures').
- Combinations of primes and of classes enter into a head-dependency relationship.
- The same phonological primes figure in the representation of vowels and consonants.
- Some primes may occur in more than one class.
- Representations are minimally specified.

We must note that these proposals are largely independent and, as such, may be shared (in part) with other approaches. The following sections

---

[1] For a more extensive discussion of DP and GP, I refer to den Dikken & van der Hulst (1988) and, specifically for DP, to van der Hulst & van de Weijer (2018b).
[2] This paper did not propose the second principle in (1), which was introduced later, following Lass (1976) and Lass & Anderson (1975).

deal with specific, characteristic topics in DP: monovalency (§ 2.2.1), the idea that vowel structure is organised in a triangular way (§ 2.2.2), segment-internal grouping (§ 2.2.3), developments in DP (§ 2.2.4) and minimal specification and polysystematicity (§ 2.2.5).

2.2.1 Monovalency

The claim that phonological primes are single-valued has a weak and a strong variant. In the weak form the claim is that only *some* features are single-valued.[3] For example, various scholars have suggested that [round] is single-valued (Steriade 1987c). Itô & Mester (1986) have argued that [voice] is a single-valued feature. Goldsmith (1985, 1987) goes further and uses a system in which both [round] and [low] are single-valued, with the proviso that the scope of [low] is extended to include mid vowels. In his system, however, [back] is binary. The strong form of the claim implies that *all* features are single-valued. This position has been defended most extensively by proponents of DP and GP (AE; KLV85).[4]

With little if any precedent in phonology, Anderson and Jones (1972, 1974) proposed, in response to the tradition of binary features (Jakobson, Fant & Halle (1952); Chomsky & Halle (1968)) that the basic building blocks of phonology are monovalent (i.e. have only one value) or unary instead of binary.[5] While DP uses the term 'component', I will here, following GP (KLV85), refer to these unary features as *elements*.[6]

An important distinction between the binary and unary approach is the fact that the binary approach allows reference to both values of a distinctive feature. For example, in the case of the feature [±voice], binary theories recognise both a class of voiced and a class of voiceless segments, whereas unary approaches only allow reference to the class that is positively specified with an element. (That is, if we disallow reference to the absence of a property in a unary model.) Given this fact, a unary approach should count as the null hypothesis because it is more restrictive, which places the burden of proof on proponents of binary features; see Kaye (1988), among others. Historically (at least in Generative Grammar), features entered the phonological arena as binary units (see again Jakobson, Fant & Halle (1952) and Chomsky & Halle (1968)) and for this reason it is often assumed that unarists

---

[3] This section is adapted from van der Hulst (2016a).
[4] There have also been claims that some or all features are multi-valued. See, among others, Williamson (1977) and Gnanadesikan (1997), who proposes that features are ternary.
[5] See van der Hulst (2016a) for an overview of the unary/binary 'debate', and van der Hulst (2016b) for references to some earlier proposals for unary features.
[6] See Sanders's (1972) simplex feature hypothesis; and see van der Hulst (2013) for some earlier precedents.

have to defend their position against the binary approach. However, from a methodological point of view, once a phonological contrast has been established, the initial hypothesis must be that that opposition is encoded in monovalent terms, thus claiming that 'the other value' is a phonological nonentity. This hypothesis cannot be falsified by facts that require reference to the other pole, which would still be represented in terms of a privative element), but it *can* be refuted by facts that require reference to both poles. Facts of the latter type necessitate an equipollent characterisation of the opposition in terms of a binary feature. There is one problem, however. If both poles of an opposition need to be entities in the phonology, it is also possible to adopt two opposing unary features. In fact, in RCVP postulating two opponent unary elements (namely |C| and |V|) is the very foundation of the whole model. For this reason, my own argument for unary features relies on more than simply not needing the opposite value. In RCVP the adoption of two opposing elements is not an ad hoc move to save unarity. Rather, because only one set of unary elements is postulated, RCVP establishes a compromise between binarity and unarity: all elements are unary, but there are two of them, forming an antagonistic pair. Apart from such overall system considerations, unarity can also be justified by delivering explanatory accounts of phonological phenomena. As I have shown in van der Hulst (2018), the assumption of unarity provides a principled explanation for certain asymmetries in the behaviour of neutral vowels in vowel harmony systems. Another example of providing an insightful account is Schane's analysis of diphthongisation in terms of unary elements; see Schane (1984).

Apart from the fact that a unary feature theory is potentially more restrictive and more explanatory, Anderson and Jones also motivate their proposal on the argument that binary features present a problem for the notion of markedness. This had in fact also been noticed by Chomsky & Halle (1968), who devoted a 'late chapter' (chapter 9) in their SPE to the fact that a theory using binary features cannot cope with certain recurrent asymmetries between the two values of some, or perhaps all, features. Comparing the vowels [ü] and [i], they note, as others did before them, that the roundness of [ü] and the non-roundness of [i] should be weighted differently, in that front vowels, in the absence of a rounding contrast, are always [−round]. Another indication of the asymmetry comes from cases of neutralisation. For example, in the domain of obstruents, where voicing is typically distinctive, voiced obstruents seem more restricted in that, if the opposition is neutralised word-finally, the voiceless obstruents emerge.[7] Unary features allow for a direct and, in fact, literal expression of markedness. The vowel [ü] is

---

[7] See Yu (2004), who discusses the case of final obstruent voicing in Lezgian.

more marked than [i] because it must bear the mark of roundness, both vowels being specified as front. Likewise, voiced obstruents are more marked than voiceless obstruents (at least in most contexts; see below), since they bear an element corresponding to [+voice] and voiceless obstruents do not.

In binary feature theories, the most straightforward expression of the asymmetry between the two values is to leave the 'expected' values literally unmarked, that is, unspecified. (Hence these values themselves became known as 'unmarked values'.) Thus, the unmarked value of [round] (for front vowels) is minus and the unmarked value for voice (in obstruents) is also minus.[8] This approach is referred to as Underspecification Theory (Halle 1959). However, for technical reasons Chomsky & Halle (1968) could not appeal to underspecification (see Stanley (1967)), but instead adopted special *m/u* values for features (alongside the plusses and minuses) and a set of markedness (and linking) conventions (see Kean (1975); van Lessen Kloeke (1982)). This theory of markedness, however, was soon abandoned and eventually underspecification made a comeback (Ringen (1978); Kiparsky (1982a); Archangeli (1984)). Kiparsky and Archangeli then proposed that unmarked values should be unspecified not only if they are redundant (i.e. in the absence of a contrast) but also when a contrast is in place. This approach, which encodes unmarkedness in terms of non-specification, came to be known as *Radical Underspecification Theory*.[9]

On one view, a monovalent approach represents an extreme form of radical underspecification. The claim is simply that unmarked or default values play no role in the phonology whatsoever. However, we must note that the issue of using under- or non-specification is not confined to binary feature systems: it is also relevant in monovalent theories (see e.g. Durand (1988) and § 2.2.5 below).

Clearly, while a single-valued system reflects the spirit of (radical) underspecification by establishing a direct correlation between markedness and complexity, it does so in a more rigorous way. Despite the fact that Radical Underspecification theories ban one value, the 'unmarked' default value, from phonological representations, the option is left open that these values are filled in at some point in the derivation, after which they may start playing a role in the phonology by taking part in rules as

---

[8] Whether voiceless for obstruents is unmarked *in all positions* could be a matter for debate, given the tendency to intervocalic voicing. Being unmarked does not correlate with having a minus specification, since that is determined by the choice of the feature name. That said, that choice itself would appear to be guided by the implicit admission that the name reflects the mark, as in [±round] or [±nasal], rather than [±spread] or [±oral].

[9] Steriade's contrastive specification theory would only leave non-contrastive values unspecified (Steriade 1987c).

targets, changes or environments. More dramatically, it has been argued that the markedness of a value may not be universal in that some languages may show a 'markedness reversal' (see e.g. Battistella (1990); de Lacy (2006)). This, then, allows for a situation in which [+voice] is the default value for (e.g. final) obstruents in some language. Monovalent theories do not allow for markedness reversals, nor do they allow the 'unmarked value' to become active in the phonology. The 'unmarked value' is a phonological nonentity.

One might ask how, if this is in fact possible, markedness can ever be contextual. Thus, how can we account for the fact that [−round] is unmarked for front vowels, requiring the specification of [+round] for front rounded vowels, while among back non-low vowels, [+round] is the unmarked value, which would suggest that [−round] must be specified for back non-round vowels in case of a contrast? A unary system that uses the unary features [front] and [round] would seem to be committed to representing the 'less marked' [u] as more complex than the more marked [ɯ]:

(2) [i]   [ü]   [ɯ]   [u]

     Front   Front   −   −
             Round   Round

I will return to this conundrum, which has haunted unary systems for a long time, below.

Overall, and leaving certain issue to be addressed, we must conclude that on methodological and empirical grounds, all things being equal, a unary approach must be preferred over a binary approach. This is evident from the growing popularity of unarism in more mainstream approaches in Generative Phonology. However, as pointed out in Harris & Lindsey (1995), in practice, when comparing different feature theories, all things are never equal. Theories can differ in terms of which specific features they recognise, what kinds of intra-segmental relations (such as head-dependency) are used, and what kinds of formal manipulations ('rules') they permit. The issue of fair comparison becomes even more complicated when monovalent approaches include primes that seem to be polar opposites. We see this in some non-DP models that use unary features, for example when two monovalent feature [ATR] and [RTR] are proposed (see Steriade (1995) and others). Van de Weijer (1992, 1993, 1996) proposed the opposite manner features [stop] and [cont], on the basis of the idea that both define recurrent natural classes. As just mentioned, RCVP embodies an approach that makes systematic use of primes that form pairs of polar opposites. Adopting apparently polar opposites is not equivalent to adopting a binary feature, however. Under usual assumptions, two values of a binary feature cannot be combined with a segment, or if they can, this must lead to phonetic sequencing (as in [−cont][+cont] proposals for affricates). Unary features, on the other hand, even when apparent opposites, may be combined to represent an intermediate category (or in some cases a sequence). This will be illustrated in the next section, where I will discuss the specific proposals for unary feature sets that have been proposed within DP. This section will also introduce the notion of intra-segmental dependency.

2.2.2 The triangular set

Moving beyond the issue of the 'arity' of features, I will now discuss the specific set of elements that has been proposed in DP, first focusing on the representation of vowels. Anderson and Jones (1972, 1974) focused on the representation of vowels. Given this limitation, this early publication did not propose a 'complete' set of phonological elements and therefore did not develop the notion of grouping elements into subsegmental units (classes, gestures). These authors introduced the characteristic and basic |a|, |i|, |u|[10] set, showing how these units can be used to represent vowels, allowing them to occur by themselves or in combinations. Let us take a closer look at the DP proposal for vowel representation.[11] Clearly, the DP system differs from the SPE system not only by using unary rather than binary features, but also by choosing different phonetic parameters for characterising the vowel space. Whereas the SPE system is bidirectional (just like, for instance, the unary feature system proposed by Sanders (1972)), since it only uses the high–low and the front–back dimensions in the description of vowels, lip rounding being superimposed on these two dimensions, the feature system of DP is tridirectional.[12]

Characteristic of tridirectional feature systems is the fact that they employ at least three basic primes in their element set, corresponding to the three extreme corners of the vowel triangle. In DP, these elements are first and foremost grounded in acoustic percepts. The three basic primes are commonly represented by the symbols |i|, |u| and |a|, after the vowels that these elements represent if they occur alone:[13]

---

[10] Various notations have been used for unary features. Here I follow DP's use of lower case enclosed in vertical lines.

[11] The following is partly based on den Dikken & van der Hulst (1988).

[12] Their choice of three units resembles the adoption of two 'colours' and 'sonority' in Natural Phonology (see Donegan (1978)), which in turn echoes Jakobson's colour and sonority axes (Jakobson 1941 [1968]). The triangular idea also resembles Stevens's (1972, 1989) quantal distinction as well as the proposals in Wood (1975, 1979)).

[13] Schane (1984) and Rennison (1984) also use this triangular set, as does GP (KLV85), which is discussed in § 2.3.

(3) The basic primes of tridirectional unary feature systems for vowels:

	Acoustic	Articulatory
|i|	acuteness/sharpness	frontness
|u|	gravity/flatness	roundness
|a|	sonority	lowness

From a phonetic point of view, these elements are clearly basic. Taken in isolation, they constitute the so-called quantal vowels (Stevens 1972, 1989), that is, the acoustically most stable vowels, of which their acoustic effects can be produced with a fairly wide range of articulatory configurations. In addition, these three vowels are maximally distinctive, both from an acoustic and from an articulatory point of view (see Liljencrants & Lindblom (1972)). Moreover, the vowels [i], [u], and [a][14] are also basic as far as phonology is concerned. As shown in several typological studies of vowels systems (see Maddieson (1984 (henceforth MD): chs 8, 9), and Sedlak (1969); Crothers (1978)), they constitute the canonical three-vowel system, and they are also typically the first vowels that children acquire (see Heijkoop (1998)). The choice of |i|, |u| and |a| as basic vocalic elements is therefore well motivated, both phonetically and phonologically. Finally, when languages with richer sets of vowels display neutralisation of vowel contrast, for instance in unstressed position, the triangular set often 'survives' in the neutralised position (see Cristófaro-Silva (1992) for the case of Brazilian Portuguese).

With the aid of these three elements, at most seven vowels can be characterised, if we bear in mind that they can be used not only in isolation, but also in combination with each other:

(4) {i}[15] [i]   {u,i}   [y]   {u}   [u]
    {i,a}   [e]   {u,i,a} [ø]   {u,a} [o]
                          {a}   [a]

---

[14] Avoiding the slant line notation for phonemes, I use square brackets for approximate phonetic values in accordance with the use of these symbols in IPA.

[15] Different notational systems have been employed by different authors, both for single elements and for combinations of elements. Here I use vertical lines when talking about elements and braces (with omission of vertical lines) when talking about classes of segments. AE adopt a specific use of the presence or absence of vertical lines. For them a set, that is, the notation '{...}', comprising elements without vertical lines refers to the set of all segments that contain these elements. If the elements are enclosed in vertical lines, {|...|}, it means that the segments making up this set must exhaustively contain these elements and no others. In other words, in their notation, '|' is an 'exhaustivity operator'. Here, when referring to vowel systems or vowel types I will *not* use the '|' notation, leaving undecided for now whether the exhaustivity interpretation is ever crucially needed.

It will be obvious that these seven representations do not cover the maximal number of different vowels that are found in the language systems of the world, or, more crucially, possibly richer (or simply different) sets of vowels that occur contrastively in specific languages. To express vowel systems containing nine or even more vowels, additional ways are needed to represent the total number of vowels in terms of (combinations of) the three basic vocalic elements. In principle, there are two ways in which this increase of the combinatorial potential of the three features could be achieved. Either elements might occur more than once in a particular representation, or one of the elements in a feature combination might enter into different degrees of prominence relative to another element (or elements). Of these two conceivable positions, the former is defended by Schane (1984) (in Particle Phonology) (henceforth PP), while DP (as well as GP) invokes the concept of dependency to arrive at a larger number of possible representations.

Compare, for instance, the DP and PP representations of the vowel [ɛ] in the partial vowel system in (5).

(5)   [i]   DP: {i}   PP: {I}
       [e]   DP: {i;a}   PP: {IA}
       [ɛ]   DP: {a;i}   PP: {IAA}
       [a]   DP: {a}   PP: {A}

Here dependency is expressed using the symbol ';', {A;B} being read as 'B is dependent on A', or 'A governs B'; see (6) for another notation.[16]

As shown, in DP, elements are not just joined in a simple, symmetrical combination, but can also enter into a relationship in which one element is relatively prominent, namely the 'head', and the other element is the dependent. If a language has just one mid series the dependency relation can remain *unspecified*. We note at this point that it is commonly assumed in phonology that contrastive use of phonetic properties involves a binary opposition, which can be expressed with a binary feature or a unary feature (versus its absence). Apparent gradual differences along a phonetic dimension can be represented with more than one feature. This can be seen in binary systems where two or more features that refer to height or aperture jointly capture a three- or four-level height distinction. In DP, such gradual effects can, to some extent, be captured by invoking combinations of elements and their various dependencies.

---

[16] Of course, many other notations can be used. In GP, for example, the head element is underlined. As we will see in § 2.3, GP expands the use of headedness by allowing elements to be headed or non-headed, independent of whether or not there is a dependent element. This in my view fundamentally alters the notion of headedness, turning it effectively into a diacritic feature of elements.

Background: Dependency and Government Phonology

In addition, in DP, two elements can even entertain a relation in which neither feature is 'dominant', a relationship which is called 'mutual/bilateral dependency'. Thus we arrive at the set of dependency relationships in (6), in two alternative notations that AE use to express dependency; the braces stand for 'a class of segments characterised by the element structure in question':

(6) a. {X;Y} or {X⇒Y} 'Y is dependent on X'
    b. {Y;X} or {Y⇒X} 'X is dependent on Y'
    c. {X:Y} or {X⇔Y} 'X and Y are mutually dependent'

By allowing the features to enter into a relationship of 'mutual dependency' with |a|, a relationship in which neither element counts as the head, DP maximally generates the following set of representations on the basis of the features |i|, |u| and |a|:

(7) The maximum number of combinations of |i|, |u| and |a| in DP:

{i}	{u,i}	{u}
{i;a}	{u,i;a}	{u;a}
{i:a}	{u,i:a}	{u:a}
{a;i}	{a;u,i}	{a;u}
	{a}	

It is not obvious on empirical grounds that the extra option of mutual dependency is required. RCVP will not allow this formal option.

Implicitly, it is assumed that {i,a;u}, {u;a,i}, {i;a,u}, {a,u;i} do not result in phonetically distinct vowels; rather, they result in phonetically identical events. This means that the combination |u,i| behaves like a unit, such that |u| and |i| cannot occur on opposite ends of the dependency relation. In other words, this combination of elements does not seem to show a dependency asymmetry. Although the system of DP would in principle allow for the 'gradual' oppositions {i} vs. {i;u} vs. {u;i} vs. {u}, it turns out, as AE (p. 275) observe, that 'in virtually all languages, we find at each height maximally one segment containing both |i| and |u|; in other words, dependency relationships holding between |i| and |u| are not required'. Yet, although they may not be required in practice, the fact remains that nothing in the theoretical framework of DP renders dependency relations between the features |i| and |u| impossible on a principled basis. This of course is a stipulation in DP (as well as in GP[17]), which I will not follow in RCVP, which uses these two possible ways of combining the colour elements to represent, for example, the two kinds of rounded vowels in Swedish (e.g. Riad (2014)); see § 5.3.

---

[17] GP makes the same claim (see KLV85), but Kaye, Lowenstamm & Vergnaud derive it from the internal logic of their theory.

Staying with the DP proposal to not allow |i| and |u| to combine in two ways, at most eight front vowels and four back vowels can be represented, plus the low vowel. This is still, however, not enough to characterise all possible vowels and vowel systems in the world's languages. In particular, the central vowels and/or the back unrounded vowels cannot be represented on the basis of (6) alone. Here the 'and/or' refers to the fact that it is not certain that central and back unrounded are distinct phonological categories, although the former class, according to the International Phonetic Alphabet (henceforth IPA) system, allows both rounded and unrounded vowels. This brings us back to the issue raised in (2) of the representation of [u] versus [ɯ], which led to the question of how this contrast can be represented without running into a 'markedness paradox'.

A number of phonologists, notably Lass (1984) and Rennison (1986), have argued that the two 'faces' of |u| should in fact be given independent status, thus splitting up |u| into two elements, |ω| ('labiality' or 'roundness') and |ɯ| ('velarity' or 'high backness').[18] However, in this approach, whatever its motivation (which I do not discuss here), it is still the case, as shown in (8), that [u] comes out as more marked than the back unrounded vowel:

(8) /i/   /ü/   /ɯ/   /u/
    |i| |i| |ɯ| |ɯ|
          |ω| |ω|

To deal with the problem of central vowels, AE propose the following solution. To the vowel [ɯ] they assign not only two colour elements (which by itself would produce a [ü]), but also a new element: |ə|, the centrality element:

(9) The representation of [u]:   The representation of [ɯ]:
    standard DP: {u}   standard DP: {u,i,ə}

While this proposal solves the markedness asymmetry by representing central vowels as more complex (at the cost of introducing a new element), another solution that could be considered is to represent [ɯ] as devoid of any elements; this is in fact what Anderson (2011b) suggests. The idea that one vowel can be represented as the null set has other precedents, especially with regard to one of the central vowels, in particular the schwa (see e.g. S. Anderson (1982)).[19] At first sight, this makes this

---

[18] Scheer (2004) also proposes this split in the context of GP, and so does Staun (2013).
[19] In treatments of vowel harmony in Turkish the back unrounded vowel, which harmonises for both roundness and frontness, would for that reason alone be specified as 'empty'; see van der Hulst & van de Weijer (1991) and van der Hulst (2018).

vowel the least complex, but if we limit the markedness–complexity correlation to segments that are positively specified, we can add the special clause that a segment that is devoid of any property (especially having no 'colour' elements) is the most 'marked' vowel, due to the fact that it misses any perceptual salience, which is worse than mixing two perceptual images as in vowels that combine two or more elements.[20] The proposal to acknowledge the 'null option' (lacking elements) may obviate the need for the centrality element, although it is not clear how central vowels of different heights will be represented, since a null 'element' cannot engage in combinations.

Thus far, there is no general mechanism to distinguish between advanced and non-advanced vowels. While the 'height distinction' for the mid series can be interpreted as a distinction between advanced and non-advanced vowels, this leaves a similar distinction among high vowels unaccounted for, as well as for low vowels. As we will see in the next sections, DP addresses this problem by introducing an Advanced Tongue Root (henceforth ATR) element. Of course, there are further distinctions that need to be covered for vowels, such as nasality. In the next section we will see that AE add several elements to the basic triangular set, including several elements that are motivated for consonantal contrasts, beyond the use of the triangular set which is also used for consonants.

2.2.3 Grouping and elements in Dependency Phonology

The relevance of element grouping has long been recognised in DP. While it was not part of the original proposal by Anderson & Jones (1974), Lass & Anderson (1975) and Lass (1976) offer a number of specific arguments that support the view that the matrix characterising the segment should be split up into at least two submatrices, or 'gestures'.[21] This subdivision into element sets reflects the fact that phonological processes can refer precisely (e.g. delete or spread) to either of these gestures, the other gesture being unaffected (cf. the so-called 'stability effects' of Autosegmental Phonology; Goldsmith (1976a)). Lass (1976) discusses cases of reduction of full consonants to the glottal consonants [h] and [ʔ], which occur, for instance, in many varieties of Scots (cf. also Lass (1984: 113–15), demonstrating the independence of the laryngeal features vis-à-vis the oral features, a conclusion also drawn in Thráinsson (1978) on the basis of Icelandic preaspiration data, and subsequently in various versions of FG. The DP arguments for grouping are essentially analogous

---

[20] This point is also acknowledged in Anderson (2011c, 2014).
[21] Other than in this section, I will not use the latter term, which is more commonly used with reference to individual articulatory actions rather than to groupings, as for example in Articulatory Phonology (Browman & Goldstein 1986).

to the arguments that have been presented for feature classes in FG (see Clements (1985); Sagey (1986)).

In early DP work, the bipartite division into a laryngeal gesture and an oral gesture that was suggested by Lass & Anderson (1975) was replaced by the proposal in (10) for a tripartite gestural division of segments (Anderson & Ewen (1980); Ewen (1980a); Lass (1984)), by splitting the oral gesture into a gesture for major class and manner-like distinctions (the categorial gesture), and a strictly articulatory (place) gesture. The term 'gesture' here is used completely equivalently to the way in which 'class node' is used in FG.

(10)

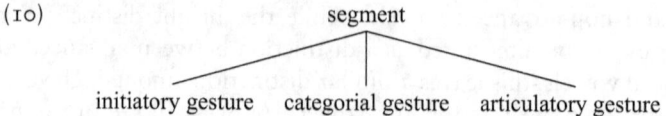

The initiatory gesture contains elements expressing airstream properties and glottal states.

Ewen (1986: 205) extends this model by recognising two major 'super' gestures, the categorial and the articulatory gesture, both of which contain two subgestures. The categorial gesture contains a 'phonatory' subgesture (for elements expressing manner or stricture properties and major class distinctions[22]) and the initiatory subgesture (as before, for airstream properties and glottal states). The articulatory gesture contains the locational subgesture (with elements for place properties) and an oro-nasal subgesture containing just one element (that is, nasal). In addition, a tonological gesture is added:

(11)

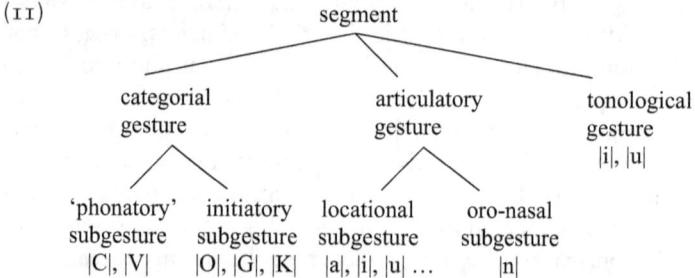

The locational elements listed in (11) are not an exhaustive set; see below.

I will now discuss the structure displayed in (11) in more detail, following AE. The proposals which AE make for the tonological gesture are sketchy, although interesting in using the two elements, |i| and |u|, that are

---

[22] The label 'phonatory' is unfortunate for this group, but it should be noted that AE include 'voicing' in the group.

Background: Dependency and Government Phonology

also found in the locational gesture (more on this below). Most attention focuses on the development of the 'phonatory' subgesture (for manner and major class distinctions) and the locational gesture (for place). I will discuss these two subgestures in turn.

The 'phonatory' subgesture contains two elements, |C| and |V| which AE define as follows:

> |V|, a component which can be defined as 'relatively periodic', and |C|, a component of 'periodic energy reduction'. (p. 151)

As mentioned above, from the start DP adopted the view that the primary interpretation of element is acoustic, a position that GP has adopted as well (see § 2.3). AE then continue:

> |V| and |C| differ from the [Jakobsonian] vocalic and consonantal distinctive features in that the presence of, say, |V| in a segment does not necessarily imply that the segment is in a simple binary opposition to an otherwise identical segment not containing |V|. Rather [...] the more prominent a particular [...] component [...] the greater the preponderance of the property characterized by that component. Notice too that |V| and |C| can characterize segments either alone or in combination. (p. 151)

As already mentioned, 'prominence', or salience, of elements is expressed in terms of a head-dependent relation.

These dependency relations provide the tools to express a number of major segment classes in terms of combinations of |V| and |C|, as shown in (12):

(12)
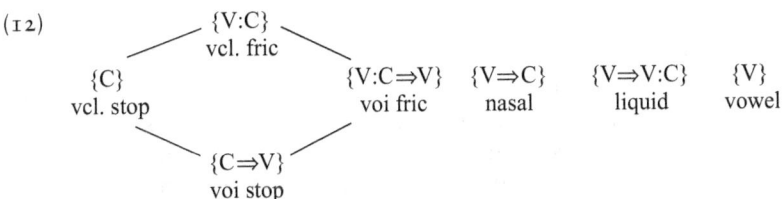

Below the actual representations, AE indicate which classes of segments they represent. AE argue that the representations reflect a *sonority ranking*, going from left to right, in which the classes of voiceless fricatives and voiced stops are claimed to have equal sonority. Further distinctions (leading to separate representations for laterals, strident fricatives, etc.) will be discussed below. Note the use of complex structures that involve 'primary (or head) structure' like |V:C| entering into a dependency with other, 'secondary' structure, another instance of using the same element multiple times (this time *within* a gesture). DP did not use the 'primary' and 'secondary' terminology, but I will use it in the context of RCVP, following Anderson (2011b).

In order to characterise the segment classes in (12) in a feature system of the SPE type (Chomsky & Halle 1968), we would need the features [voice], [consonantal], [continuant] and [sonorant], where DP uses just two single-valued features: the elements |C| and |V| and their interdependencies. However, pure reductionism was not AE's primary motivation for replacing major class and manner features by CV complexes. AE claim that their approach is more adequate than traditional binary theories in a number of respects. Firstly, as saw above, by replacing binary features with structures of varying complexity, representations more adequately reflect the relative markedness of phonological major class and manner categories. In (12), the categories 'vowel' and 'voiceless stop' are the least complex, which reflects their relatively unmarked status. Fricatives are more complex than stops and voiced obstruents are more complex than voiceless ones. This again reflects well-known and widely accepted claims regarding the relative markedness of these categories, backed up by both typological evidence (as shown in Lass (1984)) and evidence from phonological acquisition (as shown in Heijkoop (1998)), and before that in Jakobson (1941 [1968]). Secondly, as already mentioned, AE also claim that the array of structures provides an adequate characterisation of the notion of relative sonority. Degrees of sonority correspond to the amount of 'V-ness' that a representation contains. (We could likewise define strength in terms of the amount of 'C-ness'.) This is useful in the characterisation of lenition processes, which can be represented in terms of a reduction in V preponderance.[23] Thirdly, AE claim that the structures composed of |C| and |V| provide a more adequate basis for the expression of phonological processes than traditional binary systems do. With reference to (12), AE note that these structures reflect an asymmetry in the behaviour of 'voicedness', as opposed to 'unvoicedness'. If we assume (as most phonologists do) that phonological rules can only cause phonetic events by manipulating phonological units, the structures in (12) express that languages can spread 'voicing' but not the absence thereof. If this is empirically correct, representations as in (12) are superior to binary feature systems in which [+voice] and [−voice] have the same status.[24]

---

[23] John Anderson's view on processes is that these belong to the domain of historical change, rather than being part of the synchronic grammar. I have argued in § 1.5 that we must assume that there is a synchronic reflex of such processes, which then form part of the phonetic implementation system until their automaticity breaks down, which is when the synchronic reflex becomes part of the statement of allomorphy in the lexicon.

[24] In this particular case, voicing, there is a significant literature claiming that the phonology needs reference to both values of voicing. See, for example, Wetzels & Mascaró (2001) and Chapter 6 of this book.

Finally, the CV constellations are constructed in such a way that affinities between the phonological categories that they represent are formally expressed. For example, in the structures in (12), an ungoverned |V| can be glossed as [(+)sonorant], whereas a governed |V| forms the equivalent of [(+)voice]. This particular example reveals that DP manages to express distinct but clearly related phonological categories in terms of a single primitive appearing in different structural positions, where traditional feature systems must stipulate a relation in the form of redundancy rules like [+sonorant] → [+voice]. In DP, [+sonorant] and [+voice] are manifestations of one and the same element, namely |V|. The relation between these two categories is therefore intrinsic to the basic vocabulary. This reduction strategy is fundamental to RCVP, as we will see in Chapter 3.

Before I turn to a further discussion of the syntax of the categorical elements |C| and |V|, I will briefly discuss the other 'gestures' (element classes) in (11). Firstly, I turn to the second subgesture of the categorial gesture, that is, the initiatory subgesture. DP advocates the idea that the traditional concept of phonation (involving glottal states and vocal fold vibration) is relevant to two different gestures. Vocal fold vibration (voicing) is, as we have seen, expressed within the 'phonatory' subgesture of the categorial gesture, whereas glottal state distinctions are incorporated into the initiatory gesture.[25] This latter subgesture contains the 'glottal opening' element |O| ('aspiration') and two elements used for the description of different types of airstream mechanisms: |G| (for 'glottalicness', i.e. 'constricted glottis') and |K| (for 'velaric suction').

AE argue that the use of |O| is called for in three types of languages (AE p. 188):[26]

– Languages that have a voice distinction that involves more than two categories (usually voiced, voiceless and aspirated)
– Languages that do not seem to use voice but rather aspiration (i.e. voiceless non-aspirated vs. voiceless aspirated)
– Languages that have an opposition between voiced and voiceless sonorants[27]

---

[25] It is noteworthy that AE include voicing in the same class that also characterises major class and manner distinctions. This is in part motivated by the fact that both voicing and continuancy contribute to relative sonority and also result from intervocalic weakening.

[26] I will provide examples of such languages in Chapter 6.

[27] This has also been suggested in other work, such as Lombardi (1991), and it is supported by the fact that languages that have a voicing contrast for sonorants invariably also have an aspiration contrast for stops, as well as by the fact that in English, approximants are partially devoiced in clusters of voiceless stops followed by an approximant: aspiration in vowels (*key, tin*) is phonetically similar to devoicing in approximants (*clean, twin*).

The |O| element corresponds, of course, to the '+' value of the binary feature [±spread glottis], which has been used in binary systems for similar reasons. The |G| element plays a role in the characterisation of implosives and ejectives (AE p. 203ff.). The element |K| represents the velaric ingressive airstream for clicks. |O|, |G| and |K| can all enter into dependency relations with the phonatory subgesture to accommodate airstream differences as well as so-called 'accompaniments' for clicks. While the particular proposals were never further developed, the structures proposed by AE anticipate the notion that clicks are complex segments of some kind.

Proceeding with this sketch of DP, let us turn to the daughters of the locational subgesture. AE introduce the place elements in (13):

(13)   DP place elements:

|i| 'palatality, acuteness/sharpness' |l| 'linguality'
|u| 'roundness, gravity/flatness' |t| 'apicality'
|a| 'lowness, sonority' |d| 'dentality'
|ə| 'centrality' |r| 'Retracted Tongue Root'
                                               (henceforth RTR)
|ɑ| 'ATR' |λ| 'laterality'

Not all these elements play an equally important role in the theory. The heart of the set of place elements is formed by the familiar 'aiu' subset, which plays a key role in the representations of vowels *and* consonants. Two further elements are added for vowels: centrality (already discussed above and perhaps redundant) and ATR. Here I will focus on the elements which are mainly or exclusively used for consonants (the right-hand column).

|l|, linguality, was motivated by Lass (1976) to capture the natural class of high front vowels and tongue blade and tongue body consonants, which he claims recurs in sixteen processes in the history of English. This property, which in a sense correlates with [−labial], has not been expressed in any binary feature as a positive value, as far as I know, while proposals to incorporate labiality in FG models adopt a unary feature [labial].[28]

|t| is meant to capture the contrast between apical and laminal coronals, while |d| distinguishes dentals from alveolars. Systems that have dentals and alveolars frequently also distinguish these places in terms of apical and laminal, although no system seems to have an apical/laminal distinction at either the dental or alveolar place of articulation (see Ladefoged & Maddieson 1996 (henceforth LM): 20–3[29]), which is

---

[28] However, in the model of FG in Clements & Hume (1995), a unit 'lingual' is used; see § 11.2.

[29] 'In general, if a language has only a dental or an alveolar stop, then that stop will be laminal if it is dental and apical if it is alveolar' (LM p. 23).

why the SPE feature set covers both in terms of [±distributed]. However, AE argue that in certain cases both |d| and |t| seem necessary (AE p. 240), mainly because they require an adequate characterisation of the phonetic properties of consonants; they wish to be able to represent the dental/alveolar distinctions and the laminal/apical distinctions directly, even if these two distinctions cannot co-occur within a single consonant system. This raises the question of whether or not elements need to be restricted to those that capture contrast. Lass (1984) explicitly states that contrast is not the only criterion. For him, an adequate set of elements can capture phonetic differences between related dialects. RCVP limits its attention to contrast.

|r| is introduced to represent pharyngeal consonants. AE also consider using this element in vowels to capture a Tongue Root (TR) distinction in systems in which retracted is the dominant property (AE pp. 243–5). However, given the evidence that in harmony systems the advanced value is (often) dominant, AE suggest that *two* separate elements are needed.[30]

|λ| (correlating with [±lateral]) is introduced simply to capture laterality. Laterals are also captured in the phonatory gesture,[31] but |λ| is independently needed for lateralised segments such as lateral fricatives. Below, we note a similar duplication for nasality.

Turning to consonantal place representations, (14) shows the way in which the major places of articulation are represented:

(14) {u}   {l}   {l,i}   {l,u}   {l,u,a}

      labials   dentals,   palatals   velars   uvulars
                alveolars

We must note that the variety of elements that is used here in the representations for consonants (cf. the right-hand column in (13) above) somewhat weakens the idea that elements are used across the board, that is, for both consonants and vowels (see the fourth assumption in (1) above).[32] As we will see, in RCVP, the original idea that elements and their combination generalise over both consonants and vowels is fully restored.

---

[30] I refer to van der Hulst (2018: chs. 7 and 8) for an extensive discussion of tongue harmony systems which does *not* lead to the conclusion that 'RTR' is a necessary phonological prime; see also § 5.3.

[31] In (17) liquids are characterised as {V⇒V:C}. A further distinction into laterals and rhotics is made by representing the former with a further dependent C element (see AE p. 164).

[32] In various DP-inspired approaches (Smith (1988); van de Weijer (1996); Staun (1996b), among others) various proposals have been made to reduce the set of locational elements to the basic 'aiu' set (see § 11.3.1).

The oro-nasal subgesture contains precisely one element, |n|, for 'nasality'. Recall that there also is a phonatory characterisation of nasals {V⇒C}; see (12). This is comparable to the case of laterality for which DP also proposes a phonatory representation (for laterals proper) as well as an element (for lateralisation). AE motivate the dual characterisation of nasality, arguing that nasal consonants not only form a natural class with other sonorant consonants by sharing certain characteristics in their categorial (particularly phonatory) representations, but also form a natural class with nasalised segments, which may have different specifications in the categorial gesture (such as nasalised vowels). In order for this latter natural class to be reflected by the DP representations of the segments in question, AE argue that we need a separate component, |n|. This argument is parallel to the dual characterisation of laterality.

Let us finally consider AE's proposals for the tonological gesture. As mentioned earlier, in their excursus on representations for tonal distinctions, AE make the intriguing suggestion that the elements |i| and |u| (as part of the tonological gesture) could be employed for high and low tone, respectively.

> we propose that the appropriate representations for the two tonal components are [...] |i| and |u|. In other words, we are suggesting that |i| and |u| in the tonological gesture bear the same relation to |i| and |u| in the articulatory gesture as |V| in the categorial gesture does to |a| in the articulatory gesture [...] That is, |i| involves (relatively) 'high frequency' and |u| (relatively) 'low frequency'; whether this is interpreted as high (or low) F_0 or as concentration of energy in the higher (or lower) regions of the spectrum depends on the context – i.e. gesture – in which it occurs. (p. 273)

What is most noticeable in this proposal is the idea of using the same elements, namely |i| and |u|, in two different gestures. To emphasise that this strategy is present in the AE proposals, we will here also quote AE on their suggestion concerning the identity of |a| and |V|.

> there is clearly a relationship between |a|, as a component within the articulatory gesture, and |V|, as a component of the categorial gesture. Consider the acoustic glosses which we have given the two components: |V| corresponds with maximal periodicity, and |a| with maximal sonority. Vowels, by virtue of their periodicity, are the most sonorous of the categorial segment-types, while open vowels are the most sonorous within the class of vowels. [...] The open unrounded vowel, then, might have {|V|} both as the representation of the categorial gesture and of the articulatory gesture. (p. 215)

The importance of these quotations is to show that AE suggest the strategy of employing the same elements *in different (sub)gestures* (which

Background: Dependency and Government Phonology   53

needs to be distinguished from using the same element more than once *within* a gesture), thus deriving similarities in phonetic interpretation, while attributing the differences to the fact that the '(sub)gestural location' of an element has a bearing on the phonetic interpretation as well.

This review shows that DP employs three strategies for reducing the number of primes. Firstly, due to the unarity claim fewer phonological primes are needed. Secondly, fewer primes are needed due to the dependency relation. Two traditional features can be replaced by the dependent and head occurrence of a single prime, for instance |V| for [voice] and [sonorant]. Thirdly, fewer primes are needed given grouping. One particular element may occur in various groups, each time with a different phonetic interpretation, and thus replace two or more features.

I will conclude this section by returning to the 'phonatory' subgesture to make the case that the 'syntax' of CV combinations is not clearly defined in AE's version of DP, a point also emphasised in den Dikken & van der Hulst (1988), who offer an alternative which can be seen as an important step in the development of RCVP (van der Hulst (1994), (1995c), (2005a)).

For convenience, in (15) I repeat the set of distinctions built from |C| and |V| given in (12), which AE propose as a kind of core set:

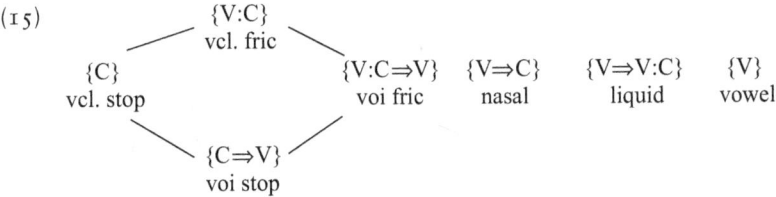

(15)
{C}   {V:C}
vcl. stop   vcl. fric
              {V:C⇒V} {V⇒C} {V⇒V:C} {V}
              voi fric nasal liquid   vowel
              {C⇒V}
              voi stop

The core of this set is formed by the five different basic structures that are composed of two elements:

(16) {C}   {C⇒V}   {V:C}   {V⇒C}   {V}
      stop voi stop fricative nasal   vowel

As we see in (17), this set can be expanded by adding a 'secondary' instance of a basic structure in (mutually) dependent position:[33]

(17) {V:C⇔V}   {V⇒V:C⇒C} {V:C⇔V⇒C}   {V:C⇒C}
      fricative lateral   voiced lateral   non-sibilant
      trill   fricative   fricative

---

[33] In the second and third case AE do not indicate whether the (mutual) dependency relations are hierarchically ordered.

Here we see the use of three levels of structure for the two categories in the middle. The argumentation that AE provide in favour of these representations is based on attested natural classes. Fricative trills may pattern with voiced fricatives in conditioning phonological processes (as an example AE give Aitken's Law, a historical process that occurred in the late sixteenth to the early seventeenth century in many Scots dialects, which groups [r] with voiced fricatives). Given the representations in (15 and 17), the relevant natural class can be represented as in (18):

(18) {V:C⇒V}

Lateral liquids, of course, must be distinguished from r-sounds, which motivates the second structure in (17). AE write:

> laterals are phonetically unique, as far as the phonatory sub-gesture is concerned, in having effectively two manners of articulation. While there is a stricture of open approximation at one or both sides of the mouth (at least for sonorant laterals), there is also closure in the centre of the oral tract. [...] Essentially, then, the |C| node characterizes a secondary [...] stricture type within the phonatory sub-gesture. (p. 163)

The dependent |C| in laterals expresses the fact that laterals may pattern with stops. In traditional feature systems, there is no direct way to express such a class without introducing the feature [continuant] in laterals, which is redundant since laterals are already uniquely characterised as [+lateral].

The extra dependent |C| in the third representation in (17), then, also adds laterality to the fricatives (AE p. 164).

The fourth structure reflects the distinction between sibilant and non-sibilant fricatives.

> /s/ may be interpreted as the optimal fricative phonetically; acoustically it shows the 'simplest' combination of consonantal and vocalic properties, while the other fricatives involve energy reduction in various frequency bands. In comparison with the sibilants, then, the other fricatives display extra /C/-ness. (p. 166)

While these various proposals are well motivated, one would like to know, from the viewpoint of generative power, exactly what the set of possible C/V combinations is that includes primary and secondary structures. AE do not address this issue explicitly. Rather, as seems motivated by the attestation of manner contrasts, they continue to add new structures, more or less in an ad hoc way (even though they provide reasonable arguments for each individual structure that they propose). In conclusion, even though AE carefully motivate the various structures, formally capturing many relations between different sound classes that must be stipulated in traditional feature theories, questions can be raised concerning the restrictiveness of their approach. The 'syntax' underlying combinations of components (|C| and |V| in this case) is not explicitly defined; that is, we do not know what the total set of possible dependency structures is. Clearly, AE assume that the syntax is, in a sense, *recursive*, so that structures that have been formed can be input to further combinatorial structures. However, given that this recursive syntax allows, in principle, many other structures, we must conclude that AE make no attempt to come to grips with the notion 'possible phonological segment'. Arguably, the notion of possible segment does not play a decisive role for AE. Their approach allows one to conceive of structures of various degrees of complexity, and the only relevant concern would then be to predict that more complex structures imply structures of lower degrees of complexity within a given language (within a given position). To some extent, RCVP adopts this viewpoint, although it delimits the required complexity is a manner that is less ad hoc.

It can also be noted that AE do not aim to reveal a similar set of structures in the different gestures. In contrast with this, RCVP pushes a structural analogy between the structural possibilities with each 'class node'.

In an attempt to find a principled syntax, den Dikken & van der Hulst (1988) make a proposal with respect to the use of the components |C| and |V| that imposes a general limitation on the complexity of CV structures. The initial idea in this proposal (based on van der Hulst (1988a, 1988b) and discussed in § 2.4) is that each component can occur *at most* twice. I will not discuss den Dikken & van der Hulst's proposal here in detail, adding that RCVP pursues the spirit of their approach by formulating an explicit syntax for CV combinations, which, since C and V occur in every grouping, is proposed as a general syntax for all these groups, which reflects the notion of structural analogy within the segmental structure.

The theory proposed in this book differs from DP in a number of ways. I adopt a 'gesture' grouping that is different from Anderson and Ewen in some respects, and more like the 'geometry' proposed in Clements (1985). I also push a high degree of structural analogy between the class nodes in terms of the structural possibilities for element combinations. However, the most salient property of my theory is to push the use of the same elements in different classes to its logical endpoint: in my proposal each class contains the same (two) elements, |C| and |V|, suggesting the name of the theory: Radical CV Phonology.

2.2.4 Developments in Dependency Phonology

In this section I discuss several developments that have taken place in DP with respect to the set of elements and their grouping.[34]

Standard DP used the possibility of allowing subgestures to enter into dependency relations (as in their treatment of airstream mechanisms and glottal states), but this was not fully exploited and it is unclear why AE use some dependencies but not others. For example, the variable dependency between the two subgestures of the articulatory gesture is used to account for two degrees of nasality (claimed to occur in Palantla Chinantec; Ladefoged (1971: 35)). Arguably, one could be sceptical about the two distinctive degrees of nasalisation, however (LM pp. 299–300[35]). In an attempt to restrict the DP model, Davenport & Staun (1986) argued to dispense with inter-subgesture dependency. I refer to that work for further discussion of this point, and the ramifications of their proposal for the DP framework. RCVP shares the idea of abandoning variable dependency between its 'gestures' ('class nodes').

Noting that DP expresses nasality in two ways (see above), Davenport (1995) proposes dispensing with the nasality component |n| altogether. This implies that the categorial characterisation of nasality 'survives', although Davenport's proposal is that nasality is expressed not in the Major class/Manner ('phonatory') subgesture (i.e. not in terms of specific |C|/|V| combination), but as a separate component |N| in the initiatory subgesture. I refer to Davenport's article, which claims that the dual representation of nasality leads to unsatisfactory results in DP.[36] The expression of nasality in RCVP has varied in my articles that have led up to the present account. In Chapter 4 ('Manner') I will make a proposal that restores the original duality idea of DP.

In their restructuring of the DP element geometry, Davenport & Staun (1986) maintain an initiatory subgesture, which contains elements for airstream distinctions: |I| 'egressive airflow' (not present in AE), |G| 'glottalicness' and |K| 'velaric suction'. The |O| element which forms part of this subgesture in AE has been moved to the phonatory subgesture in Davenport & Staun's model. Furthermore, we have just seen that Davenport (1995) proposes adding a component |N| 'nasal' to the initiatory subgesture:

---

[34] For a more extensive discussion of developments in DP see den Dikken & van der Hulst (1988) and van der Hulst & van de Weijer (2018b). This section is adapted from sections in both articles. Also of course see Anderson (2011c).

[35] A better description of the three Chinantec contrasts might be as being between oral vowels, oral-nasal diphthongs and nasalised vowels' (LM p. 300).

[36] Interestingly, a proposal for dual expression of nasality can also be found in Rice & Avery (1989) and Piggott (1992), who adopt a Spontaneous Voicing node and a Soft Palate node, which can both dominate the feature [nasal].

(19)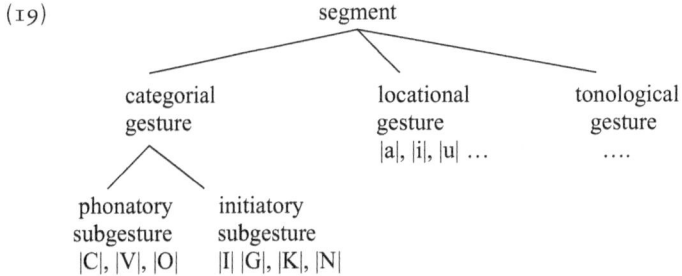

It is noteworthy that work in DP has not developed a separate 'laryngeal' gesture that would capture voicing, aspiration and glottalic constriction, as well as tonal distinctions (as in most FG models). It is also noteworthy that FG proposals have generally not proposed a class node with features for initiation, that is, for ingressive sounds like implosives and clicks, or egressive sounds like ejectives. Segments of the latter type are usually expressed with laryngeal features or as complex segments with a double articulation (see Sagey (1986)). RCVP, as we will see, restores the phonatory subgesture (as the 'manner class') with only the elements |C| and |V| and it does not adopt an initiatory subgesture. Instead, it adopts a laryngeal class that covers phonation and tone distinctions. There will be no elements for airstream direction, while clicks will be represented as complex segments

Staun (2013), inspired by earlier formulations of RCVP, has proposed another revision of the categorial and articulatory gestures, arguing to replace the |V| element by the element |a| in the former, reflecting the suggestions discussed earlier in AE concerning the affinity between |V| and |a|. In his system, |a| occurs in both the categorial and the articulatory gesture, and the latter also includes elements that capture coronal (his |t|) and peripheral (his |w|), the latter 'splitting' into two further elements: dorsal (|k|) and labial (|p|). Staun unfolds a detailed proposal to account for the element characterisation of consonants and vowels, which I will not discuss here. RCVP adopts a single element |V|, which subsumes the old |a| element, and also incorporates the coronal/peripheral division in the place class.

Earlier I mentioned work by Norval Smith and his students (e.g. Humbert (1996); Li (1996); Botma (2004, 2009); Botma & Smith (2006, 2007); Smith (1988)) which pursued the rigorous idea of representing locational properties of vowels and consonants solely in terms of the triangular 'aiu' set, developing the idea of using an element more than once in a representation proposed in van der Hulst (1988a).[37] In a related line

---

[37] Norval Smith and I collaborated on this work and presented an early proposal at a colloquium talk at MIT ('Features and dependency') and on 9 October 1989 at an

of work Ewen & van der Hulst (1985, 1987, 1988) and van der Hulst (1989, 1990b) explored a hierarchical organisation for the 'aiu' elements which contained a proposal for a new element |y| that dominates both |i| and |u| to express their commonality. Van der Hulst & Smith (1988c, 1990) explored similar ideas.[38] The |y| element returns in RCVP as the |∀| element in the manner class.

The developments just discussed reflect changes that are to be expected when a model is developed; we see a similar flurry of proposals in the domain of mainstream FG (see den Dikken & van der Hulst (1988); McCarthy (1988); Phillips (1994) for reviews).

In this section I conclude with Anderson (2011c), who discusses RCVP as proposed in van der Hulst (2005a), a close precursor of the model presented in this book. While criticising certain aspects of the model, Anderson also embraces some aspects of it. He does not present a complete outline of his current view of DP elements and their structures, but, in the structures that he proposes, he more *explicitly* recognises a distinction between primary and secondary occurrences of elements, which represents an innovation compared to AE. Revising the combinatorial system proposed in AE, Anderson proposes representing nasality and voicing in terms of secondary occurrence of the C and V elements (using lower case for the secondary elements):

(20)   {V;C{c}}   {V;C}   {V;C{v}}
       nasal   lateral   rhotic

(Anderson (2011b: 114))

(21)   {C;V{v}}   voiced fricative
       {C{v}}   voiced stop

(Anderson (2011b: 362))

The RCVP model explores the use of secondary elements for all three element classes, as will see in subsequent chapters.

2.2.5 Minimal specification and polysystematicity

Even though the adoption of unary features pre-empts the notion of underspecification in many ways, underspecification does not become inapplicable. As we have seen in § 1.3.4, Anderson advocates a strong minimalist view with respect to the specification of phonological

---

MIT conference; this paper ('On the structure of complex consonants') was never published.

[38] See van Nice (1991) for similar proposals within Schane's particle theory (Schane 1984).

information, which must be strictly contrastive. All redundant, predictable properties should be eliminated from the representation. Underspecification becomes relevant when we consider positional phonotactic restrictions, as for example in the well-known case of English initial clusters. In a trisegmental cluster like /spr/ the initial segment, if consonantal, can only be /s/, which means that all properties of this segment, except its consonantality, are predictable. Likewise, the second segment (a voiceless stop) and third segment (an approximant) also have many predictable properties. Without spelling out what the minimal representation in terms of components would be, it seems clear that very few elements are required.

As also discussed in § 1.3.4 (in general, not just in DP), the use of underspecification undermines the traditional notion of the phoneme as a unit that generalises over allophones that occur in different positions, being in complementary distribution. Such a rejection is masked by the use of terms like 'archiphoneme'. Rather, it leads to a type of analysis in which each position in the string of segments has its own contrastive set of oppositions (its own segment system, so to speak). This means that phonology is polysystematic (as recognised in the Firthian approach (Firth 1948)). For example, if a language limits syllable-final consonants to plain voiceless stops, the relevant position only allows a contrast between whatever the plain voiceless stops are that the language allows in terms of place. If these are labial, coronal and dorsal, for instance, then a final 'k' can simply be represented as {consonantal, dorsal}. However, an initial 'k' might contrast with all other consonants and might therefore have a richer representation, for instance {consonantal, voiceless, stop, dorsal}. The polysystematic view holds that these two sets of features are independent and not unified under a joined concept of 'the phoneme /k/'. Nevertheless, these two sets are mapped onto phonetic events which are very similar. The classical notion of the phoneme formally expresses this phonetic similarity, which, as argued by Pike (1947), provides a natural basis for an economical alphabetic writing system. However, Anderson sees this traditional notion of phoneme that generalised over positions that have different contrastive sets as not being a genuine phonological entity (see Anderson 2014).

In conclusion, Anderson postulates that segments in different positions have their own sets of oppositions. Segments in a given position are specified minimally to distinguish them from other segments that can occur in the same paradigmatic slot. Furthermore, in any such system one member can always be specified as the null option (i.e. without any elements).

Anderson extends the use of underspecification to linear order. I return to this point in § 3.2.2, where we discuss the DP approach to syllable structure.

2.3 Government Phonology

In this section, I will make some brief remarks about the approach to segmental structure taken in GP.[39] The foundations for this approach were laid in work presented by Jean-Roger Vergnaud in 1982 at a GLOW conference (based on collaboration with Jonathan Kaye and Jean Lowenstamm). The first full statement of this theory, offered in KLV85, is extensive and explicit. A proposal was made for a set of elements that would be shared by and sufficient for both consonants and vowels, although KLV85 only discusses vowel structures in detail. The GP approach, though apparently developed independently from DP, has important characteristics in common with the latter approach.[40] Apart from adopting the same basic primes that DP adopted, GP then also proposed that these primes could be 'fused', and that in each combination, one prime is the head, while the other is an 'operator'.[41] In KLV85 all elements were characterised in terms of a feature matrix, with one feature being the 'hot' feature, that is, the most characteristic property of that element and the one it would add to another element if fused with it as an 'operator'. For example, the hot feature of the element [U][42] would be [+round]. Combining [U] as an operator with [I], the head, would produce a [+round] [i] vowel, namely [ü].[43] Since 1985, GP has undergone significant further development, mostly involving simplification and reduction in the set of elements, as well as elimination of the idea that elements consist of a feature bundle. At the present time, there is a proposal to allow just six elements. The most explicit account of GP's representation of vowel and consonant contrast is offered in Backley (2011).[44]

---

[39] I discuss some of the latest development, leading to 'Government Phonology 2.0', in § 11.3.7.

[40] The author of this book pointed out this 'resemblance' to J. R. Vergnaud in 1982 when he presented these ideas at a GLOW workshop in Paris. A statement in KLV85 (p. 310) that their 'molecular' approach to segmental structure bears some degree of resemblance to earlier work by Anderson and Jones which has developed into 'dependency phonology' strikes me as somewhat of an understatement. In 1987, Norval Smith and I organised a workshop in Leiden (The Netherlands) with both John Anderson and Jonathan Kaye as invited speakers. Theoretical resemblances were acknowledged, but GP and DP, having been developed independently, continued to be so.

[41] The notion of operator corresponds to what DP calls the dependent. For some reason (unknown to me), KLV85 did not see fusion as involving a head-dependent relation, structurally identical to suprasegmental head-dependency relations.

[42] A common GP notation for elements uses capital letters between square brackets.

[43] The fusion of these two elements with [U] being the head also produces [ü], which is intended because KLV85 do not want the difference to be distinctive (see KLV85 pp. 315–16). They share this claim with DP, as we have seen in § 2.2.2.

[44] Many GP phonologists have made valuable contributions to the evolution of this model; see Scheer & Kula (2018), Scheer & Cyran (2018a, 2018b) and Ritter (to appear).

Below I will return to the specifics of Backley's version of GP and point to a certain convergence between RCVP and GP.[45]

Here I will discuss two particular aspects of the KLV85 proposal, referring for a detailed review to den Dikken and van der Hulst (1988).

Firstly, in addition to the 'aiu' set KLV85 propose two other elements, namely [v] ('the cold vowel') and [ɨ] ('ATR'). Both elements were eventually removed from the theory. I will discuss how they function in the original KLV85 proposal so that I can refer back to them when introducing the RCVP model. The cold vowel, which is somewhat similar to the centrality element in DP, has no 'hot feature', which means that when applied as an operator to another element it has a vacuous effect; it returns the head element and thus functions as an 'identity element'. Given the feature bundles of [v] and [I], [U] or [ATR], applying the last three as operators to [v] also produces a result that is identical to these three elements.[46] The only instance where fusion of an element with the cold vowel is not vacuous is in the case of the combination of [v] and [A], with [A] as operator, which results in a [-round, +back, -high, -low, -ATR] vowel (i.e. a 'raised' 'a' that KLV85 represent as [ə]); see KLV85 p. 310 for details.

The role of the element ATR is, obviously, to allow a distinction between two sets of vowels that differ in tongue advancement. As an example, consider the vowel system of Kpokolo, an African language discussed by KLV85 themselves.[47]

(22) /i/ /i̘/ /u/
     /ɪ/ /ɨ/ /ʊ/
     /e/ /ɐ/ /o/
     /ɛ/ /ɜ/ /ɔ/
          /a/

The system of Kpokolo makes distinctive, phonological use of a five-way contrast along the height dimension,[48] and it will be clear that the GP framework cannot accommodate this system without the introduction of an additional element. The element in question is ATR. With the aid of

---

[45] More recently, a new version of GP, called GP 2.0, has been proposed, which I will discuss in § 11.3.7.
[46] This is because the cold vowel has no hot feature. When [I], [U] or [ATR] impose their hot feature value on the cold vowel, they simply produce a feature column that is identical to the one they have; see KLV85 for details.
[47] In the present discussion of KLV85 I maintain the slanted lines for 'phonemes' as used there.
[48] However, the need for distinguishing between /ɜ/ and /a/ as contrastive vowels is not obvious. KLV85 provide several arguments that these sounds are in near-complementary distribution.

the ATR element and the cold vowel [v], GP can accommodate the vowel system of Kpokolo as in (23). In this diagram the underlining indicates headhood (a common practice in GP):

(23)
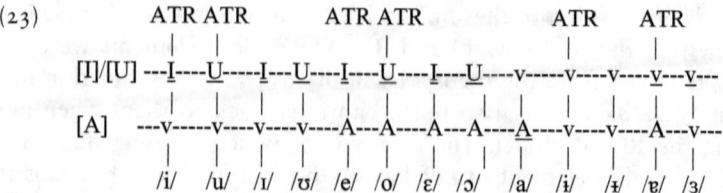

A difference between the systems of DP and GP involves the use of '(quasi-)autosegmental tiers'. However, in the GP system, the element ATR never resides on a tier or line of its own. This property of ATR is taken to give formal expression to the stipulation that this element can never be the head of a complex expression. In addition, it should be noted that in (23) the elements [I] and [U] occur on the same autosegmental line. This 'line fusion', according to KLV85 (p. 368), is 'an unmarked option of vowel systems' (KLV85 p. 308), and will obtain in any language lacking front rounded vowels, whose presence is effectively excluded by [I]/[U] line fusion: when these two lines are fused, combinations of [I] and [U] are rendered impossible. Both these aspects of lines or tiers (i.e. the fact that an element can lack a line of its own, namely ATR, and that lines can be fused) are specific to GP.

Looking back at the DP system, as well as at the GP system discussed so far, we note that there is no possibility of formally expressing the relative markedness of particular element combinations. That is, there is no formal property associated with the elements that renders it intrinsically unfavourable for two elements to combine in the representation of a given segment. In principle, all elements can freely combine with one another. Yet, as KLV85 (p. 371) point out,

> even a cursory look at segmental structure [...] shows that there do exist classes of elements sharing a particular property. This property has an impact on the combinations of elements that may exist and on their organisation into segmental systems (vowels or consonants).

In the feature system of GP this property is hence given formal status, and is called *charm*. It is assumed that there are positively and negatively charmed elements, and that a combination of elements with like charm is strongly dispreferred, whereas there is an attraction between elements of opposite charm. GP's proposal for positive and negative charm among its vowel elements is as in (24).

(24) Positive charm: Negative charm:
     [A]+   [I]–
     [ATR]+   [U]–
     [N]+   [v]–

KLV85 (p. 371) correlates the property of charm with a resonating cavity (the oral cavity for [A], the pharyngeal cavity for [ATR], and the nasal cavity for [N]). In general, the charm of a compound expression, that is, a combination of two elements, is the charm of its head. This is different when the ATR element is involved. The result in that case is said to be charmed, independent of whether this element is a head or dependent; here I will not detail KLV85's motivation for this stipulation.

From (24) we may now derive the extent to which certain combinations of elements are preferred. We can divide these possible combinations into two classes, preferred and dispreferred ones, as in (25):

(25) Preferred combinations: Dispreferred combinations:
     [A] + [I]   [A] + [ATR]
     [A] + [U]   [I] + [U]
     [A] + [v]   [I] + [v]
     [I] + [ATR]   [U] + [v]
     [U] + [ATR]   [N] + [A]
     [v] + [ATR]

It would seem, though, that of the set of dispreferred combinations the last three are not obviously dispreferred. In fact, two of these ([I] + [v] and [U] + [v]) are found in the vowel system of Kpokolo discussed above, while [I] + [U] occurs in vowel systems containing front rounded vowels such as [ü]. Finally, the claim that [N] prefers not to combine with the element [A], forming a nasalised low vowel, seems completely wrong, especially since nasalisation has a lowering effect on vowels (cf. Italian *vino* with [i] and French *vin* [with [ɛ̃]).

What the GP feature system, embodying the notion of charm, is able to express successfully, however, is that fusion of [A] and [ATR] is not highly valued in a vowel system. This is taken to account straightforwardly for the absence in most ATR vowel systems of a [+ATR] counterpart of the low vowel /a/. In vowel systems in which /a/ does have a [+ATR] counterpart, such as Kpokolo, where /ə/ is the [+ATR] variant of the low vowel, a special procedure must be followed. KLV85 (p. 377) argue that

> in situations where the positively charmed ATR element seeks to fuse with [A+] there are apparently two possibilities: the positive charm of [A+] prevents association; the roles of operator and head are reversed and a negatively charmed expression is formed, to which the positive ATR element can associate.

In languages in which /a/ has a [+ATR] counterpart, then, the second strategy will be adopted. In particular, the expression (v–.A̱+)+ is replaced by (A+.v̱–)–, which is subsequently combined with [ATR+] to form (ATR+.(A+.v̱–))+:

(26)
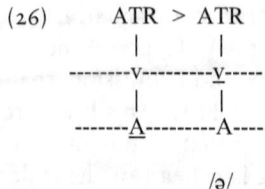

/ə/

The concept of head–operator reversal introduced for the description of the [+ATR] variant of the low vowel is clearly ad hoc. Yet the intuitive idea behind the notion of charm is a sound one, albeit that the way in which KLV85 chose to capture it may not be the most felicitous. As shown in the discussion of (25), charm theory did not make the correct predictions (in either the first version in KLV85 or the second version in KLV90[49]) and this notion was eventually abandoned in GP. Interestingly, a comparable notion falls out naturally from the RCVP theory in which all elements are classified as being either 'V' or 'C'. The V bias of elements corresponds more or less to the notion of positive charm, which, intuitively, correlates with high sonority or, as GP puts it, 'voweliness'.

Let us now return once more to the elements [ATR] and [v], which both GP and DP seem to require. It should be noted that these two elements differ from the other three elements [I], [U] and [A], in particular because they are clearly not as basic as the other three elements. The different status of [ATR] and [v] as compared to [I], [U] and [A] is formally recognised in the system of GP. There, as we saw above, [ATR] and [v] are assumed not to occupy tiers of their own, in contradistinction to the other GP elements. [ATR] and [v], in addition, differ among themselves as well, in that the latter, even though it does not have its own tier, always occurs on some other autosegmental line, where it fills up the gaps, whereas [ATR] is never placed on any line at all, and as a consequence can never be the head of a complex expression, as opposed to the cold vowel [v]. In addition, the ATR element functions in a peculiar way with respect to charm. It attributes charm to an expression even when it occurs as an operator (which it typically or always does). In addition, the ATR element has a hot feature (namely [+ATR]), while the cold vowel, faithful to its name, has no hot feature.

---

[49] In KLV90 charm theory was modified and a third category, neutral charm, was introduced. These details do not concern us here, since my focus is on the general idea behind charm, which I think is valid.

Given that these two elements had specific (stipulated) properties, over time, in an attempt to simplify the element system, GP abandoned the cold vowel and the ATR element. As we will see, RCVP recognises an element, symbolised as |∀| (shorthand for |C| in the head manner class of vowels), which shares certain similarities with the cold vowel. Also, RCVP will recognise an ATR element (without ad hoc properties) which naturally emerges from its basic principles.

KLV90, mainly dealing with syntagmatic structure ('syllable structure'), introduce a tentative, more complete set of elements, adding those in (27) to the five already discussed ('[A], [I], [U], [v], [ɨ]'):[50]

(27) [H] 'stiff vocal cords, that is, high tone or voicelessness'
 [L] 'slack vocal cords, that is, low tone or voice'
 [h] 'narrow constriction, continuant, release'
 [ʔ] 'full constriction, stop'
 [R] 'coronal'
 [N] 'nasal'

Even though I have here provided articulatory descriptions, it should be clear that GP, like DP, emphasised that elements are primarily acoustic images, placing articulatory properties effectively outside the phonological grammar.[51] KLV90 adopt the above eleven elements, but not much information is given on their full use. The first two elements, H and L, are obviously used for tonal distinctions and phonation. We may assume from later work (cf. Kaye (2000)) that H and L can enter into combinations, giving (HL), but whether differences in headedness among these two elements can be exploited (e.g. to generate a four-way distinction) is not clear. It must be borne in mind that GP does not recognise gestures or class nodes. Hence a vowel, let us say [a], with a midtone is specified as (H,L,A̲). Apparently, tonal elements do not, then, enter into combinations among themselves. Rather, they are operators to the head of the segment, which is likely to be a place element. Indeed, in Kaye (2000), three tonal specifications are possible: (H,A), (H,L,A) and (L,A). The absence of a tonal specification is contrastively used as a fourth choice.

---

[50] For detailed discussion of the acoustic and articulatory correlates of all GP elements see Harris (1990, 1994) and Harris & Lindsey (1995). I here ignore the charm values. In KLV90, charm theory was altered compared to KLV85, due to additional motivations based on the need to establish a principled relationship between syllabic positions and elements that may or can, or cannot, appear in these positions. This idea to correlate charm with syllabic positions also finds a counterpart in RCVP in the notion of 'harmony', which is discussed in Chapter 8.
[51] See AE, Harris (1994), Harris & Lindsey (1995) and Backley (2011) for arguments for this position. RCVP takes a more 'nuanced' view on this matter, giving a role to both acoustic and articulatory correlates; see § 1.3.1.

The use of the elements [h] and [?] in KLV90 seems to suggest that stops, nasals and laterals have [?], while fricatives and presumably affricates have [h]; the latter may also contain [?]. Harris (1990, 1994) is more complete in his characterisation of the use of these 'manner' elements. For him, released stops have both [?] and [h], while unreleased stops have only [h], just like fricatives:

(28) /p/: [U̲, ?, h]
 /f/: [U̲, ?]
 /w/: [U̲]

I refer to Harris (1994) for a fuller discussion of the representations for consonants.[52]

Subsequently, GP embarked on a 'minimalist programme' of its own, aiming to eliminate various properties of the original KLV theory. Charm theory was discarded and various elements were also deemed unnecessary (not only the cold vowel but also the [R] and the [h] elements). One proposal that allowed the elimination of the stop element was to adopt the idea that elements can be headed or non-headed independently of the occurrence of an element that is dependent on them. Headedness in this proposal attributes a property to the element (such as stricture or being advanced) which the non-headed occurrence lacks (see Harris (1994); Ritter (1997)). Thus headedness effectively becomes a *diacritic*, which effectively introduces a doubling of the number of elements.[53] RCVP does not use headedness as a diacritic.

---

[52] See Ritter (1997) for another perspective on differentiating these segment types, using 'contrastive headedness'; see below.

Several other studies apply the principles of GP to specific languages, introducing various developments and proposals. See, for example, Cyran (1997, 2003, 2014). Remarkably, all work in GP was done by European phonologists or in Europe by several international students (from Japan, Brazil) who graduated at the School of Oriental and African Studies, and by Ritter (1995), who graduated at New York University. For a more thorough review of GP work I refer to Scheer (2004), Scheer & Kula (2018), Scheer & Cyran (2018a, 2018b) and Ritter (to appear).

[53] In GP, an element occurring by itself would be headed, that is, be the head of the construction that it forms. This is a standard assumption in head/dependency-based theories. The non-headed occurrence of an element is taken to be a combination of this element with the 'cold vowel element', which is the head. In this proposal, headedness is not a diacritic, but it presupposes the cold vowel element, which GP came to abandon. This makes the non-headed property in Backley (2011) a diacritic. Backley (2012) also discusses a possible use of non-headed element combinations in GP, which he compares to the element combinations that in DP have 'mutual dependency'; see (6) on p. 43.

The overall result of this reduction programme was a set of six elements, which Backley (2011) discusses and applies to segmental inventories and processes: he proposes a system of six elements with no further structure imposed on this set; also see Scheer & Kula (2018) and Backley (2012). GP continues to do without any concept of element grouping. However, in his last chapter, Backley discusses two ways of informally classifying the six elements.

(29) | Variable | Relevant values | Elements | |
| --- | --- | --- | --- |
| | | dark | light |
| resonance | resonant vs. non-resonant | [A] | [?] |
| frequency | low vs. high frequency | [L] | [H] |
| colour | dark vs. bright | [U] | [I] |

By grouping the elements in *antagonistic* pairs, Backley says we reveal 'three variables that are even more basic than the acoustic patterns associated with the elements themselves' (2011: 195):

> We can think of the perceptual variables in [(29)] as the fundamental properties of spoken language – properties which humans instinctively pay attention to during communication. Now, because contrast is based on acoustic differences, it makes sense for languages to exploit cues that are maximally different, since these are the easiest to distinguish. The cues that are relevant to phonology are therefore the cues that identify the most extreme values of the three variables. In other words, the elements in each pair are opposites.

Backley asserts that the variables are not formal units of grammar and nor are the labels 'dark' and 'light'. As we will see when we discuss RCVP, this is an important aspect in which this model differs from GP element theory. In Chapter 3 I show that (29) correlates with two fundamental properties of the RCVP structure. This structure adopts the three-way class distinction that was also part of Clements's (1985) FG model in which the three classes correspond to Backley's variables (added in parentheses in (30)). Within each class, RCVP will locate the same two elements, C and V, which correlate with the 'light/dark' distinction. Thus, RCVP, in a way, delivers a six-way distinction which corresponds to the six elements that GP ended up with:[54]

---

[54] In fact, informally I will use the 'traditional' element labels, only replacing the element |ʔ| by the element name |∀|.

(30) The 'geometry' of elements in RCVP

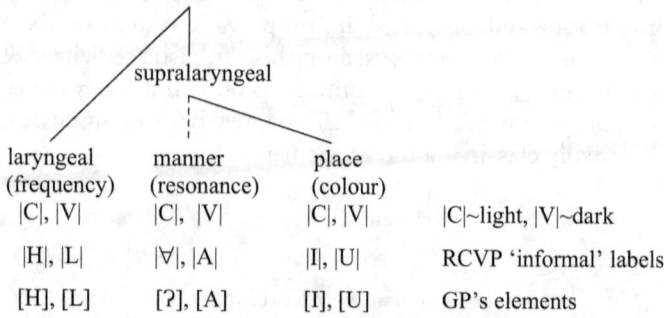

	laryngeal (frequency)	manner (resonance)	place (colour)	
	|C|, |V|	|C|, |V|	|C|, |V|	|C|~light, |V|~dark
	|H|, |L|	|∀|, |A|	|I|, |U|	RCVP 'informal' labels
	[H], [L]	[?], [A]	[I], [U]	GP's elements

I note that if Backley had recognised grouping and the light/dark distinction formally in his system, his theory would have ended up being very close to the RCVP model, as it was proposed in my previous articles, which as such, of course, long predate his monograph. An apparent difference between RCVP and GP (including Backley's version) lies in RCVP's adoption of the element |∀| (|C| in manner), which is the antagonistic counterpart of |A| (|V| in manner), although KLV85 originally proposed an element very much like it, [ɨ], which was abandoned in favour of contrastive use of headedness, as mentioned above. In GP, there is no theoretical reason for pairing up the element |A| with an antagonistic partner, as there is in RCVP. The crucial availability of the element |∀| for vowels is supported in van der Hulst (2018), an extensive study of vowel harmony systems. As shown in (30), Backley pairs |A| up with the [?] element, but the latter element does not really represent a counterpart to |A| since it only captures 'occlusion', which is mostly relevant for consonants, and for vowels only as glottalisation. In RCVP |∀| takes the same place as the GP [?] element, making the latter superfluous. The adoption of |∀| makes explicit that the 'closure' element has an equal role to play in vowels (representing high or 'non-low') and in consonants (representing 'non-continuancy').

Finally, I need to highlight a specific aspect of element theory that is adopted in GP, which is the claim that each element is supposed to be independently pronounceable. This means that each element, occurring alone, characterises a complete segment. While this was certainly also the case in the DP approach, at least for the 'aiu' set, DP does not adopt this requirement for all elements, at least not explicitly.

(31) | Element | Stand-alone interpretation |
|---|---|
| [A] | [a] |
| [I] | [i] |
| [U] | [u] |

[v]	[i]
[ɨ]	? (this element was replaced by the notion 'headedness')
[H]	?
[L]	?
[h]	[h]
[?]	[?]
[R]	[ɾ]
[N]	[n]

As indicated, I do not know what the stand-alone interpretation of [H] and [L], which correlate with high and low fundamental frequency, was meant to be. However, details aside (which changed, of course, as the set of elements was reduced), the stand-alone requirement brings to the surface a crucial difference between elements and binary features. While features are *attributes* of phonological segments, elements *are* independent '*substances*' that can be phonological segments, at least in principle. In RCVP, the stand-alone properties of elements only apply to the head occurrence of elements.

2.4 Towards Radical CV Phonology

Van der Hulst (1988a) elaborates on the DP idea that elements in head position contribute more strongly to the resulting vowel than the same element in dependent position; indeed such elements have greater perceptual and thus cognitive salience, which is a hallmark of headship. This idea implies that phonetic interpretation is sensitive to the head or dependent status of an element. Van der Hulst (1988a, 1988b) pushes this one step further by proposing that elements in their head and dependent status have different, albeit phonetically related, interpretations, as summed up in (32), using articulatory rather than acoustic labels:

(32) Interpretation of |u| Head: Velar constriction
                                              |
                            Dependent: Rounding

      Interpretation of |i| Head: Palatal constriction
                                              |
                            Dependent: ATR

      Interpretation of |a| Head: Pharyngeal constriction
                                              |
                            Dependent: Openness (RTR)

The specific aspects of this proposal are not replicated in the current RCVP model.[55] However, the idea that ATR is a manifestation of the |I| element in dependent position is incorporated in the RCVP model; see § 5.3.2. What does not carry over is that this proposal allows for contrastive use of the occurrence of an element alone and this same element occurring with itself as a dependent, among other things to distinguish between back rounded and back unrounded vowels:

(33) /i/ /ü/   /ɯ/ /u/
     |i| |i| |u| |u|
          |u| |u|

We must note that this system, which is similar to proposals to split up the old u-element discussed earlier (see (8) on p. 44), also does not solve the markedness issue discussed in § 2.2.2, since [u] is still represented as more complex than [ɯ]. In RCVP, contrastive use of a dependent that is identical to its head is not adopted in this form. Van der Hulst (1988a, 1988b) proposed that an identical dependent is the default case when there is no contrast, but in RCVP this predictable dependent is taken to be universally present, so that a difference between presence and absence of an identical dependent can never be contrastive; see Chapter 3 for details.

The proposal in van der Hulst (1988b), which only deals with vowel representations in terms of the elements |a|, |i| and |u|, allows for a controlled set of representations, which, when applied to the categorial gestures, delivers the following eight representations (see den Dikken & van der Hulst (1988: 64)):

(34) C   C   C   C   V   V   V   V
      | /\ | | | /\ | |
      C   C V   V   C   C   C V   V   V
     vcl vcd vcl vcd   nas liq glide vowel
     stop stop fric fric

Two crucial further steps were taken in van der Hulst (1995c). Firstly, I propose that the elements |C| and |V| are used in all element groups. Secondly, I propose a system which bans the contrastive distinction between a bare element and that element with an identical dependent, which leads to a four-way distinction, here given in two notations:[56]

---

[55] It was adopted and further developed in various dependency based articles (van der Hulst (1989) and also in work by Norval Smith and students; e.g. Smith (1988), Botma (2004, 2009), Botma & Smith (2006, 2007). A somewhat different proposal is made in Ewen & van der Hulst (1991)).

[56] An unpublished manuscript ('The book of segments', van der Hulst (1990a)), distributed on a limited scale, formed an intermediate step in the development of

(35) a. C   C   V   V
              | |
              V   C

b. C   C;V   V;C   V

However, since this only provides four choices for each element group, I proposed that each of these four structures can have the four basic structures as a dependent, albeit headed with the 'opposite' element:

(36) C   C   C;V   C;V   V;C   V;C   V   V
      | | | | | | | |
      V   V;C V;C   V   C   C;V   C   C;V

This proposal, while also not preserved in RCVP in this form, is a precursor to an important distinction in RCVP between the notions primary and secondary element class. Van der Hulst (1995b) deals with both manner and laryngeal distinctions. An application to place distinction is van der Hulst (1996c). Van der Hulst (2005a) presents the first complete formulation of RCVP.[57] In Chapter 3 I offer a detailed review of the RCVP model in its current form, which will be elaborated in Chapters 4–7 with empirical support.

2.5 Summary and concluding remarks

In this chapter, I have reviewed the initial proposals and later developments of the element theories of DP and GP. This review serves a purpose in its own right as a history of how various theories have developed. However, I also provided this amount of detail to be able to situate my own model (RCVP) more clearly, in terms of both what it owes to previous proposals and how it differs. I concluded with some articles of my own which lead up to the ideas that are presented in this book.

RCVP shares with previous approaches:

- the use of unary primes (DP, GP)
- the use of dependency relations between primes (DP, GP)
- the use of grouping (DP)
- a unified set of elements for both consonant and vowels (DP,GP)
- a classification of elements in two 'kinds' (GP's charm theory)

RCVP. This manuscript aimed to have the same scope as the present book, covering manner, place and laryngeal distinctions, albeit in a rudimentary form. This proposal did not yet use the same two elements in all element classes.

[57] Van der Hulst (2000b) also applies the RCVP approach to sign language phonology; see Chapter 10 for an updated proposal.

- representations as minimal (DP,GP)
- the occurrence of elements in more than one group (DP)

In particular, the last point, for which the seeds were planted in AE, is pushed to the extreme in RCVP.[58]

In the chapters to follow, I will offer a detailed presentation of RCVP, starting in Chapter 3 with a comprehensive outline of the RCVP 'syntax'.

---

[58] The idea to use one set of elements in all elements groups was suggested to me by Petra Kottman, who proposed to use |I| and |U| in all groups.

3

Radical CV Phonology

3.1 Introduction

In this chapter, I present an introduction to the RCVP model, focusing on the 'syntax' of C/V combinations but without providing details of the segmental structure or empirical underpinning.[1] In the following chapters, I will then go into the details for each class of phonological elements (manner, place, laryngeal) and provide empirical support from typological studies of segmental contrast and inventories, notably reported in MD, LM, Gordon (2016) and various databases that are available online. I show how the two RCVP 'C' and 'V' elements are phonetically interpreted by providing a set of interpretation functions. In this chapter, I will also provide the RCVP model of the syllable and discuss how segmental structure and syllable structure are connected.

3.2 An outline of Radical CV Phonology

3.2.1 *The segmental model*

RCVP is an approach based on both *DP*) (AE) and *GP* (KLV85, KLV90; Harris & Lindsey (1995)).[2] Roughly, RCVP shares its basic principles, as expressed in (1), with DP:[3]

---

[1] This chapter does not presuppose familiarity with Chapters 1 and 2.
[2] Related work, also based on the notion of dependency and unary elements, is Botma (2004, 2009), Botma & Smith (2006, 2007) and Smith (1988).
[3] RCVP is not the same theory as 'strict CV', a theory of syllable structure that has been developed by Jean Lowenstamm (see Lowenstamm (1996)), but there is a similarity in the idea of reducing the building blocks of phonology to two antagonistic units. Lowenstamm pursues this idea at the level of *structure*, while RCVP pursues this idea with reference to phonological *content* (as well as structure, but differently from Lowenstamm's theory).

(1) Fundamental principles:
   a. Phonological primes are unary (they are called *elements*[4]).
   b. Elements are grouped into units ('gestures' or 'class nodes').[5]
   c. Each class is populated by the same two elements, C and V.
   d. When combined, elements enter into a head-dependency relation.
   e. All elements are used for both consonants and vowels.
   f. Some primes may occur in more than one class.
   g. Representations are minimally specified.

In (2) I represent the full RCVP geometry:[6]

(2) The 'geometry' of elements in RCVP

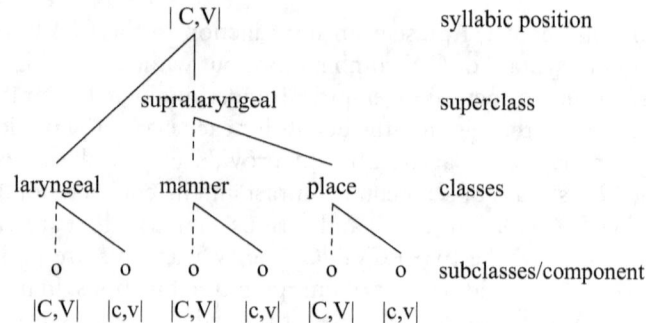

- Vertical broken lines dominate heads.
- Vertical closed lines indicate subjunction (showing the same unit to be a head multiple levels).
- Slant lines connect dependents to their heads.

---

[4] DP uses the term *component*, but I adopt the GP term *element*. Schane (1984) uses the term *particle*.

[5] The idea of acknowledging element classes occurs in the earliest version of DP (e.g. see Anderson & Jones (1974)). The same idea later led to versions of what was called 'FG' (see Clements (1985)). In Chapter 11 I discuss various FG models.

These element classes are similar to the *dimensions* proposed in Avery & Idsardi (2001). These authors propose a theory of features which also introduces the notion of antagonistic pairs, referring to Sherrington (1947), who claimed that muscles are organised in antagonistic pairs. In Avery & Idsardi's theory (unlike in RCVP), members of a pair cannot both be active in a single segment, nor can they both be distinctive in a single language.

[6] The left-to-right arrangement in this diagram does not imply any notion of linear order.

This geometry deviates somewhat from the one adopted in AE and bears a close resemblance to the original geometry that was proposed in Clements (1985). In Chapter 11 this model is compared to other models with which it shares certain properties.

The notation |C,V| or |c,v| stands for 'C or V'; it does *not* represent a combination of C and V.

I will refer to element specification in head subclasses as primary specifications and specifications in the dependent class as secondary specifications.[7] Both subclasses contain the two elements C and V; for convenience, the elements in the dependent are given in lower case when we explicitly consider them in secondary subclasses; when I refer to elements in general I will use upper case. Within each class, elements can occur alone or in combination (with dependency). A general characteristic of elements that are heads is their perceptual salience.

The motivation for regarding manner as the head class comes from the fact that manner specifications, specifically primary specifications, are determinants of the syllabic distribution of segments and of their sonority (which is of course related to syllabic distribution). Their relevance for sonority also correlates with the role of head in perceptual salience. Additionally, taking mobility ('spreadability') to be characteristic of dependents, I suggest that relative stability (resistance to 'spreading') is also a sign of heads.[8] This same criterion then also motivates the laryngeal and place classes as dependent classes, given the 'mobility' of laryngeal elements (specifically tone) and place elements.[9] Another property of heads is obligatoriness. All segments have a manner property. The laryngeal class is taken to be the outer dependent ('the specifier') because of its greater optionality (especially when interpreted as tone) and its greater mobility than the place elements, again clearly evident not only from the mobility of tonal elements, but also from phonation properties like voicing. Clements (1985) also proposed the three classes that RCVP acknowledges. In later work in 'FG' the manner node was removed on the argument that there are no processes that treat manner features as a group (see, e.g. McCarthy (1988)). However, group behaviour can also be demonstrated by relevance to phonotactic distribution and in this respect manner features do act like a group. I thus reject the argument that only 'processes' support grouping.[10]

In § 3.2.2 I discuss the question as to whether we need a separate C/V characterisation for major class distinctions. For the moment I will assume that these distinctions are encoded in terms of the syllabic structure.

[7] In terms of formal power, one might argue that GP's distinction between headed and non-headed elements is comparable to RCVP's distinction between primary and secondary elements. However, the details of how these distinctions are applied to distinctive properties are very different.

[8] See Gordon (2016: ch. 6) for a study showing that spreading processes involving major class or manner features are rare.

[9] In autosegmental approaches, mobility amounts to 'spreading' (adding association lines). My own approach to mobility in as far as it falls within phonology proper uses the notion of licensing (of variable elements); see van der Hulst (2018).

[10] In fact, if automatic processes are accounted for in the phonetic implementation, their relevance for grouping is dubious.

While (2) contains labels for element classes, a proper representation of segmental structure can omit all the labels that were provided in (1); that is, the various labels for the classes are for convenience only, having no formal status in RCVP. Each unit in the structure can be defined in purely structural terms:

(3)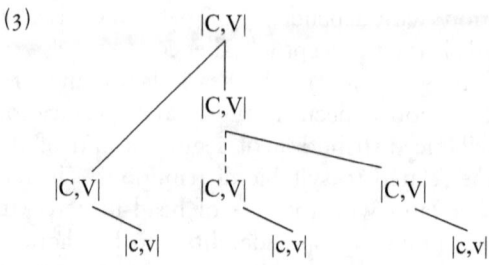

It is important to see that (2)/(3) is a pure dependency structure and thus not a constituent structure.[11]

The two elements C and V[12] (upper or lower case) are strictly formal units, which, depending on their position in the segmental structure (and their role as head or dependent), correlate with specific phonetic properties (as encoded in a set of interpretation functions; see (9) on p. 83). Additionally, their interpretation is also dependent on the syllabic position of the entire segmental structure, which means that both elements have different (albeit related) interpretations for each syllabic position in all three classes. The choice of the symbols ('C' and 'V', rather than, say 'א' and 'ע') for the two basic primes is motivated by the fact that within each class node, one element is favoured in the syllabic onset head position (the preferred locus of Consonants), while the other is favoured in the rhymal head position (the preferred locus of Vowels). In other words, the labels are mnemonic aids to the traditional idea that consonants and vowels are optimal segments in onset and rhymal head positions, respectively. (In § 3.2.2, I show how the C/V notation extends to syllable structure.) Since vowels are more sonorous than consonants and thus have greater perceptual salience, we can interpret the C/V opposition as standing for relative

---

[11] It is worth pointing out that in a dependency approach (which does not recognise constituents) there is no distinction between 'merging' and 'labelling'. In a dependency approach, the unit that a dependent adjoins to is automatically the head of the construction, which thus has the identity of the head unit. The issue of labelling simply does not exist in a dependency approach and is thus a non-issue.

[12] When referring to these two elements, I will not *consistently* place them between vertical lines (the exhaustivity operator). Nor do I use the brace notation, unless reference to the notion of a set of elements is necessary, which occurs when a distinction must be made between primary and secondary elements. See fn. 15 in Chapter 2 on the 'proper' use of these two notations.

Radical CV Phonology

perceptual salience, with V indicating higher perceptual salience. Indeed, this interpretation of the element opposition makes the C/V labelling notation arbitrary, which becomes especially clear when I apply RCVP to sign language phonology (see Chapter 10). Nevertheless, I will continue to use the C/V labelling, having taken note of the notational arbitrariness.

It cannot be left unnoticed that RCVP derives the traditional classes of 'features' (laryngeal, manner, place and major class) from an 'X-bar' type macrostructure. I speculate that this particular organisation, which appears to be shared between (pre-Merge versions of) syntax and phonology, in which heads can have two types of dependents ('complements' and 'specifiers/modifiers'), is perhaps not accidental, but rather reflects a 'deep' structural analogy between syntax and phonology; see den Dikken & van der Hulst (2020) for a strong defence of this view. X-bar theory was introduced as a constituent-based theory, augmented with the notion of headedness; see Kornai & Pullum (1990) for a critical discussion of some aspects of this idea, albeit with acceptance of the central notion of headedness. Following DP (AE), the head-dependency relation in RCVP is seen not as an augmentation of a constituent structure, but rather as replacing constituent structure.

Within each of the six subclasses in (2), in principle, an element can occur alone or in combination. This allows for a four-way distinction in which two structures are formally complex in combining two elements:[13]

(4)   C   C;V   V;C   V

In earlier accounts of RCVP, I would say that the maximal set of four structures results from a two-way splitting of the phonetic space that correlates with a phonological element class:

(5)   a.

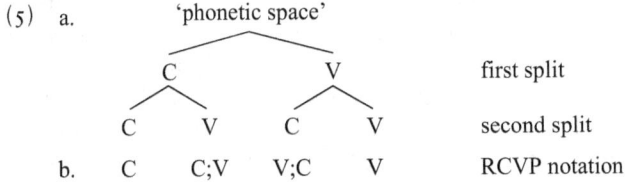

The first split produces two opposed categories that can be characterised with a single element, C or V. For example, in the head manner class for onset heads (when occupied by obstruents[14]), this split would produce stops and fricatives. A second split creates two 'smaller' categories, one of

---

[13] Recall that DP uses 'x;y' to indicate that x is the head and y is the dependent.
[14] In § 3.2.2 I discuss the theoretical position which allows only obstruents in the onset head position.

which is chacterised by an element combination. For example, still within the same class, a second split of the C category delivers plain stops, C, and fricative stops (affricates), C;V.

Even though this older notation has intuitive appeal, it is important to note that this two-way splitting diagram is *not*, as such, part of the representation of the segmental structure. It merely depicts how the splitting procedure *recursively* delivers four potentially distinctive phonetic categories that are formally represented as a single C or V or as combinations of these two elements, with a dependency relation imposed. Recursive splitting is due to what van der Hulst (2015b) calls *the Opponent Principle*. As was discussed in § 1.3.2, this principle (which is rooted in categorical perception; Harnad (1990)) directs a specific categorisation of phonetic substance that 'produces' feature systems for spoken and signed languages in the course of ontogenetic development.[15]

The question could now be asked whether the two simple structures in (4) and (5b), given the diagram in (5a), are not in actual fact complex by having two instances of the same element, which would in fact be suggested by the diagram in (6):

(6) C;C   C;V   V;C   V;V

While one could conceivably allow this to be the case, I will argue that no contrast is needed between a single and a double occurrence (which was actually used in an earlier version of RCVP; see § 2.2.4). Hence, RCVP is here defined to not allow the six-way contrast in (7), which can be expressed by the constraint that within each (sub)class each element can occur only once:

(7) C   C;C   C;V   V;C   V;V   V[16]

To express that the two outer categories in (7) are 'unmarked', in comparison with the two mixed structures, we could say that the dependent occurrence of the same element in (7) is universally implied. However, there is no specific gain in saying that, because, as we will see, while elements as heads or dependents have different phonetic interpretations, the phonetic interpretation of C as a dependent is included in the interpretation of C as a head, unless a V dependent is specified.

---

[15] Theoretically, each of the four categories could be split once more into two opponent categories. The phonetic differences between categories would then become very subtle and it is apparently the case that natural languages do not require going into such subtle differences to achieve phonemic contrast. Additionally, it may be that such subtler differences will be increasingly hard to distinguish perceptually, and to make articulatorily.

[16] See den Dikken & Dékány (2018). These authors discuss a general restriction on recursion which would precisely exclude the {X;X} cases.

As shown in (2) and (3), the two elements can also occur in a secondary (dependent) subclass in each class, which, if we allow a four-way distinction there as well, leads to the following set of possible structures for each element class:

(8) a. Plane primary (head) structures:

      C   C;V   V;C   V

   b. Primary structures with added secondary (dependent) structures:[17]

{{C}c}	{{C;V}c}	{{V;C}c}	{{V}c}
{{C}c;v}	{{C;V}c;v}	{{V;C}c;v}	{{V}c;v}
{{C}v;c}	{{C;V}v;c}	{{V;C}v;c}	{{V}v;c}
{{C}v}	{{C;V}v}	{{V;C}v}	{{V}v}

Note that RCVP admits, as one would expect, that the absence of a dependent *secondary* specification can be contrastive with the presence of such a specification. Dependents are never obligatory by default.[18] The 'option' of having structures that *lack* a head class element, which would create four additional possibilities, is simply not available as part of the RCVP syntax (because dependents cannot be more complex than heads and, moreover, because dependents need a head). As a consequence, elements in dependent nodes can only be activated when elements in corresponding head nodes have been activated.[19] RCVP also rules out a completely unspecified class node as a contrastive option.[20]

In (8a), the four-way distinction regards the combinations of elements within the head class, while (8b) represents a combination of each of

---

[17] Recall that as a matter of notational convention, I will use lower case symbols for the dependent class elements, following Anderson (2011b). I will also use the brace notation when a distinction between primary and secondary elements is made.

[18] In specific segmental systems it is possible in principle that a dependent is required in a certain class, although in such cases the presence of the dependent is always predictable and thus absent in a minimal-contrastive representation. An example would be the requirement that high vowels are advanced. See Chapter 9 where 'underspecification' is discussed.

[19] The idea that *within a class*, the head component elements must be activated before we get to the dependent elements correlates with the fact that within the segmental structure as a whole the manner class (more specifically its head elements, which account for aperture) must be activated before we get to the place component elements. It has been shown in typological studies of vowel systems that a minimal system would use only manner (i.e. aperture), leading to a so-called *vertical vowel system*, found in some northwest Caucasian languages (Kabardian, Adyghe); see Lass (1984). But there are no vowel systems that only use place distinctions. This further motivates the head status of the manner class (which expresses aperture for vowels and stricture for consonants).

[20] See § 7.2.1.1 for a discussion of the notion 'empty nucleus' which might qualify as a possible candidate for the representation of a completely unspecified segment.

these four options and one or two elements in the dependent class. The full array of structural possibilities in (8b) is unlikely to be exploited in any language. Moreover, as we will see, there is a strong tendency for the dependent class to only require the two simple structures c and v. The only reason for formally permitting complex dependent structures is that this may be required in the manner class for obstruent consonants and vowels (both syllabic heads), as I will show in Chapter 4. This means that the two middle rows in (8b) are mostly not used.

Structures for vowels are much more restricted than structures for consonants,[21] with one exception. There is only limited use for a dependent class in vowel place, and secondary vowel manner is typologically rare. However, in the case of the laryngeal class, consonants are more limited than vowels. In consonants, as we will see in Chapter 6, element combinations are excluded in *both* the head and the dependent dimension. For vowels, tonal properties do require combinations of the head laryngeal elements, which can be supplemented by a dependent class element (representing register differences[22]). These various points about dependent structures will be more fully explained and motivated in subsequent chapters.

The fact that combinations are (typically) allowed in head classes but not in dependent classes is perfectly 'natural' in a dependency approach, where, in fact, we expect to find complexity asymmetries between heads and dependents of precisely this kind. Heads allowing greater complexity than dependents is a typical manifestation of head/dependent asymmetries (Dresher & van der Hulst 1998). For example, as just mentioned, while manner and place allow complex structures in their head classes, this is not required for the laryngeal class, at least for consonants.[23] Both laryngeal and place are dependent classes, but the place class is included in the super class supralaryngeal. Thus, the fact that the place class (especially for consonants) will be shown to allow more structures than the laryngeal class is, once more, an example of an expected head/dependent asymmetry.

---

[21] This correlates with the fact that universally there are many more consonant distinctions than vowel distinctions, which in turn correlates with the greater role that consonants play in lexical phonemic contrast.

[22] The notion of register has also been invoked to explain the occurrence of four tone heights in Yip (1980). I restrict the use of register to the dependent class elements; see § 6.3.

[23] It should be noted that this does not square with the fact that consonants generally allow more contrast (see fn. 19). The fact of the matter is that languages can allow a four-way tonal contrast in the primary laryngeal class, especially Asian tone languages. This richness is not matched by phonation contrasts among consonants, at least not given the way in which RCVP represents phonation contrast, where the primary class only contrasts voicing with 'non-voicing' (which I refer to as 'tenseness'); see Chapter 6 for details.

In van der Hulst (2015b), it is proposed that the limitation of the set of elements to two units per subclass can be seen as resulting from a basic principle of categorisation, called *the Opponent Principle*, mentioned above in conjunction with the notion of successive splitting of phonetic spaces. Assuming that each subclass in (1) correlates with a 'phonetic space or dimension', C and V correlate with (and phonologise) opposite phonetic categories within such a dimension.[24] The opposing categories comprise two non-overlapping 'intervals' within which certain 'prototypical' phonetic events are optimal in terms of achieving maximal perceptual contrast with minimal articulatory effort.[25] While the elements are thus strictly formal cognitive units, they do correlate with phonetic events (or phonetic categories, covering a subrange of the relevant phonetic dimension). In fact, we can think of elements as (subconscious) cognitive percepts and proprioceptsthat correlate with such phonetic categories.[26]

It is important to stress that while the Opponent Principle delivers the maximally opposed elements C and V for each phonetic dimension, it does not as such deliver all the phonological categories that are needed for the analysis of all possible contrasts. For that, we need not only the two opposed elements, but also their combinations. This clearly shows that to explain phonological categorisation more is needed than the Opponent Principle alone. Crucially, we also need a Combinatorial Principle, and, moreover, a Dependency Principle, the last as an obligatory aspect of 'combinations'.

The proposal to represent contrastive segments in terms of element structures does not entail that phonemic[27] contrast must always be represented in terms of different, positively specified C/V structures. One might

---

[24] A question that could be asked is why the Opponent Principle (or an extended version thereof) does not enforce four phonetic spaces rather than three. I would argue that this principle regulates the element choices as the microlevel of the segmental organisation. With respect to the macrostructure, the 'omnipresent' tripartite X-bar principle comes into play.

[25] A phonetic category thus has a prototype character with optimal members, i.e. prototypes, and suboptimal members. This prototype functions as a perceptual magnet; see Kuhl (1991).

[26] As mentioned, I assume that elements have both an acoustic correlate (a percept) and an articulatory plan (a propriocept).
We could also call these mental units *concepts*, but because that term is usually associated with 'semantic' concepts, I will use the term *percepts* for mental units that correlate with phonetic substance.

[27] Since I use the term 'phonological' as comprising the study both of contrastive or distinctive units at the cognitive level and of phonetic categories (as well as the relation between them) at the utterance level, I will often refer to the level of cognitive ('symbolic' or 'formal') representations as 'phonemic', whereas the utterance level will be called 'phonetic'; this follows the terminological practice of American structuralists; see van der Hulst (2013, 2015b, 2016b).

argue that a strictly minimal way of representing contrast can make use of the 'zero option', that is, the absence of an element specification. Thus, a contrast within a given class could perhaps be expressed in terms of C versus zero or V versus zero, and one would expect that this choice would have implications for which category is deemed 'marked'. For example, if a language has a simple tonal contrast between H (= C in the laryngeal head class) and L (= V in the laryngeal head class), one could conceivably specify only one of them. In many analyses of tonal systems, phonologist have argued that only the H tone is literally marked. I will discuss the use of non-specification in this sense in Chapter 9. However, I will mention here that in RCVP use of the zero option is limited in various ways; for example, the zero option cannot be used in the head manner class, since a manner specification is obligatory for each segment.

While the elements are formal and as such 'substance-free', elements do of course correlate with phonetic 'events' (phonetic categories); in John Anderson's terms, the primes of phonology are *substance-based* (see Anderson (2011c)); see § 1.3.3. The relation between formal units such as elements and phonetic events is often referred to in terms like 'phonetic implementation', although phonetic implementation comprises much more by also accounting for co-articulatory, allophonic effects. Here I focus on the phonetic correlates of elements as they occur in syllabified segments, assuming that elements, given their structural context, have more or less invariant phonetic correlates.[28] Since the elements C and V occur in many different structural positions, they correlate with several different (albeit related) phonetic events. I will refer to these correlates as the phonetic interpretations or simply correlates of elements; other phonological approaches use the term 'exponents'. I do not think that it is possible to assign a very global 'phonetic meaning' to C and V 'out of context'. Rather, out of context, these two elements account for a general bias that each occurrence of them shares. The bias of C is that each occurrence of this element is preferred in a syllable position that itself has this label ('a syllabic onset') and the reverse holds for the V element ('a syllabic nucleus'). I will explain this further after having discussed the RCVP account of syllable structure in § 3.2.2; Chapter 8 is mostly devoted to this idea of preference. Also, as mentioned earlier, an even more abstract interpretation of the C and V categories refers to their relative perceptual salience, with C being less salient than V.

We will see that each of these two elements has a variety of phonetic 'meanings' or interpretations that in traditional binary feature systems are usually associated with different distinctive features. It is in this sense

---

[28] One reason for not excluding articulations as correlates of elements is that in several cases, while there is an invariant articulatory correlate, an invariant acoustic property can be hard to find locally in the segment; see Taylor (2006).

that RCVP provides a 'metatheory' of phonological features, albeit unary features and not binary ones.[29] Of course, RCVP cannot accommodate 'all features that have ever been proposed'. My claim is that it accommodates precisely those feature proposals that are the best motivated empirically and therefore most widely used.

In (9), I indicate some of these interpretation functions. The inclusion of, 'onset head' or 'nucleus head' implies that interpretation is dependent not only on the elements subclass (the head class in (9)), but also, as mentioned, on syllabic position:

(9) Phonetic Interpretation (PI) functions for elements in manner (Man) and laryngeal (Lar) *head* classes when occurring in syllabic head positions:[30]

PI (Man: C, head class, onset head)	= ⟦stop⟧
PI (Man: C, head class, nucleus head)	= ⟦high⟧
PI (Man: V, head class, onset head)	= ⟦fricative⟧
PI (Man: V, head class, nucleus head)	= ⟦low⟧
PI (Place: C, head class, onset head)	= ⟦palatal⟧
PI (Place: C, head class, nucleus head)	= ⟦front⟧
PI (Place: V, head class, onset head)	= ⟦labial⟧
PI (Place: V, head class, nucleus head)	= ⟦round⟧
PI (Lar: C, head class, onset head)	= ⟦tense⟧
PI (Lar: C, head class, nucleus head)	= ⟦high tone⟧
PI (Lar: V, head class, onset head)	= ⟦voiced⟧
PI (Lar: V, head class, nucleus head)	= ⟦low tone⟧

The phonetic details of interpretations are, to some extent, language-specific. The property 'rhotic', for example, which will be expressed as a manner distinction for *sonorant* consonants, has rather different phonetic manifestations in different languages, so much so that it has been argued that there is no unifying phonetic property. This issue is discussed in detail in Navarro (2018), who makes a convincing argument for the claim that

---

[29] That said, RCVP captures the idea of binarity by reducing all contrast to a binary opposition between C and V, whose phonetic interpretations often resemble the interpretation of the two values of traditional binary features.

[30] I focus here on articulatory interpretations. There are also (psycho-)acoustic interpretations; see § 1.3.1. The '⟦. . .⟧' indicate 'phonetic interpretation/implementation'. It cannot escape our attention that the labels for these phonetic interpretations look a lot like traditional binary feature labels, while the use of double brackets is borrowed from a common usage for the representation of meanings that are assigned to syntactic objects.

there is nonetheless a unifying phonological representation. Another extreme example concerns ⟦ATR⟧, which is represented in RCVP by a C element in the dependent place class of vowels (see § 5.3.2). Different languages show rather different phonetic correlates of this element, which means that the label ATR is only a rough indication of the articulatory mechanisms that can be involved. It has been observed that the acoustic goals of the expanded correlate can be achieved in multiple ways, including lowering the larynx, expansion of the pharyngeal wall or activity of the epiglottis, for example; see Lindau (1979) and Moisik (2013). This specific example is discussed in detail in van der Hulst (2018: ch. 3).

In conclusion, the phonetic interpretation of an element is dependent on:

(10) a. Being a C or V element
b. Being a head or a dependent in a subclass
c. Occurring in a head or dependent subclass
d. Its syllabic position

The reduction of a set of phonetic properties that correspond to different features in traditional feature systems to either C or V is reminiscent of reducing a set of phonetic segments to a single phoneme. Such a reduction (albeit not uncontested; see § 1.3.5) is possible when phonetic segments occur in *complementary distribution*, for instance by occupying different structural positions in the syllable, foot or word. My claim is that the phonetic interpretations of C and V are likewise in complementary distribution. For example, the elements in the head laryngeal class are interpreted as tonal properties when they occur in the syllable head (nucleus), whereas they are interpreted as phonation properties when they occur in the onset head. In this sense tonal properties and phonation properties are in complementary distribution. The idea that tonal and phonation properties are interpretations of the same set of primes was originally proposed in Halle & Stevens (1971), and RCVP accommodates this proposal in a strong form, by claiming that tone and phonation are in complementary distribution.[31] Likewise, in the manner class, stricture in consonants (as captured by the binary feature [±continuant]) is claimed to be in complementary distribution with height (aperture) in vowels.

We expect the different interpretations of elements in different positions to be phonetically related (just as allophones of a phoneme are supposed to be phonetically similar) and we also expect phonological generalisations to express correlations between instances of the same element that occur in different classes and syllabic positions. As an example, I mention the fact that V correlates with the property of being

---

[31] This claim is not without empirical challenges, which I discuss in § 6.4.4.

a sonorant in the syllabic V position ('the nucleus'), whereas it correlates with voicing in the laryngeal head class for consonants. The correlation between [+sonorant] and [+voice] has often been noted. It is captured by a redundancy rule in binary systems:

(11)   [+sonorant] → [+voice]

In RCVP the same redundancy reflects the general fact that the implied dependency holds between occurrences of the same element in different structural positions:

(12)   [Syllabic: V] → [Laryngeal: V]

A similar dependency can be observed between [+high] and [+ATR], which in RCVP are also interpretations of the same element C (in the manner head class and the dependent place class, respectively). It is thus an advantage of RCVP that it is possible to reduce to a general format redundancy statements which in a traditional feature system essentially express random correlations between formally different features, as:

(13)   X:α → Y:α

Here 'X' and 'Y' are variables for structural positions, while 'α' ranges over C and V. In Chapter 8 I will present a systematic exploitation of the 'universal redundancy or preference rule' in (13), which expresses what I call Harmony (or Bias).

As discussed in § 1.4, a guiding principle of DP is the SAA, which states that representations in phonology and syntax differ mostly due to the fact that these two planes have different sets of basic categories (the so-called 'alphabets'), given that they are grounded in different substances. Since phonology and syntax categorise different cognitive substances (phonetic percepts and semantic concepts, respectively), we expect their sets of basic categories to be different, both in number and in nature. What the SAA states is that phonological structure and syntactic structure display identical *structural relations*, such as, in particular, the relation of dependency between head and dependents, recursion and perhaps also maximal binarity of structure.[32] However, I assume that structural analogy also promotes 'replication' of the same structures *within* planes. RCVP postulates that the various classes within the segment are structurally analogous to the extent that all make use of the same C/V structures (namely those in (8)).

Before turning to the characterisation of syllabic positions, I return to the idea that the four-way array in (8a) can be seen as an instance

---

[32] See den Dikken & van der Hulst (2020) for the strong claim that there is only one type of syntax, which generalises over phonology and 'syntax'.

of *recursive splitting*, in that the category corresponding to each polar element can be split into two smaller categories.[33]

(14) a.

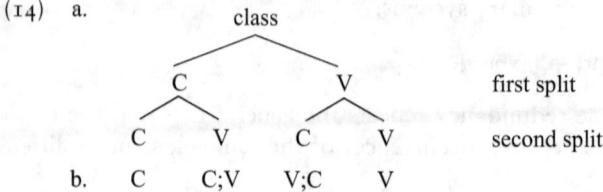

The effect of the second split is formally captured in the dependency model by allowing the polar elements to combine, as in (14b), to create complex, intermediate categories. One might now ask whether this recursive split of categories halts after one cycle. At first sight, given that we have distinguished a head and dependent subclass, one could regard the dependent class as providing a further recursive split of the head categories:

(15)

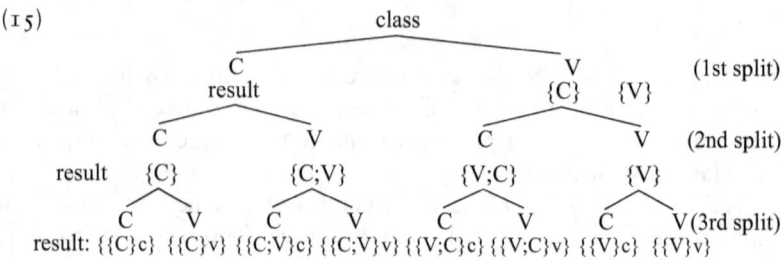

This results in twelve categories. However, note that while the structures resulting from the second split are *not* added to those of the first (which would produce six categories, namely C, V plus C;C,C;V, V;C and V;V), the structure resulting from the third split *is* added to those that result from the second split (leading to the sixteen categories in (8b)). This means that splitting *within* a subclass is not additive (it literally divides a category into two new categories, giving four categories), whereas the 'splitting' that produces a secondary class is additive (it adds an optional set of specifications to the categories we already have). I take this to mean that the addition of secondary properties is *not* the result of a third recursive split, but rather that splitting within the head and

---

[33] Salting (2005) proposes a model, 'the nested subregister model', which also represents phonological categories in terms of a double split. He applies this to vowel height and location categories and discusses the parallels of his model with RCVP; see § 11.3.2. Staun (2013) refers to this notion of splitting as 'fission'.

dependent class is separate and that the head/dependent subclass split is indeed a subclass division.

Let us now return to the question of whether the dependent class itself allows a recursive second split (as in fact we assumed in (8b)):

(16)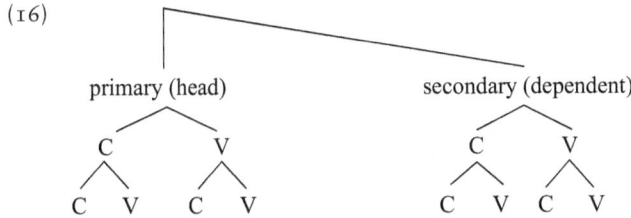

As mentioned earlier, the utility of *complex* secondary structures (c;v, v;c) is very limited. This finding squares with the overall head/dependency asymmetry discussed in Dresher & van der Hulst (1998), which states that a lesser degree of complexity is a hallmark of dependent units. Perhaps it is only in the manner class (more convincingly so for consonants than for vowels) that the dependent class is allowed to engage in combinations. I refer to Chapter 4 where I discuss manner contrast.

Having outlined the RCVP model, I will now draw attention to some specific differences between RCVP and (standard) DP and GP, as well as some commonalities, summarising points made more extensively in Chapter 2. Firstly, the three models employ different sets of elements (and different versions of each approach may have different elements as well). Secondly, as I have shown in § 2.3, there is a sense in which the choice of only two elements in RCVP converges with a particular version of GP that only adopts six elements (as assumed in Backley 2011). I here repeat (30) from that section as (17):

(17) The 'geometry' of elements in RCVP

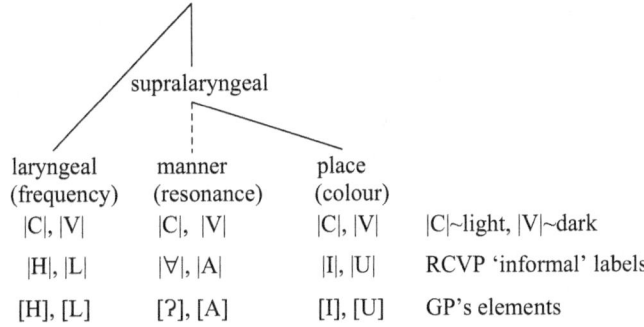

RCVP can reduce the set of six to a set of two, because, unlike GP, RCVP adopts the notion of element grouping. I here also remind the reader that I will be using the informal labels on the second line to avoid more cumbersome sequences of C's and V's as well as reference to the classes. For example, |H| is used as a short head for [Lar: C, head class, nucleus head]; see (9). Thirdly, it is thus crucial that RCVP formally recognises element *classes*, as does DP, while GP does not. The RCVP macrostructure differs from that of DP and is more in line with the one originally proposed in Clements (1985). Fourthly, the idea that elements generalise over vowels and consonants is shared with both DP and GP, and restores a tradition in phonology that was started in Jakobson, Fant & Halle (1952), but abandoned in Chomsky & Halle (1968), although DP and GP differ from Jakobson, Fant and Halle's proposal in exclusively capitalising on the acoustic nature of elements.[34] RCVP also shares with KLV85 a notational system in which elements are represented on 'lines' (which are similar to the 'autosegmental tiers' of Goldsmith (1976a, 1976b),[35] as well as the idea that, for instance, vowel harmony is accounted for in terms of a lateral licensing relation between elements in adjacent syllable heads, where an element in some privileged position *licenses* the same element in other nuclei under strict locality. These aspects of the theory are extensively used in van der Hulst (2018).

We have also seen that DP and GP make somewhat different usage of the dependency relation. RCVP rigidly applies the head-dependency relation, which means that I do not recognise structures in which elements stand in a relationship of 'mutual dependency', as is possible in DP, nor do I use the diacritic headed/non-headed distinction of GP. Thus, I only allow (18a) and (18b) and exclude the possibilities in (18c):

(18) a. A is the head of B.
 b. B is the head of A.
 c. i. DP: A and B are 'mutually dependent'.
  ii. GP: Elements can be headed or non-headed.

In contrast to (18c), RCVP uses headedness *obligatorily* to acknowledge the asymmetry that arises from merging (maximally two) elements per class node; mono-elemental structures are headed by default. Thus, in RCVP, |A| (or its RCVP 'full' equivalent) cannot be distinct from |A̲|, nor is |AI| distinct from either |A̲I| or |AI̲|.

---

[34] The idea of having a unified set of primes has also been pursued in work within the model of FG (see, for example, Clements (1991a)); see Chapter 11.
[35] However, this notational system, which is not used in this book, is used for convenience in van der Hulst (2018); it does not actually have a theoretical status in the RCVP model.

3.2.2 Syllable structure

Having outlined the general framework of RCVP, and before turning to a more detailed account of the phonetic interpretations of intra-segmental C/V structures in each of the three classes in subsequent chapters, I will briefly discuss the way in which RCVP represents syllable structure. This is necessary because, as discussed above, the interpretation of intra-segmental C/V structures is sensitive to the syllabic positions of a segment. Faithful to the basic premise of RCVP, the syllable itself is a combination of the C and V units, which, if no further splitting applies, delivers the core CV syllable structure that all languages have. If languages exceed this minimal CV syllable, this results from splitting the C and/or V unit, which produces binary branching onsets and rhymes, respectively:

(19) a.   syllabic positions

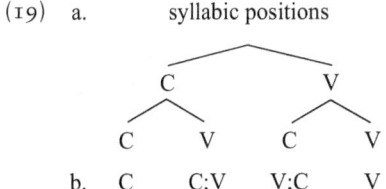

b.   C   C;V   V;C   V

While the four-way division as such implies no linearisation, when combined into a syllable structure, linear sequencing will be dictated by some version of the well-known 'Sonority Sequencing Generalisation', according to which the sonority level rises towards the nucleus and then lowers (see Clements (1990a) for a detailed discussion and references):

(20) a.   syllabic positions, linearised

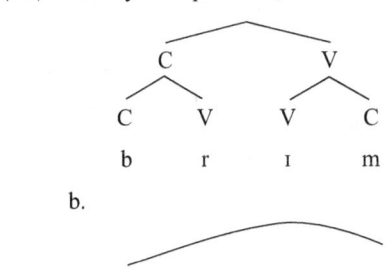

A proper dependency representation of a syllable structure that contains all four syllabic categories is as follows (adding convenient unit labels for each construction and for each of the four segmental positions, although the labels have no formal status; they are just used for convenience when I refer to syllabic units):

(21) a.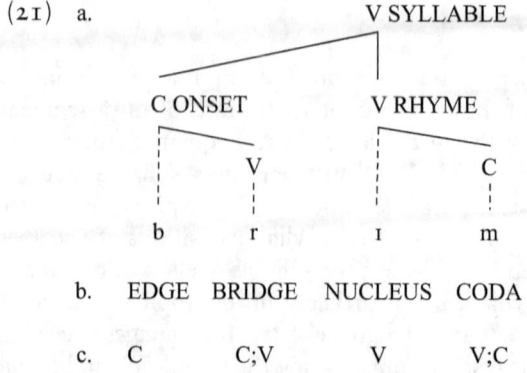

b.   EDGE   BRIDGE   NUCLEUS   CODA

c.   C   C;V   V   V;C

I assume a strict dependency model, which means that there is no 'constituent structure'.[36]

We should note that the C/V units that make up syllabic nodes are associated with interpretation functions that assign phonetic implementations that correspond to the traditional major class features [consonantal] and [sonorant], as in (22):[37]

(22)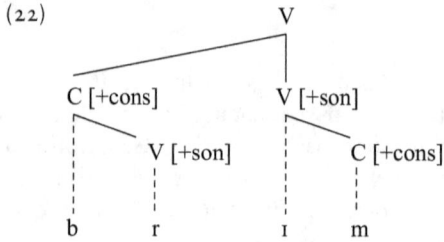

This approach to syllable structure does not appeal to a skeletal tier (as in Clements and Keyser (1983)), but in effect the C and V labels in (22) function like a skeletal tier, which allows, for example, multiple 'association' of a segmental structure to more than one skeletal position; see § 4.5. Example (22) mimics the so-called onset/rhyme approach to syllable structure and is thus radically different from the moraic approach (see Hayes (1986b)). The notion 'syllable weight' (with reference to stress) appeals not to counting morae, but rather to the complexity of the rhyme unit. I refer to van der Hulst (in prep.) for further discussion.

---

[36] Perhaps there is a resemblance between seeing all syntagmatic relation in terms of dependency and seeing them in terms of 'lateral licensing', as in Scheer (2004), among others.

[37] The structural expression of major class is similar in spirit to proposals in Golston & van der Hulst (1999).

As we will see in subsequent chapters, we can often associate the interpretation of elements as heads or dependent with different traditional feature labels. Moreover the head and dependent interpretation correlate with the plus and minus value of a single traditional feature (see (5) in § 4.2.1.1). In the case at hand, this is not so for the interpretation of the head occurrences. Onset segments share being consonants, and rhyme segments share being sonorants. There is no single traditional feature that can cover the oppositions between consonants and sonorants. Also, I cannot come up with a single feature for the dependent occurrence labels. The reason for this is that all sonorant consonants can occur in both positions. This, then, results in (23), which captures the specifications in (22).[38]

(23)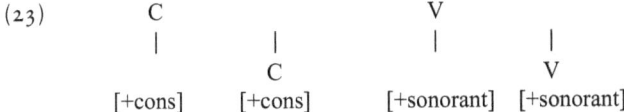

Hence, in (22)/(23) I have assigned the same interpretation to both C and V in their different roles as heads or dependents. We must then assume that in both cases the presence of a dependent, a sonorant consonant, forces the head to 'polarise' in order to be consistent with the Sonority Sequencing Generalisation. This means that, effectively, the onset head is interpreted as [–son] and the nucleus as [–cons] when these units have a dependent. The notation in (22) might suggest that an onset head in the absence of a dependent can be any consonant, including obstruents and sonorant consonants, while the nucleus, in the absence of a dependent, can contain any sonorant, including vowels and sonorant consonants. While this is true in both cases, I will argue below that sonorant consonants in onset head position or rhyme head position cannot be represented as bare C or bare V. Instead sonorants as onset head or rhyme heads must be represented as C,V structures (just as when they are dependents) albeit with subjunction; see (26) and (27) below.

[38] There is a difference in preference for sonorants in the edge and the coda. In the edge position, nasals seem to be dispreferred, whereas a case could be made for saying that nasals are preferred coda (see VanDam (2004) and see § 4.3.3). This would result in:

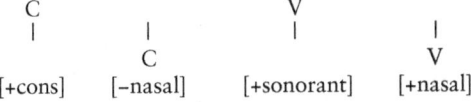

I will not adopt this because the interpretations for C and V are not meant to be tendencies. Moreover, we still use two different features for the head occurrences. We cannot assign [–sonorant] to C as a head, because that incorrectly says that edge consonants are [–sonorant]. For whatever reason (which I cannot 'pin down'), things work a little differently for the syllabic major class distinctions.

In 'classical' GP (KLV90), it was assumed that a syllable with four positions represents the universally maximal expansion of a syllable that can occur freely (i.e. word-internally, as well as at the word beginning and end, although the edges may allow 'extra segments'[39]). This would once more seem to indicate that there is, in fact, a maximal two-way split that universally limits the degree of complexity within each domain, whether an element class or a structural unit like the syllable. Whereas element groups represent paradigmatic dimensions and the syllables represent the syntagmatic dimension, the structural possibilities are the same, indeed structurally analogous. It is significant that both dimensions, whether paradigmatic or syntagmatic, are subject to the same system of categorisation as captured by the C/V syntax.

The claim that syllables maximally contain four 'core' positions faces problems because syllables that occur at the word edges may display additional complexity. In English and Dutch, for example, the left edge can have triconsonantal structures of a limited variety. They have to start with [s] followed by an obstruent + liquid cluster (see Fudge (1987); Trommelen (1983); van der Hulst (1984)). On the right edge, we find so-called superheavy rhymes containing a tense vowel followed by a consonant, or a lax vowel followed by two consonants.[40] If we follow the RCVP syntax which distinguishes between a head and dependent class, we could allow a secondary class of syllabic positions (which, I will assume, does not allow combinations):

(24) syllabic positions

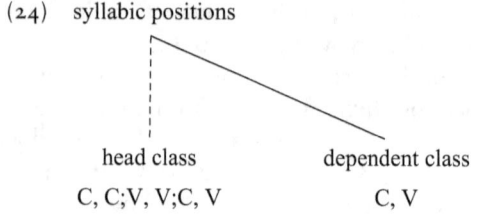

head class   dependent class
C, C;V, V;C, V   C, V

In the syllable structure, these extra positions occur as *adjuncts* to the units that contain the primary structures:[41]

---

[39] These extra segments of course need an account. GP opts for allowing syllables with empty nuclei, while DP allows 'adjunction'; see below.

[40] In English and Dutch, a further word-final syllabic unit (called the 'appendix') is possible. We do not discuss this unit, an additional rhymal adjunction, here (see Fudge (1987); van der Hulst (1984)). See Anderson (2011c) for a similar treatment of syllable structure, with some extra notation that is omitted here.

[41] I choose the 'unusual word' 'splonk' because it shows a maximal structure. It is a frequently used onomatopoeic word, but it is also a brand name of a spam eliminator on the Internet.

(25)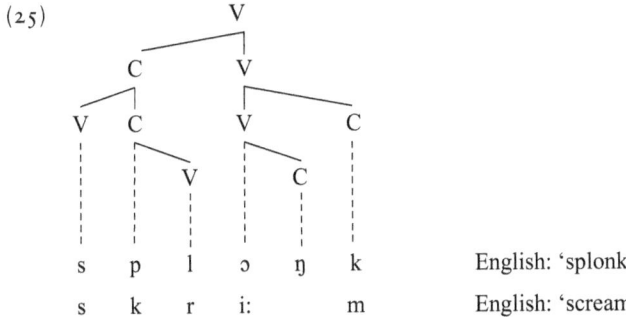

English: 'splonk'
English: 'scream'

A polysystematic view on segmental inventories holds that each syllabic position can have its own contrastive set of segments; see § 1.3.5. The onset head adjunct has a singleton set in English and Dutch, namely [s].[42] The rhymal adjunct comprises all consonants, but is limited to obstruents if they occur after a sonorant consonant; for Dutch see Trommelen (1983) and van der Hulst (1984).

It is interesting that the C/V structure for the onset dependent is C;V, while the structure for the coda is V;C. This suggests that the onset dependent is 'stronger', that is, more C-like than the coda position, which comes out as weaker (and more 'sonorant'). I will argue in the next section that both positions are universally reserved for sonorant consonants. The difference between the C/V structures of the two positions suggests that sonorant consonants are phonetically stronger in the onset than the rhyme, which is empirically shown by the difference, for example in English, between liquids in the onset and in the coda, where the latter have a much weaker constriction. It might be suggested that the difference between the bridge and the coda position, apart from having an effect on the phonetic implementation of sonorant consonants, may also lead to the latter only allowing a subset of sonorant consonants. I return to this issue in the next section.

Let us now return to the obvious point that it is not the case that only obstruents can appear in the edge position. Sonorant consonants can also form onsets by themselves and in that case they occupy the edge position. Likewise, we must be able to represent syllabic consonants, which means that the nucleus must be able to contain consonantal segments. To address these necessities, in (26a) and (26b) I propose two different structures for sonorant consonants when occurring as onset heads (26a) and as onset dependents (26b):

---

[42] It has also been proposed that /s/+obstruent clusters should be regarded as a kind of complex segment, i.e. 'reversed affricates' (see Ewen (1980a); van de Weijer (1996) for discussion, and references cited there). I will not here try to evaluate the different predictions these different approaches make.

(26) a.

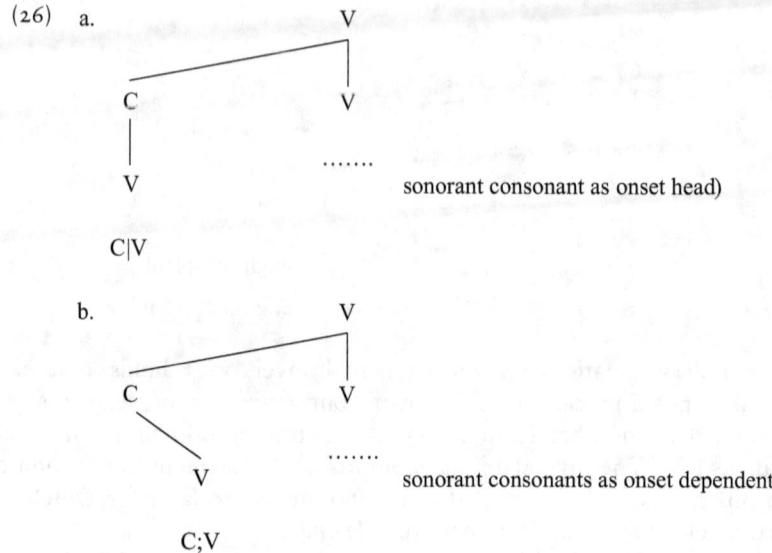

sonorant consonant as onset head)

b.

sonorant consonants as onset dependent

In both cases V is dependent on C and yet the syllabic position will reflect the difference between V being subjoined or adjoined to C. In (26a) I represent the former structure notationally as C|V, indicating that V is subjoined to C, rather than being adjoined as in (28b). The essential difference between X|Y and X;Y is that the latter leads to a linear order of both nodes, while the former does not.

Likewise, there are two different structures for syllabic sonorant consonants and coda sonorant consonants:

(27) a.

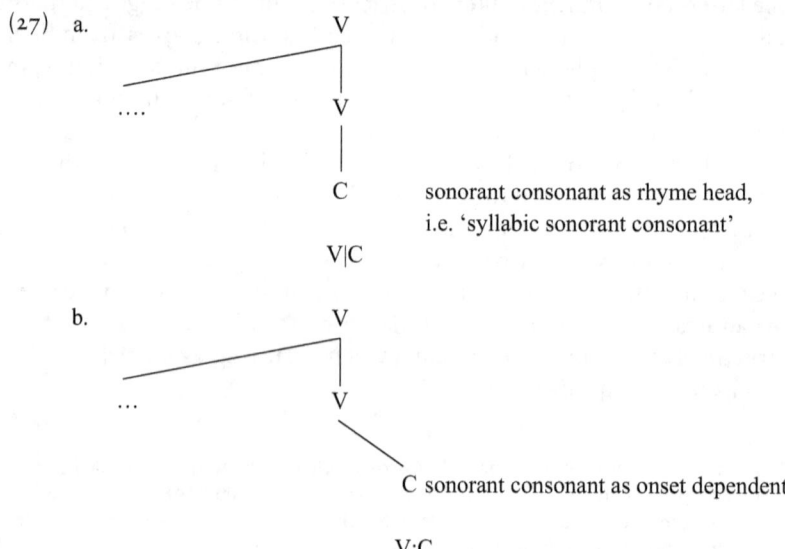

sonorant consonant as rhyme head, i.e. 'syllabic sonorant consonant'

b.

C sonorant consonant as onset dependent

Radical CV Phonology   95

The distinction between subjunction and adjunction has already been used in the representation of the syllable as a whole, in which the V node is subjoined to itself so that the onset and the coda can be dependents at two different levels.[43] I refer to Böhm (2018) for a discussion of the distinction between adjunction and subjunction and the legitimacy of both in a dependency approach.[44]

Anderson (1987a) questions the necessity of specifying the linear order of segments in the lexicon, if segments are organised in a syllabic structure. The argument is that an onset that groups an obstruent and a sonorant consonant will necessarily order these two consonants in that order if we assume that linear order can be predicted from the Sonority Sequencing Generalisation. The same point applies to segments that form a rhyme. Golston & van der Hulst (1999) accept this point, stating that if lexical representations are syllabified, the linear order of segments is predictable. These authors cite various arguments for why syllable structure is present in lexical representations, both linguistic and psycholinguistic. Linguistic evidence comes from the representation of geminate consonants and long vowels, which require two syllabic terminal positions, assuming a standard non-linear account. Also, standardly minimality requirements and templatic morphology make reference to prosodic, including syllabic, structure. Psycholinguistic evidence comes from tip-of-the-tongue phenomena and various kinds of speech errors. In the RCVP model I will therefore also assume that segments within a syllabic unit are not linearly ordered.[45] The linear order of onset sand rhyme can also be predicted given that the rhyme contains the sonority peak. Formally, the way in which the syllabic distribution of segments is stored amounts to specifying the syllabic affiliation for each segment in terms of a syllabic C/V specification conforming to (22), (26) and (27):

(28) a.   C C;V   V   V;C
            b   r   ɪ   m

      b.   C|V   V   V;C
            r   ɪ   m

      c.   V|C
            (bott)   m

---

[43] I will also invoke this distinction in § 3.2.5 where I discuss recursion in syllable structure.
[44] In the syntactic plane, Anderson (2011a) uses the subjunction structure to represent category conversion in the lexicon, e.g. from noun to verb or vice versa.
[45] I will leave open here whether we can extend the elimination of linear order above the level of the syllable, although it is easy to see that syllables forming a foot can also be ordered, given that the foot type is fixed for the language as a whole.

Given that major class distinctions are interpretations of syllabic positions and given that segments in the lexicon are syllabified, meaning they come with a piece of syllable structure, there is no need for an independent layer of major class specifications; the piece of syllabic structure that segments 'wear on their sleeves' is the major class specification. Still, the syllabic specifications in (28) are not the same as major class features that in some proposals are specified 'in the root node' (see McCarthy (1988)), because in these proposals the major class specifications are not meant to be a direct encoding of the syllabic distributions of segments. In the present framework it does not make sense to think of the syllabic specification as being specified 'in the root node'. Given that manner specifications are the head of the segmental structure, it will be those specifications that are projected upwards and will be visible on the root node, so that they can interact directly with the syllabic affiliation specification.[46] Thus, the syllabic specification is independent of the segmental structure and one can think of the metaphor 'wearing on the sleeve' as referring to an association relation.

(29)   C   C;V   V   V;C
       :   :   :   :
       b   r   I   m

In this proposal, syllable structure is not a projection of segmental structure. Rather it is specified in a separate 'tier' in association with the segmental structure.

3.2.3 Empirical issues

The proposal in the previous section makes very strong predictions about the maximal complexity of syllables and which segment types can occur in syllabic positions. Both onset and rhyme can be maximally binary branching. In addition, we disallow onsets consisting of two obstruents, two sonorant consonants and sonorant consonant followed by an obstruent. We also disallow obstruents to function as nuclei and as codas.

---

[46] Alternatively, I point out that the syllabic specifications can be formalised in terms of the slash notation from categorial grammar. The two ways in which sonorant consonants as syllabic dependents could be represented using that notation would be as follows:

    C   C\C   V   V\V
    b   r   I   m

The slash notation is independently useful to represent lax vowels in Germanic languages, which must be followed by a tautosyllabic consonant: V/C. I will here not explore this formalism; see also Anderson (2011c).

A similarly strict view was adopted by proponents of GP (see KLV90). The GP view is in line with the specific formulation of the Sonority Sequencing Generalisation that is proposed in Clements (1990a), who suggested that the ideal sonority profile for the syllable involves a sharp rise and then a smooth decline in sonority. But this strict view obviously faces a host of empirical problems. For example, this position requires a reconsideration of so-called syllabic obstruents in Tashlhiyt Berber (see Dell & Elmedlaoui (2002)) and other languages (see Bell (1978)). It also needs to deal with the fact that in languages such as English and Dutch obstruents would appear to occur in codas almost as freely as sonorant consonants. Finally, consideration should be given to numerous cases in which consonant clusters in apparent onsets are not a sequence of an obstruent followed by a sonorant consonant, or cases in which the number of onset consonants exceeds two; see Morelli (1999) and Kreitman (2008).

There is a way to accommodate a more liberal view on the relationship between syllabic positions and segment types. To allow, for example, obstruents in the syllabic nucleus or in onset dependent position, it would be necessary to distinguish between a major class specification and a syllabic affiliation, which, as we would expect,[47] can both be expressed in terms of the same set of C/V specifications.

In this view, the relationship between major class specification and a syllabic affiliation specification can be said to involve a *preference ranking*, as in (29), which states that the 'bias' or 'preference' of each syllabic position involves a complete match between both specifications. As for other major classes that need to be allowed, the most liberal view would allow all three major classes in each position in a particular order of preference, as determined by the C/V specification of the syllabic positions. The top choice involves a complete identity between the syllabic position and the major class specification:

(30) syllabic position   C   C;V   V   V;C
                          :   :   :   :
     major class   C   C;V   V   V;C
                          C;V   V;C   V;C   C;V
                          V;C   C   C;V   V
                          V   V   C   C

---

[47] I have just argued that the syllabic C/V labelling encodes major class differences. Hence we would specify major class information twice, once as a syllabic template and once as a major class property of segments.

In this book it has not been my intention to decide on the choice between the liberal and the strict viewpoint on the relation between syllabic positions and segment types, but I will proceed here on the assumption that the strict view leads to productive inquiries into the specific nature of segmental sequences that deviate from this view. This means that I do not need major class specifications as an independent layer of information.

Given this strict view on syllable structure, we have to recognise that some languages may impose restrictions that narrow down even this restricted set of options. Indeed, there are languages that disallow high sonority consonants (specifically liquids and glides) from onset head position; see Gordon (2016), Smith (2002) and Flack (2007a). If, for example, only nasals are allowed to be onset heads, we have to specify that only sonorant consonants that exhaustively contain C in their *manner* class are allowed, in other words, the most C-like sonorant consonants. Indeed, in this case we are also dealing with preferences which, as I will show in Chapter 8, can be stated in terms of preference rankings between syllabic specifications and manner specifications.

While it is perhaps expected in this section, I postpone a discussion of the representation of long vowels, diphthongs and geminates to § 4.5, since we will first need to have discussed manner specifications, which are the subject of Chapter 4.

3.2.4 *The segment–syllable connection*

In this section I discuss two views on the relationship between the segment and syllable level, one assuming an integration, and the other a separation of both levels.

Kehrein & Golston (2004) and Fulop & Golston (2008) adopt the idea that laryngeal and place properties are properties of syllable nodes, which they take to be onset, nucleus and coda (see also Golston & Kehrein (1998)). The reason for this proposal is that these authors' typological studies show that members of these syllabic categories cannot have different laryngeal or place specifications.[48] Moreover, these properties are typically manifested on the head of these units. The latter does not automatically follow from assigning these properties to the nodes that dominate these units without a notion of headedness and a 'percolation convention' that would trickle these properties down to head nodes. In the spirit of this idea, the first view on the segment–syllable connection that is consistent with RCVP would be to assume that laryngeal and place properties are specified as properties of onset and rhymes:

---

[48] For onset clusters, a similar point is made in Hirst (1985, 1995).

(31)

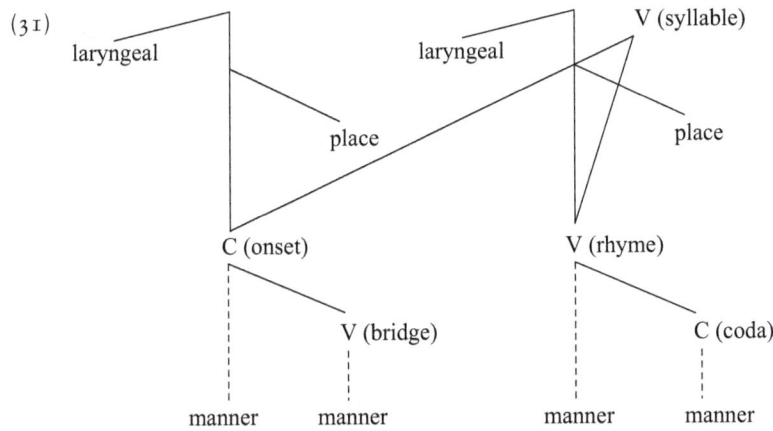

In this model, onset dependent and rhyme dependents cannot have distinctive specifications for place or laryngeal elements. These positions only allow distinctive manner elements. This structure does allow sonorant consonants in onset head and rhymal head to have laryngeal and place specifications. The proposal in (31) abandons 'segmental integrity'.

Another way to formalise the same restriction is to maintain segmental integrity and say that the segmental structure for dependent nodes is less complex and can only contain a manner node. Such an asymmetry between the rhymal heads and dependents is to be expected:

(32)

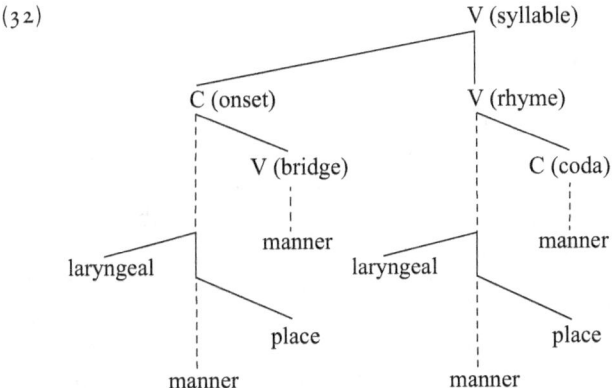

As we will see in Chapters 4 and 5, we need to make some special provisions for the bridge and coda positions because both seem to require limited place distinctions while the coda position can have tonal distinctions. Both necessities, if convincing, would argue in favour of the second alternative, which maintains a strict segregation between segmental and syllabic structure, so that the possibility remains open of providing the bridge and coda with non-manner specifications.

3.2.5 Recursivity in syllables or foot structure in Radical CV Phonology

In this section,[49] I will briefly extend the RCVP approach to foot structure. My goal here is not to discuss notions of accent and rhythm (see van der Hulst (in prep.)). Rather, I want to discuss the possibility of recursion in syllable structure, here understood as the possibility of embedding syllables inside syllables, that is, self-embedding recursion. A commonly held view in theoretical linguistics is that the formal organisation of phonology is fundamentally different from that of syntax. Claims to that effect in the literature concern either representational aspects or derivational ones (cf. Bromberger & Halle (1989): phonology has extrinsic rule ordering, syntax does not). In the representational domain, it is customary to state that whereas recursion is a fundamental property of syntax, phonological structure is non-recursive:

> Recursion consists of embedding a constituent in a constituent of the same type, for example a relative clause inside a relative clause [...]. This does not exist in phonological structure: a syllable, for instance, cannot be embedded in another syllable. (Pinker & Jackendoff (2005: 10))
>
> syntax has recursive structures, whereas phonology does not. (Neeleman & van de Koot 2006: 1524)
>
> syllabic structure is devoid of anything resembling recursion. (Bickerton 2000)

Neeleman & van de Koot (2006: 1524), as well as Scheer (2013), reject the idea that phonological organisation appeals to any notion of *constituency;* see also Carr (2006) for scepticism regarding syntax–phonology parallelism. Indeed, it should be noted that discussions about phonological structure and recursion are always carried out in a constituency-based approach. In this book, I have adopted a dependency approach which does not involve constituency. Nevertheless, it seems to me that the issue of recursion can also be addressed in a dependency approach. Elsewhere, I have argued that there is no good reason to deny phonology the formal option of recursion; see van der Hulst (2010). This argument was carried out with reference to a constituency view of phonological structure, augmented with head-dependency. An extension of this proposal, which pushes analogies between phonology and

---

[49] This section is partly based on van der Hulst (2010) and den Dikken & van der Hulst (2020).

current theories of syntax, can be found in den Dikken & van der Hulst (2020). In these two articles, several proposals are discussed by linguists who have pushed for structural analogies between syllable structure and sentence or phrasal structure (Kuryłowicz (1947); Pike & Pike (1947); Fudge (1987)):

(33) a.

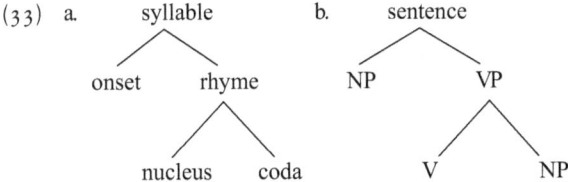

More recent claims to the same effect can be found in Levin (1985), Carstairs-McCarthy (1999) and Völtz (1999), among others.

Whatever the merit of these parallels, no mention is made in these works of a potential further parallelism that would involve recursion. Most writers, while acknowledging that phonotactic structure is constituency-based (and making reference to X-bar(ish) organisation of syllables), propose that phonological (often called 'prosodic') constituency is 'strictly layered', which means that no constituent contains a constituent of the same type. This explicitly bars (self-embedding) recursion. With reference to 'higher' phonological/prosodic structure, recursion *has* been recognised, but here it is then said to reflect the recursive structure of syntax, at least to some extent (Ladd (2008); Wagner (2005); van der Hulst (2010); Hunyadi (2010)).[50] Limiting recursion in phonology to units that have morphosyntactic structure is tantamount to saying that no recursion will be found *within* morphemes (or simplex words), where whatever structure exists cannot be a mapping from morphosyntactic structure.

However, some phonologists – whose proposals differ in several ways that will not concern us here – have argued that syllable structure can display recursion (Smith (1999); N. Smith (2003); Garcia Bellido (2005); van de Weijer & Zhang (2008); van der Hulst (2010)). Following van der Hulst (2010), the present section will support the idea that syllable structure shares non-trivial properties with syntactic structure (parallels that cannot have been inherited from syntactic phrasing), including, crucially, recursion. I will resolve certain problems that arise for my original proposal. While van der Hulst (2010) does not adhere to a dependency

---

[50] The claim of strict layering which prevents recursion has been 'officially' abandoned in later work in prosodic phonology, albeit that the driving force behind recursive structures in prosody is still morphosyntax; see Selkirk (2011) and Itô & Mester (2013).

approach in the strictest sense (using constituency, augmented by headedness), I will here use the dependency notation that has been used in this book.

The point of departure is the syllabic model that was introduced in the preceding section:

(34)
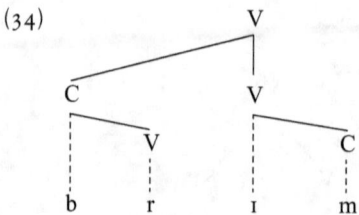

The crucial point in van der Hulst (2010) involves the idea that the coda position can form an entire syllable, making the coda the recursive node in syllable structure, just like the complement position in an X-bar-type organisation. Adopting the C/V notation, I propose in van der Hulst (2010) that the structure for the traditional notion of a trochaic foot in (35a) can be recast as the structure in (35b) with significant explanatory gain. This is illustrated with the Dutch word *káno* 'canoe':[51]

(35) a.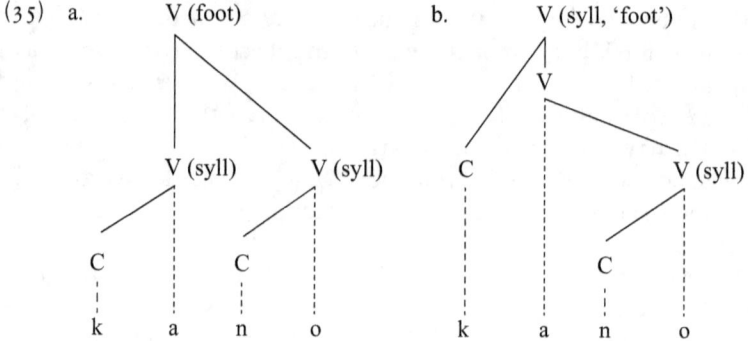

The embedding of syllables inside syllables does not have to stop here. A full structure of a so-called dactylic 'ternary foot', sometimes referred to as a 'superfoot' (as in English *vanity*), displays degree-2 embedding.

---

[51] The representation of both syllables requires a V node in (35a), which seemingly goes against the expectation that V heads take C dependents, and vice versa. The same problem arises in (35b), however. I address this issue below.

(36)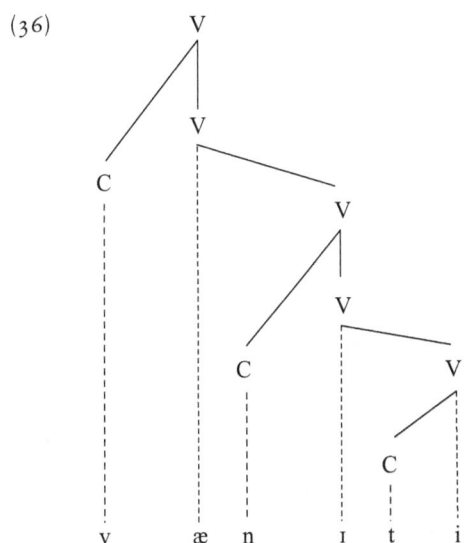

This structure is a perfectly legitimate object also in, for example, English _Winnipesaukee, hippopotamus_. An interesting consequence of this proposal is that it is now immediately clear why in poetic rhyme the initial onset is ignored, but not the second (or indeed the third, in forms like _sanity ~ vanity_). The initial consonant of such structures is external to the whole sequence that forms the rhyming unit in the proposal made here. The recursive structures capture the special position of the initial onset (which can or must be different), as opposed to the other more deeply embedded onsets (which must be identical). In the structures proposed here the rhyming subpart of the string forms a unit, which is not the case in a traditional foot structure in which all syllables are separate units.

This proposal faces two problems that went unnoted in van der Hulst (2010). Firstly, the recursive node (the coda) is a 'bare' C position in a 'closed' syllable that has no embedded syllable, while it seemingly must be a V position, when the coda is an embedded syllable. The dual nature of the coda labelling has been recognised in syllable templates that subsume CVC and CVV under CVX (as for example in Duanmu's (2008) syllable model). The second problem is that the matrix syllable can itself be a 'closed syllable', as in a word like [tɛmpo] in (37b) (in either English or Dutch), which would seem to imply 'double occupancy' of the coda position).

To solve both problems, I will assume that the embedded syllable is the 'complement' of the C node in both cases in (37), which means that the embedded syllable is the dependent complement of the 'coda':

(37) a.   b.

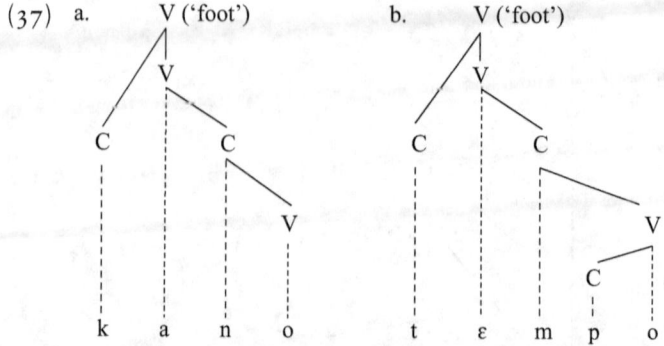

The embedded syllable is thus a C;V-type syllable, which accounts for its 'weaker' status in comparison to the head matrix syllable; this then also accounts for its lower degree of salience (and 'stress').[52]

Accepting that recursion is available to phonology does not entail that phonology will display the same amount of recursive structure as morphosyntax. The kinds of structures that are employed in both modules do not exist in a vacuum, but rather are formed to accommodate the substances that these structures are grounded in. As den Dikken & van der Hulst (2020) point out, syntax displays more recursive structure than phonology due to the lack of a parallel to morphosyntactic functional categories in the latter. A second reason why recursion is less pervasive in phonology was discussed in van der Hulst (2010). If we accept the fact that semantic, conceptual substance is inherently recursive, we expect morphosyntax to be isomorphic to this semantic, conceptual structure as much as possible. Nevertheless, recursion in morphosyntax is curtailed by processing factors. Phonological structure, on the other hand, accommodates phonetic-perceptual substance, which arguably is not inherently recursive. Rather, it is sequential and as the result of motoric actions in articulation rhythmic. As a result, recursion in phonology is curtailed by a 'flattening force' which causes disrhythmic structures that contain lapses (sequences of weak units, 'SWWW ...' (where S = Strong and W = Weak)) to 'flatten' by breaking up into smaller rhythmic units (i.e. 'SW-SW'). The flattening force essentially limits recursion to level-3 embedding ('SWW'). As shown in Giegerich (1985), this kind of flattening also applies to higher-order prosodic structures that follow the recursive structure of morphosyntax, but tend to be flattened into sequences of rhythmically well-formed phonological phrases.

---

[52] Several other 'solutions' to the problem of double occupancy (which will not be repeated here) are discussed and rejected in den Dikken & van der Hulst (2020). This article proposes to 'enlighten' phonology with the introduction of a parallel to the syntactic notion of 'light *v*', an idea that is not adopted here.

The proposal for recursion in syllable structure provides an alternative to the representation of so-called trochaic (SW) and dactylic (SWW) feet that has been proposed in Metrical Theory. This theory has also made use of iambic feet and various proposals for a complete foot typology have been proposed (see van der Hulst (1999b, 1999c) for reviews). Here I will not discuss how RCVP can be applied to 'iambic' foot types; for some suggestions I refer to van der Hulst & Ritter (1998) and den Dikken & van der Hulst (2020).

In conclusion, the argument that recursion is unique to morphosyntax is not compelling. It is a manifestation of a syntactico-centric way of thinking that a computational device that the human mind has would only apply within one component of the grammar. It is simply not reasonable to claim that the mental power to combine units that themselves are the product of combining (thus allowing self-embedding as a logical option) is limited to grammar, let alone to one component in the grammar.

3.3 Summary and concluding remarks

In this chapter I have laid out, albeit programmatically, the structure of segments in the RCVP model. Although the focus of this book is not on syllable structure, I have shown that there is a syllable model that is consistent with the principles of RCVP. I then also made a RCVP proposal for the reanalysis of trochaic feet as recursive syllables.

The next four chapters will elaborate and support this model for each of the three classes (Manner, Place, Laryngeal) and for 'special cases', such as various kinds of complex segments. In each chapter, I will seek to assign interpretations to the structural possibilities that the model allows. The explicit aim is to allow precisely those structures that are needed to express all phonetic distinctions that can be used contrastively in languages. My main source for potential contrast will be MD, LM, Gordon (2016) and various online sources such as WALS (World Atlas of Language Structures) and the updated UPSID (UCLA Phonological Segment Inventory Database), now LAPSyd (Lyon-Albuquerque Phonological Systems Database),[53] but I will also make reference to work that is devoted to specific features or feature classes.

As I have stressed and as the reader will have come to notice, the point of RCVP is not to propose an entirely new set of phonological contrasts. In fact, as will be clear from the articulatory glosses, the distinctions will look quite similar to well-accepted distinctive feature labels. The crucial point then is that this 'classic set' of features is *derived from* the RCVP architecture, that is, from a small number of first principles that guide

---

[53] WALS: <http://wals.info>; LAPSyD: <http://www.lapsyd.ddl.ish-lyon.cnrs.fr> (both last accessed 14 February 2020).

the emergence of phonological primes in ontogeny. As such, RCVP can be seen as a metatheory of phonological (unary) features, which has a definite advantage over a 'theory' that presents the features and their groupings as 'lists'. Because the 'features' are derived from general principles which apply to all phonetic spaces that are available for phonological contrast, RCVP embodies the claim that there are striking *structural analogies* between the various element classes, and indeed between paradigmatic and syntagmatic structure. Additionally, as we will see in Chapters 8 and 9, the specific design of RCVP also provides a principled basis for the preferred co-occurrences of elements in different classes, for preferences of segment classes in syllabic positions and for recurrent phoneme inventories, as well as for notions such as markedness. In Chapter 10 I will apply the principles of this model to sign language phonology, while Chapter 11 discusses a representative number of segmental theories with which RCVP shares certain properties.

4

Manner

4.1 Introduction

In this chapter, I focus on the manner class. I take manner to be the head class of the segmental structure. As already discussed in Chapter 3, there are three reasons for this. Firstly, if manner is the head, a manner specification is *obligatory* for each segment. In syllabic head positions, segments can have only a manner specification, but not only a place or laryngeal specification. In addition, onset dependent positions only *require* manner distinctions, while not allowing specifications for place or laryngeal (with minimal exceptions). This suggests that manner specifications are the minimally required properties of segments. A consequence of the obligatoriness of manner is that segments that have no specification at all are excluded ('empty segments'), which makes the system of representations highly constrained. I will discuss this consequence in § 7.2.1.1, since 'empty segments' (or the closely related notion of empty syllabic positions) have been proposed in various models, specifically, but not exclusively, in GP (see KLV90; Scheer (1998)). The second reason for regarding manner as the head is that manner distinctions contribute to the perceptual salience (*sonority*) level of segments more than place and laryngeal distinctions. One piece of evidence for this is that when segments are ranked on a sonority (or strength) scale, usually reference is mainly or exclusively made to manner properties, although the laryngeal property of voicing is also usually deemed relevant.[1] Thirdly, manner elements are the most *stable* elements, resisting assimilation or harmony, albeit that they are not totally immune to such processes.[2] In a

---

[1] For this reason, AE represent voicing as a manner property; see § 2.2.3. See Foley (1977), who extends his 'strength' scale approach to place properties. Generalising over manner, place and laryngeal element in terms of a ranking that reflects 'salience' is achieved by using the C/V characterisation for all elements; see Chapter 8.

[2] The greater stability of manner properties is documented in a typological study of 'spreading' processes in Gordon (2016: ch. 6).

dependency approach, obligatoriness, perceptual salience (sonority) and stability are natural traits of heads.[3]

Following the notion of polysystematicity, I will discuss manner distinctions for each of the four syllabic positions and, where relevant, for the head (primary) *and* dependent (secondary) classes separately. I will first discuss the structure of segment types that are preferred in each syllabic position and then turn to the occurrence of non-preferred segment types in syllabic head positions (see § 3.2.3 on this distinction; Chapter 8 offers a systematic discussion of this notion of preference for all element classes). In (1) I repeat the RCVP syllabic structure for convenience with, added, the interpretation of the permitted major classes in each syllabic position (following the 'strict' view on what can occur in each position that was discussed in § 3.2.2):

(1)

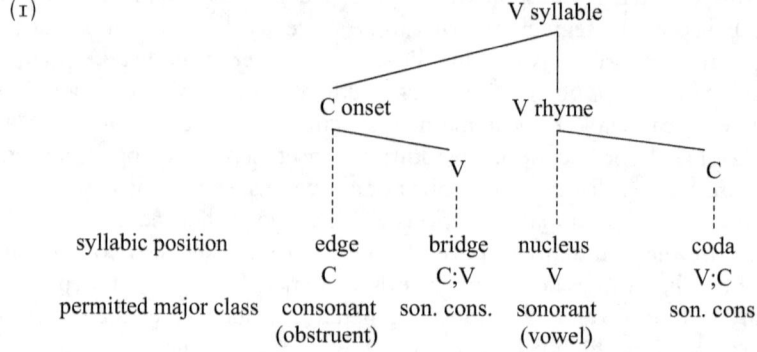

syllabic position	edge	bridge	nucleus	coda
	C	C;V	V	V;C
permitted major class	consonant (obstruent)	son. cons.	sonorant (vowel)	son. cons

In the 'strict view' (see § 3.2.2–3.2.3) both the bridge and the coda position are reserved for sonorant consonants, while the edge position and the nucleus can only contain obstruents and vowels, respectively. However, as proposed in § 3.2.2, the dependent positions (bridge and coda) can 'become' syllabic heads by subjoining rather than adjoining the V or C element to the syllabic head position:

(2) a.

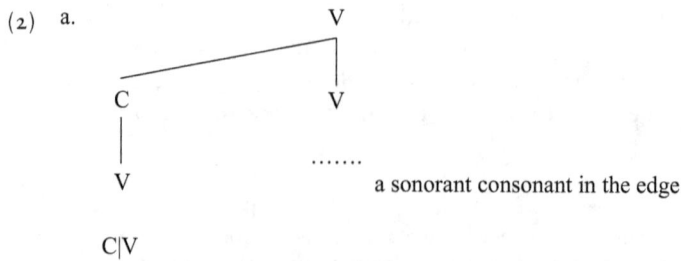

a sonorant consonant in the edge

---

[3] Interestingly, these three properties are also characteristic of the notions 'accent' or 'stress' which are associated with headhood at the word level; see van der Hulst (in prep.).

b.

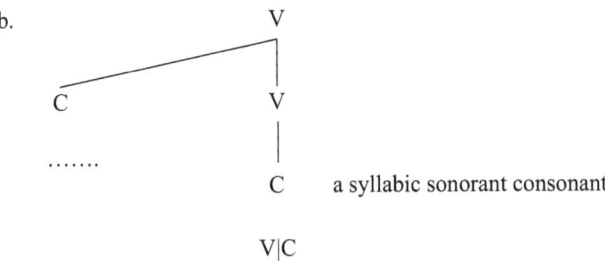

a syllabic sonorant consonant

The structure of this chapter and the following two chapters is to propose an interpretation for all permitted CV structures for manner, place and laryngeal in each relevant syllabic position, starting in each case with the interpretation of CV structures in the head subclass before turning to the dependent subclass.

4.2 Onset

In RCVP, in the onset head position (edge) obstruents are the only permitted consonants.[4] The occurrence of obstruents in the edge is typologically widely acknowledged as an observed 'preference' that is supported by the preference in this position for obstruents over sonorant consonants in all languages (see Gordon (2016) and Chapter 8)) and by the fact that obstruents are the preferred onset choice in early child language development.[5] These claims about obstruents are uncontroversially attested for stops. When we consider fricatives, we need to acknowledge the fact that nasals are more preferred than fricatives in language development, the reason for which is that they are essentially 'stops', consonants with full oral closure (albeit with nasal release) which maximally contrast with a following vowel. In addition, fricatives, with their approximate closure, pose a greater articulatory challenge in early development. As noted in LM (p. 13), it is more straightforward to characterise the place properties of stops and nasals than it is to describe the place of consonants with a lesser degree of stricture. If this is true for the linguist, we expect it also to hold for the language-learning child. Nevertheless, because fricatives,

---

[4] More precisely, *voiceless* obstruents are the most preferred consonants. I will show in Chapter 6 that this is accounted for in RCVP by the fact that voicelessness is encoded by the element C in the head laryngeal class (see also Chapter 8). Even more precisely, *coronal* voiceless obstruents are preferred and this too follows from the fact that coronal is encoded by the C element in the place class (see Chapter 5). In general, as Chapter 6 will make explicit, preference is accounted for in RCVP by assuming that C/V structures in element classes prefer to 'agree' or 'harmonise' with the syllabic C/V structure. A corollary of this top-down agreement is that C/V specifications also prefer to harmonise *across* classes.

[5] See Ingram (1989); Vihman (1996, 2013).

being obstruents, create a better sonority profile with following vowels than nasals, they are eventually, in later stages of development, generally preferred over sonorant consonants.[6]

4.2.1 Edge (onset head): obstruents

4.2.1.1 Edge (onset head): head class

I take the first manner split for the edge position to be between stops and fricatives, corresponding to the traditional feature [±continuant]. Within each category, a second split then creates a finer distinction, which corresponds to the feature [±strident].[7] The resulting four-way categorisation can be seen as following from a once-recursive two-way split:

(3) a. Edge: primary manner

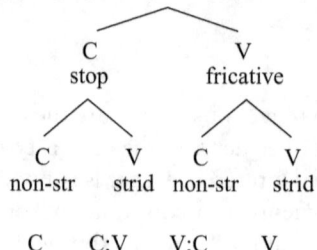

b.   C   C;V   V;C   V

In (4) I list IPA symbols that represent the four possibilities for the three major places of articulation, for voiceless obstruents:[8]

(4) | non-str | strid | non-str | strid | |
| --- | --- | --- | --- | --- |
| [p] | [pf] | [ɸ] | [f] | (with labial location) |
| [t] | [ts] | [θ] | [s] | (with coronal location) |
| [k] | [kx] | [x] | [χ] | (with dorsal location) |

Note that the sequence of segments in (3) is predicted to express a 'sonority' scale, with [p] being the least and [f] the most sonorous (for voiceless labial consonants). This makes non-strident fricatives, such as [ɸ] and [θ], less

---

[6] The fact that preferences in early development can be different from preference in more advanced, adult stages is also seen in the early preference for labial consonants, while eventually coronal consonants acquire the status of being 'unmarked'; see Paradis & Prunet (1991).
[7] AE take the secondary distinction for obstruents to be voicing, which they thus effectively treat as a manner distinction. Anderson (2011a) regards voicing as a 'secondary manner element'. RCVP does not adopt this position, with voicing being represented in the laryngeal class.
[8] Given contrastivity, languages that do not have mellow fricatives can represent the affricate as a headless combination of C and V.

'sonorous' than their strident counterparts, which correlates with the presence of the C element in the representation of the non-strident fricatives. Whether one wants to call strident segments more sonorant depends on one's definition of sonority. Sonorancy is usually said to depend on greater aperture due to lesser stricture. This does not obviously apply to strident consonants. If anything, strident consonants owe their special property to an extra barrier for the outflowing air, namely the upper teeth. The noise that this extra barrier causes makes strident fricatives more perceptually 'salient'. This could be said to make them more 'sonorant' if we take perceptual salience to be the hallmark of being 'sonorant' (rather than relative structure). I will therefore say that the scale in (4) first and foremost captures perceptual salience and not degree of stricture, although I will continue to use the term 'sonorancy' here with the understanding that this term primarily denotes perceptual salience. AE see stridency as being first and foremost a property of the sibilant [s] (AE pp. 163–4), but it is common to regard the difference between [ɸ] and [f] in the same way, involving stridency for the latter.[9] A stridency contrast is not acknowledged for dorsal fricatives by all phonologists. However, Jakobson, Fant & Halle (1952: 24) assumed that uvular fricatives are a strident version of velar fricatives (with the uvula as the extra 'edge'):

> Strident phonemes are primarily characterized by a noise which is due to turbulence at the point of articulation. This strong turbulence, in its turn, is a consequence of a more complex impediment which distinguishes the strident from the corresponding mellow consonants: the labiodentals from the bilabials, the hissing and hushing sibilants from the nonsibilant dentals and palatals respectively, and the uvulars from the velars proper.

I do not want to exclude the relevance of stridency for dorsals, although we will see that uvulars can also be represented in terms of a dependent place element.[10]

At this point it must be noted that a phonetic *place* difference is present when comparing strident and mellow coronal fricatives, with the former being labiodental and the latter bilabial. RCVP chooses to see the place difference as an 'epiphenomenon', that is, a side effect of the stridency distinction. The prediction that follows from this is that the phonetic difference between labiodental and bilabial is not available as a distinctive place difference (assuming that there is no 'room' in the place class to represent this distinction; see Chapter 5). This predicts that such a

---

[9] AE (pp. 165–6) also encode non-stridency as an extra C element, which, in their wording, captures a 'secondary articulation' (see AE p. 246ff.).

[10] In § 5.2.3, I will propose that the distinction between pharyngeal and epiglottal fricatives also suggests a stridency contrast, with epiglottal fricatives being the strident ones.

distinction is not available for other consonant types such as stops or nasals. LM (p. 17) report not personally knowing of labiodental stops in any language, although they note that such consonants have been reported among languages of Southern Africa, in Doke's (1926) study of Zulu. The existence of labiodental stops is dubious on the grounds that non-continuancy presupposes an airtight labiodental closure which is unlikely for most speakers. Such sounds could be variants (for those speakers who can make them) of affricates that end with a labiodental fricative gesture, such as the 'labial' affricate [pf] that occurs in German, in which the stop closure is bilabial, while the fricative release is labiodental.[11] I discuss affricates below in more detail.

As for nasals, LM (p. 18) report that labial–labiodental differences occurs in many languages, although 'As in Tsonga they are usually the result of coarticulation with a following labiodental fricative.' They add:

> Labiodental nasals have, however, been reported as segments contrasting with both bilabial nasals and labiodental fricatives in the Kukuya dialect of Teke. Paulian (1975: 57) describes this sound as 'realised as a labiodental nasal occlusive, invariably voiced; the occlusion is formed between the upper teeth and the lower lip, and is accompanied by strong protrusion of both lips'.

LM add that they do not know if a true occlusive could be made with this gesture, when we take into account the gaps that often occur between the incisors. Pullum & Ladusaw (1996: 112) refer to this same language as having this contrast. It would appear that to date this is the only language that would have such a segment in contrast with [m] and [n]. Paulian (1975: 57) reports that the labiodental nasal is labialised [ɱʷ] before the vowel [a], [ɱ] before [i] and [e] and non-occurring before back rounded vowels. The latter gap indicates that the relevant consonant could be analysed as a labialised labial nasal [mʷ], although labialisation is not otherwise reported for stops or fricatives in this language. Another possible analysis would be to see this segment as nasalised approximant, although this would likewise not be supported from the overall segmental system.

Assuming that there is no compelling case for the labiodental nasal as a contrastive option, I will conclude that it should not be a possible choice in the place class. As I will show in Chapter 5 there is indeed no option in that class for such a distinction. This, then, supports viewing this phonetic distinction for fricatives as a side effect of the stridency distinction.

As expected, affricates are most common for coronal place. Given that affricates require a complex manner specification (i.e. {V;C}), it is expected that such complexity is more likely to occur for obstruents that

---

[11] This actually supports the epiphenomenal nature of labiodental because affricates are 'normally' homorganic.

have a preferred place specification (i.e. C, which is preferred in the onset C position).

A noteworthy aspect of the proposal in (3) and (4) is that affricates are represented as strident stops. Indeed, this is also the proposal in Jakobson, Fant & Halle (1952), who intended this feature to cover both fricatives and stops. Chomsky and Halle introduced a dynamic feature [delayed release] to characterise affricates, arguing, as reported in McCawley (1967), that the Athabaskan language Dëne Sųłiné (Chipewyan) has a phonemic distinction among three series of anterior coronals sounds: plain stops such as [t], non-sibilant affricates such as [tθ], and sibilant affricates such as [ts]. This seemed to require a feature distinction between [tθ] ([−strident]) and [ts] ([+strident]), necessitating a different feature to differentiate the affricates from the non-affricate [t], namely [delayed release]. This conclusion was shown to be premature in Clements (1999), who analyses distinction between [t] and [tθ] in terms of the feature [±distributed], which in RCVP would be a place distinction (see Chapter 5).

Kim, Clements & Toda (2015) also discuss the 'autosegmental' proposal of representing affricates in terms of 'branching structures', that is, as a sequence of a stop followed by a continuant. If stridency can be used for affricates such proposals are unnecessary, unless strong evidence can be produced that such segment types behave like stops to their left and like continuants to their right. Kim, Clements & Toda (2015: 181): point out that affricates 'rarely if ever pattern with fricatives'. I will thus assume that the branching structure for affricates is not well motivated.

In (5), I show that the interpretation of the two elements is dependent on occurring in head or dependent position (with the manner head class):[12]

(5)
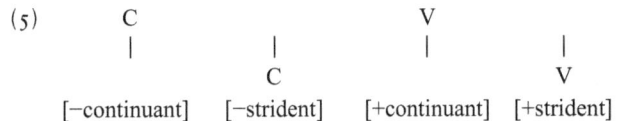

[−continuant]   [−strident]   [+continuant]   [+strident]

Plain stops and strident fricatives are represented as C and V, respectively; see (3b). Recall that the simple structures C and V redundantly contain dependent copies which we leave unspecified in (3b), as discussed in Chapter 3, to avoid allowing an extra contrastive option (i.e. C without and with dependent C, and likewise for V). This means that the strident character of strident fricatives is not actually specified since they have no dependent V element (which would be a copy of the head V element). This captures the fact that stridency is the (literally) 'unmarked' choice

---

[12] Recall from § 3.2.2 (see (22) on p. 90) that head and dependent occurrences in the syllabic structure do not get different interpretations.

for fricatives, just as non-stridency is for stops. Stridency is only (literally) marked for affricates, just as non-stridency is for fricatives. This explains why affricates and non-strident fricatives are less preferred than plain stops and strident fricatives: they are literally more marked.

The fact that we leave the dependent 'copies' unspecified, yet implicitly present, is supported by the fact that, for example in English, all affricates and strident fricatives form a natural class with respect to the choice of the 'long' form of the plural suffix possessive and third person singular suffixes ([əz]). In principle, we would expect that both head and dependent elements denote possible natural classes. In the case of (5) this is perhaps the least obvious for dependent C. While head elements C and V represent the natural classes of stops (including affricates) and fricatives, dependent C (if the 'copy' for plain stops is included) would group together plain stops and non-strident fricatives. Given the relative rarity of non-strident fricatives, it is unlikely for that reason alone that evidence for this natural class will be found.

On the subject of natural classes, stops *can* form a natural class with nasals which, as shown in § 4.2.2, follows from the fact that nasals are also specified with a C element for manner.[13]

The manner choices for the head subclass for obstruents are summarised in (6):[14]

(6)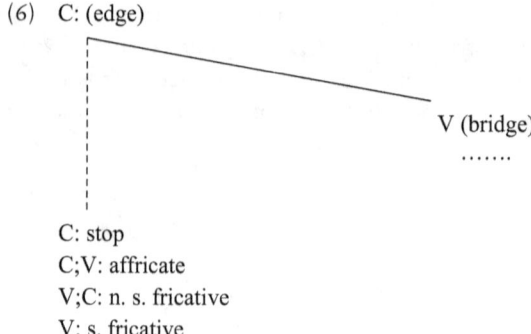

C: stop
C;V: affricate
V;C: n. s. fricative
V: s. fricative

---

[13] And sometimes with laterals, which have a head C element (like nasals and stops), but also a dependent V; see Mielke (2005) for a review of the dual behaviour of nasals and laterals. Mielke remarks that traditional feature systems cannot characterise the observed duality. In § 4.2.1.2 I will show that RCVP representations can: nasals and laterals share not only a V element with fricatives but also a C element with stops. The relative preponderance of the C and V provides a basis for explaining, for example, that nasals are more likely to pattern with stops than laterals.

[14] I assume that unreleased stops, indicated with the IPA diacritic ['], are never contrastive with released stops, which is why we do not need separate CV structures for these variants. Special types of stops such as ejectives and implosives, or aspirated stops, and so on will be represented in terms of laryngeal specifications in Chapter 6. In Chapter 5 I discuss the representation of the glottal stop [ʔ].

LM (p. 202ff.) show that there can be several additional distinctions among obstruents (such as lateral vs. non-lateral obstruents). These are treated as secondary distinctions, that is, in terms of secondary elements (see § 4.2.1.2).

At this juncture, the reader might wonder how the laryngeal consonants [h] and [ʔ] will be represented in RCVP. In terms of their major class status, these consonants have both been analysed as sonorants and as obstruents. Since I will further discuss the distinction between obstruents and sonorant as onset heads (as given in (1) and (2a)) in § 4.2.3, I will postpone my proposal for the representation of laryngeal consonants to that section.

In Chapter 5 I will claim that affrication of stops can be a phonetic effect of certain places of articulation in the palatal place region, which means that not all phonetic coronal affricates have a V-manner element that encodes stridency. Backley (2011: 108–10), in fact, claims that affrication is *always* the result of stops occurring in certain places of articulation, such as the palatal place (cf. also Kehrein (2002)). I do not deny that affrication can be a phonetic side effect of palatal place. There are in fact many examples of languages having both palato-alveolar and palatal affricates (such as Polish and Chinese), which could be seen as a place distinction, with affrication being a phonetic effect in both places. However, we cannot always predict affrication from the place specification. There are languages that have a contrast between palatal stops and affricates:

(7) Komi (MD 052[15]):
    c   tʃ   c

In fact, one could argue that affricates also occur contrastively with stops within the same coronal place in English, which contrasts [t] and [ts] where [t] and [ts] have the same location; see also MD (p. 166), who makes this point about the feature sibilant, which I take to be another name for stridency.

Another example making this point is cited in LM (pp. 35–6):

> [there are] a few reports in the literature of languages that contrast palatal, velar and uvular stops without making the first of these an affricate. The most convincing case of this kind is that of Jaqaru, a language fairly closely related to Quechua. Hardman (1966) describes this language as contrasting not only c, k, q but also ts, tʃ, t̺s̺, making it plain that the palatal stop is not an affricate, but actually contrasts with a series of affricates, as well as with velar and uvular stops.

[15] Citations in this form refer to language numbers in MD.

Another compelling reason for *not* seeing affrication as 'phonetic' in all cases is that affrication is a separate category for labial stops in German, which distinguishes [pf] from both [p] and [f] (Wiese (2000)):

(8) Pferd 'horse'
    Periode 'period'
    Fehler 'mistake'

Also, Swiss German has the contrastive velar affricate (Goblirsch (2002)).

While affricates are strident stops, it is of course clear that their phonetic realisation displays a linearisation of a stop and a fricative part which are (phonologically) homorganic with respect to their 'major place' choice, given that the stop in question has a single place specification. As noted earlier, the 'f' part of the labial affricate in German is phonetically labiodental and not bilabial.

While having just one place may allow the 'f' part of German [pf] to be labiodental and not bilabial, there are, however, apparent affricates that clearly do not have a single place of articulation that covers both the stop and the fricative part. Examples are the [tx] in Navajo and Chiricahua Apache (Hoijer & Opler (1938)) as well as affricates in various Bantu languages such as Phuthi, which has alveolar–labiodental affricates [tf] and [dv], and Sesotho, which has bilabial–palato-alveolar affricates [pʃ] and [bʒ] (Louwrens, Kosch & Kotzé (1995)). Sagey (1986, 1988) treats 'affricates' of this type as complex, multiply-articulated segments that thus have two places of articulation in which a distinction is made between a major and minor articulation that have different degrees of closure. I will return to these types of segments and this proposal in § 7.3.1.1.

Turning now to the contrast between strident and non-strident fricatives, it must be noted that this contrast is not very frequent. A well-known example of a language with a stridency contrast for fricatives is Ewe:[16]

(9) [efe] 'nail; debt'
    [eve] 'two'
    [eφe] 'year'
    [eβe] 'Ewe people'

---

[16] See Maddieson (2006a).
   LM (p. 18) also report bilabial fricatives (voiced and voiceless) for the XiNkuna dialect of Tsonga (Baumbach (1974, 1987)). MD (p. 226) reports the voiceless bilabial fricative for seventeen languages, while the voiced bilabial fricative occurs in thirty languages. However, only three languages (Ewe, Iai, Kanuari) have both [f] and [φ], while only two (Ewe, Iai) have both [v] and [β].

Bilabial fricatives (voiced and voiceless) more often occur as non-contrastive variants, either instead of labiodentals or as allophones thereof. In addition, bilabial fricatives can occur as an allophone of labial stops (Hall 1944) or of [h] (in Japanese).[17]

Turning to the coronal fricatives, we see a similar pattern. A contrast between mellow and strident coronal fricatives [θ] and [s] or [ð] and [z], all too familiar in most forms of English, is not common cross-linguistically. [θ] can be a dialectal variant of [s] (in Venetian Italian) or of [t] (in Tuscan Italian), while the voiced counterpart [ð] occurs as a dialectal variant of [z] or as allophone of [d] (see Repetti (2000)). Nevertheless, the [ð] ≠ [z] contrast occurs in a fair number of other languages.

That coronal place is more receptive to the occurrence of non-strident fricatives (just as it is for affricates) than other places is once more consistent with the idea that coronal itself is the unmarked place of articulation (place: C) for consonants; see Chapter 6.

The present proposal, as we have seen, attributes the phonetic place distinction between bilabial and labiodental fricatives to a manner distinction involving stridency, which is justified by the fact that the place distinction is virtually absent for stops and nasals. The coronal fricatives [θ] and [s] or [ð] and [z] also involve a phonetic place distinction, the non-strident consonants often being described as 'interdental'. Again, we note that a distinction between dental (or alveolar) and interdental is never reported for stops or nasals. The pattern seems to be that fricatives allow phonetic places (labiodental, interdental) that are exclusive to this category of obstruents. This in my view strongly suggests that these phonetic properties should not be acknowledged as contrastive places, but rather should be analysed as a side effect of a manner distinction (stridency) that applies to both stops and fricatives, delivering affricates for the former.

Following the logic of the C/V syntax, which allows a four-way distinction in each class, a four-way primary manner distinction is predicted. I have shown how each of the four categories can be interpreted (see (3)). Of course, it is not claimed that this four-way distinction occurs in every language. A language may only have plain stops and strident fricatives (the first 'cut' in (3)), or it may have both of these and a second cut for only one of them, in which case the second cut for C into C and C;V is the most common. In fact, we have seen that the second cut for V is rather rare. With stops being preferred over fricatives, the preference for a further division of stops into stops and affricates over a division of fricatives into mellow and strident fricatives is thus also expected. This

---

[17] According to Maddieson (2006a), the Japanese occurrence is a very different sound from the alleged same sound in Ewe.

raises the question as to whether a split into stops and affricates is likely to occur when there is no split into stops and fricatives. In other words, is it possible for a second cut to occur if there was no first cut? There are, in fact, languages that lack fricatives:

> The great majority of languages without fricatives occur in Australia, with other notable clusters in New Guinea and in the interior of South America. Outside of these areas there are only a few sporadic examples of languages without fricatives, such as Kiribati and Hawaiian (both Austronesian), the Nilo-Saharan languages Dinka and Lango, spoken in the Sudan and Uganda, respectively, and the one surviving Great Andamanese language (also known as Pucikwar), as well as Aleut, as mentioned above. (WALS online, <https://wals.info/chapter/18> (last accessed 30 January 2020)

If the absence of a first cut blocks a second cut, we would expect that none of these languages has affricates, which, I believe, is the case, although MD (pp. 39–40) does not list it as a generalisation.

One might ask what the consequence would be if there were a language in which affricates occurred in the absence of fricatives. In that case we could consider that the contrast is made in terms of the first cut, opposing C to V, allowing for the possibility that the first cut can be interpreted as a distinction between stops and affricates, rather than stops and fricatives. Effectively this means that the first cut distinguishes obstruents in terms of stridency. This, of course, would weaken the predictable relation between phonological structures and phonetic correlates, which, while necessarily 'flexible', is not expected to differ very dramatically from one language to the next. Nevertheless, some flexibility is needed. While in the presence of a contrast, mellow (bilabial) fricatives are represented as V;C and strident (labiodentals) as plain V, it would seem that if no contrast is present, fricatives are represented as plain V, which according to (3) delivers a strident fricative. However, according to the survey in MD, most languages that have bilabial fricatives do not have labiodental fricatives.[18] If mellow fricatives in the absence of contrast can be represented as plain manner V (instead of V;C), this means that the phonetic implementation module can 'add' a phonetic property that does not have a phonological presence

---

[18] The languages Hausa, Sui, Kan, Washkuk, Kewa, Fasu, Yareba, Otomi, Yuchi, Alabama, Cayapa, Ocaina, Muinane and Araucanian have a voiceless bilabial fricative, but no voiceless labiodental fricative. A contrast only occurs in Ewe and Iai. Of the thirty languages with voiced biliabial fricatives, only two also have voiced labiodental fricatives (Ewe, Iai); see MD (pp. 226–7).

(namely the property that correlates with the unspecified dependent C element). I have argued in van der Hulst (2018) that this 'power' does not lead to unwanted forms of abstractness, unlike the case in which an element that *is* phonologically present fails to be interpreted. I have thus proposed that phonetic implementation should not have the option of failing to interpret a specified element.

Considering the four obstruent manners that we have proposed, we can ask whether there is a preference of occurrence in the edge position. I have already mentioned that stops would appear to be the preferred category in the onset head position, following the principles that the syllabic C position (the 'edge') prefers the manner C element. This principle and preference of occurrence of the other obstruent types are discussed in detail in Chapter 8. There we will see that after stops, the next preferred manner category for the edge position is |V|, fricatives, rather than affricates, even though the latter contain the |C| element, which is also the characterisation of the edge itself. I will claim that this follows from an independent principle which states that simplex categories are preferred over complex categories in *syllabic head positions*, which, as I will argue, creates perceptual distance among segments in head positions, which are 'salient' positions.

Finally, we need to ask how we account for obstruents that occur in positions other than the onset head. If we adopt the 'strict' view that obstruents can only occur in the onset head, we need a different syllabic analysis of obstruents that allegedly occur in other positions, such as the coda, which seems to contain a stop in a word like *cat*, or a fricative in *miss*.[19] A more lenient view would go less far, and simply assume that the manner options given in this section can occur in positions other than the edge, perhaps with certain restrictions. I discussed these two approaches in § 3.2.2. As for onset clusters consisting of two obstruents, GP would not allow the analysis of such clusters as complex onsets, because that would entail having an obstruent in the bridge position. Where such clusters occur, they seem to prefer the stop–fricative order over the reverse, which indicates a preference for rising sonority.[20] In Chapter 3, I have

---

[19] That the final [t] or [s] in the words cannot be a coda is a position that is adopted in GP (KLV90), but GP adopts the stronger position that no coda can occur unless the coda consonant is licensed by a following onset consonant that is less sonorant. The actual view does not require the licensing onset to be more sonorant. For a more technical account in terms of intra-segmental complexity see Harris (1990). In his view an obstruent can be a coda if the following onset obstruent is not less complex; Harris (1990: 274).

[20] See Kreitman (2008). See also Morelli (1999) and Greenberg (1978).

subscribed to the strict view of GP because a strict view on what is possible forces the phonologist to look for creative solutions for cases that involve apparently impossible patterns. This may reveal regularities that would go unnoticed if 'anything goes'. An approach that simply allows anything does not go beyond descriptive adequacy, unless a theoretical basis can be found for ranking patterns in terms of their cross-linguistic likelihood or preference. For example, for onsets one could stipulate (or derive from certain principles) a ranking like this: obstruent + sonorant > stop + fricative > fricative + stop > sonorant + obstruent. Kreitman (2006, 2008) confirms that this implicational scale obtains. As discussed in Chapter 3, such an approach would be possible within the RCVP model, although this would then require us to distinguish the encoding of syllabic positions from an extra information level for major class encoding. The idea of expressing a preference ranking is used in this book with respect to the occurrence of segment types in syllabic positions, as explored in Chapter 8. In this case, for example, we want to derive that stops are more preferred as onset heads than fricatives, as mentioned above. This ranking, as noted, would follow from the RCVP practice of encoding syllabic position in terms of the same elements that are used for the segmental content.

Adhering to a strict view on syllabic structure, GP generously appeals to so-called empty nuclei to account for word–final 'coda' consonants (which are analysed as onsets followed by an empty nucleus) and consonant clusters that cannot be analysed as complex onsets or as coda–onset sequences (so-called interludes). By imposing constraints on the occurrence of such empty nuclei, this approach explains certain distributional limitations on the occurrence of such 'deviating' structures. My goal in this book is not to endorse or explore such analyses, although in general my preference would be to deal with such cases in terms of adjunction structures at word edges (with no appeal to empty nuclei), an approach which also imposes limitations on the distribution of deviating structures. In the view of John Anderson, empty nuclei are ill-formed phonological objects because they are not grounded in phonetic substance; see Anderson (2014).

4.2.1.2 Edge (onset head): dependent class

In the previous section I have proposed a set of four structures for head manner distinctions in the edge position (which is reserved for obstruents). We now turn to the dependent manner structures for onset heads, which I will also call secondary manners:

(10)

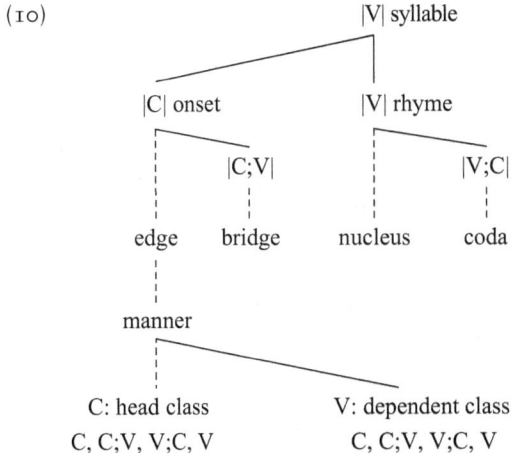

As shown in (10), the dependent class allows, in principle at least, for the same four basic structures that are permitted in the head class. I propose that the secondary manners for obstruents have a 'sonorant character'. As we will see when we discuss head manner in the bridge, the secondary manners for obstruents are in fact identical to the head bridge manners for sonorant consonants. This in itself shows that there is a close relationship between onset heads with secondary manner and onset heads that occur with an onset dependent.

In (11) I propose four secondary manners for obstruents:

(11) Edge: secondary manner

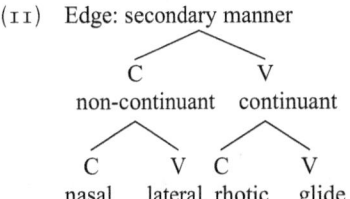

From here on, for convenience, I will follow the notational system that Anderson (2011b) employs in his dependency model:

(12) {PRIMARY DISTINCTION {secondary distinction}}

Given this notation, a stop with a secondary nasal manner (which is most likely to be interpreted as a prenasalised stop) can be written as follows:

(13) Edge: Manner {C{c}}, e.g. [ᵐb] (given that place is labial)

The four 'sonorant-type' secondary options create, in principle, four segment types for each of the four obstruent types that are distinguished in term of primary manner (see (3)). While it might be expected that the glide option in (11) would account for secondary articulations like palatalisation [C^y] or labialisation [C^w], I will account for these in terms of secondary *place* specifications (Place: {X{c}} and Place: {X{v}},[21] or in the 'traditional' element notation: secondary |I| and secondary |U|). Here, in manner, the glide option is exclusively realised as a pharyngeal 'glide', that is, as pharyngealisation or, in traditional element terms, |A|.[22]

If we cross-classify all the primary and secondary manner distinctions for the edge position, we generate twenty obstruent structures, four plain ones and sixteen with secondary manner:

(14) Primary and secondary distinctions in the edge:[23]

plain	c	c;v	v;c	v
	nasal	lateral	rhotic	pharyngeal
C stop				
C;V affricate				
V;C mellow fricative				
V strident fricative				

Starting with secondary nasality, there is good evidence for recognising this property with obstruents, resulting in prenasalised stops and nasalised fricatives.[24] LM (p. 118ff.) discuss prenasalised stops under the heading 'partially nasal consonants' in which

---

[21] The variable 'X' stands for C or V, the primary element.
[22] This is consistent with the fact that in RCVP |A| is a manner element (namely V), while |I| and |U| are place elements (namely C and V, respectively).
[23] I note here that it is somewhat misleading to label the secondary c as 'nasal(isation)'. The |c| is interpreted as a stop articulation that produces a nasal consonant because the secondary manner for obstruent has a sonorant character. As such |c| refers not to the activation of the nasal cavity, but rather to the occurrence of a full constriction in the vocal tract. Because the secondary manner is inherently 'sonorant' it follows that the full constriction must be combined with nasal release. I will return to the correlation between sonorant manner |C| and nasality in the next section.
[24] General references about prenasalised obstruents: Herbert (1986); Durvasula (2008); Feinstein (1979); Sagey (1986); Piggott (1988); Rosenthall (1992); Maddieson (2009b); Riehl & Cohn (2011); Tak (2011).
   I am here not considering the combination of prenasalisation and 'special' phonation properties (which in RCVP include implosive and ejective articulations). LM (p. 119) indicate that prenasalised glottalic consonants do not seem to occur; nor do those segments occur with voicelessness, aspiration or creaky voice. This could

the velic position is changed during their production so that for part of their duration they are nasal and for part of their duration they are oral. It is possible to imagine a much larger number of potential categories of partially nasal consonants than those which seem actually to have been observed. (LM p. 118)

In what follows here, I will try to make the case that we only need to recognise secondary nasality for plain stops and fricatives. For starters, I will assume that so-called prenasalised affricates are, phonologically, fricatives with secondary nasal manner. We could understand this effect as the intrusion of an epenthetic phonetic stop between the nasal part and the fricative part.[25] MD does not report a language that has a contrast between nasalised fricatives and prenasalised affricates at the same place of articulation. Since affricates have a complex primary manner and since we will observe multiple times that secondary manners tend to occur only with simple primary manners, it would seem reasonable to assume that affricates (as well as mellow fricatives) never occur with any secondary manner. This empirical gap, then, can be seen as caused by the avoidance of an accumulation of complexity which would result from combining a secondary manner with a complex primary manner. I will show, as we go along, that this avoidance of cumulative complexity will also be observed in the other element classes (i.e. place and laryngeal). I do not wish to propose a formal constraint to block all cumulative complexity. We can simply assume that there is no need for languages to reach into high degrees of complexity, given the overall size of segmental inventories and the many other simpler ways that are available to expand the segmental inventory.

While a nasal secondary manner for stops necessarily leads to a phonetically complex segment (which, I suggest is always a prenasalised stop; see below), nasalisation with a fricative produces prenasalised affricates. However, nasalisation of a fricative can also be phonetically co-temporal. LM (p. 132ff.) discuss 'oral continuants (fricatives and approximants) that are produced with a lowered velum so that air is also free to pass out through the nasal passage'. They add: 'These types of segments occur most often as allophonic variants of their non-nasalised counterparts in positions where nasality spreads from a nasal consonant or a nasalised vowel in the neighbourhood.' However, in some cases the nasalisation cannot be analysed as allophonic. Leaving aside the nasalised approximants which can simply be analysed as such

---

also be seen as an avoidance of cumulative complexity. (Pre)nasalised clicks will be discussed in § 7.3.2.

[25] The same kind of intrusion is found in the pronunciation [prints] for 'prince', making this word near-homophonous with 'prints'; see Clements (1985).

(see § 4.2.3) and the possibility that some alleged nasalised fricatives are in fact approximants, LM site the case of UMbundu (Schadeberg (1982)) as a genuine example of a contrastively nasalised fricative. UMbundu also has prenasalised stops. More interestingly, this language also has a palatal prenasalised affricate, which is the nasal counterpart of a palatal affricate. If accumulation of complexity resisted having secondary nasalisation on an affricate, we could insist that this prenasalised affricate is in fact a nasalised fricative. However, if Schadeberg is right in analysing [ṽ] as a contrastively nasalised labial approximant, then this language would provide a rare example of a true nasalised fricative; perhaps the case of Igbo is another example (LM p. 133).[26] I conclude that affrication of a nasalised fricative is less compelling at the labial place of articulation, which allows us to hypothesise that at the coronal place, secondary nasalisation of fricatives always produces prenasalised affricates.[27] No language contrasts these two categories, and in some languages they are allophonically realised as either (Poser (1979); van de Weijer (1996)).

Prenasalised stops need not always be stops with a secondary manner. They can be surface variants of either voiced stops or plain nasals, often depending on preceding or following nasal or oral vowels; see Anderson (1976).[28]

If such occurrences of prenasalised stops are seen as resulting from phonetic implementation, this would mean that there is no need to represent such segments as phonologically complex in the sense of having a primary and secondary manner (as in (14)). However, such an analysis is not possible if a language has a four-way contrast (e.g. [p-b-m-^{m}b]), in which case a complex structure for the prenasalised stop is required. MD (p. 206) list eighteen languages with [^{m}b]. Several of those lack [p], [b] or [m], but four languages have a four-way contrast:

- [p, b, m, ^{m}b]: Gbeya, Yulu, Sara, Ngizim
- no [b]: Luvale, Wantoat, Nambakaengo, Paez, Sedang
- no [m]: Siriono
- no [p]: Berta, Alawa

---

[26] Ohala (1975: 300) argues that voiced nasalised fricatives are 'nasalized frictionless continuants' since the nasal outflow of air makes it difficult to sustain voicing.

[27] Languages in UPSID with prenasalised affricates are Mazatec, Luvale, Sedang (although this segment is missing in the segmental inventory in MD (p. 323)), Washkuk and Siriono.

[28] LM (p. 118) mention: 'Surface "medionasal" segments – stops with an oral onset and offset, but a nasal medial portion – are reported in Kaingang (Wiesemann 1972). These are the variants of prenasalised stops that occur medially after oral vowels.'

- no [b. m]: Hakka
- no [p, b]: Washkuk, Selepet, Kewa
- no [b, m]: Apinaye, Kaliai

Irrespective of how [ᵐb] will be analysed in languages that lack the four-way labial contrast, the fact that some languages have a four-way contrast necessitates a non-derivative representation of [ᵐb].

However, a non-derivative representation does not have to be a complex segment (i.e. in this case, a single segment with a secondary property). In general, RCVP does not preclude structural ambiguity, that is, more than one theoretically permitted analysis of a 'phonetic event'. What is at issue in this section is whether in the case at hand one such theoretical analysis consists of a primary obstruent manner combined with a secondary sonorant manner. Some phonological theories also allow complex onsets consisting of an obstruent and a sonorant. As discussed in Chapter 7, perhaps some complex events may require a 'double root' analysis. This adds up to *four* possible analyses of a phonetic event that combines nasality with 'obstruent properties':

(15) a. Phonetic realisation of a simple stop or nasal
 b. An obstruent with secondary nasality
 c. A complex onset (e.g. [mb])
 d. A 'double root' cluster

If all these options are theoretically possible, the proper analysis for any language will have to be carried out with reference to the phonological behaviour (phonetically or vis-à-vis processes/rules). As pointed out in Durvasula (2008), the behaviour of such events with respect to nasal harmony (as being 'transparent' or opaque) could be a decisive factor. Analysis of the syllable template might exclude a complex onset analysis, if there is no independent evidence for complex onsets. This is in fact a common argument for analysing [ᵐb] as a single, albeit complex segment. But even if complex onsets are permitted, a complex onset analysis [mb] would be excluded on the grounds that there has to be a rising sonority distance between the onset head and the onset dependent. Indeed, in the RCVP model of the syllable discussed in § 3.2.2, 'onsets' like [mb] *are* excluded. LM devote considerable discussion to prenasalised obstruents, specifically addressing the question of whether a monosegmental or bisegmental analysis obtains. On page 120, they mention Sinhala as possibly having a contrast between these two options, citing the minimal pair lan.nda 'thicket' and la.nda 'blind'. They opt for an analysis of a single versus geminate nasal followed by a stop, for instance [mb, nd] vs. [mmb, nnd]. This would then necessitate a 'marked' onset [nb, nd]. They propose a similar analysis for Fula

(LM p. 121). In general, LM do not believe that timing differences will decide the mono/bisegmental controversy. LM also discuss the matter of voicing. While in most cases prenasalised 'segments' are voiced throughout, 'in many Bantu languages such as KeSukuma (Batibo 1976) there are both "voiced" and "voiceless" prenasalised stops. In KeSukuma the voiceless prenasalised stops are quite strongly aspirated' (LM p. 123). They conclude:

> Whatever the facts concerning articulatory timing and voicing may be in a given case, the motivation for talking of prenasalised stops, rather than of a nasal + stop sequence, is often phonological rather than phonetic (in languages which do not have a within-language contrast of the type found in Sinhala and Fula). A unitary analysis may be preferred because the language has no other consonant sequences in any position, as in Fijian (Milner 1956), or has no other consonant sequences in initial position, as in Gbeya (Samarin 1966). We note that the unitary analysis also avoids recognizing a syllable onset with the structure nasal + stop. Syllable onsets with this structure violate the expectation that more sonorous elements (in this case nasals) appear closer to the syllable nucleus than less sonorous ones (stops), in conformity with well-established ideas of the sonority hierarchy (cf. Jespersen (1897–1899), Hooper (1976), Steriade (1982)). In fact, violations of this particular kind seem to be rather prevalent.

While the last statement seems to undermine the argument that the 'preferred' sonority profile of syllable can be used as a phonological argument for a monosegmental analysis, I would agree with their overall assessment that the mono/bisegmental issues cannot be decided on phonetic grounds alone.

LM (p. 127) then mention the question of whether any distinction is implied by the use of transcriptions like both [^{m}b, ^{n}d] and [m^b, n^d], which have sometimes been distinguished as 'prenasalised stops' versus 'post-stopped nasals'. With no obvious candidate for a contrast between these two phonetic events, I will assume that post-stopped nasals can be analysed as allophonic effects of a nasal consonant preceding an oral vowel.

To make matters 'worse', there are also so-called pre-stopped nasals; see LM (p. 128ff.) and Durvasula (2008). Segments like [^{b}m] can occur as allophones of a nasal consonant following an oral vowel (Anderson (1976)). However, in some cases, LM suggest that a bisegmental analysis is the most obvious account, citing Russian as a case in point, because this language has stop–nasal sequences word-initially. Proponents of strict views on what can be a possible onset would in this case propose an analysis in which the two consonants are separate onsets, separated by an empty nucleus (as in GP; KLV90) or treat the stop as a word-initial adjunct.

LM also consider cases of pre-stopped nasals in which the stop part is voiceless. An allophonic analysis may be less likely in this case because it would leave the voicelessness of the stop unexplained. Nevertheless, an allophonic relation between a nasal and a [ᵖm] sound is suggested for the Australian language Diyari (Austin (1981)) which shows a pattern: Cáma > CáᵖMa (but not if C is nasal: náma). In Olgolo (Dixon (1970, 1980)), the distinction has become 'phonemic' because initial consonants have been dropped, leading to a contrast in intervocalic position: áᵇma ≠ áma (but note that here the stop part is transcribed as being voiced). In Arrernte (Dixon (1980)) subsequently initial vowels also got dropped, now allowing pre-stopped nasals to occur initially, creating a contrast # ᵇma =/= #ma. As reported in Maddieson & Ladefoged (1993) this language also has prenasalised stops, which allows for a three-way contrast between nasal, prenasalised and pre-stopped nasal consonants, not only initially, but apparently also medially (see LM p. 129). Clearly, we cannot represent both types of nasalised consonants as consonants with a secondary nasal manner. Since the pre-stopped nasals have, or can have, a voiceless stop it would seem warranted to analyse pre-stopped nasals as a consonant sequence of some kind. Arrente does not otherwise permit complex onsets. In fact, Breen & Pensalfini (1999) analyse this language as having no onsets. Here I refrain from providing an analysis.

A final category of partially nasalised sounds is that of segments that show a combination of prenasalisation and trilling (LM p. 130ff.), specifically prenasalised stops with a trilled release, which occur in Kele, a language spoken in the Admiralty Islands north of the New Guinea mainland (Ladefoged, Cochran & Disner 1977). The trill phase of the labial prenasalised stop has developed in front of a high back rounded vowel [u]. While it may be possible to analyse the trill as allophonic in this environment, it would seem that prenasalised *apical* trills are perhaps the result of a 'strong' reflex of the stop part regardless of the quality of the following vowel. To analyse such segments as having *two* secondary manners (nasality and rhoticism) would be a formal addition to the RCVP syntax.[29] This would then 'force' a bisegmental analysis of the nasal and stop part, which would allow the stop to have a secondary rhotic property. Hence treating the trill phase as an allophonic effect in all cases is perhaps the more obvious analysis.

After this long discussion of secondary manner v, I now turn to the second column of (14), that is, secondary manner c;v, which delivers secondary lateralisation. I suggest that we again only need secondary lateralisation for stops and fricatives, if so-called lateral affricatives are

---

[29] On page 128 and in subsequent chapters we will encounter other cases which may require double secondary specifications.

analysed as realisations of lateralised stops, given that no language has a contrast between these two phonetic options.

(16) [ɬ] [ɮ]   voiceless and voiced lateral fricative
     [tɬ] [dɮ] voiceless and voiced lateral stop (affricate)

In 'a number of languages' lateral fricatives vary with lateral affricates, but '[n]onetheless, it is possible to find language which clearly show their contrastivity' (LM p. 209). Zulu has a contrast between lateral approximants, lateral fricatives and lateral affricates at various places of articulation, all coronal. Another language rich in these consonants is Archi. Lateral affricates are common in Native American languages such as Tlingit (MD 76). In this language a contrast occurs between lateral fricatives and lateral affricates (701 in MD; see also LM p. 207). In Welsh 'a voiceless alveolar lateral fricative alternates with a voiced alveolar lateral approximant under specific morphological conditions, but because of loanwords the two segments now contrast' (LM p. 203). LM (p. 203ff.) provide other examples of lateralised consonants.

The third column of (14), secondary v;c, is less easy to link to occurring obstruents with a secondary property. Despite the prenasalised *apical* trills that were just mentioned for the language Kele, there is no clear occurrence of 'rhotic stops' or 'rhotic fricatives'. Rhoticised stops have rarely been described, but the consonant described as [dr̄] in Mapudungun (Mapuche) (Zúñiga (2000); Smeets (2008)) is a possible candidate. As for the rhoticised fricatives, LM (pp. 166–7) discuss a possible contrast between velar and uvular fricatives, remarking that the latter may occur with a vibrating uvula, which leads to a description as 'a uvular fricative trill', occurring, for instance, in Wolof. Here, then, the distinction is one of secondary v in the place class, with the fricative aspects being epiphenomenal (see (17) below). On page 228 LM mention the Czech [ř] as a type of trill that occurs with frication. They view this segment not as a primary fricative with a secondary trill, but rather as a trill with secondary frication. I will discuss this unique sound in § 4.2.3, where we will see that it is not so clear whether it should be represented as a sonorant or as an obstruent.

I suggest that the secondary category v;c can also be interpreted as retroflexion. There is an affinity between retroflexion and r-sounds. LM (p. 171) note that a retroflex [s] in Standard Swedish is, phonologically, a sequence of [r+s]. The retroflex vowel in English words like *bird*, *girl*, and so on is historically a sequence of a plain vowel followed by [r]. However, if secondary manner {X{v;c}} is interpreted as retroflexion then we need to allow for obstruents having *two* secondary manners – another instance of unexpected accumulation of complexity:[30]

---

[30] The problem here is analogous to the one we noted for prenasalised stops with a trilled release.

- Voiced retroflex lateral fricative in Ao (MD 512)
- Prenasalised voiced retroflex plosive for Alawa (MD 354)
- Nasally released voiced retroflex plosive in Aranda (MD 362)

A lesser problem is that we then also have affricates with this secondary manner (see LM p. 224).[31] This would display the above-mentioned unexpected accumulation of complexity.[32]

The idea of analysing retroflexion as a manner suggests a further possibility, which is to include 'apical' as a correlate of the v;c manner. In that case, pursuing this further we might correlate c;v not only with lateral but also with laminal. We thus get a 'cleaner' interpretation of the place elements, which, as we will see, can then exclusively correlate with the passive places of articulation and not also with the shape of the active articulator. In short, I propose that distinctions such as apical and laminal are properly understood as manners of articulation which refer to different ways in which the active articulator makes contact with the passive articulator.

I now turn to the fourth column of (14), secondary v. I propose interpreting secondary v as pharyngealisation. Pharyngealised stops and fricatives are widely reported in MD, but not, interestingly, pharyngealised affricates. I assume that the secondary element v produces pharyngealisation *or* velarisation (which have been claimed to be non-contrastive; van de Weijer (1996), following Keating (1988b)). This secondary articulation distinguishes velars from dorsals and can also be used to represent so-called 'empathic' consonants. Anticipating the discussion of place in Chapter 5, I here show the difference between dorsals and uvulars:

(17) /k g x ɣ/   /q G χ ʁ/

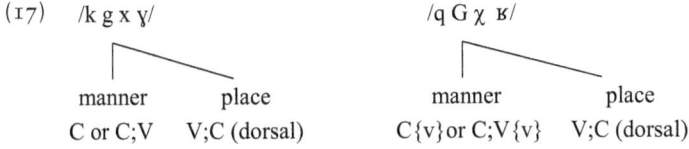

    manner   place   manner   place
    C or C;V   V;C (dorsal)   C{v} or C;V{v}   V;C (dorsal)

Velarisation and pharyngealisation are usually grouped with palatalisation and labialisation under the rubric of secondary articulations. In RCVP, however, the former is a secondary *manner* type whereas the latter two are secondary place specifications (see § 5.2.2).

---

[31] The complex case of the voiceless and voiced retroflex affricated trills in Malagasy (MD 410) could be handled by analysing such segments as retroflex affricates, with the trill as a phonetic effect.

[32] That is, that retroflexion can also occur with sonorants, but that is not a problem; see § 4.2.3.

130   *Principles of Radical CV Phonology*

Given the preceding, we can reduce the twenty-four possibilities in (14) to the eight occurring segment types in (18). The resulting three-way distinction in secondary manner thus involves the three cavities: nasal, oral, pharyngeal:[33]

(18) Primary and secondary distinctions in the edge:

plain	c	cv	v;c	v
	nasal	lateral	rhotic/retroflex	pharyngeal
C stop	prenasal stop	lateral stop (affricate)	retroflex stop	pharyngeal stop
V fricative	prenasal fricative (affricate)	lateral fricative	retroflex fricative	pharyngeal fricative

We can now summarise the manner options for the edge position with both head (primary) and dependent (secondary) specifications:

(19) C (edge)

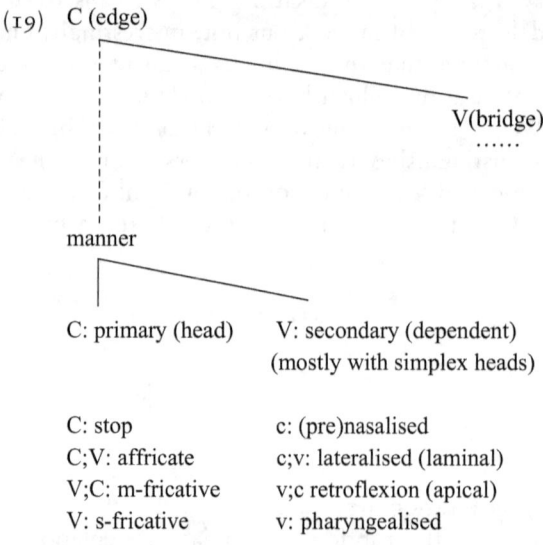

C: primary (head)   V: secondary (dependent)
                          (mostly with simplex heads)

C: stop   c: (pre)nasalised
C;V: affricate   c;v: lateralised (laminal)
V;C: m-fricative   v;c retroflexion (apical)
V: s-fricative   v: pharyngealised

One possibility that I did not anticipate in Chapter 3 is that in (19) I have labelled the primary class and the secondary class with C and V, respectively. We note that the secondary manner for obstruents has a sonorant character. It is thus in the spirit of RCVP to label both classes

---

[33] Additionally, as expected, there is as a strong tendency for secondary manners to be limited to coronal obstruents.

accordingly. However, in § 4.2.3, where we consider sonorant consonants in onset head position, we will see that a similar antagonistic relation between primary and secondary manner does not hold.

In the next section I will discuss manner options for sonorant consonants occurring in the onset dependent position (bridge), which will appear to be very similar to the secondary manner properties for obstruents that we have discussed in this section.

4.2.2 *Bridge (onset dependent): sonorants*

As proposed in § 3.2.2, the bridge position is reserved for sonorant consonants. Obstruents cannot appear in the bridge. Sonorant bridge consonants can thus combine with onset head positions that will contain an obstruent. However, sonorants can also occur in the onset head positions, when the onset is simplex (non-branching), although they are less preferred than obstruents as onset heads. I discuss sonorants as onset heads in the next section.

The fact that the onset head and the onset dependent have opposite labels, C and V respectively, indicates that the daughters of a syllabic unit (both branching onset and branching rhyme) enter into a polar, disharmonic relationship. (The same polar relationship was also observed for the head and dependent manners in the previous section; see (19)). Polarity stands in contrast to the harmonic relationship between the label of the syllabic position and the segment-internal preferred specifications. As we have seen, in the syllabic C position (the edge) C manners are preferred (and, as we will see, C locations and C laryngeal specifications).

I will now present a proposal for sonorant consonant manner distinctions as onset dependents. As in the case of obstruents, the first cut for sonorant involves the degree of continuancy, which opposes nasals and laterals, which have a stronger contact stricture to two classes of segments that have a lesser stricture and are thus the least likely, as discussed earlier, to pattern with stop obstruents (see Mielke (2005)).

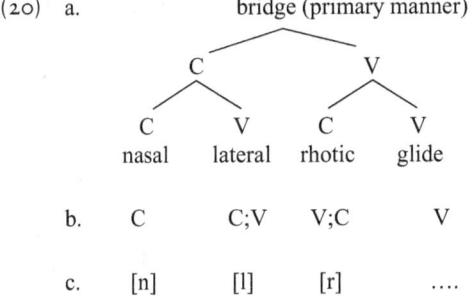

We can represent the phonetic interpretation of the two elements in their head and dependent role as follows:

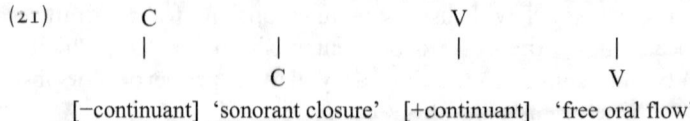

(21)

C   V
| | | |
C   V
[−continuant] 'sonorant closure' [+continuant] 'free oral flow'

[−continuant] here means full contact closure (throughout the entire segment). The gloss 'sonorant closure' refers to the fact that both nasals and rhotics have complete contact closure, although rhotics have a *repeated* full closure, interrupted by opening phases. Laterals, on the other hand, share with vowels an *uninterrupted* ('free') outflow of air, although laterals also have a simultaneous central closure. The interpretations for the dependent occurrence of C and V do not correspond to the two values of a traditional binary feature. This could mean that in this case the dependent elements do not correlate with a natural class, such as *nasals + rhotics or laterals + glides*, which are both discontinuous with respect to the sonority scale. Elements in head position do characterise continuous natural classes, such as nasals and laterals (Mielke (2005)), as well as rhotics and glides (Kok, Botma & van 't Veer (2018)). Note that given (20) all non-nasal sonorants, which are often taken together as the class of approximants, share the formal property of containing a V element. Conversely, all segments sharing a C element are true consonants, whereas glides are often denied this status because of their possible alternations with vowels (which has also prompted the term 'semivowel').

Note the resemblance between the four-way distinction for sonorant consonants and the four-way distinction for secondary manners for onset heads that was proposed in the previous section. In the latter case, the secondary v choice was interpreted as velarisation/pharyngealisation, that is, the element |A|. If we expect a parallel interpretation for the onset bridge, we would expect the V option to be a glide. Backley (2011), followed in Kok, Botma & van 't Veer (2018), takes the approximant [ɹ] to be the glide counterpart of [a].[34] Given that it will be proposed in Chapter 5 that the absence of a place specification gives us pharyngeal place, the counterpart of [a] would have to be a pharyngeal glide' [h].[35] In van der Hulst (2005a), instead of mentioning the option of a pharyngeal glide, I took the glides [j] or [w] to instantiate this slot. The idea of reserving the

---

[34] LM (p. 323) have a different view: 'for many speakers of American English, the approximant [ɹ] at the beginning of the word "red" bears the same relationship to the vowel in "bird" as the approximant j in "yes" does to the vowel i in "heed".'

[35] Helga Humbert (p.c.) suggested to me that the glide version of the vowel [a] is [h], just as [j] and [w] are the glide versions of [i] and [u], respectively.

V structure for [h] is attractive, due to the analogy with the interpretation of secondary v in the previous section. However, there is also a need to allow other glides such as [j] and [w] as bridges, which, in fact, are more likely to occur as bridges than [h].

One reason for taking at least [w] to be a possible bridge is that this glide can occur in complex onsets, such as the clusters [dw] (*dwepen* 'to rave'), [tw] (*twee* 'two') in Dutch (see Trommelen (1983); van der Hulst (1984)). Trommelen, in fact, based on this distributional behaviour, classifies the [w] as a liquid together with [l] and [r].[36] Such clusters can also occur as complex onsets word-internally as in *e.tui* [e.twi] 'case for pencils, glasses and so on'.[37] However, as Trommelen (1983) shows, a similar behaviour for [j] does not occur in Dutch. While [j] can occur as an onset bridge word-initially in rare examples (*tjalk* 'barge'), intervocalically such clusters are divided over two syllables (*at.jar* 'sweet-and-sour pickle').[38]

However, if we allow [w] to be a bridge, this implies that we also have to specify a place element (|U|), which goes against the generalisation discussed in § 3.2.4 that only syllabic heads (i.e. edges and nuclei) can have contrastive place or laryngeal properties. Indeed, I know of no evidence for place specifications for the lateral and rhotics in bridge positions in any language, although nasals may pose an issue as well if we allow nasals as bridges; see below.

To maintain the generalisation that bridges have no contrastive place properties, we could say, for Dutch at least, that if [w] is the only permissible glide, the labiality can be seen as predictable, which means it does not have to be specified.[39] Another approach would be to say that

---

[36] This would not work in RCVP because in that case the [w] needs to be distinguished from either [l] or [r] with a place specification, but specifying place for the bridge is what I try to avoid.

[37] The evidence for this syllabic parsing is that the vowel preceding the obstruent is 'lax'; see van der Hulst (1984), Trommelen (1983). When a consonant cluster is a proper branching onset the vowel preceding it is 'tense', as in *me.tro, a.pril* etc.

[38] The facts in Dutch do not straightforwardly show that word-internal sequence of obstruent followed by [l], [r] or [w] always form a branching onset, the diagnostic for which would be that the preceding vowel is tense. While obstruent plus [r] will always be preceded by a tense vowel, there are examples of obstruent with [l] or [w], especially in brand names such as Popla, Kapla and Hiswa, in which the preceding vowel is lax; see van der Torre (2003). Thanks to Bert Botma for bringing this to my attention.

[39] There are languages that only allow glides as a 'bridge'. A case in point is Korean; see Ahn (1988). Although glides are usually analysed as part of a branching onset, another possible analysis for such languages would be that they do not have complex onsets at all, the 'glide' being a secondary place articulation, or forming part of the nucleus. This avoids having to specify place of articulation for bridges if [j] and [w] need to be distinguished as such.

apparent complex onsets with [w] in the bridge are complex segments, that is, obstruents with a secondary labial articulation.[40] While both proposals might be defended for Dutch, I do not want to build on one language a case for a model that is supposed to apply to all languages. Since in other languages glides such as [j] and [w] can form genuine bridges, even word-medially, we would simply have to relax the requirement that bridge consonants cannot have place properties. As we will see in § 4.3.2, such a relaxation may also be called for in the case of coda consonants.

I now turn to the possibility of nasals as bridges. Dutch allows clusters like [kn] and [km] word-initially (the latter only in *khmer*), but if such clusters occur intervocalically they are heterosyllabic (*ac.né* 'acne', *bok.ma* 'Dutch gin'). Note that if we were to allow nasals to occur as bridge consonants, we would need a place distinction, again contradicting the idea that bridges cannot have distinctive place specifications. We can block nasals from the bridge if we require a sonority distance between the edge and the bridge which excludes the manner obstruent + nasal sequences. Again, while nasals are impossible bridges in Dutch, this is not so universally, although we must always bear in mind that solid evidence for onset clusters has to come from word-internal onsets, because at the word beginning, extra consonants can occur that do not count as forming a complex onset with the following consonant. Alternatively, we would have to take a polysystematic view and say that the set of complex onsets can differ depending on the position in the word, notably word-initial versus word-internal. In that case we have to accept that word-initial complex onsets can lift constraints that apply to word-internal complex onsets. For Dutch, then, this would mean that the constraint again nasals as bridge is lifted word-initially.

In conclusion I will assume that in principle all sonorants can be bridges at least in some languages, although liquids are likely to be preferred and nasals are the most likely to be excluded. As for glides, if [h] is analysed as a placeless glide it would seem that this option is also likely to be excluded, perhaps because apparent obstruent + [h] 'clusters' might be more obviously analysed as (post-)aspirated obstruents by language learners. I note here that if we were to allow bridges to have a place specification, we would create a three-way distinction not only for glides ([j, w, h] but also for nasals, one placeless and two with a place property. However, if placelessness implies 'pharyngeal' then this option would be

---

[40] This is the approach taken in Duanmu (2008), who argues that all alleged complex onsets, including those with liquids, are single consonants with secondary articulations. Later in this chapter I make a case for maintaining the structural option of branching onsets.

excluded for nasals on phonetic grounds.[41] Of course, we also predict different place options for liquids, but place options are extremely limited for these types of consonants due to the nature of their manner.

(22)

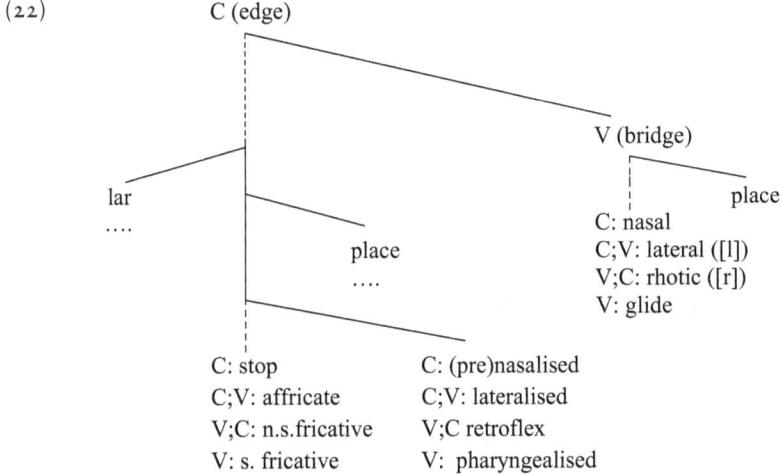

The preference for liquids can be understood by referring to the harmonic match between syllabic C;V (bridge) and the intermediate manners for laterals (C;V) and rhotics (V;C). When we consider preferences for the coda position in § 4.3.3 it will become clear that codas do not prefer liquids. Rather the preferred coda consonant is a nasal (see VanDam (2004); Krämer & Zec (2019)). To account for this fact, I will propose that the syllabic positions for the bridge and coda prefer V- and C-type manners, respectively, thus focusing on the terminal labels of their syllabic positions, which are V and C, respectively. This would then predict that the order of preference in (23):

(23) a. Bridge: V > V;C > C;V > C
     b. Coda: C > C;V > V;C > V

These rankings make nasals the least preferred bridge and the most preferred coda, both of which are correct. The only problem is now that (23a) predicts glides to be the most preferred bridge, whereas we have found that liquids form a better transition between the onset head and the rhymal head. Precisely for this reason, I suggest, liquids win over glides as optimal bridges. Formally, we could state this by adding to (23),

---

[41] LM (p. 37): 'it is logically impossible to make pharyngeal nasals (as we define nasals), since air cannot come out through the nose while the articulators make a complete closure in the pharyngeal region'.

which captures a paradigmatic form of harmony, that the intra-syllabic sequence C – C;V – V gives liquids the status of perfect bridges from a syntagmatic point of view. Here, then, the syntagmatic force prevails over the paradigmatic force. In the coda position there is no sense in which coda sonorants can be 'bridges', at least not within the syllable, which allows nasals to be preferred.[42]

We note the lack of secondary manner articulation for bridge consonants, which is expected given their dependent status. The head onset position is the position that displays the greatest array of contrasts.

It has been proposed (e.g. in Duanmu (2008) and Lowenstamm (1996)) that *all* alleged complex onsets can be analysed as complex segments, which would imply that onsets are always non-branching. Duanmu allows the rhyme to branch, while Lowenstamm has no branching constituents at all, reducing syllable structure to the first cut, resulting in a 'strict CV' approach (see Scheer (2004) for an extensive application of this approach). I maintain that true complex onsets are possible, despite the noted similarity between secondary manners and the manner of bridge consonants, which a proponent of the 'no complex onset' view might perhaps use to support this position. My 'pro complex onset' position is theoretically driven by the idea that a second cut is predicted to be possible in RCVP. How can I further motivate this choice empirically? As already discussed (with reference also to LM), it is not possible to settle the issue with phonetic evidence. We need phonological arguments. A possible argument involves the notion of intra-segmental homorganicity. For consonants that I analyse as complex, the primary and secondary specifications are 'phonetically harmonic', that is, have the same place of articulation and the same laryngeal property. We find [^{m}b] and [^{n}d], but not [^{n}g] and [^{m}d]. Likewise, we do not find [^{n}t] with a voiceless [t] and a preceding sonorant which is inherently voiced (other than as resulting from allophonic processes). Another example is that lateralised consonants are (always) coronal; see Shaw (1991).[43] We do not, however, find this kind of harmony in true complex onsets consisting of obstruent and liquid. Even though bridge consonants cannot have their own place or laryngeal specification, they do not harmonise in this way with the onset head consonant. In fact, in English and Dutch, clusters like [dl] and [tl] are excluded, arguably precisely because they are homorganic. This kind

---

[42] That said, liquids as coda sonorant consonants, when followed by an obstruent onset head, have been found to form preferred interludes, as expressed in the SCL, proposed in Murray and Vennemann (1983).

[43] However, secondary pharyngealisation can occur with consonants of all kinds of places of articulation. Here, then, the harmonicity requirement does not hold. We will also see that secondary *place* articulations need not be homorganic with the place of 'head consonant'. This puts pharyngealisation, labialisation and palatalisation 'in the same camp', even though RCVP separates them over manner and place.

of disharmony suggests a greater structural distance between the two parts of the complex onset construction. In the case of complex manner, location has scope over both parts of the manner specification, but in a complex onset that is not the case. Location and manner specification, in that case, apply to the head of the complex unit.

Of course, as discussed in this section, post-stopped nasals with a voiceless stop phrase have been reported as voiceless. I have also referred to alleged affricates that are not homorganic. If I then say that such cases are *not* complex segments, the argument from homorganicity becomes circular or, at the very best, an incentive to look for arguments that support a bisegmental analysis or an analysis in terms of allophonic variation, or even for potential transcription errors.[44]

A better type of evidence for distinguishing between complex segments and onset clusters can be found in reduplication patterns that involve cluster reduction. If the reduplicant prefix is CV-, while the base starts with a complex onset, only the head consonant is copied, but if the head consonant is a complex segment it is copied as such. Examples to demonstrate this can be found in Sanskrit and Gothic (see Zukoff (2017)):

(24) Gothic:

	Infinitive	Past tense	
a.	gretan [gret-an] 'to weep'	gaigrot [ge-grot]	(*[gre-grot])
b.	hʷopan [xʷep-an]'to boast'	haihop [xʷexʷop]	(*[xe-xʷop])

In (24a) a true complex onset is reduced in the reduplicant prefix, while in (24b) the labialised velar is copied as such.[45]

Assuming, then, that a complete reduction of all onset events to single segments is too drastic, the task of developing a comprehensive theory of syllable structure is still far from completed. The problem in evaluating the possibilities for complex onsets is that most case studies or typological studies usually do not clearly distinguish between word-initial and word-medial onsets, or only consider the former since word-medially the question of syllable division may be unclear. As discussed earlier, it is necessary to adopt a polysystematic viewpoint which accounts for

---

[44] Arguments based on child language acquisition data would not help because, I assume, children are just likely to simplify both complex onsets and complex segments.

[45] What weakens the argument is that [st] and [sk] reduplicate as 'clusters'. Example verbs are *gastaldan* 'to acquire' and *skaidan* 'to separate'. A way out would be to analyse these clusters as 'reversed' affricates, as proposed in Ewen (1982) and van de Weijer (1991).

There is of course a rich literature over the question of mono- versus bisegmental analyses of complex phonetic events. For a review see Ewen (1980b).

onsets (and syllable structure in general) relative to different positions in the word (initial, medial, final), and such factors as stress (primary and secondary) if relevant in a specific language.[46] The 'strict' view, which for onsets only permits obstruent–liquid clusters, is defensible for word-medial syllables in Dutch and other languages, perhaps allowing, in certain languages, nasals and or glides in the bridge as well, all submitting to the sonority sequence observing obstruent–sonorant patterns. However, word-initial syllables are clearly more permissive in many languages, without necessarily being completely unconstrained.[47] In some languages medial syllables can only begin with one consonant, while initial syllables can have a cluster.[48] If medial syllables can have complex onsets, initial syllables often display more combinations or even extra consonants. In Dutch, for example, word-initially, there are limited examples of obstruent + nasal and obstruent + [j], all still observing the sonority profile, hence onsets that are clearly more permissive that can occur medially (see Trommelen (1983); van der Hulst (1984)). Some conceivable and actually occurring word-initial clusters are likely to fall outside the range of any coherent theory of complex onset, such as sonorant–obstruent sequences in Slavic languages (Scheer (2004); Cyran & Gussmann (1999)) or sequences of many consonants as in Georgian (Ritter (2006)). In the works here cited, such cases are analysed with an appeal to sequences of multiple onsets with intervening empty nuclei. An alternative would be to adopt an option of word-peripheral adjunction.

4.2.3 Sonorant consonants as onset heads (including taps/flaps)

As we have seen in § 3.2.2 (see (26) in that section), sonorants can occur as singleton onsets, where, as we expect in edge position, they can have place and laryngeal properties, and even secondary properties. In this role, sonorants can be nasals, laterals and rhotics, as well as glides. Both place and laryngeal distinctions are freely possible because sonorants as onset heads can have place specifications and laryngeal specifications,

---

[46] Polysystematicity is observed in OT approaches by making constraints that govern the content of onsets, or syllables in general, relative to 'prominent positions'; see Smith (2002) and Flack (2007a).

[47] Possibly, languages such as Bella Coola, now known as Nuxalk (Bagemihl 1991) and Tashlhiyt Berber (Dell & Elmedlaoui 1985) do not have syllable structure at all at the level of grammatical phonology, and hence lack phonotactic restrictions on phoneme combinations. This still allows such languages to have a syllabic patterning at the utterance level, that is, phonetic syllabification.

[48] Hawaiian is a language with CV-only syllables; yet loanwords are permitted to start with an onset cluster. See Elbert & Pukui (2001: 13).

just like obstruents: nasals can be labial, coronal or velar; laterals can be coronal or palatal; glides can be palatal or (labio)velar. While rhotics can be coronal or uvular, no language seems to use that rather clear articulatory distinction contrastively.[49] Place distinctions for sonorant consonants in edge position are discussed in Chapter 5. As for laryngeal distinctions, while reference to voiceless sonorants occurs, one view is that such segment types are actually to be analysed as being aspirated. With the exclusion of voiceless, sonorants can have a variety of phonation types. I discuss laryngeal distinctions for sonorant consonants in edge position in Chapter 6.

Turning to secondary manner properties, we can take nasalised sonorants (other than nasals) and pharyngealised sonorants as cases of this kind, and perhaps also retroflex versions. As nasals with secondary manner qualify retroflex nasals (see MD 238 with many examples) and rarely occurring pharyngealised nasals (MD 239: !Xufi).

Staying with nasal consonants, we have seen that in plain nasals, the oral closure causes nasal release due to the fact that sonorants require a free outflow of air. In a sense, nasal release is a side effect of oral closure. This point is acknowledged in AE, who postulate two sources for nasal(ity). Nasal consonants have a manner representation (which is the manner C in RCVP), but Anderson and Ewen also postulate a separate N element.[50] In a sense, RCVP also has a dual representation of nasality: as a stricture element C for nasal consonants and as a secondary c element for segments that are nasalised. The former focuses on the complete oral stricture of nasal consonants, the latter on velic opening. Given this duality, it would seem necessary to say that plain nasals in fact have a secondary nasal articulation, albeit that this secondary articulation is a 'phonetic necessity' and thus, strictly speaking, redundant. This, however, means that retroflex or pharyngeal nasals have two secondary manners, albeit that the nasality property is, as suggested, redundant.[51]

MD groups laterals, rhotics and glides under his category of approximants. For laterals his dataset contains several velarised/pharyngealised cases (pp. 243–4) and numerous retroflex cases (p. 244). For rhotics he lists several retroflex cases (p. 241) and one pharyngealised case (p. 240: Shilha). In the category of glides there are examples of nasalisation ([j̃],

---

[49] A labial trill ('raspberry') is also possible. As discussed in § 4.2.1, it can occur allophonically as part of a prenasalised bilabial stop with trilled release. See Maddieson (1989a). A good case for three bilabial trills as contrastive segments is made for the language Mangbetu (Olson & Koogibho (2013)).

[50] In some FG models, it has also been proposed that there is a dual representation of nasality (see Avery & Rice (1990) and Piggott (1992)).

[51] This is the third time that I have had to consider the possibility of two secondary manners; see footnote 32 in this chapter.

p. 245: Yakut, Kharia; and [w̃], p. 246: Breton). Notably absent are nasalised laterals and rhotics, although a nasalised [l] is likely to be realised as [n] in a nasal context; an example of such an alternation occurs in Yoruba (Akinlabi (1985)).

While nasalised rhotics are missing in UPSID, we need to consider another secondary manner for rhotics, namely frication. On page 228, LM mention the infamous Czech [ř] as a type of trill with frication. This rhotic sound has been described as unique in the languages of the world. Historically a palatalised [r], [ř] is contrastive with [r] In Czech. Kučera (1961: 30–1) described this consonant as follows:

> /ř/ is an apical trill with simultaneous raising of the grooved blade of the tongue towards the palate which results in some lamino-palatal friction.

Scheer (1998: 52) has the following description:

> [ř] is a segment showing properties of [r] and the postalveolars [ʃ,ʒ]: on the one hand, the apex is trilling in the alveolar region exactly in the way [r] is produced. On the other hand, the tongue body position is that of the postalveolar fricatives [ʃ,ʒ], i.e., higher than that of [r].

It is important to establish whether [ř] is a sonorant or an obstruent. Kučera (1961: 31) remarks that it patterns as a sonorant, which is suggested by its occurrence as the second consonant in onset clusters.[52] A notable property is that there is an allophonic alternation between a voiced and a voiceless version. The voiceless version appears after a voiceless consonant and in final position. The fact that it undergoes both progressive voice assimilation and final devoicing strongly suggests it should be identified as an obstruent. If we analyse it as an obstruent, it must be represented as a fricative with secondary v;c (which I also designated as representing retroflexion).

Czech displays an alternation between [r] and [ř]. When the former occurs in a cluster with an obstruent, the latter appears when this cluster is followed by a front vowel (Scheer 1998: 56):

(25) Nom. Voc.
  petr petř-e 'Peter'
  kufr kufř-e 'suitcase'
  cvikr cvikř-e 'monocle'
  kopr kopř-e 'dill'

---

[52] I refer to Scheer (1998) for examples that illustrate the distribution of [ř] and the allophonic alternation between the voiced and voiceless variant. See also Bičan (2011) for an extensive 'phonemic' and phonotactic analysis of Czech.

svetr svetř-e 'pullover'
mesr mesř-e Mackie Messer (Mack the Knife), character from Brecht's *Threepenny Opera*

The ambivalent behaviour of [ř] as sonorant or obstruent is reminiscent of the similar ambiguous behaviour of labial and palatal fricative/ approximants, as well as the laryngeal [h]. All three display dual behaviour in Hungarian (see Szigetvári (1998); Siptár (1996); Ritter (1997, 2000); Blaho (2008)). The general pattern for these consonants is to act as obstruents in final, coda position, and as sonorants elsewhere. As obstruents they can engage in voicing assimilation patterns. The question is whether this duality as well as the voicing assimilation facts fall within the realm of phonology proper. Voicing assimilation in many languages has been shown to be non-neutralising and gradient. This is also the case in Hungarian (see Markó, Fráczi & Bóna (2010)). My preference would be to analyse these various segments as sonorants (for [h] see below) and relegate the obstruent appearance and behaviour to the phonetic implementation. From a phonological point of view one would not expect the coda to prefer an obstruent-like realisation if codas can only contain, or at least prefer, sonorant consonants. It is possible perhaps to analyse the alleged coda positions as (stranded) onset positions when they occur word-finally.[53] That said, I will not commit here to a further analysis. The behaviour of Czech [r] and [ř] is different because the two segments are separate phonemes, alternating as shown in (25). This alternation cannot be analysed as an implementation process given that the Instrumental suffix [-ɛm] does not trigger the appearance of [-ř] (NOM *petr* but INST *petr-em*, **petř-em*; the reason is that this suffix historically did not have a front vowel (see Scheer (1998: 56, fn. 17)). I would thus analyse this alternation as a lexical choice between the two phonemes, using the variable notation proposed in van der Hulst (2018); see also § 1.5.

This leaves unresolved the question as to whether [ř] should be analysed as an obstruent or as a sonorant. I favour the latter analysis on the basis of the phonotactic distribution of this consonant, occurring as a bridge in a complex onset. This then requires me to relegate the participation in voicing assimilation and final devoicing of this consonant,

---

[53] In RCVP, sonorants in the bridge and in the coda have a different syllabic specification. In the onset, sonorant consonants occur in a V position that is dominated by C (hence C;V), while in the coda, they occur in a C position that is dominated by V (hence V;C). This would suggest that sonorant consonants are 'stronger' in onset position, that is, more obstruent-like, especially if the sonorant occurs as an onset head. It is worth exploring whether this difference can account for the phonetic duality of sonorant consonants in general.

as mentioned, to the phonetic implementation, alongside the similar behaviour of sonorant consonants in Hungarian. Given the analysis as a sonorant, we then have to account for the specific post-alveolar/palatal tongue body position that causes the friction. The most obvious analysis (given the historical source of this consonant, as well as its current articulatory character) is to analyse [ř] as a palatalised [r], that is, in terms of a secondary place property palatal. While this might be justified for the Czech [ř], it may not be the best solution for the fricative [r] that AE (pp. 150ff.) discuss for Scots, referring to Aitken's Law. Abercrombie (1967: 54) defined this [r] as a fricative trill. In this case, there is no contrast between two r sounds, however, which makes the case for a phonemic representation that acknowledges the frication of an r sound less compelling.[54]

Nevertheless, it is possible to consider a representation of Czech [ř] that honours its fricative property directly (which, then, can also be applied to Scots [r]). This alternative attributes the frication to a secondary manner property, other than c and v which represent nasalisation and pharyngealisation, respectively. A reason for considering this alternative is that when we discuss secondary manner for vowels in § 4.3.1.2 we will find 'frication' attested as one such property, alongside stridency, retroflexion and some other phonetic properties such as 'epiglottal' or 'sphincteric'. For such cases secondary palatalisation is not an option. In § 4.3.1.2, I propose that *all* such secondary vowel manners can be represented in terms of the intermediate secondary c;v manner.[55] We could thus consider that the fricative [ř] is also characterised with the intermediate secondary manner c;v. This secondary manner then represents lateralisation for obstruents and frication for sonorants consonants and vowels.[56]

I now turn to a type of sonorant consonant that can occur as onset head that has not yet been mentioned. This is the category of taps and flaps, which can occur as onset heads in contrast with rhotics and laterals as, for example in Kurdish (MD 015), Somali (MD 258), Ngizim

---

[54] Another example of a fricative trill occurs in Dutch, where the so-called voiced uvular trill, may 'sound' like a fricative; see Collins & Mees (2003: 200). In this case there is no need for a representation that encodes frication, which can be seen as a phonetic effect, handled in phonetic implementation, and there would thus be no need for a phonemic representation.

[55] I will discuss in § 4.3.1.2 whether we must say that a distinction between c;v and v;c is potentially contrastive for vowels.

[56] Recall that for obstruents I proposed that the complex secondary manners c;v and v;c are potentially contrastive, representing lateralisation and retroflexion, respectively; see (16). It would seem that obstruents, sonorants as onset heads and perhaps vowels – all syllabic heads – dip into the maximal complexity available for secondary manners.

(MD 269), Kota (MD 903, where it is retroflex) and Basque (MD 914). In some other languages this segment seems to take the place of the rhotic consonant; see Sinhalese (MD 020), Ewe (MD 114), Luo (MD 205), Western Desert (MD 360), Selepet (MD 607), Telugu (MD 902) and so on. It can also be the sole representative of the liquid category, as in Washkuk (MD 602), Daribi (MD 616), Karok (MD 741), Amahuaca (MD 810), Chacobo (MD 811), Guarani (MD 828) and Siriono (MD 829), sometimes described as retroflex as in Pawaian (MD 612), Kunimaipa (MD 620) and Papago (MD 736). Flaps are sometimes described as being lateral (e.g. Zande, MD 130) and some other languages (see MD p. 241) or retroflex (several languages, MD pp. 241–2), or both (S. Nambiquara MD 816; Moro MD 101; Papago MD 736). All preceding examples are described as flaps in MD. A tap is given for Malayalam (MD 905) and taking the place of the rhotic in Khalaj (MD 064), Bambara (105) and Acoma (MD 749), and being the only liquid in Rotokas (MD 625).

Our interest here is in languages (that were mentioned in the preceding paragraph) that use the tap/flap segment contrastively with other sonorant consonants, especially with a lateral and rhotic liquid. No contrastive distinction between taps and flaps has been attested (see LM pp. 230–1). From an articulatory point of view, the difference is that a tap is a single light contact, whereas a flap involves curling the tongue tip and making a light contact with the underside of the tip (which produces a kind of retroflex articulation). Assuming for the moment that no distinction between tap and flaps need be made, how can this category be represented, given that it can contrast with [r] and [l] within the group of liquids?

In van der Hulst (2005a) I propose analysing these consonants as mannerless, but here I reject this proposal on the argument that manner is the head class and thus obligatory (and not as such empty). An alternative that might come to mind is that the tap/flap option is the placeless option for sonorant consonants. Since taps/flaps are typically coronal, coronality can be taken to be the default place. However, this would not be consistent with the proposal just mentioned that placelessness will be used for pharyngeal and laryngeal consonants, with the place distinction being coronal and peripheral (see Chapter 5). Therefore, it would be inconsistent to regard taps/flaps as placeless, which would then predict a pharyngeal place for those segments. Another problem for the placeless interpretation of flap/tap articulation is that taps/flaps are also reported for other places. A non-coronal flap [v] has been reported, among others for Mangbetu (see Olson & Hajek (2003, 2004) for cross-linguistic reports on this segment type).

I will here propose the following representation: taps/flaps are glides, which accounts for their 'weak' articulation, with an intermediate secondary manner articulation.[57] This makes available a distinction between taps and flaps if we separate c;v and v;c:

(26)
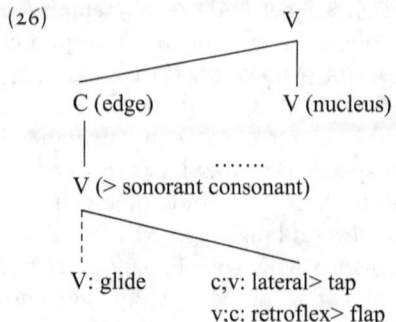

Even though the two intermediate manners do not occur contrastively, it is interesting that these two manners in fact deliver the difference between the tap and flap articulation as described above. If there is only one representation for tap and flap, we would have to assume that descriptions such as 'retroflex flap' (MD pp. 241–2) or 'lateral flap' (MD p. 242) or even 'retroflex lateral flap' (MD p. 242) merely contain phonetic descriptive elements of the articulation of these sounds, rather than contrastive categories. An argument for allowing just one intermediate secondary manner is that having both c;v and v;c predicts lateralised version of nasals, laterals and rhotics for which there appears to be no use. Allowing only the undifferentiated cv will deliver retroflex versions of all sonorant nasals and laterals. For rhotics, this would also produce a retroflex version, as well as the fricative Czech [ř], while for glides it produces the tap/flap segment type. Evidence for assuming just one secondary complex manner is that for other sonorant consonants, there is also no contrast that could correspond to the difference between c;v (lateralised) and v;c (rhotic, retroflex). In fact, what we find is only retroflex versions of nasal (MD 238), laterals (MD 244) and trills (MD 240).

In (27) I summarise the primary and secondary manner options for sonorants as onset heads discussed thus far:

---

[57] This idea bears some resemblance to a proposal in Banner Inouye (1989), who proposes an analysis in which taps/flaps are 'complex consonants' with a ternary branching structure involving a sequence of two approximant articulations flanking a stop articulation.

Manner 145

(27)

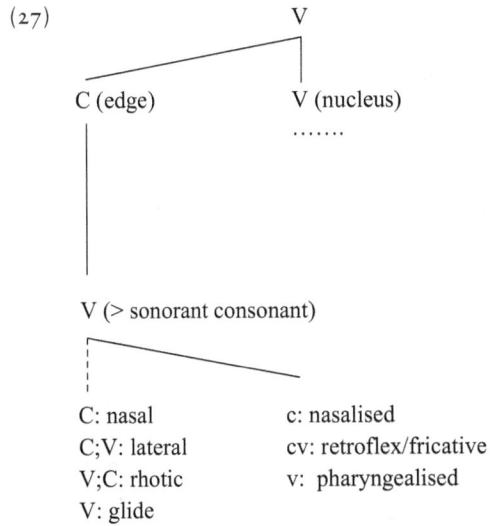

C: nasal   c: nasalised
C;V: lateral   cv: retroflex/fricative
V;C: rhotic   v: pharyngealised
V: glide

As was proposed in § 3.2.2 (see (27)), sonorant onsets require a subjunction structure with the V element immediately dominated by a C element.[58]

Recall that in the discussion of primary and secondary manner for obstruents there was a clear sense in which the primary manner and the secondary manner differed in terms of what I labelled as C versus V (see (19)). What we see in (25) is that such an antagonistic relation is largely missing (except perhaps for the rare case of the fricative [ř] in Czech). The generalisation would seem to be that secondary manner strongly tends to be of a sonorant nature. This then undermines the antagonistic labelling in (19) for obstruents.

A formal explanation for the somewhat rare occurrence of sonorant onsets with a secondary manner articulation is that sonorant onsets as such form marked structures; that is, sonorant onsets are less preferred than obstruent onsets. Again, we see that accumulations of markedness are avoided in languages. The fact is, though, that retroflexion is *not* very rare, which might be a problem for accounting for this property in the manner class.

To conclude this section, I mention the fact that even though sonorant consonants can occur as onset heads in almost all languages, there are languages which bar certain consonants from onset head position. Relevant cases are discussed in J. Smith (2002, 2003, 2007, 2008) and

---

[58] Recall that the occurrence of sonorant consonants in onset head position is structurally analogous to the occurrence of such segments in rhyme head positions (in which case we use the term 'syllabic consonant'; see § 3.2.2 and § 4.4).

Flack (2007b). The consonants that may be barred are the velar nasal [ŋ] and the laryngeal consonants [h] and [ʔ] (see Flack 2007b: 21–8). I would attribute the exclusion of laryngeal consonants to their placelessness. The velar nasal may be lacking because of its historical origin (from *[ng] in Germanic languages).[59] I here will focus on the exclusion of nasals (in general), laterals, rhotic and glides, all high-sonority consonants.

Both Smith and Flack show clearly that constraints on onset content hold either generally or, more typically, only for syllable in prominent positions. Flack suggests a hierarchy:

(28)   Utterance > word > foot[60] > syllable

The empirical observation is that the bigger the prosodic boundary the more likely it is that certain lower-sonority consonants (or the above-mentioned velar nasal and laryngeals) are barred. Both Smith (2002: 131–57) and Flack (2007a: 28ff.) focus on exclusion in word-initial position, citing cases that block only glides, both glides and rhotics or all non-nasal sonorant consonants. There is a second implicational relation here that is expected: exclusion of sonorants of some type implies exclusion of sonorants that are higher in sonority. In OT approaches, this implication is captured by a universal ranking of constraints, e.g. Smith (2007: 265):

(29)   The *Onset/X constraint family:
       *ONS/GLIDE >> *ONS/RHOTIC >> *ONS/LATERAL >>
       *ONS/NASAL >> *ONS/VOICEDOBST >> *ONS/VCLSOBST

This particular ranking is said to be functionally motivated, meaning that it is explained outside the formal theory. I take the opportunity here to point out that this ranking is formally motivated with the RCVP model:

(30)   C|V: man V >> C|V: man V;C >> C|V >> man C;V >> C|V: C >> man C: man C, Lar: V >> C: man C, Lar C

The degree of sonorance is formally determined by the preponderance of V. I cannot discuss here whether the implicational scale in (28) can also be derived from formal properties of the representation because RCVP has not been worked out up to the higher levels of prosodic structure,

---

[59] For the occurrence of the velar nasal in WALS, see Anderson (2008), who notes strong areal aspects to both the occurrence of this segment and its non-occurrence in onsets. The velar nasal can also sometimes be precluded from coda position; see § 4.3.3.

[60] The inclusion of foot structure captures the potential relevance of primary and secondary stress.

apart from 'foot structure' (see § 3.2.5), where foot-initial consonants are indeed less V-like than syllables that are foot dependents.

4.2.4 Laryngeal consonants

In this section I will discuss the representation of the laryngeal consonants [ʔ] and [h]. In the literature on FG (see § 11.2), but preceding that, in DP (Lass 1975), the proposal has been to represent these consonants as lacking a place and manner specification, thus only having a laryngeal specification, such as [+constricted glottis] for the glottal stop and [+spread glottis] for the [h]. This approach cannot be taken in the present model if all segments require a manner specification. Therefore, I propose the following structures:

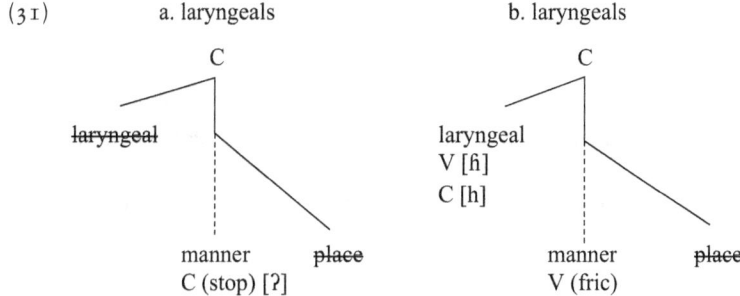

As was originally pointed out in Lass (1975) and Thráinsson (1978), the representations in (31) can account for the diachronic change ('debuccalisation') from stops like [p], [t], [k] to glottal stop (as in varieties of English (Harris 1990) and several Chinese dialects (Zhang 2006)) as the simple deletion of the place class. The same applies for a change from fricatives to [h], as in varieties of Spanish and many other languages.

There is one problem when laryngeals are represented as placeless. Labialisation can occur with the glottal stop in Kabardian (MD p. 215) and with the laryngeal [h] in Igbo, Amharic, Hupa and Siona (MD p. 234). This raises a technical problem given that these segments do not have a primary place. The same problem would arise if pharyngeal consonants with palatalisation or labialisation occurred (they do not occur in UPSID). Secondary properties, as dependents, cannot occur without a head. It would not help to then say that laryngeals are mannerless. Firstly, laryngeals can occur with pharyngealisation (as in Nootka, MD 730, p. 215), which would presuppose a primary manner, since pharyngealisation is a secondary manner. Secondly, it would still not be obvious what the place of articulation of laryngeal consonants would be, such that they can have a secondary specification. I return to this problem in § 5.2.3, where pharyngeal and laryngeal consonants are discussed.

In (31) I took the syllabic position in which the laryngeals occur to be C, which makes them 'obstruents' because their manner properties are obstruent-like, that is, stop and fricative. This is furthermore supported by the fact that laryngeal consonants make bad bridges (if they occur as such at all). However, it has also been argued that these consonants are sonorants (Odden 2013). In that case the syllabic labelling would have to be C|V (V subjoined to C). However, that would change the interpretation of the manner specification to nasal and glide, respectively. While this might work for the [h] (a placeless glide in onset head position), it does not deliver a glottal stop, but rather a 'placeless nasal' in onset head position, which is not a usable category. The decision that laryngeals are obstruent of course begs the question *why* a placeless sonorant (i.e. placeless nasal and placeless glide, if only the simple primary manner categories are considered) in onset head position is not a necessary or even usable option. The best I can offer is that sonorants in onset head position are marked, which then makes the marked option of placelessness unlikely. Nevertheless, if [h] can also be a placeless glide in onset dependent position, we end up with the conclusion that [h] is ambiguous: as onset head it is an obstruent, while as onset dependent (rare as it may be in that position) it is a sonorant.

Also note that technically complex manners (combing a primary and secondary manner) could then also occur without a place specification. Such a formal possibility is not empirically required. In the absence of a formal explanation, we would have to say the lack of place is 'marked' and that this marked option precludes a marked option for manner. In Section 4.2.1.2 I discussed the fact that marked structures preclude combinations with marked structures, in order to explain the reduction from (14) to (18). Here we need to recall that marked structures are not only those that are complex (see § 2.2.2 and § 9.5). Markedness also arises from the absence of specifications. Both mixed specification ('2' units combined) and absent specification ('o' units) undermine the perceptual salience of representations. Languages can then be said to avoid an accumulation of formal options ('2' and 'o') that undermine perceptual salience.

A voicing difference for the glottal stop is not possible. In the case of the glottal fricative, a voice contrast is phonetically possible, although this occurs rarely; Zulu (MD 126) is a possible case.[61] In the absence of a voicing contrast, oddly, perhaps, laryngeal specifications are not required

---

[61] In Zulu certain laryngeal fricatives, called voiced, act as depressor consonants, i.e. they cause tone lowering on surrounding vowels. See Strazny (2003).

for laryngeal consonants. I return to this point in § 5.2.3.

As has been pointed out in many publications, the absence of place specifications for laryngeals provides a basis for explaining their transparency in vowel harmony or vowel assimilations; see, for example, Steriade (1987a) and Stemberger (1993). This transparent behaviour can sometimes extend to so-called guttural consonants (pharyngeals and laryngeals and even uvular fricatives); see McCarthy (1994), Rose (1996), Hall (2006) and Walker & Rose (2015) for various accounts.[62]

This concludes the proposal for manner specification in the onset. Before turning to rhyme manners, I draw attention to the following predictions made by the RCVP model, which are all confirmed:

- General: simple manner structures are preferred over combinations in both the head and the dependent class.
- General: dependent structures almost always neutralise the dependency distinction for combinations, or do not use combinations at all.
- In the edge position, obstruents are preferred over sonorant consonants.
- Bridge consonants are preferably liquids (i.e. perfect transitions from onset head to nucleus).
- The absence of a secondary specification is preferred over its presence.
- For obstruent onsets, secondary specifications are more preferred for simplex primary specifications than for complex primary specifications.
- For sonorant onset heads, secondary specifications are dispreferred.
- Bridge consonants do not have, or hardly have, secondary manner specifications.
- Bridge consonants do not have laryngeal, and have only limited place, properties.

In support of the dependency approach we see overwhelming evidence for the basic head/dependent asymmetry: dependent structures display a lesser degree of complexity than head, whether intra-segmentally or in complex onsets. While the model allows a large number of possible structures, it is clear that the relative complexity of structures directly correlates with likeliness of occurrence, that is, preference. We have seen several examples of the fact that accumulation of complex structures is highly dispreferred. I will discuss this in more detail in Chapter 8. That said, we have also established that null complexity (i.e. absence of properties) creates marked, less preferred structures.

---

[62] In some cases, the guttural may be semi-transparent, i.e. exert influence on neighbouring vowels. See Walker & Rose (2015) and Mous & van der Hulst (1992). See § 7.2 for the RCVP representation of guttural consonants.

4.3 Rhyme

The discussion of rhyme structure will follow the same road map as for onset structures. Firstly, I will propose head manner structures for the rhymal head, the nucleus. This will be followed by dependent structures for the nucleus. After that, I will propose structures for the occurrence of sonorant consonants, either as rhymal heads ('syllabic sonorants') or as codas.

4.3.1 Nucleus (rhyme head): vowels

4.3.1.1 Nucleus (rhyme head): head class

Usually the notion of manner is understood as applying to consonants only, referring to aspects of segmental stricture ([±continuant]), nasality, laterality and so on. Vowels are not, then, usually thought of as having a 'manner'. RCVP draws an analogy between consonantal manner and vowel aperture (height), both involving a degree of stricture. The property 'high' for vowels is thus analogous to the property 'stop' for obstruents, both representing the highest degree of stricture within their respective realms; obviously, the highest degree of stricture for vowels must still allow for a free passage of air because this is the defining property of the class of vowels (as encoded by syllabic V position). On this assumption, RCVP proposes the following two-way split for vowel manner. The two-way split delivers the 'traditional' four vowel heights, which RCVP predicts to be the maximal number of vowel heights:[63]

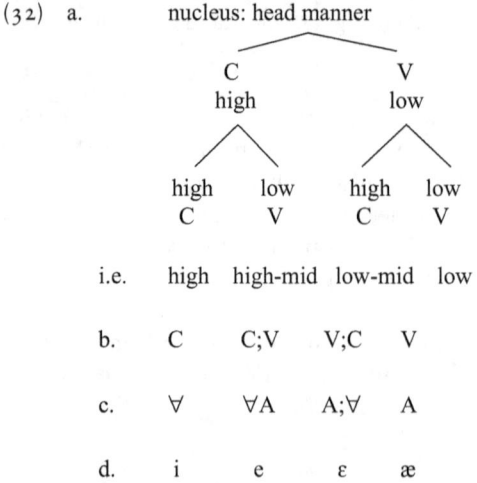

(32) a.   nucleus: head manner

                    C   V
                   high   low

              high   low   high   low
               C   V   C   V

       i.e.   high high-mid low-mid low

       b.   C   C;V   V;C   V

       c.   ∀   ∀A   A;∀   A

       d.   i   e   ɛ   æ

---

[63] This way of splitting up height is parallel to defining four tonal heights, as proposed in Yip (1980); see Chapter 6 on tone.
  On the absence of a dependency relation, see below.

As before, we see that dependent elements do not predict natural classes, since in this case this would denote discontinuous classes (high and low-mid; low and high-mid). The head element, on the other hand, denotes continuous heights (high and high-mid; low and low-mid):

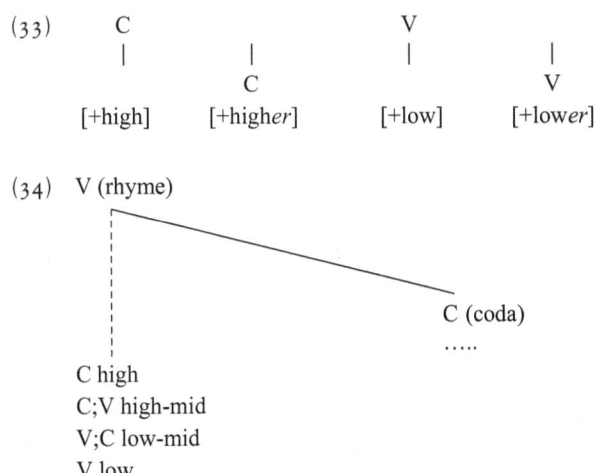

(34) V (rhyme)

C (coda)

C high
C;V high-mid
V;C low-mid
V low

The first question to ask is whether it is formally possible for a language to have no vowel contrast at all. If a manner specification is obligatory, even in that case there would have to be a 'choice' for manner. One notorious case that has been much discussed is Kabardian, as analysed in Kuipers (1960: ch. 6); on this issue see Allen (1965) and especially Wood (1991); the more popular analysis is to postulate two vowel heights for this language.[64] Of course, having no contrast is conceivable in unstressed positions which display a total neutralisation, the usual outcome being a schwa-like vowel. While in such cases the manner specification could be left unspecified, I will propose in § 7.2.1.4 that we must specify the manner as V, for which I use the shorthand symbol |A| in (32c). More commonly, a vowel system has a two-way distinction in aperture which, in the absence of a colour distinction, produces a vertical system with minimally two vowels (Abkhaz, Kabardian, Arrernte and Standard Mandarin Chinese). A vertical system can even have three vowels (Adyghe, Wichita and Irish for short vowels), perhaps even four (as in Marshallese, although that system may now have reduced to three heights; Hale (2000)).[65]

---

[64] Another such case is Moloko; see Friesen (2017).
[65] There are several typological studies of vowel systems which contain these examples: Trubetzkoy (1929, 1939); Sedlak (1969); Liljencrants & Lindblom (1972); Crothers (1978); Lass (1984); MD (ch. 8), Disner (1984); Schwartz, Boë, Vallee

Vertical systems can arise either through merger of front and round-back vowels (e.g. in Wichita, not considering length (Rood 1975)) or, more commonly, because the colour distinctions are transferred to surrounding consonants in the form of palatalisation or labialisation (Kabardian, Arrernte (Breen 2001); Marshallese (Bender (1963); Hale (2000)). In all vertical systems, vowels may end up *phonetically* with rounding or frontness, either due to consonantal influence or because 'colour' (i.e. non-height properties such as frontness and rounding) is redundantly present to prevent having central colourless vowels, which have low perceptual salience.

The fact that vowel systems can exist with height distinctions only, while systems with only colour are unattested, supports the decision to make vowel manner (height, aperture) the head of the segmental structure, analogous to the headhood of consonant manner. A vowel height specification is thus obligatory. I have also mentioned another manifestation of headhood (or lack therefore), which relates to mobility ('spreading'). The most notorious instance of spreading of vowel properties involves vowel harmony. While various types of vowel harmony exist, the most widespread cases involve either vowel colour (palatal harmony and labial harmony) or dependent manner properties (to be discussed in the next section) such as TR position or nasality. Aperture harmony (raising, lowering) does exist, however, so we cannot say that head manner specifications are completely immobile. However, van der Hulst (2018) shows that alleged height harmony is often TR harmony or, if height is involved, dependent on stress (as in metaphony in the Romance languages). Nevertheless, we cannot completely exclude height harmony, as shown in van der Hulst (2018: ch. 6).

Finally, a third argument that supports the headhood of vowel height is that differences in aperture can play a role in stress assignment in so-called prominence systems (Kenstowicz (1994b, 1995); Walker (1996); Crowhurst & Michael (2005)). If vowel height is a manner property, it follows that this property is formally visible to higher structure due to the projection of head properties to the top node of the segment.[66]

In van der Hulst (2015b, 2018) I discuss at some length the status of the C element for vowel height, which is represented with the symbol |∀|.

& Abry (1997); Gordon (2016); Hitch (2017); and https://wals.info/chapter/2, as well as the various typological databases available. In this section I will not refer to specific publication for each language that I mention as an example because, apart from one vowel system, the systems that I refer to are general and not in question.

[66] Although, probably for different reasons, tonal properties of vowels are often also included as relevant for stress (especially high tone), in this case because such properties obviously contribute to a vowel's perceptual salience; see de Lacy (2002).

The adoption of this element leads to a departure from the original DP triangular system: |A|, |I| and |U|. In RCVP, the latter two elements belong to the place class, leaving |A| as a 'lone' aperture element for 'low' or 'open'. The logic of RCVP suggests that |A| has a counterpart which represents 'closed' or 'high'. However, from an articulatory point of view, a feature such as 'high' is suspect because there appears to be no independent articulatory mechanism for raising the tongue. This is a major cause for criticism of the tongue height model of vowel aperture (see Wood (1982)). The binary categorisation of phonetic dimensions that underlies the architecture of RCVP is rooted in a cognitive principle: the Opponent Principle (see § 3.2.1). In most dimensions, there is solid phonetic grounding for the two elements that form opponent units. However, given the biological limitations of our articulatory mechanisms, discrepancies may arise between the demands of cognitive systems and the anatomy on which these systems are 'superimposed'. I have therefore suggested that, as a result, the cognitive category |∀|, which the theory predicts, lacks its own unique articulatory basis; in some sense, it is parasitic on the articulatory grounding of the |I| element, which involves advancement of the TR, leading, as a side effect, to raising of the tongue body. I also propose that this lack of phonetic identity is why the |∀| element is 'defective' in its phonological behaviour, which has led me to suggest in van der Hulst (2018) that the element |∀| cannot function as a head. This means that in combination with the element |A|, |∀| cannot be a head. Either combinations of both aperture elements are A-headed or headedness is not specified. The defective nature of |∀| is reminiscent of the defective nature of the so-called 'cold vowel' in GP, which, as a head, functions as an identity operator. The element |∀| in some sense combines properties of the cold vowel and the ATR element in GP. This latter element in GP has specific properties which distinguish it from the other elements (see den Dikken & van der Hulst (1988); van der Hulst (2015b)). For more extensive discussions of the RCVP analysis of vowel systems, I refer to van der Hulst (2018), which examines vowel structure through the lens of vowel harmony.

A challenge to the proposal in (31) could come from vowel systems that are claimed to involve more than four heights. However, in such cases it is likely that the independent dimension of TR position (advancement), creating an expanded pharyngeal cavity, has the side effect of causing differences in tongue height. Another, independent dimension is the tense/lax distinction, although I propose in van der Hulst (2018) that this phonetic property is just another exponent of the ATR element, a not uncommon claim; see, for example, Calabrese (2011). In RCVP, tenseness/laxness is thus not incorporated as an independent property. Duanmu (2016) goes so far as to claim that only a two-way difference in tongue height is universally required. Even though I do not intend here to support that proposal, his radical position suggests that exceeding four heights is far from needed.[67]

4.3.1.2 Nucleus (rhyme head): dependent class

In this section, I propose a structure for the secondary manner properties of vowels. I will start with considering two alternatives for the secondary elements c and v. I do this because, firstly, I considered one of them (that I now reject) in earlier work. Secondly, by discussing the motivations for choosing between these alternatives, we can gain a perspective on the 'logic' of RCVP, that is, the considerations that have led me to embrace certain structures and interpretations while rejecting others.

While the head manner specification accounts for aperture distinctions in the oral cavity, I propose that the simple secondary manner for vowels (c and v) involves the other two resonating cavities that our anatomy makes available: the pharyngeal and the nasal cavity. What must then be decided is the line-up between these two cavities and the c/v choice:

(35) secondary V manner (nucleus, dependent class)

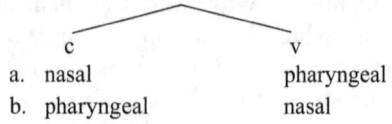

	c	v
a.	nasal	pharyngeal
b.	pharyngeal	nasal

In van der Hulst (2018) I adopt option (35a), which leads to (36):

(36) V (rhyme)

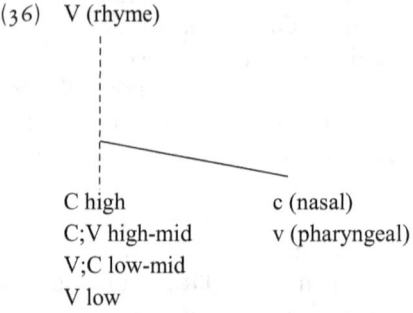

C high   c (nasal)
C;V high-mid   v (pharyngeal)
V;C low-mid
V low

---

[67] A case for five-vowel height is made in Traunmüller (1983), mentioned in LM (pp. 289–90). However, this language has just four heights for front unrounded, front round and back rounded vowels. In addition, it has a central vowel [a], but apart from phonetic motivations, there is no reason to distinguish five heights because the central vowel is lower than the lowest vowel in each series. This low vowel forms a four-way contrast with the lowest vowel in each series.

Manner   155

My reason for rejecting the proposal in (35b) in this book lies in the fact that it destroys the analogy that has been established between the interpretations of the manner structures for sonorant consonants in the bridge and coda (37a),[68] as well as the sonorant secondary articulation for obstruents (37b):

(37) a. Primary manner   C   C;V   V;C   V
        bridge/coda   nasal   lateral rhotic   glide

     b. Secondary manner   c   v
        edge   nasal   pharyngeal

     c. Secondary manner   c   v
        nucleus   i. nasal   pharyngeal (35a)
                       ii. pharyngeal   nasal (35b)

As can be observed in (37b), the secondary manner property v has been correlated with secondary pharyngealisation when it occurs with consonants in the edge position. As a primary element manner in the bridge and coda in (37a), V has been designated as representing a 'placeless glide', but we considered this to be a possible representation of the laryngeal consonant [h], if acting like a sonorant. Clearly, the choice of nasal for secondary v manner of vowels in (35b)/(37cii) would deviate from the interpretations of C/c in (37a) and (37b). Therefore, we have to adopt (35a), which achieves perfect analogy across the cases in (37).[69]

If we then apply secondary v to vowels, we expect it to represent pharyngeal constriction, popularly known as RTR. As such, it can represent pharyngealised vowels. It can also be used as such to deal with certain

---

[68] Codas manners are discussed in § 4.3.2.
[69] A second 'argument' for identifying nasality with 'v' could be that it achieves a convergence with proposals in GP in which nasality is identified with the L element when it is non-headed (see § 2.3). When L is headed, it represents voicing in obstruents and tone in vowels, while when non-headed it represents nasality. This then establishes a close connection between voicing and nasality; see Nasukawa (2005) and Backley (2011). If RCVP represented nasality with the v element it would also establish such a correlation, since the primary V element in the laryngeal class expresses voicing (for obstruents) and low tone (for vowels). Below, I discuss in detail why nasality and voicing cannot be identified with the same element in RCVP. In defence of designated nasality with c I mention the fact that the opening of the nasal cavity results from an oral action of the velum, which causes closing the oral cavity so that air flows out through the nasal cavity.
   To support correlating c with nasality: nasality prefers high vowels: nasalisation from the assimilation of a nasal consonant tends to cause a raising of vowel height, whereas rhoticity prefers low vowels. However, nasality can certainly occur with vowels of all heights, and may even be preferred for low vowels in some cases (e.g. in Thai). See Beddor (1982) and Haspelmath, Dryer, Gil & Comrie (2008: ch. 10).

kinds of vowel harmony systems. In van der Hulst (2018: § 10.1–3) I discuss a group of languages that have a so-called 'double triangular system', for which it has also been claimed that RTR is the active and often 'dominant' feature in terms of harmony, making them 'diagonal harmony systems' (a term used in Kim (1978)):

(38) double triangular system

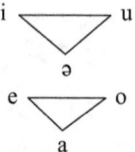

In van der Hulst (1988a), double triangular systems are analysed in terms of the primary element V (i.e. as 'A harmony'). In van der Hulst (2018) I accept this as a possible analysis within the current RCVP model, but I note that diagonal systems could also be analysed in terms of the secondary v element. It is possible that these two types of analyses refer to different situations. The mid vowels in (38) are sometimes transcribed as 'ɪ' and 'ʊ'. It is thus possible to say that if the mid vowels are [e] and [o] harmony involves the primary element V (|A|), whereas the transcription 'ɪ' and 'ʊ' might be a pointer to an analysis in terms of the secondary v as the harmonic element. But perhaps we should not make too much of differences in transcriptions in this case. Various studies of African harmony systems note that the two transcriptions are often both used by different authors for the same languages; see van der Hulst (2018: § 6.3.1.2.1 on Kikuyu).

However, by accepting the proposal in (36), we run into a problem that can be referred to as the 'mysterious (if not dubious) phonetic ambiguity of the secondary element v'. This problem arises when we consider other kinds of harmony systems that have been analysed with 'ATR' being the dominant property. Based on a broad typological study of tongue harmony in African languages, it has been convincingly shown in Casali (2003, 2008) that languages with TR harmony in which there is a TR contrast among high vowels are best analysed by taking the advanced vowels as possessing the harmony property. In van der Hulst (2018) I refer to this as 'Casali's Correlation'. Casali then also argues that languages that only have a contrast for mid vowels require activation of the feature RTR because in those cases the lower mid vowels act as the dominant class; see also Leitch (1996), who confirms this approach in a typological study of vowel harmony in Bantu languages. These proposals are discussed in great detail in van der Hulst (2018: ch. 7). The question is now whether Casali's Correlation requires the adoption of a new element, alongside secondary v (RTR), that correlates with ATR, which is required for languages that have a TR contrast for high vowels. After all, (36) does not accommodate an ATR element.

In previous work on RCVP (e.g. van der Hulst 2005a), I have considered the structure in (39), which makes room for an ATR element, at the expense of nasality:

(39)   V (rhyme)

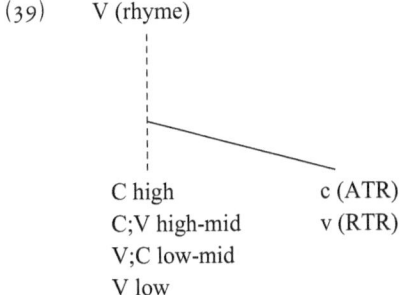

C high   c (ATR)
C;V high-mid   v (RTR)
V;C low-mid
V low

Apart from making room for an ATR element, an additional motivation for the structure in (39) is that it expresses a direct and formal correlation between tongue height and TR advancement: high (C) correlates with ATR (c) and low (V) correlates with RTR (v). These correlations are well motivated because high vowels prefer to be advanced while low vowels prefer to be retracted. In Chapter 8 I show in detail that these kinds of correlations are expected given the RCVP notation. However, there are two problems with (39). Firstly, it does not reserve a place for nasality. Secondly, it allows for a contrast between RTR and ATR vowels which remains unattested.[70] This seems to bring us back to the proposal in (36), but there is a catch. By accepting the proposal in (36) and by accepting Casali's Correlation it would appear that the secondary element v is phonetically ambiguous, in that it correlates with two opposing articulatory actions, namely advancement of the tongue (in languages that have a TR contrast among high vowels) and retraction of the TR in all other situations. As shown in Wood (1979, 1982) these two actions involve different muscles: the genioglossus and the hyoglossus, respectively.

In van der Hulst (2018) I accept this consequence of allowing the element v to be phonetically ambiguous. I took the phonetic distinction between ATR and RTR to be a non-contrastive *phonetic split* of the pharyngeal element, with ATR representing a *phonetic* c element and RTR a *phonetic* v element, the choice being determined by the structure of the vowel system, following Casali's Correlation. To make matters more complicated, I did not accept Casali's proposal that languages that

---

[70] Certain Kru languages might qualify, however, for using both ATR and RTR; see Newman (1986) and Singler (2008); but the nature of the vowel contrast and the harmony facts in these languages are not entirely clear to me.

have harmony only among mid vowels appeal to the RTR interpretation of the secondary v element. Instead I analyse such systems as follows: the mid vowels are A-headed (i.e. V;C or A;∀), whereas high-mid vowels are non-headed (CV or ∀A). In the presence of low-mid vowels, high-mid vowels will become A-headed, which accounts for the harmony. I refer to van der Hulst (2018: ch. 7) for further discussion, but I will add here that an analysis in terms of secondary v would also be possible. It is not clear to me why I did not consider this alternative in van der Hulst (2018).

Returning to the ambiguity of the element v, which is clearly undesirable, it is also not clear to me why I did not consider an 'old' idea that I had proposed in van der Hulst (1988a, 1988b), which was to identify ATR with a dependent usage of the I element (in the place class). There is good reason to link ATR to the I element, since both draw on activity of the genioglossus muscle which pulls the tongue forward as a consequence of raising and fronting the tongue body.[71] Also note that the affinity with high vowels, C mannered, is expressed because the I element is also a C element (in the place class).[72] I will thus propose in the chapter on place that ATR is the interpretation of a secondary I element (see § 5.3.2).

A consequence of this proposal is of course that we no longer rule out a language having both pharyngeal harmony and ATR harmony, at least not on formal grounds.

One issue now remains to be addressed. As explained in Lindau (1979), phonetically speaking, a distinction between the relative size of the pharyngeal cavity can be made in three different ways:

(40)   Set 1: larger pharynx: Set 2: smaller pharynx:
   a. Advanced = dominant   neutral
   b. Neutral   retracted = dominant
   c. Advanced   retracted

This finding has led some phonologists to the conclusion that if (40a) obtains, the relevant phonological category is ATR, which is the common choice for African languages. In contrast, if (40b) obtains, the active feature would be RTR. Various authors writing on vowel harmony in Asian languages belonging to the Tungusic and Mongolian language

---

[71] This affinity is perhaps also the cause of a shift from palatal harmony to ATR harmony which has been said to occur in some Mongolian languages; see Svantesson (1985). Ko (2011) argues for the opposite development.

[72] See van der Hulst (2016a) for a discussion of the correlations with reference to Wood (1975, 1979, 1982). In Wood's system, his feature [palatal] applies to all high vowels, not just [i]. In my proposal, this would only be the case for the secondary use of the element I ([ATR]).

Manner   159

families have established that a TR distinction is made in terms of tongue retraction, (40b); see van der Hulst (2018: § 9.2.). In the theory proposed in van der Hulst (2018) the interpretation of a difference such as that between (40a) and (40b), in terms of activating two different features (ATR and RTR, respectively), is rejected, on the grounds that adopting two different features (or elements) to account for TR harmony in these different groups of languages would make predictions about the behaviour of so-called neutral vowels in both types of systems that are not borne out by the data. I show that the facts regarding the behaviour of neutral vowels in *both* African and Asian languages must lead to the conclusion that the set with the larger cavity (whether positively resulting from advancement of the tongue or negatively resulting from the absence of TR retraction) is the dominant set in all vowel harmony systems that fall under Casali's Correlation, that is, in which there is a TR contrast for high vowels.

Given the current proposal, namely to analyse ATR as secondary |I|, all these languages must be analysed with harmony in terms of this element. For Tungusic and Mongolian languages in which the non-ATR vowels have active TR retraction, I would argue that this retraction merely enhances the phonetic difference between advanced and non-advanced vowels. Such enhancement might, in fact, also occur in African languages, as shown in Lindau (1975, 1976).

Tying the various considerations and findings together, while accepting the structure in (36), as well as the treatment of ATR in terms of secondary |I|, we no longer need to say that the secondary element v correlates with two opposing phonetic properties. This secondary element always correlates consistently with TR retraction (pharyngealisation). It is active in diagonal systems and possibly African harmony systems in which a tongue contrast only exists among the mid vowels; we note, however, that in both cases an alternative is available, namely A harmony (primary manner V) and 'headedness' harmony, respectively. To avoid allowing multiple analyses we could appeal to the idea that the A element as a head manner element is resistant to harmony, or we could simply ban the mechanism of headedness harmony as a formal possibility in the theory.

While the present proposal is different from what is proposed in van der Hulst (2018), it does not alter the analyses of TR harmony systems proposed there. The net consequence of this new proposal is 'replacing' the notation for the ATR-element from 'P-∀' (i.e. the phonetic ATR choice for the secondary pharyngeal element in the manner class) to 'I' (i.e. the secondary palatal element in the place class). But this is not just a notational switch. The crucial gain is that we get rid of the phonetic ambiguity of the secondary v element. We can now say that the secondary element v in (36) always correlates with TR retraction, as it does in the

160 Principles of Radical CV Phonology

secondary manner class for consonants in the edge position. For further discussion of these issues I refer to van der Hulst (to appear-b).

I now turn to the question of whether intermediary secondary manner for vowels is required:

(41) V (rhyme)

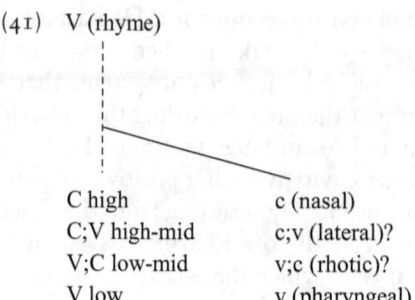

C high   c (nasal)
C;V high-mid   c;v (lateral)?
V;C low-mid   v;c (rhotic)?
V low   v (pharyngeal)

I will start the discussion by returning to pharyngealisation. LM (p. 306ff.) discuss pharyngealised vowels for which we already have a place, that is, secondary v. They remark: 'This gesture takes several different forms, resulting in vowels that are variously called pharyngealised, epiglottalised, sphincteric or strident' (p. 306). Interestingly, they add that among 'the languages which have been described as having pharyngealised vowels is Even, a Tungusic language of North-Central Siberia (Novikova 1960).' And:

> it is interesting to note that the two sets of vowels in Even also constitute vowel harmony sets in much the same way as the two sets in Akan: roots must contain vowels that are all of one set or the other. Despite these similarities, both the examination of the x-ray tracings and Novikova's comments on the acoustic characteristics of these vowels suggest that there is a greater degree of pharyngeal narrowing in Even than in Akan.

This confirms what was mentioned earlier, namely that TR harmony in (at least some) Tungusic languages seems to involve TR retraction as the active gesture. 'We will therefore consider these vowels to be characterised by pharyngealisation rather than by ATR' (LM p. 306).[73] I have argued that this conclusion is not supported by the fact that in both Asian and African languages, neutral vowels display the same behaviour as being either transparent or opaque, depending on whether they are

---

[73] Languages that have been described as having pharyngealised vowels differ in the precise articulatory and acoustic details. To illustrate this, LM discuss Caucasian and Khoisan, which have an even stronger retraction than the Tungusic languages (LM p. 306).

compatible or incompatible with the harmonic feature. We only make the correct predictions about the behaviour of neutral vowels if in all of them ATR is the active element.

Turning to 'strident' vowels, LM state (p. 310):

> The Khoisan pharyngealised vowels that we have been discussing so far are not the so-called strident vowels of these languages. Traill (1985) suggests that the strident vowels may be regarded phonologically as pharyngealised breathy voiced vowels. He goes on, however, to emphasize that the vocal tract shape is not the same as in the pharyngealised vowels, and the laryngeal action is very different from that in breathy voiced vowels. It is clear that from a phonetic point of view strident vowels are best considered as involving a distinct articulatory mechanism of their own, which he has labelled 'sphincteric' (Traill 1986).

This brings into focus that vowels can have phonatory properties which, when mixed with secondary manner (like pharyngealisation), can deliver a separate category of vowels. Phonatory properties of vowels are discussed in § 6.4.3. LM conclude that the 'strident' vowels in Khoisan may not be pharyngealised breathy vowels because of differences from pharyngealised and breathy vowels in other languages. However, it does not seem advisable to adopt new elements whenever the precise details of articulation (and acoustic effects) differ. It is widely acknowledged that phonological elements can have different phonetic correlates (within limits) in different languages. I would thus suggest that the Khoisan vowels in question can be analysed as combining pharyngealisation and breathiness. The alternative would be to recruit a complex secondary manner (c;v or v;c), although the choice would be difficult to make.

LM (p. 313) conclude:

> We have discussed ATR, pharyngealised and strident vowels as if they were characterized by separate properties. However, as we noted, [–ATR] vowels are very much akin to pharyngealised vowels, and strident vowels might be regarded as a more extreme form of pharyngealised vowels. All these vowels are characterized by some degree of pharyngeal narrowing and larynx raising. Languages seldom use more than one of the three possibilities. We cannot reduce these three possibilities to a single binary contrast because of the contrastive use of plain, pharyngealised and strident vowels in !Xóõ. But the most suitable phonological parameters to use in describing these vowels are not clear to us at this moment.

It seems to me that the three-way contrast in !Xóõ is best analysed in terms of pharyngealisation for both non-plain vowels, with breathiness added for strident vowels. While the latter are described as 'a more extreme form of pharyngealised vowels', it does not seem possible to characterise them with an intermediate secondary manner. Neither c;v (lateralised) nor v;c (rhotic, retroflex) is applicable here under a reasonable assumption of the phonetic correlate (no matter how variable) of these intermediate element combinations.

LM discuss two other categories of vowels with secondary manner: rhotic (r-coloured, also often called 'retroflex') vowels and 'fricative' vowels. Sounds like this occur in English in words such as 'bird' (Ladefoged (2001) regards this as a separate vowel phoneme, which he refers to as a retroflex), and in Mandarin Chinese (Duanmu 2002). There is at least one case with rhotic harmony (Yurok: Smith, de Wit & Noske (1988)). While the secondary property here could be v (pharyngealised), it is tempting to analyse this vowel with secondary v;c because it typically emerges in the context of an overt r sound which is 'overlaid' on the vowel articulation. I have previously proposed that this category also covers the notion of retroflexion which squares with the fact that r-coloured are often called 'retroflex'.[74]

LM discuss the Dravidian language Badaga, as reported in Emeneau (1939):

> [Emeneau] suggests that in this language there are five vowel qualities, i, e, a, o, u, each of which can be 'normal, half-retroflexed, (or) fully retroflexed.' The half-retroflex vowels are described as being 'produced with the edges and tip of the tongue retroflexed or curved upward to approach the alveolar ridge, but without touching or causing friction at any point; the front of the blade of the tongue seems to be raised also in this manner of vowel production'. His description of the fully retroflexed vowels is as follows: 'In the vowels with fully-retroflexed resonance the whole tongue is strongly retracted, the edges are curved upwards towards the hard palate well behind the alveolar ridge but without touching or causing friction at any point, and a channel is left in the center of the tongue well visible at the tip in a V-formation.' (LM pp. 313–14)

Based on this I would say that the fully retroflex vowels are pharyngealised (secondary v), while the half-retroflex vowels can be analysed with secondary v;c, which is also applicable to 'rhotic'/retroflex vowels. The various 'rhotic' vowels differ in their articulatory properties. Rhotic vowels are also described as having an RTR, in addition to having certain tongue positions (curled tongue tip and 'bunched' tongue body) which, in fact, might be the cause of TR retraction. Collapsing these into one category is perhaps justified on acoustic grounds. The variability is quite

---

[74] MD reports a retroflex vowel (high, central, unrounded) for Tarascan (MD 747).

reminiscent of the variability in the articulation of r consonants, where the unifying factor is not only in the acoustic properties, but also, perhaps mainly, in the phonotactic distribution (see Navarro (2018)).

Finally, LM discuss 'fricative vowels'. It is not clear whether this is a separate, potentially contrastive vowel type, because such vowels are typically allophones of high vowels, or syllabic variants of fricative or rhotic consonants. They are sometimes called 'apical vowels' (a term that LM reject; see Lee-Kim (2014)).[75] I suggest that if this vowel type can be contrastive, which would be the case if these vowels cannot be analysed as contextual or positional allophones, it is probably defensible to subsume this secondary articulation under the secondary cv specification. If no contrast is ever found between rhotic, retroflex and fricative vowels we can regard them as different phonetic realisations of a single intermediate category c+v. While these various possibilities are rather different in articulatory terms, it may be that there is a unifying acoustic 'signature' that is shared by them, which would justify this grouping.

Hamann (2003: 27) refers to Catford (1988: 161f.), who distinguishes between retroflexed and rhotacised vowels on phonetic grounds, describing the latter as vowels that are articulated with 'a redrawn tongue tip or with a bunched, retracted tongue body' and thus not as being retroflex articulation. However, Hamann also mentions that Trask (1996: 310) unites both articulations, grouping them as having the distinct acoustic quality of a lowered third formant.

In conclusion, certain vowels in the rhotic category can be analysed as being pharyngealised, while other perhaps fit the bill of being retroflex. I will assume that there is in fact reason to separate those two categories, at least for some languages. As we have seen in this section, pharyngealisation is certainly a required specification, while those vowels that are articulated with a curled tongue tip would be best analysed as retroflex (although this phonetic property is itself also somewhat fluid, with consonants being described as 'rhotic' or as 'retroflex' sometimes *not* having a curled tip but instead a bunched tongue body).[76]

---

[75] For fricative vowels, which tend to be high vowels for obvious reasons because these have the highest degree of stricture to begin with, see Hu & Feng (2015, or 2014) and Connell (2007). For a case where non-high vowels also participate, see Sloos, Ran & van de Weijer (2018).

[76] LM (p. 26): 'The term "retroflex" has been used for a variety of different articulations, which are linked as much by the shape of the tongue involved as the region on the upper surface of the mouth. A retroflex articulation is one in which the tip of the tongue is curled up to some extent. In addition to the sub-apical palatal articulations that occur in Toda, there are also retroflex gestures in which the tip of the tongue is curled only slightly upwards, forming an articulation in the alveolar or, more usually, post-alveolar region.' They note (p. 28) that no language uses these different types of retroflex manners contrastively.

164   Principles of Radical CV Phonology

We end up with having to distinguish three secondary manner vowel specifications:

(42)

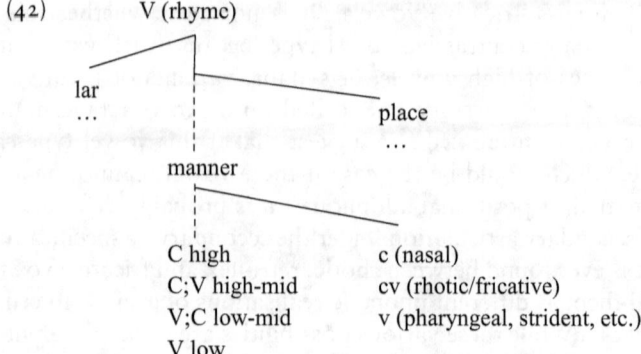

```
            V (rhyme)
           /       \
        lar         place
        ...         ...
             |
           manner
           /     \
     C high          c (nasal)
     C;V high-mid   cv (rhotic/fricative)
     V;C low-mid    v (pharyngeal, strident, etc.)
     V low
```

For secondary manners, other than nasal and clear cases of pharyngealisation, I take the proposals made here are as rather tentative.

This completes the account of manner specification for vowels. I now turn to manner representations of coda consonants, which in the RCVP scheme must be sonorant consonants.

4.3.2 Coda (rhyme dependent): sonorants

For the coda, I propose the same four sonorant consonant types as for the bridge:

(43)

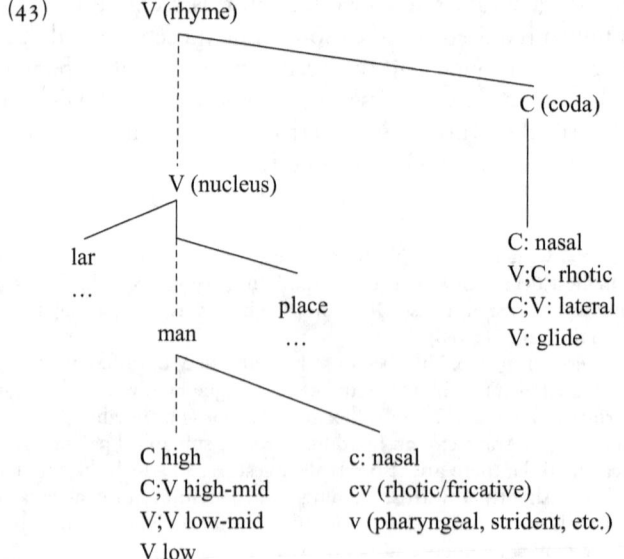

```
              V (rhyme)
             /        \
                       C (coda)
                       |
                       C: nasal
                       V;C: rhotic
                       C;V: lateral
                       V: glide
          V (nucleus)
         /     |     \
       lar         place
       ...    |    ...
             man
              |
      C high          c: nasal
      C;V high-mid   cv (rhotic/fricative)
      V;V low-mid    v (pharyngeal, strident, etc.)
      V low
```

Manner 165

In (43) I express the fact that sonorant codas do not have secondary manners, for which I have been unable to find candidates. As mentioned, there appear to differences in preferences. I turn to this issue in the next section.

4.3.3 Coda conditions

While sonorant consonants are thus viable codas, we have to ask which types of sonorants can occur in this position, considering also distinctions in place and laryngeal properties. At this point the astute reader might remember that in § 3.2.2 I assumed that the coda (as well as the bridge) only requires manner specifications, the idea being that these positions never need a contrastive specification for place or laryngeal. Complete exclusion of place and laryngeal specification from the bridge and coda is the strongest possible distributional condition on place and laryngeal specification: total absence. We have already seen that this view cannot be upheld for bridge. In § 4.2.2 we had to accept that a specification of different glides [j] and [w], if needed, would require place elements, and possibly in some language for nasals as well. With respect to the coda, there can be no doubt that place distinctions need to be made. In Dutch, and many other languages, nasals of different places can occur in the coda, although medially they have to be homorganic with the following consonant. Likewise, [j] and [w] occur in this position as well, on the assumption that, when occurring in that position, they form a diphthong with the preceding short vowel, which involves certain restrictions since Dutch has only three diphthongs.[77] (I am here only considering syllables with a branching rhyme, VC, and not so-called superheavy rhymes (VXC), which can only occur word-finally, with rare exceptions.) Another area which indicates that codas may have laryngeal specification involves sonorant consonants in the coda that are tone-bearing units. This is only possible if these coda consonants can have their own laryngeal (tonal) specification. Separate tone specifications for nucleus head and coda are reported in Gordon (2002), which is a typological study of the occurrence of contour tones, in the following order of preference: on long vowels, closed syllable with sonorants, closed syllables with obstruents and short vowels.[78] As, we will see in § 5.4 and § 6.3, these and other examples show that the strong view (banning all place and laryngeal

---

[77] For this analysis of diphthongs, see van der Hulst (1984: 91–4). This work offers a full analysis of Dutch syllable structure, as does Trommelen (1983).

[78] See also Hyman (2012) for effects of coda consonants on tone in Asian tone systems. Of course, the finding that coda obstruents can have tonal specifications, or have an effect on the tones for the nucleus, is inconsistent with the complete exclusion of obstruents in the coda.

specifications) from the coda cannot be fully maintained. For this reason, Kehrein & Golston (2004) allow non-manner specifications for onsets, nuclei and codas. I would not go that far, since place and laryngeal distinctions in coda are still very limited.

While place (and laryngeal) distinction may be required for the coda, many languages impose restrictions on the type of sonorant coda that can occur.[79] Languages have coda restrictions which can refer to manner, place and laryngeal properties, or indeed to the coda position itself.[80] Laryngeal coda restrictions occur when phonation differences are neutralised in syllable-final position. Final devoicing in Germanic languages (if not analysed as a gradient phonetic process; see § 1.5) testifies to blocking laryngeal specification such as voice from the coda. In Korean, which has a three-way contrast for obstruent phonation, syllable-final obstruents are 'plain' (Cho 2016). Place conditions apply when certain places are blocked. For example, the Australian language Lardil allows only coronals in coda position (Round 2011). Japanese allows nasals, but only placeless nasals; Japanese also allows the left halves of geminates, including obstruent geminates (Labrune 2012). Below, I will discuss examples of manner conditions that block certain consonants, such as all sonorants except nasals. In other cases, only liquids are allowed.[81]

Note that the above-mentioned coda condition for Lardil is consistent with complete exclusion of place, if it is assumed that coronal place is a default place that need not be specified.[82] The requirement that Japanese only allows placeless nasals or the left half of geminates is also consistent with this position.[83] Likewise, neutralisation of phonation oppositions

---

[79] Coda restrictions are a subtype of distribution restrictions. We have seen in § 4.2.3 that languages may impose restrictions on onset head consonants (as well as bridge consonants). Beyond the common exclusion of the velar nasal [ŋ] in onsets, we discuss cases in which onset head position excludes certain types of sonorants due to their high sonority.

[80] The most extreme coda condition is the disallowance of any coda, which thus permits only open syllables. If, in such a case, both short and long vowels are permitted, we have to ask whether the second half of a long vowel is a 'coda of sorts'; see below.

[81] For coda restrictions see Itô (1986, 1989), Fonte (1996), Lombardi (2001) and Beckman (1998). Instead of speaking of restrictions, it is also common to refer to the coda as licensing only certain features; see Goldsmith (1989, 1990) and Wiltshire (1992). In OT, the theoretical device for coda conditions is positional faithfulness; see Beckman (2004).

[82] In § 9.2 I discuss the notion of 'default' as it can be used in RCVP. Absence of place means pharyngeal only if this absence is in contrast with the presence of place as coronal and labial.

[83] As reported in Piriyawiboon (2007), Italian allows place-bound segments and coronals /s, l, r/ in the coda while Menominee allows placeless obstruents /h, ʔ/ and /s/ in the coda. These cases too are consistent with disallowing place specifications. In many other languages, coda consonants must share place of articulation with

can also be understood as resulting from a complete ban on laryngeal specification in the coda.

In § 5.4 and § 6.5, I will return to coda conditions involving place and laryngeal specifications. In this section the focus is on manner restrictions. I note firstly that in contrast to the bridge, there is no strong preference in the coda for the intermediate options (liquids).[84] Rather, as we will see, nasals are preferred, being sometimes the only sonorants that are permitted.[85] The reason for this greater tolerance could be that coda consonants are not 'squeezed' in between obstruents and vowels (as bridge consonants are). They merely contribute to a moderate falling sonority profile in the rhyme. As observed in Clements (1990a), there is a preference for a moderate fall (as opposed to a steep rise in the onset), which results from the fact that consonants other than liquids, specifically nasals, can occur in this position.

In studying coda conditions, we perhaps have to consider the word-medial and word-final position separately, just as we did for onsets, where we have seen that medial onsets and word-initial onsets can differ. This is the polysystematic viewpoint (see § 1.3.5).[86] This is especially important when we consider the possibility of having complex codas, which in RCVP are not allowed at all, medially or finally. However, finally, extra consonants can occur, which requires additional mechanisms such as empty nuclei or adjunction (see § 3.2.3). Of course, the very presence of a coda can also differ in this respect, when languages allow final codas, but not medial codas, or vice versa (see Kaye 1990). We also find that medial codas and final codas differ in terms of the specific segments that can occur in these positions, where medial codas show more limited choices than final codas. This can be explained by considering that medial codas, just like bridge sonorants, are also subject to contextual assimilatory pressure, albeit not within the syllable itself. A factor that plays a role here is the so-called 'Syllable Contact Law' (SCL) (Murray & Vennemann (1983); Vennemann 1988); Seo (2011); Gouskova (2004)), according to which a coda–onset sequence (a so-called interlude) in which the coda is high in sonority and the onset low in sonority is cross-linguistically preferred. This would suggest

---

the following onset consonant (e.g. Diola Fogny (Steriade 1982), Lardil (Wilkinson 1988) and Axininca Campa (Black 1991)).

[84] Krämer and Zec (2019) report that in their typological study they did not encounter a single language that only allows liquids in the coda.

[85] The preference of nasals over liquids is also noted in the occurrence of syllabic sonorants; see § 5.3.3.

[86] See Côté (2011) for an extensive discussion of the special case of word-final consonants as compared to medial coda consonants.

With respect to word-medial position we also need to separate morpheme-internal and cross-morphemic interlude clusters.

preference for a steeper sonority fall for the word-internal rhyme than for word-final rhymes. Fonte (1996) discusses the distinction between word-final and word-medial codas explicitly, and Gouskova (2004) also discusses the interaction between coda and onset conditions and interlude conditions. It could perhaps be argued that, apart from assimilatory processes which may limit word-medial coda options, there is no need for separate interlude conditions (like the SCL). After all, the preferred maximal sonority contrast between coda and onset that the SCL captures could be said to follow from the fact that codas prefer high-sonority consonants while onsets prefer low-sonority consonants.[87] However, it turns out that the most sonorous consonants are in fact not the most preferred codas; rather, nasal consonants are the most preferred codas. I now turn to some studies that provider example of the situations discussed in this section.[88]

A relevant early study is in Itô (1986, 1988), who gives examples of a ban on non-sonorant consonants in Italian and Japanese, which, however, do allow the left half of obstruent geminates. In an OT approach such a ban has been adopted as a universal constraint, although in that model this does not mean that all languages must adhere to it, since faithfulness constraints that outrank the coda constraints can permit violations. More comprehensive studies of sonority coda conditions are offered in VanDam (2004), Fonte (1996) and Krämer & Zec (2019).[89]

Fonte discusses Diola Fogny[90] and Ponapean, which also both ban obstruents, while lacking the 'escape' clause of allowing the left half of obstruent geminates (as in Italian and Japanese). Both VanDam (2004) and Krämer & Zec (2019) contain systematic, broader typological studies of coda consonants. The former considers both manner and place restrictions. This study is based on eighteen languages (one from each of the eighteen families identified in Ruhlen (1991)) and focuses on word-final codas of different complexities. I will here only consider the findings that are reported for simplex codas. VanDam establishes that all languages that impose limits on coda consonants at least allow

---

[87] In GP, the effect of the SCL is derived from the requirement that an onset consonant must be able to license a coda consonant, which is only possible if specific segmental properties of both are in place. Initially such conditions involved the notion of 'charm', which resembles 'sonority' see KLV85; Kaye (1990); Harris (1994). Harris (1990) reformulates the required properties in terms of the notion of 'complexity'.

[88] Another source for investigating distributional restrictions is the World Phonotactics database). I have not accessed this useful system (which reports on 3,000 languages), since my remarks on distributional restrictions in this book were not my primary concern.

[89] Fonte (1996: ch. 3) also discusses various examples of 'sonority conditions'.

[90] In this language nasals must be homorganic with the following onset, showing a place condition. This language is also discussed in Itô (1986).

nasals, followed by liquids, followed by glides and obstruents. VanDam establishes two implicational scales, one for manner and one for place:

(44) a. nasal >> liquid >> obstruent >> w,j
     b. alveolar >> velar >> retroflex, tap[91]

In his group of languages, there are cases in which liquids appear to be skipped, thus allowing nasals and obstruents (Inupiaq, Nama-Hottentot), assuming that these languages have liquids.

The data reported, considering also the small number of languages considered in this study, perhaps do not warrant the ranking of obstruents over glides. In fact, if we take into account that diphthongs forms branching rhymes, the option of glides most likely will outrank that of obstruents. What is noteworthy in (44a) is the cross-linguistic preference for nasals, which was of course also noted in previous studies, at least based on specific languages, such as Japanese (see Itô (1986)). No convincing case has been reported in which liquids are the only possible sonorant in the coda. The same result is obtained in Krämer & Zec (2019) based on a much larger sample of languages – 218, to be precise. Generally, word-final position is more tolerant than word-medial positions, but each position allows the same sets of consonants across languages. Ninety-seven languages have fewer than the four major categories that Krämer and Zec consider, namely nasals, liquids, fricatives and stops, while 120 languages have a restricted inventory word-medially.[92] The authors compare languages that allow three, two or one out of these four classes and find that nasals are always among the possible coda consonants. If two classes are permitted, we see again that liquids can be skipped, given a fair number of languages that have either nasal and fricatives or nasal and stop; we must note that allowing fricatives does not imply allowing stops. Even if three of Krämer and Zec's categories are permitted, liquid can be omitted since some languages allow nasals, fricatives and stops.

One important conclusion that these authors draw is that there is no preference ranking based on relative high sonority, since that would predict a ranking (glides) > liquids > nasals > fricatives > stops. I refer to their work for various alternative accounts of the preference that we actually find, which are essentially that nasals are preferred over all other

---

[91] Here I will not discuss this place hierarchy, which makes no mention of labials. Fonte (1996) discusses various place preferences in different languages, considering also facts from language acquisition, and, taking into account the effect of place assimilation in the interlude, concludes that there are conflicting data about which place is banned or favoured in the coda.
[92] I refer to Krämer and Zec's study for their motivation for not considering laryngeal consonants or glides.

categories. Given that in the two-category group nasal plus liquids is much higher in frequency than nasal + either fricative or stop, one might perhaps conclude that liquids are preferred over obstruents.

I will assume here, in accordance with the 'strict view', that obstruents cannot occur in the coda (with the exception of the left half of geminate obstruents; see below).[93] The claim that obstruent consonants cannot be codas is 'extreme', given the occurrence of obstruents in what most linguists would analyse as the coda position (as in the two typological studies discussed here). I already mentioned that this condition is better adhered to in word-medial codas than in word-final codas, although Krämer and Zec's study does not convincingly show that this is likely to be an effect of the SCL. Government Phonologists have argued that alleged word-final codas aren't codas at all, but rather onsets followed by an empty nucleus (KLV85; Kaye (1981)). My own preference would be to analyse such segments as syllabic adjuncts, preferably restricted to word peripheries. This, at least, would allow right-peripheral obstruent codas (as well as further 'extra' consonants for superheavy rhymes and the so-called coronal appendix).[94] The apparent coda obstruent in *at.las* would then require a different syllabic analysis, perhaps with an empty nucleus: *a.tØ.las*. It is also possible to allow unexpected medial codas only if they are homorganic with the following onset, which would allow at least certain cases of obstruent codas (such as [t.l]).[95] I refer to Harris (1985) for extensive discussions of such ideas[96] and for how GP principles apply to English phonology, and to van der Hulst (2003) for a government-style analysis of Dutch syllable structure.

If, then, we can separate the matter of obstruent codas from the matter of sonorant codas, how can we explain the preference ranking for codas in (45)?

(45)   nasal > liquid > glide

---

[93] As one of the first, Itô (1986, 1988) formulates a ban on obstruents for Italian and Japanese, although not as a universal constraint. In OT approach such a constraint has been adopted as universal, but in that model that does not mean that all languages must adhere to it, since faithfulness constraints that outrank the coda constraints, can permit violations.

[94] There is evidence from diminutive formation in Dutch for s structural distinction between obstruents and sonorants, with the former taking the short form (*kat-je* 'little cat') and the latter the long form (*kam-etje* 'little comb'); see van der Hulst (2008).

[95] This leaves non-homorganic obstruent–obstruent interludes as problematic. There are only a few examples of these in Dutch (and English), such as *reptiel* 'reptile', *wodka* 'wodka'

[96] See also Fonte (1996: 36) as well as Gouskova (2004). It seems clear that homorganicity between the coda and the onset allows the coda consonant to 'violate' coda conditions that would otherwise be in place.

To approach this, I return to the labelling of syllabic position in the syllable 'template' in (1), repeated here for convenience:

(46)

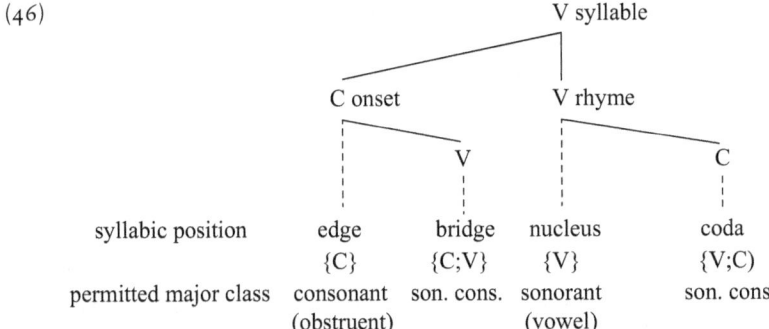

I propose that the key to understanding the different preferences in the bridge and the coda is that we have to consider the terminal labels for the bridge and coda position, which are V and C respectively. Given the sonority ranking of sonorant manners that was established in § 4.2.2 (shown in (20a)–(20b) in that section, here repeated as (47)), we can derive the different preferences for the bridge and coda position.

(47) a. bridge (primary manner)

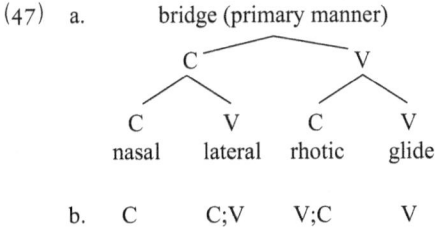

b. C   C;V   V;C   V

As shown in (48), the bridge, with the terminal label V prefers ranking from high sonority to low sonority, while the coda has the reverse order:

(48) a. Bridge (V): glides > rhotic > lateral > nasal
     b. Coda (C): nasal > lateral > rhotic > glide

The result that we obtain is not perfect. The ranking for the coda seems accurate, putting aside that the position of glides (lowest in VanDam (2004)) is perhaps not conclusive. Recall that Krämer & Zec (2019) did not study the coda occurrence of glides. My conjecture is that glides *are* indeed low in preference because of their proximity to the nucleus, which 'forces' them to form diphthongs with resulting restrictions that lower their frequency. The scale for the bridge suggests that glides are preferred over liquids, but again I would suggest that while they are preferred for 'sonority reasons', they are dispreferred because of their proximity to the nuclear vowel, which makes liquids the 'perfect' transition between the onset head and the nuclear head. Example (48) also suggests different preferences for laterals and rhotics. As mentioned previously (see fn. 42), van der Torre (2003) reports asymmetries between [l] and [r] in Dutch which suggest that [r]'s form better bridges than [l]'s, which is what (48a) would predict.

In Chapter 8 I will return to preference scales for the occurrence of manner, place and laryngeal properties in all syllabic positions, where preference can involve absolute conditions (as discussed in this section), lexical frequency, order of acquisition and so on.

Before turning to syllabic consonants, I point out here that the idea that bridge and coda can in principle dominate the same consonants, although not always the same set or with the same preference, does not necessarily imply that these consonants will be phonetically realised in the same way in both positions. In fact, given that two positions have different syllabic encoding (C;V for bridge and V;C for coda), the model predicts that coda consonants are phonetically 'weaker', being articulated with less severe constrictions. This prediction is correct. Coda consonants are more prone to weakening and vocalisation. This can be clearly seen in the articulations of [r] and [l] in many, perhaps all, languages, with frequent vocalisation of especially [l] (cf. English *old* with Dutch *oud*), or of [r] (as in Bostonian English and other so-called r-less dialects), as well as in the tendency for nasal consonants to weaken, while nasalising the preceding vowel. Glides in post-nuclear positions are also more weakly articulated then when occurring in the onset head or bridge. In § 4.2.3 I have suggested that the difference in 'strength' between the onset position and the coda position may also be responsible for the ambiguous status of sonorant consonants, which may shows signs of obstruent behaviour when occurring as onset heads, although the match is not perfect (or even problematic). This is an issue to be explored further. The differences in articulation of sonorant consonants due to the difference in syllabic position are an example of how the syllabic C/V encoding has an impact on phonetic implementation.

The effect that the two syllabic positions have on the phonetic realisation of sonorant consonants is 'phonetic'. As such this effect does not contradict the point I have just made about the preferences for sonorant consonants in the bridge and coda. While the terminal labels C and V favour 'stronger consonants' in the coda than in the bride, the bias of these labels (as being part of a syllabic C or V unit) determines their phonetic realisation.

We also need to ask whether the exclusion of coda obstruents includes the laryngeal consonants [ʔ] and [h]. As obstruents, laryngeal consonants are dispreferred for (or, in the strict view, excluded from) the coda position. Nevertheless, whatever special provision is made for obstruents

Manner   173

in apparent coda position (adjunction, empty nuclei) can also be used for laryngeal consonants. We must also reckon with the possibility that apparent occurrences of laryngeals following a vowel could be instances of secondary laryngeal articulations (see § 6.4.3). The exclusion of [h] (Dutch does not have phonemic [ʔ]) in Dutch codas (medially and finally) would need independent motivation given that other obstruents can occur as apparent codas. As we have seen, an argument has been made for including at least laryngeal [h] in the category of glides, which would suggest that they can occur in the bridge and the coda, although in both positions glides are not preferred or are even excluded (see (48)). The impossibility of laryngeals (which by definition are placeless) sharing a place with the following onset may also contribute to their dispreferred occurrence in the coda. I will admit that the analysis of laryngeal consonants offered here is not entirely conclusive.

4.4 Syllabic consonants (sonorants)

I now turn to the analysis of so-called syllabic consonants. This case arises when the nucleus head is occupied by a segment that is not a vowel. In § 3.2.1, I have suggested that only sonorant consonants be permitted in the nuclear head position, which gives rise to syllabic nasals, laterals and rhotics. In this case the syllabic terminal V, which normally represents the coda, is subjoined to the nuclear label V, instead of being adjoined. As in the coda position, sonorant consonants in nuclear head position do not allow secondary manners.

(49)

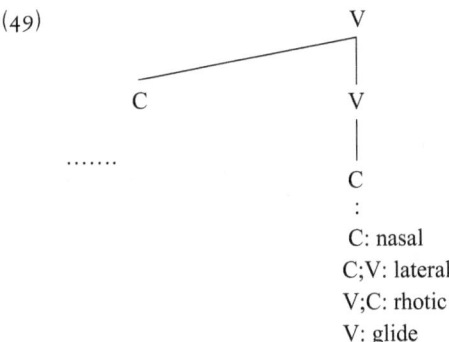

C: nasal
C;V: lateral
V;C: rhotic
V: glide

We have to wonder what the result is of having V manner in the nuclear head position. How is that different from a vowel? I here suggest that this possibility could account for so-called 'weak vowels', for instance the vowels that English has in unstressed syllables, which, in accordance with Bolinger (1981), can have |I|, |U| as their place elements or be placeless. This gives rise to the unstressed vowels in *happy, hollow* and *mica*.

In accordance with the 'strict view' obstruents are not permitted to be syllabic. This flies in the face of notorious reports on syllabic obstruents in languages such as Bella Coola, now known as Nuxalk (Bagemihl 1991), and Tashlhiyt Berber (Dell & Elmedlaoui 1985). I have suggested in fn. 47 that such languages lack syllable structure at all at the level of grammatical phonology, and hence lack phonotactic restrictions of phoneme combinations. My point here is that the main raison d'être for syllable structure is phonotactic restrictions, which may be missing in Nuxalk and Tashlhiyt Berber.[97]

4.5 Long vowels, diphthongs and geminates

In this section I offer a brief discussion of how RCVP represents long vowels, diphthongs and geminate consonants.

A long vowel can be represented with both syllabic positions sharing one 'root node':

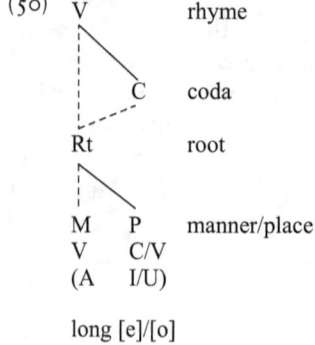

(50)   V   rhyme
             C   coda
        Rt   root
        M   P   manner/place
        V   C/V
        (A   I/U)

        long [e]/[o]

Common diphthongs, such as [ai]/[au], have a glide in the coda position, which, as mentioned earlier, implies that the coda position can have location properties:[98]

---

[97] Some authors do not accept this argument; see Steriade (1999), who explicitly argues that phonotactic restrictions do not require reference to syllable structure. And then there are those who do not see a use for the syllable at all; see Kohler (1996). Hyman (1985) makes the case for syllable structure not being universal.

[98] The representation of so-called short diphthongs is discussed in § 7.3.3.1.

(51)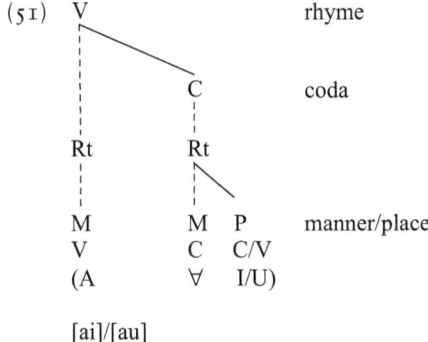

Diphthongs like [ei] and [ou] have colour elements in the nuclear position:

(52)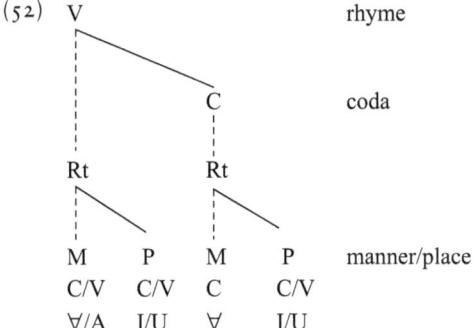

To represent diphthongs like [ei], [ou] or [œy], the place elements are shared:

(53)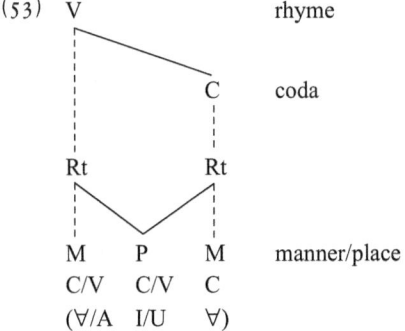

176 *Principles of Radical CV Phonology*

A centralising diphthong, one ending in a schwa-like vowel, can be represented with the manner V option, for instance for [iə]:[99]

(54)

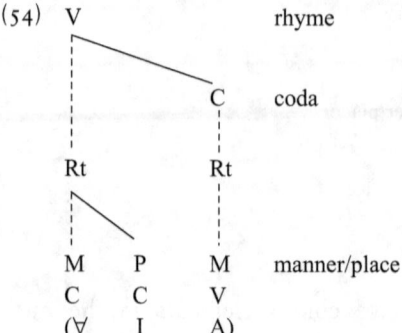

Turning to geminate consonants, I propose the following structure:

(55)   geminate consonant

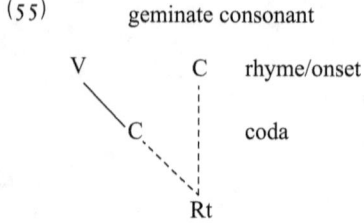

While geminates of all major classes are thus allowed, including obstruents, I maintain that the coda position does not support obstruents as independent segments.

4.6 Summary and concluding remarks

In this chapter, I have provided interpretations for CV structures in the manner class. Here I summarise the structures for four syllabic positions in two formats:

---

[99] The schwa vowel cannot be represented as totally unspecified, given the mandatory presence of a manner element. I will propose in § 7.2.1 that the element A, without place elements, occurring in weak positions such as unstressed nuclei in English and unstressable nuclei in Dutch, or in the coda position, is interpreted as schwa [ə].

Manner 177

(56) Manner (edge): head and dependent structure:

```
C    C+c    C+cv    C̶+̶c̶v̶    C+v
CV   C̶V̶+̶c̶  C̶V̶+̶c̶v̶  C̶V̶+̶c̶v̶  CV+v
CV   C̶V̶+̶c̶  C̶V̶+̶c̶v̶  C̶V̶+̶c̶v̶  CV+v
V    V+c    V+cv    V̶+̶c̶v̶   V+v
```

| | c | c;v | v;c | v |
	nasal	lateral	rhotic/retroflex	pharyngeal
C stop				
C;V affricate				
V;C m-fric				
V s-fric				

Head: full range of four possibilities (even though the contrast between mellow and strident fricatives is infrequent)
Dependent: limited application to the intermediate structure in the head manner

(57) Manner (nucleus): head and dependent structure:

```
C     C+c    C+cv    C̶+̶c̶v̶    C+v
C;V   C̶V̶+̶c̶  C̶V̶+̶c̶v̶  C̶V̶+̶c̶v̶  C̶V̶+̶v̶
V;C   C̶V̶+̶c̶  C̶V̶+̶c̶v̶  C̶V̶+̶c̶v̶  C̶V̶+̶v̶
V     V+c    V+cv    V̶+̶c̶v̶   V+v
```

| | c | cv | v |
	nasal	fricative/rhotic/retroflex	pharyngeal
C high			
C;V high-mid			
V;C low-mid			
V low			

Head: full range of four possibilities (setting a limit of four vowel heights)
Dependent: reduction to three-way contrast (although the cv option is infrequent, perhaps even questionable)

(58) Manner (bridge and coda): no secondary specifications at all:

```
C     C̶+̶c̶    C̶+̶c̶v̶    C̶+̶c̶v̶    C̶+̶v̶
C;V   C̶V̶+̶c̶   C̶V̶+̶c̶v̶   C̶V̶+̶c̶v̶   C̶V̶+̶v̶
V;C   C̶V̶+̶c̶   C̶V̶+̶c̶v̶   C̶V̶+̶c̶v̶   C̶V̶+̶v̶
V     V̶+̶c̶    V̶+̶c̶v̶    V̶+̶c̶v̶    V̶+̶v̶
```

C nasal
C;V lateral
V;C rhotic
V pharyngeal

Head: four-way contrast
Dependent: sonorants only occur with secondary manner, unless the sonorant occurs in the onset head position

The constraints that exclude the structures that are not required are not ad hoc. It is my hope that this chapter has demonstrated to the reader how the 'logic' of RCVP has led me to the proposed permitted structures, as well as those that are excluded. While I expect the objection that the overall design of the manner class is 'overly complex', I want to emphasise that this structure follows from basic principles of categorisation, such as the Opponent Principle (which generates two elements for each class), the Combinatorial Principle and the head-dependency principle, which allows asymmetric combinations of these two elements, albeit mostly in head classes. Where restrictions apply, we usually see the head/dependent asymmetry at play: dependents cannot be more complex than heads and are, in fact, typically less complex. We will see in the next two chapters that the logic that has been demonstrated in this chapter, as per the SAA, applies there as well, with only minor differences.

5

Place

5.1 Introduction

This chapter proposes CV structures for the place class. I use the term location, as well as place and sometimes colour. Place elements are mostly relevant for the syllabic head positions, because syllabic dependents (bridge, coda), as has been proposed and motivated in the previous chapter, have limited distinctive location. Liquid consonants in the bridge do not require distinctive place specification, but we have seen in Chapter 4 that glides and perhaps nasals may require a distinction between coronal and labial. This would also appear to be needed for the coda position. In this chapter, I follow the same structure as for the chapter on manner (which I will also follow in the next chapter when I discuss the laryngeal class).

5.2 Edge (onset head): obstruents

As usual, I first introduce the structure for the head class, starting with consonants in onset head position, recognising major places (labial, coronal, dorsal), albeit with a division of coronal into posterior and anterior. This, of course, is not new at all, but what is important is that this four-way distinction can be broken down in a double two-way split that is predicted by the RCVP model. (Pharyngeal consonants will be represented as lacking a major place in § 5.2.3.) I then proceed with the dependent class, which essentially accounts for finer distinctions, including what are traditionally called 'secondary articulations'.

5.2.1 Edge (onset head): head class

The head class, as we expect, allows for four place options. The first split is that between coronal and peripheral,[1] each of which can be subject to a further split:[2]

(1) a.

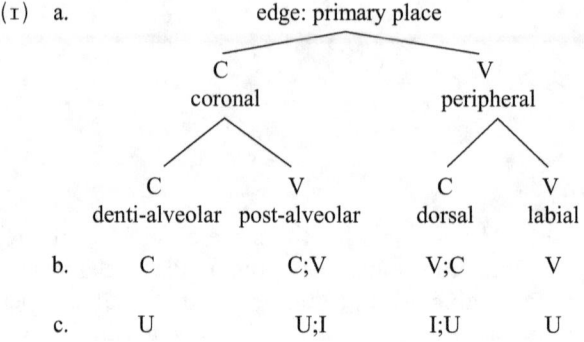

```
b.        C           C;V         V;C         V
c.        U           U;I         I;U         U
```

While languages usually have consonants at the coronal, dorsal and labial places of articulation, the typical fourth places are palato-alveolar/palatal or uvular, according to Gordon (2016: 46). A division between front coronals and back coronals is made with the second split in the coronal area. However, the front–back distinction can take different forms, as long as there is a relative difference along the front–back axis. A broad denti-alveolar contact (which practically implies that the articulation is laminal) can contrast with post-alveolar, but dental can thus contrast with alveolar.

Within the coronal area a further distinction is necessary, which is captured in the SPE feature system with the feature [distributed], to create a potential four-way distinction which can be found in Australian languages, such as Wubuy and Arrernte (Dixon (1980); Butcher (1993); Fletcher & Butcher (2014)).[3] In (2), I represent this four-way distinction with the traditional terminological designations in the feature system of SPE:

---

[1] This distinction corresponds to the division between [–grave] and [+grave] in Jakobson, Fant & Halle (1952). The SPE system did not have the feature [±grave], making a distinction in terms of [±anterior], where [+anterior] covers labials and 'front' coronals, whereas [–anterior] covers 'back' coronals and dorsals. This approach produced unnatural classes, as has been widely recognised.
[2] LM (p. 20) note that the interdental articulation does not occur in contrast with dental articulation.
[3] A similar four-way distinction also occurs in several Dravidian languages; see Krishnamurti (2003).

Place   181

(2)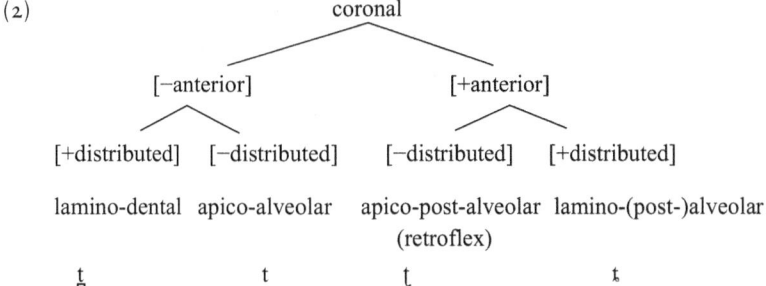

To mimic this classification we would have to add a third C/V split in (1), which would go against the idea that each class node only has two splits. In van der Hulst (2005a) I tried to cover this extra division by recruiting the secondary place distinction c, which correlates with palatality, but that idea will not be adopted here. In § 4.2.1.2 I have proposed that the laminal/apical distinction could be analysed as a manner distinction. This approach was suggested because a retroflex articulation, which is often represented as an anterior coronal apical articulation, found a natural place in the category that also correlated with a secondary rhotic manner v;c. I then suggested that the other complex secondary manner, c;v, which correlates with laterality, could correlate with laminal.[4] With this proposal, the four-way distinction that occurs in Australian languages can be represented as follows:

(3)   t̪   t   ʈ   t̪
    Place   C   C   C;V   C;V
    Manner   c;v   v;c   v;c   c;v

The retroflex [ʈ] would thus be represented as follows:

(4)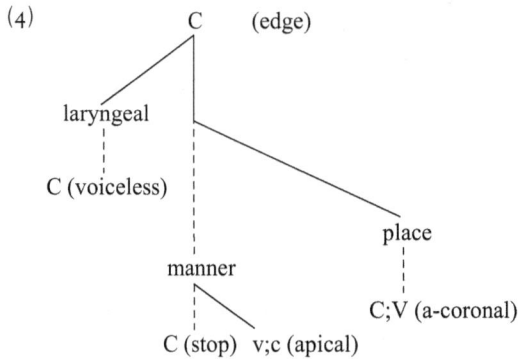

---

[4] LM (p. 24) also remark that if a language has both an apical and a laminal stop consonant, then the laminal consonant is likely to be more affricated.

In the peripheral class in (1), the C/V distinction correlates not with a 'front/back' distinction, as it does in the coronal class, but rather with a lingual (dorsal)/labial distinction:

(5)
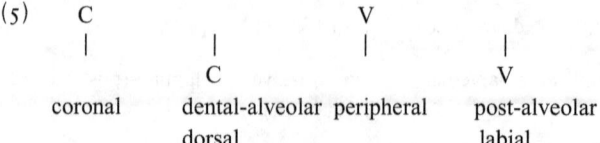

        coronal   dental-alveolar peripheral   post-alveolar
                        dorsal   labial

Given the different interpretations for C and V as dependents, the dependent elements once more do not seem to predict natural classes; that is, we do not expect to find a natural class consisting of front coronal and dorsal. Up to this point, the only case in which a dependent element denotes a natural class was in the case of dependent V manner, which refers to the class of strident obstruents, including affricates and strident fricatives (see § 4.2.1.2).

While the interpretation of C and V in the manner class was, for the most part, rather straightforward, given that C naturally correlates with relative closure or stricture, with V correlating with relative opening, which in turn correlates with a difference in sonority or perceptual salience, I need to address more carefully why I take the C and V options to be coronal and peripheral, respectively, and also what motivates the choices in the second split. Indeed, the critical reader might object that it is not clear why the C/V elements apply to place properties to begin with. Yet pursuing this possibility lies at the heart of RCVP.[5] I start with motivating the identification of coronal as a C element, which is 'easier' than identifying labial as a V element.

The choice for place C as coronal is motivated by the fact that coronal has been widely taken to be the unmarked place of articulation for consonants (Paradis & Prunet (1991)); this motivates its C nature, since we are here dealing with place in the onset head, which is a syllabic C position. Paradigmatic harmony predicts that C place is preferred in the syllabic C location (see Chapter 8).

I take this opportunity to briefly discuss the various reasons that phonologists have used for establishing the markedness status of a phonological category:[6]

---

[5] Applying the C/V elements to all classes is, in a way, reminiscent of Foley's (1977) proposal of applying the notion of strength to manner, place and laryngeal properties.
[6] For a longer discussion of such markedness criteria, see Rice (2007), but see also Haspelmath (2006), who considers the whole notion of markedness problematic. The argument that claims about markedness are circular ('what is unmarked is

(6) Common criteria for markedness:

    a. Occurrence in the absence of contrast in (subsets of) the segmental system
    b. Occurrence in the absence of contrast in a specific position
    c. Occurrence in all languages
    d. Lexical frequency
    e. Early appearance in language acquisition
    f. Resilience in language loss due to aphasia

I will offer some further explanation for each point (which will be discussed in detail in Chapter 8 along with similar predictions for manner and laryngeal specifications):

1. We predict that in the absence of a contrast between coronals and peripheral, coronals are the preferred choice. While the absence of both labial and dorsals for obstruents does not occur in any language, when looking at the subsystem of nasal consonants, with only one nasal consonant present, such a consonant would typically be coronal. MD (p. 62) has seven languages that have only one nasal, five of which have [n]: 'Tlingit (701), Chipewyan (703), Wichita (755), Yuchi (757) and S. Nambiquara (816). Taoripi (623), with /m/, is an exception, as is Mixtec (728) with /ŋ/).' Also, if a language only has one fricative, this is likely to be the coronal fricative [s].
2. Here we consider positional neutralisation, that is, syllabic positions where a contrast is missing. We find ample evidence for a preference for coronals. In English and Dutch (and other Germanic languages), so-called extra-syllabic consonants are always coronals, such as the initial [s] and the final 'appendix'; see van der Hulst (1984) for Dutch and Fudge (1987) for English. Languages that restrict the coda position to coronal consonants were mentioned in § 4.3.3 (the Australian language Lardil allows only coronals in coda position.).
3. As for occurrence in all languages, the situation is that all languages have coronal consonants for both obstruents and sonorants, whereas labials or velars may be missing Gordon (2016: 46) reports for voiceless stop consonants that dentals/alveolars are the most common

---

preferred, what is preferred is unmarked') loses force when different kinds of preferences converge on the same conclusion; this was the original point in Jakobson (1941), who also considered preference patterns in language change, which I have not mentioned here.

    The same criteria apply to the categories that qualify as (un)marked in the manner class.

(found in 97.5 per cent of all languages[7]), after velars (89.3 per cent) and bilabials (82.9 per cent). In UPSID, coronals represent the biggest class of segments, making of 44.5 per cent of segments in this database (see Stefanuto & Vallée (1999)).
4. Another indication of the unmarked status of coronals is their lexical frequency. In American English, seven of the most frequent consonants are all coronal (n > t >r > s > l > ð > d in that order of frequency (Hayden (1950)).[8]
5. Whereas labials can make an early appearance, arguably due to their visible articulation, coronals quickly take over the status of being predominant in early speech.[9]
6. The famous Broca's patient 'Tan' was only able to articulate one syllable, with two coronal consonants (Sheehan & van der Wal (2018)).

In addition to these criteria (which are for the most part observation-driven, hence inductive), there are also approaches that correlate markedness directly with phonetic properties of segments in production or in perception (see Hayes & Steriade (2004)) or with formal aspects of phonological structure, where complex structures (i.e. branching structures or combinations of elements) or lack of specification (van der Hulst & van de Weijer (2018a)) are correlated with markedness. These approaches then take a more deductive approach towards markedness, deducing markedness from phonetic considerations or from formal-phonological considerations.[10]

Based on complexity as reflection in the CV structures that RCVP uses, we can derive a markedness scale for places of articulation as follows:

---

[7] If we add the fricative [s], we get to 100 per cent.
[8] See also Gordon (2014: § 3.6).
[9] McLeod & Crowe (2018) provide an extensive overview of the results of the acquisition of consonantal systems. While there is much variation, labials often precede coronals.
[10] Hayes & Steriade (2004: 3) write: 'Lindblom (1990: 46) observes that the study of distinctive features can proceed in two ways: inductively and deductively. The inductive approach in the study of features is to introduce a new feature whenever the descriptive need arises. The deductive approach, e.g. Stevens' Quantal Theory (1989) or Lindblom's Dispersion Theory (1986), proceeds not from a question of description ("What are the features used in language?") but from a principled expectation: "What features should we expect to find given certain assumptions about the conditions [under which] speech sounds are likely to develop?" (Lindblom & Engstrand 1989: 107).' I here suggest that reasoning from the formal structure of a phonological theory (which is grounded in cognitive considerations that involve principles of categorisation) is another instance of the deductive approach.

(7) a. {C, V} > {C;V, V;C}

b. {dental, labial} > {alveolar, dorsal}

The reason behind (7a) is that simple structures are preferred over complex structures due to their greater perceptual salience; this point is worked out in detail in Chapter 8. We can differentiate between the structures in each set in (7a) by adding that C place in the onset head is unmarked because onset heads are labelled C; we then predict the following complete ranking:

(8) a. {C > V > C;V > V;C}

b. {dental > labial > alveolar > dorsal}

Interestingly, this scale correlates with another scale, based on perceptibility, that is proposed in Jun (2004) (which does not differentiate between two types of coronals):

(9) coronal > labial > dorsal

An argument for the ranking of consonantal places can also be based on differences in weakening (lenition) processes. It has been argued that labials are the most resistant to intervocalic weakening, followed by coronals, with dorsal the most likely to weaken, that is, to spirantise (Foley 1977: 28). This produces the following scale, which switches the order of labials and coronals:

(10) labials > coronal > dorsal

Flemming (2004) provides a phonetic explanation for the ranking in (10). He views consonant weakening in terms of *effort reduction*. Given that the neutralisation of a voice contrast between voiceless and voiced obstruents is an aspect of weakening, he points out that preserving this contrast is easiest for labials and the most difficult for dorsals, given the decreasing volume behind the stricture that is necessary to build up the pressure that allows vocal fold vibration. Resisting reduction of dorsals thus requires a greater effort, relatively speaking. This, then, makes dorsals more prone to weakening (loss of voice contrast) than labials, with coronals in between. The weakening difference and the articulatory explanation for it leads to a scale that is different from the one in (9), which is primarily based on the *acoustic affinity* between labials and dorsals, both being 'grave' (or V in the RCVP notation). Despite the fact that my phonetic glosses of elements and element structures are usually stated in articulatory terms, I am not claiming that acoustic properties take a back seat. That said, I do not share with DP and GP the view that acoustic properties always dominate over articulatory properties.[11] Often both are in harmony, but in this particular case, they are not. While the two scales in (9) and (10) agree on the vulnerability and markedness of velars, there is 'disagreement' with respect to labials and coronals. The RCVP model sides with the scale in (9) and thus does not provide an immediate explanation for the scale in (10). In Chapter 8, I will return in some detail to how scales of preference can be deduced from the RCVP structures for *all* the phonological categories. However, we will see that there are other cases where a single scale cannot account for 'everything'.[12]

If then, the claim that coronal is the appropriate interpretation of the C element (in the place class for onset heads) is correct, it follows that V must be peripheral. One might ask whether there is, in addition to being 'not-C', a positive property that correlates with labials and dorsals being V. In the previous chapter on manner I have proposed that the property V correlates with a higher perceptual salience (or 'sonority'). Jakobson, Fant & Halle (1952) describe peripheral consonants (which they call [+grave]) acoustically as having a concentration of energy in the lower spectrum. Does this suggest that dorsals and labials manifest a higher 'sonority' or perceptual salience as a positive manifestation of their V-hood? Not according to Jun (2004) (see (9)), who argues that coronal is the most salient place from a perceptual point of view. For the moment, then, we must be satisfied with analysing peripheral consonants as having a V-place property on the argument that they are opposed to coronals, for which a C status is firmly established on the grounds that coronal is widely considered to be the unmarked place of articulation.

With respect to the second split, we must also ask whether front coronals (C) are more preferred (more common) than back coronals (V); see (1). If so, this would justify their representation in terms of the C choice. In UPSID, which does not distinguish between dental and alveolar, the combined dental/alveolar location is overwhelmingly the more frequent place compared to other (post-alveolar) coronal places (see MD p. 32). This supports the prediction that dental/alveolar is more common than post-alveolar. If the front/back distinction is made within the

---

[11] The view of Roman Jakobson (e.g. (1941)) was that acoustic properties are shared by speaker and hearer and are therefore more important than articulatory properties. In § 1.3.1 I have advocated a balanced view which denies absolute dominance for either articulation or perception, also suggesting that acoustic properties may prevail for vowels, whereas articulatory properties may prevail for consonants.

[12] Krämer & Zec (2019) also arrive at this conclusion in their study of restrictions on coda consonants in terms of manner properties.

dental-alveolar region, we predict that dentals are more preferred than alveolars. I do not have clear data to confirm this prediction.[13]

What about velars(C) and labials (V)? Are labials more common than velars? MD (p. 32) does not report a notable difference: 99.1 per cent of languages have bilabial as a place for stops while 99.4 per cent have velar place.

We can also again ask whether labials and velar differ in terms of perceptual salience. Indeed, as per (10), labials are more perceptually salient than velars. The scale in (9), which is based on perceptibility, thus seems to support the V choice for labial.

Finally, if the onset head position favours C choices we might expect that within the class of peripherals, dorsals (C;V) are preferred over labials (V), just as denti-alveolars are preferred over post-/palato-alveolars in inventories that have only one coronal and in languages that have both. In Kessler & Treiman (1997), who studied the distribution of English phonemes in 2,001 uninflected CVC words, labials 'beat' velars in terms of occurrence in both onset and coda, with coronals beating both.[14] In Chapter 8 I will argue that labials beat velars because they are not a mixed category. Velars combine C and V and this, I will argue, makes them less preferred in the onset head position.

5.2.2 Edge (onset head): dependent class

As might be expected, given their interpretation in the head class, for the dependent class I will take C and V to represent the secondary articulations of *palatalisation* and *labialisation*:

---

[13] With respect to a correlation between dental vs. alveolar and laminal vs. apical, LM (p. 23) note: 'In general, if a language has only a dental or an alveolar stop, then that stop will be laminal if it is dental and apical if it is alveolar. [...] There are comparatively few languages in which a dental stop is required to be apical. This is, however, the case in Temne, a West Atlantic language spoken in Sierra Leone, which breaks the generalisation that languages that contrast dental and alveolar stops have laminal dentals and apical alveolars. In Temne the stop made on the teeth is articulated with the tip of the tongue, and the one made on the alveolar ridge, which is slightly affricated, involves the blade of the tongue.'

The laminal/apical distinctions is represented as secondary manners c;v and v;c, respectively. This means that the model predicts that since laminal is more c-like, this manner is less marked than apical in a C-syllabic position. This contradicts the preference that LM note for alveolars being apical if alveolars are less marked than dentals, for which the evidence is not clear. However, the correlation between dental and laminal on the one hand and alveolar and apical on the other hand is also broken in languages such as Spanish and French in which the alveolar coronals are laminal.

[14] Coronals are also frequent in the 'coda' given the occurrence of the coronal appendix in many English words.

188 Principles of Radical CV Phonology

(11)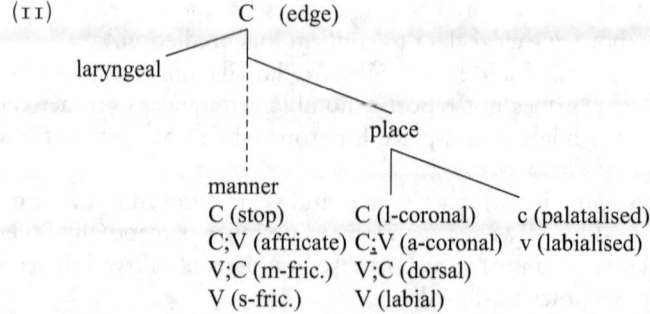

Recall that the third traditionally recognised secondary articulation, pharyngeal, has been treated as a manner distinction in the previous chapter, that is, as secondary manner v. We note that the secondary locations in the place class appeal to two simple structures, namely c and v. I do not see a need for complex secondary structures. Allowing simpler structures but no complex structures in a dependent unit is of course precisely the asymmetry that is expected in the current model:[15]

(12)

	c palatal	v labial
C front coronal/apical)		
C;V back coronal/laminal		
V;C dorsal		
V labial		

This allows four 'plain' locations (i.e. without a secondary articulation) and eight categories with a secondary articulation, leading to a total of twelve. While palatalisation and labialisation are extremely frequent in UPSID, we do not, of course, expect any single language to use all the potentially contrastive options. In the MD index of segment types, labialisation and palatalisation occur over fifty times, with all major places of articulation (here including both obstruents and sonorants; see § 4.2.1.2).

These two cases of secondary articulation are straightforward and attested phonemically in a large group of languages, especially with respect to labialisation (LM p. 354ff.). There may also be other types of secondary articulation, such as labiodentalisation (LM p. 366), which could involve a [ü]-like superimposition, that is, secondary cv. However,

---

[15] Notwithstanding the possibility that we do need one intermediate complex structure in the dependent manner node, albeit marginally, as we have seen in § 4.2.1.2 and § 4.3.1.2.

there is no secondary articulation, for instance, that corresponds to the vowel '[e]', which cannot be represented as a combination of place elements, but rather would require both secondary place (I) *and* secondary manner (C;V).

The following table illustrates all twelve possibilities *for stops* with IPA symbols:[16]

(13) C locations (for stops):

Head	Dependent		
C (front coronal)			dental coronal[t̪ d̪]
	c (palatal)	{C{c}}	palatalised coronal
	v (labial)	{C{v}}	labialised coronal [tʷ]
CV (back coronal)			(post-)alveolar coronal [t d]
	c (palatal)	{C;V{c}}	palatalised alv. [tʲ]/ alveo-palatal. [ɕ, ʑ] (palato-alveolar)
	v (labial)	{C;V{v}}	lab. coronal [tʷ]
CV (per./dorsal)			plain dorsal [k g]
	c (palatal)	{V;C{c}}	pal. dors. [kʲ]/ palatal [cɟ][17]
	v (labial)	{V;C{v}}	lab. dorsal [kʷ]
V (per./labial)			plain bilab [p b]
	c (palatal)	{V{c}}	pal. labial [pʲ]
	v (labial)	{V{v}}	lab. labial [pʷ]

The anterior coronal with secondary palatalisation covers a range of articulations, including not only a palatalised [tʲ] but also the intermediate alveo-palatal or palato-alveolar articulations. The labelling and IPA transcriptions of posterior coronal sounds are not consistent in the literature. For example, LM (p. 146) note that the more posterior sibilant in English, symbolised 'ʃ' in the IPA tradition, has been variously

---

[16] I here refrain from specifying a similar table for fricatives or intermediate manners like affricates. Also, I have not included the possibilities for stops with secondary manner. We expect that intermediate primary manners as well as stops with secondary manners will occur less frequently, if at all, with secondary place properties. Palatalised and labialised affricates do occur; see MD (pp. 221–4).

[17] LM (p. 31): 'When places of articulation are grouped according to the active articulator used, palatal articulations, which use the body of the tongue rather than the blade, fall outside the Coronal class of articulations. Rather, they are connected to the velar and uvular places. We use the term Dorsal for this group.'

described as palato-alveolar, alveolo-palatal, palatal, lamino-alveolar or lamino-domal.[18]

Labiodental is not represented as a location distinction. As proposed in § 4.2.1.1, labiodentals differ from bilabials in being strident, a manner distinction, which also accounts for affricates. This leaves open that C-headed stops (alveo-palatals/palato-alveolars and palatals) are likely to be phonetically produced with affrication (see Kehrein (2002)), which means that affrication would sometimes be phonological and sometimes phonetic, as discussed in § 4.2.1.1.

An issue that arises, since the strident distinction is not applied to sonorant consonants, is that there are reports of languages that distinguish between [m] and [ɱ], a distinction that can thus not be made in RCVP. The prediction that RCVP makes is that labiodental nasal never occurs contrastively. This issue was also discussed in § 4.2.1.1, where I suggested alternatives for cases in which the labiodental nasal cannot obviously be analysed as a contextual allophone.

In any given language with just the usual three major places, the representation in (14) will be sufficient:[19]

(14)   place   in onset head position

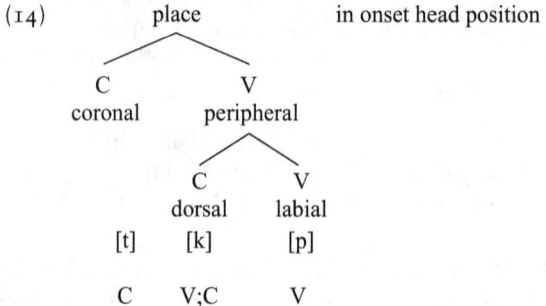

Hawaiian (MD 424) has a simpler system, with a contrast between

---

[18] The palato-alveolar place could be grouped with palatal. LM (p. 31): 'Languages seldom distinguish between sounds simply by one being a palatal and the other a palato-alveolar, preferring instead either to have affricates in the one position and stops in the other, or in some other way to supplement the contrasts in place of articulation with additional variations in the manner of articulation.' See also Lahiri & Blumstein (1984).

[19] LM (p. 43ff.), finding that 'Thus a typical stop inventory is far more likely to contain p, t, k rather than ʈ, t̪, t̟ or c, k, q', provide functional explanations for this fact (pp. 45–6). I would not say that such functional factors are irrelevant, but I would not conclude that these explanations render a formal account unnecessary. While segmental inventory may be shaped by such factors over historical time, language learners must, in my view, be equipped with an evolved, innate categorisation system that delivers a mental system of segmental contrasts.

labial and velar for stops, although nasals have a labial/coronal contrast. However, [k] is in free variation with [t]. For nasals, there are reports that [n] varies with the velar nasal.[20] I suggest that this system can be analysed with a split only at the first level, leading to an interpretation of C as lingual, instead of coronal:

(15)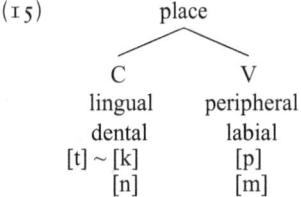

```
              place
            /      \
           C        V
        lingual  peripheral
        dental    labial
        [t] ~ [k]  [p]
          [n]     [m]
```

The dental and labial articulation would be the default interpretation of the first split, which makes the appearance of [k] unexpected.

LM (pp. 18–19) discuss linguo-labials, which involve a contact between the tongue and the upper lip. Consonants with this place of articulation occur with stops, fricatives and nasals 'in a group of languages from the islands of Espiritu Santo and Malekula in Vanuatu (Maddieson 1989b). These languages have stops and nasals with a linguo-labial gesture, contrasting with bilabial and alveolar gestures' (LM p. 18).[21] My analysis of this place will represent it as a compound structure which combines coronal and peripheral. Compound structures are proposed in § 7.3.2, including for MACs and clicks.

In the previous chapter we have seen that the secondary *manner* element v delivers pharyngealisation, which is how uvulars can be distinguished from velars:

(16)   dorsal: [k g x ɣ]   uvular: [q G χ ʁ]

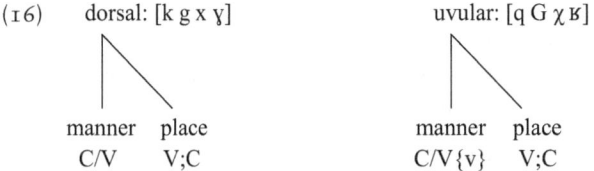

```
        manner  place              manner    place
         C/V    V;C                C/V{v}    V;C
```

With the option of having palatalised dorsals (which represent not only a palatalised dorsal [kʲ] but also plain palatals), RCVP can thus represent a three-way contrast for dorsals. LM discuss the contrast between palatal, velar and uvular, remarking that

---

[20] See Schütz (1994).
[21] This type of articulation can take the place of a plain labial; see Olson, Reiman, Sabio & da Silva (2009).

We have not ourselves heard any language that contrasts palatal stops with both velars and uvulars. Usually, when there are three stops in this area the most forward of the three is a laminal post-alveolar (palato-alveolar) affricate rather than a palatal stop as is the case in Quechua. [...] There are, however, a few reports in the literature of languages that contrast palatal, velar and uvular stops without making the first of these an affricate. The most convincing case of this kind is that of Jaqaru, a language fairly closely related to Quechua. (LM p. 35)

Pharyngeal consonants will be discussed in the next section. I will propose that these segments are obstruents that *lack* a location specification. In this section I will also return to the representation of laryngeal consonants, which likewise lack a place specification, as already proposed in § 4.2.4.

5.2.3 Post-velar consonants: pharyngeals and laryngeals

In RCVP, pharyngeals do *not* have a place specification. They share this property with laryngeals. The proposal is that the absence of a place element is phonetically interpreted as pharyngeal. It turns out that there is a substantial number of pharyngeals which perhaps need to be represented as potentially contrastive. Due to the work of Esling ((1999, 2009); Edmondson & Esling (2006); Moisik, Czaykowska-Higgins & Esling (2011)), two classes of pharyngeals, one of which needs a subdivision, can be distinguished on phonetic grounds:[22]

(17) Upper pharyngeals (involving TR retraction):
  Fricative voiceless [ħ]
         voiced [ʕ]

  Lower pharyngeals (aryepiglottal[23])
   Stop   voiceless [ʔ] (has full closure as geminate)
         voiced 'X'[24]

   Fricative voiceless [ʜ]
         voiced [ʢ]

We see that 'deep down' in the vocal tract there is an area of possible constrictions that traditional treatments of consonantal places often

---

[22] After completing this book, I received Esling, Moisik, Benner & Crevier-Buchman (2019), which contains much additional material.
[23] Produced by contracting the aryepiglottal folds of the larynx against the epiglottis.
[24] LM (p. 38) assume that there is a voiced stop counterpart for which there is no IPA symbol. It occurs in Dahalo in their analysis.

do not deal with. The distinction between radico- (upper) pharyngeals and epiglotto- (lower) pharyngeals, and even plain glottals is difficult to observe, but instrumental studies have confirmed these articulations (see references given above). LM (p. 38) report that S. Kodzasov (p.c.) describes a dialect of Agul that may contain four pharyngeals: a voiced and voiceless pharyngeal ([ʕ] and [ħ]) and a voiceless epiglottal fricative [H], as well as a voiceless epiglottal stop [ʡ]. According to Catford (1983) there is a fifth pharyngeal, namely [ʢ]. In addition, this language has the two laryngeal consonants [h] and [ʔ]. Despite Catford's claim, I will here assume that at most four segment types need to be represented.

Let us now see how the pharyngeal consonants, which, as I propose, all lack a place element, can be represented in RCVP,. We can obviously make use of the head manner C/V distinction to separate stops (like voiceless [ʡ]) from fricatives ([ħ], [ʕ] and [H], [ʢ]). In each pair of fricatives there is a voiced/voiceless distinction, so the critical issue is how to separate the two pairs of fricatives that are referred to in (17) as upper and lower pharyngeal, respectively. Since we are dealing with fricatives the most obvious choice is to invoke stridency. LM describe epiglottal fricatives as 'noisier'. These authors in fact propose analysing the alleged pharyngeal fricatives in Semitic as epiglottal:

> In our experience there is audible local turbulence in the sound that Catford symbolizes as [ħ], but, as he notes, it is very seldom apparent in what he symbolizes as [ʕ]. We would also suggest that these Semitic fricatives might more properly be called epiglottal rather than pharyngeal. (LM p. 168)

If we accept this suggestion, the upper pharyngeals would be non-strident, hence in head manner: V;C:

(18)   a. radico-pharyngeal fricatives   b. epiglotto-pharyngeal fricatives

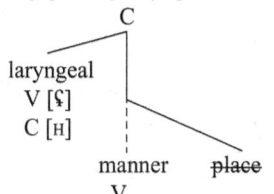

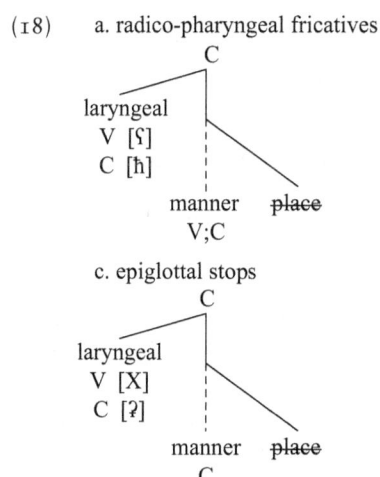

194 Principles of Radical CV Phonology

The laryngeal elements V and C represent voicing and lack of voicing (or 'tense'), respectively; see Chapter 6.[25]

There is one remaining issue. In § 4.2.4 I have proposed that laryngeal consonants too are represented as placeless, divided into the fricative [h] and the stop [ʔ] in terms of the manner elements V and C.[26]

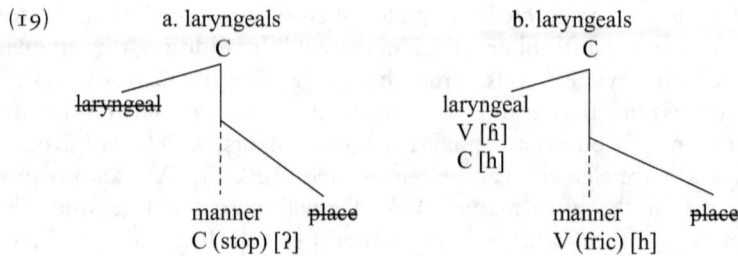

However, we must note that these representations for laryngeals are the same as those for the epiglottal pharyngeal in (18c) and (18b). Hence when a language has *both* the laryngeal consonants and the epiglottal pharyngeal consonants, one of these would have to be specified with an additional element. The most obvious possibility is to represent epiglottal pharyngeals with a secondary manner v specification, with the usual interpretation of pharyngealised:

---

[25] Moisik, Czaykowska-Higgins & Esling (2011) provide some information about processes concerning pharyngeal genesis, discussing the change from uvular ejectives and uvular fricatives into the pharyngeals [ʕ] and [ħ], respectively, which can be seen as the loss of the dorsal manner, suggesting perhaps the obstruent nature of the resulting sounds, which are sometimes described as 'approximants'. This change did not affect the plain uvular stops (see (16) for the RCVP representation of uvulars), but that in itself could be a restriction on the process that does not immediately need to follow from a representational difference between uvular stops and fricatives, although the model that Moisik, Czaykowska-Higgins & Esling (2011) propose makes a representational difference between uvular stops and fricatives.

[26] The laryngeal fricative [h] can have a voiced counterpart [ɦ], although this distinction has not been reported as being contrastive; see § 4.2.4. Zulu (MD 126) is a possible case where the laryngeal fricative behaves as a depressor consonant. LM (p. 76) discuss two cases where there is a phonological distinction between a voiced and voiceless glottal stop. In Gimi, a Papuan language of the Eastern Highlands, Papua New Guinea, two glottal consonants have developed from a [k]/[g] pair and one of these 'behaves' as a voiced consonant. LM assume that this sound has creaky voice. They mention that 'Another language which has been reported to have a voiced glottal stop is Jingpho (Maran 1971), but in this case it seems to us preferable to regard the contrasting forms as being distinguished by tonal differences' (p. 77).

(20)   a. (upper) pharyngeal fricatives   b. epiglottal fricatives

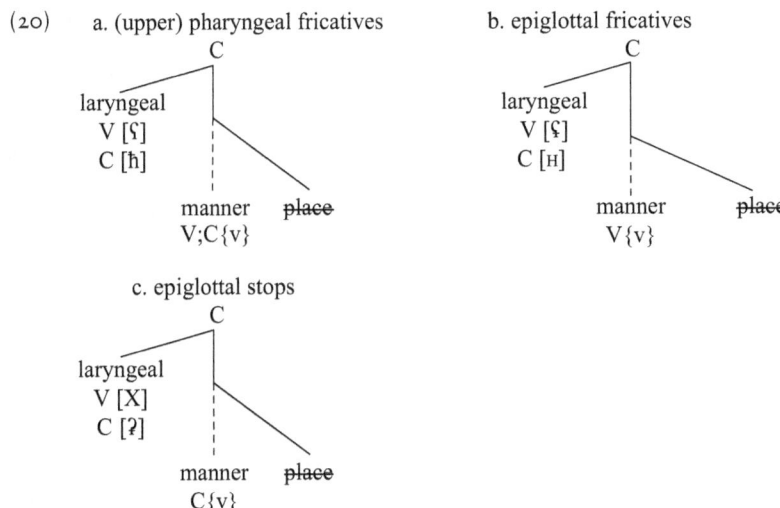

Recall that uvular consonants are represented as dorsals with a secondary manner specification v:

(21)   uvular consonants [q G χ ʁ]

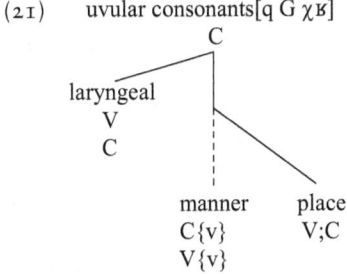

McCarthy (1990) proposes the natural class of gutturals, which may comprise uvular consonants and pharyngeals. This class can now be captured with reference to the secondary manner specification v.[27]

There is only one remaining problem, which is that the class of gutturals can also sometimes include the laryngeal consonants. If we were to assign the secondary manner {v} to these laryngeal consonants, we would be back to the problem of differentiating between laryngeals and epiglottals. I would have to assume that in the relevant cases, there is in

---

[27] The model proposed here does not, however, provide a basis for explaining why pharyngeal consonants can have an effect of 'fronting' a low vowel [a] to [ae]. I suspect that the label fronting for the '[ae]' is a misnomer and that this vowel is really a retracted low vowel.

fact no contrast between laryngeals and epiglottals, so that the laryngeals adopt the representation of epiglottals.[28]

As a final note, in addition, to pharyngealisation, we might then also expect that the class of pharyngeal consonants could occur with the secondary manner specification c, which causes nasalisation. I am not aware of reports of such segments. What might prevent such segment types is that they would require two secondary manner specifications: v for pharyngeal and c for nasal, although we have previously seen that such complexity cannot be completely ruled out. However, nasalisation has been reported as occurring with laryngeals, for instance in Nenets:

(22) nʔ   prenasalised glottal stop
      h̃   nasalised [h]

In § 4.2.4 I noted a problem for the placeless view of laryngeal consonants, namely that laryngeal consonants have been reported that have a secondary place specification. Secondary specifications are not supposed to occur in the absence of primary specifications. While only very few examples have been reported, there could also be cases of pharyngeal or epiglottal consonants with secondary place specifications, which creates the same problem. The treatment of laryngeal as a positive place of articulation is shared by many FG models (see § 11.2). Models that recognise a pharyngeal node have been proposed in McCarthy (1994) and Rose (1996). Moisik, Czaykowska-Higgins & Esling (2011) discuss such earlier models and propose their own model that reckon with the rich array of post-velar consonants that have been discussed in this section; see also Moisik (2013) for an even more extensive discussion. I will return to possible developments of the RCVP model, such as in (23), in Chapter 12.

In this section I have reviewed place distinctions for obstruents. The following table contains all the locations in (20) and adds pharyngeal and laryngeal consonants:[29]

---

[28] This would also be the approach to the pharyngealised glottal consonants in Nootka (MD 730, p. 25).

[29] Backley (2011) uses the term 'palatal' for post-alveolars, while he glosses the symbols that are usually used for 'palatals' in the IPA as palato-*velars*.

Place 197

(23) Consonantal location structures and IPA:

		bilabial	labio dental	dental	alveolar	postalv	alveo palatal	retro flex	palatal	velar	uvular	phar	epigl	lar
		ɸ β	f v	θ ð	s z	ʃ ʒ	ɕ ʑ	ʂ ʐ	ç j	x ɣ	χ ʁ	ħ ʕ	ʜ ʢ	h ɦ
Man	Head	V;C	V	V;C	V	V	V	V	V	V	V	V;C	V	V
	Dep						v;c		−	v	v	v		
		p b	− −	t̪ d̪	t d	− −		t̢ ɖ	c ɟ	k g	q ɢ		ʡ ?	ʔ −
Man	Head	C		C	C	C	C	C	C	C	C		C	C
	Dep						v;c		−	v				
Pla	Head	V	V	C	C;V	C;V	C;V	C;V	V;C	V;C		−	−	− −
	Dep						c		c					
Lar	Head	C V	C V	C V	C V	C V	C V	C V	C V	C V	C V	C V	C V	C V
	Dep													

5.2.4 Place distinctions for sonorant consonants in the edge

Sonorant consonants can occur as onset heads and in this position they can have distinctive place properties. In principle, the place distinctions that are possible for obstruents also are available for sonorant consonants:

(24)

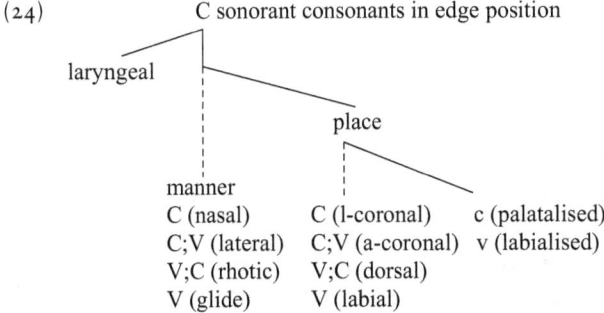

```
                C sonorant consonants in edge position
   laryngeal
                  place

        manner
        C (nasal)      C (l-coronal)    c (palatalised)
        C;V (lateral)  C;V (a-coronal)  v (labialised)
        V;C (rhotic)   V;C (dorsal)
        V (glide)      V (labial)
```

The full array of primary locations can certainly be found for nasals, with many languages barring the velar nasal [ŋ] while permitting this nasal in the coda (see § 4.3.2). MD (p. 66) concludes that

> no nasal with a secondary articulation occurs unless a simple nasal occurs at the same place of articulation, and none occurs unless consonants of another type also occur with the same secondary articulation and in the same place of articulation.[30]

[30] See also Crothers (1975).

Place differentiation is more limited for the other three types of sonorant consonants. Laterals are dental/alveolar in the great majority of cases (87 per cent in UPSID). Retroflex laterals, the next most frequent type, is represented with a secondary manner v;c in RCVP (see § 4.2.1.2). Next come palatal laterals. Velar laterals only occur in Yagaria (609). MD (p. 77) mentions some other cases including in the New Guinea languages Melpa, Mid-Waghi and Kanite and the Chadic language Kotoko.

Rhotics are typical of the dental/alveolar region. The uvular rhotic is said to be restricted to 'prestige dialects of Western European languages' (MD p. 81). It is remarkable that no languages use the difference between the coronal and uvular rhotic as distinctive. Retroflex rhotics occur in two languages in UPSID.

Glides (called vocoid approximants in MD) occur mostly as [j] (in 86.1 per cent of the UPSID languages) or [w] (only in 75.5 per cent). A velar approximant occurs in five languages, while the labial-palatal occurs in four cases. These four places of articulation for glides match the four high vowels [i], [ü], [ɨ] and [u] that we will discuss in the next section on vowel place.

Secondary locations are more limited for sonorant consonants in comparison to obstruents, and labialised and palatalised nasals occur multiple times in UPSID (MD p. 235ff.; and Paez (MD 804; p. 242). For laterals, palatalisation occurs in several languages (MD pp. 242–4), but secondary labialisation is not attested for laterals, or for rhotics. A palatalised rhotic occurs in Lithuanian (MD 007, p. 240). Both secondary articulations are unattested for plain glides, although a palatalised flap occurs in a few languages (MD p. 241).

5.3 Nucleus (rhyme head): vowels

We now turn our attention to place properties of vowels. As proposed in Chapter 3, vowel place is specified with the same elements that are used for consonantal place. In RCVP terms, this means 'C' and 'V', which is not a big surprise since these are the only two elements. The parallelism between the consonant and vowel realms becomes extra clear if we use the usual mnemonic element labels 'I' and 'U'.

In van der Hulst (2018) I analyse a large number of vowel harmony systems, many of which involve the elements I and U. In that work, I present the RCVP model of vowel structure in great detail and provide exemplification of the theory by discussing different kinds of vowel systems. I will not repeat that extensive discussion here and limit myself in this section to the 'bare bones' of the RCVP account of vowel place elements.

5.3.1 Nucleus (rhyme head): head class

Location elements in the nucleus represent the vowel 'colours', round and front:

(25)

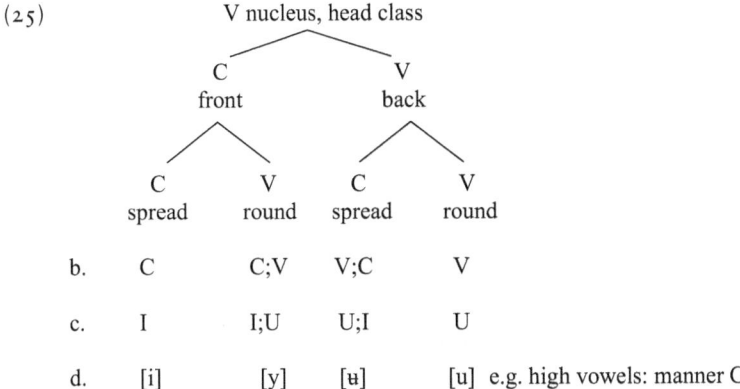

```
                V nucleus, head class
                 C            V
               front         back
              /   \         /    \
             C     V       C      V
           spread round  spread  round

    b.      C     C;V     V;C      V

    c.      I     I;U     U;I      U

    d.     [i]    [y]     [ʉ]     [u]   e.g. high vowels: manner C
```

Both C and V as heads denote natural classes, of front and back vowels respectively. As for the dependent occurrence, it would seem that the dependent occurrence of V denotes a natural class.[31]

(26)
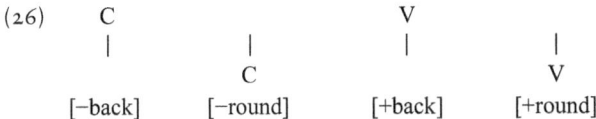

```
        C                V
        |                |
        |       C        |      V
        |       |        |      |
     [−back] [−round] [+back] [+round]
```

The divisions and their phonetic correlates in (26) are very similar to the categorisation of locations for onset heads (i.e. consonants), at least as far as the unmarked choice in the second cut is involved:

(27)

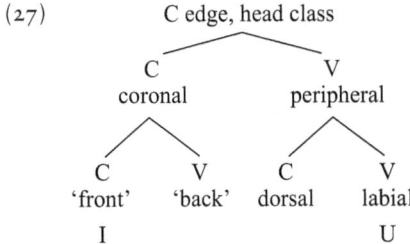

```
              C edge, head class
              C              V
           coronal        peripheral
          /    \          /     \
         C      V        C       V
       'front' 'back'  dorsal  labial
         I                       U
```

However, with respect to the marked choice of the second cut, the parallels are 'weaker'. While dorsal–labial mirrors back unrounded–back

---

[31] This is like the dependent V element in obstruent manner which denotes the class of strident obstruents; see § 4.2.1.1.

rounded vowels, the spread/round difference seems to have nothing in common with the denti-alveolar vs. post-alveolar distinction.

If we cross-classify manner and location for vowels, we can generate the following table, which includes vowels that are 'colourless' (i.e. central) vowels:

(28) Vowel distinctions:

	C	C;V	placeless	V;C	V
C	i/ɪ	y/ʏ	ɨ~ɯ	ʉ	u/ʊ
C;V	e	ø	ɘ~ɤ	ɵ	o
V;C	ɛ	œ	ɜ~ʌ	ɞ	ɔ
V	æ	Œ	a	ɑ	ɒ

In (29) we find the same table, this time with the mnemonic element labels:

(29)

	I	I;U	Placeless	U;I	U
∀	i/ɪ	y/ʏ	ɨ~ɯ	ʉ	u/ʊ
∀;A	e	ø	ɘ~ɤ	ɵ	o
A;∀	ɛ	œ	ɜ~ʌ	ɞ	ɔ
A	æ	Œ	a	ɑ	ɒ

(30)[32] VOWELS

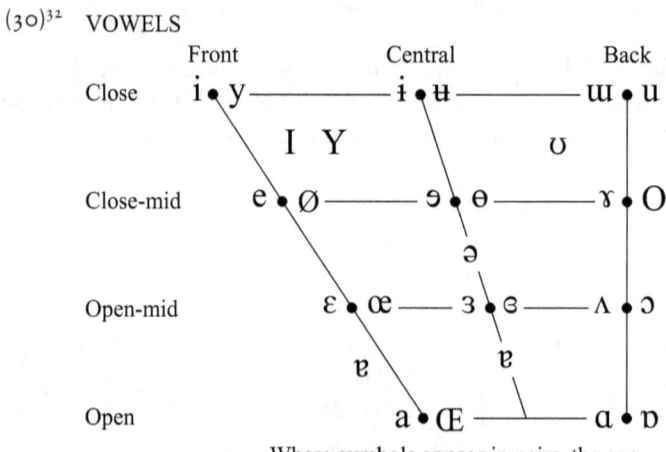

Where symbols appear in pairs, the one to the right represents a rounded vowel.

[32] <https://www.internationalphoneticassociation.org/IPAcharts/IPA_Kiel_2018_vowels_1200.png> (last accessed 14 February 2020).

A few comments are in order regarding the relation between (29) and (30). First, the IPA chart represents 'a' as front and 'æ' as slightly higher, while in my tables 'a' is analysed as colourless, with 'æ' being its front counterpart. Clearly, the goal of a phonological theory should not be to characterise each and every IPA symbol in terms of a unique element structure. What matters (in my view) is rather which sound types can occur contrastively in languages. Thus, by placing different phonetic symbols together in one cell, I make the claim that these phonetic units cannot occur contrastively in any language. Another possible mismatch between the phonology and the IPA chart is that certain IPA symbols might correspond to different phonological structures in different languages or even in the same language (when different phonological objects receive the same phonetic interpretation). I refer to van der Hulst (2018: § 4.4), where I argue that phonetic [i] may have different representations depending on whether it triggers palatal harmony or not. Likewise, the short vowel [ɛ] displays similar ambiguity in how it behaves in the harmony systems. In general, ambiguity in the behaviour of a certain segment may be due to this segment having two different structural representations.

Compared to DP and GP, I permit the element U and I to occur in two combinations, with either U being the head or I; see (25). This point was discussed in § 2.2 and § 2.3, respectively, and in van der Hulst (2018: § 2.2.3) I use the two structures for front so-called 'outrounded' vowels and for central 'inrounded' vowels, which occur contrastively in Swedish; see Riad (2014).

5.3.2 Nucleus (rhyme head): dependent class

If a secondary specification for vowels was needed, we would expect it to provide the option of 'palatal' or 'labial'. An option to consider would be to explore the idea that I and U as secondary specifications can account for vowel harmony. The second row in (29) and (30) shows two vowels (e.g. i / ɪ). The difference here involves ATR. As proposed in § 4.3.1, I take the position in this book that ATR is the correlate of a dependent occurrence of the element I. That proposal deviates from the model in van der Hulst (2018) for reasons explained in that section.

This then raises the question as to whether secondary usage of the U element delivers a property of vowels that is needed, either for contrast or for a form of vowel harmony. No such usage has been identified. Palatal harmony is treated in terms of the primary element I, while labial harmony is treated with the primary element U. In specific vowel harmony processes, each element may be a head or a dependent. As shown in van der Hulst (2018: ch. 5), the two place elements do not behave in the same way in harmony processes, with U harmony often being 'parasitic' on the occurrence of I harmony. It is perhaps worth exploring whether this might be due to labial harmony involve secondary U, rather than primary U. Here I will not explore this possibility, however. This would be more at place in a 'second edition' of van der Hulst (2018).

For the time being, I conclude that vowels, unlike consonants, do not appeal to 'secondary articulations' as much as consonants do. Given the fact that languages have more consonants than vowels (due to the fact that consonants are mostly responsible for encoding phonemic difference between morphemes and words), it follows that consonants, especially those in the onset head position, make use of more structural options.[33]

5.3.3 Syllabic consonants (sonorants)

We now turn to place distinction for syllabic consonants. Sonorant consonants in head positions (edge or nucleus) can have distinctive place properties. For syllabic sonorant consonants such distinctions seem to only occur when nasals occur as syllabic. Such syllabic nasal consonants do not occur with secondary manner or secondary place properties. My impression is that the occurrence of consonants in the nucleus is less preferred than sonorant consonants in the onset head position. A formal explanation for this difference is that the nucleus is V headed, which makes this location inherently more resistant to consonants than the onset, which is C headed. Also, we can again refer to the overall tendency to have fewer distinctive options in the nucleus than in the onset, given the functional role in the lexicon of especially onset consonants.[34]

In English, the nasals [m] and [n], as well as the liquids [l] and [r], can occur as syllabic consonants (*bottom, button, bottle, butter*). Bell (1978) offers a typological study of syllabic consonants based on eighty-five languages.[35] Historically, syllabic consonants often derive from vowel loss, with a consonant filling the nucleus left vacant. Sonorants are preferred over obstruents and within each class nasals are preferred over

---

[33] The astute reader might have noted that in treating ATR as dependent I predict that central vowels, which are placeless, cannot be advanced. This is analogous to the problem noted for laryngeal and pharyngeal consonants, also placeless, if those consonant types can occur with secondary palatalisation and labialisation. I discuss this issue in § 12.5.

[34] I discussed in § 3.2.2 the fact that RCVP prohibits syllabic obstruents

[35] See also Toft (2002); Dell & Elmedlaoui (1985, 1988); Fougeron & Ridouane (2008). For a GP analysis of the Slavic languages Czech and Polish, see Scheer (2008). He does not see syllabic consonants as being in the nucleus, but rather as 'spreading to' the nucleus position from a consonantal position.

liquids, and fricatives over stops. The preference for nasals runs counter to the sonority preference for nuclei, which would be expected to favour liquids over nasals. Only one language in Bell's corpus only allow liquids as syllabic (Lendu),[36] against thirty-five languages that only have syllabic nasals. This asymmetry clearly shows that the likelihood of occurring as syllabic is not simply a function of sonority. We have to look at the historical processes that give rise to syllabic consonants, and here I suggest that nasals are more likely to interact and fuse with a preceding vowel than liquids, given the natural occurrence of nasalisation of vowels before nasals. While this may give rise to the nasal disappearing, it is likely that the emergence of syllabic nasals is a result of the reverse process. If syllabic sonorants emerge from coda sonorants, the higher frequency of syllabic nasals follows from the higher frequency of nasals as codas (see § 4.3.3).

Among nasals, syllabic [m] and [ŋ] are preferred over syllabic [n], which may be a sonority effect, given that peripheral nasals are more sonorous, which correlates with their place being V. Bell does not indicate whether among liquids there is a preference for rhotics over laterals, or vice versa, although he does remark that 'there are a few hints that dark laterals are favoured as syllabic' (1978: 172) (but that could be meant as applying within the class of laterals).

Turning to syllabic obstruents, we note that Trubetzkoy (1939 [1960])[37] did not admit obstruents as possible syllabic consonants, and is followed in this regard by Chomsky & Halle (1968).[38] That said, Bell's corpus contains thirty-four languages with syllabic obstruents, ten of which do not have syllabic sonorants. Bell discusses a number of factors that play a role in the distribution of syllabic consonants, such as morpheme status (root, affix), word-medial or peripheral syllable, stress and the overall complexity of the syllable. Bell attests fricatives of all places of articulation as syllabic. He also finds a syllabic occurrence of the laryngeal [h] in Akan and a syllabic glottal stop (in Koryak).

We cannot draw firm conclusions from Bell's survey, useful as it is. With respect to the possibility of obstruents being syllabic it is crucial to know all the details of the syllabic analysis, and also whether reports on the syllabicity of obstruents are based on phonotactic analysis or on surface syllabification in utterances.

---

[36] 'Sanskrit also only had syllabic liquids, while PIE had both syllabic liquids and syllabic nasals (Bell 1978: 171).

[37] 'It should be noted that in the case of the consonants only the so-called sonorants, that is, the nasals and liquids, are considered independent syllabic nuclei' (Trubetzkoy (1939 [1960]: 171)).

[38] 'Obstruents would by definition be excluded from forming a syllabic peak' (Chomsky & Halle (1968: 354)).

5.4 Bridge and coda

Thus far, I have dealt with place specifications in syllabic heads, that is, the edge and nucleus, respectively. Place specification for syllabic dependents has been claimed to be absent in § 3.2.2. However, I remind the reader that we did have to acknowledge that bridge consonants would need a place specification if different places can occur for glides and nasals; see § 4.2.2.

In § 4.3.3, in the context of discussing coda conditions on manner, I also mentioned examples of such conditions involving place, which presupposes that, while limitations apply, place distinction are possible in the coda. This then means that the coda position may require place elements as well, although we only need I and U. This accounts for place distinctions among nasals or for the distinction between [j] and [w] in coda position; these correspond to the C and V manner for sonorant consonants, respectively.

Assuming, then, that place distinctions are possible, quite often restrictions apply. It is my impression that sonorant consonants in coda position do not need secondary place specifications (palatalisation, labialisation). As for primary place distinctions, I suspect that languages that have place distinctions for laterals do not allow them in coda. Beckman (2004) discusses the case of Tamil, which has a five-way distinction for nasals and a three-way distinction for laterals and rhotics. These segment types are avoided as codas by rules of epenthesis or rules of place assimilation.

A study of coda conditions involving place based on several languages is offered in Fonte (1996). It does not seem possible to establish one single preference ranking for places of articulation that accounts for all attested types of place coda conditions. Fonte concludes that there is no universally unmarked place (p. 35). The problem, as she notes, is that coda conditions can be different depending on whether we consider the word-final or word-medial position. In the latter case she argues for 'a constraint which enforces, rather than "allows", place identity between a coda and a following onset'.[39]

In Chapter 8 I will return to preference rankings for the coda (and all other syllabic positions).

5.5 Summary and concluding remarks

In this chapter I have provided interpretations for location structures. Unlike manner, we find that location makes only modest use of secondary

---

[39] See also Gouskova (2004) on this point.

articulations. Consonantal place uses palatalisation and labialisation, that is, only the simplex structures C and V:

(31) Location (edge):

C	C+c	C+cv	C+cv	C+v
C;V	CV+c	CV+cv	CV+cv	CV+v
V;C	CV+c	CV+cv	CV+cv	CV+v
V	V+c	V+cv	V+cv	V+v

	c palatalisation c;v v;c	v labialisation

C anterior coronal
C;V posterior coronal
V;C dorsal
V labial

The location distinctions for the nucleus are even more modest:

(32) Location (nucleus):

C	C+c	C+cv	C+cv	C+v
C;V	CV+c	CV+cv	CV+cv	CV+v
V;C	CV+c	CV+cv	CV+cv	CV+v
V	V+c	V+cv	V+cv	V+v

	c (ATR)	c;v c;v v

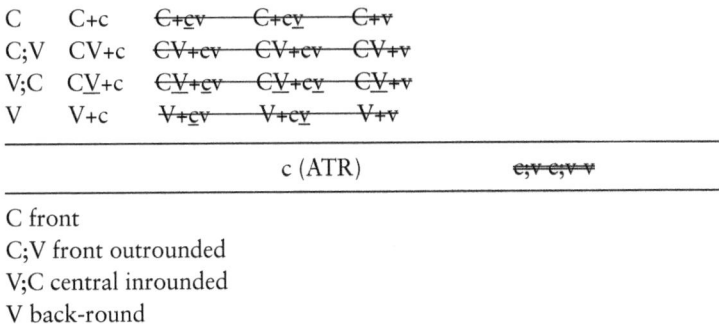

C front
C;V front outrounded
V;C central inrounded
V back-round

In this chapter, I have outlined the possibilities for place specifications for both consonants and vowels. I draw attention to the fact that RCVP offers a 'unified approach to place', which means that the same two elements, namely I and U, are used for both consonants and vowels. These two elements can characterise place by themselves or in combination, with the possibility of a dependency relation. As secondary specifications, these elements are only fully required for consonants, providing mostly what is traditionally referred to as secondary articulation, but they also represent some finer distinctions among the primary places. For vowels, I have proposed that secondary I accounts for ATR.

We must note that whereas the manner class is obligatory for segment structure, the place class is not. This means that the absence of place can be contrastive with the presence of place elements. This is a formal possibility that we have used in this chapter. For example, laryngeals were analysed as placeless obstruents (but not without considering an alternative approach; see (23)). This creates a contrast between consonants like [p], [t], [k] and [ʔ].

In the next chapter, I will discuss the third class of elements, namely those that characterise laryngeal properties for vowels and consonants. Again, we will see a unified set, which accounts for tonal distinctions among vowels and phonation distinctions among consonants.

6

Laryngeal: phonation and tone

6.1 Introduction

In this chapter, I will discuss the laryngeal class as needed for phonation types in consonants and for tone in vowels. After discussing the proposed RCVP structure, I turn to a special topic, namely the notion of laryngeal realism with specific reference to the analysis of phonation types in different Germanic languages. Despite its apparent abstractness, RCVP is committed to a notion of phonetic realism: elements are interpreted phonetically, taking into account their structural position and occurrences of the elements that are structurally close (such as those that occur in the head or dependent subclass of an element class). After discussing a specific instance of phonetic realism, namely laryngeal realism, I turn to a number of issues that arise in typologies of phonation types and phonation on vowels. I then review correlations between tone and phonation, and finally turn again to bridge and coda.

6.2 Edge (onset head): consonants (phonation)

I treat the head and dependent specification for phonation in one section, rather than spreading them out in two section, as I did for manner and place. The reason is that both subclasses are very closely connected, more so than in manner and place.

For consonants, the most common phonation distinction is that between voiced and voiceless (MD p. 28). However, there are additional phonation types that are possible, such as aspiration. In this case the opening between the vocal cords is 'extra wide', which causes a delay in the onset of voicing in the next segment: the aspiration effect.[1] When the

---

[1] Aspiration is often expressed in terms of Voice Onset Time (VOT); see Lisker & Abramson (1964). When a voiceless stop is followed by a vowel, the voicing of the vowel will 'ideally' start right after the release of the stop. But if a stop is produced with spread glottis, the onset of voicing is delayed and the vowel will start voiceless, which causes the aspiration effect. Reluctant to build the notion of 'time' into

vocal folds are tight together, the result is glottalisation as a phonation type. In addition, there are two further phonation types, called creaky voice and breathy voice. It has been claimed that these six types are sufficient as a basis for all possible phonemic contrasts that are attested in the world's languages (MD p. 30), with some languages allowing perhaps all of them.

There is a considerable amount of literature about phonation features that I cannot do justice to here. Important work on potentially contrastive distinctions can be found in Ladefoged (1973), Halle & Stevens (1971), Keating (1984) and Gordon & Ladefoged (2001). In Halle & Stevens (1971) phonation (and tone) distinctions are captured with the features [±constricted glottis]/[±spread glottis] and [±stiff vocal folds]/[±slack vocal folds], each creating a three-way distinction. A noteworthy property of the Halle & Stevens system is that they proposed a unified set of features for phonation and tone. This, of course, is also the aim of RCVP.

In later works, when referring to phonation, [±stiff vocal folds]/[±slack vocal folds] were sometimes replaced by the 'older feature' [±voice] (see Kenstowicz (1994a)):

(1) Voicing   Glottal width/constriction
     [±voice]   [±constricted glottis], [±spread glottis]

These features produce the following array of possible combinations and interpretations:[2]

(2)

	[−voice]	[+voice]
[+constricted] [−spread]	pʔ / p' glottalised (ejective) ʔp pre-glottalised	bʔ= IPA ɓ̥ creaky (laryngealised) ɓ implosive
[+constricted] [+spread]	---	---
[−constricted] [−spread]	p voiceless	b voiced (modal)
[−constricted] [+spread]	pʰ aspirated	bʰ = IPA b̤ breathy (murmur)

phonemic representations, I adopt the view that the onset delay of voicing could be seen as an effect of the wider glottal opening, which takes more time to close and thus 'spills over' into the vowel.
[2] Preglottalisation is specified as [+c.gl] and [+slack v.c.] in Halle & Stevens (1971).

Laryngeal: phonation and tone 209

The two glottal width features allow three, not four, options because the combination [+constricted, +spread] is impossible (just as the vowel height features [+high] and [+low] cannot be combined); this reflects a recurrent case of overgeneration in binary feature theories, which we also encounter with features for major classes, vowel height and tone height. There is perhaps nothing wrong in principle with allowing formal structures that cannot receive a coherent phonetic interpretation. However, if this situation can be avoided by altering the theory, this should be preferred. Alternatively, one could actually give an interpretation to combinations like [+high, + low] or [+constricted, +spread] (see Liberman (2017)), adopt different features (see below) or abandon binary features (see below).

In Halle and Stevens's system, implosives are [–stiff, –slack], differing from creaky voice, which they analyse as [–stiff, +slack]. With only [±voice], creaky voice and implosive have to be put in the same category and thus be seen as phonetic variants.³ These authors analyse ejectives (and variants) as [+stiff, –slack], which is the third combination of the features [±stiff] and [±slack]. In this case too, the combination of two plus values is deemed uninterpretable. Clearly, recognising two features [±stiff] and [±slack] allows more options than a system with only [±voice]. Arguably, and this is the argument for adopting the latter feature, Halle and Stevens's system allowed too many categories.

A further development, anticipated in Ewen (1980a) and AE, was the proposal that phonation features are unary. This view was later adopted in various other works (Lombardi (1991, 1995a, 1995b); Iverson & Salmons (1995); Avery (1996); Avery & Idsardi (2001); Kehrein & Golston (2004)).⁴ The use of unary primes such as [spread], [constricted] and [voice] limits the set of possible phonation types to six (three for sonorant consonants which are inherently voiced) as follows:

(3)	Voiceless	aspirated	breathy (murmur)	modal	creaky (laryngealised)	glottal
	-	spread	spread voiced	- voiced	constricted voiced	constricted
Obs	+	+	+	+	+	+
Son	*	*	+⁵	+	+	*

³ Unless additional features are adopted for the raised or lowered position of the larynx; see Trigo (1991) and Avery & Idsardi (2001).
⁴ The system parallels that of AE, who also use three unary features: |V| for voice, |O| for [spread] and |G| for glottalic. As we saw in Chapter 2, AE regarded voice as a manner feature.
⁵ This option represents what is often called a 'voiceless sonorant'. In other proposals (AE; Lombardi (1991)), voiceless sonorants are represented as aspirated, as they are in RCVP. LM (p. 69) confirm this type of analysis: 'Burmese has many pairs of

LM (p. 49ff.) consider phonation distinctions as a continuum of how closely the vocal folds are held together; LM include aspiration because

> in at least some cases voiceless aspiration involves a wider opening between the vocal folds than occurs for open voicelessness. This position can be considered as yet a further step along the continuum of vocal fold opening. However, aspiration involves matters of relative timing (VOT [...]) between laryngeal and oral articulations, and the wider opening can be viewed as an aspect of the control of this timing.

In the account presented here, timing will not be a factor that will be directly encoded. LM (p. 67) report that in Eastern Armenian aspirated stops can occur word-finally, which means that a VOT account is not possible anyway. For one recorded speaker:

> the difference between the voiceless aspirated and unaspirated stops [...]is in the strength of the release. The voiceless unaspirated stops are weakly released or (in other data from this speaker) not released at all, whereas the aspirated stop has a shorter closure and a noticeable burst followed by noisy airflow that is sustained for some considerable time.

Aspiration can also take the form of preaspiration:

> In Gaelic the preaspirated stops occur only in medial and final position, where they are the counterparts of the aspirated stops which occur in initial position. In Icelandic and Faroese, where preaspirated stops also occur only in medial and final position, they are realisations of long (geminate) voiceless aspirated stops. All these languages have a contrast between voiceless unaspirated and voiceless aspirated stops in initial position. (LM p. 70)

LM add (p. 73):

> we do not know of any language in which it is necessary to regard preaspiration as a feature required for distinguishing underlying forms. Stops of this kind always occur intervocalically or finally; there are no occurrences of initial pre-aspirated stops that we are aware of.

> verbs and adjectives that show a morphological alternation between simplex forms with voiceless unaspirated stops and causative forms with voiceless aspirated stops. The parallel alternation in nasals and laterals is usually described as being between voiced and voiceless counterparts. [...] Patterns such as these have suggested to a number of phonologists that aspirated stops and voiceless sonorants share a common feature of aspiration (or [spread glottis]) (Cho (1990), Steriade (1993b)).'

LM (p. 50) also recognise a category of modal voice which 'occurs in ordinary voiced vowels and in voiced continuant consonants such as nasals' and which is 'normally maintained in stops that are phonologically voiced. It is well known that in some languages, English being a familiar example, the vocal folds may not vibrate throughout the closure for a voiced stop.' They add (p. 51): 'In contrast, to English and several other Germanic languages, a considerable number of languages have voiced stops which require more energetic efforts to produce sustained vocal fold vibration. Such languages include well-known ones such as French and Thai.' The distinction referred to here will play an important role in § 6.4.2, where it will be proposed that 'voicing' indeed can have a different formal status in the languages referred to here. 'Voiceless' may also have different representations, since

> In some languages, such as the Polynesian group (Hawaiian, Maori, Tongan, etc.) actual vocal fold opening seems to be required; in others, such as most of the Australian languages, the stops may be produced with no actual opening required, with vibration ceasing due to lack of efforts to sustain it. (LM p. 53)

I will suggest that the voiceless consonants in Polynesian languages are specified [tense] (laryngeal C), while Australian languages simply miss a laryngeal specification.

Breathy voice results from a compromise between voicing and aspiration, resulting in 'sounds that have a higher flow rate and a looser form of vibration of the vocal folds' (LM p. 57).

Turning to creaky and glottalised phonation, I will take larynx raising to be a side effect of glottal stricture. To equate ejectives with voiceless glottalised consonants is common in the phonation literature (see Kenstowicz (1994a)). It is tempting, as suggested in (1), to say that implosives are phonetic variants for 'creaky/laryngealised phonation', so that we do not have to adopt an extra feature pair, creating undesirable overgeneration (Ahn & Iverson (2004)).[6] Thus, RCVP does not make room for elements for different airstreams (ingressive, egressive, resulting from laryngeal lowering or raising). Voiced ejectives do not occur (LM p. 80), but implosives, while usually voiced, can also occur as

---

[6] LM (p. 53), in surveying creaky voice phonation for stops, remark: 'we are not sure if each of them uses what we would term creaky voice. The published descriptions suggest that there is some variation: in some of these languages the series of stops in question is described as preglottalised, while in others they are compared to implosives.' They add (pp. 54-5): 'A creaky voice type of vocal fold vibration persisting through the closure of a stop is often observed in Fula, a language quite closely related to Serer.' And (p. 55): 'The difference in the amplitude patterns may indicate more cavity expansion in the creaky voiced stop than in the modally voiced one, perhaps with larynx lowering playing a role.' These remarks suggest an affinity between creaky voice and implosives.

voiceless (e.g. in Igbo). I propose analysing voiceless implosives as glottalic consonants, with the same representation that is used for 'ejectives'. This implies that larynx raising or lowering is not the basic property of glottalic consonants; rather, voicing is.[7]

Glottal closure can accompany an obstruent as a phonation type, or it can occur 'by itself' as a glottal consonant. Glottal closure is not compatible with voicing.

Indo-Aryan languages such as Hindi and Marathi show a rich display of phonation types, with voiceless unaspirated, voiceless aspirated, voiced and voiced aspirated (breathy), thus cross-classifying voicing and aspiration. Owerri Igbo is a language with an especially rich array, adding two types of implosives, voiced and voiceless, to the four types that occur in the Indo-Aryan languages. I will argue below that the so-called voiceless implosive will get the same representation as ejectives in other languages. Rather than listing further examples here, I refer to various studies offering typological surveys of phonation systems (Avery (1996); Kehrein & Golston (2004); LM pp. 47–81), making arguments for feature systems that capture potential contrasts.[8]

---

[7] LM (p. 60) claim that Owerri Igbo has a voicing contrast for implosives. A problem for regarding the voiceless sounds as a possible manifestation of the glottalised/ejective category is that LM's table (p. 101) suggests that 'Igbo' (presumably another dialect) has a *three*-way contrast between voiced implosives, voiceless implosives and ejectives, but I have not been able to find a source that reports ejectives for this language. Another problem case is Lendu, which according to Demolin (1995) has a distinction between voiced and voiceless implosives (rather than between voiced implosives and creaky voice implosives). The voiceless implosives have also been described as 'preglottalised' or even 'ejectives' (see Demolin (1995: 368)). Demolin shows that the voiceless implosives (which are an innovation only found in Lendu) have larynx lowering followed by a sudden raising of the larynx to the original position (1995: 372). The voiceless implosives thus really seem to be implosive. However, since Lendu does not have ejectives, it is still possible to place the voiceless implosive in this same category. Combining glottal closure and voicelessness then has two different phonetic side effects: larynx raising (the usual effect) or larynx lowering (in Igbo and Lendu).

[8] LM also include the category of 'slack' and 'stiff' voice (on either side of 'creaky voice), the former with 'a slightly increased glottal aperture beyond that which occurs in modal voice, and a moderate increase in flow' (p. 63), while the latter denotes 'a slight degree of laryngealisation' (p. 55). 'Just as it is convenient to distinguish between stiff voice and creaky voice, so it is also convenient to distinguish between slack voice and breathy voice, using the term breathy voice to describe sounds that have a higher flow rate and a looser form of vibration of the vocal folds than occurs in the sounds with slack voice, which will be described in the next §' (p. 57). However, I will not try to represent these distinctions as separate potentially contrastive categories. LM refer to a phonation type in Korean that has been subject to different interpretations as 'stiff voice', occurring along with voiceless/lenis and voiceless aspirated obstruents, and being described

Arguably, the fact that in (3) three options are blocked (*) points to an imperfection of the feature system. Also, to specify sonorant consonants as [+voiced] runs counter to the idea that sonorants have 'spontaneous voicing'. Avery & Idsardi (2001) return to the Halle and Stevens features in a unary form, using the unary feature pair [stiff]/[slack] and [constricted]/[spread]. These authors also introduce a unary pair [raised]/[lowered] to account for glottal height in ejectives and implosives. Avery & Rice (1990) and Rice (1993) propose that obstruents have a laryngeal node (dominating the features [laryngeal voice] and [spread glottis]), whereas sonorant consonants have a so-called spontaneous voicing node (which dominates 'sonorant manner features' such as for nasality, laterality, etc.). This proposal, then, avoids assigning a redundant feature [voice] to sonorants. These authors also use unary features.

Here I cannot do justice to a comparative discussion of all feature systems that have been proposed for phonation, but in Chapter 11 I will present a more extended comparison between the RCVP models and other models, such as those mentioned here. It is an understatement to say that glottal distinctions are very complex, as are the interactions between glottal states and other aspects of sound structure (see Miller (2012); Esling, Moisik, Benner & Crevier-Buchman (2019)). I will take the view that *minimally* three different articulatory dimensions (all no doubt complex in their own right) are necessary to express the phonation distinctions that can be linguistically relevant (i.e. potentially distinctive). The feature [±voice] regulates the stretching (elongating) of the vocal folds. [–voice] means that the folds are stretched or 'tense'. [+voice] means that the folds are less stretched (and therefore more likely to vibrate). (Elongation causes 'stiffness' and lack of elongation 'slackness'.) Instead of using a binary feature, this contrast can also be expressed in terms of [voice] versus 'zero' or, as in Avery & Idsardi (2001) and in fact AE, by two unary features [stiff] and [slack]. The opening of the glottis is controlled by the arytenoid cartilages (ACs) which are attached to one side of the vowel folds. Their action can change glottal width by outward and inward movement (ad/abduction) and they can 'rotate inwards' at their top, bringing the vocal folds together 'in the middle':

(4)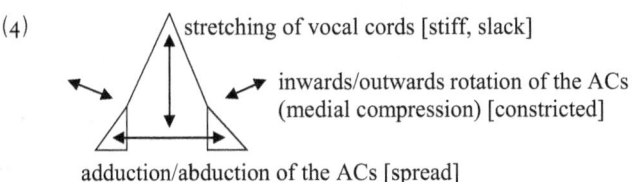
stretching of vocal cords [stiff, slack]

inwards/outwards rotation of the ACs
(medial compression) [constricted]

adduction/abduction of the ACs [spread]

as 'fortis', which is precisely how I will analyse it; see Kim, Maeda, Honda & Crevier-Buchman (2017).

As shown, while the presence (or absence) of [voice] captures the 'stretching' (slacking or stiffening) of the vocal cords (corresponding to activity of the vocalis muscle, which impacts the thickness of the vocal cords, and the cricothyroid muscle, which elongates the vocal cords, respectively[9]), the two glottal width features can be taken to refer to the two different activities of the ACs. At first sight this seems to warrant a single element for voicing and two elements for glottal width. Nevertheless, I will show in this chapter that the voicing dimension also requires two elements. The RCVP logic suggests that we supply [voice] with an opponent counterpart, here labelled [tense].[10] The element [tense] is thus enforced by the principle of RCVP that does not allow 'lone' elements; each element has an antagonistic counterpart, but I will show that the extra element that is forced upon us can be justified empirically.[11]

In van der Hulst (2015a), I propose that the laryngeal class (just like the manner and place classes) has two subclasses, here called *folds* and *glottis*, the head and dependent class, respectively.[12] What seems to be special for phonation is that the head class (folds) does not allow combinations. For the 'folds' class, I suggest the interpretations 'voiced' for V and 'tense' for C. I take the folds class to be the head class because the voicing opposition is the most common phonation opposition, which frequently occurs in the absence of other phonation distinctions. In § 6.4.1, I will discuss systems that seem to lack the voiced category, having a binary contrast between voiceless and aspirated. The dependent glottis element expresses 'glottal spreading' (V) and constricted glottis (C):[13]

---

[9] Bao (1990: 157) cites Sawashima & Hirose (1983: 21–2), who propose correlating these two muscles with 'stiff' and 'slack'.

[10] In van der Hulst (2015a) I use the label 'fortis'. Interestingly, Hubers & Kooij (1973) propose using both the feature [±voice] and the feature [±tense] in their analysis of voicing assimilation in Dutch.

[11] In Chapter 4 we encountered another case of a 'forced element', namely the height element C for vowels.

[12] Unlike Avery and Idsardi's Dimension Theory, RCVP does not, in general, disallow combinations of elements that belong to one subcomponent (or 'dimension' as they call it) since this possibility is crucial in the location and manner class. However, we will see that combinations actually *are* excluded in the laryngeal class.

[13] The division between folds and glottis is also made in the laryngeal geometry in Bao (1999), He applies it to tonal distinctions too.

(5) a. laryngeal

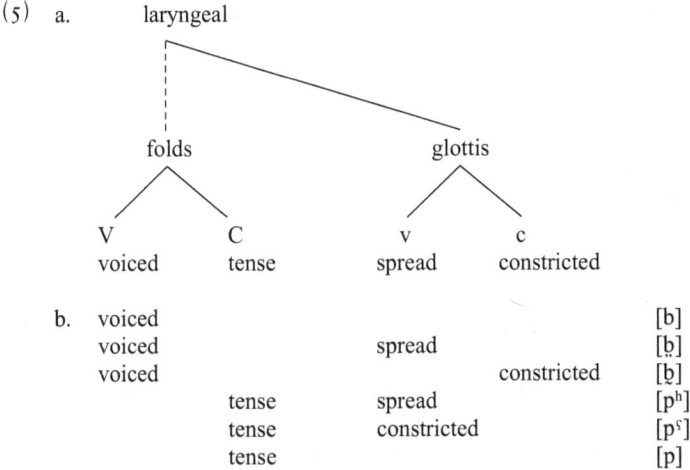

b.

voiced			[b]
voiced		spread	[b̤]
voiced		constricted	[b̰]
	tense	spread	[pʰ]
	tense	constricted	[pʼ]
	tense		[p]

To reduce the number of available options to the six that we need, we have to assume that the syntax of the phonation gesture does not allow combinations within *both* subclasses. This, then, permits the six structures in (5b) and (6):[14]

(6)

Head/Secondary	no secondary element	c (constricted)	v (spread)
C	tense [p]	ejective [pʼ]	aspirated [pʰ]
V	voiced [b]	creaky [b̰]/ implosive [ɓ]	breathy [b̤]

In van der Hulst (2005a) I consider an alternative which is actually more in line with the structure in other classes, namely by allowing the elements in the head class to combine, although in that case, too, I end up concluding that we do not need the intermediate structure in the head class. I will briefly recapitulate the argumentation that I provided there. Allowing intermediate structures in the head laryngeal class allows for an eight-way contrast, giving creaky voice and implosives a different

---

[14] Gordon (2016: § 3.2.1) reports that a two-way contrast between 'voiced' and voiceless stops is the most common contrast (51.1 per cent of languages). In 15.5 per cent there are only voiceless stops, while 24 per cent have a contrast with more than two distinctions. Voicing in stops is more difficult to maintain for dorsal consonants for aerodynamic reasons, and easiest for the labial stop. The latter fact can even lead to a language having a [b], but no [p], as in some Afro-Asiatic, Nilo-Saharan and New Guinea languages (MD p. 37). For fricatives, voicing is dispreferred overall.

structure, but creating an extra slot that is suitable for breathy voice, here assuming that secondary elements only occur with the simple head structures C and V:

(7)

		c (constricted)	v (aspirated)
C	tense	ejective	aspirated
C;V	breathy	–	–
V;C	creaky	–	–
V	voiced	implosive	breathy

The reason I prefer the first option (in 6) is that it gives us a tighter fit with the attested phonation categories and, also, that it does not treat breathy and creaky phonation as more basic than, for example, aspiration, which (7) represents as having a secondary specification. This seems problematic, given that after voiceless and voiced, voiceless aspirated is the most likely next choice. I thus opt for the proposal made in van der Hulst (2015a), which is adopted here. This proposal is not really different from the one in (7), except for the fact that the intermediate categories in the head class are 'blocked', while implosive and creaky are taken to be phonetic variants of the same phonological category:[15]

(8) (= 6)

		c (constricted)	v (aspirated)
C	tense	ejective	aspirated
C;V	*	–	–
V;C	*	–	–
V	voiced	implosive/creaky	breathy

That a lower degree of complexity is found in the laryngeal head class (as compared to the manner and place head classes) is in line with the general fact that dependent units tend to display a lower complexity than head units; here we see that a complexity asymmetry also obtains between the place class and the laryngeal class, which squares with the fact that the place class, while a dependent class, is part of the supralaryngeal superclass of which the laryngeal class is a dependent. While the occurrence of simpler structure in the laryngeal dependent class thus need not be too surprising, it remains a fact that there is no apparent formal explanation for blocking the intermediate structures.

---

[15] That the intermediate options cannot be universally barred from the head laryngeal class follows from the fact that we need them for tonal distinctions where we must allow the head class to allow element combinations, in addition to needing secondary specification; see § 6.3.

6.3 Nucleus (rhyme head): vowels (tone)

As in the case of consonantal phonation, I treat the head and dependent distinctions for tone in one section.

All languages use pitch modulation in their intonational system. So-called tone languages use pitch differences contrastively in the lexicon to distinguish morphemes and to express morphological categories such as past or present tense. When pitch is used in these ways (i.e. contrastively in the lexicon) we call it tone.[16] Minimally, a tone language has a two-way contrast between high and low tone. There are also languages with three tones and even four.[17] IPA uses two systems for tone notation.

(9) TONES AND WORD ACCENTS

LEVEL		CONTOUR	
ə̋ or ˥	Extra high	ě or ˩˥	Rising
é ˦	High	ê ˥˩	Falling
ē ˧	Mid	e᷄ ˦˥	High rising
è ˨	Low	e᷅ ˩˨	Low rising
ȅ ˩	Extra low	ê̌ ˧˦˧	Rising-falling
↓	Downstep	↗	Global rise
↑	Upstep	↘	Global fall

We see that more distinctions can be made than 'high' and 'low' (tone). In particular, vowels can have intermediate level tones as well as contour tones (rising, falling, etc.). Languages that predominantly use level tones (e.g. African tone languages) are sometimes called level tone languages.[18] Asian tone systems often use contour tones and they are then called contour tone systems; see Weidert (1981) and Yip (2002) for extensive introductions to tone.[19]

---

[16] According to Yip (2002) some 70 per cent of the world's languages use tone (or pitch). See also <https://wals.info/chapter/13> (last accessed 2 February 2020). I will here not discuss the distinction that is often made between tone and pitch accent; see van der Hulst (2011c) for an extensive discussion.
[17] A number that can be doubled in so-called register languages; see below.
[18] Sometimes level tone systems are also called register tone systems; I avoid this term because the use of different 'registers' is typical of contour tone systems.
[19] There are many overview articles on tone; see e.g. Hyman (2011).

The formal representation of tones has been the subject of a lot of theoretical debate. Two important (and as we will see interrelated) issues have been addressed:

- Which features are needed?[20]
- Is tone part of the vowel phonemes or somehow independent?

As for tone features, many different proposals have been advanced (see Fromkin (1972) for a review of early proposals and Yip (2002: ch. 3) for later proposals). A simple view that would use two tone features ([±high] and [±low] will not work because it only allows three meaningful combinations, [+high, +low] being uninterpretable.[21]

(10) +high tone   v́   'H'
      −low tone

      −high tone   v̄   'M'
      −low tone

      −high tone   v̀   'L'
      +low tone

(The capital letters are often used as abbreviations of the tonal specifications.) However, if we assume that a level tone language can distinguish up to four different tone levels, we need a different system, unless one of the mid tones is formally represented as unmarked. The question of whether having four level tones presents a maximum is contested by languages that are claimed to have more level tone distinctions. IPA allows for five level tones. Odden (to appear) writes (about African languages): 'Five levels are quite rare, occurring in Benchnon and the Santa dialect of Dan, and only Chori is reported to have six.' In Dihoff's analysis, three of those either result from tone sandhi or are in fact contour tones.[22] See also Odden (to appear) and Dihoff (1976).

---

[20] See Clements, Michaud & Patin (2011), who critically exam the need for features for level tones, and conclude that the different tone levels could perhaps be treated as primitive, rather than in terms of a set of universal tone features. These authors do not exclude, however, the possibility that the language learner could come to such an analysis based on language-specific data. In that case, I would argue, RCVP logic guides the learner.

[21] A parallel problem arises with vowel height if four heights need to be distinguished. One could of course change the 'semantics' of the feature values and allow [+high, +low] to have an interpretation.

[22] Black Miao, an Asian language, has been claimed to have five level-tone contrasts; see Kuang (2013). Here I would suggest that we also have to include register specifications. See Snider and van der Hulst (1993: 2) for some additional examples, including the often-mentioned case of Copala Trique (Hollenbach 1988).

Laryngeal: phonation and tone 219

The distinction between level tones and contour tones raises additional issues. Prior to Autosegmental Phonology, contour tones required additional features like [±falling tone] and [±rising tone]. However, in an autosegmental model such features are not necessary because one tone-bearing unit can be associated with two sequentially distinct tonal specifications (see Goldsmith (1976a)).

My focus here will be on more recent so-called 'register' proposals which use two features [±high tone] and [±high register] (Yip 2002):[23]

(11)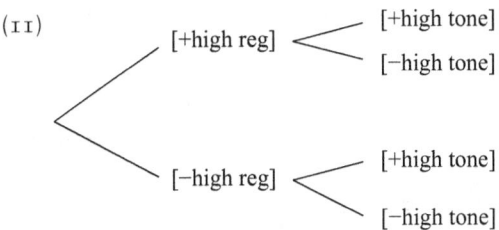

Clements (1990b: 59) defines register as the 'frequency band internal to the speaker's range, which determines the highest and lowest frequency within which tones can be realised at any given point in the utterance'.[24] It would seem that at first sight, Yip's proposal can straightforwardly be incorporated into RCVP:

(12)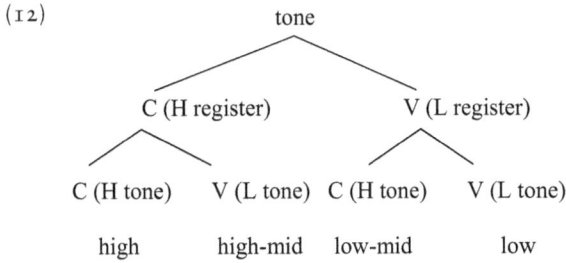

---

[23] Yip (2001) discusses some problems for the register aspect of tone, which seem to require a greater role for phonetic implementation algorithms.
[24] As mentioned, especially with reference to Asian tone languages, the notion 'register' is usually understood as involving not only pitch distinctions, but also phonation distinctions, vowel length, pharyngeal expansion and others. See Trigo (1991), Yip (1999) and § 6.4.4. See also Abramson & Luangthongkum (2009), who distinguish tone from 'voice register', the latter being a phonatory matter, although they argue that many languages combine the two; see also Gordon & Ladefoged (2001) and Brunelle & Kirby (2016), who find the concepts 'tone' and 'register' not fully adequate to deal with the diversity of tonal systems in Asian languages.

Here the proposal is that the first split is a 'register' split, while the second split makes a 'tonal' distinction within each register; of course, both aspects involve the phonetic property of 'pitch' (i.e. Fo), although, as we discuss below, the notion 'register' may come with additional phonetic properties. While this seems like a sensible way to interpret the two cuts, when we turn to contour tones we realise that we need to rethink this. Yip's proposal was primarily motivated by tonal systems in Asian languages, which have traditionally been described as having two tonal 'registers' (with the notion 'register' comprising more than only pitch distinctions, as they involve phonation-type distinctions). Within these registers, it is possible to have an array of tonal distinctions, including tonal contours. For African tonal systems, the notion of register (as being used in the analysis of Asian tone systems) has not been invoked, at least not with reference to lexical tonal distinctions. For lexical tonal contrast in African languages, a maximal four-way distinction of level tones has usually been suggested, which can be represented in terms of Yip's proposal (see, for example, Hyman (1986); Pulleyblank (1986)), given the definition in Clements (1990b). However, the notion of register has also been used for African languages to account for postlexical tonal effects (including downstep and downdrift); see van der Hulst & Snider (1993) for an overview of proposals and several case studies.

To accommodate these various requirements, I will represent 'register' in terms of the secondary (dependent) class elements:

(13)

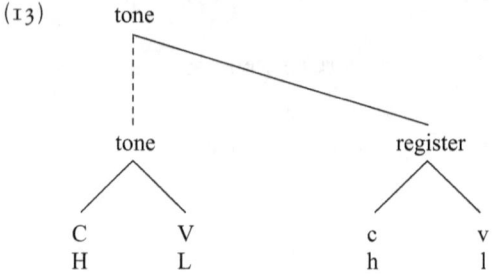

I will then assume that in African languages, at the lexical level, only the head class is activated, maximally allowing a four-way distinction, as in (14):

(14) High   C   H
     High-mid   C;V   H;L
     Low-mid   V;C   L;H
     Low   V   L

The register class would then only come into 'action' at the post-lexical level, as proposed in Snider (1999).

The same four-way distinction is allowed in Asian languages, but in this case, typically, the register class would be active at the lexical level, which creates two registers, also often called 'voice registers'. I suggest that if such languages allow combinations in the head class, the register split enforces a *sequential interpretation* which produces contour tones within each register. This, I suggest, is due to the fact that multiple level tones within a register would jeopardise the perceptual contrast between level tones that are too close in terms of their pitch level:

(15) An eight-way tonal contrast in a contour tone/register language:

H + h	high tone in high register	high
H;L + h	falling tone in high register	high falling
L;H + h	rising tone in high register	high rising
L + h	low tone in high register	mid-high
H + l	high tone in low register	mid-low
H;L + l	falling tone in low register	[low falling]
L;H + l	rising tone in low register	low rising
L + l	low tone in low register	low

Cantonese has seven contrastive tones, indicated in the third column, missing the low-falling tone; see Zsiga (2013).

Activating the register class *at the lexical level* is thus a property of so-called 'register tone languages', whereas, as mentioned, register in African languages can be active post-lexically to account for processes of downdrift (see Snider (1988, 1990a); Hyman (1993)). A proposal that details the treatment of these phenomena is offered in Snider (1999).

When comparing the proposed structure in (13) to the phonation structure for consonants (here repeated in (16)), we conclude that the only difference is that we have not seen evidence for allowing combinations in the head class for phonation, while such combinations are necessary for tone. Of course, for African-type systems we could adopt (13) and allow register to distinguish tones at the lexical level (as in Hyman (1986); Pulleyblank (1986); Bao (1999); Snider (1999); see 18), but my account of the Asian-type system would still need combinations for the 'folds' class:

(16)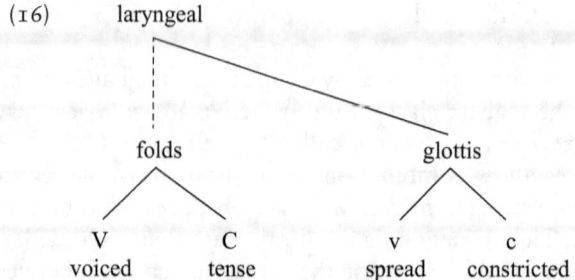

Various variants of Yip's original proposal have been developed (in Bao (1990, 1999), Snider (1990b, 1999), Duanmu (1990) and Hyman (1993), among others). Bao (1999) offers an extensive overview and Yip (2002: 52ff.) also discusses various FG models of tone. The models proposed in Bao (1990, 1999) and Snider (1988, 1990a, 1999) are very similar to the proposal made here (minus headedness):

(17) 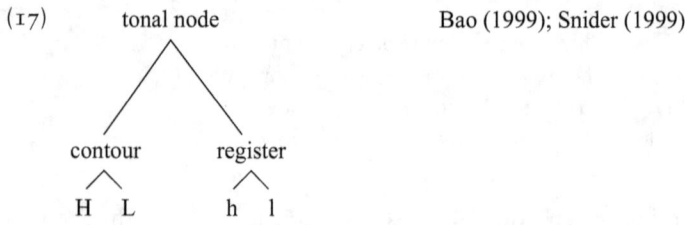 Bao (1999); Snider (1999)

In principle, the node 'contour' could allow for the specification of tonal contours, that is, sequences of H and L (as in the RCVP model), However, in the model proposed by Bao and Snider, the distinction between four level tones is represented as a combination of a tonal element and a register element. There are two ways to do that, however:

(18) High   H ({h})
     High-mid   H {l}
     Low-mid   L {h}
     Low   L ({l})

This proposal allows natural classes in terms of register, for instance high and low-mid grouping into high register. It is not clear that such classes are well motivated. An alternative would be:

(19) High   H ({h})
     High-mid   L {h}
     Low-mid   H {l}
     Low   L ({l})

The second option also makes dubious natural class predictions, such as the discontinuous class of high and low-mid, or high-mid and low. I conclude that register should not be invoked to create intermediate level tones.

Hyman (1993) uses unary features H/L which can attach to two different levels in the structure of the tonal node, such that their phonetic interpretation depends on the levels that they occur at:

(20)

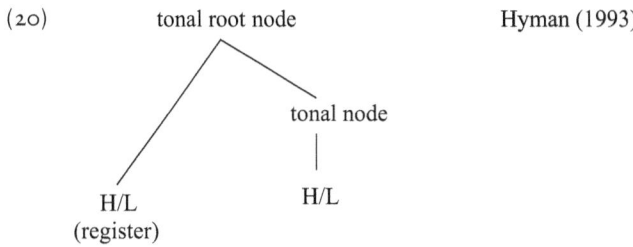

Hyman (1993)

A register distinction results from adjoining H/L under the tonal root node. There is again a similarity with the RCVP structure, in using the same elements with different interpretations and analysing mid tones as combinations under the tone node. Here too there is no notion of headedness.

Special attention has been given by various authors to a formal distinction between two types of contour tones (see e.g. Hyman (2011), Yip (1989, 2002), etc.): unitary contour tones (as in Asian languages), with one tonal root node, and compound tones (as in African languages), with two tonal root nodes. With respect to the former, Yip (2002: 203) reports careful instrumental investigation (Gandour (1974); Gandour, Tumtavitikul & Satthamnuwong (1999)) which has shown that the five-way tonal contrast of Thai (including a HL contour tone) is preserved in such shortened syllables. The same kind of rule occurs in Dschang (Pulleyblank (1986)). Duanmu (1994) has suggested, however, that contour tones on short vowels do not exist, but it would seem that the data mentioned in Yip (2001) do not support this claim. Duanmu's claim also regards tonal contours in African languages. However, ample evidence has been provided for cases in which short vowels are associated with two tones, either because the tonal melody needs to be completed in the last vowel or due to 'dumping' a tone of a deleted vowel onto a preceding vowel that already carries a tone. In this case the standard autosegmental representation is to associate two independent tones to one tone-bearing unit. Indeed, Yip (1989) also points out that African contours, which she calls 'tone clusters', result from two level tones (dominated by separate tonal root nodes) associating with a single short vowel, arising on final vowels for example when a HL sequence cannot be associated with two consecutive vowels in right-to-left association. She points out that Asian contour tones do not similarly decompose into two level tones, nor are such tones restricted to final vowels. Various authors propose different ways for making a formal distinction between these two types of contour tones, which I will not discuss here.

RCVP captures the 'unitary' nature of Asian contour tones and accounts for non-unitary contours in terms of compound structure (two primary tonal structures), which I will discuss in more detail in § 7.3.3.2:[25]

(21)

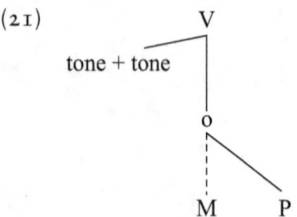

In conclusion, RCVP claims that phonation and tone are 'in complementary distribution': the former occurs in the onset head and the latter in the rhymal head. The secondary tonal specification represents the notion of 'register', which is relevant lexically in Asian tone languages that can have up to four contrastive tones in both registers (Yip 2002). In these languages contour tones are unitary contour tones, where {C;V} and {V;C} refer to rising and falling tones rather than intermediate level tones. African tone systems do not employ register for lexical contrast and in these languages the intermediate structures refer to different level tones. Tonal contours in African language are represented in terms of two tonal class nodes. The different usage register is an example of an areal difference in the phonetic interpretation of element structures, although, additionally, it is likely that the Asian usage of register involves so-called voice register.

6.4 Four issues

In this section, I address some consequences and potential problems concerning the proposals made in the preceding sections. Firstly, I examine the status of the laryngeal class as being obligatory or not.

---

[25] There is perhaps an alternative way of thinking about tone as an autosegmental property. If tones are the only truly autosegmental units then we would have to assume that, as in traditional Autosegmental Phonology, one-to-many associations are possible even though within the segment structure as such there cannot be a linear sequence of tones. Such a view would entail a mechanism that 'raises' tone out of the segmental structure to a separate tier. I will not develop this possibility here, but return to it in § 12.5.

Laryngeal: phonation and tone 225

Secondly, I discuss the notion of 'laryngeal realism' with reference to voicing oppositions in various German languages and in French. Thirdly, I discuss cases which seem to require non-tonal phonation properties in the nucleus. Fourthly, I take a closer look at the correlation between tone and phonation, as predicted in RCVP.

6.4.1 *Phonation oppositions in obstruents and sonorants*

In this section, I discuss an issue that arises when we compare the use of structures in the place class and in the laryngeal class.

In the place class I have suggested that the absence of a place property delivers consonant articulations that are neither coronal nor peripheral (labial or dorsal), which are both suprapharyngeal (and supralaryngeal). Absence of place thus delivers consonantal articulations that are either pharyngeal or laryngeal. For vowel articulations, absence of place delivers a pharyngeal vowel [a] (or in metrically weak positions a schwa):

(22) (Place)[26]   Place   Place

                     C   V

     Laryngeal   coronal labial
     Pharyngeal

       [a]   front   round

When looking at the laryngeal class it would seem that a comparable three-way distinction should not be made; a three-way distinction is undesirable because it would allow for a three-way 'voicing' contrast, which is unattested:

(23) (Lar)   Lar   Lar

             C   V

    ???   tense voiced
    ???   high   low

There is, I believe, a substantive reason for disallowing the absence of a laryngeal specification to be contrastive with the specification of C and V. While perhaps one might be inclined to say that the absence of a laryngeal specification represents 'modal voice', it does not seem justified to recognise this category as distinctive. A language that would contrast voiceless, voiced and modal voice obstruents does not seem to exist.

---

[26] I use parentheses here as an informal device to indicate absence.

We can give an independent interpretation to being placeless which simply means that there is 'no place in the oral cavity', which then implies that the place is in the pharyngeal cavity or is laryngeal.[27] For the laryngeal class, however, it makes no sense to interpret its absence as being contrastive with the laryngeal elements C and V, on the assumption that all segments necessarily involve the larynx (i.e. folds and glottis). The only interpretation that can be given to a non-specified laryngeal node is that laryngeal distinctions are non-contrastive entirely. Hence, for a non-tonal language, we do not need to specify a laryngeal class. (Vowels in such a language would have a neutral, low-a pitch level, unless otherwise specified in terms of intonational tones.) If a language were to have no phonation distinctions (for all obstruents or a subclass), the same would apply. Such a language would come across as only having voiceless obstruents. MD (p. 27) reports that forty-nine out of fifty languages that lack a voicing contrast for stops have voiceless stops; the one reported exception is Bandjalang (368), which Maddieson doubts is correct.

Nevertheless, we can think of one case in which the absence of a laryngeal specification can be used contrastively, namely if we oppose it to only *one* laryngeal specification. In my analysis of various languages that have a 'voicing contrast' in § 6.4.2 I propose that the contrast can often be represented in terms of C versus the absence of C. (In principle, the other option, V versus the absence of V, is also a formal possibility.) In this particular case, the non-specification stands in contrast with the specification of an element. To not specify an opposing category brings in the notion of under- or non-specification. One might say that only specifying one element when there is a contrast is tantamount to underspecifying the other element. While this is true, RCVP does not allow non-specification of a class node as a different formal structure from absence of a class node. In other words, RCVP does not allow the following three-way contrast for place:

(24) a. (Place)   b. Place   c. Place
                      |
                      C

The place node labels are not formal primitives that can exist in the absence of elements for that class. Hence, the structure in (24c) is incoherent, a formal impossibility. This means that a two-way contrast in phonation cannot be represented as in (25):

---

[27] In § 12.5 (4) I consider an alternative that would not appeal to the absence of place for pharyngeals and laryngeals.

(25) a. lar   b. lar
              |
              C

The only way to invoke underspecification would thus be to oppose (25b) to the absence of the laryngeal node. The empirical prediction that follows from underspecification in the laryngeal class is that the non-specified member in the opposition has a phonetic target that is more variable than the target of a specified element. Keating (1988c) refers to the former case as underspecification that persists into the phonetic implementation. I will argue below that in fact all cases of non-specification work that way, which is why I prefer the term 'non-specification' over 'underspecification'. The latter term is often taken to mean that a feature or element can be filled in before implementation. I wish to exclude that possibility, but I refer further discussion of this point to Chapter 9.

As for the manner class, given that this class cannot be absent at all, non-specification (because it formally means absence of a manner node) is excluded.

In conclusion, non-specification in the laryngeal class does not create an independent category. However, it can be used as standing in contrast with a laryngeal element if, and only if, only one laryngeal element is specified in the segmental system (or in a natural class of segments within the segmental system).[28] Non-specification will always imply that the phonetic interpretation is variable or contextual.

I now turn to a second issue that arises for the laryngeal class. We have seen that for obstruents there is a maximal six-way contrast:

(26)
	Voiceless	aspirated	breathy	modal	creaky	glottal
	–	spread	spread voiced	–	constricted voiced	constricted
Obs	+	+	+	+	+	+
Son	*	*	+	+	+	*
	C	C{v}	V{v}	–	V{c}	C{c}

However, sonorant consonants see this set reduced to a three-way contrast, which seems to follow from the fact that sonorants cannot have

---

[28] This is similar to requiring that in a binary feature system zero can be used along with one of the two values, but not both. This condition protects the so-called radical underspecification approach from falling into the trap of turning a binary system into a ternary system; see Kiparsky (1982a) and Archangeli (1984).

the laryngeal C element. In fact, one could argue that sonorants do not even need the laryngeal V element. While there is no formal account that I can think of, we could add a constraint (a stipulation) that sonorant consonants do not have a laryngeal specification; the non-specification of a laryngeal element leads to sonorants being produced with 'spontaneous voicing'. (Vowels also have spontaneous voicing, even when laryngeal specifications are present, which would get a tonal interpretation.) But this is too strong a constraint, given that languages can have sonorants with contrastive phonation properties, such as voiceless sonorants (which have been analysed as aspirated sonorants, with many examples in MD) and nasals with breathy/laryngealised voice or glottalisation (creaky voice; see MD pp. 236–40), laryngealised rhotics (MD p. 240) and flaps (MD pp. 241–2), breathy voice laterals (MD p. 243) and laryngealised glides (MD pp. 245, 247).

Arguably, it would be precisely the contrastive use of secondary phonation properties which would enforce the specification of the head element V. The proper constraint would thus be that sonorant consonants cannot have contrastive laryngeal head elements. This constraint is a formal stipulation, just like the stipulation that the absence of the laryngeal class cannot be contrastive with specifying both C and V. In the latter case, I proposed a substantive explanation. That sonorant consonants have spontaneous rather than contrastive voicing can also be explained on substantive grounds. Voicing is the natural state of segments that are produced with a free outflow of air, which naturally causes vocal cord vibration. Only in obstruents, due to the full or partial stricture, is it possible to subdue voicing by blocking or impeding the outflow of air.

The idea that a non-contrastive head element can occur if required by the occurrence of secondary properties is independently needed for languages that contrast voiceless obstruents with either aspirated or glottalised obstruents (as in the Mayan language K'ekchi; see Ahn & Iverson (2004)) or in several northern Californian languages (Haynie (2012)). This calls for the following representations:

(27) K'ekchi, and various Northern Californian languages:

Phon –   Phon {C{c}}   Phon {C{v}}
[p]   [p']   [pʰ]

In this case we are perhaps inclined to specify the head element for the voiceless [p]. However, precisely because there is no contrast, we do not have to do that. For the glottalised and aspirated obstruents, on the other hand, we *must* specify the head C element because its presence is required for the dependent secondary properties.

In conclusion:

- In the case of a voicing contrast, obstruents are specified as C or nothing (where nothing is passive voicing) or as V vs. nothing (see § 6.4.2).
- Plain sonorants are specified without a laryngeal specification (which correlates with spontaneous voicing).
- Sonorants get non-contrastive V if there is a secondary laryngeal property.
- Non-contrastive head elements can be enforced by the contrastive occurrence of secondary elements.

A further issue regarding laryngeal specification involves the possible use of laryngeal V for sonorants with the interpretation of nasality. Indeed, in some accounts, nasality is included in the set of phonations (Laver (2009)). Since laryngeal V for obstruents means voiced, using laryngeal V for nasality in sonorants suggest an affinity between nasality and voicing in terms of a single element. In most versions of GP, it is indeed argued that voicing and nasality are possible exponents of the element L (with voicing being the interpretation if this element is marked as 'headed' and nasality when it is not marked as headed; see § 2.3).

However, this idea is incompatible with the suggestion just made that sonorant consonants do not have laryngeal elements. In response to that, one could say that they can have laryngeal head elements, but that the interpretation of V is not voiced (because all sonorants are spontaneously voiced), which opens up a way to say that for sonorants the element V has a different interpretation (that one might call 'nasal voice'). There are problems with this idea, however. Firstly, we then also need to ask how the laryngeal C element is interpreted when occurring in a sonorant consonant. One could say that it makes the sonorant voiceless, but we already have an account of 'voiceless sonorants', namely as being aspirated, an analysis that is empirically supported (see AE and Lombardi (1991)). This problem could be handled by a narrower constraint which only blocks C for sonorants. Another, bigger problem is that this idea predicts that vowels will acquire low tone when preceding nasals, because the V element for vowels gets a tonal interpretation. This is unheard of; vowels become nasalised before nasal consonants. A third reason for rejecting this idea is that we already have a representation for nasal, namely secondary v in the manner class.

The empirical argument for interpreting V as nasal is that V for obstruents can sometimes involve nasality, such that a contrast between C (tense) and V (voiced) produced [p] and [ᵐb] or even [m]. But this does not require the proposal that V is nasal for sonorants. Rather, we can say that laryngeal V for obstruents can be manifested as oral voice or as a combination of oral voice and 'nasal voice', where the recruitment of the nasal passage functions as a phonetic enhancement of the laryngeal contrast.[29]

6.4.2 Laryngeal realism

This section focuses on the proper specification of voicing contrasts.[30] It has been argued that the laryngeal representation for English and French must be different because the two languages realise the 'voice' contrast between 'p' and 'b' very differently. In French, there really seems to be a voicing contrast, but in English the burden of differentiating 'b' and 'p' (at least in the onset of a stressed syllable) is on 'p' being aspirated (while 'b' is not as strongly voiced as its counterpart in French). In the model that I propose here we could capture this fact by specifying these languages as in (28) below, where in French the specified element is V/[voice], whereas in English the specified element is C/[tense]. An implication of this is that the aspiration for non-voiced consonants in English (which appears in the onset of stressed syllables) must be an 'added' property, which raises the question of whether this property is added as an actual element 'in the phonology' (along the lines of the class of enhancement rules that is proposed in Stevens, Keyser & Kawasaki (1986) and Stevens & Keyser (1989)) or in the phonetic implementation component. A further question is then whether we actually want to make such a difference in the first place. In van der Hulst (2015a, 2018) I proposed making such a difference, which led me to place enhancement rules at the 'word level', a pre-implementation level where 'redundant' elements can be activated. Contrary to that proposal, I will propose here that all predictable properties, whether apparently corresponding to an element or 'sub-elemental', will be handled in the phonetic implementation component. Below, such properties are introduced by a double-shafted arrow and the property will be placed between square brackets; the single bracket notation simply represents the phonetic interpretation of the elements:

(28) Binary phonation contrast in French and English:

		'b'	'p'
a.	French	V/[voice]	–
b.	English	–	C/[tense] ($\Rightarrow$ [aspirated]/onset[31])

---

[29] For further comparison between RCVP and GP regarding nasality, see van der Hulst (to appear-b).
[30] This section is based on van der Hulst (2015a).
[31] The context for aspiration is here indicated in a simplified manner. I also ignore the fact that no aspiration is assigned when the obstruent is preceded by [s], or perhaps in other positions.

In this analysis, the 'voiced' character of obstruents transcribed with the IPA symbol 'b' would not be due to an element [voiced]. Rather, voicing in English would be contextual, that is, a result of what is sometimes called *passive voicing* which arises in the phonetic implementation. The proposal in (28) suggests that the aspiration of tense stops is not contextual in the same manner if indeed we postulate an allophonic rule that literally adds the aspiration element in the phonology. Below I will return to this potential difference between enhancement properties that feed into the phonetic implementation and properties that are directly attributed to the phonetic implementation.

However, in the domain of phonation it has been argued in various publications that the distinction between French and English should be expressed as in (29), where the lower case 'v' indicates that [spread] would correspond to a secondary laryngeal element in RCVP:

(29) Binary phonation contrasts:

		'b'	'p'
a.	French	V/[voice]	–
b.	English	–	v/[spread]

This viewpoint has been widely accepted in the phonation literature (see Iverson & Salmons (1995, 2003); Avery & Idsardi (2001); Honeybone (2002); see especially Cyran (2017) for discussion and further references), where the general claim is that Germanic languages (except in some cases, such as Dutch; see below) are '[spread] languages', whereas the Romance languages are '[voiced] languages'.

If this approach, which Honeybone (2002) refers to as *Laryngeal Realism*, is correct, it seems to follow that English has a phonation system that does not activate the vocal fold head element class at all, as in (29b). However, this analysis of English (and other alleged [spread] languages) violates the restriction in RCVP that a phonation contrast must involve activation of the head class in the laryngeal class. This could be salvaged by adding a head element for the English case:

(30) Binary phonation contrasts:

		'b'	'p'
a.	French	V/[voice]	–
b.	English	–	C{v}/ [tense] {[spread]}

However, once the head element C needs to be specified, we might just as well adopt the representation in (31), which attributes aspiration to phonetic implementation.

(31) French 'b/v'   'p/f'
                V/[voice]   –

       English 'b/v'   'p/f'
                –   C/[tense] (⇒ ⟦aspiration⟧/onset)

The representation in (31) is also 'realistic' in that this captures the difference between English and French in terms of different element specifications too. This representation correlates with a common view, especially in phonology textbooks, that aspiration is allophonic in English.

I would now like to consider an alternative to (31), also consistent with RCVP, in which *all* non-voiced obstruents are specified as [tense], which would entail that the phonation contrasts in French and English do not differ at the lexical level at all. In this analysis, we say that *all* these languages make a lexical contrast between tense and non-tense phonation, and that the differences between them are accounted for in the phonetic implementation, which attributes stronger voicing to the non-tense obstruents in French than in English:[32]

(32) French 'b/v'   'p/f'
                – (⇒ ⟦strong voicing⟧)   C/[tense]

       English 'b/v'   'p/f'
                – (⇒ ⟦weak voicing⟧)   C/[tense] (⇒ ⟦aspiration⟧/onset[33])

With this alternative in mind, let us now consider the analysis of Dutch obstruents. The literature cited above classifies Dutch, another Germanic language, as a [voice] system, like French, because it lacks the typical aspiration that other Germanic languages have. Apparently, Dutch has drifted away from the Germanic pattern, probably under the influence of French. However, given the analysis in (32), in which aspiration is a predictable property in English, it would be possible to maintain that Dutch drifted away from the Germanic group not in its element specification, but by not having predictable aspiration. Since the Dutch 'b' is 'more voiced' than the English 'b', it would then have to be assumed that passive voicing is stronger in Dutch than in English (due perhaps to the historical influence of the voiced 'b' of French).[34]

---

[32] Note that in this analysis, the lexical specification is the 'unmarked' one (in onset head position, which is a C position), namely |C|. I return to this issue in Chapter 8.

[33] The aspiration property does not, however, emerge on fricatives. Aspiration in fricatives is uncommon. LM (p. 178) mention Burmese as a rare example with voiced, voiceless and voiceless aspirated fricatives.

[34] Stronger voicing in Dutch, and in French, for the unmarked obstruents, compared to English, is perhaps also due to the fact that in English the contrast between 'voiced' and 'voiceless' stops is enhanced by predictable aspiration.

Laryngeal: phonation and tone   233

There is, however, a difference between French and Dutch. Dutch 'voiced' fricatives are not as strongly voiced as stops. To account for this, Iverson & Salmons (2003) analyse Dutch as a 'split system' with presence versus absence of voicing being contrastive for stops, while the contrast in fricatives is specified equipollently in terms of [voiced] versus [spread]. In other words, fricatives display the 'legacy' of Germanic aspiration. In this connection these authors refer to a generalisation concerning fricatives proposed in Vaux (1998), according to which non-voiced fricatives in a [voice] system display redundant [aspiration]. The Dutch non-voiced fricatives, according to Iverson and Salmons, display this aspiration as a legacy specification, which means that this property has remained lexically specified, even after the obstruent system had switched over to using contrastive [voice]. To me it is not obvious that voiceless fricatives in Dutch are aspirated. Nevertheless, accepting the idea of a split system, we can say that phonetic voicing for stops and fricatives is different in Dutch:

(33)   Dutch 'b'   'p'
        – (⇒ ⟦strong voicing⟧)   [tense]

        'v'   'f'
        – (⇒ ⟦weak voicing⟧)   [tense]

        French 'b/v'   'p/f'
        – (⇒ ⟦strong voicing⟧)   [tense]

        English 'b/v'   'p/f'
        – (⇒ ⟦weak voicing⟧)   [tense](⇒ ⟦aspiration⟧/onset)

Assuming, then, that both phonetic voicing and phonetic aspiration can be recruited to enhance the phonation distinction between obstruents, a language might also choose to apply both types of enhancements. This is what happens in Swedish (as analysed in Helgason & Ringen (2008)). Swedish is a candidate for this 'overdifferentiation' of the two contrasting obstruent groups. In (34) I summarise these three possibilities for enhancement (omitting their contextual conditions):

(34)   Dutch 'b'   'p'
        – (⇒ ⟦strong voicing⟧/onset)   [tense]

        'v'   'f'
        – (⇒ ⟦weak voicing⟧)   [tense]

        French 'b/v'   'p/f'
        – (⇒ ⟦strong voicing⟧)   [tense]

        English 'b/v'   'p/f'
        – (⇒ ⟦weak voicing⟧)   [tense](⇒ ⟦aspiration⟧/onset)

Swedish 'b/v'   'p/f'
− (⇒ ⟦strong voicing⟧)   [tense](⇒ ⟦aspiration⟧/onset)

The approach presented in this section is 'traditional' in that all languages with a binary phonation contrast have the same phonological specification, but it is 'realistic' in that the enhancement properties account for the fact that this basic contrast is realised phonetically in different ways. However, the choice of representing the binary contrast as '[tense] vs. Ø' deviates from the usual choice of taking the voiced series as being phonologically marked. I will motivate this choice further in Chapter 8. One consideration given here is that marking obstruents as C/tense vs. zero makes their laryngeal specification almost complementary to that of sonorant consonants, which are universally voiced, thus laryngeally specified with the head element V. As proposed in § 6.4.1, if we take the presence of laryngeal V as the identifying property of sonorant consonants, the complementarity is complete.

The question that remains (in my mind at least) is whether a distinction is needed between enhancement (involving the addition of a voice or aspiration element) and 'passive voicing'. The latter occurs when obstruents are 'more voiced' in, for example, intervocalic position. I suggest that both types of processes can be handled in the phonetic implementation. This proposal agrees with Cyran (2017), who proposes a 'systemic module' (i.e. phonetic implementation) which handles both enhancement and passive voicing. An argument for attributing predictable properties to the phonetic implementation is that aspiration of stops in English is not equally strong in all positions. Stops preceding a primary stress are more strongly aspirated than before a secondary stress (see Davis & Cho (2003)).

The potential argument against using C/[tense] in all the languages discussed is that there is no account of voicing assimilation, where voiced obstruents impose voicing on neighbouring obstruents. My reply to this argument is that voicing assimilation processes have generally been claimed to be gradient and thus, in my view, part of the phonetic implementation.[35] It has been clearly shown that voicing assimilation rules in Dutch have the property of 'variable' rules, with voicing being gradient rather than categorical (see in particular Slis (1986)). The fact that in Dutch, voiced stops cause regressive voice assimilation while fricatives undergo progressive devoicing is in accordance with the fact that non-tense stops are more strongly voiced than non-tense fricatives, which are thus likely to be voiceless when preceded by a voiceless obstruent.

---

[35] Snoeren & Segui (2003) show that voice assimilation in French is a gradient process. This is a general claim for voicing assimilation processes in many other languages.

6.4.3 Phonation in the nucleus

In § 6.3, I proposed that the laryngeal classes, when applied to vowels, deliver tonal distinctions. The implied complementary distribution between phonation (in the onset head position) and tone (in the rhymal head position) predicts that consonants in onset head position cannot bear tone,[36] while vowels cannot have phonation distinctions. While the former claim is undisputed, there are languages in which vowels have phonation distinctions (see Gordon (1998)). If such languages are non-tonal, we can simply say that the phonation properties are in fact interpretations of the same structures that are usually be interpreted in terms of pitch (i.e. as tones). Recall that the register distinction *as voice register* involved phonatory distinctions (see Abramson & Luangthongkum (2009)). If vowels are reported as breathy, it is also possible to regard this as an exponent of the ATR specification in the place class (see Lindau (1979)). As an example, of a voice register system, I consider the language Jalapa Mazatec (LM p. 317), which has a rich set of vowels that are distinguished in terms of phonation:

(35) Jalapa Mazatec vowels:

Modal voice
Breathy voice
Creaky voice

Modal nasal
Breathy nasal
Creaky nasal

Nasality in RCVP is accounted for as a vowel manner, which leaves a three-way 'phonation' distinction. In terms of the RCVP structure this leads to:

(36)   laryngeal (nucleus)

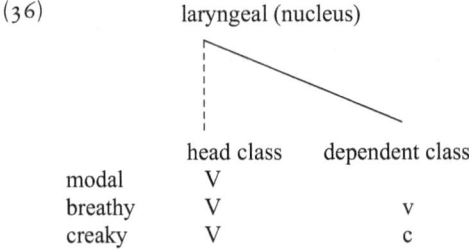

	head class	dependent class
modal	V	
breathy	V	v
creaky	V	c

---

[36] A refinement of this view is that tonal distinctions are possible in the coda position; see § 6.5.

This proposal is justified by the fact that there is in many tone languages a close (and synergistic) relationship between phonation and tone, in which certain tones are associated with non-modal phonation that presumably serves to aid in the realisation of tonal contrasts (see § 6.4.4).

Nasality is sometimes subsumed under the notion phonation (see Laver (1994)). This view is echoed in GP, where nasality is an exponent of the L element (as a dependent; see Botma (2004) and Backley (2011)). However, the case of Jalapa Mazatec shows that the V element in the laryngeal node for vowels cannot accommodate nasality, because it is needed for the 'phonation' contrasts in (36). It is also the case that many languages have a nasal contrast combined with contrastive tone (e.g. Kalabari; Otelemate (2004)), which is hard to square with the alleged double function of the L element.

A problem for taking vowel phonation to be 'just' another way that tonal elements can be interpreted might be the case of the Sino-Tibetan language Mpi, which has a six-way tonal contrast on plain and laryngealised vowels, according to LM (pp. 315–16), giving a twelve-way contrast:[37]

(37) Phonation on Mpi vowels:

	Plain (modal voice)	laryngealised (stiff voice)[38]
high		
high rising		
mid rising		
mid		
low rising		
low		

This system seems to tell us that the laryngeal class for vowels cannot be used for tonal distinctions, since that would preclude this cross-classification of six tonal distinctions with two phonation distinctions. I suggest that in this case the phonation distinctions are interpretations of register specifications. This, as in the maximal Asian tonal system, gives us only an eight-way distinction, which I repeat here in (38):

---

[37] Matt Gordon (p.c.) also mentions Dinka as a case in which tonal distinctions and phonation distinctions (breathy vs. laryngealised) appear to be cross-classified. Kuang (2013) is a comprehensive study of languages that combine tonal and phonation on vowels. For Mpi, see Silverman (1997) and Blankenship (2002).

[38] LM (p. 316) uses the labels 'modal' and 'stiff voice'.

Laryngeal: phonation and tone   237

(38) An eight-way tonal contrast in a contour tone/register language:[39]

H + h	high tone in high register
HL + h	falling tone in high register
LH + h	rising tone in high register
L + h	low tone in high register
H + l	high tone in low register
HL + l	falling tone in low register
LH + l	rising tone in low register
L + l	low tone in low register

However, this eight-way distinction does not seem to translate into the twelve-way contrast in Mpi. At this point, we need to consider a representational possibility that was not addressed in our discussion of tonal structures. In a register language, low and high register are active. I did not address the question as to whether register specification could be in contrast with the absence of register. We would expect this to be possible, given that in other classes the presence of secondary properties can be contrastive with their absence. For example, obstruents can have the secondary properties of nasalisation and pharyngealisation, but with such secondary properties present, we also find plain versions of obstruents. If we then assume that the low/high register distinction can co-occur with tonal specifications that do not have a register specification, we increase the number of possible distinctions to twelve.

(39) A twelve-way tonal contrast in a contour tone/register language:

H + h	high tone in high register
HL + h	falling tone in high register
LH + h	rising tone in high register
L + h	low tone in high register
H + l	high tone in low register
HL + l	falling tone in low register
LH + l	rising tone in low register
L + l	low tone in low register
H	high tone
HL	high-mid tone
LH	low-mid tone
L	low tone

---

[39] But see Zsiga (2013), who distinguishes between high, mid, low, mid rising, low rising and falling; the latter 'falling' case replaces the high rising option.

238 Principles of Radical CV Phonology

To allow the twelve-way contrast in (39) is unattractive, however, because it predicts tonal systems that oppose high, low and no register. Register seems to be a property that does not allow for a 'third option' (i.e. no register). Moreover, it is not even clear how the system in (39) would account for the Mpi vowel contrasts in (37).

The only way that I can see to account for this system is to analyse the rising tones as resulting from a second H tone, forming a 'tone cluster':

(40) Phonation on Mpi vowels:

plain: l   laryngealised: h

high	H
high rising	H + H
mid	HL
mid rising	HL + H
low	L
low rising	L + H

I will discuss the option of 'tone clusters' in § 7.3.3.2.

6.4.4 The correlation between tone and phonation

The phonetic relationship between phonation and tone has been of interest in Generative Phonology since Halle & Stevens (1971), who proposed a unified set of binary features for both domains, and prior to that in many studies of tonal genesis, which often show that tonal distinctions on vowels can arise as phonemisations of allophonic effects caused by surrounding consonants (see Hyslop (2007, 2010); Lee (2008); Tang (2008); Kingston (2011)). Halle and Stevens proposed the feature [+stiff vocal folds] for voiceless consonants and high tone, while [+slack vocal folds] is associated with voiced consonants and low tone. They also proposed the features [spread glottis] and [constricted glottis] as phonation features, but these do not have a non-tonal interpretation. Subsequent models (Duanmu (1990) and Bao (1990)) have pursued the idea of Halle and Stevens in an FG model; see § 6.3.

In the present proposal, phonation and tone are expressed by the same elements:

Laryngeal: phonation and tone 239

(41)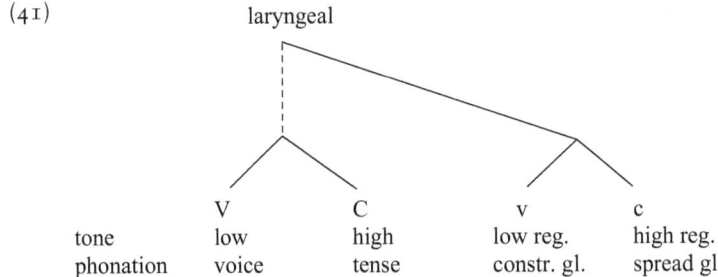

This correspondence suggests that glottal states and register should be subsumed under a more general category. A conflation of this kind has already been proposed in § 6.4.3, where it was suggested that the register distinction on vowels can be interpreted as phonation, which is supported by the fact that in several Asian languages what is called voice register is associated not only with relative pitch, but also with phonation-type properties and pharyngeal properties (see Trigo (1991)):[40]

(42) Low register   High register
     (Chest register)   (Head register)
     spread glottis   constricted glottis
     slack vocal folds   stiff vocal folds
     ATR   RTR
     Laryngeal lowering Laryngeal raising
     Breathiness/murmur creakiness

Trigo (1991: 113–14):

> The so-called 'chest' register has been variously described as involving all or some of the following articulatory traits: spread vocal cords, tongue root advancement, higher and fronter dorsal placement, slack vocal cords, dilated pharyngeal walls, lowered larynx; the 'head' register is said to involve the opposite characteristics: constricted vocal cords, tongue root retraction, lower and retracted dorsal placement, higher pitch, contracted pharyngeal walls, raised larynx.

I conclude that 'register' is a phonological dimension that involves a variety of articulatory pharyngeal and phonation parameters. In consonants, the register distinction gives rise to the various phonation

---

[40] Here I include terms like 'murmur/breathiness' and 'creak'. ATR often is said to correlate with 'breathiness'. Creakiness refers to constriction combined with voice; I have equated creaky with implosive, which also correlates with these two dimensions plus laryngeal lowering.

types, with one or the other perhaps more predominant, maybe most typically glottal width, while in vowels there can be a mixed effect on tone register and voice register, the latter including a variety of phonetic effects (see Gordon (1998) for a typological study). In RCVP, both types of register are subsumed under the same secondary laryngeal elements: c and v.

6.5 Bridge and coda

We have assumed at first that the bridge and coda positions do not have distinctive laryngeal properties. This position has been maintained for the bridge (granted that disharmonic obstruent clusters are analysed as not involving a branching onset). For the coda position, we can also maintain this position for consonants, granted that the phonation contrasts in obstruents do not falsify this position, if obstruents are not analysed as proper codas. However, we do have to reckon with tonal distinction on coda consonants. I refer to Hyman (2012) for a discussion of coda tones. It would seem that codas need a limited amount of tonal specification (as well as a limited amount of place specification, as established in § 5.4) My conjecture is that the tonal specification for coda will never be completely independent from the tonal properties of the vowel, perhaps only differing in terms of the head tone specification, but not in terms of register where this applies.

6.6 Summary and concluding remarks

The following tables summarise the proposal for laryngeal elements:

(43) Laryngeal (edge) > phonation:
      C   C+c   ~~C+c;v~~   ~~C+v;c~~   C+v
      ~~C;V~~ ~~C;V+c~~ ~~C;V+c;v~~ ~~C;V+v;c~~ ~~C;V+v~~
      ~~V;C~~ ~~CV+c~~   ~~V;C+c;v~~ ~~V;C+v;c~~ ~~V;C+v~~
      V   V+c   ~~V+c;v~~   ~~V+v;c~~   V+v

Laryngeal, edge:

	c [constr. gl.]	~~c;v~~	~~v;c~~	v [spread gl.]
C [tense]				
~~C;V~~				
~~V;C~~				
V [voiced]				

Laryngeal: phonation and tone 241

(44) Laryngeal (nucleus) > tone:
```
C      C+c    C+c;v   C+v;c   C+v
C;V    C;V+c  C;V+c;v C;V+v;c C;V+v
V;C    CV+c   V;C+c;v V;C+v;c V;C+v
V      V+c    V+c;v   V+v;c   V+v
```

Laryngeal, nucleus:

	c [high register]	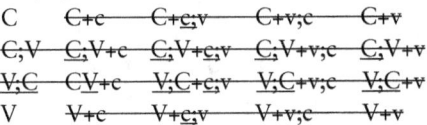	v [low register]
C [high tone]			
C;V [high-mid]/[falling]			
V;C[low-mid]/[rising]			
V l[ow tone]			

(45) Laryngeal (coda)
```
C      C+c    C+c;v   C+v;c   C+v
C;V    C;V+c  C;V+c;v C;V+v;c C;V+v
V;C    CV+c   V;C+c;v V;C+v;c V;C+v
V      V+c    V+c;v   V+v;c   V+v
```

Tone, nucleus/coda:

	c	c;v	c;v	v
C high				
C;V				
V;C				
V low				

In this chapter, I have proposed an RCVP structure for the laryngeal class. I started out by adopting the view that tone and phonation are in complementary distribution, the former occurring on rhyme heads and the latter on onset heads. This is apparently contradicted by the occurrence of phonation (or voice quality) distinctions on vowels, sometimes co-occurring with tonal distinctions. A crucial step in understanding this contradiction lies in the recognition that the secondary specifications in the laryngeal class can have a variety of interpretations, which range from pitch to voice quality. Hence, phonation can occur on vowels as an expression of secondary laryngeal elements.

For a summary of all structures that have been proposed in Chapters 4, 5 and 6, I refer to the Appendix at the end of this book.

7
Special structures

7.1 Introduction

In this chapter, I propose both 'incomplete' and 'overcomplete' structures for specific segment types. Incomplete structures are structures that miss one of the element classes. We have already seen examples of this, in the sense that a non-tonal language does not use the laryngeal node for vowels. We have also seen that the place class can be missing, as in central vowels and pharyngeal and laryngeal consonants. What cannot be missing is the manner class, because this class, being the head class, is obligatory. This, of course, is a theoretical decision that follows the idea that headedness plays a role and the claim that the manner class is the head class. One might ask whether RCVP allows a formal difference between the non-presence of a class and the presence of a class without any element. This issue has already been discussed in § 6.4.1. The answer is *no* for dependent classes, that is, the laryngeal and place class, and also *no* for secondary classes: a segment cannot have a secondary element in the absence of a specified primary element in any class. The simplest and most general answer would of course be that empty class nodes are not allowed at all, but I will consider below whether the manner class, being obligatory, can be 'empty'. I will, however, provide an approach that does not require this kind of option, which means that, indeed, RCVP bars empty class nodes entirely. I then turn to overcomplete structures, which are necessary for various classes of so-called complex segments such as clicks, consonants with multiple articulations, short diphthongs and some other types of segments.[1]

---

[1] I will also return to cases discussed in Chapters 4–6 where the apparent need was noted to allow a segment to have two secondary specifications in some classes; see, for example, §§ 4.2.1.2, 4.2.3 and 5.2.3.

7.2 Incomplete structures

7.2.1 *No content at all*

Let us first consider the possibility of allowing a so-called 'empty nucleus', that is, a nucleus position that is not associated with any segmental structure. In GP it is assumed that every 'syllable'[2] must have a nucleus position, this being the obligatory unit in the syllable. In this theory, this allows for the option to have no content in this nucleus position, which is then a 'skeletal point' that does not dominate segmental content. Such an empty nucleus will remain silent (if governed) and must otherwise be filled and thus realised, or 'just realised' (in the phonetic implementation). This proposal underlies the treatment of vowel/zero alternations in this theory (KLV90; Scheer (2004); van der Hulst (2006b)), which will be discussed below.

Referring back to § 3.2.2, in which I developed the RCVP approach to syllable structure, let us ask whether the 'empty nucleus' option is coherent in RCVP. At first sight, an empty nucleus could be represented as follows:

(1) empty nucleus in closed syllable

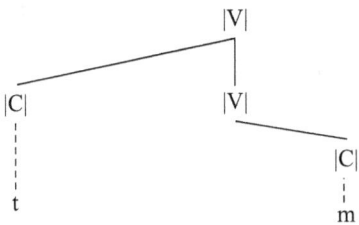

(2) empty nucleus in open syllable

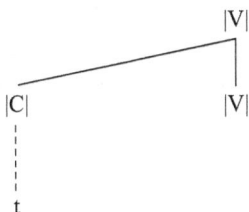

---

[2] GP actually does not recognise the syllable as a 'constituent', although it still acknowledges that onsets and rhymes come in 'OR' (onset rhyme) pairs.

Note that the structure in (1) would be intended to be different from the representation that was chosen to represent a syllabic consonant:

(3)

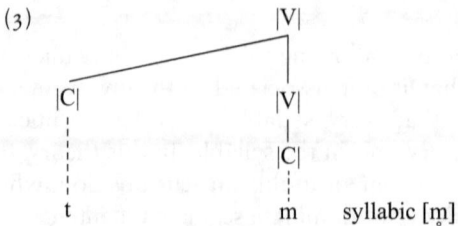

However, the structures in (1) and (2) are *in*coherent in a dependency approach where nodes are projections of contentful units (whether words in syntax or segments in phonology).

Having thus 'blocked' the theoretical option of empty nuclei, I question that whether we actually need such structures to account for vowel/zero alternations. GP employs empty nuclei not only for such alternations but also to account for consonant sequences that seem to exceed what a restrictive view on syllable structure (i.e. onset, coda–onset sequences or codas) can accommodate. I will first discuss alternative ways of analysing such cases without an appeal to empty nuclei, and then turn to some other related issues (namely consonant clusters, initial geminates, the representation of schwa, consonant/zero alternations, so-called ghost consonants and morphological templates).

7.2.1.1 Vowel/zero alternations

In GP, empty nuclei are recruited to account for vowel/zero alternations. The central idea is that if an empty nucleus position is licensed (or 'properly governed') by a full vowel to its right,[3] it can remain 'silent'; otherwise is it realised (see KLV90). In cases where the unlicensed vowel always has the same vowel quality, this vowel quality can simply result from 'phonetic interpretation' (which I take to be the same as phonetic implementation). For example, in Yowlumne the non-licensed nucleus always sounds like [i]. A 'traditional' GP account runs as follows (using a C/V notation for skeletal positions and nuclei;[4] the arrow represents the proper government relation):[5]

---

[3] The question as to whether the location of the governor is subject to parametric variation is raised in Rowicka (1999b), who employs 'trochaic government'.

[4] In a dependency notation we would not have such a skeleton. Rather, the segments would be associated with syllabic nodes.

[5] See Kenstowicz & Kisseberth (1979: 83ff.) for a traditional generative analysis and Kaye (1990) for a GP account.

Special structures   245

(4)   Yowlumni in GP

a.

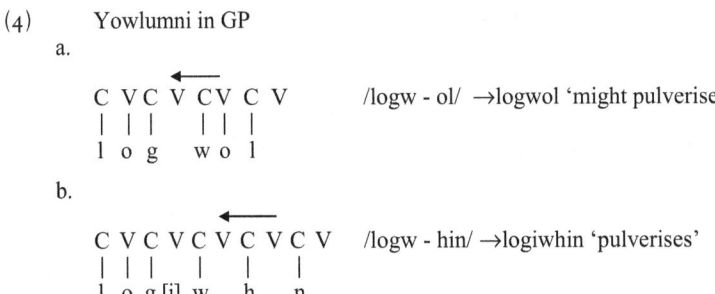

C V C V CV C V   /logw - ol/ →logwol 'might pulverise'
| | | | | |
l o g   w o l

b.

C V C V C V C V   /logw - hin/ →logiwhin 'pulverises'
| | | | | |
l o g [i] w   h   n

There are various empty nuclei in these representations. The final ones are licensed by a special constraint called 'final licensing'. In (4a) the second vowel [o] licenses the preceding empty nucleus, which can therefore remain silent. In (4b), there are two internal empty nuclei. The rightmost (non-final) one is not licensed[6] and is thus realised as [i]. Being realised, it can now license the preceding empty nucleus. Note that, given that an [i] that results from an empty nucleus that is not licensed can itself function as a licenser, the emergence of [i] cannot simply be a matter of phonetic implementation.

As we have seen, an account in RCVP cannot appeal to 'empty nuclei'. Given a morpheme such as /logw/ and a constraint that prohibits complex onsets, the two forms have different syllabic representations:

(5)   Yowlumne in RCVP

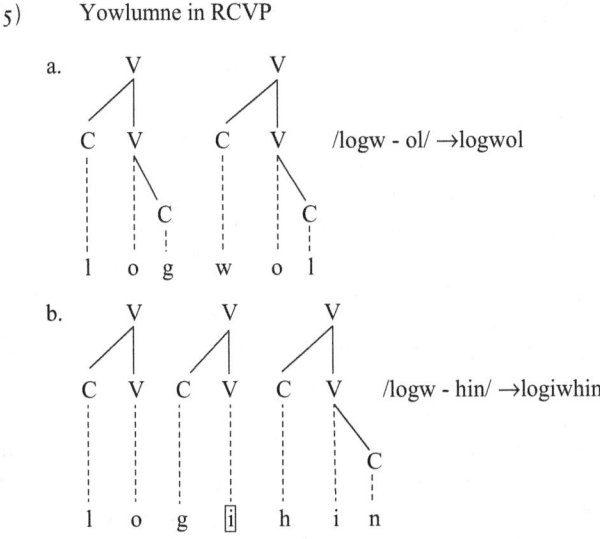

---

[6] This assumes that a licensed final empty nucleus cannot be a licenser of a preceding empty nucleus. Exceptions to this have been proposed in some cases in the GP literature.

We thus need an account for the appearance of the vowel [i] in the form in (5b). I will consider two possible approaches.

Assuming a syllable structure constraint which prohibits complex onsets, the [w] in (5b) will remain 'stranded' in front of a consonant-initial suffix. We can then say that the insertion of [i] is a 'repair strategy' which leads to the syllabic structure in (5b).

A second approach would be to make the 'epenthetic' [i] a part of the underlying morpheme as a 'variable' vowel, the idea being that a variable vowel can surface in some cases but not in others, the condition being that it occurs when syllabification would otherwise fail:

(6) a. /log(i)w/
    b. /l o g i w – h i n/ > [logiw-hin]
    c. /l o g (i) – w o l/ > [log-wol] and not [logiwol]

While in (6c) syllabification with [i] is possible, syllabification is also possible without it.

The use of the variable notation essentially implies that both allomorphs are listed, but conflated to the extent that they are identical, in such a way that only the difference is indicated as a choice. I also use the variable notation in van der Hulst (2018) for the treatment of allomorphy that results from vowel harmony. The principle here is that if the variable element is licensed it is realised, which causes the effect of harmony. Clearly, in the case of vowel/zero alternations we need a different kind of licensing. What kind of licensing would apply with reference to (6) to ensure the occurrence of [i] in (6c), but not in (6b)? The simplest answer would be that, rather than invoking licensing, we assume that a variable segment will only be necessary when otherwise syllabification fails; but this does not always work, as we will see below when considering some data from Czech; see (13)–(14). Alternatively, we could distinguish two types of licensing. Scheer (2004) makes a distinction between licensing of content (which would apply in the case of vowel harmony) and proper government, which is the mechanism to 'license' silence (i.e. the lack of content). If we transfer this distinction to the RCVP model, we could say that the variable (i) in (6a) remains silent if it is 'properly governed', which means licensed to be silent. It would thus seem that Scheer (2004) is right to distinguish licensing (licensing of content) from proper government (licensing of the absence of content). In summary, I will assume that there are two types of licensing; licensing which permits the presence of a variable element, and thus harmony, and licensing which silences a variable element. For the latter, which is the reverse of *licensing* content, I will use the term *silencing*.[7] If we employ the variable notation for

---

[7] As a mnemonic aid, the reader might note that the first two consonants are 'reversed'.

both situations (i.e. harmony and vowel/zero alternation) this would mean that this notation itself is neutral with respect to what enforces the variable element to be present or absent. Rather, this would follow from specifying the nature of the licensing relationship.[8] To explain the difference between (6b) and (6c) we could say that silencing is only possible in (6c) due to locality, that is, the fact that only one consonant intervenes. In support of the second analysis (lexical specification of the 'epenthetic vowel' as variable and thus not by using a repair rule), I cite two cases of vowel/zero alternation which only work if we use lexical specification.

As a first example, I give the nominative singular and genitive singular of the words in Cezch for 'dog' (*per, psa*) and 'brain' (*mozek, mozku*):[9]

(7)
C	V	C	V	~	C	V	C	V
:	:	:			:		:	
p	e	s			p		s	a

(8)
C	V	C	V	C	~	C	V	C	V	C	V
:	:	:	:	:		:		:		:	
m	o	z	e	k		m	o	z		k	u

Much has been written about whether the *yer*-alternation should be handled as insertion of [e] or deletion of an underlying [e]. Scheer (2011: 2938) dismisses the insertion approach:

> Among the arguments in favour of deletion, the following are decisive. In those languages, such as Russian, where more than one vowel alternates with zero, it cannot be predicted which vowel will appear in which morpheme. That is, the presence of an alternating e in *d'én* – *dn'-á* 'day (nom sg/gen sg)', against alternating o in *són* – *sn-á* 'dream (nom sg/gen sg)', is a lexical property of the root. An insertion-based analysis would not know which vowel to epenthesize into which root. The second reason is that there is no context for insertion. The motor for insertion is held to be the avoidance of heavy clusters [...]: the genitive plural of Russian *lásk-a* 'weasel (nom sg)' and *bobr-á* 'beaver fur (nom sg)' is *lások* and *bob'ór*, respectively; the genitive plural forms are supposed to undergo epenthesis in order to avoid final -sk# and -br# clusters. This cannot be the reason, though, since Russian happily tolerates these clusters in *lásk-a* – *lásk* 'caress (nom sg/gen pl)' and *bobr-á* – *bóbr* 'beaver (gen sg/nom sg)'. The same situation is found in other Slavic languages.

---

[8] We could explore whether licensing applies when a single element is variable, while silencing applies when the entire segment is variable. I will leave that line of research unexplored here.

[9] See Scheer (2004) for extensive reviews and analyses of the so-called *yer*-alternations in Slavic languages.

How would the variable vowel approach work in this case? The lexical representation that underlies the alternation contains a variable segment '(e)':

(9) / m o z (e) k /   / p (e) s /

Pursuing the first approach for Yowlumne (the one using a variable vowel, rather than an epenthesis rule), the silencing principle (like proper government) would suppress realisation of the variable vowel if licensed by an overt vowel one nucleus to its right. As Scheer notes, in the case of yer-alternations there is a compelling argument for lexical encoding of the non-zero vowel. While Czech, like other Western Slavic languages (except for Slovak), has merged the two historically present yers into one vowel [e], two yer realisations occur in Eastern Slavic languages. Below I present his examples from Russian, where we find an alternating e in *d'én'– dn'-á* 'day (nom sg/gen sg)', against alternating o in *són – sn-á* 'dream (nom sg/gen sg)', as a lexical property of the root (Scheer 2011: 2039).

(10) d'én' – dn'-á   'day (nom sg/gen sg)' > e/o
     són   – sn-á   'dream (nom sg/gen sg)' > o/o

In such cases, then, we cannot assume that there is one empty nucleus for both, nor can we adopt an epenthesis rule. We need to encode whether the overt form of the yer vowel is [e] or [o] in the morphemes in question.

(11) [e/o] d'(e)n' – d(e)n'-a   'day (nom sg/gen sg.)'
     [o/o] s(o)n   – s(o)n-a   'dream (nom sg/gen sg.)'

The appearance of the yer follows from silencing.

Another argument for lexical encoding comes from cases where epenthesis breaks up an ill-formed word-final cluster. We first consider the case of Turkish. In Turkish, final clusters involve a high vowel (which follows the pattern of vowel harmony for fronting and rounding):

(12) Turkish (Hankamer 2010):
     akıl   'intelligence'   akl-ı   akıl-da   ak(ı)l
     oğul   'son'   oğl-u   oğul-da   oğ(u)l
     beyin   'brain'   beyn-i   beyin-de   bey(i)n
     ağız   'mouth'   ağz-ı   ağız-da   ağ(ı)z

This can be dealt with given that the 'epenthetic' vowel always and only appears to break up otherwise ill-formed final clusters. Both a GP

Special structures 249

account with empty nuclei and an epenthetic rule can handle this case, and so can an analysis with a variable vowel. The case remains undecided based on the Turkish data.[10]

However, in Czech we find cases where epenthesis occurs even if the cluster is well formed in the final position, as in the following examples (Scheer 2010):

(13) a. kvart-a ~ kvart 'quart NOM-SG, GEN-PL'
     b. kart-a ~ karet 'card NOM-SG, GEN-PL'

An epenthesis rule approach cannot account for this minimal pair. This means that the two forms must have different representations such that the occurrence of epenthesis in (14b) is encoded:

(14) a. /kvart/
     b. /kar(e)t/

Once more, silencing accounts for the appearance of the variable vowel when it is not locally licensed.[11]

In conclusion, all vowel/zero alternations can be handled with a variable vowel (combined with silencing). I will admit that if the occurrence of a vowel involved in a vowel/zero alternation is fully regular (as in Yowlumne and Turkish), an epenthesis repair rule is perhaps the most straightforward treatment. However, in cases where such a rule approach fails, vowel/zero alternations can and must be handled in terms of a variable vowel combined with silencing. This leads me to suggest the variable analysis for all cases. In this way we dismiss empty nuclei and we also remove a derivational step of applying repair rules. It should be noted that in this account there is no empty nucleus when the variable vowel is silenced. If silenced, there is no vowel and hence no syllabic position (nucleus) will be projected.

7.2.1.2 Consonant clusters
Staying with the empty nucleus notion, we note that GP makes abundant use of this option, even beyond the cases where languages display vowel/zero alternations. Empty nuclei are also postulated in cases where

---

[10] In both this case and the Yowlumne case, an argument *against* lexical specification of the 'epenthetic vowel' is that lexical specification in principle would allow variable vowels to occur in different positions which would also allow proper syllabification. For example, in (6a) we could take as the lexical form /logw(i)/, which produces *lowgwihin* for (6b).

[11] The Czech examples show that the appearance of the variable vowel cannot be explained as a rescue for syllabification because a form without the variable vowel is phonologically well formed, as (13a) shows.

consonant clusters seem to exceed what can be regarded as well-formed onsets, codas or onset–coda sequences.[12]

An inspection of Dutch syllable structure (as found in Trommelen (1983) and van der Hulst (1984)) reveals that Dutch 'onsets' (like those in English and other Germanic languages) can exceed the number of two at the left word edge, where triconsonantal clusters are allowed consisting of [s] + obstruent + liquid:

(15) stronk   'trunk'
      splijt   'split'
      sprong   'jump'

However, when such a triconsonantal cluster is found word-internally (between two vowels), without the interference of a strong morpheme boundary, it is usually split by a syllable break:

(16) mis.tral   'mistral'
      es.planade   'esplanade'
      Cas.tro   'Castro'

For Dutch, we can tell that the [s] syllabifies to the left because the preceding vowel is lax. In Dutch, lax vowels must be followed by a tautosyllabic consonant (see van der Hulst (1984, 1985, 2006b)).

The claim that word-initial clusters need not be clusters that can occur as onsets word-internally can even be shown on the basis of seemingly well-behaved biconsonantal clusters consisting of an obstruent and a sonorant:

(17) a. gnoom   'gnome'   b. Ag.nes   'Agnes'
        slaaf   'slave'   Os.lo   'Oslo'
        tjiftjaf 'chiffchaff'   at.jar   'atjar'

The possible initial clusters [gn], [sl], [tj] are split up intervocalically (again indicated by the preceding vowel being lax). This shows that the only 'real' branching onsets are those consisting of an obstruent (excluding [s]) followed by a liquid and /w/ (see Trommelen (1983)).[13]

---

[12] This is even more relevant to a version of GP known as 'strict CV' (Lowenstamm 1996), which does not allow branching onsets or branching rhymes.

[13] For a government-based analysis of Dutch syllable structure, see van der Hulst (2006b).

For Dutch words such as *paprika*, opinions differ as to whether the pronunciation is pa-prika (with tense 'a') or pap-rika (with lax 'a'). In the latter case, I would argue that the /p/ is analysed as a virtual geminate, otherwise known as an

The apparent fact that certain types of clusters are tolerated as onsets word-initially but not word-medially is reinforced by the fact that such alleged onsets do not occur medially when the preceding vowel is tense in Dutch. So, while *metro* (with tense 'e') is fine, *mestro* (with tense 'e') is not. The question thus arises of how such clusters are represented when they occur word-initially. Looking back at § 3.2.2, we noted that we could simply allow the [s] consonant to be adjoined to a 'well-behaved' branching onset:

(18)
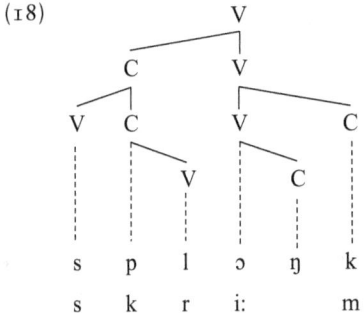

In this example, I have also added an extra consonant at the end, creating a so-called superheavy rhyme, which can only occur word-finally, with few exceptions. However, the issue is whether adjunction at the word periphery is limitless. Proponents of GP argue that limitations can be established once we postulate empty nuclei to break up initial clusters into sequences of well-formed onsets that are separated by an empty nucleus. Given that empty nuclei are subject to proper government, this, in principle, restricts the occurrence of consonants in an onset to two:[14]

(19)
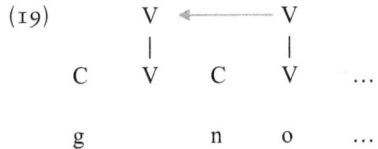

ambisyllabic consonant. That said, clusters that form proper onsets tend to resist having an initial ambisyllabic consonant (see van der Hulst (1985, 2006b)).

I noted in § 4.3.3 that some clusters that can occur word-internally as proper onsets can in some words still be split up. While obstruent + [r] cluster behave like proper onsets word-medially, obstruent + [l] tend to be split up; see van der Torre (2003: 149ff.).

[14] As mentioned, the postulation of empty nuclei has proliferated in the so-called strict CV version of GP (Lowenstamm (1996)), which does not allow branching onsets at all.

In this approach, more than two consonants might be possible if both onsets can be complex. This does not occur in Dutch. A possible explanation for this could be that proper government cannot apply across a complex onset. This means that at best only the first onset can be complex. However, Dutch does not have clusters that consist of a complex onset, say [pl], which is followed by a simplex onset, say [r]. One could then say that empty nuclei cannot 'license' complex onsets.[15]

But such auxiliary hypotheses may be moot because there *are* languages that have word-initial clusters that combine a simple onset with a complex onset. Such a language is Polish (Cyran & Gussmann (1999); Rubach & Booij (1990); Rowicka (1999a)):

(20) pstry   'mottled'
     bzdura   'nonsense'
     z'dz'bl-o 'blade'   [z'z'bwo]
     tknąc   'touch'

To accommodate these cases, different auxiliary mechanisms are required. Cyran and Gussmann propose the following representation for the last two examples in (20):

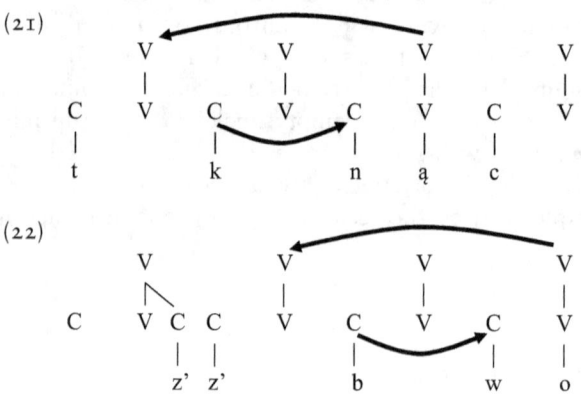

These authors propose two different licensing relations for both examples. The top one is proper government, which allows the first empty nucleus to remain silent. Note that proper government is here allowed to 'skip' the intermediate empty nucleus because this one is 'shielded' by an *inter-onset licensing* relation (indicated by the lower arrow), which is possible because [k] is less sonorous than [n]. This second relation creates a 'pseudo complex onset' which observes rising sonority but is not possible as a 'proper onset' (which only allows liquids as onset dependents).

---

[15] Onset licensing is another type of licensing in GP; see KLV90.

For the form for 'blade', Cyran and Gussmann need to make the further assumption that the first [z'] projects a nucleus by itself, turning this into a syllabic consonant in a sense.

While ingenious, analyses of this kind actually do not explain why the very complex consonant clusters only occur word-initially. Another approach would be to simply acknowledge that constraints on syllabic organisation are more liberal at the word margins, following the notion of polysystematicity. This could mean different things. Firstly, constraints on onset dependents could be relaxed (while still making rising sonority obligatory). Secondly, adding 'extra' consonants like [s] or [z'] could be allowed as adjuncts to word-initial onsets only. (The sibilant /z'/ in the second word is comparable to the /s/ in English /spr/.) Thirdly, an additional consonant could also be adjoined to the syllable node, on either the left or the right edge:[16]

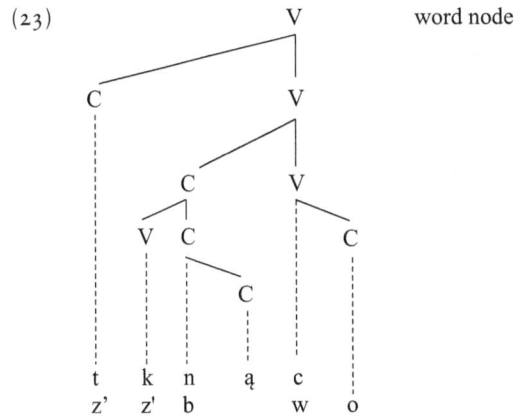

Evidence for the word-internal syllabification of consonant clusters is hard to obtain, given their scarcity in underived words, but this is in itself an indication that the clusters may be restricted to the word-initial position. Rubach & Booij (1990) note that the options for word-internal onsets are considerably restricted, suggesting that a cluster like [-rt-], which is allowed word-initially, is heterosyllabic word-internally: *kar-ty* 'cards'. This is very similar to what I reported for Dutch above.

It is not obvious, perhaps, that allowing multiple adjunctions at the word periphery is inferior to postulating empty nuclei and a host of special licensing principles. It is of course correct to argue that there are limitations on the number and nature of the consonants that can go beyond the internal 'core' syllable, and the proposals in Cyran & Gussmann (1999) are

---

[16] In RCVP, obstruents are not allowed as codas. Hence this consonant is here represented as being adjoined to the rhyme, analogous to /z'/ being adjoined to the onset.

quite coherent in this respect. But we can instead formulate 'reasonable' constraints on adjunction by, firstly, permitting only one adjunction at each level in the syllabic structure, that is, at the onset or rhyme level and at the syllable level, and, secondly, by restricting adjunction to word edges. After all, it is one thing to add a layer to a unit that is already formed, but it would be a stretch to add a layer to a unit that is internal to a bigger unit. With these restrictions in place, the structure in (23) goes a long way to 'making sense' of these complex clusters in Polish.[17]

Many phonologists who do not employ the GP model have treated the extra options at the left edge of words by allowing an 'extra-syllabic' consonant in that position (cf. Rubach & Booij (1990) for Polish), treated as stranded onsets by some (cf. Kuryłowicz (1947)). Others have suggested that the apparent sequence of two consonants may in some case involve complex segments (s+C clusters; cf. Ewen (1980b, 1982); van de Weijer (1996)). Some of these options are perhaps not mutually exclusive and may be compounded in a language like Georgian, leading to initial clusters of excessive complexity.[18] The commitment of RCVP is such that the mechanism of empty nuclei can be left out of the set of tools that we use to explain complex consonant clusters, following the principle that phonological structure is based on substance.

As already shown in (18), complex consonant clusters can also occur on the right side of words. Languages such as Dutch, English and many others allow word-final codas that are rather complex:

(24) Dutch: English:
 oogst 'harvest' sixth [ksθ]
 ernst 'seriousness' blast
 vreemd 'strange' paint
 prompt 'prompt'

In a view, such as proposed here, that only allows sonorant consonants in the coda position, even a single non-sonorant consonant would require special measures. A possible approach would be to lower the sonority threshold for word-final codas, but that as argued requires a revision of the syllable model. However, 'codas' with multiple consonants would require other measures. In Dutch and English, we find lax/short vowels followed by up to four consonants ($V_{lax}CCCC$), or tense/long vowels followed by up to three consonants ($V_{tense}CCC$). An inspection of word-internal

---

[17] Another formal option which may be relevant for the Georgian case (see below) is to analyse consonantal sequences as 'double-root' segments; see § 7.3.4.

[18] Other languages that permit special word-initial consonant clusters have also been reported; see Ritter (1995) and Törkenczy & Siptár (1999) for initial clusters in Hungarian. A particularly complex case occurs in Georgian (see Nepveu (1994), Bush (1997), Vogt (1958) and Ritter (2005)).

Special structures 255

syllables demonstrates that such very complex rhymes are rare when they are not word-final. This leads us to the descriptive generalisation that syllables ending in 'overcomplex' codas are limited to the right edge of words. As expected, GP analyses postulate empty nuclei, whereas others employ adjunction of extra-syllabic consonants, or propose a special unit to accommodate these consonants, called the appendix (see Fudge (1987)).

(25)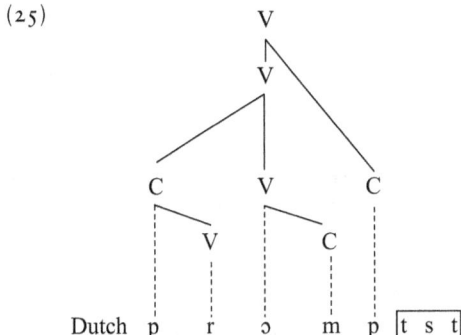

The [tst] sequence contains the [st] superlative suffix.[19] In this case, my proposal would be that the appendix forms a special syllabic constituent that can be adjoined to the word node (like a 'clitic'):

(26)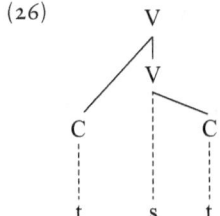

Some languages seem to challenge the claim that certain complexities occur at edges only, by allowing words that consist of sequences of consonants only:

(27) Nuxalk (formerly called Bella Coola; Bagemihl (1991)):
xsc'c   'I'm now fat'
lxwtlcxw 'you spat on me'

Imdlawn Tashlhiyt Berber (Dell & Elmedlaoui 1985):
tftkt   'you suffered a sprain'
ssrksxt   'I hid him'

[19] Phonetically, the [t] or even [pt] before [st] can be left unpronounced.

With respect to the Nuxalk facts, it has been suggested that such sequences should be taken as evidence for the claim that syllables can consist of just onsets (Hockett (1955)), that the segmental string lacks syllable structure (Newman (1947, 1971)), that there is only partial syllable structure (Bagemihl (1991)), or that syllables can have obstruents as their peaks (Hoard (1978)). Dell & Elmedlaoui (1985) suggest that in the Berber dialect that they analyse, any type of segment (including all consonants) can form a syllable peak. An alternative analysis of similar facts in another dialect is found in Guerssel (1990), who postulates empty nuclei.[20] The point of these examples is to suggest, however, that apart from complexities regarding consonant clusters at edges, the total absence of phonemic vowels throughout a word is a phenomenon that we must also reckon with.[21] I do not have a specific proposal for how to handle cases of this kind. One could perhaps seriously entertain the idea that languages of this kind indeed do not have syllable structure, which would then imply that there are no phonotactic constraints on segment sequences. In that case I would qualify that the kind of 'syllable structure' that Dell & Elmedlaoui (1985) detect in Berber would be located in what I call the utterance phonology and what others might call the phonetic representation. In any event, the grouping that occurs in Berber would be caused by the phonetic implementation.

As a final remark in this section, I draw attention to the fact that in the languages where the complexities only occur at the edges, we have to take into account the morphological composition of words. Historically, complexities at edges may be the result of consonantal affixes that may have become synchronically opaque as independent morphological units. This means that we have to expect mismatches between morphological structure and phonological structure. Phonotactic constraints on syllable structure hold within a certain domain; let us call it the phonological word. Compounds typically consist of multiple phonological words, which means that compounds can have word-internal clusters that one would not find internal to the phonological word. This is commonly accepted. However, morphological structure may not be recognisable in some 'frozen' compounds, which may then be regarded as one morphological word while still reflecting phonological complexities that do not fit a single phonological word. In that case, there is a mismatch in that one morphological word contains two phonological words. An example is the Dutch frozen compound *aalbes* 'currant', which contains a word-internal superheavy rhyme. In this case a compound

---

[20] A complication in evaluating the different analyses involves subtle differences in the emergence of schwa-like epenthetic sounds.
[21] Non-phonemic, epenthetic vowels may appear as a result of transitions between consonants.

analysis is tempting because of the recognisable second part *bes* 'berry', which makes *aal* a 'cranberry' morpheme; indeed, *aalbes* is similar to *cranberry*. In the Dutch word *loempia* 'spring roll' (borrowed from Indonesian), any attempt to construct a compound analysis is doomed; still, this word has to be analysed as two phonological words. My reference to the syllabic appendix as a 'phonological clitic' should be taken in the same spirit.

In this book I do not intend to offer analyses of the syllabic organisation in all these different situations and languages. My goal would be to analyse all these cases without the use of so-called empty nuclei, on the assumption that syllabic nodes can only be projections of segments.

7.2.1.3 Initial geminates

Another case in which GP would be forced to postulate empty nuclei is when languages are described as having word-initial geminates. Clearly, geminates do not fit the pattern of well-behaved onsets. A case that has received much attention is Leti. In van der Hulst & van Engelenhoven (1995) and van der Hulst & Klamer (1996), an analysis is provided of Leti initial geminates which uses the GP approach involving empty nuclei. While this analysis elegantly accounts for a large set of data in the language, the analysis could not (I'm inclined to say 'unfortunately') be maintained if empty nuclei are abandoned. I can't here provide an alternative analysis which is as elegant as the original GP analysis. That said, it is possible that some cases of alleged initial geminates in certain languages involve fortified, tense consonants (see LM p. 95), which of course raises the question of which feature accounts for this – presumably a laryngeal feature. LM compare the initial geminates in LuGanda with the fortis consonants in Korean, where the latter have been analysed as involving a laryngeal property such as constricted glottis. Another option is to 'simply' allow adjunction at the left word edge, but that would then have to be constrained to only allow adjunction of a consonant that is identical to the onset following it, which would be a suspicious constraint. Thirdly, initial geminates in Tashlhiyt Berber would be possible if there are no phonotactic constraints to begin with (see Ridouane & Hallé (2017)). For different theoretical proposals for the representation of initial geminates see Kraehenmann (2001), Topintzi (2008)[22] and Hamzah (2013), as well as Kubozono (2017) for many studies on the general issue of geminates.

---

[22] Topintzi (2008) proposes treating initial geminates as involving a moraic position. This predicts geminate onsets can also occur word-medially, for which she finds evidence in Marshallese and Trique.

7.2.1.4 Schwa

Having 'condemned' the use of empty nuclei, the question naturally arises of how RCVP would represent the vowel schwa when this vowel occurs in unstressed syllables, either underlyingly or as the result of vowel reduction, rather than as a distinctive vowel that can occur in all positions where other vowels can occur.

The option that I have proposed in § 4.3.1 is of a segmental nucleus structure with only a manner specification, which, in fact, would be the only obligatory specification for any segment type:[23]

(28) Nucleus: Manner, but no Place, no Laryngeal:
V   (Nucleus)
|
|
V   (Manner specification)

One might think that the representation in (28) cannot be the representation of a schwa vowel (or of an empty nucleus for that matter), because the manner V specification by itself, unaccompanied by place or laryngeal elements, is also taken to represent the vowel [a]. However, if we adopt the polysystematic view of phonemic contrast, which would focus on the fact that the vowel set that occurs in unstressed syllables is a separate vowel class with its own set of contrasts, we can in fact represent the schwa with the manner element |V|, which would be interpreted not as [a], but as [ə] in metrically weak position.[24]

7.2.1.5 Consonant/zero alternations

Languages may also display consonant/zero alternations. A typical case occurs in French:

(29) petit garcon – petit ami   'small boy' – 'small friend'
     tres garçons – tres amis   'three boys' – 'three friends'

---

[23] Conceivably, one could entertain this option as a representation of empty nuclei, but only in those cases in which the silent nucleus alternates with a minimal vowel, like schwa, which would allow the phonetic implementation of this structure to be 'silence'. This is also something that RCVP will not allow for reasons that have not been discussed here. In van der Hulst (2018) I argue at length that we cannot allow the phonetic implementation to *not* realise specified phonological elements because this would allow the kind of abstractness that was argued against in Kiparsky (1968), for good reasons.

[24] Bolinger (1981) shows that English has three unstressable vowels: schwa and the final vowels in *happy* and *hollow*. The latter two would have |I| and |U| as place elements.

Special structures   259

The nature of the consonant that appears is not predictable. For such cases, the 'latent' final consonant can be represented as a variable segment:

(30) /peti(t)/
      /tre(s)/

The non-realisation can be said to be due to licensing, the local licenser being the immediately following vowel.

7.2.1.6 Ghost consonants

Having provided alternatives to analyses (or suggestions for alternatives) that use empty nuclei in GP, I now turn to questioning the use of 'empty onsets'. Besides empty nuclei, it has also been proposed that there can be empty onsets. In GP, every rhyme is by definition preceded by an onset position. Such empty onsets do not really have a specific function, so in my approach I will not assume that every rhyme is preceded by an onset node that has no content; in fact, given that syllabic positions are based on segmental content, such empty nodes are incoherent. There is, however, another type of empty onset, while less widely used, that some phonologists have proposed: so-called 'ghost consonants', such as the *h-aspiré* in French, which is postulated in words that audibly lack a consonant while *behaving as if* they start with a consonant:

(31) la hache   *l'hache   'the axe'

RCVP rejects the use of empty syllabic positions, since syllabic positions are projections of overt segments. In this case, there is no consonant/zero alternation, so no variable consonant can be postulated. In my view, the use of the empty onset specification for *h-aspiré* 'feels' like the *diacritic use of phonological means*. I see no other option than to mark *h-aspiré* words as learned exceptions to the kinds of processes that respond to vowel-initial words. This is a lexical kind of marking, but not one that is disguised as a phonological unit.

There are cases, however, in which a morpheme can be said to have an empty onset, which, when a consonant-final word precedes, delivers a geminate due to spreading of said consonant to the following empty onset position. In this case, while an empty onset position is postulated to explain the gemination effect, the onset does not remain empty in the surface form. A case of this kind is presented in Marlett and Stemberger (1983).[25] The rejection of empty structure would not

---

[25] Marlett & Stemberger (1983: 631): 'We have shown that there is a group of verbs that behave in relation to every relevant rule as if the verb roots began with a

be meant to ban such an analysis since in such cases there is an alternation between the presence of an onset consonant and its absence, although I would propose representing that onset position as 'variable', meaning it would be licensed by a preceding consonant, resulting in the interpretation of this consonant in two positions. This approach would be analogous to the approach that I suggested for vowel/zero alternations.

7.2.1.7 Morphological templates

Finally, one might wonder how morphemic templates can be represented as lexical items if such templates are 'mere syllable structure', devoid of segmental content. Since templates can represent a morphological category, as in Arabic and other Semitic languages, they have been treated as morphemes in their own right, just like the vocalic and consonantal melodies that fill the syllabic positions:

(32)
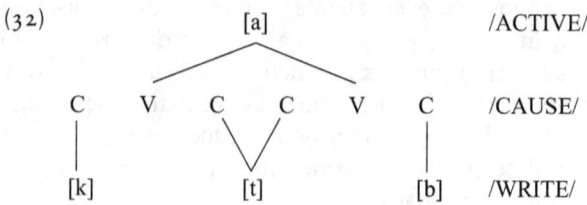

The question is now whether in RCVP it is coherent to allow morphemes that are templates, that is, a sequence of syllabic positions. One might argue that it is possible to represent a templatic morpheme like 'CVCCVC' as a syllabic organisation that can be merged with morphemes that consist of a sequence of vowels and a sequence of consonants, although this might then lead to the argument that there is no problem in including a piece of syllable structure (like an empty nucleus or an empty onset) that is interspersed in a consonant–vowel sequence. There is a difference, however, between postulating contentless syllabic structure which is specifically meant to be unrealisable as such, and allowing contentless syllabic units to occur *as part of* a well-formed complete representation. We can exclude the latter while allowing the former. Morphological templates (not only in root-and-pattern morphology but also including reduplicative templates) are not as such realisable; they are not meant to be well-formed, complete phonological expressions, even under special circumstances. Templates are comparable to

consonant, even though they apparently begin with a vowel. All these verbs are associated with one other phenomenon in Seri: gemination of any consonant that immediately precedes the root.'

Special structures 261

having morphemes that consist of 'tone only' or just one property such as 'nasality' or 'palatality' (e.g. umlaut in Germanic/Old English), which are likewise not meant to be complete, realisable phonological expressions. When we compare this to empty nuclei, we realise that such empty positions are well formed as such, under the special circumstance of being governed by a specified nucleus.

In conclusion, given the need for morphemes that consist of a single element, like an element for nasal, we can then also accept morphological templates as legitimate lexical entries, while at the same time maintaining the rejection of empty nuclei and empty onsets, which are claimed to exist in the representation of words without having to merge with phonological material that makes the representation complete.

7.2.2 Partial content

7.2.2.1 No 'no manner'
Since manner is the head class, it would be inconsistent to allow location or laryngeal specifications without a manner specification (unless in the case of morphemes that consist of partial content that needs to be merged with other content, as discussed in the previous section).

7.2.2.2 Manner only
In the preceding section, I proposed representing the schwa as a manner-only vowel. In § 5.2.3 I discussed representations for pharyngeal and laryngeal consonants, which share the property of being placeless. The glottal stop even lacks a laryngeal specification, which makes it a manner-only segment. Also, the glottal fricative [h] can be represented with just a manner V element:

(33)   laryngeals

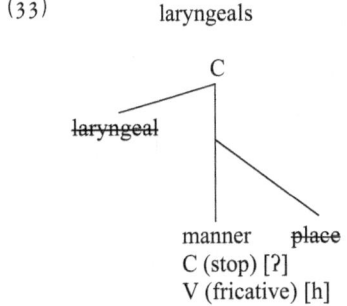

manner   place
C (stop) [?]
V (fricative) [h]

A laryngeal specification can differentiate between a voiceless [h] and a voiced [ɦ]; see (31b) in § 4.2.4.

262   Principles of Radical CV Phonology

As shown in Chapter 6, pharyngeals combine the structure in (33) with a secondary manner v for pharyngealisation, although they typically also have laryngeal properties:[26]

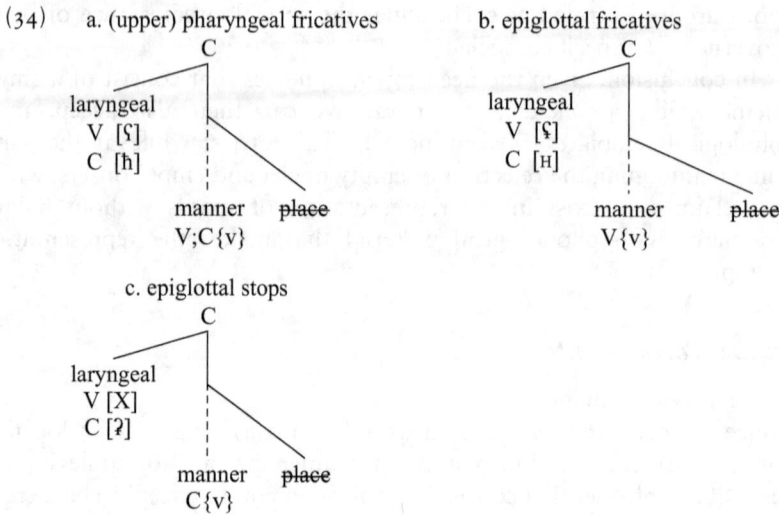

This concludes the discussion of incomplete structures. In Chapter 9 I discuss the notion of *minimal specification*, which deals with the question as to whether representations should eliminate all element specifications that are not strictly necessary for the expression of contrast. This refers to elements that could be considered redundant, in the sense of being predictable and non-contrastive. For example, in the class of pharyngeals, it may not be necessary to specify the voicing of the pharyngeal if a language does not have a voice contrast. In binary feature theories, use has been made of another type of non-specification, namely 'radical underspecification', which promotes the non-specification of contrastive features. For example, if there is a contrast between oral and nasal vowels, one could mark the latter as [+nasal] and leave the former unspecified, postulating a default rule that will fill in [−nasal] at some point prior to phonetic implementation (or perhaps leaving the interpretation of such segments entirely to the phonetic implementation). In a single-value system, most instances of radical underspecification are 'built in' (see § 2.2.1). Given that nasality is expressed in terms of an element, while non-nasal is not, there is simply no sense in which an oral vowel is underspecified for nasality. However, in RCVP, given that each element class contains two elements, there is a sense of binarity

---

[26] Recall that an IPA symbol for a voice epiglottal stop is missing; see (17) in § 5.2.3. Whether a voiced segment of this type is phonetically possible is questionable.

that is, in fact, fundamental to the system. So, when obstruents display a voicing contrast, one could mark voiceless obstruents as C and voiced obstruents as V, but one could also leave one of the two unspecified, treating it as a 'default' element (see Ewen & van der Hulst (1987), where this practice is suggested for a unary element system). In § 6.4.1 I discussed the use of this kind of non-specification, showing that this can only be allowed if non-specification for a certain class does not have an independent interpretation that is potentially contrastive with the presence of both elements in that class. I will continue this issue in Chapter 9 because I myself have violated this restriction in van der Hulst (2018), where I followed Dresher (2009) in adopting a 'successive division algorithm' which delivers minimal representations. However, as I will show in Chapter 9, the resulting minimality cannot be maintained in some cases given that, in the current model, non-specification of an element is formally indistinguishable from the class node itself being absent. This then creates a problem when the absence of a class has its own phonetic interpretation, different from the alleged unspecified, default element (as in the case of pharyngeal place).[27] In Chapter 9 I will address this problem and propose a resolution.

7.3 Overcomplete structures

I now turn to how RCVP represents segments, specifically consonants, that have traditionally been designated as being 'complex segments'.[28] We have already dealt with several of these, but we will see that there are certain kinds of complex segments that require structural options that have thus far not been used.

7.3.1 Complex consonants

In previous chapters, I have discussed the structure of segments and syllables in the RCVP framework, which involved representations for many segment types that are traditionally called complex, such as 'contour' segments (in the sense of Sagey (1986)) and segments with secondary articulations (for manner or place[29]). The term 'contour segment' is traditionally used for affricates and prenasalised consonants because in one type of analysis in binary systems both get two opposite specifications

---

[27] In § 12.5 I consider an alternative class organisation which would represent pharyngeal consonants in a 'positive' way; see (4) in that section.
[28] This section is based on § 5 in van der Hulst & van de Weijer (2018a).
[29] I note here that the term 'secondary articulation' was not invoked to represent laryngeal properties that activate the secondary element class for 'complex' phonation types such as breathy or creaky voice.

for the same binary feature ([continuant] and [nasal], respectively; I am here sidestepping the question of whether similar contouring is also possible for other features, or if it is not, why not (see van de Weijer (1991, 1996)).

Hence, I have already accounted for most segments that are traditionally called complex, with the exclusion of (35c) and (35d):

(35) a. Contour segments:
 – affricates (complex primary manner) (§ 4.2.1.1)
 – prenasalised consonants (secondary manner) (§ 4.2.1.2)

 b. Secondary articulations:
 – pharyngealisation (secondary manner) (§ 4.2.1.2)
 – palatalisation (secondary place) (§ 5.2.2)
 – labialisation (secondary place) (§ 5.2.2)

 c. Multiple articulations:
 clicks
 k͡p, t͡p, t͡k

 d. Compound (i.e. non-unitary) contour tones on short vowels

This leaves me with proposing a representation for clicks and other so-called MACs, as well as segment types such as short vowels with multiple tones.

The representation of these segment types has been the subject of much discussion, ranging from single complex segments, to double-root segments, to branching onsets. For clicks, van de Weijer (1996) adopts a so-called two-root solution, a structure in between complex syllabic constituents and complex segments.

Before we turn to the cases in (35c)–(35d), I first summarise the accounts in (35a)–(35b).

7.3.1.1 Affricates

Affricates result from a combination within the head manner class (§ 4.2.1.1):

(36) affricates Complex primary manner: C;V

Non-strident fricatives are V;C. They thus have the same complexity as affricates although they are not phonetically complex in the sense of requiring phonetic sequencing.

I mention here once more that affricates may also arise as the phonetic realisation of palatal or alveo-palatal places or articulation; see for instance Lin (2011) and references cited there, as well as LM (ch. 3).

Special structures   265

Clusters in languages such as Dutch or English that start with an [s] followed by a stop have been analysed as 'reversed affricates' (see Ewen (1980a, 1982); van de Weijer (1996)). I have not followed this proposal, instead suggesting an adjunction analysis (see § 3.2.2 and (18) on p. 251). Non-homorganic stop–fricative sequences such as [px] or [ks] also cannot be analysed as affricates, nor can they be analysed as proper onsets, this requiring a double-root analysis (see § 7.3.4).

7.3.1.2 Consonants with secondary manner

In all of the cases below, a primary manner is accompanied by a secondary manner. I have suggested that mostly only simple primary structures occur with a secondary manner:[30]

(37) a. Prenasalised consonants   Secondary manner c
                                    Prenasalised stops: Manner {{C}c}
                                    Prenasalised fricatives: Manner {{V}c}
      b. Lateralised consonants   Secondary manner c;v
                                    Lateralised stops: Manner {{C}c;v}
                                    Lateralised fricatives: Manner {{V}c:v}
      c. Retroflex consonants   Secondary manner v;c
                                    Retroflex stops: Manner {{C}v;c}
                                    Retroflex fricatives: Manner {{V}v;c}
      d. Pharyngealisation   Secondary manner v
                                    Pharyngealised stops: Manner {{C}v}
                                    Pharyngealisedfric: Manner {{V}v}

All these segment types have been extensively documented in Chapter 4, especially § 4.2.1.2.

7.3.1.3 Consonants with secondary place

While velarisation, uvularisation and pharyngealisation have been analysed as a secondary manner v, the other two traditional cases of secondary articulation involve secondary place:

(38) 'Secondary articulations':

    Palatalisation   Secondary location: Place {{..}c}
    Labialisation   Secondary location: Place {{..}v}

I refer to (13) in § 5.2.2, which provides the interpretation of all the secondary place articulations. In that table, the primary structures produce

---

[30] It would seem that the extra complexity of the secondary subclass is 'compensated for' by adding secondary properties only to simple head structures to avoid an abundance of complexity.

the four-way major place distinction in the first column, while secondary c and v add secondary articulations, which in some cases deliver segments that would not necessarily be regarded as phonetically complex (but see e.g. Keating (1988a) on palatals).

7.3.2 Consonants with two major places (clicks and multiply-articulated consonants)

I now turn to other classes of complex segments that have not been, and cannot be, represented in terms of structures developed in the previous chapters. The proposals that follow are tentative, offered because it is important to show how, in principle, RCVP can deal with all segment types, even if that requires an extension, or as yet unexplored structural possibility.

Both clicks and MACs seem to combine *two* major places of articulation. The evidence for designating one or the other as the head is inconclusive. [k͡p], for example, can neutralise to either a labial or a dorsal (see Danis (2015)). Regarding clicks, different researchers have treated either the coronal or the dorsal place as 'central'.[31] I suggest that the special option of combining places does not use headedness distinctively, which allows different languages to fix headedness in the phonetics in different ways. I will call structures that combine two major (primary) places *compound structures*.

First turning to MACs, one might expect two options, on the assumption that the places that are combined in a compound structure have to be 'sisters' in the CV structure for place (which seems to be the 'first and most natural choice' for element compounding):

(39)   compounds with sister place structures

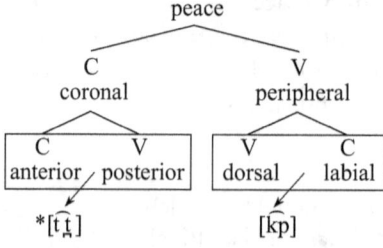

---

[31] The coronal part is taken to be the primary location (as suggested by Trubetzkoy (1939 [1960]), Jakobson, Fant & Halle (1952) and Chomsky & Halle (1968)). Danis (2015) shows that clicks reduce or neutralise to or alternate with dorsals in Fwe and Yeyi.

References on clicks include Bennett (2008, 2009, 2014); Bradfield (2014); Jakobson (1968); Ladefoged & Traill (1984, 1994); Miller (2017); Miller, Namaseb & Iskarous (2007); Sagey (1986); Traill (1993, 1995); Wright, Maddieson, Ladefoged & Sands (1995).

Arguably, combining the two coronal places does not produce a viable MAC because, both being coronal, it is not possible for the tongue crown to be in two places at the same time.[32] This is different for the two peripheral places, which can be combined to produce the only MAC that has been reliably attested, namely labial-velar [k͡p]:

> by far the most common double stop articulation is a bilabial and velar one. Languages with bilabial-velar stops are especially common in West Africa and northern Central Africa, where they occur in several different families. Idoma, Yoruba, Gwandara, Logbara and many other African languages exemplify the Labial-Dorsal category [...]. Sounds of this type are also found in several New Guinea languages, such as Kate, Ono, Mape, Dedua and Yeletnye. (LM p. 333)

As argued in Bennett (2014), claims for labial-coronals as single segments are not strong: these events are more likely better analysed as consonant clusters.[33] We must note that such combinations would include compounding non-sisters. As I will argue now, such combinations may have a purpose, however, for the analysis of clicks.

If both clicks and multiple articulated segments are in some sense complex place-wise, how do we derive the 'click effect'? In virtually all feature systems that have been proposed, separate features are adopted that refer to airstream mechanisms that deviate from the predominant pulmonic egressive airstream, which, being the default, is assumed to need no feature. Such feature sets including features for 'larynx lowering' (which induces a glottalic ingressive airstream for implosives), 'larynx raising' (for ejectives) or 'velar suction' for clicks.[34] In § 6.2 I have proposed analysing implosives in terms of voicing and constricted glottis (Laryngeal: {V{c}}), which delegates the ingressive airstream resulting from larynx lowering as a phonetic variant of 'creaky phonation'.

This leaves clicks, and here too I do not want to resort to an element that is interpreted as a specific airstream, such as 'velic suction'. There is no natural place for such an element in the RCVP architecture. I will therefore suggest that clicks are MACs of a particular kind, viewing the velaric suction as a phonetic effect. Rather than combining two sister places, I propose that clicks involve a compound structure consisting of a coronal place (either C or C;V, to recognise the fact that the coronal

---

[32] This shows, as also emphasised in Bennett (2014), that the phonology can produce structures that do not have a 'sensible' phonetic interpretation.
[33] Of course, we still need to account for such 'clusters', since they cannot be proper onsets. I will suggest a two-root approach below (§ 7.3.4).
[34] Usually there is also a feature for 'larynx raising' (for ejectives) which as such does not correlate with a 'special' airstream.

part can differ contrastively) and a 'peripheral place', with dorsal being the most likely choice:

(40) compounds with sister place structures

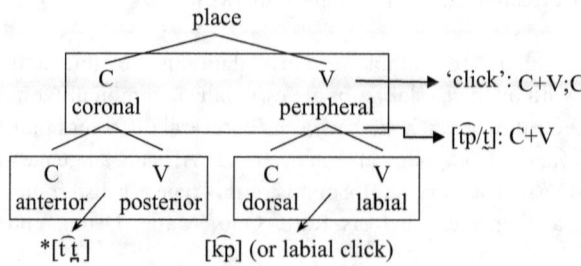

A click consonant thus results from combining the coronal element C with the peripheral-dorsal element combination V;C, which provides the dorsal component.

Interestingly, a candidate may present itself for combining the coronal element C with the peripheral-labial element V. In § 5.2.2 I mentioned linguo-labial consonants which involve a contact between the tongue and the upper lip. Such consonants occur contrastively in Tangoa (LM pp. 18–19) and in a group of languages from the islands of Espiritu Santo and Malekula in Vanuatu (Maddieson 1989b). Such sounds can be represented as in (42), while clicks fit the representations in (41). In both cases the coronal place can vary, although this is not reported as contrastive for the linguo-labial:

(41) {{C} + {V;C}}   dental coronal click
      {{C;V} + {V;C}} alveolar coronal click

(42) {{C} + {V}}   linguo-labial
      {{C;V} + {V}}   linguo-labial

We have not yet provided a representation for the labial click. There is just one possible labial click [ʘ], which has a dorsal efflux. Labial clicks are very rare (Bennett 2014), but that in itself does not mean that we should not have a representation for them. Interestingly, Ladefoged (1968) notes that bilabial clicks are allophones of labial-velar stops in some West African languages. This suggest the possibility of representing bilabial clicks and labial-velar stops in the same terms, again seeing the difference in airstream as 'phonetic'; see Bennett (2014) for a critical evaluation of this idea and important discussion. Alternatively, it would also be possible to represent labial clicks in the same way we analysed linguo-labials. LM (p. 353) cite Traill (1985: 106), who notes that cavity expansion for labial clicks is achieved 'by a lowering and retraction of the front part of the tongue'. Traill also observes that labial clicks have a tongue front contact as well as the labial and velar contacts and thus have 'three points of articulation'. These observations suggest that labial clicks combine a labial and a lingual gesture, the latter covering coronal and dorsal. Both proposals can be seriously entertained. No language contrasts labial clicks and labial-dorsal or linguo-labials (for the former claim see Bennett (2014: 119)).[35]

In (43) I summarise my proposals for MACs and clicks:

(43)   [k͡p] or [ʘ]   {{V} + { V;C}}

       dental coronal click   {{C} + {V}}
       alveolar coronal click   {{C;V} + {V}}

       labio-lingual or [ʘ]   {C(;V)} + {V}

In conclusion, in the RCVP model, there is no need for independent airstream elements.

I did not here consider the distribution of clicks. Clicks, in languages that have them, are not rare. As LM (p. 246) report, over 70 per cent of the words in a !Xóõ dictionary (Traill 1994) have clicks. Clicks do not occur as codas, while as onsets they predominantly occur at the left edge of the word. This falls in line if codas do not permit obstruents and clicks are universally analysed as obstruents. However, if word endings are more tolerant in that respect, clicks could occur there; but they do not. We expect of course that clicks, being very complex, will have a limited distribution. This, then, could explain the fact that clicks only occur syllable-initially and perhaps, as such, only word- and root-initially (see Miller (2011: 431–5)).

Another noteworthy property of clicks is that they can occur with a great number of secondary articulation and phonation types. LM spend an entire chapter on clicks (ch. 8), with a twenty-page discussion of 'click accompaniments', namely the properties that are associated with the efflux part of the click, which is the dorsal part. Following LM's detailed discussion, I will here offer a likewise detailed analysis of how the accompaniments that they find fit within the RCVP model. As it turns out, there is a perfect fit between attested accompaniments and the array of possibilities that is predicted by the model. LM note that there are three types of variations in the accompaniments of clicks:

---

[35] Bilabial clicks can also be nasalised, as in Ndau, a Bantu language spoken in Mozambique (Jones (1911)). Jones suggests that these nasal clicks are variants of a labialised nasal [m^w].

270   *Principles of Radical CV Phonology*

(44) Click accompaniments:
   a. those associated with activities of the larynx;
   b. those associated with the oro-nasal process; and
   c. those associated with the place and manner of release of the back closure.

The language !Xóõ has five types of click articulation in terms of the place of the influx; there are bilabial, dental, alveolar, lateral and palatal clicks. Each click has one of seventeen possible accompaniments, which are exemplified in their table 8.4, which I reproduce here:

(45) Clicks in !Xóõ:[36]

	Bilabial	dental	alveolar	lateral	palatal
1	gʘòõ (type of worm)	gǀáá 'work'	gǃàã 'accompany'	gǁàã 'beg'	gǂàa 'exploit'
2	kʘôõ 'dream'	kǀâa 'move off'	kǃàã 'wait for'	kǁãã 'poison'	kǂàã 'bone'
3	kʘʰoū 'ill fitting'	kǀʰáa 'be smooth'	kǃʰàn 'inside'	kǁʰàã 'other'	kǂʰàa 'stamp flat'
4	ɢʘòo 'be split'	ɢǀáá 'spread out'	ɢǃá̰ã 'brains'	ɢǁàa 'light up'	ɢǂàa 'depress'
5	qʘóu 'wild cat'	qǀàa 'rub with hand'	qǃa̰ẽ 'hunt'	qǁáã 'thigh'	qǂàa 'conceal'
6	ŋʘò̰õ 'louse'	ŋǀãa 'see you'	ŋǃãã 'one's peer'	ŋǁáã 'grewia berry'	ŋǂàa 'peer into'
7	ŋʘâʔã 'be close together'	ŋǀûʔi 'be careful'	ŋǃâʔm 'evade an attack'	ŋǁâʔm 'be damp'	ŋǂûʔã 'be out of reach'
8	ʔŋʘâje 'tree'	ʔŋǀàa 'to suit'	ʔŋǃa̰n 'lie horizontal'	ʔŋǁàhã 'amount'	ʔŋǂaũ 'right side'
9	ŋʘʰòõ 'smeared with dirt'	ŋǀʰáa 'look for spoor'	ŋǃʰài 'fall'	ŋǁʰáa 'carry'	ŋǂʰàa 'ahead'
10	kʘˣóõ 'walk slowly'	kǀˣâa 'dance'	kǃˣáa 'go a distance'	kǁˣàa 'scrape'	kǂˣáa 'mind out'
11	gʘkxàna 'make fire with sticks'	gǀkxáá 'splatter water'	gǃkxàn 'soften'	gǁkxáʔn 'calf muscle'	gǂkxáʔã 'sneeze'
12	kʘʼqʼóm 'delicious'	kǀʼqʼàa 'hand'	kǃʼqʼáa 'spread out'	kǁʼqʼâã 'grass'	kǂʼqʼàũ 'neck'

[36] LM have the final form, ɢǂhâẽ, in the lateral column, which I assume is a mistake.

Special structures 271

	Bilabial	dental	alveolar	lateral	palatal
13	gʘq'óõ 'fly'	g|q'àā 'chase'	g!q'áā 'cry incessantly'	g||q'áā 'tumor'	gⱡq'àa 'ground to powder'
14	gʘhòō 'sp. bush'	g|hâa 'stale meat'	g!hàa 'thorns'	g||hàā 'bone arrow tip'	gⱡháa 'cut'
15	kʘʔòo 'be stiff'	k|ʔàa 'die'	k!ʔáā 'be seated' [pI.]	k||ʔàa 'not to be'	kⱡʔāa 'shoot you'
16	qʘ'ûm 'close mouth'	q|'án 'small' [pI.]	q!'àma 'stickgrass'	q||'úɲa 'turn one's back'	qⱡ'àn 'lay down' [pI.]
17	–	ɢ|hàô 'put into'	ɢ!ʰâɲa 'grey haired'	–	ɢⱡʰâẽ 'push away'

The accompaniments are described in LM (pp. 265–73) as follows (unless indicated as uvular, all accompaniments are velar):

(46) Description of !Xóõ clicks:

1. Voiced
2. Voiceless
3. Voiceless aspirated
4. Voiced uvular
5. Voiceless uvular
6. Nasal
7. Voiceless nasal
8. Preglottalised nasal
9. Voiceless aspirated nasal
10. Voiceless affricate
11. Sequences of two consonants: a voiced velar click [g|] (as in item 1 in this list), followed by a voiceless velar fricative [x] or affricate [kx]
12. Sequence of a voiceless click followed by uvular ejective[37]
13. Voiced version of item 12 in this list
14. Voiced aspirated (breathy)
15. Voiceless glottalised
16. Voiceless glottalised uvular
17. Voiced aspirated uvular

---

[37] LM remark that this analysis is further supported by the fact that !Xóõ has a uvular ejective in its consonant inventory, making these sequences more plausible. A similar point has been made recently by Traill (1993). Here I do not adopt the bisegmental analysis.

272   *Principles of Radical CV Phonology*

In (47) I provide the RCVP representation for these seventeen accompaniments. The first column indicates the laryngeal distinction, while the other columns provide manner distinctions in the head manner and the dependent manner, respectively. For head manner I specify the difference between stops (C) and affricates (C;V), whereas secondary manner allows us to specify uvulars (v) and nasality (c). If uvular is not marked, the place of the efflux is velar:

(47) RCVP encoding of accompaniment in !Xóõ clicks:

		LAR	MAN-Head	MAN-Dep	
				c: nasal	v: uvular
1.	Voiced	V	C		
2.	Voiceless	C	C		
3.	Voiceless aspirated	C{v}	C		
4.	Voiced uvular	V	C		v
5.	Voiceless uvular	C	C		v
6.	Nasal	V	C	c	
7.	Voiceless nasal	C[38]	C	c	
8.	Preglottalised nasal	C{c}	C	c	
9.	Voiceless aspirated nasal	C{v}	C	c	
10.	Voiceless affricate	C	C;V		
11.	(Item 1 of (46)) + [x]/[kx]	V	C/C;V		
12.	(Item 2 of (46)) + [q']	C{c}	C		v
13.	(Item 1 of (46)) + [q']	C{v}	C		v
14.	Voiced aspirated	V{v}	C		
15.	Voiceless glottalised	C{c}	C		
16.	Voiceless glottalised uvular	C{c}	C		v
17.	Voiced aspirated uvular	V{v}	C		v

As shown, there is no need for a sequence analysis of types 11–13. All three 'click events' fit the range of possibilities for laryngeal specification of the accompaniments. We also note that the only phonation type that is missing is 'creaky' (V{c}). The cross-classification of phonation and manner can be expressed in the following table:

(48) Cross-classification of laryngeal and manner element structure:

Lar\Man	–	C;V	c	v
V	1	11	6	4
C	2	10	7	5

[38] Since there is a contrast between 7: voiceless nasal and 9: voiceless aspirated nasal, the voiceless nasal accompaniment has only the head C element for tense/voiceless.

Special structures 273

Lar\Man	–	C;V	c	v
V{v}	14	–	–	17
V{c}	–	–	–	–
C{v}	3	–	9	13
C{c}	15	–	8	12~16

We note that types 12 and 16 'compete' for the same slot. If we analysed 12 as a sequence (as suggested in LM), we should do the same for 13, which then creates a voiceless aspirated uvular. However, we should take note of the fact, as LM add (p. 271), the accompaniments in both rows 12 and 13

> are pronounced with more velar friction in other dialects of !Xóõ. Instead of the sequence of two ejectives kl'q' [...], there is a single ejective affricate with a less uvular quality, more appropriately transcribed as k!x'; and instead of the prevoiced version glq', there is a sequence that could be transcribed gk!x. These more affricated dialectal pronunciations correspond to the standard pronunciation in Zhul'hoasi.

I take this to mean that we can analyse types 12 and 13 as affricates (and without uvular). This leads to the following table:

(49) Cross-classification of laryngeal and manner element structure:

Lar\Man	–	C;V	c	v
V	1	11	6	4
C	2	10	7	5
V{v}	14	–	–	17
V{c}	–	–	–	–
C{v}	3	13	9	–
C{c}	15	12	8	16

These types occur for all places, except that bilabial and the lateral option lack the option of voiced aspirated uvular (see the table in (49)). This allows !Xóõ to have eighty-three different clicks.

LM (p. 274ff.) also discuss Zhul'hoasi, which is a dialect of !Xū, based on work by Snyman (1978) (see more references in LM), and data of their own. This language has a slightly smaller number of clicks than !Xoo, mainly because it does not have bilabial clicks, and no uvular accompaniments. The following table provides the RCVP encodings for this language:

(50) Zhul'hoasi (following LM p. 275, table 8.5):

	–	C;V	c	v
V	1	7	4	–
C	2	8	5	–
V{v}	10	–	–	–
V{c}	–	–	–	–
C{v}	3	11	12	–
C{c}	6	9	–	–

LM note a sequence that does not occur in !Xóõ, but does occur in Zhul'hoasi, namely a voiced velar nasal and voiceless aspirated velar nasal (no. 12 in their table 8.5, p. 275: ŋŋ!ʰ). I placed this type in the slot C{v} + c (nasal) in the table for Zhul'hoasi. However, !Xoo has ŋ!ʰ (type 9) which I analysed as the same category in (47)–(48).

LM then produce a table (p. 278, table 8.6) with *all* attested click types in Xhosa, Nama, !Xóõ, and Zhul'hoasi. In (51) I provide the RCVP interpretation of this table. LM's table 8.5 for Zhul'hoasi also shows /g!ᵡ/, which does not occur in their table 8.6. I have added /g!ᵡ/ here as (11b). LM say that they do not know of any language that contrasts the !Xóõ clicks g!kx (or g!x) with the typical Zhul'hoasi click g!ᵡ, adding that in Zhul'hoasi the comparable click is not always fricative (p.274). Nevertheless I have separated the [g!ᵡ] from [g!kx] (or [g!x]), simply because RCVP provides two separate representations corresponding to this phonetic difference. Hence in my table, there are separate slots for (11a) and (11b).

(51) Clicks and their accompaniments:[39]

1. g!	Voiced velar plosive	!Xóõ, Zhul'hoasi	V	
2. k!	Voiceless unaspirated velar plosive	all four	C	
3. k!ʰ	[Voiceless] Aspirated velar plosive	all four	Cv	
4. ŋ!	Voiced velar nasal	all four	V	c

---

[39] LM (p. 279) add the following points: types 12/13 and 19/20 are dialectal variants in !Xóõ. With respect to 14 and 15: 'There are no strong arguments for regarding these non-contrasting sounds as distinct at a phonetic classificatory level.' Types 10, 11, 13, 14, 19, 20 and 21 are taken to be sequences.
   With respect to 11a: see LM (p. 274), and note that both gk!ˣ (p. 278) and g!kˣ (p. 274) are used in LM. Here I take voiced + voiceless to be voiced aspirated. This click does not occur in LM table 8.5, which has g!ᵡ instead. On p. 274 LM say this is similar to !Xóõ g|kx (*sic*: this should be g!kx; see (11) in their table 8.12).
   With respect to 13: LM use both gk!ˣ' (pp. 278–9) and g!kˣ' (p. 275).

Special structures 275

5. g!	Breathy voiced velar plosive	Xhosa	Vv		
6. ŋ̈!	Breathy voiced velar nasal	Xhosa	Vv	c	
7. ŋ̥!ʰ	Voiceless aspirated velar nasal	Nama, !Xóõ, Zhul'hoasi	Cv	c	
8. k!ʔ	Voiceless velar plosive and glottal stop	Nama, !Xóõ, Zhul'hoasi	Cc		
9. k!ˣ	Voiceless affricated velar plosive	!Xóõ, Zhul'hoasi	C	C;V	
10. g!h	Voiced velar plosive followed by aspiration	!Xóõ, Zhul'hoasi	Vv		
11a. gk!ˣ or g!ˣ	Voiced velar plosive followed by voiceless velar fricative or affricate	!Xóõ, Zhul'hoasi	Vv	V C;V	
11b. g!ˠ	Voiced velar fricative	Zhul'hoasi	V	V	
12. k!ˣ'	Affricated velar ejective [voiceless]	Zhul'hoasi	Cc	C;V	
13. g!kˣ'	Voiced velar plosive followed by voiceless affricated ejective	Zhul'hoasi	Cv	C;V	
14. ŋŋ̥!ʰ	Voiced velar nasal followed by voiceless aspirated velar nasal	Zhul'hoasi	Cv	c	
15. ŋ̥!	Voiceless velar nasal	!Xóõ	C	c	
16. ʔŋ!	Preglottalised velar nasal	!Xóõ	Cc	c	
17. ɢ!	Voiced (optionally prenasalised) uvular plosive	!Xóõ	V		v
18. q!	Voiceless unaspirated uvular plosive	!Xóõ	C		v
19. k!'q'	Voiceless velar ejective, followed by uvular ejective	!Xóõ	Cc		v
20. g!q'	Voiced velar plosive, followed by uvular ejective	!Xóõ	Cv		v
21. ɢ!h	Voiced uvular plosive, followed by aspiration	!Xóõ	Vv		v

The encoding in (51) can be condensed as (52):

(52) Click accompaniments:

	–	C;V	c	v
V	1	11b:g!ˠ	4	17
C	2	9	15	18

276   Principles of Radical CV Phonology

	–	C;V	c	v
Vv	5/10	11a: gk!ˣ	6	21
Vc	–	–	–	–
Cv	3	13	7/14	20
Cc	8	12	16	19

In the two cases where two types from the list are placed in the same slot, these phonetic types do not occur within the same language, as can be seen in (51). I take it to be supportive of the RCVP approach that all combinations of laryngeal specification and manner specification are attested, with the exception of creaky voice/laryngealised phonation (which I take to be also 'implosive'). What is the phonetic reason for this gap? Here is what LM say on p. 297:

> Combinations using additional phonation types would be possible. We should also consider other airstream mechanisms that might be used. It is comparatively easy to produce a voiced velar implosive while producing a click. In fact, it is probably easier for most non-Khoisan phoneticians to say ɠ!a than it is to say g!q'a. But implosives never occur as click accompaniments.

We can now propose a detailed RCVP structure for clicks:

(53)

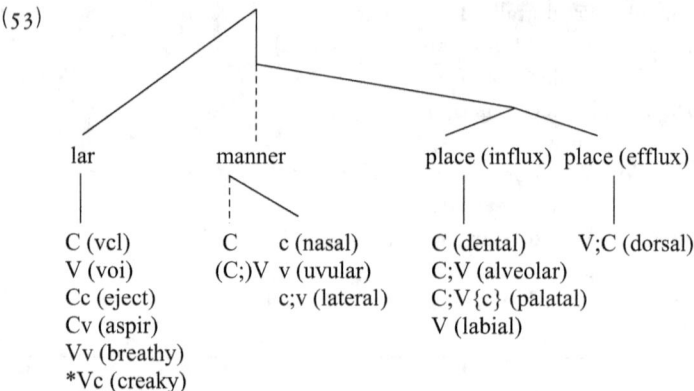

```
    lar           manner        place (influx)  place (efflux)
    |               |                |                |
  C (vcl)         C   c (nasal)   C (dental)      V;C (dorsal)
  V (voi)        (C;)V v (uvular) C;V (alveolar)
  Cc (eject)          c;v (lateral) C;V{c} (palatal)
  Cv (aspir)                        V (labial)
  Vv (breathy)
  *Vc (creaky)
```

The manner and laryngeal properties are implemented in the efflux, which is always dorsal (or uvular is there is a secondary manner {v}). In (53) I also included the secondary manner lateral, which LM include as a 'place' in their table 8.4 (here reproduced as (48)). Since lateral clicks can be uvular or nasal, we have to conclude that such click types have two secondary manner specifications.

Special structures

We must now ask whether we also need compound place structures for vowels. Below, in § 7.3.3.1, I will explore the use of such structures for representing so-called short diphthongs.

Another question is whether, if compound structures are allowed in the place class, such structures are also required in the manner and the laryngeal class. Turning to the manner class first, it would seem that compound combinations of sister manner structures for obstruents do not create results that produce viable phonetic events:

(54) C (stop) + C;V (affricate)
V (strident fricative) + V;C (non-strident fricative)

The first structure would essentially be an affricate, for which the structure {C;V} is sufficient (and simpler), while the second structure does not lead to a coherent phonetic event if a stridency contour simply cannot be realised phonetically.

Combining non-sister manners leads to yet another representation for affricates which we probably do not need, unless there is empirical evidence for distinguishing different kinds of affricates. We have already allowed for affricates to be 'phonetic' as realisation of palatal place, in addition to the {C;V} manner representation for obstruents.

(55) C (stop) + V (fricative)

Summarising, allowing compound structures for manner only leads to new possibilities for affricates, and also for strident fricatives:

(56) compounds with sister manner structures

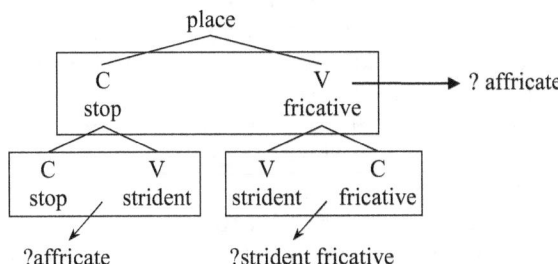

We must accept that the two additional representations for affricates are available, given the use of compound structures in place; the principle of structural analogy requires us to accept this. However, if indeed affricates can be represented in multiple ways, it seems reasonable to expect that languages will go for the simplest representation first, which would be {C;V}. If there is no empirical evidence for different structures being contrastively used, the most reasonable explanation is that the phonetic interpretations of these different structures is simply too close.[40] One possibility that could be explored is whether [s] + obstruent clusters, for which several phonologists have proposed complex structure status (see van de Weijer (1996)) or a status as 'reversed affricates' (see Ewen (1980b, 1986)) could qualify as structures with compound manners. I will not explore that option here, but it is worth considering.

Turning to the laryngeal class, it is unlikely that there will be a need to combine two head laryngeal options (tense and voiced) for obstruents, given that voicing does not even allow contours in obstruent clusters. Here too, then, this formal possibility is not exploited, due to the impossibility of assigning it a phonetic interpretation that the vocal cords can realise.

Whether compound structures are of any use for the laryngeal (i.e. tonal) specification of vowels is discussed in § 7.3.3.2 below.

In conclusion, compound structures (which involve an extension of the RCVP syntax) within the head classes provide an insightful perspective on MACs (including linguo-labial place) and clicks, when applied to the head place class for consonants. In all other classes, using this option leads to combinations of structures that are too close phonetically, although in some cases (short diphthongs and contour tones on short vowels), this option could be explored further; see §§ 7.3.3.1 and 7.3.3.2.

I would like to conclude this section with a speculative remark about compound place structures. It is tempting to regard clicks in particular as 'syllable-like' structures. The two places (coronal and dorsal) represent, as it were, both edges of a 'CVC' unit, with the very prominent click noise representing the saliency peak V. Within the RCVP approach, these click 'syllables' would be 'intra-segmental', that is, occurring within the segment that we call a click. As I will show in Chapter 10, where I propose an RCVP structure for signs (in sign languages), the notion of intra-segmental syllable is also recruited there. There is no paradox in allowing intra-segmental syllables on the argument that sequential structure is the hallmark of syllable structure. To speculate even more, given the widely recognised 'ancient' nature of click languages (see Sands & Güldemann (2009); Huybregts (2017)), as possibly representing the earliest forms of human language, it is perhaps possible to think of clicks as having been syllables in their own right at first, only to be later incorporated into another sequential CV(C) structure that we normally think of when discussing syllable structure. This way of looking at clicks

---

[40] To make matters worse, yet another representation would become available if we allowed 'double-root' structures; see § 7.3.4.

suggests a compromise between the segmental analysis advanced here and the idea that clicks can be reduced to sequences of consonants (see Bradfield (2014) for a recent defence of this approach).

7.3.3 Complex vowels

In this section, I (very) briefly deal with 'complexity' in vowels. Here I refer to place complexity (as in (short) diphthongs, § 7.3.3.1), tonal complexity (as in contour tones on short vowels, § 7.3.3.2) and vowels with special phonation (§ 7.3.3.3) or manner of articulation types (§ 7.3.3.4).

7.3.3.1 Short diphthongs

As proposed in § 4.5, diphthongs are branching VC rhymes, but what, then, are so-called short diphthongs? These segments have created some controversy in the analysis of some languages, such as Old English (see e.g. Bauer (1956); Hogg (1992); White (2016)). It is possible in RCVP to represent short diphthongs as having two place specifications (analogous to two-place consonants, discussed in the previous section) if indeed such vowels can occur contrastively with other short vowels and with ordinary diphthongs. In some languages, such as Modern Icelandic, Fijian and Sami, short diphthongs are said to exist, but it is questionable if there is a phonemic short/long contrast in these cases, which means that such vowels could be analysed as occupying two rhymal positions. One language that stands out as a clear case of having contrastive long and short diphthongs is Thai (see Abramson & Rent (1990); Tingsabadh & Abramson (1993)). I will leave the proper representation of short diphthongs for further, future exploration, suggesting the compound place analysis as a possibility.

7.3.3.2 Vowels with contour tones

Recall that RCVP assumes that phonation and tone are, by and large, 'in complementary distribution', the former occurring in the onset head and the latter in the rhymal head. As proposed in § 6.3, the secondary tonal specification represents the notion of 'register' as occurring lexically in Asian tone languages, which can have up to four contrastive tones in both registers. I proposed that in these languages contour tones are unitary contour tones where {C;V} and {V;C}, as head laryngeal structures, refer to rising and falling tones rather than intermediate level tones. I have suggested that the register split forces a linear interpretation of the combined tonal element in the head class. The contrastive, lexical use of register is a property of Asian tone languages. African languages can use register post-lexically in processes such as downstep and downdrift.

In Chapter 6, a distinction was made between contour tones resulting from associating two tones with a tone-bearing unit (typical of African tone languages and called tone clusters) and so-called 'unitary contour tones' (typical of Asian tone languages). The latter were represented as combinations of the primary elements C and V in register languages. If compound tones are to be recruited, they could provide an account of contour tones on short vowels in African languages.[41]

7.3.3.3 Vowels with special phonation
As sonorants, vowels are usually voiced. In this case, voicing is simply implied by these segments being sonorants and no laryngeal specification of voicing is required. If the laryngeal node for vowels provides tonal structures, specification of voicing is not even possible. Voicelessness in vowels is thus predicted to be allophonic, for instance as in Modern Standard Japanese, which devoices high vowels between voiceless consonants and word-finally after voiceless consonants (see e.g. contributions to van de Weijer, Nanjo & Nishihara (2005) and references cited there). However, voiceless vowels are argued to occur contrastively in Turkana (Dimmendaal (1983); Gordon (1998)). Vowels can also have breathy or creaky voice contrastively (MD p. 132ff.).[42] It would seem that such cases would require a phonation interpretation of their laryngeal elements, which, then, would exclude tonal interpretations. However, in some cases, it appears that such vowels can have (contrastive) tonal properties as well. In § 6.4.3 I have discussed cases of this type, showing that the phonation distinctions can be analysed as phonetic realisations of register distinctions.

7.3.3.4 Vowels with special manner
A final type of complexity occurs in vowels that have 'consonantal aspects' of articulation, which were analysed at some length in § 4.3.1.2 as secondary manner elements. Qualifying as such are nasalised vowels (secondary c), pharyngealised vowels (secondary v) and a class of manners including retroflex or rhotacised vowels and fricative, strident and sphincteric vowels, which I took to be phonetic realisations of the intermediate secondary manner cv.

---

[41] I note here that Duanmu (1990, 1994) claims that contour tones (in all languages) always occur with long vowels, although this necessitates also postulating long vowels when no short/long contrast is present.

[42] MD (p. 132ff.) also mentions 'pharyngealisation' on vowels, which lends some support to the idea that pharyngealisation is different from place of articulation (see above).

7.3.4 Branching syllabic constituents or 'two-root structures'

Since RCVP allows branching onsets (and branching rhymes), this model accepts the traditional view on the structure of prevocalic (and tautosyllabic) [kl], [br] and so on in languages such as English as branching onsets. In some approaches, branching onsets (or any branching syllabic units) are banned.[43]

Another theoretical possibility that could be explored is whether certain complex events can be analysed as *two-root structures*. This theoretical option is explored by van de Weijer (1996), where it is suggested that clicks have two independent root nodes. While we do not, perhaps, need this option for clicks (for which we have suggested compound place structures of non-sister places), van de Weijer points out that multi-root representations may also be useful in other cases. For example, nasalisation on vowels may have a different status in different languages; van de Weijer refers to Polish (Rowicka & van de Weijer (1992)), where nasalisation may involve a two-root structure resulting from *compression* of independent segments (possibly as an intermediate step between oral vowels + nasal consonant and fully nasal vowels). While perhaps no language will distinguish two types of nasal vowels (but see Ladefoged (1971: 35) for a possible case in point), it may be 'realistic' to allow representations that reflect different degrees of intimacy between the vowel and the nasal element. What this would mean is that although being contrastive in a single language is the main criterion for proposing structure, it need not be the only criterion if we wish to represent 'transitional' stages.

Another conceivable use of double-root structure could lie in providing an account for 'improper' onsets such as [pt] (if not analysable as a compound structure with two non-sister places) or, for that matter, initial 'onsets' such as Dutch [kn] or [xn], or any instance of onsets that cannot occur word-medially, including all [s+C] clusters and complex and contour segments for which we have already proposed formal structures. If thus used, we could perhaps do away with initial adjunction, as discussed in § 7.2.1.2. I will leave the exploration of the potential use of double-root segments, which seems like a very powerful formal device, for another occasion, assuming for the moment that no appeal needs to be made to this option within the current RCVP model.

---

[43] Lowenstamm's strict CV approach outlaws all branching units, allowing CV as the only syllable structure (Lowenstamm (1996)). Alleged branching onsets are analysed either as two onsets with an intervening empty nucleus or as complex segments, which could be analysed as /p^r/. Duanmu (2011), who suggests CVX is the universal syllable structure, proposes analysing all alleged branching onsets as complex segments.

7.4 Summary and concluding remarks

In this chapter, I have considered two types of special structures, namely ones that miss certain class nodes (which, in fact, had been encountered in preceding chapters) and ones that seem to call for extra structures. I considered the potential use of empty segments, remaining sceptical that such entities are required. Turning to segment types that seem to require extra complexity, I proposed using compound structures, which combine the two options for the primary C/V split, finding the strongest motivation for this option in coronal clicks and multiply-articulated segments. Finally, an option of two-root segments was considered, which may be useful as a half-way house between branching syllabic constituents and compound structures.

8

Predictability and preference

8.1 Introduction

The discussion in this chapter will be framed by the following issues and questions:

- Predictability of elements: are some element specifications of segments predicted to be unmarked based on the C/V nature of syllabic positions? (§ 8.2)
- Preference of occurrence (lexical or token frequency): does RCVP predict preference ranking of segment types, with reference to position in the syllable? (§ 8.3)
- Preferred segmental systems (system typology, type frequency): does RCVP predict the shape of preferred phoneme systems? (§ 8.4)

Throughout the preceding chapters, I have occasionally indicated how RCVP addresses some of these questions, but in this chapter I will offer a systematic account.

In § 8.2, I will show how RCVP embodies a notion of bias (which I will also call paradigmatic harmony), meaning that syllabic positions favour elements in primary classes and to some extent also in the secondary classes that are identical to, or 'harmonic' with, the labelling of the syllabic position; for example, the syllabic C position (the edge) favours primary C elements in the manner, place and laryngeal classes. In § 8.3, I take this issue one step further and ask whether RCVP, given an inventory of segments in some language, predicts a preference ranking of these segments for each syllabic position. This question, which concerns token frequency, is usually addressed by focusing on lexical frequency in general, but I will explore the polysystematic route and discuss preferences of segment types for each syllabic position. In § 8.4, I show how bias can also be a predictor for the preferred structure of segmental inventories of a certain size, given the additional principle of economy ('fewest elements'). While it is common to account for system preference with respect to the segment inventory as a whole, given the notion of polysystematicity, one should actually address inventories separately for different phonotactic positions. However, since the available typological information on inventories reports data on inventories as a whole, I will not develop a polysystematic account of segment inventories, save for a few remarks. On the whole, this chapter has a rather programmatic character in that it will lay out predictions without reporting extensive support for each. I take this to be a task for future work.

8.2 Harmony

8.2.1 *Paradigmatic and cross-class harmony*

I will start by restating some basic properties of RCVP. Classes maximally allow a four-way contrast:

(1) C C;V V;C V

These options result from a two-way split of a particular phonetic space:

(2)

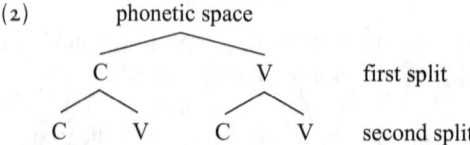

               first split

 C V C V   second split

The first split produces two opposed categories that can be characterised with a single element: C or V. For example, in the head manner class for onset heads (which is reserved for obstruents), this split would produce stops and fricatives. A second split creates two additional (sub)categories. For example, a second split of the C category delivers plain stops, C, and 'fricative stops' (i.e. affricates), C;V.

It is important to note once more that this two-way splitting diagram is *not*, as such, part of the representation of the segmental structure. It merely depicts how the Opponent Principle *recursively* delivers four potentially distinctive phonological categories, which are formally represented as a single C or V or as combinations of these two elements, with a dependency relation imposed, as in (1). While two categories in a four-way split are thus represented with a simple occurrence of C or V, the figure in (2) might suggest that these 'simple' categories seem to contain a copy of themselves as a dependent:

(3) C;C C;V V;C V;V

The syntax of RCVP does not, however, allow (by stipulation, encoded in (5) below) a contrast between X and X;X. In other words, the six-way contrast in (4) is not permitted: within each class each element can occur only once. For this reason, the dependent 'copy' can remain unspecified, as in (1).

(4)   C   C;C   C;V   V;C   V;V   V

In § 3.2.1 I considered the position that the apparently identical dependent element in X;X, which we regard as simply X, might be said to be predictable, perhaps to be specified at some point in the phonology, which would of course break with the constraint that only one element can occur in each (sub)class. If we assume that the dependent specification is never actually specified, this predicts that the stridency of strident fricatives cannot be referred to in the phonology, but it also says that we cannot make reference to the class of strident obstruents (affricates and strident fricatives). This is contradicted by the allomorphy of the English plural suffix, which is [əz] after strident obstruents (*bush-es*, *match-es*, *kiss-es* vs. *roof-s*, *moth-s*). We might thus be forced to conclude that dependent copies *can* be referred to in the phonology, assuming that the alternations in the plural suffix are handled in the grammatical phonology. As proposed in van der Hulst (2018), there might be a necessity to refer to predictable elements 'at the word level', where predictable elements *can* become active.

Another reason to specify predictable elements could be that they have to be referred to by the phonetic implementation. The manner specification V means fricative, but more than that: it means strident fricative. If stridency is the interpretation of dependent V, then it would seem that the predictable dependent V element has to be added before phonetic implementation can take place. There is, however, a different perspective on the non-contrastivity of the structures X and X;X, which is to say that the phonetic interpretation of an element as a dependent is subsumed under the phonetic interpretation of the head occurrence of this element, unless a dependent to the contrary is specified. This idea is expressed in KLV85 by designating the dependent interpretation as one of the features that characterises the head interpretation. Backley (2011) also assumes this inclusiveness of phonetic interpretation. In this case, one might say that it follows that the representations X and X;X cannot be contrastive, since they have the same phonetic interpretation. This perspective is compatible with the idea that the redundant copies can be active in the word-level phonology.

To formally encode the non-contrastivity of X and X;X I postulate the following constraint, or redundancy rule, which applies obligatorily within every element class:

(5) Universal Harmony Rule (UHR):

  X(head) ⇒ X(dependent)   (within each head class)

Effectively, (5) encodes the constraint that an element can be contrastively used only once in each (sub)class. The various instances of the UHR are spelled out in (6) in two steps:

(6) a. Universal harmony rules (general):

  C ⇒ C;C
  V ⇒ V;V

  b. Harmony rules for each element class:

  Edge manner:
  C (obs) ⇒ C;C (stop; non-strident)
  V (fric) ⇒ V;V (fricative; strident)

  Edge place:
  C (coronal) ⇒ C;C (coronal; dental)
  V (peripheral) ⇒ V;V (peripheral; labial)

  Edge laryngeal:[1]
  C (tense) ⇒ C;C (tense; tense)
  V (voiced) ⇒ V;V (voiced; voiced)

  Nucleus manner:
  C (high) ⇒ C;C (high; high-mid)
  V (low) ⇒ V;V (low; low-mid)

  Nucleus place:
  C (front) ⇒ C;C (front; spread)
  V (back) ⇒ V;V (round; back)

  Nucleus laryngeal:
  C (high reg) ⇒ C;C (high tone; high-mid)
  V (low reg) ⇒ V;V (low tone; low-mid)

We also find this rule in the bridge and coda position:

(7) Bridge/Coda Manner:

  C (non-continuant) ⇒ C;C (nasal; non-continuant)
  V (continuant) ⇒ V;V (glide; continuant)

---

[1] This case is not relevant since I have argued (Chapter 6) that the laryngeal head class for consonants does not allow combinations, so there is no separate interpretation for dependent occurrence of laryngeal C and V.

Given the predictability of the identical dependent, single elements – that is, plain C and V – are literally the unmarked category. For example, consonant manner C (a plain stop) is unmarked in comparison to C;V (a strident stop, i.e. an affricate). Here, the notion of markedness thus corresponds directly to complexity; the relationship between complexity and markedness is further discussed in § 9.5.

I will now suggest that the relevance of the UHR as a rule of preference rather than as an obligatory rule extends to specifying a number of other paradigmatic relationships. I will first clarify the kinds of relationships that can be explored and then discuss them one by one.

As a point a departure, I repeat the full 'geometry' of elements in the model:[2]

(8) The 'geometry' of elements in RCVP

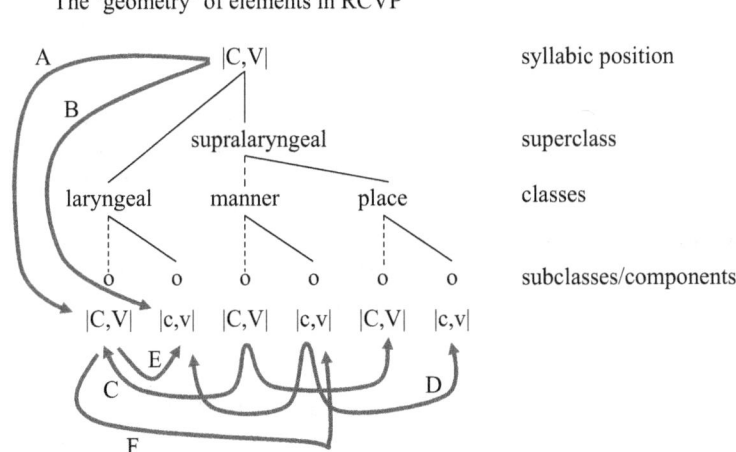

I will describe each relationship in turn:

A and B: paradigmatic harmony:

A. This is a relation between the C/V encoding of the syllabic position and the element choice in the head class of each element class.
B. This is a relation between the C/V encoding of the syllabic position and the element choice in the dependent class of each element class.

---

[2] This geometry deviates somewhat from the one adopted in AE and bears a close resemblance to the original geometry that was proposed in Clements (1985). In Chapter 11 this model is compared to other models with which it shares certain properties.
  In § 3.2.3 I discuss the question as to whether we need a separate C/V characterisation for major class distinctions. For the moment I will assume that these distinctions are encoded in terms of the syllabic structure.

C–F: cross-class harmony:

C. This is a relation between the element choices in the different head classes.
D. This is a relation between the element choices in the different dependent classes.
E. This is a relation between the element choices in the head class and the dependent class within each element class.
F. This is a relation between head elements in one class and secondary elements in another class.

All these relationships are called 'harmony relationship' because the expectation is that in each case the unmarked relationship is one of identity:

(9) X ⇒ X

Rule (5) is a specific instance of this general 'identity' rule, which has the status of an obligatory rule (to achieve the exclusion of a contrast between X and X;X within head classes). In all relationships A–D, the rule in (9) is not an obligatory rule, but rather a rule that expresses what is the preferred, unmarked correlation.

I will discuss these various relationships, with the proviso that for each paradigmatic relationship I will discuss the interaction with one of the cross-harmony relations. For example, we will quickly see that correlations A and C interact.

As indicated in (8), I assume that the correlations are unidirectional, meaning that paradigmatic harmony is top-down, whereas the cross-class harmonies go from heads to dependents. Another point of interest is that the correlations predict not only the unmarked choice in cases of contrast, but also which choice obtains in cases of no contrast.

Correlation A: between the C/V encoding of the syllabic position and the element choice in the head class of each element class

As per correlation A, we predict the following unmarked (or 'preferred') element choices in each head class. Note that 'unmarked' here does not mean that the other element choices are not permitted; whether they are or are not depends on whether a specific language has a contrast between the two choices. In (10) I provide the preferred element head choices for the edge and the nucleus:[3]

---

[3] I will discuss the bridge and coda preferences for the element choices separately later in this section. Recall that, with exceptions, these syllabic positions only need manner head elements.

(10) A. Syllabic position ⇒ manner, location, laryngeal head element:

  a. Edge C   ⇒ manner C (stop)
  b. Edge C   ⇒ place C (coronal)
  c. Edge C   ⇒ laryngeal C (tense)
  d. Nucleus V ⇒ manner V (low)
  e. Nucleus V ⇒ place V (round)
  f. Nucleus V ⇒ laryngeal (low tone)

Clearly, there is harmony between the preferred categorical specification of the syllabic head positions and the manner elements. Another 'verbal' way of stating the predictions in (10) is given in (11):

(11) a. Obstruents prefer to be stops over fricatives.
  b. Obstruents prefer to be coronal over peripheral (labial, dorsal).
  c. Obstruents prefer to be tense (voiceless) over voiced.
  d. Vowels prefer to be low over high.
  e. Vowels prefer to be round over front.
  f. Vowels prefer to be low toned over high toned.

As for the syllabic head position, there is general consensus that the preferred onset head consonant is a voiceless, coronal stop [t] (Paradis & Prunet 1991). In this case, the unmarked element choice for all three head classes is C.

For the nucleus position, harmony for all elements predicts a low-toned, rounded low vowel. Let us first look at the correlation between vowel height (or vowel quality in general, including colour) and tone. A correlation is expected to exist given that low vowels have an intrinsically lower pitch than high vowels; see Lehiste (1970) and Whalen & Levitt (1995). However, as reported in Köhnlein & van Oostendorp (2017), such a correlation has in fact been denied (Hombert (1977, 1978); Hombert, Ohala & Ewan (1979)).[4] Nevertheless, Becker & Jurgec (2017) discuss a correlation between low tone and high vowels in Franconian dialects. An explanation for such an unexpected correlation might be that precisely because of the intrinsic correlation between vowel height and pitch, a high tone on a low vowel, as well as a low tone on a high vowel, is perceptually more salient. However, in view of the scarcity of information, I will refrain from discussing correlations between tone and vowel quality.

As for the correlation between low vowels and rounding, we should note that low vowels actually 'do not like' to be rounded, given that the

---

[4] Köhnlein & van Oostendorp (2017) also note that low(er) vowels are more prone to attract stress, whereas high tone also attracts stress. Yet low vowels intrinsically correlate with lower pitch.

height degree of aperture prevents clear lip rounding (as observed in Kaun (1995, 2004) on rounding harmony and vowel height; see also van der Hulst (2018: § 5.3.3)). This would be an example of a phonetic factor overriding a prediction that follows from correlation A. The resistance of low vowels to rounding is part of a broader phenomenon whereby the lowest vowel resists *both* colour elements, due to the fact that the open jaw position blocks lip rounding as well as the tongue advancement that is needed for front vowels.

The dispreference of low vowels both for low tone (if genuine) and for rounding illustrates the fact that the predictions that can be derived from the RCVP systems are not claimed to be the only factors that play a role in preference choices.[5] Apart from the fact that, as we will see, different correlations may make contradictory predictions, we also have to reckon with purely phonetic factors that may have the upper hand, such as in the resistance of low vowels to being rounded.

At this point the reader may wonder whether the RCVP system makes predictions about the preferred height of mid vowels, in case there is just one such series, being high-mid [e] and [o] or low-mid [ɛ] and [ɔ]. KLV85 suggest that [e] and [o] are preferred over [ɛ] and [ɔ], and the overview in Hitch (2017) also refers to five-vowel systems with intermediate [e] and [o] as the most common systems, although this may just be a transcription preference in the sources.

Given that correlations predict not only the unmarked choice in cases of contrast, but also the choice when there is no contrast, correlation A predicts a preference for V;C, that is, low-mid vowels, because of the headedness of V being preferred in the syllabic V position. Five-vowel systems with low-mid vowels are certainly not uncommon, but I do not have the evidence for deciding whether low-mid vowels are more frequent than high-mid vowels.

Correlation C: *between the element choices in the different head classes*

As just stated, the preference for coronal and voiceless can be understood in two different ways. As captured in (10), each class independently prefers the C element in a C-syllabic position. However, as per correlation C, we predict that element choices in the different head classes harmonise. This means that we expect C manner to harmonise with C place and C laryngeal, and likewise for V manner, V place and

---

[5] One might object that the potential preference of high tone for low vowel (and vice versa) could also be applied to the resistance of low vowels to rounding, making the point that rounding on such vowels would then be more salient. I think the two situations are not quite parallel, assuming that there is no phonetic conflict between vowel height and tonal choice, as there is with vowel height and rounding.

V laryngeal. However, this cross-class harmony also follows from paradigmatic harmony since C syllabic will prefer C manner, C place and C laryngeal, and likewise for V syllabic. Whether cross-harmony plays an independent role can be established if a non-harmonic manner occurs in a syllabic position. Let us suppose that a fricative (manner V) occurs in the syllabic head position. In this case, we can ask which place and laryngeal elements are most preferred. If the preferred place and laryngeal element harmonise with the syllabic C position (as per correlation A), we predict that [s] is preferred, having a C place (coronal) and a C laryngeal (voiceless). However, if cross-class harmony (i.e. correlation C) prevails, we expect that a fricative which has V manner would prefer to also have V place (labiodental) and V laryngeal (voiced). This points to [v] as the preferred fricative.

It seems clear that the evidence points to the fricative [s] being preferred over [v], which suggest that paradigmatic harmony prevails (correlation A) over cross-class harmony (correlation C). I will assume that this ranking is universal.[6]

We can then also ask what the preferences are in cases where the manner in onset head position is of an intermediate nature (C;V or V;C), which would also deviate from the unmarked correlation A. Given the scarcity of mellow fricatives, I will not pursue this issue for this manner. As for the affricate obstruent (C;V), in this case cross-class harmony would predict the same structure C;V for place, which would be a posterior coronal.[7] In this case bias and cross-class harmony are not in conflict and it would seem that cross-class harmony has an independent effect, since affricates are likely to be posterior coronals (i.e. palatals or palato-alveolars).

To investigate the role of cross-class harmony for the nuclear position, the non-harmonic choice for vowel manner (as per correlation A) would be C (high vowel), which predicts that high vowels are likely to be front (place: C) and have high tone (laryngeal: C). I have already addressed the reverse correlation between vowel height and tonal height. This leaves us with asking whether high vowels are more likely to be front than back.

If cross-class harmony prevails, the preferred high vowel (manner C) is predicted to be front [i] (place C). If, on the other hand, syllabic bias prevails, we predict the high vowel to be preferably labial [u] (place V). If [i] is more preferred, this means that the unmarked V choice (round) is never shown to be correct because we have just seen that, albeit for phonetic reasons, it does not hold for low vowels either. Potential evidence

---

[6] While I accept ranking as a legitimate theoretical device, I try to stay away from OT-style language-specific ranking, which lowers the predictive capabilities of any theory to below zero.

[7] There is no C;V option for laryngeal, which does not have C/V combinations.

for a preference for high vowels that are front can come from vertical vowel systems that only use vowel height contrastively. Which vowel acts as the high vowel is often unclear because, as in Kabardian, the high vowel will take on the colour properties of surrounding consonants (see Wood (1991)). Hockett (1955: 85) reports vertical systems with a high vowel for Adyge and possibly for Abkhaz and Ubykh, which have a high central vowel, thus showing no colour preference. A recent typological study of vowel systems is Hitch (2017), who reports Kabardian as having a non-low central vowel and a low vowel, and Margi as having a high central vowel and a low vowel. He also refers to the Australian languages Enindhilyagwa~Anindilyakwa and Kaytetye~Kaititj, again with a high central vowel. The same situation applies to Marshallese. He only mentions Wichita as having a front high vowel, although this language may actually have a vertical three-height system, with the front vowels [i] and [e]. Other three-height systems would appear to have central vowels.

Another type of evidence might come from epenthetic vowels. However, in this case one would not expect such a vowel to be the optimal vowel; rather, one would expect an epenthetic vowel to adopt the less salient choice.

In conclusion, it is not clear on empirical grounds whether high vowels prefer to be front rather than back (and round). Correlation A predicts round, while correlation C predicts front. If this conflict is resolved by ranking A over C (as we established for the onset head), we expect the preference to be round.

We can also consider what we expect on phonetic grounds. A phonetic expectation for high vowels to prefer fronting is that they are necessarily produced by advancing the TR (see Wood (1979, 1982)). This suggests an immediate phonetic relation between high vowel position and fronting, which is predicted by cross-class harmony, even though paradigmatic harmony prefers round vowels (as shown in (10e)), which would agree with correlation C. I will leave the ranking of A and C for vowels unresolved.[8]

As in the discussion of consonantal manner references, once the manner choice is the one that is not preferred (i.e. V in the edge for fricatives and C in the nucleus for high vowels), there is conflict between paradigmatic harmony (which prefers C and V place and laryngeal elements, respectively) and cross-class harmony (which prefers V and C place and laryngeal elements, respectively). For consonantal manner we have seen that in that case paradigmatic harmony prevails (given the

---

[8] Of course, accepting C>A would make the ranking distinct from that in the onset. This could still be a universal ranking, given that ranking can be dependent on the syllabic position.

preference for voiceless, coronal fricatives). In the case of vowels, accepting that there are perhaps no clear preferences for tonal properties, it is not clear which of the two harmonies prevails for high vowels.

One might now also ask whether preferences can be detected for vowels of intermediate height, again leaving tone aside. I am not aware of evidence for any preference based on cross-harmony correlations; that is, it does not seem warranted to say that low-mid (V;C) prefers to be central-rounded ('inrounded'; V;C) and high-mid (C;V) prefers to be front-rounded ('outrounded'; C;V). However, if harmony is paradigmatic, we would predict all vowels of intermediate height to prefer rounding. A third possibility is that preference is only based on the head element of the intermediate height. In that case low-mid vowels would favour rounding (due to manner V being the head) while high-mid vowels would favour fronting (due to manner C being the head):

(12)   a.   Low-mid vowels: [ɔ] > [ɛ]
       b.   High-mid vowels: [ɛ] > [ɔ]

I am not aware of typological generalisations concerning vowel systems that would support the preference rankings in (12). If supporting evidence can be found it would suggest that for the nucleus, correlation A ranks over correlation C.

In conclusion, while paradigmatic harmony makes the correct prediction regarding unmarked manners, the independence of cross-class harmony can be examined when we consider cases in which marked manners are chosen. Here, for obstruents, correlation A makes the right prediction for place and laryngeal properties ([s] > [v]), while the situation for vowels is unclear, due to lack of typological information.

It is important to stress that it is a virtue of the RCVP model that it makes all these very specific predictions which are, in principle, testable, given sufficient typological resources. While such testing may actually be possible given the available resources, I am here deferring rigorous testing to future work.

Correlation B: *between the C/V encoding of the syllabic position and the element choice in the dependent class of each element class*

We will now ask whether preferences can be detected for secondary elements, based on paradigmatic harmony. To be clear, paradigmatic harmony does not predict that the presence of harmonising secondary properties is preferred over the absence of such properties. Secondary specifications contribute to complexity and thus markedness, which implies that plain place specifications are always preferred. Let me spell out what the predictions are:

(13) In onset head position (C):

    a. Obstruents prefer nasalisation (c) over pharyngealisation (v).
    b. Obstruents prefer palatalisation (c) over labialisation (v).
    c. Obstruents prefer glottalisation (c) over aspiration (v).

In rhyme head position (V):

    d. Vowels prefer pharyngealisation (v) over nasalisation (c).
    e. [For secondary place there is no secondary v element.]
    f. Vowels prefer to be low register (v) over high register (c).

MD's survey supports the preference for prenasalised obstruents and palatalised secondary articulations, which confirms (13a) and (13b). As for phonation preference, a preference for glottalised phonation may exist. The UPSID database does not clearly support prediction (13c), but does not contradict it either.

One might of course ask whether the predictions in (13a)–(13c) are more obvious for stops than for fricatives. If so, this would be due to correlation E, which we discuss below. I will suggest that in fact E outranks B, which means that the predictions for fricatives would indeed run in the other direction.

Turning to predictions (13d)–(13f), it would seem that (13d) is not correct: nasalisation on vowels strikes me as more common than pharyngealisation, but this depends on the analysis of vowel systems that have a TR distinction. If such a distinction were marked with the secondary property pharyngealisation, the balance could shift to supporting (13d). However, van der Hulst (2018) opts for analysing the majority of TR systems in terms of TR advancement being dominant.

With respect to (13f) I do not have evidence that goes one way or the other.

Correlation D: *between the element choices in the different dependent classes*

I do not expect that correlation D is testable given the unlikelihood that one segment has multiple secondary specifications. If such events were not unlikely, correlation D would lead us to expect that nasalisation (c) would correlate with palatalisation (c) and glottalisation (c) for stops (C), and that pharyngealisation (v) would correlate with labialisation (v) and aspiration (v) for fricatives (V).

For high vowels (C), we expect nasalisation (c) to correlate with ATR (c) and high register (c), while for lower vowels (V) we expect correlations between RTR (v) and low register (v). (Recall that we did not find a use for secondary v in the place class.)

Apart from the difficulty of testing these predictions due to the unlikely co-occurrence of secondary specifications, we have to reckon with the fact that secondary specifications are also predicted by correlation B, which would favour, for example, palatalisation correlating with nasalisation and glottalisation for the onset head, and pharyngealisation (v) with low register (v) for the rhyme head, which contradicts correlation D for fricatives and high vowels. Even more importantly, we also have to consider the role of correlation E, which, unlike B and D, favours a 'local' harmony between the primary and the secondary element, due to which it is likely to outrank both.

Correlation E: *between the element choices in the head class and the dependent class within each element class*

According to this correlation, secondary specifications would prefer to harmonise with the primary specification *within* each class:

(14) Harmony rules for head and dependent elements:

Onset head position:

a. *Edge manner: primary element C (stop)* ⇒ secondary element c (nasal)
b. *Edge manner: primary element V (cont.)* ⇒ secondary element v (phar.)
c. *Edge lar: primary element C (tense)* ⇒ secondary element c (glottal)
d. *Edge lar: primary element V (voiced)* ⇒ secondary element v (asp.)
e. *Edge place: primary element C (coronal)* ⇒ secondary element c (palatal)
f. *Edge place: primary element V (labial)* ⇒ secondary element v (labial)

Rhyme head position:

g. *Nucleus manner: primary element V (low)* ⇒ secondary element v (RTR)
h. *Nucleus manner: primary element C (high)* ⇒ secondary element c (nasal)
i. *Nucleus lar: primary element V (L)* ⇒ secondary element v (l reg.)
j. *Nucleus lar: primary element C (H)* ⇒ secondary element c (h reg.)
k. *Nucleus place: primary element V* ⇒ [none identified]
l. *Nucleus place: primary element C* ⇒ secondary element (ATR)

The prediction of correlation E can be verbally stated as follows:

(15) Onset head position:

    a. Stops prefer nasalisation over pharyngealisation.
    b. *Fricatives prefer pharyngealisation over nasalisation.*
    c. Tense (voiceless) obstruents prefer glottalisation over aspiration.
    d. *Voiced obstruents prefer aspiration over glottalisation.*
    e. Coronal obstruents prefer palatalisation over labialisation.
    f. *Peripheral (labial, dorsal) obstruents prefer labialisation over palatalisation.*

Rhyme head position:

    g. Low vowels prefer RTR over nasalisation.
    h. *High vowels prefer nasalisation over RTR.*
    i. Low tone prefers low register over high register.
    j. *High tone prefers high register over low register.*
    k. [not applicable]
    l. *Front vowels prefer ATR.*

The expected elements for the cases where the primary element harmonises with the syllabic position are precisely those that are based on correlation B. The independence of correlation E comes into play when the primary element is disharmonic with the syllabic position. These are the correlations that are italicised in (14) and (15). It is not clear that all the italicised correlations can be confirmed. All of them are of course in conflict with correlation B, and there is also a potential conflict with correlation D (which however, was deemed insignificant).

While several of these predictions need to be tested against typological surveys, none of them seems outrageous to me. In fact, most of them seem quite plausible.

A further elaboration could consider preference when the primary specification is an intermediate choice such as C;V or V;C. I will illustrate this with the example of vowel height. We can ask whether mid vowels have preferences for either place or laryngeal properties. Again leaving laryngeal/tonal correlations aside, and assuming that only the head element is relevant here, we predict that high-mid front vowels have a preference for ATR, whereas back vowels would have no such preference.

Correlation F: *between head elements in one class and secondary elements in another class*

I will only address the correlation for consonants, first considering a possible harmonic relation between the head manner choice and the dependent laryngeal and place choices:

(16) Head manner ⇒ laryngeal, place dependent:

    a. Manner C (stop) ⇒ laryngeal c (constricted)
    b. *Manner V (fric)* ⇒ *laryngeal v (aspirated)*

    c. Manner C (stop) ⇒ place c (palatalised)
    d. *Manner V (fric)* ⇒ *place v (labialised)*

Again, we first have to note that the independent role of correlation F can only be seen in the cases that are italicised, since in the other two cases the correlation also follows from correlation B.

Nevertheless, I point to evidence for both (16a) and (16b):

(17)   a. Stops reduce to glottal stops in syllable 'final' position (Harris (1990, 1994)).
      b. Fricatives have been claimed to be redundantly aspirated (Vaux & Samuels (2005)).[9]

The cross-class harmonies involving secondary place elements are less clear. While stops are more likely to be palatalised than labialised (as per correlation B), it is not obvious that the reverse holds for fricatives (which would then mean that correlation B prevails over correlation F).

In conclusion, we have discussed five instances of harmony:

(18) Harmony rules:

    A. Syllabic position ⇒ manner, location, laryngeal head element
    B. Syllabic position ⇒ manner, location, laryngeal dependent element
    C. Head elements ⇒ head elements (across classes)
    D. Dependent elements ⇒ dependent elements (across classes)
    E. Head elements ⇒ dependent elements (within the class)
    F. Head elements ⇒ dependent elements (across classes)

As shown, the harmony rules make a host of predictions, which in some cases are contradictory. When contradictions arise, I would expect that in all cases a universal ranking can be applied. Needless to say, the proposals made here, while having initial plausibility, need more rigorous testing. The merit of RCVP is that it makes predictions that can be now tested, using typological resources. But there is work to be done here.

An important part of this work is to establish the ranking where correlations make contradictory predictions. I have not explored this

---

[9] In § 6.4.2 I have questioned the validity of this correlation.

systematically, but throughout the preceding discussion, I have suggested rankings of the following kind:

(19) [A >> C] >> [E >> B, D, F]

Both correlations in the first group regard the predictability of head specifications, and here it would seem that the top-down paradigmatic correlation is stronger than the correlations across classes. All correlations in the second group regard dependent specifications, and here the most local one, E, seems stronger than the other three, with D and F probably being of little significance.

The discussion thus far has only talked about preferences in syllabic head positions, that is, obstruents and vowels. Typically, consonantal systems will also contain sonorant consonants (glides, liquids, nasals). Sonorant consonants can occur in all four syllabic positions. In (20a) and (20b) I include the bridge and coda position, but sonorants can also occur in the syllabic head positions (as in (20c) and (20d)). There are thus four possible positions for sonorant consonants, and for each we can ask which segment type is preferred:

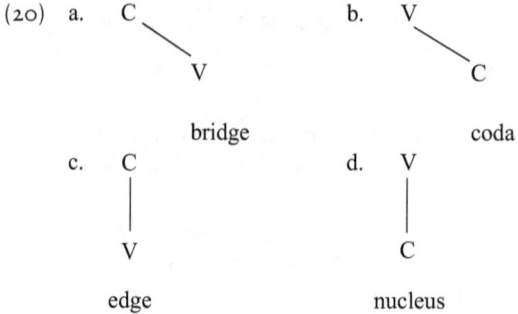

The bridge (20a) presupposes the option of a branching onset, while the coda (20b) occurs when closed syllables occur. Sonorants occurring in the edge (20c) are quite common, while syllabic sonorants (20d) are widely attested. In all cases, the C label indicates a consonant, while the V label indicates a sonorant. This means that all four positions characterise 'a sonorant consonant'. The question is now whether a specific manner is preferred.

In § 4.2.2 and § 4.3.3 I have discussed preferences for the bridge and the coda, respectively. Based on typological studies regarding coda conditions (especially VanDam (2004) and Krämer & Zec (2019)), we found that nasals are the preferred codas. If we want this manner preference to follow from correlation A, we have to conclude that what determines the manner preference is the terminal label of the syllabic position, which is C in the case of the coda. Given the sonorant manners that I proposed in § 4.2.2, here repeated as (21), we then correctly predict that nasals are the preferred coda manner, as per correlation A:

(21)   C   nasal
      C;V   lateral
      V;C   rhotic
      V   glide

For the bridge position, which has the terminal element V, we then predict glides as the optimal manner. As I suggested in § 4.3.3, bridge preferences may also depend on the syntagmatic pressure to literally form a perfect transition between the obstruent onset head and the vowel. I took this to be a reason to prefer liquids over glides, with nasals as the least attractive bridge.

Turning now to the structures in (20c) and (20d), we must ask whether the same preference applies here as in the bridge and coda, respectively. With respect to syllabic sonorants it would seem that nasals are preferred (Bell (1978)), which can be explained by the fact that they originate as codas. With respect to sonorant onset head it does not seem to be the case that high sonority sonorants are preferred over low sonority ones. In fact, the opposite holds. As we have seen in § 4.2.3, both Smith (2002: 131–57) and Flack (2007a: 28ff.), focusing on exclusions in word-initial position, mention languages that block only glides or both glides and rhotics or all non-nasal sonorant consonants in onset head position. It is undoubtedly significant that these exclusions are found in word-initial position. Following the polysystematic view, we need to take into account the possibility that onset constraints that are predicted by correlation A at the syllable level are overruled by correlations between higher phonological units such as the (phonological) word.

In this section, I have focused on which elements or element structures are preferred in syllabic positions, based on the notion of bias/harmony. Asking these questions leads to predicting which segment types are preferred in syllabic positions. To say that the manner element C is biased towards the onset head position implies that in this position obstruent coronal stops are preferred. What I did not address was the matter of the preference rankings of all segments that can occur in each syllabic position. While preference in the onset head for C elements implies a lower preference for V elements or indeed combinations such C;V or V;C, we also need to ask whether the model predicts an overall ranking of C, V, C;V and V;C. In § 8.3, the notion of bias, as well as other factors, will be used to make predictions about the ranking of preferred segment types in syllabic positions.

8.2.2 Disharmony

Before we turn to overall preference rankings, I want to draw attention to the fact that whereas preferences that regard the internal structure of segments reflect harmony, preferences that hold at the syntagmatic level of the syllable reflect disharmony. It is well known that there is disharmony rather than harmony between the members of complex syllabic constituents. Onset heads and onset dependents are opposites (C versus V), and so are the nucleus and the coda (V versus C). This preference for disharmony also affects the choice of place and laryngeal specifications, which is a logical consequence of the fact that such specifications are rare for syllabic dependents. Nevertheless, the exclusion of [t/d] + [l] in English and other Germanic languages suggests a dislike for place harmony in onset clusters.

It is perhaps significant that we find disharmony with complex syllabic constituents and, as a tendency, in consonants that have secondary properties, because in both cases we see a linearisation of the different units, albeit only a phonetic linearisation in the case of secondary specifications. This suggests that linear sequencing invites disharmony, whereas simultaneity invites 'harmony'.

8.3 Preference rankings of segments per syllabic position

In the previous section, I discussed which elements are unmarked in specific syllabic positions, as per correlation A. We can also ask, for any given system in any given position, which segments are preferred more than others. Preference rankings are implicit in the correlations that have been discussed in the previous section, which is evident from the way in which many of the predictions were formulated (i.e. see (11), (13) and (15)). In most cases, the preference ranking was established with respect to the polar choice C and V. In this section I will consider preference rankings for all four structures – that is, C, C;V, V;C and V – where this applies, mostly only in head classes, which are the ones that I will discuss here.[10] One might think at first sight that intermediate structures (C;V and V;C) will be less preferred than the simple structures due to their complexity, but this is not always obvious, as we will see.

---

[10] I do not, then, discuss preference rankings for secondary manners where, both for consonants and for vowels, I have also used intermediate categories. Of course, intermediate categories will also be ranked lower than the simple categories.

One criterion for preference is token frequency, which may be indicative of a preference ranking.[11] As in the previous section, my focus here is on laying out the predictions that follow from the RCVP model and not on exhaustive testing. Nevertheless, I will mention relevant data in many cases.

8.3.1 Two determining principles: harmony and dispersion

I now turn to the predictions that can be derived from RCVP with respect to the *preference* rankings for segment types in specific syllabic positions. Preference ranking can be relative or absolute. Relative ranking is manifested by some segment types having a higher relative token frequency in the relevant position. We call this *lexical token frequency* (see Gordon (2016: ch. 3)). Secondly, preferences may take an absolute character, which means that these positions only allow certain phoneme types, while excluding others. To set the stage, a familiar kind of absolute restriction is that the coda position only allows a subset of the sonorants that can occur in the onset position (see § 4.3.3). In phonological accounts, such facts are expressed by distributional constraints (in this case often called coda conditions). However, in the polysystematic view adopted here, in this example the coda position simply has a different consonant system from, for example, the onset position. This means that absolute distributional restrictions regard which types of segmental systems occur in different syllabic positions, and this question is addressed in the next section, which deals with preferred segmental systems. As pointed out in Gordon (2016: § 3.6), a correlation between system preference and preference of occurrence (token preference) is to be expected, and in fact is largely confirmed. Nevertheless, there could be other factors that influence the nature of distributional restrictions and the structure of segmental systems. I will further discuss this issue in the next section.

Turning now to token preference, we have, in the preceding section, already discussed which element choices (and thus segment types) are *top-ranked* in syllabic positions. Thus, in the onset head (C), C manner (stops) is unmarked (whether or not there is a contrast with V manner (fricatives)):

---

[11] Other criteria can also be considered, such as substitutions in speech errors, in first or second language acquisition or in language change. Another criterion for ranking can be derived from system typology, that is, from the preferred occurrence of segment types in systems in the absence of contrast. For example, if a language does not contrast between [l] and [r], we may try to establish which liquid is more likely to appear. I will consider this angle in the next section.

(22) Harmony (correlation A):

    syllabic position A ⇒ head element A (cf. (10))

    (where A = C or V)

Let us now see whether harmony can also be used to establish relative preference when there is a three- or four-way contrast in categories. If there are only two categories we already know that C is preferred over V in a syllabic C position; that is, if C is top-ranked, then if there is a binary contrast, V must be less preferred in the onset head position:

(23)   C > V

Given that four categories imply a scale from 'most C' to 'least C' (or vice versa for V), one might expect that in edge position we would find the following ranking of preference, if there is a full four-way contrast:

(24) Ranking according to harmony: C   >   C;V >   V;C   >   V
                                                          stops   affric.   m-fric   s-fric

This may seem 'reasonable' since the intermediate categories are more C-like (in harmony with the syllabic onset position) than the 'bare' V category. But this predicts that languages which, for example, have stops, affricates and fricatives prefer affricates over fricatives in the edge position, which is not the case, at least not in English (Hayden (1950)). Likewise, the strident coronal fricative [s] has a greater lexical frequency than the non-strident [θ] as a simplex onset. In complex onsets, plain stops and strident fricatives are also more likely to occur. In fact, in English, affricates cannot be the head of a complex onset, although the non-strident [θ] can. All in all, it is clear that strident fricatives are more likely to occur in onsets than the two intermediate categories.[12] While plain C (stop) is unmarked, a further preference ranking is not determined by the preponderance of the C element. Rather, it would seem that the second preferred category after stops is fricatives.[13]

(25) Actual ranking: C   >   V   >   C;V / V;C
                           stops   s-fric   affric. / m-fric

---

[12] This of course also depends on the fact that affricates are generally more limited in their distinctive place of articulation.

[13] If we take into account polysyllabic strings, fricatives could be more frequent than stops due to 'intervocalic weakening' effects, which prevent stops in intervocalic position. In this section, the focus is on preference within the confines of a single syllable.

Whether the two intermediate categories can be ranked among themselves will be discussed below.

How can we derive the ranking of V over the two intermediate categories? Two explanations come to mind: complexity and dispersion. Dispersion has been recruited to explain the structure of segmental inventories (see Liljencrants & Lindblom (1972)). However, the reason why dispersion is relevant is that more dispersed sounds provide for better contrast when they can occur in the same position. Dispersion as relevant to segmental systems is thus inherently a paradigmatic force. If stops are the biased segment type in the onset head, the segments that would most clearly contrast within the class of obstruents with stops are fricatives, because these two categories do not share any manner element in common. Hence, in this sense dispersion favours fricatives over the intermediate categories, leading to the following overall ranking:

(26) Ranking according to dispersion: C / V > C;V / V;C

To derive the ranking in (26) one might say that instead of dispersion an appeal could also be made to complexity:

(27) Ranking according to complexity: C / V > C;V / V;C

The principles in (26) and (27) both extensionally lead to the same result and cannot really be distinguished from each other because complex structures necessarily undermine dispersion by combining elements.

Focusing on the edge position, it would seem that the dispersion ranking outranks top-down, paradigmatic harmony (i.e. correlation A). I take this ranking to be universally fixed but I will argue below that dispersion is only relevant for syllabic head positions, which, I assume, are the more salient positions where maximal contrast is thus most crucial. Paradigmatic harmony still plays a role by predicting the ranking of C over V and of C;V over V;C.

In the next subsections, I will systematically spell out which preference rankings are now predicted for the various element classes.

8.3.1.1 Manner preferences

8.3.1.1.1 *Manner preferences: edge*
As we have already established, in head positions, dispersion and harmony, in that order, impose a complete order on the four manner categories in the edge position, given that dispersion is ranked over harmony:

(28) Dispersion C, V > C;V / V;C
    Harmony   C > C;V > V;C > V

               C > V > C;V > V;C

    Edge: stops-fric affr. ns-fric
               [p] > [f] > [ɸ] > [pf]
               [t] > [s] > [ts] > [θ]
               [k] > [x] > [kx] > ...[14]

To test the claim that affricates are preferred over non-strident fricatives, we need to examine languages that have both categories. English is such a language, and in it the affricates [tʃ] and [dʒ] are more frequent than the non-strident fricatives [θ] and [ð] (Hayden (1950)).

In support of the ranking of affricates over non-strident fricatives we can also refer to the fact that in the absence of a contrast, affricates are more likely to be part of the segmental system than mellow fricatives; this point will be taken up in the next section where we look at inventories.

If, however, there is no convincing evidence to rank the two complex categories when contrastive, we could say that harmony only applies to simplex categories, which then leads to a partial ordering:

(29) Dispersion   C, V > C;V / V;C
    Harmony (simplex)   C > V

                        C > V > C;V / V;C

    Edge: stop s-fric ns-fric / affr.
            [p] > [f] > [ɸ]   / [pf]
            [t] > [s] > [θ]   / [ts]
            [k] > [x] > -   / [kx]

In (30) I graphically summarise the two versions of positional preference:

---

[14] I am assuming here that the stridency opposition does not apply to dorsal obstruents.

(30)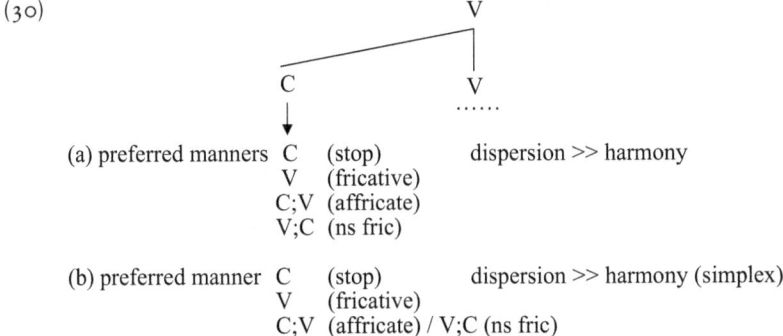

    (a) preferred manners C (stop)   dispersion >> harmony
                                    V (fricative)
                                    C;V (affricate)
                                  V;C (ns fric)

    (b) preferred manner C (stop)   dispersion >> harmony (simplex)
                                  V (fricative)
                                C;V (affricate) / V;C (ns fric)

The only apparent problem with the prediction made here is that, at least in word-initial position, [s] is the most frequent consonant in English and in other languages (such as Spanish) as well. It has, however, been argued that initial [s] occupies a special adjunction position which lies outside the onset as such and which is not available to stops. Since in this special position only [s] can occur, this explains that the frequency of [s] is a result of the frequency of the 'prepindix' unit.

8.3.1.1.2 *Manner preferences: nucleus*
For nucleus manner, I will also assume that dispersion outranks harmony. As for harmony, we have the same two options that we considered in the preceding section.

(31)   Dispersion C, V > CV / CV
       Harmony   V > C;V > V;C > C

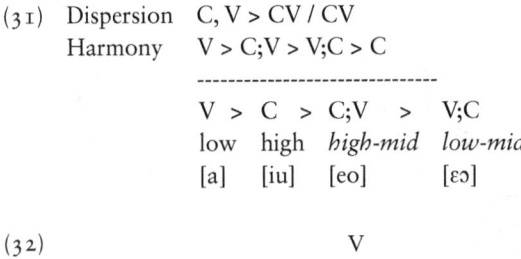

(32)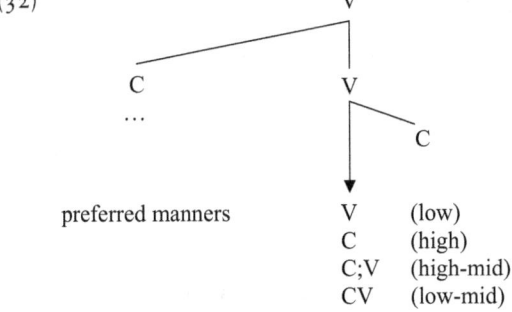

    preferred manners   V   (low)
                              C   (high)
                              C;V (high-mid)
                              CV (low-mid)

In (33) we do not predict a relative ranking for mid-vowels by applying 'harmony (simplex)', which only ranks the simple structures C and V:

(33) Dispersion   C, V > C;V / V;C
     Harmony (simplex) V > C

                       V > C > CV   / CV
                       low   high   high-mid / low-mid
                       [a]   [iu]   [eo]   / [ɛɔ]

(34)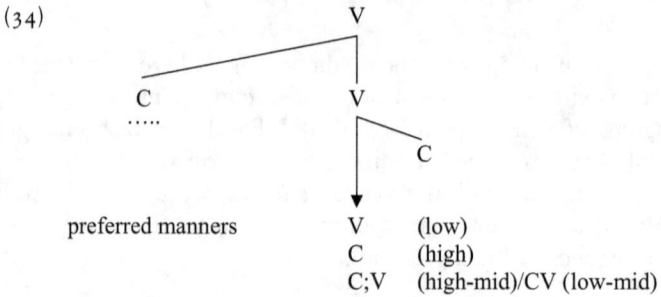

     preferred manners   V   (low)
                          C   (high)
                          C;V   (high-mid)/CV (low-mid)

It is not obvious that high-mid vowels are preferred over low-mid vowels or vice versa in languages that have both. Thus, as in the previous case of onset head manner, it may be the case that harmony only applies to simplex categories.[15]

8.3.1.1.3 Manner preferences: bridge and coda

Let us now address the dependent syllabic positions (bridge and coda). I will assume that in the syllabic dependent positions, which are less salient and thus less sensitive to dispersion, dispersion is not a factor. This means we only take into account harmony, but recall that harmony refers to terminal labels, which means V for the bridge and C for the coda. This produces the following full ranking:

(35) a. Bridge: V   > V;C > C;V > C
                 [j] > [r] > [l] > [n]
     b. Coda: C   > C;V > V;C > V
                 [n] > [l] > [r] > [j]

---

[15] In § 8.2.1 I mentioned that KLV85 make the claim that in systems with one mid series, high-mid vowels are preferred. However, five-vowel systems with high-mid vowels and with low-mid vowels are both widely attested.

Predictability and preference 307

Recall that in the bridge another factor comes into play which favours liquids over glides, since liquids form the perfect transition from the onset head to the rhyme head.

Parker (2012b) offers a typological study which has a direct bearing on the issue at hand. In this study, Parker compares two theories concerning complex onset clusters: the Minimum Sonority Distance approach and the Sonority Dispersion Principle. His work is best explained by quoting extensively from his abstract:

> Minimum Sonority Distance is a general tendency by which specific languages may impose a parametric requirement that sonority rise by at least x ranks from C_1 to C_2 in a syllable-initial consonant cluster (Steriade (1982); Selkirk (1984)). Assuming the typical five-category sonority scale (vowel > glide > liquid > nasal > obstruent), sonority distance favours glides as the default (unmarked) class of segments in C_2 position since glides are higher in relative sonority than all other consonants.[16] In contrast to this, the Sonority Dispersion Principle posits that in a C_1C_2V sequence, these three segments should be maximally and evenly dispersed (separated) from each other in terms of sonority, all else being equal (Clements 1990a). This results in a preference for liquids rather than glides in C_2 position since liquids are halfway between obstruents and vowels in most sonority scales.

It would seem that the prediction of the Sonority Distance approach, which favours glides in the onset dependent position, is captured in (35a), which means that the determining factor here is top-down harmony. Parker's (2012b) abstract continues:

> I report here the findings of a survey of 122 languages containing onset clusters, designed to shed fresh light on this topic. The results partially validate both generalisations simultaneously: glides are the preferred C_2 segments in some languages, while other languages require all syllable-initial clusters to end with a liquid. Therefore, neither the Minimum Sonority Distance model by itself nor the Sonority Dispersion Principle alone can account for all languages exhibiting onset clusters; i.e., neither of them holds true as an absolute statement of markedness concerning preferred sequences of onset consonants in all cases.

In fact, Parker (2012b, 2016) reports the following percentages based on a search in the World Phonotactics Database (Australian National University), which contains phonotactic information on 3,798 languages[17] (his term 'offset' refers to the onset dependent, i.e. the bridge):

---

[16] My note: for this reason, the name 'Minimum Sonority Distance' is not meant to imply that 'minimum; is good; in fact, as we see, 'maximal' is good.

[17] During completion of this book the website was shut 'for maintenance'.

total languages with glide offsets: 489
total languages with liquid offsets: 346
consonant-glide (CG) only: 259 languages (43 per cent); consonant–liquid (CL) only: 112 languages (19 per cent)
both CG and CL: 230 languages (38 per cent)

These numbers show that there is a clear preference for glides, especially witnessed by the 259 languages that only have such complex onsets. This is confirmed by Parker's search in the Lyon-Albuquerque Phonological Systems Database (LAPSyD),[18] which contains 623 languages:

total languages with glide offsets: 89
total languages with liquid offsets: 65
CG only: 58
CL only: 34

These results confirm the RCVP prediction that glides are unmarked bridges. The issue, then, is how to account for languages that only permit liquids (CL), since the ranking (35a) suggest that CL implies CG. Parker's study does not distinguish between the two types of liquids, [r] and [l], but if maximal sonority distance is what matters, we would expect Cr to do better than Cl.

To account for CG-only languages, Parker appeals to the second theory, Sonority Dispersion, which captures the idea that liquids form a more perfect transition to the nucleus than glides.[19] Following Parker, we can thus refer to the relevant factor as Sonority Dispersion, with the understanding that dispersion here applies along the syntagmatic axis, rather than the paradigmatic axis as in the previous discussion. To make this clear I will refer to Parker's second theory as syntagmatic dispersion. If syntagmatic dispersion outranks paradigmatic harmony, we derive the result that liquids are preferred over glides:

(36) Bridge:
Syntagmatic dispersion: V;C / C;V > V / C
Harmony: V > V;C > C;V > C

                          V;C > C;V > V > C
                          [r] > [l] > [j] > [n]

[18] <http://www.lapsyd.ddl.ish-lyon.cnrs.fr> (last accessed 14 February 2020).
[19] An additional advantage of liquids as bridge segments, also noted in Parker (2016), is that these consonants are coronal, which makes it unnecessary to supply the bridge with place elements. I noted in § 5.2.2 that clusters with glides may require a place distinction, which then runs counter to the generalisation that onsets have only one place specification, which is implemented on the onset head.

Predictability and preference 309

It remains to be determined whether the complete ranking in (36) can be validated. Is [r] a better bridge than [l]? Recall that van der Torre (2003) reports evidence which shows that in Dutch [r] is indeed more preferred as a bridge than [l], as predicted in (35a). It would seem that [j] is certainly a better bridge than [n]. Both facts indicate that harmony plays a role.

The question is then how to reconcile both theories with the facts that support (and contradict) both. The key to this is that (maximal) sonority distance, which favours CG, targets the onset, whereas (syntagmatic) sonority dispersion targets the onset plus the vowel (which Clements (1990a) referred to as a demisyllable). Languages that favour CG would then simply not activate the syntagmatic dispersion constraint, which, I will assume here, targets the syllable (since RCVP does not recognise the demisyllable as a unit). There is thus no paradox here. CG-only languages do not activate syntagmatic sonority dispersion, which is a syllable-level constraint, while CL-only languages do. In the latter case, as shown in (36), the constraint on the larger domain outranks the constraint on the lower domain.[20]

Parker's typological studies show that paradigmatic dispersion is not a factor in bridges. Paradigmatic dispersion would suggest that after glides, nasals are preferred, thus skipping liquids. That runs counter to the fact that languages that allow consonant–nasal (CN) onsets also allow onsets with bridges of higher sonority.

(37) Bridge:
Paradigmatic dispersion: C / V > C;V/ V;C
Harmony: V > V;C > C;V > C

                           V > C > C;V > V;C
                           [j] > [n] > [l] > [r]

As mentioned above, we expect paradigmatic dispersion to be relevant only for syllabic heads, which are salient. We can conclude that paradigmatic dispersion and syntagmatic dispersion are in complementary distribution, the former applying to onset heads, and the latter to the syllable as a whole.

---

[20] We could also consider an alternative. Paradigmatic harmony predicts the preference for glides because, I have assumed, this correlation only looks at the terminal level V for bridges. To explain CL languages we could perhaps say that harmony looks at the complete C;V labelling of the bridge. However, harmony would then favour laterals (manner C;V), rather than liquids in general. For this reason, we must reject this alternative.

Let us now ask whether syntagmatic dispersion is relevant for the coda. If the domain of this constraint is the syllable, we expect implications for the rhyme, namely favouring of a preferred maximal distance between the vowel and the coda. This would strengthen the preference for nasals.

In considering preferences for codas, we should perhaps also consider the following onset for word-medial codas, as per the SCL (Murray & Vennemann (1983)). We could then say that in between the vowel and the following onset, assuming that this is an obstruent, again liquids would form the best transition:

(38) Coda:
 Syntagmatic dispersion: V;C / C;V> V /C
 Harmony: C > C;V >V;C> V

                           C;V > V;C > C > V
                           [l] > [r] > [n] > [j]

However, while consideration of word-medial and word-final codas is important, the evidence seems to suggest that nasals are preferred codas in both positions, as explicitly stated in Krämer & Zec (2019). More importantly, syntagmatic dispersion cannot refer to the rhyme plus following onset because this is not a unit in the RCVP syntax (even if we accept the recursive structure discussed in § 3.2.5).

We have not yet dealt with preferences for sonorant consonants as onset heads. We have seen in §§ 4.2.3 and 8.2.1 that both Smith (2002: 131–57) and Flack (2007a: 28ff.) mention languages that block only glides, both glides and rhotics or all non-nasal sonorant consonants in onset head position. These (dis)preferences are exactly opposite to what we have found for the bridge, where glides are preferred. This reversal is due to the fact that sonorants as onset heads occupy a syllabic C position:

Let us recall the difference between sonorants in the edge and in the bridge (see § 3.2.1):

(39) a.

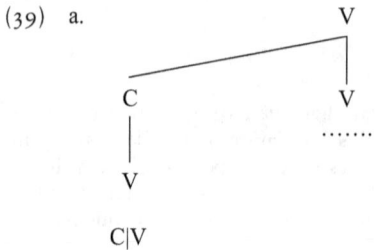

Predictability and preference 311

b.
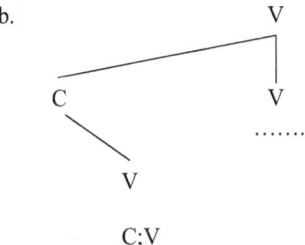
C;V

In both cases, V is dependent on C, and yet the syllabic position will reflect the difference between V being subjoined or adjoined to C. We must conclude that in cases of the subjoined structure, harmony ignores the subjoined V. Thus while a sonorant in the bridge is truly a V, sonorants in the onset head are Vs that have been converted into Cs:

(40)
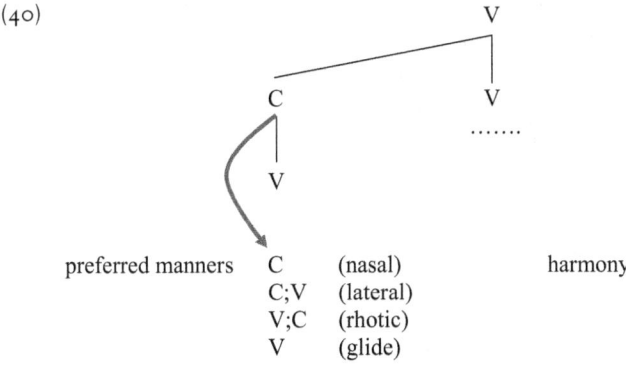

preferred manners C   (nasal)   harmony
                   C;V (lateral)
                   V;C (rhotic)
                   V   (glide)

There is, however, a further point: to achieve the ranking that follows from the findings of Smith and Flack, which put glides at the bottom of the list, we must assume that the preference ranking for sonorants is not subject to dispersion, which would put glides in second place. We achieve the desired result by ranking harmony over dispersion:

(41) preferred manners C   (nasal)   Harmony >> paradigmatic
                                                  dispersion
                        C;V (lateral)
                        V;C (rhotic)
                        V   (glide)

(42) Harmony   C > C;V > V;C > V
     Dispersion C / V > C;V / V;C

                 C > C;V > V;C > V
                 [n] > [l] > [r] > [j]

The different ranking of harmony and dispersion is not universal, however. It applies to sonorants that have been converted to onset heads only, not to obstruents. Of course, a more straightforward account is to say that dispersion does not apply to syllabic positions that are 'mixed' (i.e. contain a C and a V). Since I will make this claim for the bridge and the coda, we might just as well extend it to the other two mixed positions, that is, sonorant onset heads and syllabic sonorants.

We arrive at the following generalisation concerning the edge:

(43) Edge:
Obstruents: paradigmatic dispersion >> harmony
Sonorants: harmony

In conclusion, the syllabic position of sonorants as onset heads is inherently mixed, which I take to be the reason why dispersion plays no role.

We also need to establish the preference for sonorant consonants in the nucleus. If we assume that here, too, dispersion is irrelevant because the syllabic category is mixed, and that harmony is dependent on the V label (because syllabic sonorants are consonants that are converted to rhyme head), we predict the following ranking:

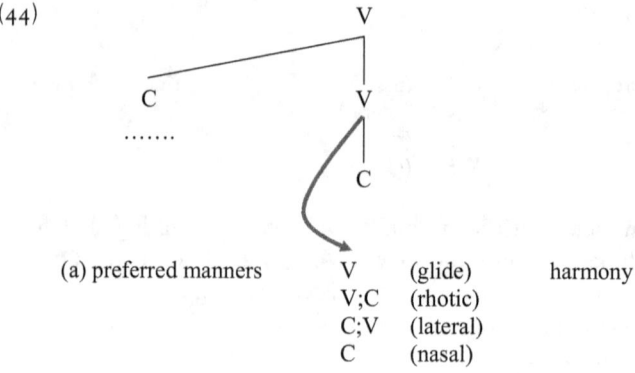

(a) preferred manners   V   (glide)   harmony
                               V;C   (rhotic)
                               C;V   (lateral)
                               C   (nasal)

This ranking does not square with Bell's (1978) finding, discussed in § 5.3.3 above, that nasals appear to be the preferred syllabic consonants, given that in his corpus there are thirty-five languages that only have syllabic nasals. Before we except the difference between sonorants as onset heads and syllabic sonorants as involving a contradiction (and thus an internal inconsistency in RCVP), let us ask what it would mean for a glide to be syllabic. Arguably, there would be no way to distinguish syllabic glides from fully fledged vowels.[21] This would allow us to ignore glides

---

[21] In § 4.4, I have suggested the non-stressable vowels in English *pity*, *pillow*, *Nina* as candidates for a syllabic glide.

Predictability and preference 313

as top-ranking syllabic sonorants. In § 5.3.3 I have provided a possible explanation for the popularity of syllabic nasals, pointing to the historical processes that give rise to syllabic consonants and suggesting

> that nasals are more likely to interact and fuse with a preceding vowel than liquids, given the natural occurrence of nasalisation of vowels before nasals. While this may give rise to the nasal disappearing, it is likely that the emergence of syllabic nasals is a result of the reverse process.

For the moment, then, I will maintain that the ranking in (44) is tenable. It is consistent with the RCVP approach followed thus far. We have to accept, I suppose, that actual preference orders that are found can in some cases be due to additional factors.

8.3.1.2 Place preferences
Location preferences only need to be established for syllabic heads, given that syllabic dependents do not have place properties (or laryngeal properties).[22]

8.3.1.2.1 Place preferences: edge
In the onset head position, harmony correctly orders the polar opposites, given that paradigmatic dispersion takes precedence:

(45) Dispersion   C/V > C;V / V;C
     Harmony   C > V > C;V > V;C

                  C > V > C;V > V;C
     Edge: acor labial pcor dors[23]
                  [t̪] > [p] > [t] > [k]

(46) Dispersion   C / V > C;V / V;C
     Harmony (sim) C > V

                    C > V > C;V / V;C
     Edge: acor labial dors / pcor
                    [t̪] > [p] > [k] / [t]

---

[22] Here I ignore the fact that bridge and coda can have limited place distinctions; see § 5.2.2.
[23] Here I distinguish anterior coronals (acor) and posterior coronals (pcor), as proposed in § 5.2.1.

314 Principles of Radical CV Phonology

The prediction is that anterior coronals are preferred and that labials are the second-ranked category. In (45) the ranking indicates that systems that have two types of coronals (anterior and posterior) are both more preferred as onsets than [k]. I do not have evidence in favour of or against this ranking. Given that systems with only three places overwhelmingly have one coronal, one labial and one dorsal consonant, this might suggest that ranking the two kinds of coronals higher than the dorsal in systems that have a four-way distinction is not correct. However, we have to separate preferences within a given system and preferences for what occurs in systems of a certain size. I will return to this issue in the next section. In (46), where harmony only applies to the simplex place categories C and V, we stay on the safe side by making no preference distinctions between the posterior coronal and the dorsal.

We also need to check the proposed rankings for fricatives and sonorant consonants. Preference for place may be dependent on manner and major category. While relevant lexical frequency data are no doubt available for many languages that would allow me to check the relative frequencies of all consonant types, I have to leave such testing for future work, once more stressing that my goal in this chapter is to lay out the predictions that RCVP makes, with slightly varying assumptions about the scope of paradigmatic harmony, and not a full-scale, rigorous testing. That said, I believe that in many places convincing supporting evidence has been provided.

8.3.1.2.2 Place preferences: nucleus

If we follow the same principles for the rhyme head, we predict the following preferences:

(47)   Dispersion   V / C > C;V / V;C
       Harmony   V > C > V;C > C;V

                    V   > C   > V;C   > C;V
                    ba-ro   front   ba-unro   fro-ro
                    [u] > [i]   > [ɯ]   > [y]

(48)   Dispersion   V / C > C;V / V;C
       Harmony (sim)   V > C

                    V   > C   > C;V   / V;C
                    ba-ro front   fro-ro / ba-unro
                    [u] > [i]   > [y]   / [ɯ]

The full ranking in (47) makes [ɯ] more preferred than [y]. Turkish has both vowels but according to Kemaloğlu, Kamışlı & Mengü (2017) the

Predictability and preference 315

front rounded vowel is reported as more frequent than the central/back unrounded vowels in various sources.[24] However, among the low vowels the preference is reversed, with [a], not surprisingly, being the most frequent vowel in all these authors' sources. This suggests once more that place rankings might be different for different manners.

8.3.1.3 Laryngeal preferences

8.3.1.3.1 Laryngeal preferences: edge (phonation)
The order of preference for phonation in the edge is straightforward, because the head elements are not allowed to occur in combinations (see Chapter 6); this bleeds the relevance of dispersion:

(49) Dispersion C, V (= vacuous because head elements do not combine)
      Harmony   C > V

                 C > V
                 tns voi

Tense (voiceless) obstruents are preferred over voiced obstruents, which I take to be uncontroversial. Here we need to take into account the finding that, for labials, [b] may be preferred over [p] in different languages (such as Yoruba and Arabic), due to aerodynamic factors that cause velars to resist voicing (as in Dutch, which has no [g]), while labials favour it. This shows, once more, that the ranking that can be derived from the RCVP system cannot be the only factor in determining preference rankings.

In the case of phonation types it would be interesting to explore the preferences when we take secondary specifications into account. I pointed out in § 8.2.1 that, according to correlation B, secondary c (glottalisation) is preferred in the onset head over secondary v (aspiration), which would suggest that glottalised consonants are preferred over aspirated consonants in languages that have both. This is, obviously, another prediction that can be tested with the appropriate databases.

8.3.1.3.2 Laryngeal preferences: nucleus (tone)
In the tonal domain, low tone is preferred over high tone, while the choice between the two mid-level tones is not clear, given that not many languages have this contrast:

---

[24] In contrast with this, MD (p. 254) reports twenty languages with [ɯ] and only three with [y] (p. 249). This of course does not regard preference in a system that has both, which makes this observation relevant to the next section.

(50) Dispersion V, C > C;V / V;C
      Harmony   V > C, C;V > V;C

      V > C > C;V > V;C
      low   high   low-mid   high-mid

(51) Dispersion   V, C > C;V / V;C
      Harmony (sim)   V > C > C;V > V;C

      V > C > C;V   / V;C
      low   high   low-mid / high-mid

We noted above that if tone languages distinguish high from low tone, the high tone is usually assumed to be literally marked, which makes low tone unmarked, as predicted by harmony.

8.3.1.4 Concluding remarks

In conclusion, dispersion (or complexity) plays an important role in predicting preference for both syllabic head positions (onset head and nucleus), supplemented by paradigmatic harmony. In dependent positions (bridge, coda), only harmony applies, which I have justified by claiming that these positions, being non-head positions, are less perceptually salient. However, preference in the bridge position can be affected by syntagmatic dispersion at the syllable level, which creates a preference for liquids. I have only looked at segments without secondary properties, but for those we would certainly expect that such 'complex' segments have a lower preference, both in systems as a whole (see the next section) and in specific positions. Nevertheless, it would be possible to differentiate preference for segments with secondary specifications within the same subclass.

The following table summarises the token preference predictions for each syllabic position. The categories separated by a double line are unordered if harmony (sim) is used; otherwise harmony imposes the ordering given:

(52)

						Dispersion	Harmony
ons head	manner	C	V	C;V	V;C	yes	yes
		stop	fric	affr	m.fric		
	location	C	V	C;V	V;C	yes	yes
		cor	lab	p.cor	vel		
	laryngeal	C	V	–	–	yes	yes
		vcl	voi				

						Dispersion	Harmony
rhy head	manner	V low	C high	C;V h.mid	V;C l.mid	yes	yes
	location	V labial	C cor	C;V dorsal	V;C cor-lab	yes	yes
	laryngeal	V low	C high	C;V h.mid	V;C l.mid	yes	yes
ons dep	manner	V gli	V;C rho	C;V lat	C nas	---	yes
rhy dep	manner	C nas	C;V lat	V;C rho	V gli	---	yes

I have mentioned several times that I do not claim that the preferred rankings that are predicted, based on the RCVP systems and the additional principles of paradigmatic and syntagmatic dispersion and harmony, are the only relevant factors. Other factors also play a role. One factor that would certainly have to be taken into account when looking at token preference concerns the surrounding segments. For example, in complex onsets, the preference for [l] is low when the preceding obstruent is a coronal (*[dl], *[tl] in English), although this, being the result of a distributional constraint, means that in a post-coronal position, the set of contrasting segments is reduced in an absolute manner. But one can imagine that in contexts where both [l] and [r] are allowed, certain preceding consonants in the onset may favour or disfavour one of them, without imposing an absolute restriction. Following vowels can also impose absolute or non-absolute preferences. With respect to coda consonants, we may need to consider the influence of a following onset head. It is possible that the preference for nasal codas could result from the fact that nasals typically allow a strong bond with the following obstruents due to place agreement.

As mentioned, we could also relate the preference ordering of segments to the process of phonological acquisition. Segments that are more preferred are expected to be acquired before less preferred segments. The reverse ordering would be expected to be relevant in language breakdown. Thirdly, we expect relevance of ordering in language change and in loanword adaptation. To connect these various types of preference is of course the programme of Jakobson's 'Kindersprache' (Jakobson 1941 [1968]). I have not discussed all these areas. However, such facts would better fit into the next section, which addresses the preferred structure of vowel and consonant systems, given a certain number of segments, and thus, in a sense, the order in which segments 'enter' a system when it grows in size.

8.4 Preferred segmental systems

The preferences discussed in the previous section do not predict that all language have the same segmental system. The prediction is that, given a segmental system that is relevant to a certain position, preferences of occurrence are predicted, both in a relative way (token frequency) and in an absolute way (distributional constraints), although the latter involve the relation between segmental systems in different positions. In this section the focus is on the structure of preferred segmental systems of a certain size.

8.4.1 *The overall structure of segmental systems*

In segmental systems we expect less preferred segments to imply the presence of more preferred segments. The programme of Liljencrants & Lindblom (1972) assigns a central role to dispersion. As mentioned in the preceding section, the fact that contrast among maximally opposed segment types is preferred can also be captured in terms of the notion of complexity. This means that segments with a combination of elements in a primary class imply the presence of segments that are simple (C or V). This also applies to the secondary classes. In addition, the mere presence of a secondary specification implies the occurrence of the corresponding plane segment.[25] Thus, mid vowels cannot occur without the occurrence of peripheral vowels.[26] This means that within each class the following implication holds:

(53) a. C;V, V;C ⇒ C, V
     b. X;Y   ⇒ X, Y

The reason, as we saw in the previous section, is that mixed structures undermine perceptual salience. The idea that vowel systems display maximal dispersion amounts to the same result.

The idea of dispersion when applied to vowel systems works reasonably well for smaller vowel systems. As shown in various studies (for

---

[25] Here 'corresponding' could be applied loosely, i.e. saying that the occurrence of prenasalised stops implies plain stops. But MD notes in various places that the occurrence of consonants with secondary properties implies the occurrence of those same consonants without the secondary specification. Hence [^{m}b] implies [b]. The implication between [^{m}b] and [b] does not hold when the former is 'merely' a phonetic realisation of a voiced [b].

[26] The following statement in MD (p. 124) is curious: 'Vowels in the mid-range are a little more common than high vowels, namely 1032 to 994, or 40.5% of the sample to 39.0%. However, the reason is that for mid vowels we have two potential series, low-mid and high-mid.'

example, Vaux & Samuels (2015)), there are problems with the predictive power of dispersion for larger systems in which the impact of processes of change is greater. In any event, there is agreement that of the two vowel systems in (54) the triangular system is more preferred:

(54) a. i u a
 b. ö e o

In fact, (54b) is less preferred because it uses an element combination to characterise the intermediate height (CV), leaving the simple options of C and V unused.

The principles that determine what is preferred in systems have been implicit in the preceding section. We expect segments with harmonic elements to be more preferred than segments with non-harmonic or less harmonic elements. Hence occurrence of the latter implies occurrence of the former:

(55) Harmony:
 Onset head: C > V
 Rhyme head: V > C

Harmony impacts all three element classes. Given the preference rankings uncovered in the previous sections, we expect segmental systems to 'grow' by working their way down the ranking, 'adding' less preferred segments after more preferred segments.

We also expect elements in head classes to be more preferred than elements in dependent classes:

(56) The choice of which elements to activate follows from the hierarchical organisation of the element classes:

Manner > Place > Laryngeal[27]

This ranking is supported by the facts that there are vowel systems that recruit manner only (vertical systems) and that not all languages use tonal distinctions.

This ranking does not imply that all element structures in higher-ranked classes *precede* all element structures in dependent classes. I here suggest a notion of *balance*, which means that expansion of the segmental set goes back and forth between the different element classes. Balance, as I argue below, is fed by dispersion and avoidance of complexity.

---

[27] In consonantal systems, the priority of having a distinction in manner among obstruents is not fulfilled in Australian languages that only have stops, yet have a rich inventory of distinctive locations.

Arguably, we also need to postulate the notion of *feature economy*, developed in the work of Martinet (1948) and, later, in Clements (2003), which explains why element structures, once 'activated', are put to *maximal use* before other element structures are activated.

Consider the following example. One could distinguish five vowels in the following way:

(57) Vowel 1: low and nasal
Vowel 2: low and high toned
Vowel 3: low and low toned
Vowel 4: high and round
Vowel 5: high and front

This requires the activation of manner, distinguishing two apertures: C (high) and V (low). Within the low category, a three-way distinction is made using the two different tonal elements C (H) and V (L), as well as the nasal element (secondary v). The high vowels are differentiated in terms of two additional elements: C (front) and V (round). Clearly, it would be more economical to differentiate five vowels using only the manner elements and the colour elements. This suggests the following principle of economy:

(58) Economy:

For any number of vowels, choose the smallest number of elements to differentiate them

The principle in (58) adds to the ranking of classes in (56) that before a lower-ranked element is activated within a class, any previously activated elements in the same or in other classes are put to maximal use. This explains why, if colour elements are activated, they are applied to the different vowel heights that have been distinguished in terms of manner.

However, economy is counteracted by dispersion. Consider three-vowel systems. Surely the most economical way would be to distinguish just three heights, which produces a vertical system. However, a majority of three-vowel systems use two apertures and colour. Economy is also counterbalanced by avoiding complexity. Adding a complex structure in a head class may be less preferred than adding a simple structure in a dependent class. Distinguishing three heights, one needs C, V and CV. Arguably, the CV option contributes a form of complexity that can be avoided by the activation of a colour element. Thus, economy is held back by both dispersion and complexity avoidance, acting independently, but both feeding into the notion of balance that was just mentioned.

To illustrate the fact that different languages can 'choose' to develop classes differently, consider Turkish, which distinguishes only two heights, but then also uses two colours and element combinations to arrive at an eight-vowel set. Turkish, then, is 'colour heavy' as opposed to a five- or seven-vowel system that distinguishes more than two heights but makes no use of colour combinations.

(59)   Turkish: colour heavy:

manner (C, V) + location (C, V and CV):
/i,ü,ɪ,u,e,ö,a,o/

Spanish: aperture heavy:

Manner (C, V and CV) + colour (Cm V)

Likewise, phonation and tone specifications can be activated for smaller vowel systems that only modestly exploit all the possible manner or place distinctions. An extreme example is Chinese languages that are tone heavy, while not having overly rich vowel systems in terms of place and manner.

The idea of balance is not only driven by dispersion ('perceptual ease') and complexity avoidance. In addition, 'articulatory ease' will also play a role. This explains why no three-vowel system will have one colourless high vowel and two low vowels that have contrastive colour. Distinctive colour is more difficult to articulate on low vowels, which in turn produces a less salient effect from a perceptual point of view. We discussed this when considering the fact that low vowels avoid rounding (see Kaun (1995, 2004)). In this case, both 'ease' factors prefer [a, i, u], with colour on high vowels rather than low vowels.

Articulatory ease also relates to complexity. Combinations of primary elements lead to more complex articulations, while at the same time they lead to a decrease of perceptual salience, as was discussed earlier.

As mentioned, it is not a simple matter to determine which phonetic properties contribute to maximal dispersion when systems get bigger. There is no measure for determining which of the two systems in (59) is more preferred:

(60)   a.   i   u   e   o   æ   a
       b.   i   u   a   í   ú   á

The system in (60b) has a tonal distinction and three simple vowels. Such systems are less frequent than those in (60a). The question is why. Why is having a mid-vowel better than distinguishing the three corner vowels in terms of tone? It is of course well known that for each number of vowels over three, several alternative vowel systems regularly occur, not only because of different ways to guarantee articulatory ease and maximal dispersion, but also due to the fact that umlaut processes, vowel mergers and other historical processes can add properties to a vowel system that contradict the shape of patterns that are expected on purely system-internal grounds. Useful discussion of the role of complexity in segmental structure and inventories can be found in Maddieson (2006b, 2007, 2009a, 2010).

8.4.2 Polysystematicity

In surveys of vowel and consonant systems (e.g. MD), it is usually the case that systems are discussed that apply to the language as a whole. Given the polysystematic approach, we need to look at systems relative to syllabic, prosodic or morphological position. As mentioned earlier, different vowel systems may obtain for different types of syllables, depending on degree of stress or position with respect to the stressed syllable. For example, in Brazilian Portuguese (Da Silva (1992)), the stressed syllable has a contrast among seven vowels (aeoɛɔiu), pretonic syllables have five vowels (aeoiu) and post-tonic syllables allow three vowels (aiu). Hyman (2018) shows how the consonantal inventories in Bantu languages differ between roots and affixes. Nevertheless, we expect that each relevant position in a segmental system follows the patterns that have been established for 'holistic' inventories. An extreme case of specific positions having their own segmental system involves the bridge and coda position. We have seen that both positions have a limited consonantal inventory, typically only allowing sonorant consonants. This could possibly be a universal limitation of inventories in these syllabic positions. Adopting the liberal view that all sonorant consonants are in principle allowed, specific languages may narrow down this set to a smaller one, for instance by allowing only liquids or only glides in the bridge or only nasals in the coda.

There is one final observation that needs to be made, which possibly imposes a condition on taking a polysystematic approach. We would not expect to find a language that allows certain consonants to occur as a bridge or coda while disallowing these consonants in the more liberal onset head position. In other words, segmental sets that generally occur in a position that allows fewer segments should be properly included in segmental sets that can occur in positions that allow more segments. This is what motivates the holistic approach to segmental systems. The system as a whole is permitted in at least one position, while positions that have smaller sets impose limitations on the larger set. However, there are exceptions. For example, the velar nasal in English and many other languages can occur as a coda (the more restricted position), but not in the onset. Another exception, already mentioned, is that in languages that have a schwa vowel, this may be the only vowel to occur in an unstressed syllable, while it cannot occur in the stressed syllable.

8.4.3 Conclusions

There is of course a close connection between system preference and token preference that was discussed in this section. This connection is shown to hold in Gordon (2016: ch. 3). In general, we expect segment types that occur first in systems also to be preferred tokens in the lexicon. In general, one would expect that the token ranking is similar to the ranking of segments in terms of their 'entrance' into segmental systems of increasing size. Hence if a language can have [t] without [d], but not vice versa, we would expect [t] to be more preferred than [d] in a language that has both. The similarities between preference ranking and system preference follow from the fact that both are rooted in bias/harmony and dispersion.

8.5 Summary and concluding remarks

In this chapter we have seen that the RCVP notation provides not only a metatheory of phonological primitives, but also a formal grounding for approaching preference rankings of segments in specific syllabic positions and of segmental systems as a whole. We have seen that dispersion and harmony play a fundamental role in positional preference rankings. Preferences for segmental systems show the relevance of both these principles, as would be expected, but need to take into account additional principles such as balance, economy and complexity.

My main point in this chapter has been to show that the two fundamental principles of harmony (both paradigmatic and syntagmatic) and dispersion find a natural formulation in the RCVP notation, which intrinsically connects syllabic positions and elements in terms of the overarching C/V primitives, which leads to harmony. Dispersion can be stated in a principled manner because each element class is composed of antagonistic units that, as such, maximise perceptual distance and thus dispersion.

Additionally, the consistent recruitment of head-dependency relations provides a further basis for deriving a ranking of element classes and element structures in terms of preference. Feature models that lack the use of dependency and that encode all features in terms of formally unrelated labels cannot provide the same grounding and must thus be supplemented with scales that are unrelated to the feature model.

9

Minimal specification

9.1 Introduction

Given an inventory of segments and a set of features, there are two ways to perform the feature analysis. Either all segments are specified for all features (maximal or full specification) or the feature specification is kept maximally simple (minimal or impoverished specification). RCVP subscribes to minimal specification, because it is my assumption that the distinction between contrastive and non-contrastive[1] properties is foundational to phonology. Using Occam's razor, we might then see how far we can push minimal specification, possibly also omitting contrastive properties in some circumstances. Of course, any specification, whichever view is adopted, must be correlated with phonetic properties. In a full specification approach this correlation is rather straightforward: every feature specification is implemented in terms of a phonetic correlate and these correlations must be subject to co-articulation, which creates the overlap that is characteristic of speech (and sign), and other local and global influences on phonetic implementation, such as in tonal domain, downstep and declination. When we adopt minimal specification, the question arises whether, prior to phonetic implementation, feature specifications are filled in so that we arrive at a full specification, or whether phonetic implementation can bypass that step, doing all the work that is necessary to arrive at a phonetic representation.

What counts as a minimal specification depends on certain assumptions regarding exactly what can be left unspecified, with a major difference between assuming that only non-contrastive, redundant specifications count as such (contrastive underspecification) and that, when a contrast exists, one specification, referred to as a default specification, can also be left out (radical underspecification).[2] With respect to the choice of the

---

[1] I will use the terms (non-)contrastive and (non-)distinctive interchangeably.
[2] Here the term 'radical' is not associated with the use of 'radical' in the name of the current model, although there is, as we will see, a 'family resemblance' in the sense that using unary primes is a radicalisation of radical underspecification.

feature system, a major difference exists between using binary features and using unary features (or elements). See § 2.2.1 for a discussion of these various distinctions.

An important issue is also how exactly one arrives at a minimal specification, given that, as we will see, there is not always only one way to get there. This means that we need a procedure or algorithm that guides the way to a minimal specification.

This chapter investigates these various issues, and related ones, with particular attention to the possibility of using radical underspecification in a unary system, and how, within such a system, we can arrive at a minimal representation.

To set the stage, § 9.2 starts with a typology of redundant properties. § 9.3 introduces radical underspecification, while § 9.4 explains how both contrastive and radical underspecification apply to RCVP. § 9.5 briefly revisits the notion of markedness in relation to complexity. § 9.6 discusses and illustrates the idea (advanced in Dresher (2009)) that elements are specified in accordance with a ranking of elements. I will show that Dresher's algorithm is compatible with the logic of RCVP and I will also (contra Dresher) argue that there is no cross-linguistic variability in the ranking of features or elements; rather, a universal ranking will be shown to be implicit in the RCVP segmental architecture. In § 9.7 I ask whether redundant elements can be active in the phonology. Finally, in § 9.8 I discuss a typology of constraints which limit the universally possible segmental inventories to those that occur in actual languages. I will also discuss the format of constraints (as negative or positive) and the issue of how constraints are learned.

9.2 A typology of redundant properties

In binary feature theories, it has long been suggested that we need to distinguish between contrastive and non-contrastive or redundant specifications. A widespread idea has been that redundant properties can be left unspecified (cf. Halle (1959)). Their presence, late in the phonology, just before phonetic implementation, can be handled by the application of redundancy rules that fill them in (Steriade (1995)). It has also been suggested that redundant properties can remain unspecified in the phonology, leaving it to the phonetic implementation to spell out the phonetic details (Keating (1988c)). It has been argued that, given the assumption that redundancy rules can be extrinsically ordered among phonological rules that account for allophonic and allomorphic alternations, leaving out redundant properties can be problematic and lead to an apparent ternary system (Stanley (1967)).

Several kinds of redundancy can be distinguished. I will start the discussion with a typology of redundant properties, indicating how redundancy has been dealt with in binary feature theories. Then I will turn to the account in RCVP, which uses unary primitives.

(1) A typology of redundant properties in a binary feature system:[3]

Non-contrastive properties are left out ('contrastive specification').

a. Paradigmatic contextual neutralisation: a feature F that is used contrastively in a segment system in some segment classes is not used in other segment classes; for example:
   i. Mid front vowels like [e] are redundantly [−round], while rounding is contrastive among high front vowels ([i] vs. [y]), for instance in a system [i y u e o a].
   ii. The low vowel is redundantly [+back] while backness is contrastive among non-low vowels, for instance in a five-vowel system [i u e o a].
   iii. High vowels are redundantly [+ATR] and the low vowel is redundantly [−ATR], while ATR is distinctive for mid-vowels in a system [i u e o ɛ ɔ a].

b. Syntagmatic contextual neutralisation: a feature is used contrastively in a segment class, but not when that class occurs in a specific position (either in terms of syllable or word edge, or due to stress):
   i. Obstruents are redundantly [−voice] in word-final position, whereas the voice difference between obstruents is distinctive in other positions.
   ii. Obstruents are redundantly [+voice] in intervocalic position, whereas the voice difference between obstruents is distinctive in other positions.
   iii. The second consonant in a complex onset can only be a liquid, that is, is redundantly [−sonorant, −nasal, . . .].

c. Syntagmatic contextual allophonic variation:
   i. Vowels preceding a nasal consonant are 'nasalised'.
   ii. Voiceless stops are redundantly [+aspirated] in pre-stress position.

d. Absolute, that is, context-free neutralisation: a feature is not used contrastively at all in a given language, nor is it involved in (perceptually salient) allophonic variation:
   i. In a five-vowel system [i u e o a], back, non-low vowels are redundantly [+round] and the low vowel is redundantly [−round].
   ii. In a five-vowel [u, i, e, o, a] system, ATR is not used: high and mid vowels are redundantly [+ATR].

---

[3] Within each type, we could make finer distinctions, but I will refrain from going into too much detail.

iii. All obstruents are redundantly [−continuant] (if there are no fricatives).
iv. All obstruents are redundantly [−voice] (if there are no voiced obstruents), and voicing is predictable in sonorants.
v. All vowels are 'central' and [−round] (in a vertical vowel system).
vi. All vowels are toneless (there is no contrastive tone).
vii. All consonants are non-aspirated and non-glottalised.

In cases of paradigmatic neutralisation (neutralisation based on intrasegmental context) and syntagmatic neutralisation (neutralisation based on surrounding context), most phonologists would write a rule that expresses the predictable value, this rule being a redundancy rule (if the feature specification is predictable in some context, but not in others) or a 'phonological rule' (if the neutralisation causes allophonic variation, as in the case of final devoicing). The cases in (1c) would be accounted for by allophonic rules.

The distinction between (1b) and (1c) rests on the claim that in (1b) there is, in fact, a neutralisation of a contrast that obtains in some context. However, it has been shown for cases like (1bi–ii) that there may not be neutralisation in such cases. For the example of final devoicing it has been shown that in many languages there is in fact no complete neutralisation; see Brockhaus (1995) and van der Hulst (2015a); this may apply to all so-called automatic cases of neutralisation. An argument has thus been made for treating those cases along with the allophonic processes in (1c) together, possibly as part of the phonetic implementation (see § 1.5). In this sense (1biii) is different, because here the lack of segments other than liquids in the onset dependent position is an aspect of distribution, which means that a redundancy rule would be formulated, unless an alternation is involved. However, languages typically do not have morphological contexts in which some non-liquid consonant changes into a liquid when the prefixation of an obstruent gives rise to a complex onset.

With respect to (1ci-ii), a phonologist would write an allophonic rule, although for nasalisation, being a gradient phenomenon, it might be more appropriate to relegate this to the phonetic implementation (see Krämer (2019) for discussion).

In the case of (1d), absolute neutralisation (complete neutralisation with respect to some feature that may be distinctive in some other language), redundancy rules would again be the most usual analysis. However, in the case of (1dvi–vii), which involve manner or place features, no such rules would be written. For these cases, it would seem that *a whole feature class* is simply 'irrelevant' in the language at issue, and no redundancy rule would or could be formulated that would specify a predictable value. Tone features in English are simply irrelevant at the lexical level and it does not even make sense to formulate a redundancy rule. Of course, vowels do get realised at a certain pitch level, which may vary depending on context, but such phonetic details would be relegated to phonetic implementation.[4]

Whether or not predictable properties are filled in late in the phonology or in phonetic implementation, the idea would be that leaving them unspecified up to some point in the derivation, broadly construed, explains that these properties cannot play a role in (most of) the phonology. An alternative approach is to specify all feature values (as proposed in Stanley (1967), and adopted in SPE), which then requires a set of redundancy *conditions*. Another full specification model is proposed by Calabrese (2005). He assumes that redundant feature values *are* specified, but somehow marked as 'invisible'. However, his full specification approach would presumably not assume specification for 'irrelevant features classes', however precisely defined. In summary, there are thus three approaches to predictable feature specifications:

(2) Predictable feature specifications are:
   a. not specified in the phonology at all, accounting for all of them in the phonetic implementation (as suggested in § 1.5);
   b. specified at some point in the phonology, when there is evidence for activity (see § 9.7); or
   c. always specified but somehow represented as predictable, for example by having the property of being 'invisible'.

Which approach is preferable depends on whether the predictable specifications can be active in the phonology (at some late level). Another factor is that when the phonetic output is variable, no feature value can be inserted, which means that the phonetic implementation has to step in. This argument is made in Keating (1988c). The third option, specifying all values from the start, might solve a technical problem if one were to argue that any system that uses the zero option runs the risk of being 'ternary' (see Stanley (1967)), although his reasons for rejecting underspecification were countered by Ringen (1975) and Kiparsky (1982a).

9.3 Radical underspecification

A further step towards impoverished specification is that, even in the case of contrast, one of the values, called the default (or complement)

---

[4] In vertical vowel systems it is also the case that an element class is irrelevant, namely the place class (at least for vowels); this, then, may also discourage writing redundancy rules, in particular since in those cases the vowels are central (see § 4.3.1.1), unless there are consonantal influences that give colour vowels.

Minimal specification 329

value, can be left unspecified (Archangeli (1984); Kiparsky (1982a)). Proponents of this approach have assumed that there are different cases of such radical underspecification:

(3) a. The same value is left out for the entire language (although what is the specified value and what is the default value could differ from language to language).
 b. The choice may depend on other feature specifications (paradigmatic).
 c. The choice may depend on the position in the word (syntagmatic).

The first case (3a) would result in leaving all voiceless obstruents in all positions unspecified for voice, when voicing is contrastive. Here the question is whether it is universally the same value that is left unspecified, or whether the choice could be language-specific. The second case (3b) would apply when, for example, the plus value for the feature [ATR] is left unspecified for high and mid ATR vowels, even though ATR is contrastive in those classes, but not for the low vowel, where it is not contrastive. In that case there would be a default rule assigning [+ATR] to non-low vowels and a redundancy rule assigning 7[-ATR] to low vowels. Case (3c) would apply when [+voice] for obstruents is left unspecified intervocalically, while in other positions (e.g. word-initial onsets) [-voice] would be unspecified, with voicing being contrastive in all these positions. As in the case of predictable properties, complement properties can also be handled in the three ways in (4):

(4) Default (or complement) feature specifications are:
 a. not specified in the phonology at all;
 b. specified at some point in the phonology, when there is evidence for activity; or
 c. always specified but somehow represented as predictable, for example by having the property of being 'invisible'.

Combining contrastive and radical underspecification would surely lead to phonological representations that are minimally specified.

However, it has long been noticed that underspecification of redundant specification based on predictability from other, feature values may run into the problem that the direction of predictability is not always obvious (as in the co-occurrence of back and roundness in non-low vowels in a five-vowel system; see Schane (1973)). Hence in such cases there is ambiguity in arriving at a unique minimal representation (see Ewen & van der Hulst (2001) for further discussion). The problem is exacerbated in radical underspecification approaches, especially when the choice of which value is the default/complement value is not universally fixed.

A proposal for how to arrive at minimally specified representations, using binary features in a completely deterministic way, avoiding ambiguities, was made in Dresher (2009). Dresher adopts an underspecification algorithm that refers to a hierarchy of features. This procedure is made explicit by the adoption of the following algorithm:[5]

(5) Successive Division Algorithm (SDA):

   a. In the initial state, all sounds are assumed to be variants of a single phoneme.
   b. If the set is found to have more than one phoneme, a binary distinction is made on the basis of one of the universal set of distinctive features; this cut divides the inventory into a marked set and an unmarked set. The selected feature is *contrastive* for all members of these sets.
   c. Step (b) is repeated in each set with the next feature in the hierarchy, dividing each remaining set until all distinctive sounds have been differentiated.
   d. If a feature has not been designated as contrastive for a phoneme, then it is *redundant* for that phoneme.

I will illustrate this approach with reference to the vowel system of Nez Perce (see Dresher (2009: 186)):[6]

(6) a. Nez Perce: [low] > [round] > [ATR]

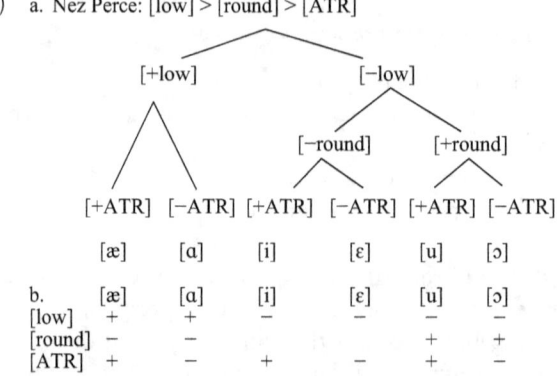

b.

	[æ]	[a]	[i]	[ɛ]	[u]	[ɔ]
[low]	+	+	−	−	−	−
[round]	−	−		−	+	+
[ATR]	+	−	+	−	+	−

---

[5] This algorithm is similar in spirit to the notion of recursive splitting that was discussed in § 3.2.1. Dresher (2009: 6, fn. 7) clearly indicates that the C/V splitting method of RCVP stands in the tradition that he follows.

[6] I analyse the vowel harmony system of this language in van der Hulst (2018: § 10.3.1), adopting a somewhat different interpretation of this vowel system.

It would seem that Dresher's approach would not disallow non-specification of one of the minimally required contrastive specifications (which then achieves radical underspecification). I believe that this possibility is not explicitly exploited in Dresher's model, although in some examples he would use 'non-low' instead of [−low], which suggests a unary usage of the features, which then leads to a radically underspecified representation. Applying that strategy to (6) would deliver (7):

(7) a.   Nez Perce: [low] > [round] > [ATR]

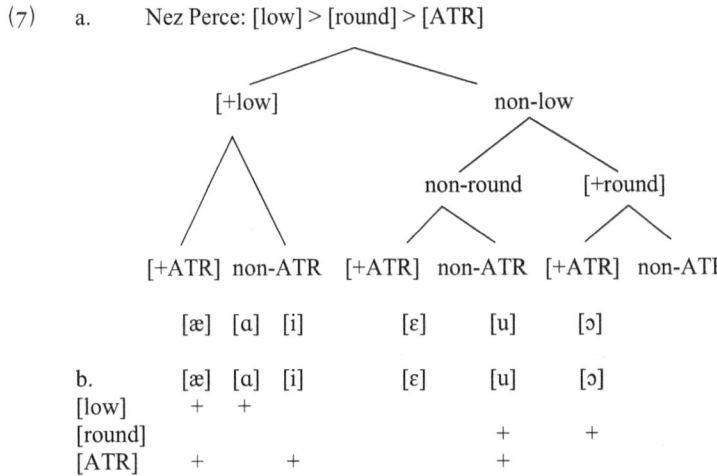

b.
	[æ]	[ɑ]	[i]	[ɛ]	[u]	[ɔ]
[low]	+	+				
[round]					+	+
[ATR]	+		+		+	

I discuss his proposal in § 9.6 with reference to the unary features that are proposed in this book, making the point that in RCVP his algorithm for arriving at a minimal specification is, in fact, built in, but I will also propose that the ranking of features is universally fixed.

9.4 Contrastive and radical underspecification in a unary framework

When we use unary 'features', most cases of radical underspecification as used in a binary system simply do not arise (see § 2.2). For example, if a language has no voicing contrast for obstruents, and assuming that the phonetic distinction at play is encoded by the presence of a positive element for voice, there is no sense in which the voiceless obstruents could be specified with an element that represents voicelessness.[7] It seems clear that unarism 'radicalises' radical underspecification by banning one 'value' for each feature from the phonology completely (see van der Hulst (2016a)).

---

[7] Arguably, one might say that the neutralised obstruent bears the element C (tense), since in RCVP head element classes contain two antagonistic elements. I will return to this point below.

I will now examine the same cases as in (1), assuming a unary system that corresponds to the RCVP elements, using the familiar, shorthand labels instead of the C/V notation:

(8) A typology of redundant properties in a unary system:

a. Paradigmatic contextual neutralisation: a feature F that is used contrastively in a segment system in some segment classes is not used in other segment classes; for example:
   i   Mid front vowels are redundantly [−round] while rounding is contrastive among high front vowels ([i] vs. [y]), for instance in a system [i y u e o a].
       - The element U would combine with I to form [y] and there would not be a mid front vowel that has the same combination;[8] there is no formal object '[−round]'.
   ii. The low vowel is redundantly [+back] while backness is contrastive among non-low vowels, for instance in a five-vowel system [i u e o a].
       - The low vowel would have the element A and there would be no low vowels that combine this element with either I or U.
   iii. High vowels are redundantly [ATR] and the low vowel is redundantly [−ATR], while ATR is distinct for mid vowels in a system [i u e o ɛ ɔ a].
       - An ATR element would occur on mid vowels but not on high and low vowels; that high vowels are phonetically advanced and the low vowel is non-advanced would be a matter of phonetic implementation.[9]

b. Syntagmatic contextual neutralisation: a feature is used contrastively in a segment class, but not when that class occurs in a specific position; for instance, voicing is contrastive for obstruents, but not word-finally; this is called positional neutralisation:
   i. Obstruents are redundantly [−voice] in word-final position, whereas the voice difference in obstruents is distinctive in other positions.
       - Final obstruents would be represented without the voice element.

---

[8] This assumes that we have constraints on element co-occurrences as part of the phonological grammar; see § 9.6.
[9] In the cases in (8ai–ii) there would be nothing to phonetically implement, while in case (8aiii), since high vowels would be phonetically advanced, phonetic implementation 'adds' the property of advancement. I argue in van der Hulst (2018) that phonetic implementation can add phonetic properties that are not backed up by specified elements, but it cannot ignore implementation of specified elements. In § 9.7 I will discuss whether, in those cases where I claim that phonetic implementation adds a phonetic property, a case can be made for adding the property as an element late in the phonology instead, particularly in cases where such properties seem to be phonologically active.

ii. Obstruents are redundantly [+voice] in intervocalic position, whereas the voice difference between obstruents is distinctive in other positions.
   - Intervocalic obstruents are voiced due to phonetic implementation.
iii. The second consonant in a complex onset can only be a liquid, that is, is redundantly [−sonorant, -nasal, . . .].
   - Consonants in this position would only have manner elements that characterise the class of liquids.

c. Syntagmatic contextual allophonic variation:
   i. Vowels preceding a nasal consonant are 'nasalised'.
      - Nasalised vowels would be nasalised due to phonetic implementation.
   ii. Voiceless stops are redundantly [+aspirated] in pre-stress position.
      - Aspiration is due to phonetic implementation.

d. Absolute, that is, context-free neutralisation: a feature is not used contrastively at all in a given language:
   i. In a five-vowel system [i u e o a], back, non-low vowels are redundantly [+round].
      - In the 'aiu' system there is no element for back, so non-low vowels that do not have the element I (which would make them front) instead have the element U.
   ii. In a five-vowel [i u e o a] system, ATR is not used: high (and mid) vowels are redundantly [+ATR].
      - High and mid vowel are advanced due to phonetic implementation.
   iii. All obstruents are redundantly [−continuant] (if there are no fricatives)
      - No obstruents have the element for continuancy, because a stop is due to phonetic implementation.
   iv. All obstruents are redundantly [−voice] (if there are no voiced obstruents).
      - No obstruents have the voice element, because voiced is due to phonetic implementation.
   v. All vowels are 'central' and [−round] (in a vertical vowel system).
      - The colour elements U and I are not active; colour, if present, is due to phonetic implementation.
   vi. All vowels are toneless (there is no contrastive tone).
      - Tonal elements are not active; pitch levels are due to phonetic implementation.
   vii. All consonants are non-aspirated and non-glottalised.
      - There are no elements for these special phonation types to be interpreted.

Of course, just as in binary systems, properties that are predictable can be 'represented' in several ways:

(9) Predictable elements are:
   a. not specified in the phonology at all; phonetic implementation takes care of 'everything';
   b. specified as elements at some point in the phonology, when there is evidence for activity (see § 9.7); or
   c. always specified but somehow represented as predictable, for example by having the property of being 'invisible'.

Even though the use of unary elements pre-empts radical underspecification in most cases, the zero option can be used in an element system. For example, as shown in Ewen & van der Hulst (1987)), if vowels are specified in terms of the element A, I and U, it is always possible to represent one vowel as lacking an element. In principle, then, the use of the zero option *as a contrastive category* is also available within the RCVP approach. This applies in the primary classes when there is a polar contrast between the two simple primary elements.[10] I will here consider the cases of contrast between primary elements:

(10)		Consonant	Vowel
	Manner	C (stop) vs. V (fricative)	C (high) vs. V (low)
	location	C (cor) vs. V (lab)	C (front) vs. V (round)
	laryngeal	C (tense) vs. V (voiced)	C (H) vs. V (L)

In each case, a contrast C vs. V could be specified as C vs. o or V vs. o, with the null option representing the 'complement' element (V and C, respectively). But what might determine the choice between these two ways of employing 'radical underspecification'? Consider the case of obstruents in a language with a contrast between stops and fricatives (in onset head position). We have seen in § 8.3 that the harmonic value for obstruent manner is C (stop), because it agrees with the nature of the onset head position (C). Thus, fricatives are less preferred, which is one way of saying that they are 'marked'. This could suggest that fricatives have to be *literally* marked with the V element, leaving stops literally unmarked, making the preferred element the complement (or default) choice.

---

[10] This cannot be done for secondary elements because here the absence of a specification does not imply the presence of the other secondary elements; rather, absence means that there is no secondary specification; see (18) below, where I explain that secondary specification for vowels (register) may be a difference in this respect.

The alternative would be that contrast is instead marked by the element that is the harmonic element, that is, the element that is the most typical (best) element for that position since it caters to the syntagmatic contrast between consonants and vowels (or onsets and rhymes). In favour of this alternative, one could say that the harmonic element is, in a sense, the 'cheapest way' to encode the contrast, precisely because it is expected, given the nature of the syllabic position. An objection to this alternative is that we now formally present the harmonic (i.e. 'unmarked') element as marked, that is, as more complex. However, we will see in a moment that there is a way of regarding the fixed specification of the harmonic C element as formally simpler than the non-marking of the 'marked' V. One would then assume that by marking the preferred choice, we predict that segments that have the preferred choice are phonetically realised with a well-defined phonetic target, while the unmarked member in the opposition gets its phonetic details from phonetic implementation, predicting variability or context-sensitivity.

The following table summarises the biased element choices (following the paradigmatic correlation A that was introduced in § 8.2.1):

(11)

	Consonant	Vowel
Manner	C (stop) vs. V (fricative)	C (high) vs. V (low)
location	C (coronal) vs. V (labial)	C (front) vs. V (round)
laryngeal	C (tense) vs. V (voiced)	C (H) vs. V (L)

We have noted in § 8.2.1 that the preferred harmonic relations for obstruents (stop, coronal and tense) are supported by the observation that [t] is the preferred onset cross-linguistically (after an initial stage in acquisition where labial perhaps take centre stage). We also noted that it is not clear that the preferred properties for vowels (low, round, L) are likewise supported, and I refer to the discussion in that section for factors that may prevent rounding and low tone being the expected elements for vowels.

Adopting the view that harmonic properties are specified (in cases of contrast), leaving the phonetic interpretation of their absence to the phonetic implementation, predicts a specific 'learning path' that guides the postulation of segmental representations.

I will demonstrate the progression and specification of the emergence of contrast with obstruent manner. The initial assumption of the learner is that there is no contrast (Dresher (2009) also makes this assumption), which means that there is only one class of obstruents, namely stops (marked with C):[11]

---

[11] This is after the learner has decided that there is a sequential syllabic CV structure, which of course is the first step in the acquisitional process.

(12) No contrast   C (Onset)
                               |
                         [man: C] (i.e. stop)

Here, we run into an apparent problem. Why would the manner be specified as C, while there is no contrast between stops and fricatives at this point in the development? Why not simply leaving the stop unspecified for manner? The reason for being suspicious of such underspecification is, as I have argued in Section 7.2, that manner is the obligatory unit in the segmental structure and, moreover, that a class node without an element is meaningless, that is, ill-formed in the present model. To resolve this issue, I appeal to a proposal made in van der Hulst (2018), namely that elements that are predictable due to the absence of contrast are represented as 'variable'. In that work, I recruited the variable notation to account for allomorphic alternations in vowel harmony (but meant as a mechanism for all allomorphic alternations) and also for predictable properties of vowels that behave ambiguously, such as neutral vowels (for example, the vowel [i] in Hungarian or Finnish), which can occur in both back and front environments; see van der Hulst (2018: § 3.6.2.2). The shared property of alternating vowels and neutral vowels that occur with both harmonic classes is 'duality of behaviour'. I will now add to this idea that we can represent all non-contrastive elements as variable, thus preventing the problem just noted, assuming that a variable specification is a specification. This loosens the criterion of duality, although I hypothesise that variable properties display phonetic variability, which is also a kind of duality. We can thus replace (12) with (13):

(13) No contrast   C (Onset)
                               |
                         [man: (C)] (i.e. stop)

The variable notation not only expresses that there is no contrast, but also formally captures the potential phonetic variability of the obstruents in question.[12]

Once a contrast between stops and fricatives is acquired, the harmonic C specification for stops becomes fixed, while fricatives receive variable (V). Assuming that a variable specification (being essentially a disjunction of an elements specification and 'zero') is more complex than a fixed

---

[12] I am here assuming that variable elements have a looser phonetic interpretation, i.e. a less clear phonetic target, than fixed elements. This corresponds to Keating's (1988c) suggestion that features that are not specified in the phonology do not have a clear phonetic target.

specification, the result is that the harmonic specification of stops is in fact formally simpler than the specification of fricatives:

(14)   C (onset): manner

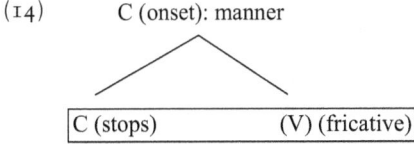

The next step could be that the learner detects an intermediate manner category. If the new category is a mellow fricative, this necessitates the specification of the fixed V element as a head, and this means that the element is now also fixed for plain (strident) fricatives. In support of this, I hypothesise that the inclusion of mellow fricatives entails a phonetic dispersion between the two fricatives types so that the strident fricative is no longer *phonetically* variable:

(15)   C (onset): manner

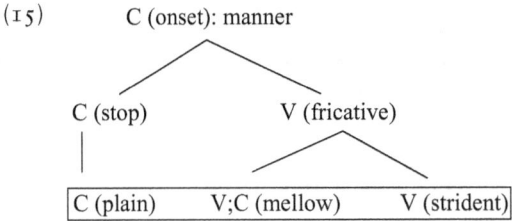

However, if the new category is an affricate, this requires the V element as a dependent, and this might not necessitate specifying plain strident fricatives with a fixed V:

(16)   C (onset): manner

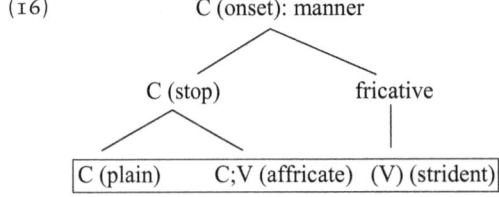

I will leave this last point unresolved.

Thus far I have discussed the specification of head elements. Before we turn to the next section, where I will relate the view on underspecification that was developed in this section to the one proposed in Dresher (2009), we need to discuss the specification of secondary elements. In the RCVP model, contrast, or lack of it, arises at two levels in the structure:

(17) Two levels of potential contrast:[13]
   a. within the head class: contrast between C and V (and combinations thereof); and
   b. within the secondary class: contrastive presence of c and/or v.[14]

We have just discussed case (17a), claiming the harmonic element carries the burden of encoding the contrast, with the other, opposite element being variable. I now turn to (17b): the presence or absence of a contrastive secondary property. The secondary class is only activated if there is a contrastive secondary property. Thus, when a contrast involves a secondary element, the element that encodes the secondary property is specified. With respect to secondary elements, the presence of one or two (or even more) properties is contrastive with their absence. It is important to note that absence of a secondary property is not represented in terms of a variable element. The reason is that the availability of secondary properties is not a binary choice, since the third choice is simply that there is no secondary property. The only exception here regards the secondary laryngeal properties for vowels that involve the register distinction. The reason for this is 'phonetic'. The two secondary properties for manner do not form part of the same phonetic dimension (RTR and nasalised), nor do the secondary properties for place (palatalised and labialised). However, once register is active, *all* tonal specification must have a register element (see § 6.3). Thus, all the three-way contrasts in (18) are permitted, except the one in (18Bc):

(18) A. Secondary properties for consonants (examples):

   a. Manner: C (stop)   Manner: C (stop)   Manner: C (stop)
                          + c (pharyngeal)   + v (nasal)

   b. Place: C (coronal) Place: C (coronal)   Place: C (coronal)
                          + c (palatalised)   + v (labialised)

   c. Laryngeal: C (tense) Laryngeal: C (tense) Laryngeal: C (tense)
                            + c (glottal)   + v (aspiration)

   B. Secondary properties for vowels (examples):

   a. Manner: C (high)   Manner: C (high)   Manner: C (high)
                          + c (nasal)   + v (RTR)

   b. Place: C (front)   Place: C   Place: C
                          + c (ATR)   + v [not defined]

---

[13] The absence or presence of a class node cannot function contrastively.
[14] I have suggested that the contrastive presence of c/v combinations is rare and perhaps only necessary in the manner class.

c. *Laryngeal: C (H)   Laryngeal C (H)   Laryngeal C (H)
                          + c (high reg)   + v (low reg)

Only in cases of register distinctions can the variable notation be used for the register level that is not harmonic, namely low register (v), which is harmonic with the syllabic nucleus (V).

The development of contrast progresses in the way outlined here for each element class that is relevant in the language. While it is reasonable to assume that the initial development of the manner class comes first, other element classes can develop before all manner contrasts are developed. In the previous chapter I referred to this back-and-forth between the development of contrast in the different element classes as balance (see § 8.4).

In this section I have laid out the ground rules for when and how elements are specified. I have proposed that in cases of contrast, harmonic elements are specified as fixed for head elements, while non-harmonic elements are specified as variable. In the absence of contrast, the harmonic element is specified as variable. With respect to secondary elements, variable specification is only justified for register.

9.5 Markedness, complexity and salience

The term 'markedness' has been used in many different ways.[15] Markedness in most unary systems is taken literally, much as in the original sense in which Trubetzkoy (1939 [1977]) intended it. A phoneme's markedness is literally determined by the number of its marks. Taken in this sense, markedness correlates with complexity. That bearing a mark contributes to complexity and markedness is evident when we consider element combinations in the head classes; C;V and V;C are more complex, and more marked, than C and V. With regard to secondary elements, marking likewise correlates with greater complexity and being more marked.

In the preceding section I first advocated the view that harmonic elements, which I had thus far been referred to as 'unmarked', are in fact formally marked. However, I then suggested that the difference between having a fixed mark and having a variable mark *can* be seen as a complexity difference, because the variable specification, which involves a disjunction, is more complex than a fixed specification. While the variable notation is obviously a way of capturing what in other systems is treated as underspecification, the variable notation is thus advantageous, since non-specification could never be called more complex than specification.

---

[15] This leads some linguists to say that the notion is meaningless; see Haspelmath (2006).

However, there may still be another problem if we equate markedness with complexity. There are cases of apparently undisputed non-specification which do *not* correlate with being unmarked. A case in point concerns central vowels, which lack a place specification in comparison with non-central vowels. Arguably, colourless non-low vowels, while less complex, are less preferred than colourful vowels, and the reason is obvious: colourless non-low vowels do not have clearly perceptible properties; they have no colour identity and this makes their identification more difficult. The theory of vowel dispersion, which explains the occurrence of the triangular [a i u] vowel system in terms of dispersion, is based on the fact that the triangular vowels have identifiable properties. If, then, colourless non-low vowels are represented as lacking place elements, this lack of element specification does not translate into being unmarked. Van der Hulst and van de Weijer (2018a) conclude that markedness thus does not always correlate with complexity; it does in some cases, but not in others. It would seem that markedness is the result of a deviation from '1': bearing a clear, single mark in an element class is what causes a segment to be unmarked because having precisely one element (in some class) is maximally perceptually salient. Clearly, both having a mixture of elements (C;V, V;C, or indeed C{c}, C{v}, V{c}, V{v}) and having no mark lead to lower salience. While the preceding reasoning strikes me as sound, it is perhaps not a good idea to see markedness as resulting from 'o' or 'more than 1' in all cases. For starters, the zero option cannot occur in the manner class, where a manner specification is obligatory. Hence for this class markedness always correlates with complexity. Secondly, we do not want to say that vowels in a language that has no lexical tone are more marked than vowels with tone in a tone language. It would thus seem that the reasoning that having no mark at all leads to being 'marked' only applies to the place class: central vowels (except for the low vowel) and pharyngeal consonants miss a place element and are considered marked in comparison with vowels or consonants with a place element.

In conclusion, the correlation between markedness and complexity is almost perfect. It only needs to be amended as resulting from non-specification in the place class when non-specification is contrastive with the specification of one or two place elements.

9.6 Examples of minimal specification

To achieve minimal representation within the proposed RCVP model, van der Hulst (2018) uses the approach to underspecification developed in Dresher (2009) that I discussed here in § 9.3. The approach sketched in § 9.4 is fully compatible with Dresher's model. What I did not make clear in van der Hulst (2018), but what became evident in § 9.4, is that

Minimal specification 341

there is actually no need to formulate the SDA as an independent module in RCVP. The SDA is, as it were, built into the 'logic' of RCVP, which predicts a path (both a learning path for the child and an analytic path for the phonologist) for 'successively' specifying elements up to a point where all segments are distinguished. This leaves the issue of feature/element rankings as a real difference between Dresher's model and mine. Contra Dresher's proposal, in van der Hulst (2018) I claim that ranking differences are not necessary. Rather, a universal ranking of elements can be derived from the element geometry, by assigning an asterisk to each head at both levels:[16]

(19) a. V syllabic V position, i.e. nucleus

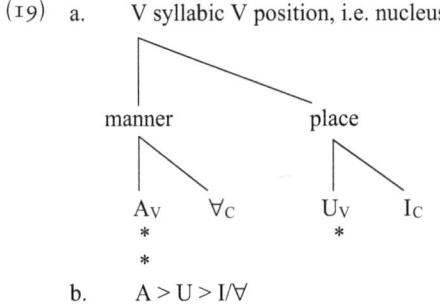

b.   A > U > I/∀

In these structures the harmonic elements A and U are represented as 'harmonic heads', being V elements in the syllabic V position. In this ranking the elementa I and ∀ have equal 'prominence'. In van der Hulst (2018: 75), I assume that

> I, which denotes a more salient phonetic event, takes precedence over ∀, unless this element is non-distinctive and/or occurs in a 'mixture' with the U element (as in Finnish, where [i] and [e] are so-called neutral vowels and front rounded vowels [ü] and [ö] are present).

See van der Hulst (2018: 88–9) for further discussion, including of the cases in which Dresher finds that different rankings are called for.[17]

Given (19), if there is no vowel contrast, the expected default is A. If a contrast is detected, it will be a contrast between A and ∀. The first binary contrast is thus a manner contrast; place does not yet come into

---

[16] The method for assigning asterisks is the same that Liberman & Prince (1977) propose for deriving a grid from a metrical tree: at the lowest layer assign an asterisk to each head; at the next layer assign another asterisk to the ultimate head of each head, etc.
[17] In particular, see § 4.2.2 in van der Hulst (2018), which analyses the vowel systems of a variety of Balto-Finnic languages in which neutral vowels behave differently.

consideration. Contrast in manner precedes contrast in place (colour), which is expected given that manner is the head class. This, however, does not mean that all manner contrasts will be exploited before turning to colour. The ranking in (19b) formally captures the notion of 'balance' that was introduced in § 8.4. After separating vowels in terms of the A element, the learner (or linguist) turns to the harmonic colour element U.

To once more illustrate the learning path, consider a three- and a five-vowel system:[18]

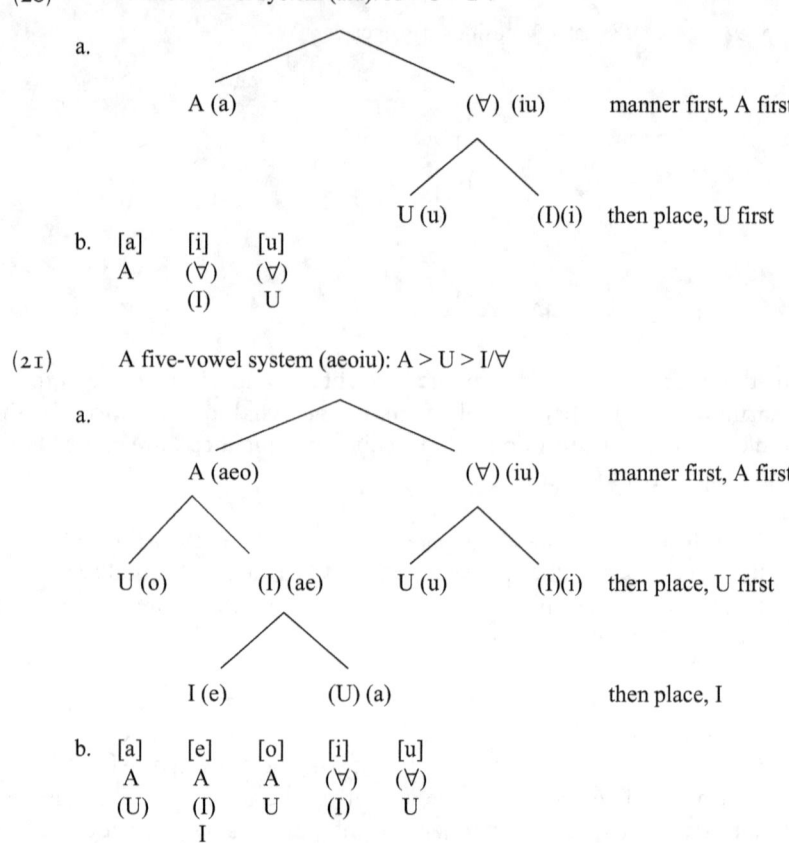

(20)   A three-vowel system (aiu): A > U > I/∀

a.

        A (a)   (∀) (iu)   manner first, A first

                         U (u) (I)(i) then place, U first

b. [a] [i] [u]
     A   (∀) (∀)
          (I) U

(21)   A five-vowel system (aeoiu): A > U > I/∀

a.

       A (aeo)   (∀) (iu)   manner first, A first

  U (o) (I) (ae)   U (u) (I)(i) then place, U first

       I (e) (U) (a)   then place, I

b. [a] [e] [o] [i] [u]
     A   A   A   (∀) (∀)
    (U) (I) U   (I) U
            I

---

[18] For an analysis of many more vowel systems, see van der Hulst (2018), but bear in mind that in that work I did not use the variable notation for the non-harmonic elements; rather, I used the symbol 'Ø' for underspecification. Also note that the variable specifications are placed on the same line as the harmonic opposite element that is the target of the parsing phase. An element can thus be variable on one line and fixed on its own line, in which case the element counts as fixed.

We note that the vowel [a] has a variable element U. This follows from the method that was proposed in § 8.4. Low vowels are reluctant to show variability involving rounding because rounding and low do not mix well (see Kaun (1995, 2004)).

In practice, this developmental scheme implies the following ordering of elements with respect to their activation:

(22)   Ranking:

Two-vowel system (no place): $A_V > \forall_C$
Three-vowel system without place: $A_V > \forall_C > A_V+\forall_C$
Three-vowel system with place: $A_V > U_V$
Five-vowel system: $A_V > U_V > I_C$
More complicated systems: $A_V > U_V > I_C > \forall_C$

I must stress that the 'parsing trees' do not form an independent level of representation. They merely depict how phonological segments are minimally represented, given the ranking of elements in (19b).

The preceding discussion of vowel systems has only looked at fairly simple examples; a more thorough discussion of vowel systems is offered in van der Hulst (2018), which accounts for the development of intermediate categories (different vowel heights) and some secondary properties (such as nasality or ATR), or even primary properties such as tone. It is clear that it cannot be expected that all these potentially distinctive properties will form one single ranking. Rather, while I have proposed an integrated ranking for manner and place elements, there are independent rankings for laryngeal and supralaryngeal (i.e. manner and place) properties and for primary and secondary distinctions within these, as well as higher-order rankings which may rank colour over laryngeal elements. Vowel systems (and consonant systems) can increase in complexity along these different paths and we would expect learners not to finish one line completely first and only then start the next. Rather, the increase in complexity is likely to be incorporated by the learner by switching back and forth between different lines of development. This is the notion of balance that I discussed earlier in this section and in § 8.4. Another dimension of vowel systems is that between short and long vowels and/or diphthongs, which involves an increase in complexity of the syllable rhyme.[19]

Consonant systems are of course even more complex than vowel systems. All languages have more consonants than vowels, often significantly more (MD). Nevertheless, we expect that a similar approach to

---

[19] Maddieson (2006b, 2007, 2009a) discusses similar ideas concerning the different layers of structure within which complexity may increase. These works also discuss other factors that play a role in the structure of segmental systems.

that taken to vowel systems can be developed for consonants. Starting simply, we would adopt the following ranking for obstruent manner and place, which is analogous to that for vowels in (19):

(23) a. C syllabic C-position, i.e. onset head

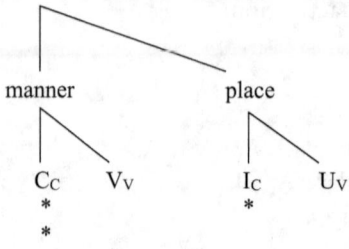

$$\begin{array}{cccc} & \text{manner} & & \text{place} \\ C_C & V_V & I_C & U_V \\ * & & * & \\ * & & & \end{array}$$

b. $C_C > I_C > V_V/U_V$

According to this ranking, and obviously after the syntagmatic contrast between vowel and consonant has been detected, the first split is that between stops and fricatives, followed by the split in terms of place:[20]

(24) A six-consonant system (ptkfsx): $C_{man} > I > U$

a.

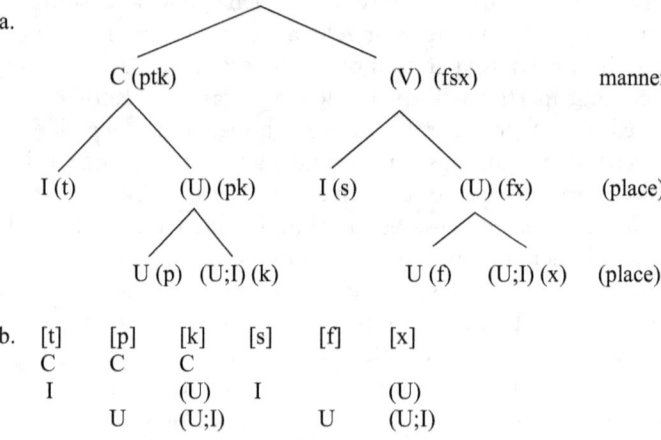

		C (ptk)			(V) (fsx)		manner
	I (t)		(U) (pk)	I (s)		(U) (fx)	(place)
		U (p)	(U;I) (k)		U (f)	(U;I) (x)	(place)

b.
	[t]	[p]	[k]	[s]	[f]	[x]
	C	C	C			
	I			I		
		U	(U)			(U)
			(U;I)		U	(U;I)

For more complex systems, further expansions take place along different dimensions, intermediate categories of manner (affricates, mellow fricatives) including phonation properties. Hence, if a system contains three series of consonants (stops, fricatives, voiced and voiceless, and nasals) with the same place of articulation, the following parsing tree applies:

---

[20] Note that at this level of parsing U (which is [place V]) stands in contrast with U;I [place V;C].

Minimal specification 345

(25) A twelve-consonant system (ptk, bdg, fsx, vzɣ): $C_{man} > I > U > C_{phon}$

a.
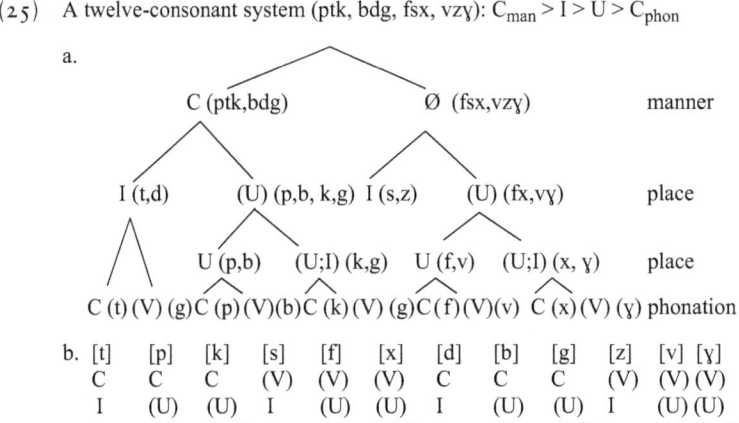

b.
[t]	[p]	[k]	[s]	[f]	[x]	[d]	[b]	[g]	[z]	[v]	[ɣ]
C	C	C	(V)	(V)	(V)	C	C	C	(V)	(V)	(V)
I	(U)	(U)	I	(U)	(U)	I	(U)	(U)	I	(U)	(U)
	U	(U;I)		U	(U;I)		U	(U;I)		U	(U;I)
C	C	C	C	C	C	(V)	(V)	(V)	(V)	(V)	(V)

It is of course likely that consonantal systems include sonorant consonants. This involves, in the RCVP model, a split in terms of the nature of the onset head position:

(26)   C   vs.   C
                          |
                          V

      Obstruent   sonorant consonant (flat notation: C|V)

The opposition between stops and nasals is reported as early in acquisition, before stops vs. fricatives. This means that the differentiation between stops and nasals precedes that between stops and fricatives.

(27) A fifteen-consonant system (ptk,fsx,bdg,vzɣ, mnŋ): $C_{man} > I > U > C_{phon}$

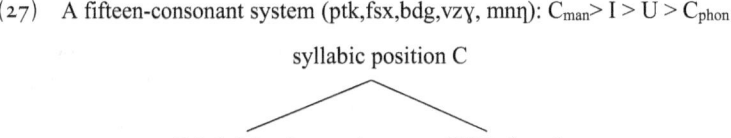

The subsequent parsing could first differentiate in term of continuancy, and place can proceed as in (25).

The phonetic implementation will be held responsible for spelling out the phonetic properties of variable elements and the absence of elements. Variable elements arise as opposites to specified harmonic elements. However, if a certain class is not active at all, we may not need or want variable specifications. For example, in a non-tonal language, we are not going to specify a variable tonal specification for vowels, although we could specify all vowels as (L), since L is the harmonic tonal specification (laryngeal V, in a syllabic V position).[21] Be that as it may, we certainly do not want to specify the absence of secondary properties as variable properties.

9.7 Can redundant elements become active?

This section is concerned with the question of whether variable (or non-specified) elements can ever be(come) active in the phonology. I can think of two reasons for assuming that such elements are specified as fixed 'late', namely in the (post-cyclic) word-level phonology.

Firstly, in van der Hulst (2018), I suggest that non-contrastive elements can become active in the word-level phonology, for example when, in a five-vowel system that lacks an ATR contrast among high vowels, [i] and [u] cause mid vowels to become advanced, producing *allophones*.[22] If such a harmony is to be treated on a par with harmony that is triggered by a contrastive element, we may want to activate the non-contrastive element for high vowels. Of course, the harmony process could also be located in the phonetic implementation.

Secondly, another reason for including non-distinctive elements in the phonology relates to the notion of enhancement. Returning to the issue of consonantal phonation, recall my proposal in § 6.4.2 to specify the contrast between 'p' and 'b' by specifying 'p' as C[tense], which is harmonic. This is in line with the idea that the harmonic phonation type C is lexically specified, as proposed in § 9.4. In this analysis, English does not activate the dependent laryngeal class. Yet voiceless stops are aspirated in the onset of stressed syllables. I suggested the possibility of attributing the aspiration to an enhancement rule, which is different from a rule of phonetic implementation. The fact that tense stops acquire aspiration in the onset of a stressed syllable (unless preceded by [s]) is a clear characteristic of English; it does not occur in Dutch, which, in my analysis, has the same lexical contrast between a tense and non-specified phonation. It strikes me as plausible in cases of non-specification that enhancement is not just a matter of implementation, but I will leave this matter open.

9.8 Constraints and learnability

The RCVP model characterises the maximal set of contrasts that are possible. Of course, no language will employ all possibilities. This means that, for any given language, there is a set of constraints that limits the

---

[21] Still, I had to specify the stopness of consonants in the absence of a contrast with fricatives as (C) to make sure that such segments are not mannerless; see (13).
[22] See van der Hulst (2018: 448–50).

inventory to what actually occurs. Since inventories can differ for different phonotactic positions, different constraint sets may obtain. I will ignore this point here and focus on the types of constraints that can be expected, taking vowels as my example.

There are four types of constraints that govern the structure of phonological segments (see van der Hulst 2018: 68):

(28) Segment-internal co-occurrence constraints:
   a. General class constraints (a1–a2 in (29))
   b. In-class constraints:
      • on the presence of dependent class elements (b1–b3 in (29))
   c. In-subclass constraints:
      • on combinations of elements (c1–c2 in (29))
      • on the use of dependency (c3–c4 in (29))
   d. Cross-class constraints (d1–d5 etc. in (29))

The last type is 'open-ended' (for the moment) in the sense that it remains to be established what the set of all such constraints is.

(29) Constraints on vowel systems:[23]

Setting	Constraint	Description	Excluded vowels
a1	¬ laryngeal	Absence of laryngeal elements	Bars tonal contrast
a2	¬ colour	Absence of colour elements	Bars all rows but middle one
b1	¬ Dep class (manner)	Absence of RTR and nasal	Bars retracted and nasalised vowels
b2	¬ Dep class (place)	Absence of ATR	Bars advanced vowels
b3	¬ Dep class (laryngeal)	Absence of register distinction	Bars register distinction and thus unitary contour tones
c1	¬ A &∀	'Line conflation of aperture element'	Bars mid vowels
c2	¬ U & I	'Line conflation of colour element'	Bars front rounded vowels

---

[23] This table is taken from van der Hulst (2018: 69), with some minor changes/corrections.

	Setting	Constraint	Description	Excluded vowels
c3		(A;∀) = (∀;A)	No dependency	Bars mid-vowel contrast
c4		(U;I) = (I;U)	No dependency	Bars inrounding/outrounding contrast
d1		colour →∀	Colour implies the ∀ element	Bars row 5, except column 3
d2		∀→ colour	The ∀ element implies colour	Bars column 3, except [a]
d3		A∀→ colour	Mid vowels have colour	Bars mid central vowels
d4		colour ∧ A →∀	Colour and A implies the element ∀	Bars row 5, except [a]
d5		¬∀→ A	Non-ATR vowels contain the A-element	Bars [ɪ] and [ʊ]

All the shaded constraints in (29), when active, suppress all the shaded cells:

(30)

	I	IU	–	UI	U
∀ + ATR	i	y	ɨ	ʉ	u
∀	ɪ (>i)	Y	ɨ̞	ʊ̈	ʊ (>u)
∀;A	e	ø	ʌ	ɘ	o
A;∀	ɛ	œ	ɐ	æ	ɔ
A	æ	Œ	a	ɑ	ɒ

Every phonological theory must employ constraints in order to define the set of contrastive phonological segments. In early Generative Phonology, such mechanisms were called *segment structure rules* (taken to be rules that fill in non-contrastive, predictable/redundant specifications; Halle (1959)), or segment structure conditions (taken to be statements that designate certain specifications as predictable; Chomsky & Halle (1968)). In GP, the equivalent of segment structure rules/conditions is called an (intra-segmental or paradigmatic) *licensing constraint*. Such constraints state the potential for each element of being a head or dependent in a given vowel system (see Charette & Göksel (1998)). Ritter (1995), also working within GP, formulates a general scheme of *licensing parameters*, which, once the parameters have been set, essentially function as segment structure constraints.

Let us now ask what the status is of these constraints, and also how they are or become part of the phonological grammar.[24]

From the view point of a linguist who performs a phonological analysis based on a phonetic IPA transcription, the usual practice is to first establish what the phonemes are (using the minimal pair test) and then, given that set, to formulate the constraints that produce that set (given a theory of features). The linguist will formulate constraints on feature/element combinations ('segment structure conditions'). Similarly, the linguist will establish 'sequence structure constraints' that account for the distributional restrictions on the occurrence or combinations of phonemes. Both analytic activities lead to the formulation of negative constraints or to implicational statements.[25] But positive constraints are also sometimes formulated, although typically with reference to *syntagmatic* syllable structure. If a language has an obligatory onset, this would normally be accounted for with a 'positive' template CV, rather than a negative constraint ¬V, which actually leaves open what is allowed.[26] The practice of formulating segmental and sequential constraints (or conditions) may vary and often all the relevant constraints are not spelled out, with many of them taken for granted, especially regarding features that are 'irrelevant' in the language at issue.

In work that deals with computational properties of phonology or that adopts a formal approach to learning, such casual practices are not tolerated. Apart from questions about the logical format of constraints, a prominent question is how a language learner comes to 'know' them.

One approach would be to assume that all constraints are innate, in the spirit of Natural Phonology (Stampe (1973)) or Prince and Smolensky's (1993) OT. If all are active, the impact is that there is no segmental inventory, or that all phonetic events that the child is exposed to count as realisations of a single segment. Learning the segmental inventory then involves deactivating constraints one by one, until the appropriate set is characterised. However, we do not need to assume that the initial state before any contrast has been established is that all

---

[24] The term 'phonotactic' is usually taken to cover sequential structure. I am using this term to refer to both segmental and sequential structure.
[25] There is a logical equivalence between negative constraints that involve more than one argument and implicational constraints; see Melis (1976) and Lambert & Rogers (2019).
[26] We also see this in the typical OT constraint ONSET, which means 'syllables must have onsets'; Prince and Smolensky (1993).

constraints are 'on', which means that all segments are disallowed. The idea that much grammatical knowledge is innate has recently been called into question. Even phonological features/elements are no longer taken to be innate. Furthermore, the idea is that segmental and sequential constraints are learned on the basis of positive evidence, although learners may have a bias towards constraints that are 'phonologically natural' (see Hayes (1999); Hayes & Wilson (2008); Hayes & White (2013)).

Rather than saying that the child expects that everything is impossible, we simply say that she is open to 'suggestions'. Constraints are learned inductively on the basis of what the child hears (or sees), coupled with a sensitivity to statistical frequencies. If constraints refer to the notion of segment (either its internal make-up or its combinability with other segments) we have to assume that constraints that establish what the segments (i.e. phonemes) are come first. While the linguist may establish phonemes on the basis of minimal pairs, it is now generally accepted that children establish phonemes based on the statistical distribution of speech sounds; see Maye & Gerken (2000), McMurray, Aslin & Toscano (2009) and Boersma, Escudero & Hayes (2003). It is now known that the child has knowledge of phonetic categories long before she has established a lexicon of sufficient size to contain minimal pairs. Children thus use statistics to establish a set of phonetic categories that match the phonemes that are used by adult speakers. While phonemes are realised in terms of a set of phonetic exemplars, these exemplars do not have a random distribution, but instead cluster around the more prototypical realisations (see also Kuhl (1991)). The statistical angle entails that not all phonetic categories will be equally 'strong'.[27] Marginal phonemes will occur less frequently and this will affect the 'importance' of the set phonetic categories that are more frequent. This is a very important result, because the whole idea of parsing the phonemic inventory in terms of a minimal representation presupposes the prior determination of the 'candidate phoneme set'. As discussed by Boersma, Escudero & Hayes (2003), phonological learning indeed proceeds in two steps, the first step being learning the 'phonetic categories' and the second involving establishing a phonological representation.[28] We do not, then, have to assume that the learner is sensitive to contrast, even though, in the end, the contrastive use of phonetic properties will solidify the categories that have been established much earlier. If we follow the division algorithm (SDA) that was discussed in § 9.6, we can conclude that the parsing of the segmental

---

[27] The same idea for constraints is formulated in van de Weijer (2014, 2019).
[28] See Dillon, Dunbar & Idsardi (2013) for a proposal to 'collapse' the two stages into one.

inventory, following a ranking of the features/elements, automatically establishes a set of positive constraints. Let us again consider the parsing of a five-vowel system:

(31) A five-vowel system (aeoiu): A > U > I/∀

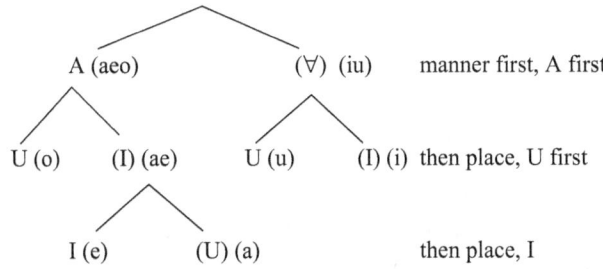

This parse establishes for the learner that the three elements A, I and U are active and that A combines with both colour elements. The parse does not validate a difference in dependency for such combinations, or for combining the colour elements. Assuming, then, that parsing follows having learned the phonetic categories, a larger and larger set of positive constraints results in an increasing size of the segmental inventory.

With respect to sequential structure, it has also been found that statistical asymmetries in sequences of phonetic segments are picked up very quickly by (young) learners; see Saffran, Newport & Aslin (1996). We must assume that sequential phonotactic constraints, formulated in terms of features/elements, *must* follow the featural parsing of the phonetic categories that reflect the phonemes of the language. It has been shown that sequential constraints can be gradient, which is caused by the strength of the statistical asymmetries that underlie them (see Hayes & Wilson (2008); Hayes & White (2013)).

This leaves us with the following question: how or when does the learner conclude what is *not* well-formed? While a set of positive constraints will reflect knowledge of what is possible, and thus well-formed, such a set leaves open what counts as ill-formed or ungrammatical given a certain language. This applies not only to establishing the segmental inventory, but also to learning what is sequentially well-formed. One answer to this question could be that learners do not make the leap from what is well-formed to the formulation of a set of negative constraints. This would mean that while the linguist is inclined to formulate negative constraints (as in (29)), the learner is not. Confronted with a word form that is alien to their language, people might quickly run this form by the set of positive constraints and decide that it is ill-formed if no constraints that they have acquired validate it. This is like being declined access to the party when the bouncer has checked that your name is not on the list of invitees. Obviously, this list will not contain the names of all the people who were not invited. In conclusion, negative constraints may not be necessary at all, at least not from the view point of the language learner.

9.9 Summary and concluding remarks

This chapter has dealt with a wide variety of notions that recur in most discussions of feature systems, such as feature (under)specification and the relation between markedness and complexity. I have shown that the RCVP notation not only provides a metatheory of phonological primitives, but also embodies a formal procedure for minimal specification. I have examined a straightforward correlation between complexity and markedness, drawing attention to the fact that markedness is primarily determined by perceptual salience, although the role of complexity is still important with respect to segments that contain head element combinations and secondary elements. Some other issues, such as phonological activity of non-contrastive properties and the status of constraints (as either positive or negative), have been discussed in a more tentative manner.

Having arrived at this point, I feel that the RCVP model has been rather exhaustively presented, discussed and supported, which is not to say that issues that call for further work have not been mentioned as well.

A crucial claim of RCVP is that features/elements are not innate. Rather, what is innate is a set of principles that allow the learner to construct a set of features/elements, including a set of hierarchical relationships among them. The set of principles is not specific to the spoken modality of languages. I will demonstrate in the next chapter that the same principles can also be applied to the signed modality.

10

Radical CV Phonology applied to sign phonology

10.1 Introduction

As explained in Chapter 1, a central aspect of RCVP is that the basic building blocks of phonology are not phonetically defined features, whether innate or not. Views on the innateness of features have shifted over recent years. The central idea of RCVP is that phonetic features/properties are correlates of abstract phonological categories that impose a categorisation on phonetic spaces, according to general principles, such as the Opponent Principle, the Combinatorial Principle, the Binarity Principle, the Head-Dependency Principle, the SAA, and Monovalency. The ultimate units in the phonological structure are the elements C and V, which are correlated with phonetic implementations (both acoustic and articulatory; see § 1.3.1) that more or less resemble the phonetically defined features that phonologists have assumed for several decades. The actual occurrence of the basic elements in the structure emerges from successive splitting during language acquisition, based on the prior recognition of phonetic categories, which are a statistical reflection of contrastive segments in the ambient language (see § 9.8). This means that there is no overall innate phonological structure for segments in any specific language. The nature of the structure that is needed is dependent on which phonetic properties in the phonetic space are used contrastively in a given language. The preceding chapters have discussed in detail how the principles of RCVP lead to a set of contrastive categories in spoken languages. However, the procedure was never meant to be specific to the spoken modality and it therefore carries over to what we can say about phonological structure in another modality: the manual-visual modality. If RCVP is a truly a-modal theory, its principles must also be appropriate for constructing a phonological organisation for sign languages. In this chapter, I demonstrate that the RCVP approach can be fruitfully applied to sign language phonology. In previous work over the last two decades, I have developed, in collaboration with others, an explicit model of sign language phonology.[1] In that previous work, I did not always emphasise how an appropriate structure for signs can be derived from the principles of RCVP, using more 'descriptive' phonetic labels for contrastive specifications, although in van der Hulst (2000b) I make an explicit comparison between the two modalities in terms of the RCVP approach. In this chapter I will show how the phonological structure of signs can be represented in terms of the basic C and V units. Admittedly, the labels 'C' and 'V' may be less felicitous to the extent that these labels were inspired by their bias for syllabic Consonantal and Vocalic positions. I have mentioned that using arbitrary labels in the model for spoken languages would make the notation even more abstract than it already is. I will adopt the C and V labelling for sign phonology as well, on the assumption that V represents perceptually salient units.

When applying the RCVP model to the phonology of signs, we do not have the advantage of being able to rely on a long tradition of proposals for feature sets and higher constructs. If linguistics is a young (and, some would say, immature) discipline, then sign linguistics has just been born.[2] The discipline essentially started in 1960 with the publication of Stokoe (1960), anticipated by some earlier work that recognised the linguistic, communicative status of signing. Even though Stokoe's goal was to analyse signs phonemically – that is, in terms of contrastive properties – there has always been a strong focus on describing the great richness of phonetic aspects of signs, including those that have not been shown to be contrastive.[3] As a consequence, many proposals for features involve rather large sets of features, minutely encoding many phonetic details, and giving the impression that the feature structure of signed languages is much richer than that of spoken languages. While, in my view, this is actually the case (see below), we should nonetheless aim at differentiating between distinctive properties and predictable properties, and, at the same time, try to formulate the rules that account for the latter. Questions about whether such rules belong to the grammatical phonology or to utterance phonology (phonetic implementation) are as relevant in the study of signs as they are in the study of spoken language phonology.

Having said this, I do not wish to downplay the enormous advances that have been made in the short period of a little over half a century by a relatively small group of linguists. Following the lead of Stokoe's (1960) seminal work, in the early 1970s we find foundational work by Klima & Bellugi (1979), reflecting the work of a group of influential

---

[1] See van der Hulst (1993b, 1995b, 1996b, 2000b); van der Hulst & van der Kooij (2006, to appear); van der Kooij (2002).
[2] See van der Hulst (to appear-a) for a historical account of the birth and development of sign phonology.
[3] Sometimes deliberately so, as in Johnson & Liddell (2011a, 2011b, 2012).

researchers. In addition, several very detailed dissertations on the phonology of American Sign Language (ASL) appeared around that time, and throughout the 1980s (for example, Friedman (1976); Mandel (1981); Battison (1978); Sandler (1989); for overviews see Wilbur (1987) and many later overview articles). In the early 1990s, when I started working in sign phonology, at that time having little insight into the subject matter based on personal empirical research, I tried to interpret detailed models that by that time had been proposed for sign language phonology in terms of the principles of DP, including binarity and headedness, and by using unary elements. The first results can be found in van der Hulst (1993b, 1995a, 1995b, 1996a, 1996b). The model proposed was well received in the field of sign phonology and it has been empirically tested and developed in subsequent and ongoing research (especially in van der Kooij (2002)). Here I discuss a proposal that follows this line of work, as also reported in van der Hulst & van der Kooij (to appear), which, however, does not stress the C/V 'logic' behind the model, as I will do here.

Since the pioneering work of Stokoe (1960), signs are said to be composed of non-manual properties and manual properties. The former can play a role at the level of lexical distinctions, but seem more active at the post-lexical level.[4] Here, I have no proposals concerning non-manual categorisation of phonological elements (see Sutton-Spence & Braem (2013)). Manual properties involve a characterisation of the handshape, the movement of the hand and a location (where the action takes place). Battison (1978) added orientation (of the hand) as a fourth manual property. Each unit in (1) can be instantiated by a finite set of values (i.e. binary features or elements):[5]

(1)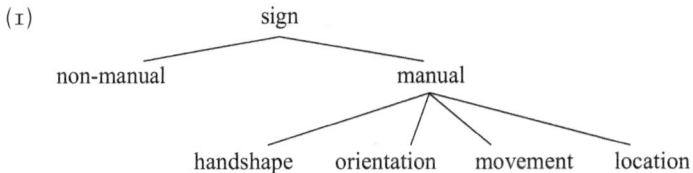

---

[4] Non-manual properties at the post-lexical level encode distinctions that, in spoken languages, are often encoded in terms of intonational tones (boundary tones, pitch accents). The functional correspondence between non-manual and laryngeal properties is supported here by a formal correspondence in terms of their place in the RCVP structure that is developed in this chapter.
[5] There is an implicit assumption here that I will make explicit later, which is that Stokoe first and foremost addressed signs that are monomorphemic, in which case the empirical observation is that such signs have one occurrence of each major unit, i.e. one place of articulation, one handshape and so on. Signs that are polymorphemic, notably compounds, can have multiple such units.

Stokoe put forward the idea that the difference between a sign and a spoken word (for example, between a sign with the meaning CAT and the English word *cat*) was that the former was essentially a simultaneous event, whereas the latter had a temporal organisation. Thus, the basic units of a sign (movement, handshape, location, etc.), which he called cheremes (and were later called phonemes by most sign phonologists) were noticed by Stokoe to be linearly *un*ordered, that is, simultaneous, whereas the phonemes of speech are linearly sequenced. Note, however, that the structure in (1) looks somewhat like an FG, comparable to FGs that have been proposed for the structure of segments in spoken language. After all, neither the class units that make up a segment (such as laryngeal, manner and place), nor the features within them (although there opinions differ; see § 7.3[6]), are linearly ordered. Hence, a comparison of (1) to single segments in spoken language would seem to indicate that the difference between spoken and signed languages is not whether or not the composing parts are linearly ordered, but rather that signs in sign language appear to be monosegmental. I made exactly this point in my earlier publications and I will develop it further below. Firstly, let us look at some more history, which we need for what is to follow (see also Corina & Sandler (1993); van der Hulst (to appear-a)).

After Stokoe's ground-breaking work, later researchers (especially Liddell (1980)) felt that it was necessary to be able to make reference to the beginning and end point of the movement of signs, for example for morphological, inflectional purposes, or to express assimilations involving a switch in the beginning and endpoint of the movement (see Sandler (1989) and van der Hulst (1993b) for a discussion of the arguments). Without formally recognising the beginning and endpoint in the linguistic representation it would be impossible to formulate rules that refer to these entities.[7] These considerations led to the adoption of some kind of skeleton with which the other units of the sign associate in an autosegmental fashion (as explicitly proposed in Sandler (1986)). Most researchers (Liddell & Johnson (1984, 1989); Sandler (1989, 1993); Perlmutter (1992); Brentari (1999)) proposed a skeleton that represented not only the initial location and final location, but also an intermediary movement:

(2)   L   M   L

---

[6] Contour tones on short vowels are an exception to this generalisation if such segments are represented in terms of level features, namely when rising and falling tones need to be distinguished. The ordering of phonetic phases within affricates and prenasalised consonants is purely phonetic, i.e. non-distinctive.

[7] I could imagine that proponents of Q-theory (see § 11.3.8) might find commonalities here between sign 'segments' and segments in spoken languages.

Several researchers have assigned a central perceptual status to the movement unit (see Perlmutter (1992), Corina & Sandler (1993), Sandler (1993, 2008, 2011) and Brentari (1999) for relevant discussions) and it then seemed obvious to refer to the LML sequences as analogous to a CVC syllable (see Chinchor (1979); Coulter (1982)). Following up on these earlier ideas, Perlmutter (1992) explicitly compares the M to the vowel in speech and also adds a moraic layer to the representation.

The model that was proposed in van der Hulst (1993b), however, denies movement as a unit on the skeleton, following several other researchers (for example Stack (1988); Hayes (1993); Wilbur (1993)), and replaces the LML skeleton with a bipositional XX skeleton; see § 10.5. Having reduced the skeleton to two positions, we could, as I suggest here, interpret these positions as the syllabic onset–rhyme (offset) structure of the sign, assuming that the second position in the skeleton is the more salient one.

Before we turn to the details of the monosegmental model of signs and the bipositional skeleton, I want to take a step back and compare the articulation of signs and the articulation of segments in spoken language. We should note that even though sign language also has an articulatory and a perceptual side, the two are closely related in sign language for an obvious reason: we see the articulation (albeit not the muscular activities).[8]

The review of sign structure that follows in the next sections cannot take the place of a full-blown introduction to sign structure. For more complete introductions, including illustrations and examples, I must refer to other publications such as Sandler (2012) and van der Hulst & van der Kooij (to appear).

10.2 The macrostructure of signs

From a production point of view, we can say that the articulation of a single segment in spoken language involves an action by an actor at some location:

(3)

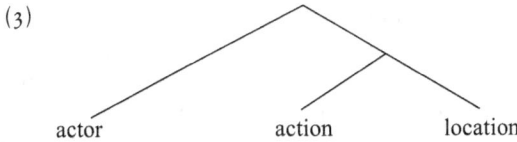

actor   action   location

---

[8] For spoken language, we can also perceive aspects of the articulation, and it has been shown in much recent work (and in the classical McGurk experiment; McGurk & MacDonald (1976)) that this factor plays a significant role in speech recognition.

In articulatory phonetics, the location is called the 'passive articulator' or the place of articulation, while the action itself is called the manner of articulation. The active articulators are the lips (perhaps more properly the lower lip) and the tongue, which is often divided into several 'sub-articulators' such as the corona (the front part), the dorsum (the back part) and the radix (the root part). Putting aside for the moment whether there are other articulators such as the epiglottis and also whether or not the larynx should be regarded as an articulator, we note that there is a fairly predictable relationship between the active articulator and the location. We also note that the active articulators overlap in the 'targets'; the teeth can be contacted by either the lower lip or the crown (i.e. corona) of the tongue. Likewise, the palatal target can be reached by the corona or the dorsum:

(4) (place)   labial - dental - alveolar - palatal - velar - uvular - pharyngeal wall

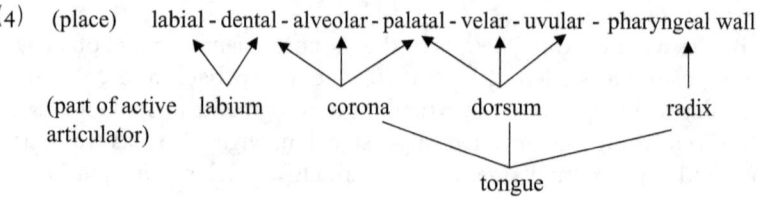

(part of active   labium   corona   dorsum   radix
 articulator)

                                       tongue

The close correlation between articulator choice and choice of location results in the fact that most phonological models for spoken segments adopt only one node that is called either 'articulator node' or 'place node'.[9] For example, in articulator-based theories (Sagey (1986); Clements (1985); Halle, Vaux & Wolfe (2000)), there are usually four articulators (labial, coronal, dorsal and radical), and to the extent that these articulators can reach more than one location, 'dependent' features are specified under the articulator feature that refers to different locations (such as [±anterior]) or to shapes of the articulator (such as [±distributed], [±retroflex] and [±lateral] as dependents of [coronal]). Other phonologists will, while still using articulator features such as [coronal], [dorsal] and so on, regard these as choices under a node labelled 'place'. As a result, phonologists have come to use 'articulator' and 'place' terminology almost interchangeably, referring to a [k] as either 'velar' (= place) or 'dorsal' (= articulator) without explicit discrimination. The point is that having both an articulator and a place/location specification, while required in the actual production of speech, introduces a significant amount of redundancy, due to the fact that many theoretical combinations are either anatomically impossible or so hard that they do not occur, such as a coronal pharyngeal (impossible)

---

[9] An exception is Gorecka (1990), who proposes a model that distinguishes between the active and passive articulator.

or a labial alveolar (difficult). In practice, then, phonological models of speech segments reduce the structure in (3) to that in (5):

(5)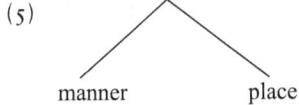

To this structure a further node is added for laryngeal distinctions, as in Clements (1985):

(6)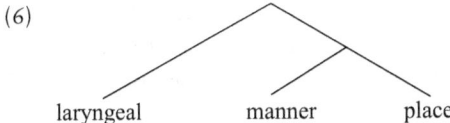

A later development was to deny status to the manner node (see McCarthy (1988) and den Dikken & van der Hulst (1988) for overviews), but I believe this to be a mistake, based on the assumption that only phonological processes provide evidence for feature classes. If we consider distribution in the syllable, manner features act as a class; it turns out that the primary manner properties are less prone to spreading (see Gordon (2016: § 5.1.3)), which is why the RCVP model essentially embraces the geometry in (5).[10]

Returning to the structure in (2), it is clear that it applies with equal force to the articulation of signs, but in this case we will see that this structure is phonologically necessary because the articulator node and the place node cannot be 'conflated'. In sign language, there is only one articulator: the hand.[11] The action of the hand is the movement of the hand. Clearly, and this is an important point, the terms 'manner' and 'movement' refer to the same aspect of articulation, namely the action of the articulator with reference to the location. Finally, the location is the body location or 'neutral space' (the space in front of the signer's body).

(7)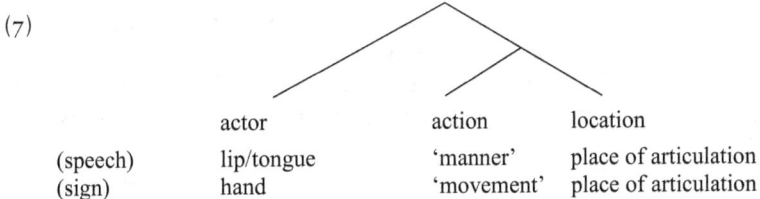

---

[10] I discuss various FG proposals in in § 11.2.
[11] I will address two-handed signs in § 10.4.

Given the similarity between both modalities, one might expect to find that formal models in both cases will be isomorphic. However, while the distinction between actor and location can be found in all sign models, this is not the case for models of segments in spoken languages, which, as we have just seen, conflate actor and location into one 'node' called either 'articulator' or 'place'. The conflation between articulator and place is not possible in sign language models. Although it may seem that specification of the articulator is redundant because there is only one articulator, there are two reasons that militate against the 'elimination' of the hand. Firstly, the hand is divided into at least six sub-articulators, namely the six 'sides' of the hand, each of which can be the part of the hand that makes contact with the place or that 'leads' the direction of the movement of the hand. It is best to visualise the hand as a flat box:[12]

(8)   The sub-articulators of the hand

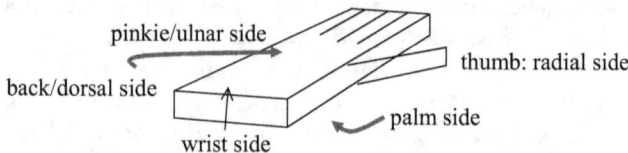

Each sub-articulator is fairly free in targeting all possible locations (although there are restrictions, e.g. the hand dorsum cannot easily target or touch the chest location). In the articulation of signs, there is thus nothing like the very restricted, mostly predictable relation between articulator and place that there is in spoken segments, as was indicated in (3).

Secondly, the hand can take many different shapes, due to the option of finger selection and finger position (bending and 'aperture') and some additional distinctions (see § 10.3.1). I will discuss this in more detail below, but for now the reader will appreciate that the hand can assume many different handshapes, as is also common in hand gestures that are used outside the domain of sign languages (e.g. pointing, thumbs up, clawing, etc.). As a result, the structure of signs, because it must distinguish the articulator and the place of articulation separately, has an 'extra' node as compared to the structure of spoken segments, as shown in (9):[13]

---

[12] If the fingers are folded into a fist, the knuckles count as the front side.
[13] An analogue to the laryngeal node would be the node that specifies non-manual information. We return to this point below; see (13).

(9)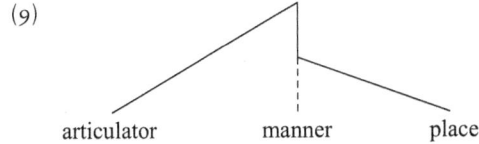
articulator   manner   place

Following the 'dogma' of a dependency approach, the main idea in van der Hulst (1993b) was to impose a head-dependency organisation on the structure of the sign as a whole. Here I take manner to be the head unit, not only because this parallels the model for spoken segments, but also because manner (aka movement) has been identified as both the obligatory and most perceptually salient unit of the sign (see Sandler (2011)). Perhaps a more intuitive choice for headhood might be to designate the hand as the central unit of the signs (as I in fact did in van der Hulst (1993b)). Signs that do not use the hand as articulator are extremely rare, so the hand seems to be an obligatory unit as well.[14] Likewise, it could be argued that all signs have a place, although, as we will see below, a case could be made for analysing signs that are made in front of the signer's body (in what is called neutral space) as placeless. The main reason for assigning headhood to manner/movement is perceptual salience. It is also important that signs that do not have a lexical manner property will nonetheless always be articulated with an 'epenthetic' movement; see Sandler (2011).[15]

The model in (9) represents a sign as a single segment in which the nodes represent so-called 'class nodes'. As mentioned, sign researchers, following Stokoe, generally compare the three units in (9) to 'phonemes'. However, it is obvious from the preceding discussion that the structure of a sign as a whole is that of a single segment, which leads to the rather surprising conclusion that (monomorphemic) signs tend to consist of a single segment.[16] Stokoe's original claim that sign language differs from spoken language in lacking sequential structure was based on the simultaneity of the units handshape, movement and location, but this would now appear to be a non-starter since the corresponding class nodes in spoken segments are also simultaneous. The striking difference between the two modalities is rather that monomorphemic signs (i.e. morphemes) lack sequential structure in being monosegmental,

---

[14] 'Handless' signs might use a head movement or a movement of the eyebrows, eyes or mouth only.
[15] Sandler (2014) reports that in the Al-Sayyid Bedouin Sign Language, a young sign language, there are signs that have no movement component. The conclusion of her work on this language is that phonology is still emerging, which is manifested in various other properties such as a greater variability among, and even within, signers, more 'sloppy' handshapes, and so on.
[16] A similar conclusion was drawn in Channon (2002).

as opposed to most morphemes in spoken languages, which consist of multiple segments.

The question now is how it could possibly be the case that 'all' monomorphemic signs are monosegmental. Surely, such a state of affairs is unheard of for any spoken language.[17] The obvious answer is that there are many more possible sign segments than there are possible spoken language phonemes, which results from three facts:

(10) a. In signs, articulator and place are independent units, each with its own set of values.
b. In signs, the articulator (in addition to its six orientations) can take many different shapes.
c. In signs, the 'manner' (i.e. movement) can take many different forms, due to its magnitude.

While the first two points were explicitly discussed above, the third point has only been implied. In spoken language, manner refers to the relationship between the active articulator and the location. This relationship involves a very small movement of the articulator towards the location, leading either to full contact or to one of two forms of approximation. The movement is so small that it cannot have any properties other than the degree of approximation or contact; for example, for obstruents this allows for the distinction between fricatives and stops. This is not the case for signs. Here the movement of the hand is large enough to differentiate between, for example, a straight path, a curved path and a path augmented by a zigzag or circular 'secondary' movement. For this reason it was not correct to suggest that the movement unit is merely a predictable interpolation between the subspecifications of the place unit, and as such redundant, as was suggested in Hayes (1993) (and adopted by van der Hulst (1993b)). Since movement can have distinguishing properties, it must correspond to a structural unit that can bear these properties. In (9) I suggest that this unit is captured by what we call the manner node in models of segments in spoken language. Unlike the lip and tongue, the hand can execute its action in multiple ways (in a straight line, in an arc, in a zigzag and so on, and, for that matter, also varying in the degree of approximation to the location, or the manner of contact with the location). This makes the movement aspect of signs much richer than the movement aspect in speech, which is what (10c) expresses. We must

---

[17] In spoken languages, vowels can constitute a morpheme by themselves, as well as consonants; the latter case is typically restricted to bound morphemes. However, given the limits on the size of phoneme inventories (with an average of thirty-one phonemes (MD)) it could not possibly be the case that a spoken language only has monosegmental morphemes.

conclude that the potential array of phonological distinctions for sign segments is many times greater than for speech segments, simply because there are many more phonetic dimensions, so much so that it is possible to represent perhaps all necessary morphemes in terms of single segments.

10.3 The microstructure of signs

In this section my aim is to discuss in some detail points (10a) and (10b) above, by showing the potentially distinctive properties that the articulator node and the place node allow. The goal of going into these details is to bring us to the level of 'distinctive features' that are required for the expression of contrast in sign language. I can then show how the feature set follows the structure that the RCVP approach would predict. It is important to repeat that the claim here is not that sign languages have the same set of features as spoken languages. Such a claim would make no sense at all, and this has been one reason for questioning the innateness of features to begin with. If there were a set of innate features such as [round], [anterior], [lateral] and [continuant], as the claim in early approaches was, the question would arise of how those features would be useful in constructing the phonology of a sign language. What I claim is that, while it is true that the phonology of both modalities can be accounted for in terms of the two basic elements C and V, there are significant differences between spoken and signed language in terms of the phonetic spaces within which phonological categories are constructed. This has immediate consequences for the phonological structure, particularly in terms of the number of class nodes, since my point will be that in terms of 'features' every class node has a binary C/V distinction, just like class nodes in spoken language phonology.

In what follows I discuss the various unary features for signs, but I do not discuss combinatorial constraints.

10.3.1 *The articulator*

The articulator must be decomposed into finger selection (FingerSelection or FingSel) and finger configuration (FingerConfiguration or FingConfig). FingSel refers to the fingers that are 'foregrounded' (selected), as opposed to the 'backgrounded' (non-selected) (see Mandel (1981: 81–4)). Mostly, foregrounded fingers are the fingers that are in a specific configuration or are the extended fingers, while backgrounded fingers are usually folded in so that the selected fingers are clearly perceptible For our present purposes, I will adopt this simplification, but when the selected fingers make contact with the thumb, the non-selected finger can be open (see Sandler (1989) and van der Kooij (2002) for a detailed discussion). Both FingSel and FingConfig have a further substructure that has been motivated in various studies (Sandler (1986, 1989, 2012); van der Hulst (1993b, 1995a); van der Kooij (2002)). The structure in (11) is a variant of the model proposed in van der Hulst (1993b, 1995a) and van der Kooij (2002):

(11)

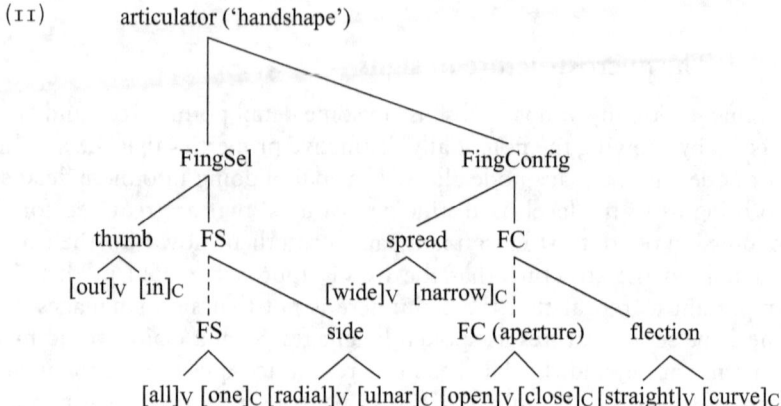

I will first motivate the FingerSelection unit and then turn to the FingerConfiguration unit. The handshape unit as a whole is claimed to have a head-dependency structure, as are the units that it consists of. The motivation for taking FingerSelection to be the head unit is that this is the obligatory unit. Also, this unit is obligatorily invariant within a sign. There can be only one FingerSelection for a (monomorphemic) sign, specified in terms of two unary features [one] and [all], identified as C and V, respectively. The feature [one] correlates with one extended finger, while [all] correlates with multiple fingers being extended. [all] is taken to be V because the selection of multiple fingers is more perceptually salient than just one finger (see Sandler (1995)). The FingerConfiguration unit is not obligatory; it is needed when signs display an 'aperture change', which is an opening or closing movement of the thumb and selected fingers, where 'closed' and 'open' will be identified as C and V, respectively, on the assumption that an open position is more salient than a closed position. Each of the two units of the articulator also requires dependent nodes (see below). The C/V subscript choice in each case is motivated by relative perceptual salience.

We will see that none of the dependent classes in either FingerSelection or FingerConfiguration allows combinations, while combinations are allowed in the head of both classes. Again, I take the possibility of allowing a combination as a sign of headhood.

10.3.1.1 FingerSelection

In accordance with the principles of DP, van der Hulst (1993b, 1995a) and van der Kooij (2002) proposed a system of unary phonological primes to characterise handshapes. In the head node there are two features, [one] and [all], which can occur by themselves or in combination; the choice of these two unary features was inspired by the proposals in Sandler (1995). If combined, a head-dependency relationship is established. This allows four possible structures, which, in conjunction with the specification of [ulnar], results in eight possible handshapes:

(12)

FingSel	one	one | all	all | one	all
	index	index and middle	index and middle and ring	all four
Side: ulnar	pinkie	index and pinkie	middle and ring and pinkie	

As shown, there are multiple handshapes which share the same finger selection but differ in other properties involving thumb extension, finger spread or finger bending. The phonetic interpretation of [one] is that one finger is selected. In principle, this could be any finger, but the default is the index finger ([radial]). The default can be overridden by specifying the Side value [ulnar] 'pinkie side'. This leaves the two options of middle finger and ring finger by themselves undifferentiated, predicting that these two either do not occur or occur as free variants of the pinkie choice.[18]

The feature [out] needs to be specified when the thumb is the selected digit, either alone or in combination with other selected fingers, where the [in] value is taken to be the 'default' choice. The thumb can also be the only selected finger, which would require [out] and a [one] specification for FingerSelection, in which case [radial] causes the suppression of the index finger choice: ☝. This leaves the so-called L-handshape unaccounted for (👆) because it has the thumb *and* the index finger extended, which then cannot also be specified as [out] and [one] because this is the specification for only having the thumb extended. This handshape must thus be a free variant of either 👆 or ☝.[19] The sets of selected fingers in (12) are found in most sign languages. Some sign languages

---

[18] The middle finger choice is avoided due to taboo.
[19] Alternatively, 👆 is analysed as an iconic handshape.

appear to have a more complex handshape inventory, and handshapes that occur in fingerspelling systems usually have handshapes that do not occur in regular signs, except as the result of initialisation.[20] However, 'meaning' can often be associated with these complex handshapes. An issue that is ignored throughout this chapter is whether signs may have phonetic properties that are iconically motivated and as such are not distinctive; see van der Kooij (2002) and van der Hulst & van der Kooij (2006).

10.3.1.2 FingerConfiguration

The central (head) unit of FingerConfiguration is taken to be Aperture, since it is the most frequent configuration of selected fingers. Aperture refers to the relation between the selected fingers and the thumb.[21] In the Aperture node we have two features, [open] and [close], which in this case allow combinations. However, unlike in the case of FingerSelection, combinations of the two aperture features do not encode intermediate degrees of opening, but rather are interpreted dynamically as opening (close to open) and closing (open to close) movement. Opening and closing movements are called local movements (Liddell (1990)).

Whether we can take the difference between the simultaneous interpretation of [one] and [all] vs. the sequential interpretation of [open] and [close] to be a manifestation of difference between the head and dependent status of FingerSelection and FingerConfiguration, respectively, is an open question. The fact that [open] and [close] can occur in two linear orders could be taken as a sign of greater complexity. This also raises another issue: are signs, as single segments, allowed to have internal linear structure? If so, this option stands in contrast with segments in spoken languages, which do not allow internal linear order, at least not in the current model. I return to this question in § 10.5.

10.3.2 Orientation

It was mentioned in § 10.2 that Battison (1978) added a fourth major unit, hand orientation, to Stokoe's list of three. As argued in Sandler (1986, 1989), orientation can be considered to be a dependent of the

---

[20] In ASL, there is a set of handshapes to represent the letters of the Roman alphabet. Signers can thus spell English words and such fingerspelled words may become part of the language, sometimes condensed, which is a form of borrowing. When the handshape of a sign is chosen as the handshape for the first letter of the corresponding English word, this is called initialisation.

[21] In closed positions the thumb can restrain the selected fingers, as in a closed fist, or be held against the index finger; these are generally taken to be allophonic variants.

articulator node. The evidence for this grouping is based on assimilation phenomena discussed in Sandler's work. In lexicalised compounds in ASL and Israeli Sign Language, we find assimilation between the parts of the compound of either the orientation by itself, or the orientation combined with the entire handshape. Since orientation can 'spread' by itself, van der Hulst (1993b) took this to be a dependent node (on the assumption that dependent nodes have greater 'mobility' than head nodes). I will assume that the orientation node can dominate a branching feature specification (e.g. [prone] and [supine]; see (13) below). A branching specification for orientation then characterises an orientation change as in ASL TO DIE, in which both hands are pointing outwards, one palm-down, the other palm-up, with both hands rotating up and down, respectively. Note that here, too, the two elements occur in linear order, as in the case of aperture change. Orientation changes, like aperture changes, are called local movements.

Admittedly, for orientation, it is hard to motivate the identification as C or V in terms of the criterion of perceptual salience. Which side is salient probably depends on the 'absolute position of the hand'. What this means is that the hand can be held with the fingers (or knuckles) pointed upward, in which case the supine choice means that the palm is facing the viewer. However, if the finger/knuckles point towards the viewer, supine means that the palm faces downwards. This suggests that there is an absolute and a relative way of talking about orientation (see Crasborn & van der Kooij (1997) for discussion of this point). That these different interpretations of the orientation features are possible suggests that we need two different orientation nodes, some version of which was proposed in van der Hulst (1993b). One of these, called Absolute Orientation (AbsOrientation), locates the leading edge (the edge that points in the direction of the movement, possibly making contact with a location at the end of the movement) of the hand in relation to three coordinates (up/down, out/in, contralateral/ipsilateral (contra/ipsi)[22]), whereas the unit called Relative Orientation (RelOrientation) specifies the palm or back side of the hand in relation to the viewer:[23]

---

[22] The absolute orientation is contralateral if the finger/knuckles point to the non-dominant side (i.e. to the left for a right-handed signer).

[23] I must also add that Relative Orientation and Absolute Orientation may be predictable in many cases, either from each other or from other aspects of the signs.

(13)

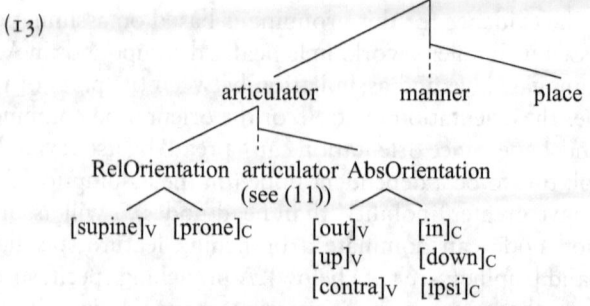

The C/V choices for orientation features are not motivated here. Intuitively, showing the palm to the viewer is more salient than showing the back of the hand. Likewise, one might say that the absolute orientation choices [out], [up] and [contra] share an attention-drawing aspect, compared to their opposites.

10.3.3 Place

Location (or place) is one of the major components of signs.[24] To motivate the claim that a monomorphemic sign has only one major location, Sandler (1986) argues that we must adopt a distinction between a major place unit and a 'setting' unit, which specifies sublocation within the major place. I first address the major place features. In several models that describe ASL we find an abundance of such features. This is due to the fact that every phonetic location that is touched or referred to by the articulator is deemed evidence for a feature specification in these models. Stokoe distinguished twelve possible values for location, based on where the hand makes contact with the body: six for the face, head and neck, one for the trunk, two for the arm, two for the hand, and one for 'neutral space'. (Signs that make no contact are assigned to neutral space as their location.) In other views, there are fewer distinctive locations; for instance, Battison (1978) suggested body (chest, trunk), hand, arm, head, neck and neutral space. It is not immediately obvious how this set can be analysed in accordance with the principles of RCVP. Kegl & Wilbur (1976) compared signs in neutral space with 'vowels' and signs that make contact with the body with 'consonants'; on the important role of contact, see also Wilbur (2010). While this suggests a tempting C/V division, this is not the obvious way to go if 'V' is taken as perceptually salient. The notion of perceptual acuity[25] with reference to location is

---

[24] The material in this section is based on van der Kooij (2002) and van der Kooij & van der Hulst (2005).

[25] Visual acuity is a measure of the ability of the eye to distinguish shapes and the details of objects at a given distance.

discussed in Siple (1978), who observed that the area of greatest visual acuity is on the face, while the area of least visual acuity is that part of the signing space monitored by the peripheral vision, which includes the space in front of the chest. Deaf people mostly fixate on the facial region of the signer (including the neck area) to pick up small, detailed movements associated with facial expression and mouth shape. Peripheral vision is used to process information outside the facial region. It is therefore striking that neutral space, which is the space in front of the signer's body, is the most frequent location, used mostly in signs that are produced in the lower visual field in front of the trunk. However, it has been found that deaf signers have a larger visual field than hearing non-signers (Bavelier et al. 2000), with a particular large extension in the lower part of the visual field, which would include the neutral space area, as well as locations on the hand and arm. This is of course important since, while movements of the hand in these lower regions are large enough to be readily observed, the handshapes and handshape changes are 'subtle' and yet crucial for sign recognition. If we take visual acuity as the primary indicator of a salience division, then a C/V interpretation of locations could be proposed, as follows:[26]

(14)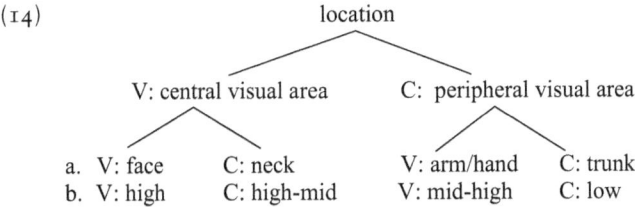

Taking up Wilbur's (2010) point about the relevance of contact, we could say that all signs that do not specify contact (and are thus not 'body-related') are by definition in neutral space, within which distinctions must be made, in higher and lower regions. This means that the four-way division in (14a) applies to body-related signs with contact, while those in (14b) apply when there is no body contact. As I argue in the next section, [contact] can be analysed as a manner property.[27]

---

[26] When the hand is the location, we need to specify its handshape. It has long been observed that the choices for the hand as location are limited to a small number of 'unmarked' handshapes; see Battison (1978) and much later work; see also § 10.4.

Since arm/hand is a more 'punctuated' location than trunk, I take it to have a higher visual salience, hence V.

The interpretation of arm/hand as mid-high and trunk as low is rather arbitrary at this point.

[27] We must also take into account (although this will not be discussed here) that the distinction between body-related and non-body-related locations correlates to a

Based on the observation that movements of monomorphemic signs stay within the major locations (i.e. those in (14)), Sandler (1989) proposed setting features to specify more specific locations within the major places of articulation. When two setting features are specified, this implies a path movement (i.e. a movement of the hand), although a single setting specification can also be used to represent a specific point within a major location. However, such single setting specifications are rarely needed; apparently, they are only needed when some specific meaning related to a 'landmark' (eye, ear, temple, heart, etc.) is expressed. Thus, setting features are usually needed to characterise path movement. By pairing up sets of settings (high–low, contra–ipsi, proximal–distal (prox–dist), etc.), simple path movements within the distinctive locations (as areas) can be formally described. In (15) I represent setting as a dependent, like FingerConfiguration, taking the major location to be its head. This accounts for the interpretation of the movement size that is implied by setting pairs as being relative to the size of the major location, that is, a downward path on the cheek may be smaller than a downward path in neutral space.

Adding the structure of the place node, we arrive at the following C/V organisation of signs:

(15)

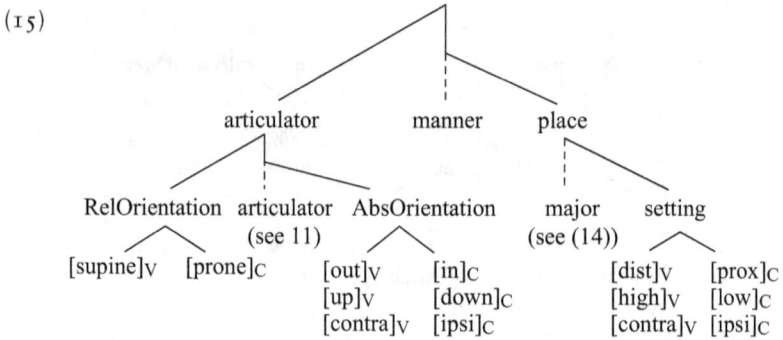

Note that the AbsOrientation and Setting oppositions are essentially the same, which means that I have associated them with the same C/V labels.

It is now time to 'flesh out' the manner unit.

10.3.4 Manner ('movement')

In the previous section, I introduced Sandler's idea that a movement of the hand results from having two setting specifications. Such a movement

> certain extent with linguistic function: the former have primary relevance in the lexical domain, whereas the latter tend to serve morphosyntactic roles.

is called a path movement. In § 10.2 I suggested that sign segments contain a manner unit which specifies properties of the movement of the hand. There are several candidates for the class of manner features, which, as a result, may be somewhat heterogeneous. Good candidates are manner features that specify the shape of the path, as well as aspects of contact, if any, between the hand and the location:

(16) A set of potential manner features:
   a. Path specification
      1. [arc]
      2. [straight]
      3. [circle]
      4. [bidirectional]
   b. Repeated
   c. Contact[28]
   d. ....

Some additional 'manner' features could relate to properties of the whole sign, such as tenseness, overall size ('whispering', 'shouting') and speed, although none of these appears to be lexically distinctive, which means that they can be accommodated in the utterance phonology, which I hold responsible for such 'pragmatic properties'. Here I will make no attempt to categorise the various manners of movement in a C/V notation.

We have also seen that there are also local movements, which involve either an open/close movement of the selected fingers (which we capture in terms of a branching finger aperture specification) or a change of orientation. This leads to the following typology of movements:

(17) Types of movement:
   a. Path movement
   b. Local movement
      i. Aperture change
      ii. Orientation change

Local movements and path movements can occur independently, or combined; in the latter case both are executed simultaneously.[29]

---

[28] There may be different kinds of contact, such as single contact, double contact, brushing, iterated contact (tapping) and perhaps others.
[29] Sandler (1993) suggests that since movement is the sonority centre of signs, different degrees of sonority can be distinguished along a sonority scale such as: path movements > internal movements > path and internal movements together.

Certain manner properties can also apply to local movements, in particular the property of repetition, although it must be indicated somehow whether this property occurs on the path or the local movement when both are combined. Local movements that co-occur with a path movement could be 'secondary movements', but this term has been reserved for a distinct set of iterated movements that co-occur with a path movement. There is a rather large variety of such iterated secondary movements, and various proposals have been made for how to formally represent them; see van der Hulst (1993b: § 2.2.2).[30] An issue that we need to consider is whether we should even try to provide all secondary movements with a unique phonological representation. In many cases, secondary movements are iconically motivated. Van der Hulst & van der Kooij (2006, to appear) and van der Kooij (2002) make the argument that the phonology cannot be held 'responsible' for all phonetic properties of signs. These authors propose that properties can often be attributed to phonetic default mechanisms and iconically motivated phonetic specifications.

Meanwhile, reckoning with the possibility that at least some secondary movements need a phonological account, I tentatively propose a further dependent node to the place unit:[31]

(18)

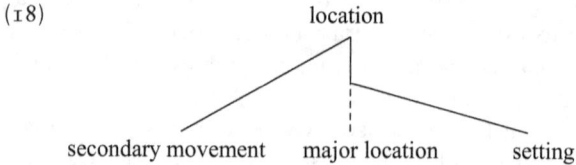

secondary movement   major location   setting

10.4 Two-handed signs

Not all signs are 'one-handed'. The other hand can, however, play two different roles. It can function as either the place for the articular or the twin of the other active articulator (which means that both hands must have the same handshape and the same movement, in phase or alternating).[32] Van der Hulst (1996b) calls the former signs unbalanced and the latter balanced. For balanced signs, in which both hands act as twin active

---

[30] Labels for secondary movements include flattening, twisting, nodding, rubbing, scissoring, pumping, squeezing, releasing, hooking, circling and so on.

[31] See Channon & van der Hulst (2011) for a proposal to represent all movements in terms of dynamic features, including non-repeated local and path movements. This proposal does not 'fit' the current account of sign structure, which avoids dynamic features in both spoken and sign phonology.

[32] This constraint was observed early on in the sign phonology literature and named the Symmetry Condition in Battison (1978). The property of two-handedness is simply a way of *enhancing* the properties of the articulator hand.

Radical CV Phonology applied to sign phonology 373

articulators, one might simply adopt the features [2-handed] and [alternating], while signs in which the hand acts as a location require [hand] to be one of the location features (see (14)). While not denying that the other hand can have two fundamentally different roles, van der Hulst (1996b) proposes that perhaps the 'other hand' deserves its own place in the structure, which requires an elaboration of the Articulator node:[33]

(19) articulator

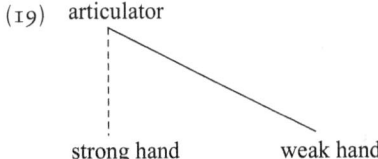

The proposal is to adopt this representation for all two-handed signs, including those in which the other hand is already specified as the place, and to argue that the dependent status of the weak hand accounts for its 'underspecification'. In balanced signs, the weak hand is fully underspecified (because it is identical to the strong hand), while the choice for unmarked handshape in balanced signs likewise correlates with a very low degree of specification.[34] We should note that the two hands cannot act as fully independent articulators. This means that the mind, when it comes to sign language, is one-handed.

We thus end up with the following sign structure:

(20)

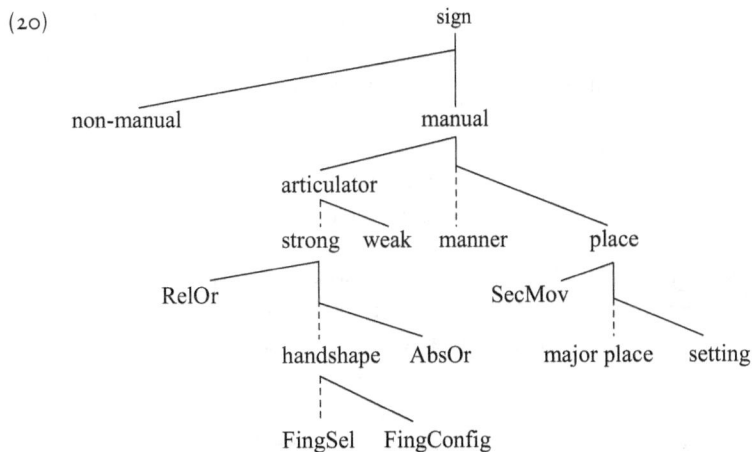

---

[33] The strong hand is usually the dominant hand of the signer.
[34] Van der Kooij (2002) observes that we may also need to specify the relation between the two hands as being in contact, crossed, below or above each other, and so on. If such specifications are required, we may have to add these to the manner unit.

In the next section, I discuss the last 'piece' of the puzzle, namely the issue of syllable structure.

10.5 What about syllable structure?

Limiting ourselves to monomorphemic signs, it would seem to follow from the monosegmental hypothesis that signs cannot have syllable structure. After all, syllable structure in spoken language presupposes a linear sequence of segments. From here, we could then investigate polymorphemic signs, which would show sequences of sign segments and thus potentially something like syllable structure. Two factors interfere with such an investigation. Firstly, we would only arrive at segment sequences resulting from concatenative morphological operations. Concatenative morphology is, however, not typical of sign languages, except for compounding. It is well known that compounds form tight phonological units in sign languages, as shown by recurrent possible processes (such as hand spreading, discussed in § 10.3.2, which seems to compress the phonological structure of the compound members into a format that conforms to the structure of single segments; see Sandler (1986)). The question is whether compounds, when not (yet) compressed, should be considered as analogues of syllables. However, an analogy with 'metrical feet' strikes me as more reasonable, especially since compounds have a prominence profile in which the second member is said to be stressed; see Friedman (1976) and Wilbur (1990).

A second factor that could make it unlikely that we will find something like a syllable structure is that in spoken languages, syllabic organisation is based on an alternation between two very different kinds of segments, namely consonants and vowels, which, in sequence, form a mandibular open/close rhythm, which perhaps ultimately underlies the recognition of syllabic units (see MacNeilage (2008)). As Sandler (2008) points out, there is no mandibular cycle in sign, or anything remotely like it.[35]

The possible conclusion that monomorphemic signs have neither syllable structure nor any other sequential phonotactic organisation, simply because there is no segment sequencing, is at odds with many other

---

[35] The closest analogue we can imagine is a distinction between signs that make body contact or refer to a body part and signs that are made in neutral space. One could argue that the former are more consonant-like, while the latter are more vowel-like, as suggested in Kegl & Wilbur (1976). However, if this difference plays a role, we would expect to see its effects in the manner in which signs are linearised in compounds or phrases. We would have to see that signs alternate between body-related and neutral space, which would make both the selection of lexical items (where there are choices) and syntactic word order dependent on a phonological principle. There is, I believe, no evidence for these kinds of effects.

claims in the literature. As already mentioned in § 10.1, after Stokoe's ground-breaking work, which stressed the simultaneity of the units that constitute a sign, later researchers (for example Newkirk (1981); Supalla & Newport (1978); Liddell & Johnson (1984)) argued that it was necessary to be able to make reference to the beginning and endpoint of the movement of signs, for example for inflectional purposes (I-GIVE-YOU as opposed to YOU-GIVE-ME), or to express assimilations involving a switch in the beginning and endpoint of the movement (see Sandler (1989) and van der Hulst (1993b) for a discussion of the arguments). This led to proposing a skeleton . which had not only the initial and final locations, but also an intermediary movement. Here I repeat (2) for convenience:

(21) L   M   L[36]

Putting aside the claim that the skeleton in (21) is formally or functionally analogous to syllable structure in spoken language (I return to this below), we cannot get around the argument that morphology needs the beginning and endpoint of movement as anchors for inflectional features. The question is whether we need a movement unit as part of this 'skeleton'. In § 10.2 and § 10.3 I argued that the presence of movement follows from a sign having two setting specifications. This opens up the possibility of taking the setting units, being dependents of the location node, as the reference points for inflection. However, the setting points must be linearised even for monomorphemic signs, because a movement can go from [high] to [low] or vice versa. Linearisation is necessary not only for setting features, but also for the features that specify orientation changes and aperture changes. As was mentioned in § 10.3.4, when a sign has more than one movement, the beginning and endpoint of each movement must be synchronised. To account for synchronisation, van der Hulst (1993b) proposed a bipositional skeleton as part of the structure of signs, albeit 'external' to the feature structure:[37]

---

[36] Liddell & Johnson (1984) had 'HMH', and Perlumtter (1992) adopts 'PMP'. These are differences in notation which I ignore here.

[37] A very similar proposal is presented by Wilbur (1993).

(22)

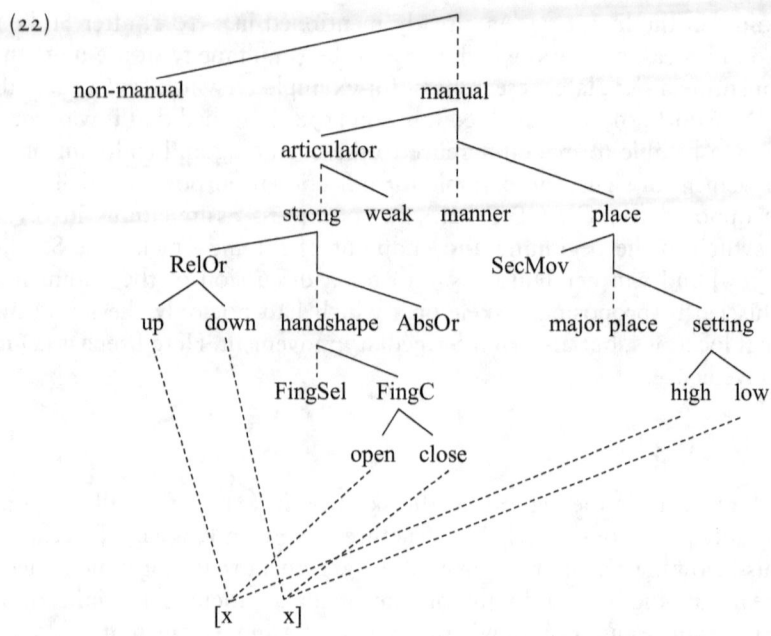

As shown, the various dynamic specifications are linearised through their association with the two skeletal points, which themselves are linearised. Thus, we come to the apparently odd conclusion that whereas signs lack suprasegmental sequencing ('syllable structure'), they do possess intra-segmental sequencing, even though, strictly speaking, there is no linearisation within the feature structure itself. Rather, linearisation is achieved through association with the skeleton, which consists of two linearised positions. This is the precise opposite of what we find in the phonological structure of spoken languages, where distinctive intra-segmental sequencing is not generally accepted.

In van der Hulst (1995b, 2000b) I have proposed explaining this difference with reference to a crucial difference between auditory and visual perception. Visual perception of signs, even if these have dynamic and apparently sequential properties, is more 'instantaneous' than the perception of auditory speech input, which is necessarily stretched out in time. Sounds reach the ear sequentially, in temporal stages. If this aspect is taken into account, it does not come as a surprise that the linear organisation of speech is perceptually salient and therefore takes precedence over the simultaneous organisation of small slices of this signal. Consequently, in the mental representation of signs, the simultaneous organisation takes precedence over linear organisation. We can understand the difference in terms of Goldsmith's (1976a) notions of vertical and horizontal slicing of the signal:

(23) Speech: Signing:
          vertical (syntagmatic)   horizontal (paradigmatic)
                    | |
          horizontal (paradigmatic)   vertical (syntagmatic)

Thus an incoming speech signal is spliced into horizontal slices, which gives rise to a linear sequences of segments. Of course, Goldsmith's point was that horizontal slicing is not absolute. Some aspects of the speech signal – notoriously, pitch in tonal languages – can be sliced off horizontally first and segmented differently from the remainder of the signal. After vertical slicing, resulting segments are further subdivided horizontally in features (which then are simultaneous). In the perception of sign language, however, the horizontal slicing takes precedence, giving rise to the simultaneous components that we call handshape, movement and place. After that, vertical slicing of each of these gives rise to linear organisation.[38]

10.6 Summary and concluding remarks

In this chapter I have shown how the RCVP approach can be applied to the phonological structure of signs in sign languages. This proposal takes into account the pioneering work of many sign linguists, adding to it the organising principles that are characteristic of RCVP. Overall, head-dependency structure is relevant to the structure of signs, involving asymmetrical relations between 'class nodes' at all levels of organisation. I have identified a number of criteria for head or dependency status, such as perceptual salience and complexity, with heads being more salient and allowing for greater complexity, which are both diagnostics of head/dependent asymmetries (see Dresher & van der Hulst (1998)). At the lowest level of structure, I made specific proposals for 'unary features', that is, C/V elements that stand in polar opposition within each phonetic space. Needless to say, much in this proposal is tentative, and only in part based on successful empirical studies of sign language structure (such as reported in van der Kooij (2002)) and, for the remainder, should function as a programme for further research. Precisely because RCVP's intention is to derive phonological structure from a small set of general principles, it is possible to develop a theoretical proposal in advance of empirical studies that lead to testable predictions, testing of which may suggest modifications or, perhaps, complete dismissal. The theory guides the researcher in looking for specific phenomena involving asymmetries of various kinds that, then, can receive a unified explanation based on RCVP's 'first principles'.

---

[38] It is tempting to relate the occurrence of intra-segmental 'syllable structure' to my speculation about clicks having an intra-segmental syllable structure; see § 7.3.2.

11

Comparison to other models

11.1 Introduction

In this chapter I offer a comparison between my model and a selection of other, prevalent models. While it will of course be important to highlight how the RCVP model differs from other models, primarily in its radical proposal of reducing all contrastive distinctions to two elements which occur in multiple roles (head, dependent) in multiple element classes and in different syllabic positions, I will be more interested in showing how the RCVP model is compatible with feature sets and FGs that have been proposed, and motivated, in other proposals. After all, to the extent that these proposals have been made on solid empirical grounds, they support the RCVP choices. What RCVP adds to these specific proposals is that it shows how they can be *derived* from a small set of basic principles. This adds an element of explanatory adequacy to these proposals. In Chapter 2 I have already extensively discussed DP and GP. Both models, but especially DP, have been highly influential in the development of RCVP and I have discussed in detail how RCVP builds on and yet differs from these two theories. This chapter will focus on a comparison between RCVP and some other models of segmental structure, but it will also include some discussion of a recent version of GP, as well as a new model, Q-phonology. I will thus focus on some striking parallels between RCVP and other proposals, which have often been developed independently from DP and RCVP and with no apparent knowledge of these models, which only adds to these proposals' value as independent confirmation of the model proposed here.

11.2 Feature Geometry models

The idea of representing segments in terms of a structured hierarchy of feature classes is fundamental to RCVP. As mentioned in Chapter 2, this idea was developed in DP and then later independently in the work of Clements (1985) and Sagey (1986), foreshadowed by some other proposals. Den Dikken & van der Hulst (1988) and McCarthy (1988) describe the emergence and development of such 'FG' models. Since then, as one would, expect, variants of this approach have been proposed by many phonologists. Phillips (1994), Morén (2007) and Duanmu (2016) provide overviews of later developments.

Note that an FG had been proposed in DP as early as 1975 (Lass & Anderson (1975)), separating an 'articulatory gesture' and 'phonatory gesture'. Lass (1976) proposed an 'oral gesture' and a 'laryngeal gesture'. AE discuss these early proposals and develop a more detailed structure, stressing (pp. 144–5) that the crucial evidence for the right structure is not strictly phonetic, but should be based on phonological arguments. The structure that they propose is given in (1):

(1)
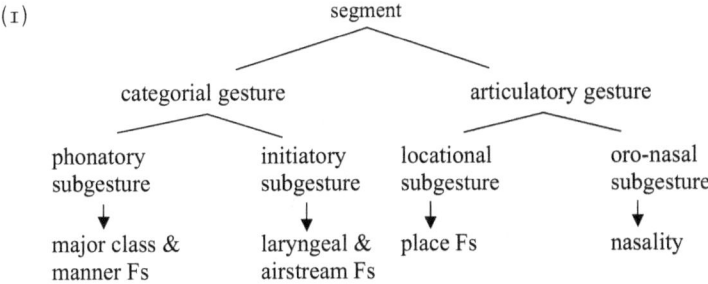

The features that are contained in each 'gesture' (i.e. 'class node') are monovalent primes.

Various alternatives to this structure have been discussed, detailed in den Dikken & van der Hulst (1988) and, to some extent, in § 2.2. When FG emerged in mainstream Generative Phonology, the DP proposals were completely ignored, despite the idea of an FG being discussed in van der Hulst & Smith (1982a), a widely read introduction to the new developments in phonology at the time.

The proposal made in Clements (1985: 266) states:

> As several writers have shown, most explicitly Goldsmith (1981), Mohanan (1983), Thráinsson (1978), and Mascaró (1984, 1986), the study of the interaction among various sets of features, as observed (for example) in the study of assimilation rules, provides prime evidence for the nature of simultaneous feature groupings. If we find that certain sets of features consistently behave as a unit with respect to certain types of rules of assimilation or resequencing, we have good reason to suppose that they constitute a unit in phonological representation, independently of the actual operation of the rules themselves.

Clements then proposes his own feature grouping structure:

(2)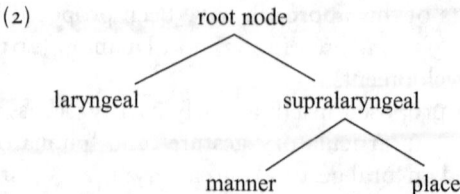

RCVP has adopted this structure, but added the idea that the 'class nodes' are organised in an X-bar style head-dependency structure (vertical lines indicate heads):

(3)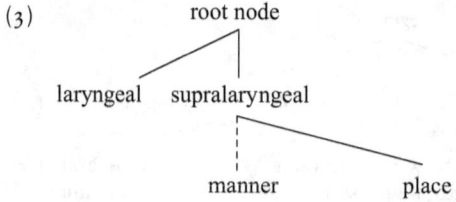

In Clements's model all features were binary.

The next development of this approach can be found in Sagey (1986) (published as Sagey (1990)). The biggest change was the elimination of the manner class, with major class and manner features now being directly and individually linked to the root node. The argument for this elimination was that few if any examples of phonological processes could be given where the relevant features were addressed as a class. Part of the problem here is that manner conflated major class and manner features, but even if major class features are set apart (or reanalysed as being 'structural', as in RCVP; see also below), it is still not clear that the remaining features ([strident], [nasal], [lateral], [continuant], etc.) ever function as a unit, as place and laryngeal features do. There are processes that delete or spread whichever features are within these latter two classes, but no such processes exist for the group of manner features as a whole. Sagey's model also introduced articulator nodes (coronal, labial, dorsal), which are effectively unary features that dominate binary features that make finer distinctions. Halle (1995) proposed a further development of Sagey's model, adding more unary nodes (such as glottal, TR in the laryngeal class, and soft palate and oral place in the supralaryngeal class). A third innovation of this model was to locate the major class feature [consonantal] and [sonorant] *in* the root node, a suggestion that goes back to Schein & Steriade (1986) and McCarthy (1988). This model explicitly advocates a close match with the articulatory system, thus following a clear example of 'substance-driven' phonology.

While various further geometries have been proposed,[1] I move on here to later work by Clements (e.g. (1991a)), who explicitly proposes using the same set of place features (i.e. the articulator units [labial], [coronal], [dorsal] and [pharyngeal]) for both consonants and vowels. Clements also introduces a distinction between a C-place and a V-place node, in which the latter is dominated by the former:

(4)
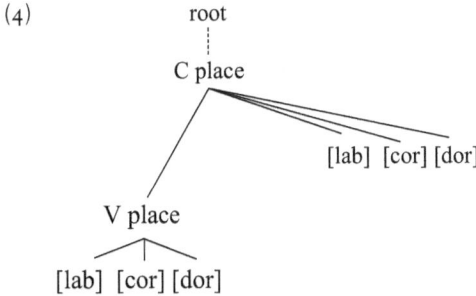

The subordinate placement of V place explains why vowels can 'communicate' (e.g. in vowel harmony) across consonants, while consonants cannot do the same across vowels. In RCVP this asymmetry is explained with reference to syllable structure: vowels are heads of syllables, which allows them to see each other at the syllable head projection level. Hence there is no need for a segment-internal account in RCVP, which has no independent motivation (see van de Weijer (1996)). The crucial innovation of Clements's model is the use of a single set of place features for both consonants and vowels. This unification, while new in the context of FG models, was also proposed in the dependency model, which uses its 'AIU' set of primes for both consonantal and vowel place, with the addition of some 'extra' unary primes that are exclusive to consonants or vowels (see §§ 2.2.1–2.2.3). The idea that consonants and vowels share the same set of features was part of the feature proposal in Jakobson, Fant & Halle (1952) and Jakobson & Halle (1956), but this programme was abandoned in Chomsky & Halle (1968), along with a switch from giving features acoustic 'meanings' (alongside articulatory meanings) to relying on articulatory definitions. This articulatory bias found its way into Sagey's model, discussed above, and Halle's, or extensions of it (Halle (1995), among others). Below I will return to the theme of unification.

---

[1] One important proposal was to introduce an articulator node 'pharyngeal'; see McCarthy (1991).

Another innovation proposed in Clements (1991b) was the introduction of an aperture node, as a sister to the V-place node. This aperture node is formally very different from other class nodes in that it dominates several layers of a single feature [open].

(5)

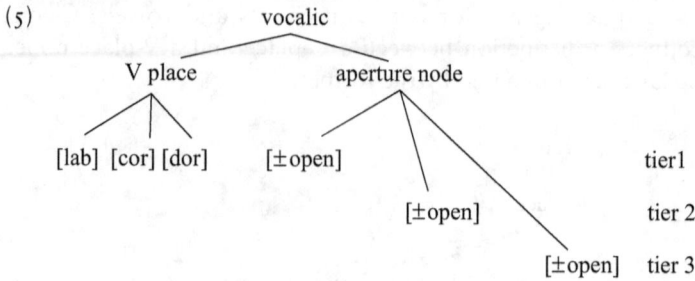

The high vowels [i] and [u] are [−open] on all three tiers, while the mid vowels [e] and [ɛ] are [+open] on tier 2, the lower mid vowels [ɛ] and [ɔ] are [+open] on tiers 2 and 3, and the lowest vowel is [+open] on all three tiers. This creates an effect of stacking '+' values to achieve an increase in openness, which is reminiscent of the particle model proposed in Schane (1984) in which more open vowels have more occurrences of the particle 'a'. This notion of stacking does not find a parallel in RCVP, however. Nevertheless, it is significant that Clements separates vowel place from vowel aperture, which in effect introduces a place/manner distinction for vowels.[2] Another interesting aspect of Clements's model is that a single feature is used to replace the three 'traditional' features [±low] (= open1), [±high] (= open2), and [±ATR] (= open3). The idea that a single prime can have different interpretations depending on its structural position is shared with RCVP, which takes this idea to its logical endpoint by adopting only two primes: C and V.

Clements & Hume (1995), based on Clements (1991a), develop a complete model of segmental structure which incorporates the idea of a C- and a V-place node (dominating identical place features) and the aperture node that combines with the V-place node under a vocalic node that is subordinate to the C-place node.

---

[2] Clements (1990a) proposes an account of major classes which uses three binary features, [±sonorant] [±approximant] and [±vocoid], in terms of which the number of '+' values correlates with an increase in sonority. Vowels have a '+' for all three, approximants for the first two and other sonorant consonants only for the feature [sonorant]. There is thus a formal resemblance (a structural analogy) between the expression of sonority in both major classes and vowel height, which I once pointed out to Nick Clements, but I do not think that he developed this analogy.

Odden (1991) also uses a vowel place node, which he splits into a Height node and a Back-Round node. This also resurrects a manner/place distinction, here only applied to vowels, which he motivates with a variety of phonological processes that address these two types of units separately:[3]

(6)

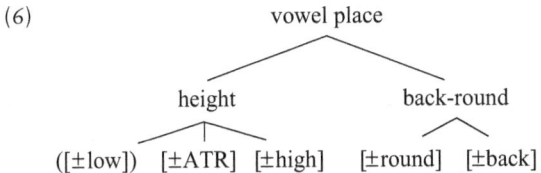

These various proposals are relevant because they introduce a bifurcation between vowel manner and vowel place, just as RCVP does. Finally, another proposal that adopts a separate aperture node was developed in Steriade (1993a, 1994). This proposal distinguishes different linear phases of aperture within segments such as stops and affricates.[4] The idea of distinguishing temporal phases within the segment is not a property of RCVP, although for reasons explained in § 10.5 temporal sequencing is used in the representation of signs, although not within the segmental organisation as such. Rather, sequencing is achieved through association with a bipositional skeletal template.

A number of interesting proposals have also been made for the representation of tone and laryngeal contrast among consonants. Some of these proposals continue the proposal in Halle & Stevens (1971) of having a unified set of features for consonantal phonation and vocalic tone, not only for reasons of economy, but also to account for consonant–vowel interactions. The latter reason also played an important role in the development of a unified set of place features in work by Clements and others. As discussed in § 6.3, various tone scholars have proposed structures for the laryngeal class that are somewhat similar to the RCVP structure (see Bao (1990); Duanmu (1990); Hyman (1993); Yip (2002); Snider (1988, 1990b, 1999)). The split between register and tone proper, proposed in Yip (1980), is incorporated, as is the division between voicing and glottal opening.[5]

Various articles have addressed the locus or validity of specific features, such as [lateral] or the major class features, either placed in the root node or eliminated in favour of a structural account (see Golston

---

[3] The location of [low] is less clear in his proposal.
[4] A development of this approach can be found in Inkelas & Shih (2016), who propose three temporal subphases in what they call their 'Q-theory'; see § 11.3.8.
[5] A critical assessment of these systems for tonal properties, or any proposal for tone features, which have been discussed in § 6.3, is Clements, Michaud & Patin (2011).

& van der Hulst (1999), who also make a structural proposal for manner features). In Chapters 4–7, where I discussed the RCVP structure for the various class nodes and complex segments, I have supplied many references to work that is similar to and/or has informed the RCVP structures.

A very important difference between all the various FG theories and RCVP (with some exceptions that are discussed in the next section) is that in the former there are no 'guiding principles'. There is no claim that the feature organisation is deductively driven by cognitive principles (involving dependency, binarity, unarity, etc.), which means, in my view, that all these models are constructed purely inductively, based on empirical observations about phonological processes and articulation. I do not wish to say that the deductive method overrules the inductive empirical method. However, without deductive guidance, empirical induction may lead to ad hoc FGs that serve the particular purpose that the proposal is focused on, which thus leads to a dense forest of feature trees, as clearly documented in den Dikken and van der Hulst (1988), which only covers the early history of FG. An example of this is the way in which the manner unit, which was originally proposed in Clements (1985), was eliminated because there are no processes that treat manner properties as a unit. As I have pointed out in Chapter 4, there is no good reason to base an FG solely on the evidence from processes, let alone if many of those processes are most likely located in the implementation system. Evidence for class units can and should also come from distributional facts, that is, the occurrence of particular segments in particular syllabic positions. Due to the lack of guiding principles, a great many different proposals for FGs have thus been made. A particular case study could lead to adding a branch or a feature, and so on, without consequences for the overall structure. Such ad hoc manoeuvres are strongly discouraged in RCVP, where the notion of structural analogy between class nodes has been an important guiding principle.

The formalisation of feature grouping in terms of tree diagrams has also been called into question. Hayes (1990) argues that the idea of representing geminates (long consonants or long vowels) in terms of a single structure that is associated with two different skeletal position makes it impossible to change only a part of it. An example concerns the rule of preaspiration in Icelandic (Thráinsson 1978), which converts geminate stops (tt, pp, kk) into a preaspirated sequence (ht, hp, hk). The preaspirated part results from deleting the place features on the first half of the geminate, but such a deletion is technically impossible if two skeletal positions share the same feature structure.[6] How can one delete the place

---

[6] This problem was also noted in Clements (1985) and Steriade (1987b). Clements suggests representing geminate and long vowels with two root nodes, which Hayes

class and at the same time maintain it? The same problem arises when long vowels diphthongise ([eː], [oː] > [ei], [ou]). Hayes proposes preserving the FG, but then associates the features at the bottom of the tree with the skeletal positions:[7]

(7)
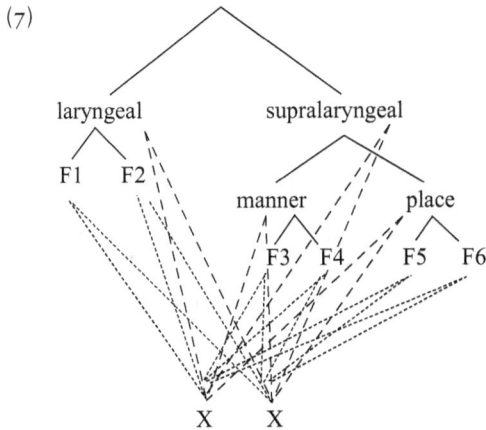

We can now cut association lines independently for the two positions that make up a geminate consonant or long vowel. However, if we want to cut a group of features from one position, for example to account for the change from [pp] to [ht] (in which case we want to remove all place features from the first position), we also need to associate each X position with the class nodes, as I have done in (7) with the thicker association lines. Hayes refers to the new model as the 'bottle brush' model.

Hayes continues to propose another formalisation, replacing the bracketing by a so-called attribute-value structure, which is essentially an alternative notation for trees:[8]

(8) Root: L: [F1]
              [F2]
         S: M: [F3]
                 [F4]
              P: [F5]
                 [F6]

rejects as going against the spirit of Autosegmental Phonology, while Steriade eliminates root nodes entirely.

[7] Actually, much as I did for the sign phonology structure in Chapter 10; see (22).
[8] See § 1.4 in Scobbie (1991).

Then, to make it possible to delete units for only one half of a geminate, Hayes proposes adding indices to co-index units in the 'tree structure' with skeletal positions:

(9) $\quad\quad\quad X_1\ X_2$
$\quad$ Root$_{12}$: $\ L_{12}$: [F1]$_{12}$
$\quad\quad\quad\quad\quad\quad$ [F2]$_{12}$
$\quad\quad\quad S_{12}$: M_{12}: [F3]$_{12}$
$\quad\quad\quad\quad\quad\quad$ [F4]$_{12}$
$\quad\quad\quad\quad\quad P_{12}$: [F5]$_{12}$
$\quad\quad\quad\quad\quad\quad$ [F6]$_{12}$

Given this notation, deletions that only apply to X_1 can be achieved by deleting the 1-index of that unit in the feature structure. I refer to Bird (1990), who discusses various problems with this proposal. The attribute-value notation may be useful in its own right as a substitute for tree structure diagrams, because, as Bird states, it has a rigorous mathematical foundation, unlike tree diagrams, which, if not rooted in a formal theory of graphs, can become 'creative drawings' of observed relationships. I also refer to Phillips (1994: § 4), who notes some other problems with Hayes's model and provides alternative solutions to the problem noted by Hayes.

Another solution to the diphthongisation problem would of course be to simply assume that geminates are represented not in terms of one feature structure, but rather as two identical neighbouring structures; this was suggested in Clements (1985). While this solves the diphthongisation problem, there is a lot of evidence against this way of representing geminates. For example, an epenthesis rule that breaks up a consonant cluster will never break up a geminate. This property of geminates is called integrity (Schein & Steriade (1986)). In fact, Hayes (1986b: 321) mentions *three* properties that have been attributed to geminates:

(10) Properties of geminates:

    a. Ambiguity: Long segments act in some contexts as if they were two segments, in others as if they were one.
    b. Integrity: Insofar as they constitute two segments, long segments cannot be split by rules of epenthesis.
    c. Inalterability: Long segments often resist the application of rules that a-priori would be expected to apply to them.

Property (a) was a problem in the SPE model, which treated geminate segments as segments that have one feature bundle containing the feature specification [+long]. As a consequence, there was no way to accommodate the behaviour as two segments. The introduction of the skeleton with two positions linked to one feature structure allowed researchers to have their cake and eat it, thus solving the ambiguity problem. Inalterability involves another problem that geminates create, even in the multilayered approach. For example, a rule turning [k] to [x] intervocalically would typically not apply to an intervocalic geminate [k:]. Hayes (1986a) and Schein & Steriade (1986), developing a suggestion by Kenstowicz & Pyle (1973), suggest that inalterability is in effect not when the rule only applies to the feature content, but only when the rule refers to the skeletal affiliation of the input or context of the rule. To take the example just given, intervocalic weakening of [k] requires the skeletal string VCV, but an intervocalic geminate [k:] occurs in the string VCCV.

While, thus, the multilayered approach can handle the three properties in (10), it cannot handle the diphthongisation problem which was addressed in Hayes (1990). Although the double association theory for geminates is well supported by processes such as epenthesis and is compatible with inalterability, it is not compatible with the diphthongisation data. This suggests that the parts of geminates are independent feature structures. However, the 'solution' of representing geminates as two separate segments runs counter to the properties of integrity and inalterability, which suggest the opposite.

So, while Hayes is correct in rejecting the double-root hypothesis, we must ask whether there is perhaps a solution to the diphthongisation problem other than the one suggested in Hayes (1990), which is not without its own problems. One would think that there is one, because it would seem that this problem has simply been ignored in the subsequent FG literature (as far as I know). However, I have seen no explicit proposal other than the one that Hayes proposes.

I would like to suggest that there is, in fact, a fairly straightforward analysis, although it does require a new formal operation, which I will call 'root meiosis'. Root meiosis is a form of fission, that is, a division of a unit into two complementary parts.[9] In cell biology, the 'normal' activity of a cell is mitosis, which is the process whereby a cell divides into two identical copies of the original cell. We could solve the diphthongisation problem by postulating a mitosis step, that is, a division of the single feature structure into two identical feature structures, each with its own root node, followed by deletion in one or both positions.[10] However, producing two identical copies of the original geminate and allowing each part to be modified misses an important generalisation, which is that in diphthongisation a single feature structure is split, such that its original parts are divided between the two new structures. This is why

---

[9] This is a simplification, because meiosis goes through various steps so that the original cell eventually produces four different cells. Meiosis applies in the formation of reproductive cells.
[10] In a sense, the Obligatory Contour Principle enforces the opposite of mitosis, by fusing two identical units into one.

the meiosis metaphor is appropriate, because meiosis involves a division of one cell into two cells, each of which contains half of the content of the original cell. One of the original advances made in theories that use unary elements, such as the AIU set, is that the diphthongisation of a vowel involves the linearisation of the elements of the monophthong (AE; Schane (1984), etc.), which typically leads to complementarity as in (11a) and (11b). The meiosis metaphor captures this complementarity:

(11) a. [e:] > [a] [i]
        [AI]   [A][I]

    b. [o] > [a] [u]
        [AU]   [A][U]

    c. [e:] > [e] [i]
        [AI]   [AI][I]

    d. [o] > [o] [u]
        [AU]   [AU][U]

However, we also have to allow for the processes in (11c) and (11d), where the colour elements occur in both halves of the diphthong, which seemingly contradicts the idea that the two halves are completely complementary. This means that after meiosis we have to allow certain elements to spread to the other position; in (12b) I indicate the spreading with arrows:

(12) Diphthongisation: R ⇒ R R (meiosis)

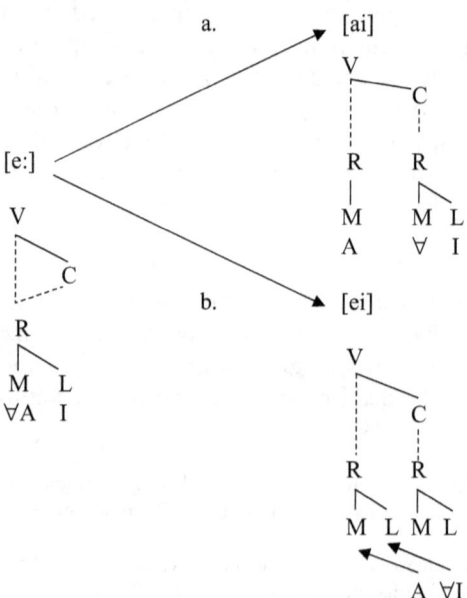

In (12) the two outcomes of diphthongising [e:] show that no new elements are introduced, nor are elements deleted. For the outcome [ei], we only need to assume that after meiosis the elements I and ∀ are copied back to the first structure. If an outcome is possible with a schwa as the second element, leading to a centralising diphthong [eə], the I element spreads to the first position and is deleted on the second.

Finally, I need to also apply the meiosis model to the consonantal case of diphthongisation cited earlier, that is, the Icelandic [kk, pp, tt] > [hk, hp, ht]. We can interpret this as a case in which all properties of the geminate are attributed to the second root, leaving the first root with a variable V-manner specification, assuming that a fricative manner without place elements is realised as [h].

The crucial point to be observed here is that traditional binary feature theories do not provide a natural basis for representing diphthongisation for what it is: a division of the properties of the monophthong over two positions. Even if the model of root meiosis is applied to a traditional FG this result can simply not be obtained, because features are not primes that have their own independent interpretation. A feature set [+high, –low, –back] for [e] cannot be split into two units that represent [a] and [i]; while [i] can be [+high, –back], the remnant [–low] does not capture the vowel [a].

11.3 Other models

11.3.1 *Dependency models*

Work on DP 'proper' was mentioned in Chapter 2. Obviously, RCVP 'owes' a lot to this approach. In this section, I mention some work that, while not located strictly within DP, uses crucial aspects of this model such as the use of (specific) unary primes and the fundamental, organising head-dependency principle.[11] DP has made some moves in the direction of using the same elements in different classes, while at the same time pursuing the idea of using the same primes for both consonants and vowels; nevertheless the programme of complete unification, using one set of unary elements (namely A, I and U) for all segmental properties, was developed in early versions of RCVP,[12] in part in joint work with Norval Smith; see van der Hulst & Smith (1987), Smith (1988) and van der Hulst (1988a, 1988b). This approach was further developed in work by Norval

---

[11] See van der Hulst (2006a) for a general review of dependency-based approaches to phonology.
[12] See van der Hulst (1990a). This manuscript was distributed on a small scale to various phonologists. The idea to only use the elements C and V occurred around 1992, as did the name 'Radical CV Phonology'.

Smith and his students; see Smith (2000), Humbert (1996), Botma (2004) (with specific attention to nasality), Botma & Smith (2006), Smith & Botma (2007) and van der Torre (2003) (on sonorant consonants); see also Poppe (2020), which builds on van der Hulst (1988a, 1988b). Specific work on vowel harmony using the AIU set is van der Hulst & Smith (1987, 1988c, 1990), which developed (eventually) into van der Hulst (2018). Another example of the generalised dependency approach, with a focus on the representation of complex segments of various kinds, is van de Weijer (1992, 1993, 1996). Ewen & van der Hulst (1985, 1988) proposed a structure in which the elements I and U are dominated by a 'Y' element which essentially represented 'high', and this approach was further developed in van der Hulst (1989), which led to the first formulation of RCVP in van der Hulst (1990b), followed by (1995c) with the C/V application to manner, in (1994) to location and in (1996c, 2000a) to syllable structure, culminating in the first full statement of this theory in van der Hulst (2005a). Dresher & van der Hulst (1998) focus on the diagnostics for head/dependent asymmetries at various levels of the prosodic hierarchy. Applications of the RCVP approach to sign phonology are van der Hulst (1993b, 1995a, 1995b, 2000b).

The notion of dependency has also played a role in other work, such as Mester (1988), but in this and related work (e.g. McCarthy (1988)), dependency is the inverse not of headedness, but of structural dominance. In this sense, in many FG works, lower features or units are said to be dependent on higher units. On these two notions of dependency, see Ewen (1995).

In this section, I also mention once more GP, which has also already been discussed in Chapter 2. Clearly, this model shares major aspects with DP. It has followed its own course of further development after the first seminal papers (KLV85, KLV90) and, as explained in Chapter 2, some of the more recent outcomes converge with RCVP in limiting the set of elements to six, which can be further divided into three sets of two elements (although this division is not formally recognised in GP). As is clear, RCVP adopts three sets of two elements, but because a formal geometry is adopted, it can then say that each set contains the same two elements.

The characteristic AIU set that plays a pivotal role in both DP and GP has also played an important role in work by Schane (1984, 1985, 1990, 1995, 2005)[13] and Rennison (1986, 1987, 1990), although neither author invoked the head-dependency relation. Schane (2005) is especially interesting for his explicit statement that the element A (which in his

---

[13] When Schane (1984) proposes his AIU approach he notes that DP has used the same elements (p. 154, fn. 28), but he deems his model to be very different from DP in rejecting 'hierarchical relations', by which he means 'dependency', which is, however, not a hierarchical relation; see Ewen (1995).

model can occur multiple times in the segmental structure, signifying an increase in sonority) covers several properties that have been attributed to different features in other models, such as vowel height, laxness and ATR. This idea, including the stacking of A's, is similar to Clements's proposal for an aperture node which also stack instances of the feature [open] (clearly similar to the A element) to cover both vowel height and ATR distinctions.

11.3.2 The nested subregister model

Salting (1998, 2004) proposes a model, 'the nested subregister model', which represents phonological categories in terms of a double split of phonetic spaces such as height or place. He applies this to the vowel height and location categories and discusses the parallels of his model with RCVP (see Salting (2005)). The two models were developed independently. The following diagram illustrates Salting's approach:

(13)

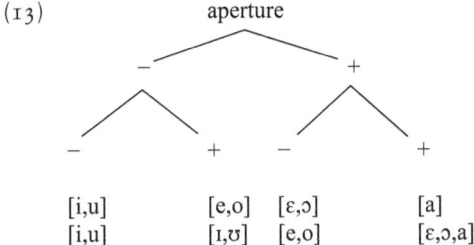

The successive split of the aperture space can group vowels differently in different languages.

Salting discusses the parallels between his model and RCVP (based on van der Hulst (2005a)).

(14)

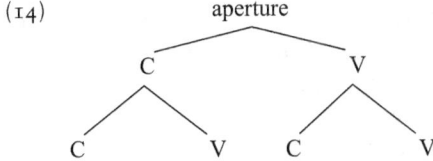

Inspired by the RCVP proposal for place, Salting shows that his subnesting approach can also be applied to place.

What emerges here as similar in both models is the application of establishing a structural analogy between different class nodes, in this case Place and Aperture. Clearly, there is no reason for not extending this model to laryngeal features, but I am not aware of work by Salting that does that. The subnested model does not incorporate the notion of dependency. We should recall that structures such as (14) are not as such part of the RCVP segmental structure. Rather, the four-way distinction results from having two opposing elements that can occur alone or in combination, with an added dependency relation in the latter case:

(15)   C   C;V   V;C   V

Thus dependency is not a guiding principle of the nested subregister model, which means that unlike (14), (15) presumably represents the partial segmental structure of vowels.

11.3.3 *The Toronto model*

Avery & Rice (1990), Rice & Avery (1990, 1991) and Rice (1992, 1995) propose an FG model that incorporates a number of new properties:

(16)

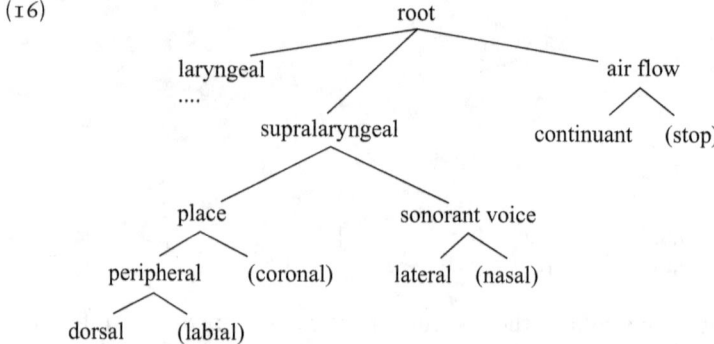

The Sonorant Voice node replaces the feature [sonorant]. Its absence marks obstruents, its bare presence identifies nasals, and if Sonorant Voice dominates [lateral] it marks laterals. The Air Flow node stands for manner features (see Rice & Avery (1991)). All features are monovalent. For each node, the feature between parentheses is taken to be the unmarked choice, which can be left unspecified. Thus, for example, a segment with a 'bare' SV node is nasal.

Like RCVP, this model restores a manner node (Air Flow), and it proposes an organisation for the place node that is shared with the RCVP place node.[14]

Interestingly, the structure of the place node as in (16) is different from the way in which Clements & Hume (1995) and Hume (1996) structure

---

[14] See also Rice (1995), who basically proposes the I/U distinction for place, referred to as 'coronal' and 'peripheral'. See also D'Arcy (2004), who applies this model to the analysis of vowel harmony.

their place node, which branches into [labial] and [lingual], with the latter dominating [coronal] and [dorsal]. The idea of adopting a unit [lingual] was also independently motivated in Lass (1976: ch. 7), and AE (pp. 235ff.) adopted it as an element in their system. In the RCVP structure this category is characterised by having a C element in the place class; see Chapter 5.

11.3.4 *The parallel structure model*

In this section, I will discuss a model that has been proposed in Morén (2003, 2007). This work is interesting because it is based on a number of explicitly stated goals that are shared with the basic principles of RCVP. The two models were developed independently.[15] Morén uses the name 'parallel structure model' to make it explicit that he wants the different class nodes in the geometry to be maximally formally identical. As the reader will realise, this is precisely the same as seeking maximal structural analogy. Morén (2003: 197) states that his objective is to show that phonological segments are composed of a limited set of identical structures, using a limited set of private articulatory-based features. The recurrent structure that he proposes is as follows:

(17)

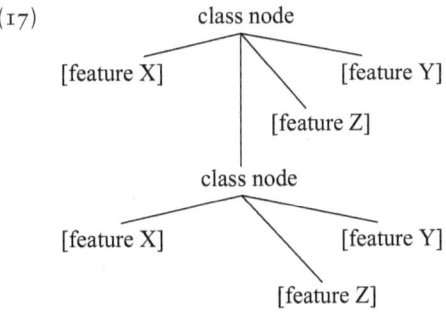

As we will see below, this general structure is replicated in the segmental structure in separate laryngeal, manner and place nodes. Subsequently, Morén proposes the same geometry as a recurrent structure in the organisation of signs. Moreover, segmental structure and sign structure are claimed to share the same macrostructure in terms of the number and types of class nodes. As for the features themselves, Morén discusses the fact that to postulate a fixed set of innate structures with innately specified phonetic definitions is difficult to maintain, given that spoken language and sign language tap into very different kinds of articulatory phonetic substances. Nevertheless, his structures for the manner and

---

[15] Morén (2007) discusses DP, but makes no reference to RCVP publications.

laryngeal nodes actually have the same feature labels in both modalities. The difference between the two modalities is mainly manifested in the features for place.

Another interesting aspect of his model is that Morén rejects major class features, arguing that major sonority class is expressed structurally. His model also adopts the position that manner distinctions apply to both consonants and vowels. Finally, he notes (p. 203):

> it is interesting that some of the current models of feature geometry (e.g. Clements & Hume (1995)) make an effort to unify the place features for both consonants and vowels, but do not do the same for the manner features [...] [T]here has been no attempt to locate a set of features that might be considered vowel manner, and we are left with a set of consonant manner features, as well as either a set of vowel heights dependent on [dor] place (e.g. Sagey (1990)) or a recursive [±open] feature on a vocalic aperture node (e.g. Clements & Hume (1995)). Is there a straightforward way to unify consonant and vowel manner?

And on page 205:

> one must ask if the same set of laryngeal features is used for both consonants and vowels, given that laryngeal features are typically used to contrast consonants (specifically obstruents) and not vowels.

It would seem that the goal of proposing a unified structure for both consonants and vowels using identical structure for all class nodes, and thus not only place, is a driving force behind Morén's model. It is quite obvious that this goal is shared with one of the goals of the RCVP model. As mentioned, an important trademark of the parallel structures model is the goal of applying the same, or a very similar, model to both spoken segments and the structure of signs. Morén complains that models for sign structure seem to diverge from models for spoken segments, although an attempt had certainly been made to achieve a far-reaching unification in (van der Hulst 1993b, 1995b, 1996b), which was further developed in the previous chapter.

Despite these various resemblances in goals, the actual model that Morén proposes is rather different from the RCVP architecture. I here display Morén's model for place properties of spoken segments (see his p. 265). In (18) I first give the highest division into four class nodes, which are presented in detail in (19) and (20):

(18)
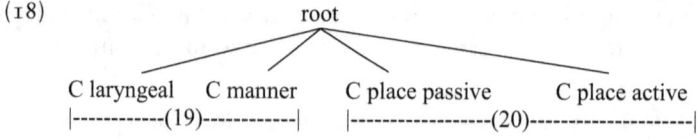

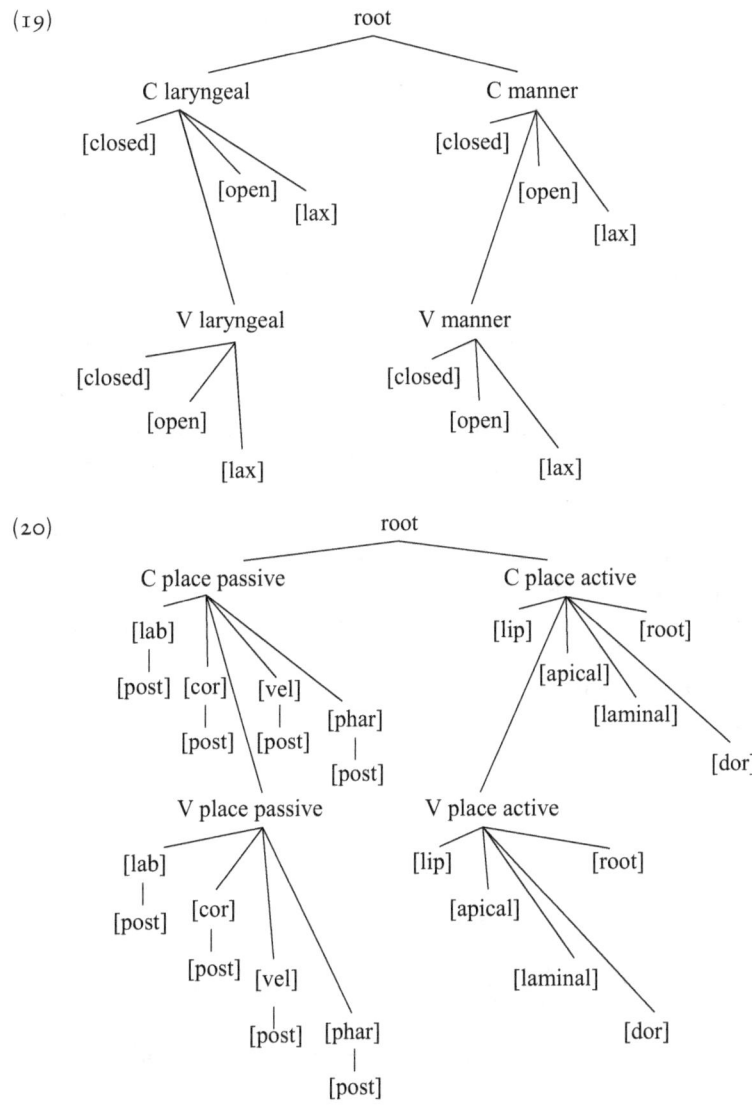

One noteworthy property is the representation of place of articulation in terms of both the passive and the active articulator. When comparing the articulation of spoken segments and signs in § 11.2 I pointed out that models of spoken language do not usually make this distinction, and with good reason. Gorecka (1990) is an exception, as is the model of Articulatory Phonology (Browman & Goldstein 1986, 1992). Morén realises that a conflation of active and passive articulators is not possible in the representation of signs, as I also argued in § 11.2. Since his goal is to establish a parallelism between segment and sign structure, he also adopts this duality for spoken segments. While the goal of establishing parallelism is good, I have not taken this to the point that the two structures must be isomorphic. What the modalities share, in my view, is a system of categorisation that leads to structures in both cases that obey the same structural principles, and not necessarily to structures that are isomorphic, because the phonetic substance of both modalities is rather different.

I will not comment on the specific place structures that Morén proposes. His system is well and cleverly designed. Distinguishing four place of articulation is shared with other articulator-based models. His use of [posterior] to create two categories for each place is interesting and elegant. RCVP represents the same distinction in a different way, in particular by distinguishing pharyngeal from the three other places.

Turning to the laryngeal and manner class, we note that Morén proposes exactly the same structure for both. The major opposition in both classes is created by the features [closed] and [open], which is motivated by the fact that in both cases the articulatory differences involve relative opening or stricture. The analogy with the elements C and V is clear, especially because he allows the two features to combine to form intermediate categories, although he does not invoke any notion of dependency.

The structure that Morén proposes for the sign adopts the same structure as in (18). The Place node for signs has a different set of places and articulators. The analogue of the laryngeal node is the non-manual node, while the label 'manner' is maintained. The non-manual and the manner node have the same structure as the analogues in the spoken segment structure:

(21)
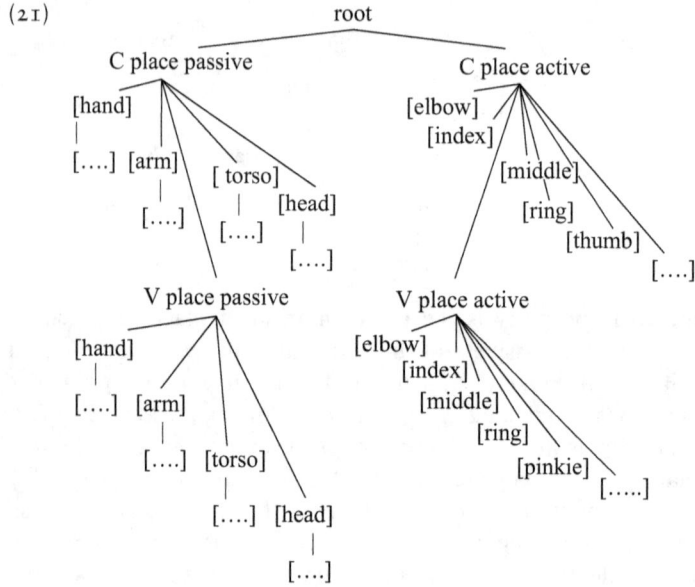

(22)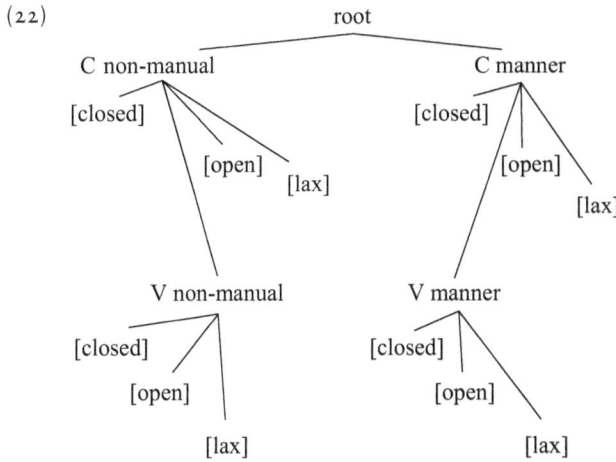

The non-manual node refers to distinctions on the face, including mouth features. Morén here simply assumes that the same structure can be used as for the laryngeal node in (20), which is reasonable since parallelism is expected even though detailed proposals for non-manual properties are not available. The sign manner node refers to the distinction that I located in the aperture node. While it may seem reasonable to equate aperture with manner, my sign model uses manner not for opening and closing movements, but rather for the manner of movement. In the case of closing and opening movements, there is no such manner, however. Manner of movement in my model only applies to path movements which are large enough to have distinguishing properties. An account of path movement seems to be missing in Morén's model.

My goal here is not to analyse Morén's sign model in greater detail. Rather, my point is to show how similar the underlying principles are. Morén's idea of using the same basic structure for different class nodes in both modalities is matched in RCVP, which structures each class node in terms of a head and a dependent class, each dominating two elements. I would say, then, that, despite the shared idea of replicating the same structure, RCVP replicates a structure that itself has a principled, binary, head-dependent organisation, as well as placing a limit on the number of contrasting options within each class node. In RCVP, class nodes do not dominate a 'random' list of features, emerging inductively from the contrastive use of the phonetic substance. Rather, each class node has exactly two 'features', namely C and V, which can occur alone or in combination.

In conclusion, while Morén's model and mine have many similarities in terms of the underlying goals and some principles, RCVP capitalises on structural analogies that follow from adopting the same principles in both modalities:

(23) Shared principles:
   a. Phonetic spaces are organised in X-bar style head-dependency macrostructures.
   b. Within all classes there are the same two unary elements: C and V.
   c. Elements can occur by themselves or combine (in the latter case a head-dependency relation holds)
   d. The phonetic correlates of the two elements differ depending on their structural location and their head or dependent status.

Given that the phonetic spaces of spoken and sign language are rather different, we do not expect that the principles in (23) will produce *overall* isomorphic structures. Morén's goal of complete isomorphism (apart from differences in the place nodes), while interesting as a daring hypothesis, is not, in my view, necessary or expected.

11.3.5 *The channel-neutral model*

Krämer (2012) supports Morén's model by adopting a parallel structure for both spoken segments and signs. In Krämer (2012: ch. 7) he pushes the idea further by proposing a structure that generalises over different modules of the grammar,

> proposing a set of features that results by and large in the same segment classes as the features of Feature Geometry but basing features on concepts used in other modules of grammar, recycling the basic categories of aspect, of deixis, of spatial adpositions and other syntactic and semantic features. These features define events of articulation which can be executed either in the vocal tract as audio signs or with the upper body as visible gestures. (p. 153)

This approach departs from the view that both spoken segments and signs can be thought of as events (as they are in Articulatory Phonology) which involve an actor (figure), an action and a location (ground). In (3) in § 10.2, here repeated as (24), I adopted a very similar viewpoint in comparing spoken segments and signs:

(24)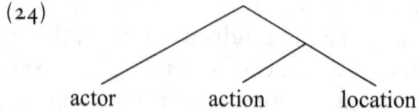

Krämer proposes adopting this perspective for spoken segments, which only requires reference to the location and the event. He adds on page 161:

With these ingredients at hand and the articulatory area determined, place of articulation can be formalised without direct reference to the articulators. Just as in discourse, once the location and the actors are set we don't need to refer to them explicitly anymore and we can use pronouns, a proper definition of where a phonological event (segment) happens saves us from specifying which body parts are involved.

Although I do not understand the reasoning here, I agree, as I have also argued that at least for spoken segments reference to the articulator is not required, given the almost 1:1 correlation between articulator and place.

The innovative aspect of Krämer's proposal is to interpret the contrastive options within the unit's location and event in terms of spatial and event concepts that are also used to describe the semantic properties of prepositions and verb types:

(25)
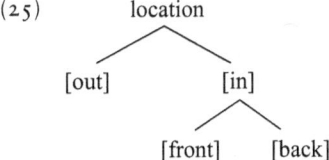

On p. 162 he writes:

For the vocal tract the division between [out] and [in] corresponds to that between [labial] (outside) and the other places of articulation. Dividing the inside of the vocal tract into a [front] and [back] area corresponds to the distinction between [coronal] and [dorsal].

Continuing:

Further potential divisions can be introduced by recursively dividing the [front] and [back] areas into a [front] and [back] subarea, i.e., specifying locations as more front in the front or more back in the front (dental and postalveolar) and more front in the back and more back in the back (palatal and uvular):

(26)
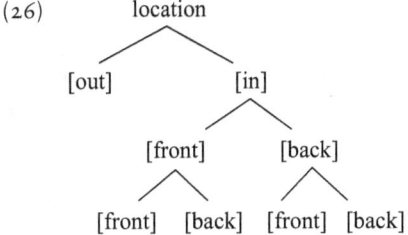

Manner distinctions are compared to event types, such as telic ('punctual') and atelic ('continuous'), which Krämer compares to stops and continuants, respectively. The differences in distance between the articulator and the location that give rise to relative stricture or relative aperture remind him of the notion of deixis (with its basic 'near/far' opposition). Krämer thus adopts the features [prox] and [dist] to represent degrees of stricture and aperture.

(27)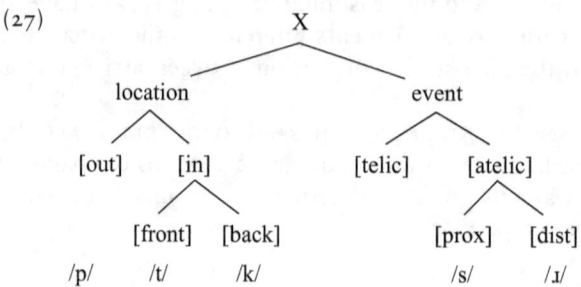

He then shows how the same features can be used for the analysis of signs, concluding that while the previously described features have obvious parallels in the analysis of signs, the two modalities, being very different in terms of their phonetic resources, cannot be expected to use exactly the same feature set (p. 169). This programmatic proposal, as Krämer realises, does not cover all the contrastive distinctions required in either spoken segments or signs. It does not cover laryngeal features, for example. Also, as I have argued in Chapter 10, sign structure does require a representation of the articulator in addition to specifying the location. But even if such gaps could be filled, Krämer does not want to claim that all modules share all their features.

Krämer certainly suggests an approach that generalises over spoken segments and signs. His approach shares with RCVP the use of unary features and the notion of recursive splitting of phonetic spaces. Beyond such parallels, and ignoring differences, his proposal has the very interesting consequence of directly linking the formal phonological properties of segments and signs to aspects of word meaning, a relationship that can be exploited for iconic or sound-symbolic purposes. For example, he notes that 'many languages display sound symbolism in their deictic particles: the particles indicating proximity often contain a high vowel while the particles indicating distance often contain a low vowel' (p. 164). He also points out the fact that in sign languages the aspectual distinction between [telic] and [atelic] very often displays a close sign–meaning correlation. For example, change-of-state verbs often involve a stop gesture.[16]

---

[16] See Wilbur (2003) for an extensive discussion of this kind of iconicity. See also Kuhn (2017).

He discusses iconicity and sound symbolism in more detail in his § 7.5 (p. 170ff.).[17]

How can we understand this proposal in relation to the RCVP model? Assuming that phonological elements are indeed correlated with articulatory instructions (as well as with an acoustic image), Krämer's proposal suggests an alternative way of thinking about these instructions by stating them at a higher level of abstraction than is usual. To see why this allows the use of features that cut across not just modalities but also different modules, in particular phonology and morphosyntax, we need to understand that features in both domains have 'meanings', that is, correlates of some kind. Phonological features (in both spoken and signed languages) have 'meanings' in terms of actual motor activity of the articulatory system, or in terms of mental simulation of such activities (as emphasised in the motor theory of speech perception). Morphosyntactic features also have meanings, and there is a way of thinking about their meanings (and about word meaning in general) which also includes mental simulations of direct perceptual and motoric experience. In so-called embodied approaches to meaning, it is claimed that meaning concepts/semantic features, or word meanings as a whole, are represented in terms of cognitive simulations[18] of motoric actions that are involved in the 'real' actions that a word refers to.[19] If we adopt this view, a morphosyntactic or semantic 'feature' like [proximal] is represented in terms of a simulation of a 'movement closely towards' (or something like that).

(28)   phonological feature   morphosyntactic/semantic feature

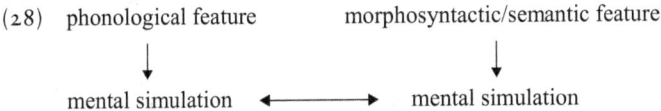

      mental simulation ⟷ mental simulation

Since there will be similarities between the mental simulations in both domains (because both involve motoric activity, among other things), it stands to reason that we can use the same feature names in both domains. We would, in fact, expect similarities between features for sign language and morphosyntactic features that refer to spatial dimensions. To link such spatial simulations to articulatory activity 'in the mouth' is less

---

[17] The direct relation between formal properties of signs and meaning concepts is also a fundamental idea in Stokoe's 'Semantic Phonology' (Stokoe 1991). In this later work, Stokoe suggested that the basic structure of signs, as in (24), is a direct expression of a semantic/syntactic subject–predicate structure. One of Krämer's earlier papers on this subject was aptly entitled 'The semantics of phonological features' (Krämer 2010).

[18] Presumably involving so-called 'mirror neurons'.

[19] See Casasanto & Lozano (2007); Bergen (2012).

obvious, unless it can be shown that at some level of motor planning, correlations are made between the motoric activities of different motor systems. The motor cortex has separate areas for different parts of the body, such as arms, fingers or tongue. Each of these organs can be moved in similar directions (up, down, forwards, etc.) and it is thus possible that these similarities are acknowledged at a higher level of cognition. This gives us a level at which articulatory descriptions of different organs can be said to be the same. There is evidence for higher-level correlations between the oral and manual articulators; see for example Woll (2001), who develops a notion of 'echo phonology' which involves the oral articulator mimicking the manual articulator:

(29)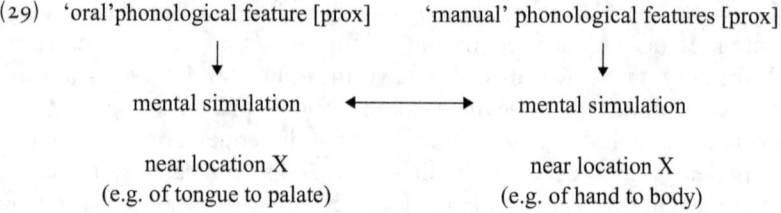

Adding up (28) and (29), there is a justification for using the same feature labels for simulations of articulation/motor movement in different modalities and in different modules.

(30)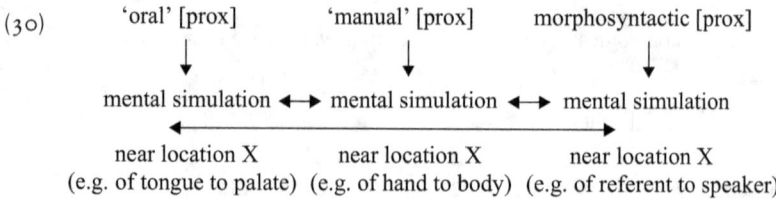

To the extent that the correlations between the 'meaning' of features across modalities and modules exist at some cognitive level, it could be argued, as I think Krämer intends to do, that in the cognitive systems that are compared here, feature systems are created from mental simulations of motor activity or sensory experience which as such provide the grounding of these features. In other words, similarities between feature systems arise because they emerge from very similar mental 'grounding domains', or even one single mental grounding domain which generalises over the various instances of, for example 'near location X'. The unification of the feature system, then, lies in the shared 'meaning' of the features.

This approach is not incompatible with the RCVP model, which, as it stands, makes no commitment to the idea that the features/primes in different modules/modalities are grounded in a shared domain. RCVP is about the manner in which features are constructed in whatever the grounding domain is. While Morén postulates a particular structure that is used to 'parse' different domains in features, including the same feature names, RCVP postulates structural principles such as the Opponent Principle and head-dependency relations, while making no commitment to feature names, since it only has two features (C and V), which represent opposing degrees of perceptual salience. By incorporating specific feature names into the model, Morén and Krämer imperil the programme of a substance-free phonology, since it would seem that the choice of features, as indicated by their names, is very much tied in with their 'substance'. This may be an unintended effect, since both phonologists subscribe to the substance-free approach. If they wish to maintain that stance, I would say that what is shared by different modules/modalities is not the features, but rather, possibly, the grounding domains at some level of cognitive abstraction. RCVP is as substance-free as I think is possible, acknowledging only an asymmetry in perceptual salience, as encoded in the C and V primes.

11.3.6 *The Duanmu model*

A recent extensive proposal for features can be found in Duanmu (2016), whose goal is to establish a minimal set of features that is sufficient to represent all possible contrasts in languages. Based on two databases of segmental systems (UPSID,[20] designed by Ian Maddieson (see MD and Maddieson & Precoda (1992)), and P-base,[21] designed by Jeff Mielke (see Mielke (2008)), Duanmu explicitly states that his feature set (contrary to earlier work in FG) is not motivated by or meant to accommodate phonological processes and natural classes. He does not suggest an 'FG', but his proposals for features and informal grouping of feature classes suggest the following classificatory organisation of binary features, and some unary 'class nodes':

---

[20] <http://web.phonetik.uni-frankfurt.de/upsid.html> (last accessed 5 February 2020).
[21] <http://pbase.phon.chass.ncsu.edu> (last accessed 5 February 2020).

(31)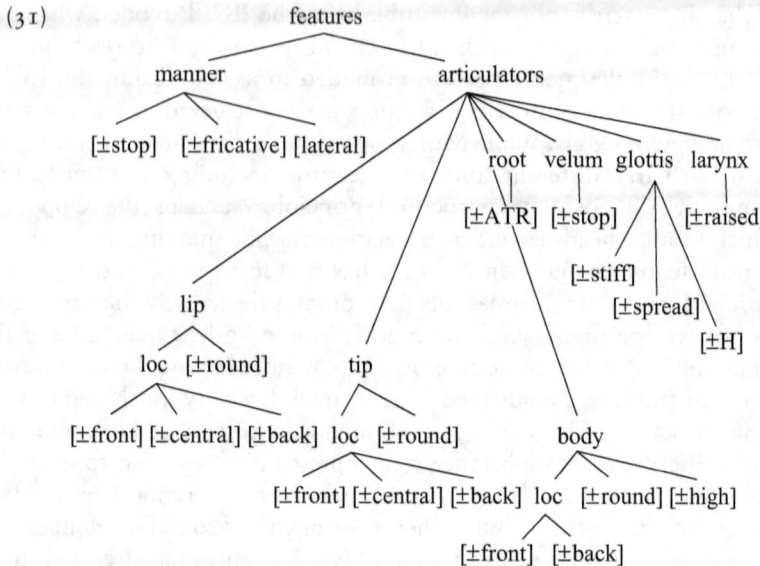

The manner features define four classes:

(32) [+stop, −fricatives]   stops
[−stop, −fricatives]   fricatives
[+stop, +fricatives]   affricates
[−stop, −fricatives]   approximants

The feature [stop] under the Velum node defines oral consonants ([+stop]) and nasal consonants ([−stop]), which contradicts the natural grouping of nasal and stops as (oral) non-continuants. Again, my goal here is not to discuss this feature system in detail. I merely point out the fact that this classification suggests a manner/articulator division, with manner being exclusively applicable to consonants. Vowel height is represented in terms of the features [±high] and [±ATR]. Clearly, this proposal is purely inductive and as such there is no intention to suggest that features emerge in a structured manner, based on phonetic substance and contrast.

11.3.7 Government Phonology 2.0

I have discussed the 'standard' version of GP (KLV85) in § 2.3. and then also developments leading up to a reduced set of six elements, noting a convergence with the RCVP model, which has three sets of two elements, which also leads to making a six-way distinction in head elements, proposed and illustrated in Backley (2011), 2012). Since then other variants of the GP element theory have been proposed, most extensively by Backley & Nasukawa ((2020b); Nasukawa & Backley (2005, 2015));

Nasukawa (2015, 2016, 2017), proposes an integration of 'melody' and 'prosody', but preserves the set of six elements. I will not discuss these proposals in details, but I note a resemblance between this approach and RCVP in that both use element labels not only for melody aspects but also for prosodic units such as rhyme, syllable and so on. This is similar to the use of C and V for segmental structure and for labelling units in the syllabic structure (see § 3.2.2) and foot structure (§ 3.2.5). Here I copy Backley & Nasukawa's representation of the word *better* (from Backley & Nasukawa (2020b: 18)):

(33)   ['betə] 'better'

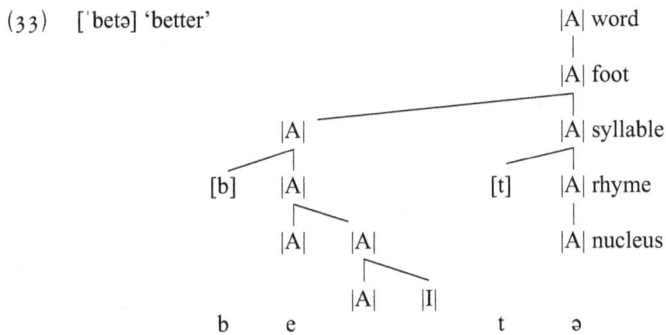

Here is another example with the element structure for a consonantal (p. 30):

(34)   Recursive structure in vowels and consonants: the CV unit [kʰi]

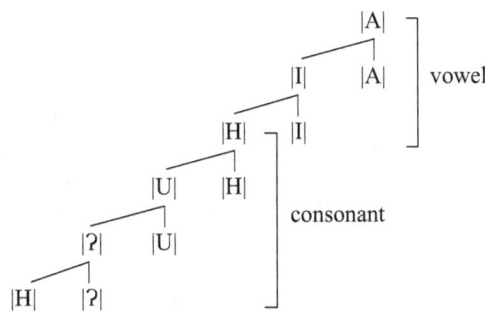

These authors thus use 'recursive structures' that use elements as labels from top to bottom.

There are some other models which also proliferate structure, not strictly stemming from the GP tradition, such as Mutlu (2020) and Schwartz (2020), which also appeal to recursive structures. In fact, the volume in which these various articles appear (Backley & Nasukawa

2020a) is entirely devoted to the use of recursive structures in phonology, and also contains den Dikken & van der Hulst (2020).

In this section I will also briefly discuss a 'new' version of GP, called GP 2.0, which has been proposed by Pöchtrager (2006, 2015, 2018, 2020) and Pöchtrager & Kaye (2013). While GP 2.0 is advocated as a new version of GP, it is, in my understanding of it, pretty much a completely different theory from the standard version, which nevertheless continues to adhere to some of the general characteristics, such as using unary elements, banning codas as legitimate syllabic units, banning extrinsic rule ordering and banning all the treatment of morpho-lexical alternations from the domain of phonology. Also, following the trend of reducing the number of elements, the authors propose that out the six elements ([H], [L], [ʔ], [A], [I], [U]), [H], [ʔ] and [A] should be replaced by 'structure'. A characteristic aspect of the theory is the use of X-bar-like structures to represent nuclei and onsets. In the notation that is used, terminal nodes of such structure are labelled 'x', with additional labels such as 'O' and 'N' indicating whether we are dealing with an onset structure or a nucleus structure. The difference between stops and fricatives, formerly made by the element [ʔ], is now made by giving stops 'more complete X-bar structure' (the arrow indicates a relation of 'control' which holds between the head and the 'complement'):

(35) a. fricatives b. stops

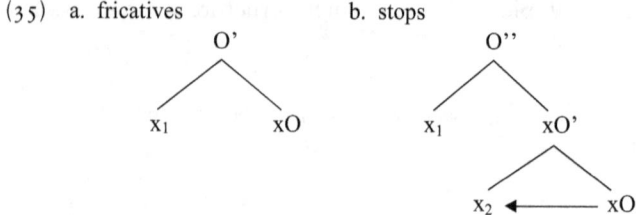

The theory also appeals to the relation of 'M-command', from the head to the specifier, which is lexically specified for some structures but not others, and which accounts for, for example, the lengthening effect that voiced obstruents have on a preceding vowel. I simply cannot do justice here to the design of the new theory, which is still very much in development.

There is a resemblance between GP 2.0 and RCVP in that in both approaches, the number of elements is reduced by adding more structure to the model, in particular X-bar-like structure. GP 2.0 reduces the set of elements to three ([L], [I], [U]), while RCVP ends up with two elements (C and V). But this is where the resemblance ends. In particular, GP 2.0 and RCVP part ways with respect to the relevance of the notion of contrast. GP has always been keen on rejecting fundamental beliefs of other phonological theories, especially the theory proposed in Chomsky

Comparison to other models 407

and Halle (1968). However, this theory also takes issue with a more traditional fundamental belief (Pöchtrager & Kaye 2013: 53):

> contrast plays no role in GP and over 20 years of research in this framework has revealed no reason why it should. The very concept of contrast is inexpressible within GP.

I can only understand this to mean that GP's goal is to represent phonetic properties of utterances, at least those that are in some sense linguistically relevant, hence presumably excluding paralinguistic properties of the speech signal. The goal of representing structures that are not based on recognising contrast is reminiscent of theories such as articulatory phonology (Browman & Goldstein (1986, 1992); Gafos et al. (to appear)), as well as the theory that I will discuss in the next section: Q-theory. We have seen in § 9.8 that it is necessarily the case that children construe phonetic categories without taking minimal pairs (and this contrast) into consideration. This, however, does not imply that contrast cannot become the cornerstone of the adult phonological grammar, after the phonetic categories have been parsed into a minimal number of phonological elements, which reveals their distinctiveness.

11.3.8 Q-theory

Q-theory (where Q stands for 'quantised subsegments') has its root in Autosegmental Phonology (Goldsmith 1976a), and in particular in the idea that contour segments like prenasalised obstruents and affricates, as well as contour tones, are represented in terms of sequences of feature specifications that are associated with one timing slot. It also follows Articulatory Phonology (Browman & Goldstein 1986), in which articulatory gestures are represented in terms of an onset phase, a target and an offset phase. Perhaps most closely, it follows aperture theory (Steriade 1993a)), in which certain segments, not just contour segments, are represented with two phases: a closure phase and a release phase. In Q-theory each segment is represented as containing three phases (Inkelas & Shih (2013, 2014, 2016, 2017); Shih & Inkelas (2014, 2019a, 2019b)):

(36) $Q(q_1\ q_2\ q_3)$

Q-theory is invoked not only for contour segments, but for all segments:

(37) a: V(a a a)   k: C(k k k)   á: V(á à à)
     ai: V(a a i) k^h: C(k k h) ǎ: V(à á á)
     ia: V(i a a) ^{n}d: C(n d d) ã: V(à á à)

The proposal of distinguishing three sequential phases is motivated by processes that affect the initial or final phase of a segment. A dramatic example of such a situation is given in Anderson (1976), who reports pre- and post-nasalised obstruents, arising from obstruents squeezed in between two nasal vowels: [ᵐbᵐ]; for other examples I refer to the various articles in which the theory is presented, applied and modified (e.g. in developments of the theory it is also possible that a segment contains two or four phases; see Inkelas & Shih (2016)). It is clear that Q-theory aims to be a phonetic theory, albeit one in which continuous representation (as in Articulatory Phonology) is quantised in discrete subsegments, each of which has its own feature bundle.

Q-theory is combined with ABC theory (Agreement by Correspondence), which focuses on processes that cause agreement between segments that already have a common set of properties. ABC constraints can apply not only to sequences of segments, but now also to sequences of subsegments.[22]

As in GP 2.0, we see here a theory that is designed to represent 'linguistically significant' phonetic properties of utterances. What count as criteria for being linguistically significant is up to the phonologist, but being contrastive is not one of them. It would seem that the representational possibilities of Q-theory are excessive, but this is perhaps only apparent. Shih & Inkelas (2019b: 29) claim that 'Q-Theory Representations are equivalent to Autosegmental Representations, in that any constraint that can be written in one theory can be written in another.' This would suggest that Q-theory is not excessively rich, unless, of course Autosegmental Phonology is also excessively rich. It most likely is so if we allow many-to-one associations from three autosegments (i.e. a sequence of three tonal units) to one unit on another tier (e.g. a tone-bearing unit). While such a situation may be warranted in the tonal domain, such structures are hardly necessary in other cases.

I conclude with a speculation, which could be understood as a defence of Q-theory of sorts. In § 7.3.2, where I proposed an RCVP structure for clicks, I very tentatively suggested that clicks can be thought of as having three phases, namely the influx, the click noise and the efflux, and I suggested that such a sequence can be seen as an intra-segmental 'CVC' structure. One might say that Q-theory generalises this kind of structure to all segments. All segments contain three phases, which, then, one might

---

[22] I note here that the notion of correspondence is similar to the notion of harmony, as applied sequentially (as in vowel harmony) and intra-segmentally as proposed in Chapter 8. The difference is that in RCVP intra-segmental 'correspondence' holds between elements of the segmental structure that are not sequentially ordered. RCVP holds the view that there is no contrastive intra-segmental linear ordering, at least not in 'spoken language phonology'.

see as an intra-segmental CVC structure. Whether or not this suggestion 'makes sense' (in general and of Q-theory), I would not be prepared to accept the rich sequential structure that this theory proposes, despite the fact that it allows elegant descriptions of many phonetic phenomena in the domain of tone, nasality and other aspect of segmental structure.

11.4 Summary and concluding remarks

The number of proposals that have been made for lists of features, with or within an explicit formal grouping, but always assuming one, is simply too large to review in this chapter. I have tried to discuss a number of well-worked-out systems in order to point out striking similarities or differences. Considering the field as a whole, various recurrent questions have been raised, which are summarised below. In (38) I add in parentheses the answers that RCVP provides:

(38) Feature issues:
   a. Is the set of features merely a list? (no)
   b. Are all or some features binary, unary or multivalued? (unary)
   c. Are features primarily articulatory units, or acoustic, or both? (both)
   d. Are features 'substance-free'? (yes)
   e. Are features innate or emergent? (emergent)
   f. Are features (formally) organised hierarchically? (yes)
   g. Can one set of features account for contrast and natural classes? (yes)
   h. Are major classes characterised with features or structurally? (structurally)
   i. Is there a manner class node? (yes)
   j. Is there a unified set of place features for both consonants and vowels? (yes)
   k. Are there unified sets for manner and laryngeal features? (yes)
   l. Are particular features/elements used in different classes? (YES!)
   m. Is the feature hierarchy organised in terms of dependency relations? (yes)
   n. Do dependency relations augment or replace constituent structure? (yes)

This list does not exhaust everything that can be asked about features and their organisation. We have also discussed the issue of full or underspecification, and here we can ask whether, for various levels of representation, all features are fully specified (no) or whether the same features are used for contrast and full phonetic specification (no). Furthermore, there are some issues that RCVP does not address as such. There is the question of whether all features are situated below the root node (which as such is associated with skeletal positions that are formed by the syllabic terminals) or whether some features associate with syllabic nodes; see § 3.2.3. There is also the 'autosegmental' issue, that is, the question of whether we need autosegmental tiers. Clements (1985) took the most extreme view, arguing that every class node and every feature occurs on its own tier.

My goal in this chapter has been to show how the RCVP answers are shared with other models, but also in what respects these other models differ. The particular grouping of primes that RCVP advocates is shared with Clements (1985) and with those models that maintain or reintroduce a manner class. The choice of unary primes, and in particular some specific primes (such as the AIU triplet,) is shared with DP, GP and PP, but also in essence with models that, following Sagey (1986), introduce unary labels for the major articulators. Proposals for unary primes are ubiquitous, sometimes limited to only certain cases, sometimes apparently meant for all primes. Hyman's (2002) set of primes for vowels (H, L, F, R) is essentially the same as the unary primes set in RCVP for manner and place. The idea of a unified set of primes for all class nodes is shared only with the parallel structure model. The use of headedness (and dependency) relations is central to RCVP and comes straight from DP, although GP adopted a similar concept. We have seen that in several models that adopt a feature grouping, the idea occurs that certain features may occur in more than one group, an idea that RCVP pushes to its logical extreme. Like several other phonologists, I assume that features are emergent, and with Morén I share the idea that, nevertheless, features are organised in a fixed structure that is not as such emergent but somehow innate. However, unlike Morén I do not postulate a 'random' recurrent structure as innate. Rather, in RCVP, the recurrent structure is the result of a cognitive categorisation system that is based on general principles such as the Opponent Principle, the Head-Dependency Principle (including its X-bar-like character that results from two types of dependents), binarity of structure and unarity of ultimate categories.

12

Conclusions

12.1 Introduction

This chapter summarises the contributions of RCVP to our understanding of segmental and syllabic representations. I will outline strengths, as well as weaknesses, and point to future research which will contribute to the advancement of models in this domain. The RCVP model was developed largely as a 'private' enterprise that helped me understand that the set of features needed for contrast, as well as their grouping and correlations between them, is neither random nor a direct mirror of articulation. RCVP was never part of mainstream Generative Phonology, a fate (or blessing) that it shares with the various models that it is most closely associated with (such as DP and GP). Nevertheless, its goals and most of its results are compatible with many proposals that have been made in mainstream models, or at least better-known models (see especially Chapter 11). In this chapter I will limit myself to some general remarks about the model, its basic properties and directions for future research.

12.2 Goals and basic principles

The most important goal of the enterprise that I report on in this book is to develop a theory of phonological structure which is in accordance with, or follows from, a set of basic 'first' principles and some further assumptions.

To start with the assumptions (see also § 1.3), I assume that there are phonological segments, which are cognitive categories that correspond to the informal notion of 'speech sound' (or 'sign'). These segments are not atomic, but can be broken up into basic primes that are organised in a hierarchical structure that corresponds to the phonetic dimensions and phonetic categories that are available for a given modality. I also assume that segments are grouped into syllables, with a basic division between onset and rhyme. A requirement for being admitted into the set of phonological categories is the possibility of occurring contrastively in some language, expectedly in more than one. Segments are minimally specified with the goal of capturing contrast. I also assume that phonology is substance-based, which means that all units and structures correlate with cognitive representations of physical events in the domain of psychoacoustics and articulation.

The first two principles that underlie these various structures is that all structures are maximally binary and headed. Headedness correlates with cognitive salience and, formally, with greater potential for complexity than dependents. Another property of heads is that they are obligatory and stable, while dependents are optional and prone to 'deletion' or 'spreading'. These two principles presuppose an even more basic principle, namely that units can occur in combinations. This is, presumably, Chomsky's notion of 'merge'.

A 'guiding' principle is that units in different parts of the overall phonological structure are 'structurally analogous' (ideally: identical). This means that particular types of organisations (in particular, X-bar types of structure; see § 12.3) are replicated throughout the phonology.[1]

I emphasise the importance of reducing traditional phonological features to phonetic implementations of the basic C/V opposition, their occurrence in different classes and in different syllabic positions. The segment–syllable connection, as we have seen in Chapter 8, allows for strong correlations between syllabic positions and preferred occurrence of particular segment types. These correlations are not independent stipulations, but rather follow from the radical use of the same elements at both levels of structure. The predictions, I argue, are one piece of the 'phonological puzzle'. Many other factors play a role in determining the structure of segmental inventories in general, and in specific syllabic positions. This is not an attempt to immunise the predictions made by the RCVP model from falsification. Rather, it is an acknowledgement of the fact that nothing in phonology follows from just 'one thing'. We need to factor out the causes that play a role and study each in great depth, as well as their interaction. Much work remains to be done.

As for its choice of basic primes, RCVP reduces the set of primes to a pair of two opposing unary elements: C and V. These are the 'ultimate constituents' of phonology. To draw on an analogy with physics, in a search for the ultimate units of structure (matter for physics, cognitive phonology for me), the conclusion is that previous claims about such units have not gone far enough. I do not know enough about physics to

---

[1] Here I will not venture to report on ideas that these structures might be replicated throughout human cognition (in other mind modules, other perceptual systems) and perhaps even in mind-external domains ('reality'). See Abler (1989) for interesting ideas concerning the shared structure of the cognitive and material world. Analogies between language as a cognitive system and the 'language of biological systems (such as the cell)' are developed in van der Hulst (1999a).

endorse string theory, but I am committed to the idea that phonology can be reduced to just two basic elements (not one!), which organise structure at the segmental and syllabic level (and perhaps beyond). Making another bold comparison, Watson & Crick (1993) started their seminal paper entitled 'Molecular structure of nucleic acids: A structure for deoxyribose nucleic acid' with the following sentences:

> We wish to suggest a structure for the salt of deoxyribose nucleic acid (D.N.A). This structure has novel features which are of considerable biological interest.

I started my 2005 article on RCVP, which was entitled 'The molecular structure of phonological segments' (2005a), with the following sentence:

> I wish to suggest a structure for the organisation of phonological primes. This structure reveals hidden properties that are of considerable phonological interest.

Clearly, my article did not quite make the same splash as the paper by Crick and Watson and I had certainly no expectation that it would, using a variant of their wording with the intention of self-mocking and relativism.

The core idea that there are only two elements follows from a principle of categorisation that I have termed the Opponent Principle, related to Aristotle's law of contrast. This principle is also related to the notion of categorical perception, but it adds that categorical perception in this case is focused on a binary distinction in some domain. As has been discussed in § 9.8, the emergence of the cognitive elements C and V is preceded by a phase of statistical learning during which the child forms phonetic categories based on statistical asymmetries in the input. The input is of course not random, but instead consists of acoustic events that reflect a grouping in clusters of speech sound exemplars that correspond to contrastive segments in the adult language. With a growing lexicon, phonetic categories are then solidified over time, leading to phonological categories that are eventually parsed into segmental internal structures in terms of elements and their grouping.

It is interesting that in a model proclaiming to propose unary elements, binarism plays such an important role. In discussions about the arity of features I have sometimes (half-seriously) remarked that RCVP offers the golden mean: all features are unary, but there are only two of them.

An important additional assumption that has been made in this work is the separation of grammatical and utterance phonology. By focusing on grammatical phonology, we are not excusing ourselves from developing a theory of utterance phonology, which, in my view, is a theory of phonetic implementation. In this work, I have said very little about this aspect of phonology, but my views here agree with those of, for example, Liberman

414 Principles of Radical CV Phonology

(2017) and Volenec & Reiss (2017). As for the grammatical phonology, I take the view that allomorphic alternations are accounted for in terms of disjunctive lexical representations. This may involve disjunctions of whole segments (perhaps even sequences of segments) in alternations that are usually highly dependent on lexical and morphological factors, and that are unproductive (which regards most of the alternations that are analysed in SPE, and which, according to proponents of DP and GP, do not even have a place in phonology). Disjunctive representations are also employed for productive alternations that involve specific elements, as in vowel harmony. For the latter I have used the variable notation in van der Hulst (2018), but we must realise that that notation captures a disjunction between the presence of an element and its absence (which in binary systems would be accounted for using underspecification). The distinction between unproductive morpho-lexical alternations, productive alternations and phonetic implementation essentially adheres to the three-way rule typology proposed in Anderson (1976).

12.3 X-bar structure everywhere

It is significant that the 'X-bar' type of structure is recurrent in RCVP. Essentially, this structure expresses the generalisation that complex units consist of a head and two levels of dependents, one more intimately connected to the head than the other. This structure is replicated not only in different classes of phonological primes, but also at the macrolevel in the structure of both spoken segments and signs:

(1)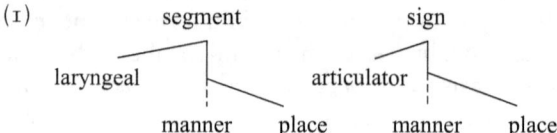

In Chapter 11 we have seen that the various class nodes in the structure of signs themselves display an X-bar-like structure.

It would, in fact, be possible, as I have not done in the previous chapters, to construe the internal structure of class nodes in terms of an X-bar configuration, as follows:

(2)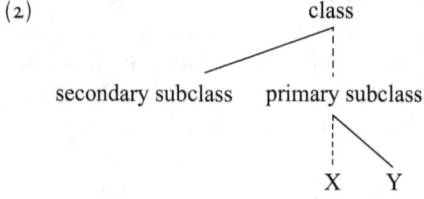

Conclusions 415

In (2) [X Y] is the primary class, which obligatorily contains one element, but can contain two, with a head-dependency relation imposed. The secondary class is generally simple, but marginally (in manner) can have a combination.

The syllabic organisation that RCVP adopts also has an X-bar structure, granted that the specifier, the onset, can be branching, but this is also the case in the structures in (1). The 'old' idea that specifiers are simplex (Jackendoff 1977) can thus not be fully maintained. In fact, in the structure of signs, the articulator node which was represented as the 'specifier' of the sign structure in Chapter 10 is the most complex of all classes:[2]

(3)
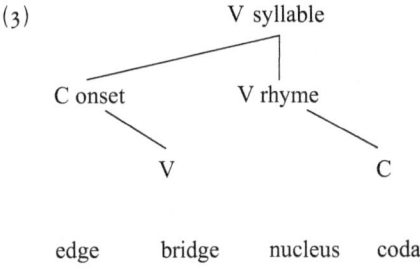

edge   bridge   nucleus   coda

X-bar structure was once heralded as a major insight into syntactic structure (Jackendoff 1977) but has recently been replaced by a simpler mode of syntactic organisation, following the minimalist programme (Chomsky 2000). Den Dikken & van der Hulst (2020), however, put X-bar structure back centre stage as a cross-modular type of organisation that is relevant in both morphosyntax and phonology. The present book subscribes to the centrality of the X-bar organisation, as will be evident from the summary above and indeed throughout all chapters.

12.4 Strengths and weaknesses

In this book, I have expanded on my 2005 article (which itself was based on a number or earlier papers, from as early as 1988, but offered the first comprehensive model in print),[3] leaving all its goals intact, as well as major aspects of the actual proposal. More than anyone else, I see the limitations of my enterprise. I can 'hear' readers (who actually managed to get through this book) thinking or telling their colleagues

---

[2] Which is why van der Hulst (1993b) regards the articulator ('the hand') as the head of the structure.
[3] The very first complete model dates from 1990a, which I worked out in a manuscript entitled 'The book of segments', which was distributed on a limited scale. Recipients of this manuscript will be surprised to see that it has emerged as a real book some thirty years later.

or students: 'This model is overarticulated and excessively rich.' This indeed is the general argument that linguists use to invalidate a theory that is not theirs. I would of course disagree with such a blanket statement, but I would not be blind to the fact that there is 'a lot of structure'. Postulating structure to achieve explanatory accounts of language data is of course what linguist do all the time. Current syntactic theories in the minimalist framework also postulate a lot of structure for sentences that are apparently simple (like 'John loves Mary'). Looking at such theories 'from the outside' leaves the reader usually with the sense that there is way too much structure being postulated for such 'simple sentences'. Of course, it may very well be that we need a simpler syntax (see Culicover & Jackendoff (2005)), and it may also be that the principles that underlie RCVP could be used to construct a 'simpler phonology'.

My own sense, however, is that RCVP cannot be further simplified, unless we give up on being able to account for contrasts that are perhaps only attested in a few languages. It is of course possible that some such contrasts can be analysed as phonetic variation of a single contrastive option, or that they turn out to be allophonic, rather than phonemic, once we know more about the languages that display them. I would maintain that the principles of RCVP are simple, and also that the model postulates a simple inventory of basic units – two, in fact. By invoking structure, the model achieves a dramatic reduction in the set of 'features' that other models propose. I have shown that the categories that are derived and represented in terms of C/V structures correspond rather closely to categories that are widely adopted in binary feature systems. I would also claim that, given the distinction between primary elements and secondary elements, the match between the set of theoretically possible structures and what we find empirically is strikingly close. From a methodological point of view, the principles of the theory prevent ad hoc addition of new structural options and categories. For example, we cannot just add a further dependent 'somewhere' to solve a problem. Changes in one part of the structure have immediate repercussions throughout the whole structure, due to adherence to structural analogy and 'X-bar structure'.

Of course, alternatives can be imagined and sometimes seem called for. Over the course of many years I have proposed revisions of earlier attempts, sometimes going back to earlier ideas. In this book I even propose certain changes to the model in van der Hulst (2018), and below I mention the possibility of accepting a separate pharyngeal/laryngeal class (which of course has been proposed in other models).

There are, as I have noted, small glitches in the structural analogy between the different element classes. The principle of binarity delivers for each class two elements that in some cases are polar, antagonistic opposites (which nevertheless can be combined to form intermediate categories). This is specifically the case in the head classes. In the laryngeal node, C and V denote [tense]/H and [voiced]/L (cf. [±voice] or [±high tone]). Here I have had to stipulate that combining these elements in consonants is not allowed. For manner, C and V denote [stop]/[high] and fricative/low (cf. [±continuant] and [±high]/[±low]), allowing combinations in both cases. For place, however, the two elements are 'less antagonistic',[4] with C and V denoting palatal/front and labial/back-round, respectively, and nevertheless allowing combinations. In two of the secondary classes, the two elements are also not obviously antagonistic (and thus in a sense more strictly 'unary'), with c and v in manner denoting nasalisation and RTR (which, however, correspond to the two non-oral spaces: the nasal and the pharyngeal cavities). In place, c and v denote palatalisation/ATR and labialisation (with no interpretation for vowels). In the laryngeal secondary class, c and v denote two states of glottal opening which could be covered with one binary feature, although usually it is not ([±constricted glottis] and [±spread glottis]). However, for vowels, high and low registers form a clear antagonistic pair. In this work, I have tried to maintain that the difference that I noted here can be explained on 'phonetic grounds', although I have not made concrete suggestions in all these cases. Perhaps, then, there is a better version of RCVP out there than the one I present here. If there is, I hope it would not deviate too much from the current version.

These kinds of differences or glitches 'bother me' ('keep me up at night'), but years of tinkering with the model have shown me that there will always be such distortions of structural analogy. Nevertheless, I have also experienced that often other glitches that I encountered could be resolved, and this has produced numerous versions of the RCVP model (going back all the way to 1990).

Another area of potential criticism regards the matter of gradience. Phonotactic distributional generalisations have been treated as absolute in three ways. Firstly, I have assumed that the predictions that can be derived from the RCVP structure of the syllable ban certain segment types from certain positions. For example, it has been repeatedly claimed that heads of complex onsets can only be obstruents, while codas can only be sonorants. The first claim flies in the face of the fact that in many languages complex onsets occur that have sonorants as their head (see Greenberg (1978); Morelli (1999); Kreitman (2006, 2008); Parker (2012a, 2016)), while preserving a rising sonority profile or a sonority plateau, thus excluding obstruents in the edge, or that have obstruents in the edge, sometimes even preceded by a sonorant, thus yielding a reversed sonority profile. I have suggested that some such cases, especially those with obstruents in second position, may require 'special' measures,

---

[4] This assessment is probably influenced by my use of articulatory terminology.

involving adjunction or, as in GP, empty nuclei. However, it would be worth exploring whether 'deviating' clusters could be accommodated by interpreting the CV structure of complex onsets in a relative rather than an absolute manner. This would mean that along a sonority scale, CV entails that the segment in the V position cannot be more sonorous than the consonant in the C position. This would conceivably even allow clusters of two obstruents or two sonorants, but it would definitely not permit clusters with a reversed sonority profile. Likewise, the strict ban on obstruents from coda might also be relative. As I have discussed in § 3.2.3, such an approach would require us to differentiate between the major class encoding in the syllable structure and a major class specification as part of a segment. It is of course more interesting to maintain strictness, because it invites looking for explanations that one might otherwise not look for. It is my impression that OT, indeed, does not care for looking for such explanations, given that any constraint is allowed to be violated in some language.[5]

A second sense in which the absoluteness of phonotactic constraints can be challenged is based on recent work that refers to the notion of gradient phonotactics.[6] This line of work reveals, and tries to model, the fact that phonotactic patterns are not simply well-formed or ill-formed, but rather more or less well-/ill-formed. It seems to me that such findings do not undermine the present approach, which has abstracted away from such statistical gradience. The important point is that one factor that determines differences in acceptability is the predictions that follow from the RCVP model, which make a binary distinction. Nothing prevents us from adding a layer of analysis which fractures the yes/no decision along a continuous scale, with factors such as lexical frequencies and relative complexity playing a role.

The third dimension that I have abstracted away from is that there are phonotactic probabilities which are sensitive to fine-grained differences between segment sequences. An example of this kind of work can be found in Hayes & Londe (2006) and Hayes, Zuraw, Siptár & Londe (2009), who use statistical methods to show the role of root-final consonants in the choice of front or back variant of suffix vowels in the vowel harmony system of Hungarian. Given access to corpora and lexica, such finer details can often be found, whatever their cause is. Without denying the factual truth of such generalisations, in van der Hulst (2018) I defended the position that one can uncover significant generalisations in vowel harmony patterns while abstracting away from these statistical tendencies.

---

[5] The OT model does allow for 'top-ranked' or 'inviolable' constraints.
[6] See Coleman & Pierrehumbert (1997); Hammond (2004); Hayes & Wilson (2008); Coetzee & Pater (2008); Anttila (2008).

In general, then, I see an account of statistical gradience as an extra layer of analysis, which is not in conflict with the categorical distinctions that I have focused on here. In a way, I am defending here what Chomsky and Halle adopted in SPE when they distinguished between the categorical nature of phonological features and a layer of analysis which would relate gradient distinctions to a phonetic component. However, the extra component that is needed here is more than phonetic implementation. We also need a statistical component, which both precedes the establishment of categorical distinctions and lingers on in terms of 'weights' that are associated with these distinctions.

12.5 Some unresolved issues

In § 4.2.2 we encountered some types of complex segments that seemed to require two secondary manner specifications, notably nasality and retroflexion or nasality and pharyngealisation or lateralisation and retroflexion. This might indicate that the decision to analyse retroflexion as a secondary manner (rather than as a secondary place property as in previous versions of the model) was not the right move. However, for the moment, I want to maintain this decision because 'it makes sense' to not see retroflexion as a subdivision of place, although this is the usual idea in binary feature theories. Allowing two secondary specifications would involve an enrichment of the RCVP syntax, which, as per structural analogy, then also creates possibilities in other classes for which we have seen no evidence. The examples of double secondary manner specifications are limited and perhaps subject to reanalysis.

Another enrichment of the RCVP was introduced in the analysis of MACs and clicks, for which I proposed a double place specification. The commonality with double specification of secondary manner is that in some circumstances a particular type of specification can occur twice. In the case of MACs and clicks, it seems inevitable that something along the lines of double specification of place elements is required.

I conclude with another problem. I have proposed that pharyngeal and laryngeal consonants are placeless. As potentially problematic for this view, I mentioned in § 4.2.4 that we now predict that laryngeals cannot have secondary place properties.

- Labialisation can occur with the glottal stop in Kabardian (MD 911, p. 215).
- Labialised can occur with [h] (MD p. 234) in Igbo (MD 116), Amharic (MD 252), Hupa (MD 705), Siona (MD 833).

In § 5.2.3, where I proposed that pharyngeal consonants are placeless, I noted that this predicts that phraryngeal consonants also cannot occur with secondary place properties. Whether such cases occur is not known to me. MD does not report them.

Before I propose a possible solution for how to represent placeless consonants with a secondary place property, I mention a parallel problem in the domain of vowels, which I mentioned in § 5.3.2. In that section I proposed analysing ATR in the place class as a dependent version of the I element (which captured an 'old' proposal in van der Hulst (1988a, 1988b)), rather than as a dependent manner element as I have done in more recent versions of the model (e.g. in van der Hulst (2018)). With this approach, RCVP makes the prediction that central vowels, which lack a primary place element, cannot display the ATR distinction, because dependent specification presupposes a head specification.

However, there is evidence to suggest that central vowels can have an ATR contrast. The low vowel [a] is notably resistant to having an advanced counterpart, and KLV85 maintain that an ATR counterpart is impossible. The apparent occurrence of an ATR version of [a], KLV85 argue, would be a low-mid central vowel that is advanced. This, then, implies that non-low central vowels can be advanced, albeit not the lowest one. KLV85 discuss the language Kpokolo, which has thirteen vowels, with high and mid central vowels having an ATR contrast; see § 2.3. Several other reports simply maintained that even the low vowel can have an advanced counterpart (see van der Hulst 2018: ch. 7). It is inevitable to conclude that advanced central vowels are possible, albeit that their occurrence is not frequent. A low ATR vowel is often missing in vowel inventories of languages with ATR harmony, and non-low advanced vowels are sometimes allophonic rather than contrastive (as in Chumburung; see Snider (1984)). An interesting test case is offered by the language Anii (Morton (2012: 71)):

> Anii has a very robust system of vowel harmony which applies to almost all affixes in the language. There are five harmonizing pairs including /a/ and /ə/, where /a/ is a [−ATR] vowel whose [+ATR] counterpart is a mid-central vowel, /ə/. There is also an eleventh vowel, a relatively high central vowel, /ɨ/. /ɨ/ is [−ATR], and only appears in words where the surrounding vowels are [−ATR], but it does not have a [+ATR] counterpart, nor does it have a [+ATR] allophone.

There is good and bad news here. On the one hand, this language does not allow an advanced counterpart of the high vowel (good news), but on the other hand, it does have an ATR counterpart of the low vowel (bad news).[7]

---

[7] Morton (2012) discusses various languages with eleven-vowel systems (reported in Casali (2003)) concluding that in such systems either the low vowel has an ATR

Conclusions 421

The problem here is analogous to the one resulting from attesting laryngeal (and perhaps pharyngeal) consonants, which are represented as placeless, with secondary labialisation (and perhaps palatalisation). The problem for vowels can be solved by returning to the proposal that ATR is secondary manner, but this does not remove the problem for laryngeal and pharyngeal consonants with secondary place properties. Moreover, expressing ATR as a secondary manner comes with its own problems, as I have shown in § 4.3.1.2, because it 'eliminates' the spot for nasalisation on vowels.

While RCVP will allow the specification of a 'redundant head element' to allow the specification of a dependent element (see § 6.4.1), we cannot simply say that laryngeal/pharyngeal consonants and central vowels have a head place element, because that head place element would be either I or U and this would then not deliver the segment types in question, which are precisely colourless.

A revision of the model that is consistent with the basic principles, which would make room for a 'positive' specification of post-velar consonants, would require a 'super' place class that splits into two major place classes, along the following lines:[8]

(4)
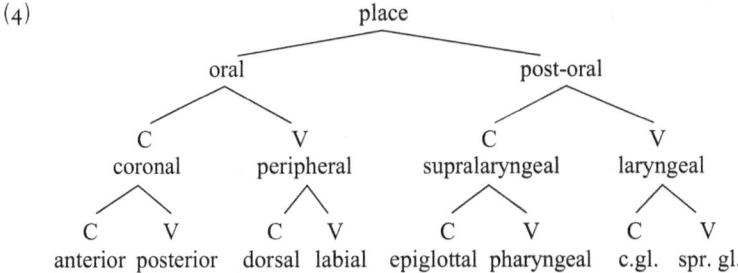

This structure allows upper and lower pharyngeals, as well as laryngeals, to be specified in terms of a place element structure, which then allows for secondary place properties. However, this structure creates overlap

---

counterpart, with an additional non-low central vowel being non-participatory in harmony (Baka, Boni, Anii), or some non-low central vowel has an ATR counterpart, with the low vowel being non-participatory (Lama, Kanembu). While both cases show that central vowels do not exhibit ATR alternation at different heights, Kpokolo exceeds such systems in having thirteen vowels with an ATR contrast among two series of non-low vowels, and possibly for the low vowel as well.

[8] Moisik, Czaykowska-Higgins & Esling (2011)) and Esling, Moisik, Benner & Crevier-Buchman (2019: 159ff.) discuss a variety of FG models that distinguish oral and post-oral place with subdivisions similar to those in (4). Unlike Moisik, Czaykowska-Higgins & Esling (2011), who propose their own FG, Esling et al. (2019) propose an entirely different type of model, the 'Phonological Potential Model'. For discussion I must refer to their exposition.

with the structure for the laryngeal class proposed in Chapter 6, which also recognises the distinction between constricted and spread glottis. Moreover, this structure, which now accommodates eight primary locations, also predicts a host of additional secondary articulations. We could consider a simpler elaboration of the place node as in (5):

(5)
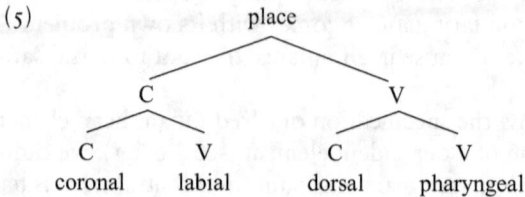

Of course, like (4), (5) undermines the strong structural analogy between the three element classes (manner, place and laryngeal). It also removes the class of peripheral places, which comprises labial and dorsal in the original proposal. Also, a further C/V split for coronals would have to be added to accommodate front and back coronals, while such a split is not required for the other three place categories. When applied to vowels, (5) essentially duplicates the head manner distinction, with dorsal corresponding to high and pharyngeal to low. Finally, both (4) and (5) destroy the structural analogy between the three classes dramatically. I thus do not find (4) and/or (5) viable revisions of the place class.

Encountering a problem of this kind can trigger three responses. The first response would be to say that the entire RCVP approach is doomed and misguided, a pipe dream that is simply not going to work. I have been there. However, I feel that this dramatic move is not called for, given the overwhelming empirical confirmation of the model. The second response is to embark on a reanalysis of the reported problematic cases. Perhaps labialised [h]'s are consonant sequences? Perhaps central advanced vowels are always allophonic? While we cannot exclude the possibility that scrutinising the relevant examples might eliminate some as problematic, it may also be the case that some of the cases are solid counterexamples to the theory. The third response would have to be to take a critical look at the theory. Such critical looks can take two forms: rejection (which is the first response mentioned) or modification. A modification may actually lead to an overall improvement of the model, or it may or may not have an ad hoc flavour (see Kuhn (1962)).

A pointer to a solution is that the place class is the only class in which I have used the absence of an element as contrastive with the presence of an element. The place elements, being I and U, were essentially reduced to a 'colour' class by removing the element A from the traditional AIU set. There was good reason for this because, going back to the basic insight of AE concerning the parallelism between their elements |A| and |V|, as well as Roman Jakobson's (1959) distinction between colour and aperture, the A element does not form a natural class with the colour elements. Locating A in the manner class is justified and this decision, as we have seen, established a perfect analogy between manner for consonants and aperture (indeed: manner) for vowels.

My proposal for the problem that we have noted is to adopt a so-called 'neutral' or 'identity' element (somewhat like the 'cold vowel' proposed in KLV85, and the 'o' element in mathematics). All laryngeal/pharyngeal consonants and central vowels have to have the 'o-element', which makes it impossible to gloss this element simply as 'pharyngeal' for both consonants and vowels. The o-element is opposed to colour properties, and as such can have different manifestations in the consonantal and vowel realms. However, the identity element is only crucially invoked as occupying the head place class when laryngeal or pharyngeal consonants have secondary place specifications or when central vowels have an ATR distinction.

Is this an ad hoc move? One might say it is, or one might suggest that we now need to investigate whether there is a need or use for the o-element in the manner and laryngeal class. We have seen that in the laryngeal domain there are cases in which languages display a contrast for secondary properties (constricted and/or spread glottis) without having a contrast for voicing (see § 6.4.1 on the language K'ekchi). In that case I proposed specifying the head element C for the consonants in question, which are voiceless. In fact, we do not want to recruit the o-element in this case, if the phonetic correlate of this element draws on a phonetic space that is opposed to the phonetic interpretations of the elements that can occur in the head class. In the laryngeal domain, I have argued, there is no such phonetic space. For manner, we do not need the o-element for the same reason, and, moreover, one might bar such an element from what is the ultimate head class of the segment. If, then, we only need the o-element for the place class (and only when there are secondary place specifications), does that make the proposal ad hoc? Perhaps not. Introducing a o-element for the place class, while specific to this class, is not ad hoc, because it captures the phonetic reality that only the place dimension comprises 'a negative area', that is, the post-oral space in the vocal tract. This fact, I note, also undermines the potential allegation that the o-element introduces ternary power into the entire system. I will leave it to more 'formal minds' to assert that the adoption of an identity element makes a complex system complete and as such is a necessity.

A final issue that I raise in this section concerns the representation of tone. The model, as it stands, analyses lexical tone as the manifestation of laryngeal elements in the syllable rhyme, specifically the nucleus. There is thus no explicit recognition of the relative independence that tones can display with respect to 'the rest' of the segmental content. Nevertheless, the original motivation of Autosegmental Phonology (Goldsmith 1976a) was precisely to find a formal basis for this relative independence. A possible extension of the current model would be to formally recognise the option of 'raising' tones from within the segmental structure to a higher structural tonal root node which is the dependent sister of the segmental root node:

(6)

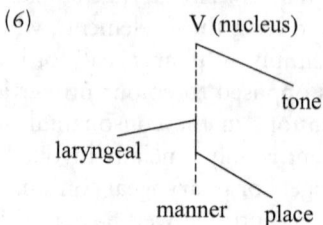

This 'raising' would be the formalisation of the older idea of 'autosegmentalisation'. In section 6.3 I have mentioned other works on tone which also make reference to a separate tonal root node (e.g. Hyman (1993). I will leave it to future work to explore this possible revision of the RCVP model.

12.6 What's next?

The programme of RCVP must be tested against a larger set of typological data than I have used in this book. In this work I have made reference to a lot of work on features and segment inventories that challenges or supports the predictions that RCVP makes. I know that there are resources (databases, typological studies in articles and dissertations) that I have not used for what I propose in this book. My excuse is that I had to finish the book at some point (which I'm glad I actually did). My next goal is thus to subject RCVP to more rigorous testing, and hopefully others will join me in this effort. In the domain of vowels, I have at least partly fulfilled this goal by a close examination of vowel systems and vowel harmony alternations in the languages of the world (van der Hulst 2018). A similar undertaking with respect to consonant systems and consonantal alternations, in relation to syllable structure, is in progress. The application of RCVP to sign structure is further developed in van der Hulst & van der Kooij (to appear). Another goal is to extend RCVP to higher levels of structure. I have already made some tentative proposals about foot structure (see § 3.2.5), but the plan is to include word and phrasal structures, with reference to the notion of stress (or accent) as heads of such units (see van der Hulst (in prep.)).

Appendix

A summary of Radical CV Phonology structures and their interpretations

(1) The 'geometry' of elements in RCVP (§ 3.2.1: (2))

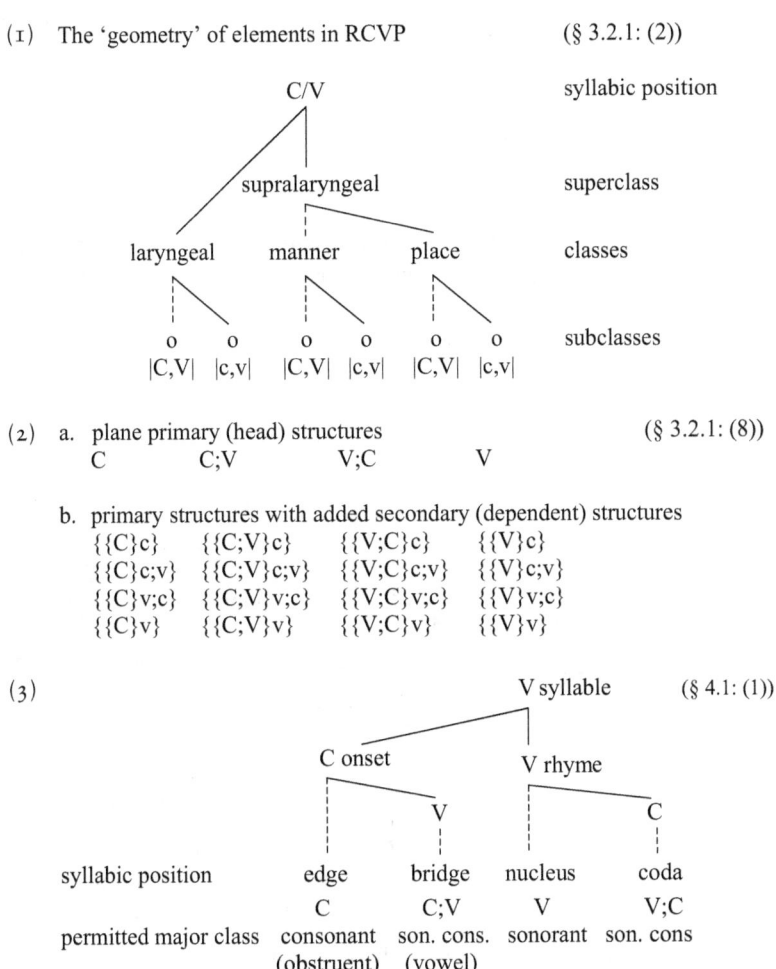

(2) a. plane primary (head) structures (§ 3.2.1: (8))
   C   C;V   V;C   V

   b. primary structures with added secondary (dependent) structures
   {{C}c}   {{C;V}c}   {{V;C}c}   {{V}c}
   {{C}c;v} {{C;V}c;v} {{V;C}c;v} {{V}c;v}
   {{C}v;c} {{C;V}v;c} {{V;C}v;c} {{V}v;c}
   {{C}v}   {{C;V}v}   {{V;C}v}   {{V}v}

(3)

426 Appendix

(4) a. A sonorant consonant in the edge (§ 4.1: (2))

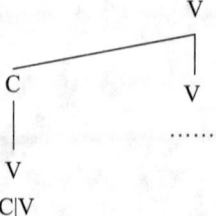

b. A sonorant consonant in the nucleus

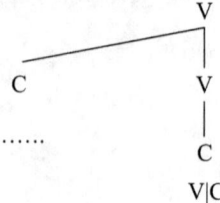

The structures in (5)–(11) summarise the proposals made in Chapters 4–6, but, for reasons of space, they do not all occur as such in these chapters.

(5) edge (laryngeal, manner, place)

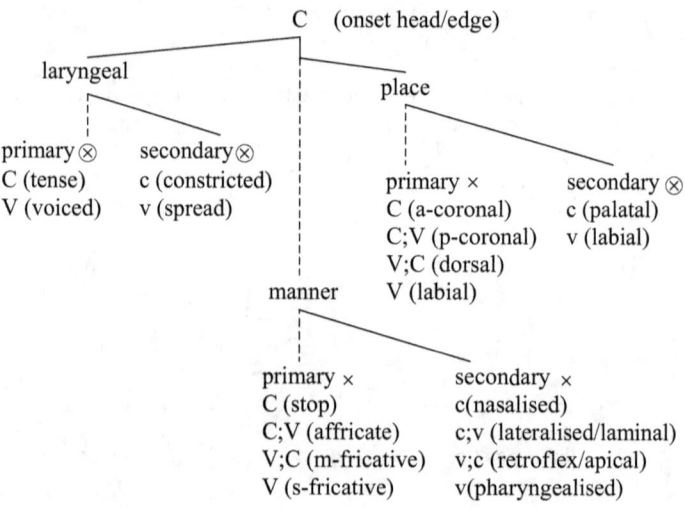

× = allows combinations; ⊗ = does not allow combinations

Appendix 427

(6) bridge (manner, place)

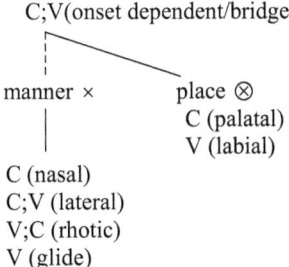

C;V(onset dependent/bridge)

manner ×   place ⊗
                           C (palatal)
                           V (labial)
C (nasal)
C;V (lateral)
V;C (rhotic)
V (glide)

× = allows combinations; ⊗ = does not allow combinations

(7) sonorant in onset head position

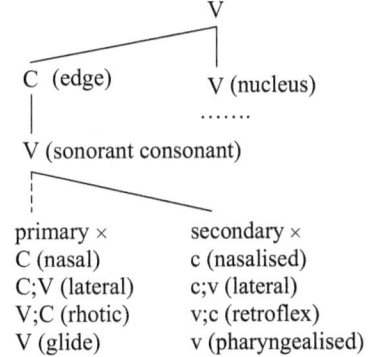

                  V
C (edge)   V (nucleus)
              ....
V (sonorant consonant)

primary ×   secondary ×
C (nasal)   c (nasalised)
C;V (lateral)   c;v (lateral)
V;C (rhotic)   v;c (retroflex)
V (glide)   v (pharyngealised)

× = allows combinations

(8) sonorant in onset head position: taps/flaps

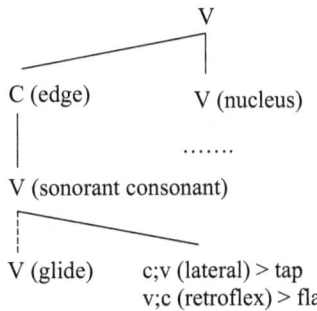

              V
C (edge)   V (nucleus)
          ....
V (sonorant consonant)

V (glide)   c;v (lateral) > tap
             v;c (retroflex) > flap

428 Appendix

(9) nucleus (laryngeal, manner, place)

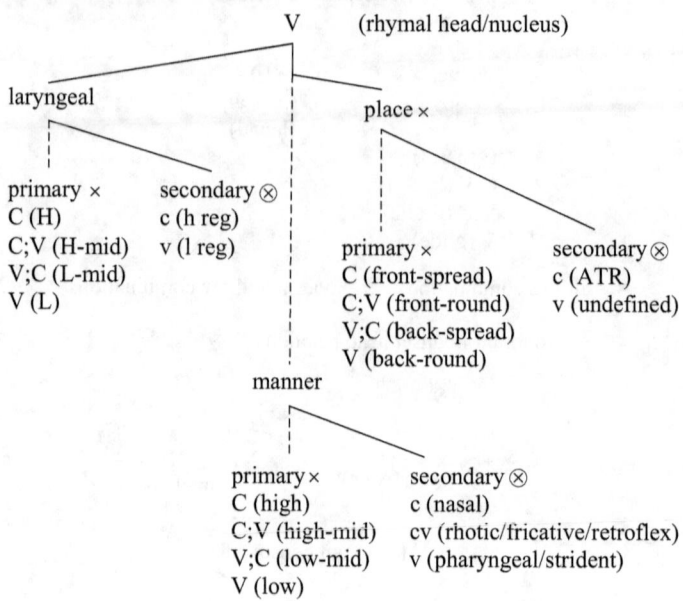

× = allows combinations; ⊗ = does not allow combinations

(10)   syllabic sonorant

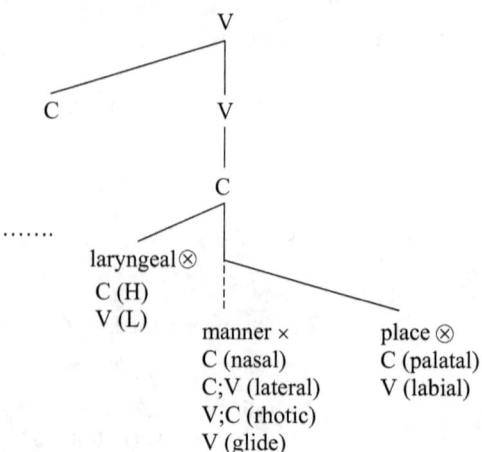

× = allows combinations; ⊗ = does not allow combinations

(11)   coda (manner, place, laryngeal)

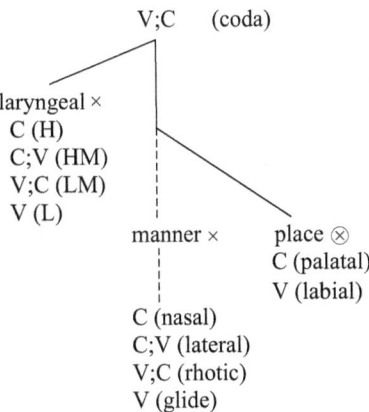

× = allows combinations; ⊗ = does not allow combinations

For (12), recall that an IPA symbol for a voice epiglottal stop is missing; see (17) in § 5.2.3. Whether a voiced segment of this type is phonetically possible is questionable.

(12)   a. (upper) pharyngeal fricatives   b. epiglottal fricatives   (§ 7.2.2.2: (34))

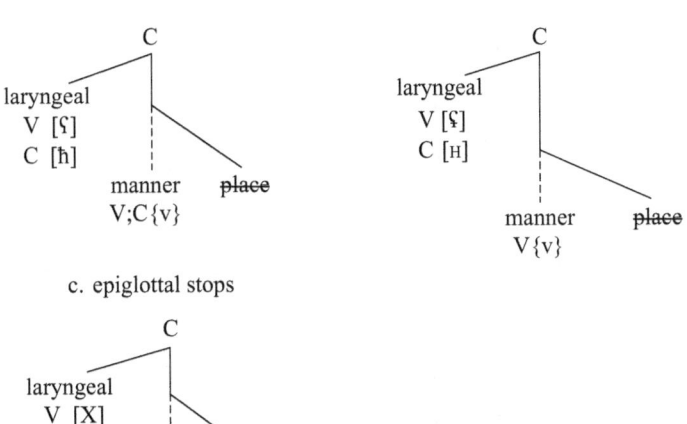

We can now propose a detailed RCVP structure for clicks:

430 Appendix

(13) compounds with sister place structures (§ 7.3.2: (40))

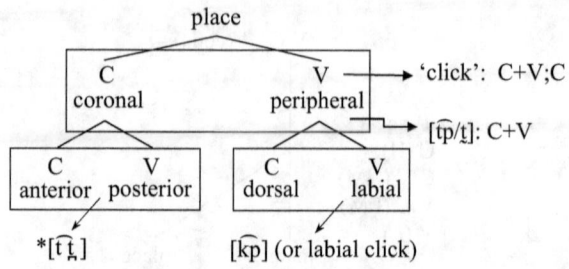

(14) RCVP structure for clicks (§ 7.3.2: (53))

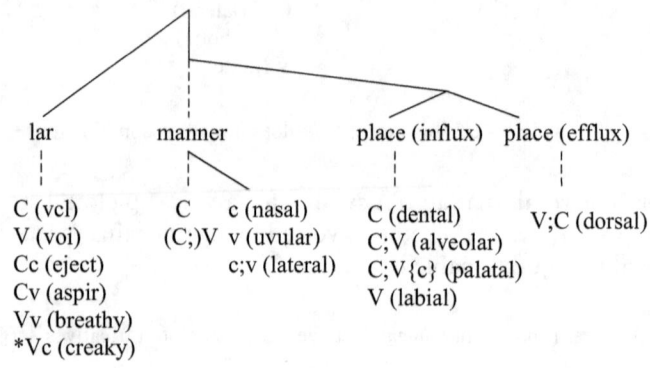

(15) The structure of signs (§ 10.5: (22))

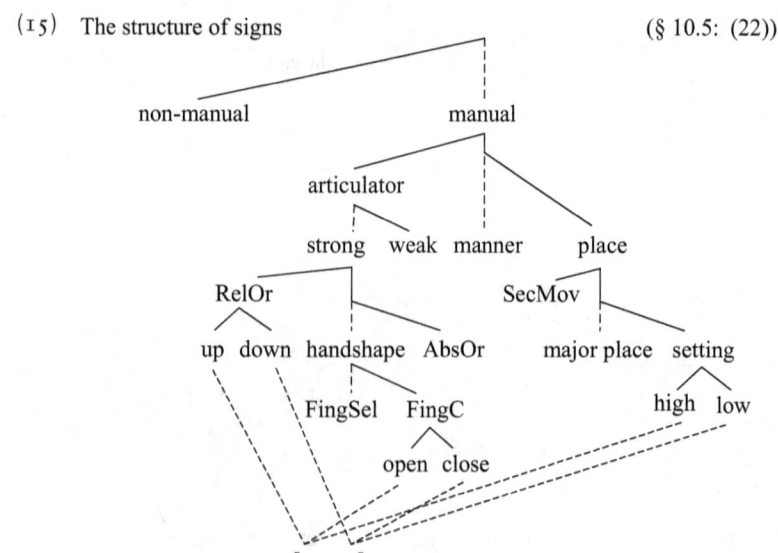

References

Abercrombie, David. 1967. *Elements of general phonetics*. Edinburgh: Edinburgh University Press.

Abler, William L. 1989. On the particulate principle of self-diversifying systems. *Journal of Social and Biological Structures* 12.1, 1–13.

Abramson, Arthur S. & Theraphan Luangthongkum. 2009. A fuzzy boundary between tone languages and voice-register languages. In Gunnar M. Fant, Hiroya Fujisaki & J. Shen (eds.), *Frontiers in phonetics and speech science*, 149–55. Beijing: Commercial Press.

Abramson, Arthur S. & Nianqi Rent. 1990. Distinctive vowel length: Duration vs. spectrum in Thai. *Journal of Phonetics* 18, 79–92.

Ahn, Sang-Cheol. 1988. A revised theory of syllable phonology. *Linguistic Journal of Korean* 13.2, 333–62.

Ahn, Sang-cheol & Gregory K. Iverson. 2004. Dimensions in Korean laryngeal phonology. *Journal of East Asian Linguistics* 13.4, 345–79.

Akinlabi, Akinbiyi. 1985. *Tonal underspecification and Yoruba tone*. PhD dissertation, University of Ibadan.

Allen, Margaret. 1978. *Morphological investigations*. PhD dissertation, University of Connecticut.

Allen, W. Sidney. 1965. On one-vowel systems. *Lingua* 13, 111–24.

Anderson, Gregory D. S. 2008. The velar nasal. In Martin Haspelmath, Matthew S. Dryer & David Gil (eds.), *The world atlas of language structures online*, <https://wals.info/chapter/9> (last accessed 20 January 2020).

Anderson, John M. 1971. *The grammar of case: Towards a localistic theory*. Cambridge: Cambridge University Press.

Anderson, John M. 1987a. The limits of linearity. In John M. Anderson & Jacques Durand (eds.), *Explorations in Dependency Phonology*, 169–90. Dordrecht: Foris.

Anderson, John M. 1987b. The tradition of structural analogy. In Ross Steele & Terry Threadgold (eds.), *Language topics: Essays in honour of Michael Halliday*, vol. II, 33–43. Amsterdam: John Benjamins.

Anderson, John M. 2004. Contrast in phonology, structural analogy, and the interfaces. *Studia Linguistica (Lund)* 58.3, 269–87.

Anderson, John M. 2011a. *The substance of language, Volume I: The domain of syntax.* Oxford: Oxford University Press.

Anderson, John M. 2011b. *The substance of language, Volume III: Phonology–syntax analogies.* Oxford: Oxford University Press.

Anderson, John M. 2011c. *The substance of language. Volume I: The domain of syntax; Volume II: Morphology, paradigms, and periphrases; Volume III: Phonology–syntax analogies.* Oxford: Oxford University Press.

Anderson, John M. 2014. Graphophonology and anachronic phonology. Notes on episodes in the history of pseudo-phonology. *Folia Linguistica Historica* 35, 1–53.

Anderson, John M. in prep. A representational grammar of English: The consequences of a substantive view of linguistic structure. MS.

Anderson, John M. & Jacques Durand. 1987. Introduction. In John M. Anderson & Jacques Durand (eds.), *Explorations in Dependency Phonology*, 1–13. Dordrecht: Foris.

Anderson, John M. & Colin J. Ewen. 1980. Introduction: A sketch of Dependency Phonology. In John M. Anderson & Colin J. Ewen (eds.), *Studies in Dependency Phonology* (Ludwigsburg Studies in Language and Linguistics 4), 9–40. Ludwigsburg: Strauch.

Anderson, John M. & Colin J. Ewen. 1987. *Principles of Dependency Phonology* (Cambridge Studies in Linguistics 47). Cambridge: Cambridge University Press.

Anderson, John M. & Charles Jones. 1972. Three theses concerning phonological representations. *Edinburgh Working Papers in Linguistics* 1, 92–115.

Anderson, John M. & Charles Jones. 1974. Three theses concerning phonological representations. *Journal of Linguistics* 10, 1–26.

Anderson, Stephen R. 1975. On the interaction of phonological rules of various types. *Journal of Linguistics* 11.1, 39–62.

Anderson, Stephen R. 1976. Nasal consonants and the internal structure of segments. *Language* 52.2, 326–44.

Anderson, Stephen R. 1982. The analysis of French shwa: Or, how to get something for nothing. *Language* 58.3, 534–73.

Anderson, Stephen R. 2000. Reflections on 'On the Phonetic Rules of Russian'. *Folia Linguistica* 34.1–2, 11–28.

Anderson, Stephen R. & David W. Lightfoot. 2002. *The language organ: Linguistics as cognitive physiology.* Cambridge: Cambridge University Press.

Anttila, Arto. 2008. Gradient phonotactics and the complexity hypothesis. *Natural Language & Linguistic Theory* 26.4, 695–729.

Archangeli, Diana. 1984. *Underspecification in Yawelmani phonology.* PhD dissertation, MIT. Published 1988, New York: Garland.

Austin, P. 1981. *A grammar of Diyari, South Australia.* Cambridge: Cambridge University Press.

Avery, Peter. 1996. *The representation of voicing contrasts.* PhD dissertation, University of Toronto.

Avery, Peter & William J. Idsardi. 2001. Laryngeal dimensions, completion and enhancement. In T. A. Hall (ed.), *Distinctive feature theory*, 41–70. Berlin: Mouton de Gruyter.

Avery, Peter & Keren Rice. 1990. Segment structure and coronal underspecification. *Phonology* 6.2, 179–200.

Backley, Phillip. 2011. *An introduction to Element Theory*. Edinburgh: Edinburgh University Press.

Backley, Phillip. 2012. Variation in Element Theory. *Linguistic Variation* 1.1, 57–102.

Backley, Phillip & Kuniya Nasukawa (eds.). 2020a. *Morpheme-internal recursion in phonology*. Berlin and New York: Mouton de Gruyter.

Backley, Phillip & Kuniya Nasukawa. 2020b. Recursion in melodic-prosodic structure. In Phillip Backley & Kuniya Nasukawa (eds.), *Morpheme-internal recursion in phonology*, 11–36. Berlin and New York: Mouton de Gruyter.

Bagemihl, Bruce. 1991. Syllable structure in Bella Coola. *Linguistic Inquiry* 22, 589–646.

Banner Inouye, Susan. 1989. The flap as a contour segment. *UCLA Working Papers in Phonetics* 72, 39–81.

Bao, Zhiming. 1990. *On the nature of tone*. PhD dissertation, MIT.

Bao, Zhiming. 1999. *The structure of tone*. Oxford and New York: Oxford University Press.

Batibo, Herman. 1976. *Le Kesukuma: Phonologie, morphologie*. Thèse de troisième cycle, Paris. Published 1985, Paris: Éditions recherche sur les civilisations.

Battison, Robbin. 1978. *Lexical borrowing in American Sign Language*. Silver Spring, MD: Linstok Press.

Battistella, Edwin L. 1990. *Markedness: The evaluative superstructure of language*. Albany, NY: SUNY Press.

Bauer, Gerd. 1956. The problem of short diphthongs in Old English. *Anglia: Zeitschrift für englische Philologie* 74, 427–37.

Bauer, Laurie. 1994. Structural analogy: An examination of some recent claims. *Studies in Language* 18.1, 1–22.

Baumbach, E. J. M. 1974. *Introduction to the speech sounds and speech sound changes of Tsonga*. Pretoria: Van Schaik.

Baumbach, E. J. M. 1987. *Analytical Tsonga grammar*. Pretoria: University of South Africa.

Bavelier, Daphné, Andrea Tomann, Chloe Hutton, Teresa Mitchell, David Corina, Guoying Liu & Helen Neville. 2000. Visual attention to the periphery is enhanced in congenitally deaf individuals. *Journal of Neuroscience* 20.17, RC931-6.

Becker, Michael & Peter Jurgec. 2017. Interactions of tone and ATR in Slovenian. In Wolfgang Kehrein, Björn Köhnlein, Paul Boersma & Marc van Oostendorp (eds.), *Segmental structure and tone* (Linguistische Arbeiten 552), 11–26. Berlin: Mouton de Gruyter.

Beckman, Jill N. 1998. *Positional faithfulness*. PhD dissertation, University of Massachusetts, Amherst.

Beckman, Jill N. 2004. On the status of CODACOND in phonology. *International Journal of English Studies* 4.2, 105–34.

Beddor, Patrice S. 1982. *Phonological and phonetic effects of nasalization on vowel height*. PhD dissertation, University of Minnesota.

Bell, Alan. 1978. Syllabic consonants. In Joseph Greenberg (ed.), *Universals of human language*, vol. 2, 153–202. Stanford: Stanford University Press.

Bender, Byron W. 1963. Marshallese phonemics: Labialization or palatalization? *Word* 19.3, 335–41.

Bennett, William G. 2008. Some interesting implications of clicks. Paper presented at Humdrum 2008.

Bennett, William G. 2009. Reconsidering nasality in nasal clicks. Paper presented at the 33rd Penn Linguistics Colloquium, University of Pennsylvania.

Bennett, William G. 2014. Some differences between clicks and labio-velars. *South African Journal of African Languages* 34.2, 115–26.

Bergen, Benjamin K. 2012. *Louder than words: The new science of how the mind makes meaning*. New York: Basic Books.

Bermúdez-Otero, Ricardo. 2018. Stratal phonology. In S. J. Hannahs & Anna R. K. Bosch (eds.), *The Routledge handbook of phonological theory* (Routledge Handbooks in Linguistics), 100–34. London: Routledge.

Bičan, Aleš. 2011. *Phonotactics of Czech*. PhD dissertation, University of Brno.

Bickerton, Derek. 2000. Calls aren't words, syllables aren't syntax. Review of: Andrew Carstairs-McCarthy (1999): The origins of complex language. An inquiry into the evolutionary beginnings of sentences, syllables and truth. Oxford: Oxford University Press. *Psycoloquy* 11, 114.

Bird, Steven. 1990. *Constraint-based phonology*. PhD dissertation, University of Edinburgh.

Black, H. Andrew. 1991. The phonology of the velar glide in Axininca Campa. *Phonology* 2, 183–217.

Blaho, Sylvia. 2008. *The syntax of phonology: A radically substance-free approach*. PhD dissertation, University of Tromsø.

Blankenship, Barbara. 2002. The timing of nonmodal phonation in vowels. *Journal of Phonetics* 30.2, 163–91.

Boersma, Paul. 1998. *Functional Phonology: Formalizing the interactions between articulatory and perceptual drives*. The Hague: Holland Academic Graphics.

Boersma, Paul, Paola Escudero & Rachel Hayes. 2003. Learning abstract phonological from auditory phonetic categories: An integrated model for the acquisition of language-specific sound categories. *Proceedings of the 15th International Congress of Phonetic Sciences*, 1013–16.

Böhm, Roger. 2018. Just for the record: Dependency (vs. constituency) for the umpteenth time – A concise guide for the confused with an appended how-(not)-to-read Tesnière's *Éléments*. In Roger Böhm & Harry van der Hulst (eds.), *Substance-based grammar: The (ongoing) work of John Anderson*

(Studies in Language Companion Series 204), 261–310. Amsterdam and Philadelphia: John Benjamins.

Bolinger, Dwight L. 1981. *Two kinds of vowels, two kinds of rhythm*. Reproduced by the Indiana University Linguistics Club.

Borowsky, Toni. 1993. On the word level. In Sharon Hargus & Ellen M. Kaisse (eds.), *Studies in Lexical Phonology*, 199–234. San Diego, CA: Academic Press.

Boston, Marisa Ferrara, John T. Hale & Marco Kuhlmann. 2010. Dependency structures derived from minimalist grammars. In Christian Ebert, Gerhard Jäger & Jens Michaelis (eds.), *The Mathematics of Language* (Lecture Notes in Computer Science 6149), 1–12. Berlin: Springer.

Botma, Bert. 2004. *Phonological aspects of nasality: An element-based dependency approach*. PhD dissertation, University of Amsterdam.

Botma, Bert. 2009. Transparency in nasal harmony and the limits of reductionism. In Kuniya Nasukawa & Philip Backley (eds.), *Strength relations in phonology*, 79–112. Berlin and New York: Mouton de Gruyter.

Botma, Bert & Norval Smith. 2006. A dependency account of the fortis–lenis contrast in Cama. In Jeroen van de Weijer & Bettelou Los (eds.), *Linguistics in the Netherlands* (AVT 23), 15–27. Amsterdam and Philadelphia: John Benjamins.

Botma, Bert & Norval Smith. 2007. A dependency-based typology of nasalization and voicing phenomena. In Bettelou Los & Marjo van Koppen (eds.), *Linguistics in the Netherlands* (AVT 24), 36–48. Amsterdam and Philadelphia: John Benjamins.

Bradfield, Julian. 2014. Clicks, concurrency and Khoisan. *Phonology* 31.1, 1–49. doi:10.1017/S0952675714000025

Breen, Gavan. 2001. The wonders of Arandic phonology. In Jane Simpson, David Nash, Mary Laughren, Peter Austin and Barry Alpher, (eds.), *Forty years on: Ken Hale and Australian languages*, 45–69. Canberra: Pacific Linguistics.

Breen, Gavan & Robert Pensalfini. 1999. Arrernte: A language with no syllable onsets. *Linguistic Inquiry* 30.1, 1–25.

Brentari, Diane. 1999. Phonological constituents in signed languages. In Martin Heusser (ed.), *Text and visuality: Word & image interactions*, 237–42. Basel: Weise.

Brockhaus, Wiebke. 1995. *Final devoicing in the phonology of German*. Tübingen: Niemeyer.

Bromberger, Sylvain & Morris Halle. 1989. Why phonology is different. *Linguistic Inquiry* 20.1, 51–70.

Browman, Catherine P. & Louis M. Goldstein. 1986. Towards an Articulatory Phonology. *Phonology Yearbook* 3, 219–52.

Browman, Catherine P. & Louis M. Goldstein. 1992. Articulatory Phonology: An overview. *Phonetica* 49.3-4, 155–80.

Brunelle, Marc & James Kirby. 2016. Tone and phonation in southeast Asian languages. *Language and Linguistics Compass* 10.4, 191–207.

Bush, Ryan. 1997. Georgian syllable structure. *Phonology at Santa Cruz* 5, 1–13.

Butcher, Andrew. 1993. *The phonetics of Australian languages*. Adelaide: Flinders University.
Bybee, Joan L. 2001. *Phonology and language use*. Cambridge and New York: Cambridge University Press.
Calabrese, Andrea. 2005. *Markedness and economy in a derivational model of phonology*. Berlin: Mouton de Gruyter.
Calabrese, Andrea. 2011. Metaphony in Romance. In Marc van Oostendorp, Colin J. Ewen, Elizabeth Hume & Keren Rice (eds.), *The Blackwell companion to phonology*, 2631–61. Oxford: Wiley-Blackwell.
Calabrese, Andrea. to appear. Constraint-and-repair strategies. In B. Elan Dresher & Harry van der Hulst (eds.), *The handbook of the (early) history of phonology*. Oxford: Oxford University Press.
Carr, Philip. 2006. Universal Grammar and syntax–phonology parallelisms. *Lingua* 116, 634–56.
Carstairs-McCarthy, Andrew. 1999. *The origins of complex language: An inquiry into the evolutionary beginnings of sentences, syllables and truth*. Oxford: Oxford University Press.
Casali, Roderic F. 2003. [ATR] value asymmetries and underlying vowel inventory structure in Niger-Congo and Nilo-Saharan. *Linguistic Typology* 7, 307–82.
Casali, Roderic F. 2008. ATR harmony in African languages. *Language and Linguistics Compass* 2.3, 496–549.
Casasanto, Daniel & Sandra C. Lozano. 2007. Meaning and motor action. *Cogsci 2007: Proceedings of the 29th Annual Conference of the Cognitive Science Society*, 149–54. Hillsdale, NJ: Lawrence Erlbaum.
Catford, J. C. 1983. Pharyngeal and laryngeal sounds in Caucasian languages. In D. M. Bless and J. H. Abbs (eds.), *Vocal Fold Physiology: Contemporary Research and Clinical Issues*, 344–50. San Diego: College Hill Press.
Catford, John C. 1988. *A practical introduction to phonetics*. Oxford: Clarendon.
Channon, Rachel. 2002. *Signs are single segments: Phonological representations and temporal sequencing in ASL and other sign languages*. PhD dissertation, University of Maryland.
Channon, Rachel & Harry van der Hulst. 2011. Are dynamic features required in signs? In Rachel Channon & Harry van der Hulst (eds.), *Formational units in sign languages* (Sign Language Typology 3), 229–60. Berlin and New York: Mouton de Gruyter.
Charette, Monik & Aslı Göksel. 1998. Licensing constraints and vowel harmony in Turkic languages. In Eugeniusz Cyran (ed.), *Structure and interpretation: Studies in phonology*, vol. 4, 65–89. Lublin: PASE.
Chinchor, Nancy. 1979. On the treatment of Mongolian vowel harmony. *Proceedings of the North East Linguistic Society (NELS)* 9, 171–87.
Cho, Young-Mee Yu. 1990. *Parameters of consonantal assimilation*. PhD dissertation, Stanford University.
Cho, Young-mee Yu. 2016. *Korean phonetics and phonology* (Oxford Research Encyclopedia of Linguistics). Oxford: Oxford University Press.

Chomsky, Noam. 1964. Current issues in linguistic theory. In Jerry A. Fodor & Jerrold J. Katz (eds.), *The structure of language*, 50–118. Englewood Cliffs, NJ: Prentice Hall.

Chomsky, Noam. 1970. Remarks on nominalization. In Roderick A. Jacobs & Peter Rosenbaum (eds.), *Readings in English transformational grammar*, 184–221. Waltham, MA: Ginn.

Chomsky, Noam. 2000. Minimalist inquiries: The framework. In Roger Martin, David Michaels & Juan Uriagereka (eds.), *Step by step: Essays on minimalist syntax in honor of Howard Lasnik*, 89–115. Cambridge, MA: MIT Press.

Chomsky, Noam & Morris Halle. 1968. *The sound pattern of English* (Studies in Language). New York: Harper and Row. Repr. 1991, Cambridge, MA: MIT Press.

Clements, George N. 1985. The geometry of phonological features. *Phonology* 2, 225–52.

Clements, George N. 1990a. The role of the sonority cycle in core syllabification. In John Kingston & Mary Beckman (eds.), *Papers in Laboratory Phonology I: Between the grammar and physics of speech*, 283–333. Cambridge: Cambridge University Press.

Clements, George N. 1990b. The status of register in intonation theory: Comments on the papers by Ladd and by Inkelas and Leben. In John Kingston & Mary E. Beckman (eds.), *Papers in Laboratory Phonology I: Between the grammar and physics of speech*, 58–71. Cambridge: Cambridge University Press.

Clements, George N. 1991a. Place of articulation in consonants and vowels: A unified approach. *Working Papers of the Cornell Phonetics Laboratory* 5, 77–123.

Clements, George N. 1991b. Vowel height assimilation in Bantu languages. *Working Papers of the Cornell Phonetics Laboratory* 5, 37–76.

Clements, George N. 1999. Affricates as noncontoured stops. In Osamu Fujimura, Brian D. Joseph & Bohumil Palek (eds.), *Proceedings of LP' 98: Item order in language and speech*, 271–99. Prague: Karolinum Press.

Clements, George N. 2003. Feature economy in sound systems. *Phonology* 20.3, 287–333.

Clements, George N. & Susan R. Hertz. 1991. Nonlinear phonology and acoustic interpretation. *Proceedings of the 12th International Congress on Phonetic Sciences*, vol. I, 364–73. Aix-en-Provence: Université de Provence, Service des Publications.

Clements, George N. & Elizabeth Hume. 1995. The internal organization of speech sounds. In John Goldsmith (ed.), *The handbook of phonological theory*, 245–306. Oxford: Blackwell.

Clements, G. N. and S. J. Keyser. 1983. *CV Phonology: A Generative Theory of the Syllable*. Cambridge, MA: MIT Press.

Clements, George N., Alexis Michaud & Cédric Patin. 2011. Do we need tone features? In John A. Goldsmith, Elizabeth Hume & W. Leo Wetzels (eds.),

Tones and features: Phonetic and phonological perspectives, 3–24. Berlin: Mouton de Gruyter.

Coetzee, Andries W. & Joe Pater. 2008. Weighted constraints and gradient restrictions on place co-occurrence in Muna and Arabic. *Natural Language & Linguistic Theory* 26.2, 289–337.

Coleman, John & Janet B. Pierrehumbert. 1997. Stochastic phonological grammars and acceptability. *Proceedings of Computational Phonology: Third Meeting of the ACL Special Interest Group in Computational Phonology*, 49–56. Somerset, NJ: Association for Computational Linguistics.

Collins, Beverley & Inger Mees. 2003. *The phonetics of English and Dutch*, 5th edn. Leiden: Brill.

Connell, Bruce. 2007. Mambila fricative vowels and Bantu spirantisation. *Africana Linguistica* 13.1, 7–31.

Corina, David P. & Wendy Sandler. 1993. On the nature of phonological structure in sign language. *Phonology* 10.2, 165–207.

Côté, Marie-Hélène. 2011. Final consonants. In Marc van Oostendorp, Colin J. Ewen, Elizabeth V. Hume & Keren Rice (eds.), *The Blackwell companion to phonology*, vol. 2, 848–72. Oxford: Wiley-Blackwell.

Coulter, Geoffrey R. 1982. On the nature of ASL as a monosyllabic language. Paper presented at the annual meeting of the Linguistic Society of America, San Diego, California.

Cowper, Elizabeth & Daniel Currie Hall. 2015. Reductiō ad discrīmen: Where features come from. *Nordlyd* 41.2, 145–64.

Crasborn, Onno & Els van der Kooij. 1997. Relative orientation in sign language phonology. In Jane Coerts & Helen de Hoop (eds.), *Linguistics in the Netherlands 1997*, 37–48. Amsterdam and Philadelphia: John Benjamins.

Cristófaro-Silva, Thaïs. 1992. *Nuclear phenomena in Brazilian Portuguese*. PhD dissertation, School of Oriental and African Studies.

Crothers, John. 1975. Nasal consonant systems. In Charles A. Ferguson, Larry M. Hyman & John J. Ohala (eds.), *Nasalfest: Papers from a symposium on nasals and nasalization*, 153–66. Stanford: Stanford University.

Crothers, John. 1978. Typology and universals of vowel systems. In Joseph H. Greenberg, Charles Ferguson & Edith Moravcsik (eds.), *Universals of human language. Vol. 2: Phonology*, 93–152. Stanford: Stanford University Press.

Crowhurst, Megan Jane & Lev D. Michael. 2005. Iterative footing and prominence-driven stress in Nanti (Kampa). *Language* 81.1, 47–95.

Culicover, Peter W. & Ray Jackendoff. 2005. *Simpler syntax*. Oxford: Oxford University Press.

Cyran, Eugeniusz. 1997. *Resonance elements in phonology: A study in Munster Irish*. Lublin: Folium.

Cyran, Eugeniusz. 2003. *Complexity scales and licensing strength in phonology*. Lublin: Wydawnictwo KUL.

Cyran, Eugeniusz. 2014. *Between phonology and phonetics: Polish voicing*. Berlin: Walter de Gruyter.

Cyran, Eugeniusz. 2017. 'Voice' languages with no [voice]? Some consequences of laryngeal relativism. *Acta Linguistica Academica* 64.4, 477–511. doi:10.1556/2062.2017.64.4.1

Cyran, Eugeniusz & Edmund Gussmann. 1999. Consonant clusters and governing relations: Polish initial consonant sequences. In Harry van der Hulst & Nancy A. Ritter (eds.), *The syllable: Views and facts*, 219–48. Berlin: Mouton de Gruyter.

D'Arcy, Alex. 2004. Unconditional neutrality: Vowel harmony in a two-place model. *Toronto Working Papers in Linguistics* 23.2, 1–46.

Da Silva, T. C. Alves. 1992. *Nuclear phenomena in Brazilian Portuguese*. PhD dissertation, School of Oriental and African Studies.

Danis, Nick. 2015. Markedness and complex stops: Evidence from simplification processes. Paper presented at the 8th World Congress of African Languages, Kyoto.

Davenport, Michael. 1995. The characterization of nasality in Dependency Phonology. In Harry van der Hulst & Jeroen van de Weijer (eds.), *Leiden in last* (HIL Phonology Papers I), 89–103. The Hague: Holland Academic Graphics.

Davenport, Michael & Jørgen Staun. 1986. Sequence, segment and configuration: Two problems for Dependency Phonology. In Jacques Durand (ed.), *Dependency and non-linear phonology*, 135–59. London: Croom Helm.

Davis, Stuart & Mi-Hui Cho. 2003. The distribution of aspirated stops and /h/ in American English and Korean: An alignment approach with typological implications. *Linguistics* 41.4, 607–52.

de Lacy, Paul. 2002. The interaction of tone and stress in Optimality Theory. *Phonology* 19.1, 1–32.

de Lacy, Paul. 2006. *Markedness: Reduction and preservation in phonology*. Cambridge: Cambridge University Press.

Dell, François & Mohamed Elmedlaoui. 1985. Syllabic consonants and syllabification in Imdlawn Tashlhiyt Berber. *Journal of African Languages and Linguistics* 7.2, 105–30.

Dell, François & Mohamed Elmedlaoui. 1988. Syllabic consonants in Berber: Some new evidence. *Journal of African Languages and Linguistics* 10.1, 1–17.

Dell, François & Mohamed Elmedlaoui. 2002. *Syllables in Tashlhiyt Berber and in Moroccan Arabic*. Dordrecht: Kluwer.

Dell, François & Elisabeth Selkirk. 1978. On a morphologically governed vowel alternation in French. In Samuel J. Keyser (ed.), *Recent transformational studies in European languages* (Linguistic Inquiry Monographs 3), 1–51. Cambridge, MA: MIT Press.

Demolin, Didier. 1995. The phonetics and phonology of glottalized consonants in Lendu. In Bruce Connell & Amalia Arvaniti (eds.), *Phonology and phonetic evidence: Papers in Laboratory Phonology IV*, 368–85. Cambridge: Cambridge University Press.

den Dikken, Marcel & Éva Dékány. 2018. A restriction on recursion. *Syntax* 21.1, 33–71.

den Dikken, Marcel & Harry van der Hulst. 1988. Segmental hierarchitecture. In Harry van der Hulst & Norval Smith (eds.), *Features, segmental structure and harmony processes*, vol. 1, 1–59. Dordrecht: Foris.

den Dikken, Marcel & Harry van der Hulst. 2020. On some deep structural analogies between syntax and phonology. In Phillip Backley & Kuniya Nasukawa (eds.), *Morpheme-internal recursion in phonology*, 57–114. Berlin and New York: Mouton de Gruyter.

Dihoff, Ivan R. 1976. *Aspects of the tonal structure of Chori*. PhD dissertation, University of Wisconsin.

Dillon, Brian, Ewan Dunbar & William Idsardi. 2013. A single-stage approach to learning phonological categories: Insights from Inuktitut. *Cognitive Science* 37.2, 344–77.

Dimmendaal, Gerrit J. 1983. *The Turkana language*. Dordrecht: Foris.

Dingemanse, Mark. 2012. Advances in the cross-linguistic study of ideophones. *Language and Linguistics Compass* 6.10, 654–72.

Disner, Sandra. 1984. Insights on vowel spacing. In Ian Maddieson, *Patterns of sounds*, 136–55. Cambridge: Cambridge University Press.

Dixon, R. M. W. 1970. Oglolo syllable structure and what they are doing about it. *Linguistic Inquiry* 1, 273–6.

Dixon, R. M. W. 1980. *The languages of Australia*. Cambridge: Cambridge University Press.

Doke, Clement M. 1926. *The phonetics of the Zulu language* (Bantu Studies special number). Johannesburg: University of the Witwatersrand Press.

Donegan, Patricia J. 1978. *On the natural phonology of vowels*. PhD dissertation, Ohio State University. Published 1985, New York: Garland.

Dresher, B. Elan. 2009. *The contrastive hierarchy in phonology* (Cambridge Studies in Linguistics 121). Cambridge: Cambridge University Press.

Dresher, B. Elan & Harry van der Hulst. 1998. Head-dependent asymmetries in phonology: Complexity and visibility. *Phonology* 15.3, 317–52.

Dresher, B. Elan & Harry van der Hulst (eds.). to appear. *The handbook of the (early) history of phonology*. Oxford: Oxford University Press.

Duanmu, San. 1990. *A formal study of syllable, tone, stress and domain in Chinese languages*. PhD dissertation, MIT.

Duanmu, San. 1994. Against contour tone units. *Linguistic Inquiry* 25.4, 555–608.

Duanmu, San. 2002. *The Phonology of Standard Chinese*. Oxford: Oxford University Press.

Duanmu, San. 2008. *Syllable structure: The limits of variation*. Oxford: Oxford University Press.

Duanmu, San. 2011. The CVX theory of syllable structure. In Charles E. Cairns & Eric Raimy (eds.), *Handbook of the syllable*, 99–128. Leiden: Brill.

Duanmu, San. 2016. *A theory of phonological features*. Oxford: Oxford University Press.

Durand, Jacques. 1988. An exploration of nasality phenomena in Midi French: Dependency Phonology and underspecification. *Occasional Papers: University of Essex, Department of Language and Linguistics* 32, 30–70.

Durvasula, Karthik. 2008. Obstruent nasals exist! Paper presented at Penn Linguistic Colloquium 32.

Edmondson, Jerold A. & John H. Esling. 2006. The valves of the throat and their functioning in tone, vocal register and stress: Laryngoscopic case studies. *Phonology* 23.2, 157–91. doi:10.1017/S095267570600087X

Elbert, Samuel H. & Mary K. Pukui. 2001. *Hawaiian grammar*. Honolulu: University Press of Hawai'i.

Emeneau, Murray B. 1939. The vowels of the Badaga language. *Language* 15, 43–7.

Esling, J. H. 1999. The IPA categories 'pharyngeal' and 'epiglottal': Laryngoscopic observations of pharyngeal articulations and larynx height. *Language and Speech* 42.4, 349.

Esling, J. H. 2009. Pharyngeal consonants and the aryepiglottic sphincter. *Journal of the International Phonetic Association* 26.2, 65–88.

Esling, John H., Scott R. Moisik, Allison Benner & Lise Crevier-Buchman. 2019. *Voice quality: The laryngeal articulator model*. Cambridge: Cambridge University Press.

Ewen, Colin J. 1980a. *Aspects of phonological structure, with particular reference to English and Dutch*. PhD dissertation, University of Edinburgh.

Ewen, Colin J. 1980b. Segment or sequence? Problems in the analysis of some consonantal phenomena. In John M. Anderson & Colin J. Ewen (eds.), *Studies in Dependency Phonology*, 157–204. Ludwigsburg: Strauch.

Ewen, Colin J. 1982. The internal structure of complex segments. In Harry van der Hulst & Norval Smith (eds.), *The structure of phonological representations*, vol. II, 27–67. Dordrecht: Foris.

Ewen, Colin J. 1986. Segmental and suprasegmental structure. In Jacques Durand (ed.), *Dependency and non-linear phonology*, 203–22. London: Croom Helm.

Ewen, Colin J. 1995. Dependency relations in phonology. In John Goldsmith (ed.), *The handbook of phonological theory*, 570–585. Oxford: Blackwell.

Ewen, Colin J. & Harry van der Hulst. 1985. Single-valued features and the nonlinear analysis of vowel harmony. In Hans Bennis & Frits Beukema (eds.), *Linguistics in the Netherlands 1985*, 39–48. Dordrecht: Foris.

Ewen, Colin J. & Harry van der Hulst. 1987. Single-valued features and the distinction between [–F] and [oF]. In Frits Beukema & Peter Coopmans (eds.), *Linguistics in the Netherlands 1987*, 51–60. Dordrecht: Foris.

Ewen, Colin J. & Harry van der Hulst. 1988. [high], [low] and [back] or [I], [A] and [U]? In Peter Coopmans & Aafke Hulk (eds.), *Linguistics in the Netherlands 1988*, 49–58. Dordrecht: Foris.

Ewen, Colin J. & Harry van der Hulst. 1991. Major class and manner features. In Pier Marco Bertinetto & Michele Loporcaro (eds.), *Certamen phonologicum II*, 19–42. Turin: Rosenberg and Sellier.

Ewen, Colin J. & Harry van der Hulst. 2001. *The phonological structure of words: An introduction.* Cambridge: Cambridge University Press.

Fabb, N. 1988. English suffixation is constrained only by selectional restrictions. *Natural Language & Linguistic Theory* 6.4, 527–39.

Feinstein, M. H. 1979. Prenasalization and syllable structure. *Linguistic Inquiry* 10.2, 245–78.

Firth, J. R. 1948. Sounds and prosodies. *Transactions of the Philological Society* 47.1, 127–52.

Flack, Kathryn G. 2007a. *The sources of phonological markedness.* PhD dissertation, University of Massachusetts, Amherst.

Flack, Kathryn G. 2007b. Templatic morphology and indexed markedness constraints. *Linguistic Inquiry* 38.4, 749–58.

Flemming, Edward. 1995 [2002]. *Auditory representations in phonology* [revised version of the author's PhD dissertation (1995), University of California, Los Angeles]. New York: Routledge.

Flemming, Edward. 2001. Scalar and categorical phenomena in a unified model of phonetics and phonology. *Phonology* 18.1, 7–44.

Flemming, Edward. 2004. Contrast and perceptual distinctiveness. In Bruce Hayes, Robert Kirchner & Donca Steriade (eds.), *Phonetically based phonology*, 232–76. Cambridge: Cambridge University Press.

Flemming, Edward. 2017. Dispersion theory and phonology (Oxford Research Encyclopedia of Linguistics). Oxford: Oxford University Press.

Fletcher, Janet & Andrew Butcher. 2014. Sound patterns of Australian languages. In Harold Koch & Rachel Nordlinger (eds.), *The languages and linguistics of Australia: A comprehensive guide* (The World of Linguistics 3), 91–139. Berlin and Boston: Mouton de Gruyter.

Foley, James. 1977. *Foundations of theoretical phonology.* Cambridge: Cambridge University Press.

Fonte, Isabel. 1996. *Restrictions on coda: An Optimality Theoretic account of phonotactics.* PhD dissertation, McGill University.

Fougeron, Cecile & Rachid Ridouane. 2008. On the phonetic implementation of syllabic consonants and vowel-less syllables in Tashlhiyt. *Estudios de Fonética Experimental* 18, 139–75.

Friedman, Lynn A. 1976. *Phonology of a soundless language: Phonological structure of ASL.* PhD dissertation, University of California, Berkeley.

Friesen, Dianne. 2017. *A grammar of Moloko.* Berlin: Language Science Press.

Fromkin, Victoria A. 1972. Tone features and tone rules. *Studies in African Linguistics* 3.1, 47–76.

Fudge, Erik. 1987. Branching structure within the syllable. *Journal of Linguistics* 23.2, 359–77.

Fulop, Sean A. & Chris Golston. 2008. Breathy and whispery voicing in White Hmong. *Proceedings of Meeting on Acoustics: 155th Meeting of the Acoustical Society of America*, vol. 4. doi:10.1121/1.3033931

Gafos, Adamantios I., Jens Roeser, Stavroula Sotiropoulou, Philip Hoole & Chakir Zeroual. to appear. Structure in mind, structure in vocal tract. *Natural Language & Linguistic Theory*.

Gaifman, Haim. 1965. Dependency systems and phrase-structure systems. *Information and Control* 8.3, 304–37.

Gandour, Jack. 1974. Consonant types and tone in Siamese. *Journal of Phonetics* 2, 337–50.

Gandour, Jack, Apiluck Tumtavitikul & Nakarin Satthamnuwong. 1999. Effects of speaking rate on Thai tones. *Phonetica* 56.3–4, 123–34.

Garcia Bellido, Paloma. 2005. The morphosyntax and syntax of phonology: The svarabhakti construction in Spanish. *Estudios de Lingüística del Español* 22, <https://raco.cat/index.php/Elies/article/view/195615> (last accessed 20 January 2020).

Giegerich, Heinz J. 1985. *Metrical Phonology and phonological structure: German and English*. Cambridge and New York: Cambridge University Press.

Glanze, Walter D., Kenneth Anderson & Lois E. Anderson. 1990. *Mosby's medical, nursing, and allied health dictionary*, 4th edn. Maryland Heights, MO: Mosby.

Gnanadesikan, Amalia. 1997. *Phonology with ternary scales*. PhD dissertation, University of Massachusetts, Amherst.

Goblirsch, Kurt Gustav. 2002. On the development of Germanic consonants: The Danish shift and the Danish lenition. *Beiträge zur Geschichte der deutschen Sprache und Literatur* 124.2, 199–232.

Goldsmith, John A. 1976a. *Autosegmental Phonology*. PhD dissertation, MIT.

Goldsmith, John A. 1976b. An overview of Autosegmental Phonology. *Linguistic Analysis* 2.1, 23–68.

Goldsmith, John A. 1981. Subsegmentals in Spanish phonology: An autosegmental approach. In William W. Cressey & Donna Jo Napoli (eds.), *Linguistic symposium on Romance languages*, 1–16. Washington, DC: Georgetown University Press.

Goldsmith, John A. 1985. Vowel harmony in Khalkha Mongolian, Yaka, Finnish and Hungarian. *Phonology Yearbook* 2, 253–75.

Goldsmith, John A. 1987. Toward a theory of vowel systems. *Parasession on autosegmental and Metrical Phonology: Chicago Linguistic Society (CLS)* 23, 116–33.

Goldsmith, John A. 1989. Autosegmental licensing, inalterability, and harmonic rule application. *Chicago Linguistic Society (CLS)* 25, 145–56.

Goldsmith, John A. 1990. *Autosegmental and Metrical Phonology*. Oxford: Blackwell.

Golston, Chris & W. Kehrein. 1998. Mazatec onsets and nuclei. *International Journal of American Linguistics* 64.4, 311–37.

Golston, Chris & Harry van der Hulst. 1999. Stricture is structure. In Ben Hermans & Marc van Oostendorp (eds.), *The derivational residue in phonological Optimality Theory*, 153–74. Dordrecht: Reidel.

Gordon, Matthew K. 1998. The phonetics and phonology of non-modal vowels: A cross-linguistic perspective. *Berkeley Linguistics Society (BLS)* 24, 93–105.

Gordon, Matthew K. 2002. A typology of contour tone restrictions. *Studies in Language* 25.3, 423–62.

Gordon, Matthew K. 2014. Disentangling stress and pitch accent: A typology of prominence at different prosodic levels. In Harry van der Hulst (ed.), *Word stress: Theoretical and typological issues*, 8–118. Cambridge: Cambridge University Press.

Gordon, Matthew K. 2016. *Phonological typology* (Oxford Surveys in Phonology and Phonetics 1). Oxford: Oxford University Press.

Gordon, Matthew K. & Peter Ladefoged. 2001. Phonation types: A cross-linguistic overview. *Journal of Phonetics* 29.4, 383–406.

Gorecka, Alicja. 1990. *Phonology of articulation*. PhD dissertation, MIT.

Gouskova, Maria. 2004. Relational hierarchies in Optimality Theory: The case of syllable contact. *Phonology* 21, 201–50.

Greenberg, Joseph H. 1978. Some generalizations concerning initial and final consonant clusters. In Joseph H. Greenberg, Charles A. Ferguson & Edith A. Moravcsik (eds.), *Universals of human language*, vol. 2, 243–79. Stanford: Stanford University Press.

Griffen, Toby D. 1976. Toward a nonsegmental phonology. *Lingua* 40.1, 1–20.

Griffen, Toby D. 1985. *Aspects of dynamic phonology*. Amsterdam and Philadelphia: John Benjamins.

Guerssel, Mohamed. 1990. On the syllabification pattern of Berber. MS, Université du Quebec à Montréal.

Hale, Mark. 2000. Marshallese phonology, the phonetics–phonology interface and historical linguistics. *The Linguistic Review* 17, 241–57.

Hale, Mark & Charles Reiss. 2000. 'Substance abuse' and 'dysfunctionalism': Current trends in phonology. *Linguistic Inquiry* 31.1, 157–69.

Hall, Jr, Robert A. 1944. Italian phonemes and orthography. *Italica* 21.2, 72–82.

Hall, Tracy A. 2006. Derived environment blocking effects in Optimality Theory. *Natural Language & Linguistic Theory* 24.3, 803–56.

Halle, Morris. 1959. *The sound pattern of Russian*. The Hague: Mouton.

Halle, Morris. 1995. Feature Geometry and feature spreading. *Linguistic Inquiry* 26.1, 1–46.

Halle, Morris & Kenneth N. Stevens. 1971. A note on laryngeal features. *Quarterly Progress Report of the MIT Research Laboratory of Electronics* 101, 198–213.

Halle, Morris, Bert Vaux & Andrew Wolfe. 2000. On feature spreading and the representation of place of articulation. *Linguistic Inquiry* 31.3, 387–444.

Halle, Morris & Jean-Roger Vergnaud. 1987. *An essay on stress*. Cambridge, MA: MIT Press.

Hamann, Silke R. 2003. *The phonetics and phonology of retroflexes*. PhD dissertation, Utrecht University.

Hammond, Michael. 2004. Gradience, phonotactics and the lexicon in English phonology. *International Journal of English Studies* 4.2, 1–24.
Hamzah, Hilmi. 2013. *The acoustics and perception of the word-initial singleton/geminate contrast in Kelantan Malay*. PhD dissertation, University of Melbourne.
Hankamer, Jorge. 2010. Turkish vowel epenthesis. In Eser Erguvanlı Taylan & Bengisu Rona (eds.), *Puzzles of language: Essays in honour of Karl Zimmer* (Turcologica 86), 55–70. Wiesbaden: Harrassowitz.
Hardman, Michael J. 1966. *Jaqaru: Outline of phonological and morphological structure* (Janua Linguarim, Series Practica 22). The Hague: Mouton.
Harnad, Stevan (ed.) 1990. *Categorical perception: The groundwork of cognition*. Cambridge: Cambridge University Press.
Harris, John. 1987. Non-structure-preserving rules in Lexical Phonology: Southeastern Bantu harmony. *Lingua* 72.4, 255–92.
Harris, John. 1990. Segmental complexity and phonological government. *Phonology* 7.2, 255–300.
Harris, John. 1994. *English sound structure*. Oxford: Blackwell.
Harris, John & Geoff Lindsey. 1995. The elements for phonological representation. In Jacques Durand & Francis Katamba (eds.), *Frontiers of phonology: Atoms, structures, derivations*, 34–79. London: Longman.
Haspelmath, Martin. 2006. Against markedness (and what to replace it with). *Journal of Linguistics* 42.1, 25–70.
Haspelmath, Martin, Matthew S. Dryer, David Gil & Bernard Comrie. 2008. *The world atlas of language structures online*. Oxford: Oxford University Press, <http://wals.info> (last accessed 20 January 2020).
Hauser, Marc D., Noam Chomsky & W. Tecumseh Fitch. 2002. The faculty of language: What is it, who has it, and how did it evolve? *Science* 298.5598, 1569–79.
Hayden, Rebecca E. 1950. The relative frequency of phonemes in General American English. *Word* 6.3, 217–23.
Hayes, Bruce. 1980. *A metrical theory of stress rules*. PhD dissertation, MIT.
Hayes, Bruce. 1986a. Assimilation as spreading in Toba Batak. *Linguistic Inquiry* 17.3, 467–99.
Hayes, Bruce. 1986b. Inalterability in CV Phonology. *Language* 62.2, 321–51.
Hayes, Bruce. 1990. Diphthongisation and coindexing. *Phonology* 7, 31–71.
Hayes, Bruce. 1993. Against movement: Comments on Liddell's paper. In Geoffrey R. Coulter (ed.), *Current Issues in ASL Phonology*, 213–26. New York: Academic Press.
Hayes, Bruce. 1999. Phonetically driven phonology: The role of Optimality Theory and inductive grounding. In Michael Darnell, Edith A. Moravcsik, Michael Noonan, Frederick J. Newmeyer and Kathleen Wheatley (eds.), *Functionalism and formalism in linguistics*, vol. 1, 243–85. John Benjamins.
Hayes, Bruce & Zsuzsa Cziráky Londe. 2006. Stochastic phonological knowledge: The case of Hungarian vowel harmony. *Phonology* 23.1, 59–104.

Hayes, Bruce & Donca Steriade. 2004. The phonetic bases of phonological markedness. In Bruce Hayes, Robert Kirchner & Donca Steriade (eds.), *Phonetically based phonology*, 1–33. Cambridge: Cambridge University Press.

Hayes, Bruce & James White. 2013. Phonological naturalness and phonotactic learning. *Linguistic Inquiry* 44.1, 45–74.

Hayes, Bruce & Colin Wilson. 2008. A maximum entropy model of phonotactics and phonotactic learning. *Linguistic Inquiry* 39.3, 379–440.

Hayes, Bruce, Kie Zuraw, Péter Siptár & Zsuzsa Londe. 2009. Natural and unnatural constraints in Hungarian vowel harmony. *Language* 85.4, 822–63.

Haynie, Hannah J. 2012. *Topics in the history and geography of California languages*. PhD dissertation, University of California, Berkeley.

Hays, D. G. 1964. Dependency theory: A formalism and some observations. *Language* 40, 511–25.

Heijkoop, Anita C. 1998. *The early acquisition of segment specification: The evolution of the child's phonological system, in particular the development of the articulatory and categorial gesture, with reference to English and Dutch*. PhD dissertation, University of Edinburgh.

Helgason, Pétur & Catherine O. Ringen. 2008. Voicing and aspiration in Swedish stops. *Journal of Phonetics* 36.4, 607–28.

Herbert, R. K. 1986. *Language universals, markedness theory, and natural phonetic processes*. Berlin: Mouton de Gruyter.

Heringer, J. T. 1967. Review of Haim Gaifman (1965). Dependency systems and phrase-structure systems. Information and Control 8.3, 304–37. *Ohio State University Research Foundation: Working Papers in Linguistics* 1, 128–36.

Hirst, Daniel. 1985. Linearisation and the single-segment hypothesis. In Jacqueline Guéron, Hans Obenauer & Jean-Yves Pollock (eds.), *Grammatical representation*, 87–100. Dordrecht: Foris.

Hirst, Daniel. 1995. Macro segments. Paper presented at Current Trends in Phonology: Models and methods, Royaumont.

Hitch, Doug. 2017. Vowel spaces and systems. *Toronto Working Papers in Linguistics* 38.

Hjelmslev, Louis. 1943 [1953]. *Prolegomena to a theory of language*. Baltimore, MD: Waverly Press.

Hoard, J. E. 1978. Syllabification in northwest Indian languages, with remarks on the nature of syllabic stops and affricates. In Alan Bell & Joan B. Hooper (eds.), *Syllables and segments*, 59–72. Amsterdam: North-Holland.

Hockett, Charles F. 1955. *A manual of phonology*. Baltimore: Waverly Press.

Hockett, Charles F. 1960. The origin of speech. *Scientific American* 203, 88–111.

Hogg, Richard M. 1992. Phonology and morphology. In Richard M. Hogg (ed.), *The Cambridge history of the English language. Vol. 1: The Beginnings to 1066*, 67–168. Cambridge: Cambridge University Press.

Hoijer, Harry & Morris E. Opler. 1938. *Chiricahua and Mescalero Apache texts* (University of Chicago Publications in Anthropology; Linguistic Series).

Chicago: University of Chicago Press. Repr. 1964, 1970, Chicago: University of Chicago Press; 1980, under H. Hoijer, New York: AMS Press.

Hollenbach, Barbara. 1988. The asymmetrical distribution of tone in Copla Trique. In Harry van der Hulst & Norval Smith (eds.), *Autosegmental studies on pitch accent*, 167–82. Dordrecht: Foris.

Hombert, Jean-Marie. 1977. Development of tones from vowel height. *Journal of Phonetics* 5, 9–16.

Hombert, Jean-Marie. 1978. Consonant types, vowel quality, and tone. In Victoria Fromkin (ed.), *Tone: A linguistic survey*, 77–111. New York: Academic Press.

Hombert, Jean-Marie, John J. Ohala & W. G. Ewan. 1979. Phonetic explanations for the development of tones. *Language* 55.1, 37–58.

Honeybone, Patrick. 2002. *Germanic obstruent lenition: Some mutual implications of theoretical and historical phonology.* PhD dissertation, University of Newcastle upon Tyne.

Hooper, Joan B. 1976. *An introduction to Natural Generative Phonology.* New York: Academic Press.

Hu, Fang & Ling Feng. 2014. Fricative vowels as an intermediate stage of vowel apicalization. Paper presented at Sound Change in Interacting Human Systems; 3rd Biennial Workshop on Sound Change, Berkeley, CA.

Hu, Fang & Ling Feng. 2015. On the fricative vowels in Suzhou Chinese. *Journal of the Acoustical Society of America* 137.4, 2380.

Hubers, G. A. C. & Jan G. Kooij. 1973. Voice assimilation in Dutch. *Acta Linguistica Hafniensia* 14.1, 25–33.

Hudson, Grover. 1974. The representation of non-productive alternations. In John M. Anderson & Charles Jones (eds.), *The First International Conference on Historical Linguistics*, vol. 2, 203–29. Amsterdam: North-Holland.

Humbert, Helga. 1996. *Phonological segments: Their structure and behaviour.* PhD dissertation, University of Amsterdam.

Hume, Elizabeth. 1996. Coronal consonant, front vowel parallels in Maltese. *Natural Language & Linguistic Theory* 14.1, 163–203.

Hunyadi, László. 2010. Cognitive grouping and recursion in prosody. In Harry van der Hulst (ed.), *Recursion and human language* (Studies in Generative Grammar 104), 343–70. Berlin and New York: Mouton de Gruyter.

Hutchinson, Larry G. 1972. Mr. Chomsky on the phoneme. MS, distributed by the Indiana University Linguistics Club.

Huybregts, Riny. 2017. Phonemic clicks and the mapping asymmetry: How language emerged and speech developed. *Neuroscience and Biobehavioral Reviews* 81, part B, 279–94. doi:10.1016/j.neubiorev.2017.01.041

Hyman, Larry M. 1985. *A theory of phonological weight.* Dordrecht: Foris.

Hyman, Larry M. 1986. The representation of multiple tone heights. In Koen Bogers, Harry van der Hulst & Maarten Mous (eds.), *The phonological representation of suprasegmentals: Studies on African languages offered to John M. Stewart on his 60th birthday*, 109–52. Dordrecht: Foris.

Hyman, Larry M. 1993. Register tones and tonal geometry. In Harry van der Hulst & Keith L. Snider (eds.), *The phonology of tone: The representation of tonal register*, 75–108. Berlin and New York: Mouton de Gruyter.

Hyman, Larry M. 2002. 'Abstract' vowel harmony in Kalong: A system-driven account. *Théories Linguistiques et Langues Sub-Sahariennes* 8, 1–22.

Hyman, Larry M. 2011. The representation of tone. In Marc van Oostendorp, Colin J. Ewen, Elizabeth V. Hume & Keren Rice (eds.), *The Blackwell companion to phonology*, vol. 2, 1078–1103. Oxford: Wiley-Blackwell.

Hyman, Larry M. 2012. Coda constraints on tone. Berkeley: UC Berkeley Phonology Lab Annual Report.

Hyman, Larry M. 2018. Positional prominence vs. word accent: Is there a difference? In Rob Goedemans, Jeffrey Heinz & Harry van der Hulst (eds.), *The study of word stress and accent: Theories, methods and data*. Cambridge: Cambridge University Press.

Hyslop, Gwendolyn. 2007. Toward a typology of tonogenesis. MS, University of Oregon.

Hyslop, Gwendolyn. 2010. Sonorants, fricatives, and a tonogenetic typology. *Extended Abstracts from the Annual LSA Meeting*. doi:10.3765/exabs.v0i0.521

Ingram, David. 1989. *First language acquisition: Method, description and explanation*. Cambridge: Cambridge University Press.

Inkelas, Sharon & Stephanie S. Shih. 2013. Contour segments and tones in (sub) segmental Agreement by Correspondence. Paper presented at Manchester Phonology Meeting.

Inkelas, Sharon & Stephanie S. Shih. 2014. Unstable surface correspondence as the source of local conspiracies. *Proceedings of the North East Linguistic Society (NELS)* 44, 191–204.

Inkelas, Sharon & Stephanie S. Shih. 2016. Re-representing phonology: Consequences of Q Theory. *Proceedings of the North East Linguistic Society (NELS)* 46, 161–74.

Inkelas, Sharon & Stephanie S. Shih. 2017. Looking into segments. In Karen Jesney, Charlie O'Hara, Caitlin Smith & Rachel Walker (eds.), *Proceedings of the 2016 Annual Meeting on Phonology*. Washington, DC: Linguistic Society of America.

Iosad, Pavel. 2013. *Representation and variation in substance-free phonology: A case study in Celtic*. PhD dissertation, University of Tromsø.

Itô, Junko. 1986. *Syllable theory in Prosodic Phonology*. PhD dissertation, University of Massachusetts, Amherst.

Itô, Junko. 1988. *Syllable theory in Prosodic Phonology*. New York: Garland.

Itô, Junko. 1989. A prosodic theory of epenthesis. *Natural Language & Linguistic Theory* 7.2, 217–59.

Itô, Junko & R. Armin Mester. 1986. The phonology of voicing in Japanese: Theoretical consequences for morphological accessibility. *Linguistic Inquiry* 17.1, 49–73.

Itô, Junko & R. Armin Mester. 2013. Prosodic subcategories in Japanese. *Lingua* 124.0, 20–40. doi:10.1016/j.lingua.2012.08.016

Iverson, Gregory K. & Joseph C. Salmons. 1995. Aspiration and laryngeal representation in Germanic. *Phonology* 12.3, 369–96.

Iverson, Gregory K. & Joseph C. Salmons. 2003. Legacy specification in the laryngeal phonology of Dutch. *Journal of Germanic Linguistics* 15.1, 1–26. doi:10.1017/S1470542703000242

Jackendoff, Ray. 1977. *X-bar syntax: A study of phrase structure* (Linguistic Inquiry Monograph 2). Cambridge, MA: MIT Press.

Jakobson, Roman. 1941. *Kindersprache, Aphasie und allgemeine Lautgesetze*. Uppsala: Almqvist & Wiksells.

Jakobson, Roman. 1941 [1968]. *Child language, aphasia and phonological universals* [originally published (1941) as *Kindersprache, Aphasie und allgemeine Lautgesetze*], trans. A. Keiler. The Hague and Paris: Mouton.

Jakobson, Roman. 1968. Extrapulmonic consonants: Ejectives, implosives, clicks. *Quarterly Progress Report of the MIT Research Laboratory of Electronics* 90, 221–7.

Jakobson, Roman. 1968 [1941]. *Child language, aphasia and phonological universals* (Originally published as *Kindersprache, Aphasie und allgemeine Lautgesetze*). The Hague: Mouton.

Jakobson, Roman, Gunnar Fant & Morris Halle. 1952. *Preliminaries to speech analysis: The distinctive features and their correlates*, 2nd edn. Cambridge, MA: MIT Press.

Jakobson, Roman & Morris Halle. 1956. *Fundamentals of language*. The Hague: Mouton.

Jespersen, Otto. 1897–9. *Fonetik*. Copenhagen: Det Schuboteske.

Johnson, Keith. 2007. Decisions and mechanisms in exemplar-based phonology. In Maria-Josep Solé, Patrice S. Beddor & Manjari Ohala (eds.), *Experimental approaches to phonology*, 25–40. Oxford: Oxford University Press.

Johnson, Robert E. & Scott K. Liddell. 2011a. A segmental framework for representing signs phonetically. *Sign Language Studies* 11.3, 408–63.

Johnson, Robert E. & Scott K. Liddell. 2011b. Toward a phonetic representation of hand configuration: The fingers. *Sign Language Studies* 12.1, 5–45.

Johnson, Robert E. & Scott K. Liddell. 2012. Toward a phonetic representation of hand configuration: The thumb. *Sign Language Studies* 12.2, 316–33.

Jones, Daniel. 1911. *The pronunciation and orthography of the Chindau language*. London: University of London Press.

Jun, Jongho. 2004. Place assimilation. In Bruce Hayes, Robert Kirchner & Donca Steriade (eds.), *Phonetically based phonology*, 58–86. Cambridge: Cambridge University Press.

Kahn, Daniel. 1976. *Syllable-based generalizations in English phonology*. PhD dissertation, MIT.

Kang, Yongsoon. 1991. *Phonology of consonant–vowel interaction with special reference to Korean and Dependency Phonology*. PhD dissertation, University of Illinois at Urbana-Champaign.

Kaun, Abigail. 1995. *The typology of rounding harmony: An Optimality Theoretic approach*. PhD dissertation, University of California, Los Angeles.

Kaun, Abigail. 2004. The phonetic foundations of the rounding harmony typology. In Bruce Hayes, Robert Kirchner & Donca Steriade (eds.), *Phonetically based phonology*, 87–116. Cambridge: Cambridge University Press.

Kaye, Jonathan. 1988. The phonologist's dilemma: A game-theoretic approach to phonological debate. *GLOW Newsletter* 21, 16–19.

Kaye, Jonathan. 1990. 'Coda' licensing. *Phonology* 7, 301–30.

Kaye, Jonathan. 2000. A user's guide to Government Phonology (GP). MS, University of Ulster.

Kaye, Jonathan, Jean Lowenstamm & Jean-Roger Vergnaud. 1985. The internal structure of phonological elements: A theory of charm and government. *Phonology Yearbook* 2, 305–28.

Kaye, Jonathan, Jean Lowenstamm & Jean-Roger Vergnaud. 1990. Constituent structure and government in phonology. *Phonology* 7.2, 193–231.

Kean, Mary Louise. 1975. *The theory of markedness in Generative Grammar*. PhD dissertation, MIT.

Keating, Patricia A. 1984. Phonetic and phonological representation of stop consonant voicing. *Language* 60.2, 286–319.

Keating, Patricia A. 1988a. Palatals as complex segments: X-ray evidence. *UCLA Working Papers in Phonetics* 69, 77–91.

Keating, Patricia A. 1988b. *A survey of phonological features* (UCLA Working Papers in Phonetics 69). Bloomington: Indiana University Linguistics Club.

Keating, Patricia A. 1988c. Underspecification in phonetics. *Phonology* 5.2, 275–92.

Kegl, Judy A. & Ronnie B. Wilbur. 1976. When does structure stop and style begin? Syntax, morphology and phonology vs. stylistic variation in American Sign Language. *Chicago Linguistic Society (CLS)* 12, 376–96.

Kehrein, Wolfgang. 2002. *Phonological representation and phonetic phasing: Affricates and laryngeals*. Tübingen: Niemeyer.

Kehrein, Wolfgang & Chris Golston. 2004. A prosodic theory of laryngeal contrasts. *Phonology* 21.3, 325–57. doi:10.1017/S0952675704000302

Kemaloğlu, Yusuf Kemal, Gurbet Şahin Kamışlı & Güven Mengü. 2017. Phonemic analysis of Turkish monosyllabic word lists used for speech discrimination (word recognition) tests. *Kulak Burun Bogaz Ihtis Derg* 27.4, 198–207. doi: 10.5606/kbbihtisas.2017.06791

Kenstowicz, Michael. 1994a. *Phonology in Generative Grammar*. Oxford: Blackwell.

Kenstowicz, Michael. 1994b. Sonority-driven stress. MS, MIT.

Kenstowicz, Michael. 1995. Quality-sensitive stress. MS, MIT.

Kenstowicz, Michael J. & Charles W. Kisseberth. 1979. *Generative Phonology: Description and theory*. New York: Academic Press.

Kenstowicz, Michael & Charles Pyle. 1973. On the phonological integrity of geminate clusters. In Michael Kenstowicz & Charles Kisseberth (eds.), *Issues in phonological theory*, 27–43. The Hague: Mouton.

Kessler, Brett & Rebecca Treiman. 1997. Syllable structure and the distribution of phonemes in English syllables. *Journal of Memory and Language* 37.3, 295–311.

Kim, Chin Wu. 1978. 'Diagonal' vowel harmony? Some implications for historical phonology. In Jacek Fisiak (ed.), *Recent developments in historical phonology*, 221–36. The Hague: Mouton.

Kim, Hyunsoon, George N. Clements & Martine Toda. 2015. The feature [strident]. In Annie Rialland, Rachid Ridouane & Harry van der Hulst (eds.), *Features in phonology and phonetics: Posthumous writings by Nick Clements and coauthors*, vol. 21 (Phonetics and Phonology), 179–94. Berlin and New York: Mouton de Gruyter.

Kim, Hyunsoon, Shinji Maeda, Kiyoshi Honda & Lise Crevier-Buchman. 2017. The mechanism and representation of Korean three-way phonation contrast: External photoglottography, intra-oral air pressure, airflow, and acoustic data. *Phonetica* 75, 57–84.

Kingston, John. 2011. Tonogenesis. In Marc van Oostendorp, Colin J. Ewen, Elizabeth V. Hume & Keren Rice (eds.), *The Blackwell companion to phonology*, vol. 4, 2304–34. Oxford: Wiley-Blackwell.

Kiparsky, Paul. 1968. *How abstract is phonology?* Bloomington: Indiana University Linguistic Club.

Kiparsky, Paul. 1982a. From cyclic phonology to Lexical Phonology. In Harry van der Hulst & Norval Smith (eds.), *The structure of phonological representations*, vol. 1, 131–75. Dordrecht: Foris.

Kiparsky, Paul. 1982b. Lexical Phonology and morphology. In In-Seok Yang (ed.), *Linguistics in the morning calm I*, 3–91. Seoul: Hanshin.

Kisseberth, C. 1970. On the functional unity of phonological rules. *Linguistic Inquiry* 1, 291–306.

Klima, Edward S. & Ursula Bellugi (eds.). 1979. *The signs of language*. Cambridge, MA: Harvard University Press.

Ko, Seongyeon. 2011. Vowel contrast and vowel harmony shift in the Mongolic languages. *Language Research* 47.1, 23–43.

Kohler, Klaus J. 1996. Is the syllable a phonological universal? *Journal of Linguistics* 2.2, 207–8.

Köhnlein, Björn & Marc van Oostendorp. 2017. Introduction. In Wolfgang Kehrein, Björn Köhnlein, Paul Boersma & Marc van Oostendorp (eds.), *Segmental structure and tone* (Linguistische Arbeiten 552), 1–10. Berlin: Mouton de Gruyter.

Kok, Kenneth D., Bert Botma & Marijn van 't Veer. 2018. Glides and laryngeals as a structural class. In Bert le Bruyn & Janine Berns (eds.), *Linguistics in the Netherlands 2018*, 51–64. Amsterdam and Philadelphia: John Benjamins.

Kornai, András & Geoffrey K. Pullum. 1990. The X-bar theory of phrase structure. *Language* 66.1, 24–50.

Koutsoudas, Andreas, Gerald Sanders & Craig Noll. 1974. On the application of phonological rules. *Language* 50.1, 1–28.

Kraehenmann, Astrid. 2001. Swiss German stops: Geminates all over the word. *Phonology* 18.1, 109–45.

Krämer, Martin. 2010. The semantics of phonological features. Paper presented at the 18th Manchester Phonology Meeting, Manchester, 20–2 May 2010.

Krämer, Martin. 2012. *Underlying representations*. Cambridge and New York: Cambridge University Press.

Krämer, Martin. 2019. Is vowel nasalisation phonological in English? A systematic review. *English Language and Linguistics* 23.2, 405–37. doi:10.1017/S1360674317000442

Krämer, Martin & Draga Zec. 2019. Coda manners and hierarchies. MS, University of Tromsø.

Kreitman, Rina. 2006. Cluster buster: A typology of onset clusters. *Chicago Linguistic Society (CLS)* 42.1, 163–79.

Kreitman, Rina. 2008. *The phonetics and phonology of onset clusters: The case of Modern Hebrew*. PhD dissertation, Cornell University.

Krishnamurti, B. 2003. *The Dravidian languages*. Cambridge: Cambridge University Press.

Kuang, Jianjing. 2013. *Phonation in tonal contrasts*. PhD dissertation, University of California, Los Angeles.

Kubozono, Haruo (ed.). 2017. *The phonetics and phonology of geminate consonants* (Oxford Studies in Phonology and Phonetics). Oxford: Oxford University Press.

Kučera, Henry. 1961. *The phonology of Czech*. The Hague: Mouton.

Kuhl, Patricia K. 1991. Human adults and human infants show a 'perceptual magnet effect' for the prototypes of speech categories, monkeys do not. *Perception & Psychophysics* 50.2, 93–107.

Kuhn, Jeremy. 2017. Telicity and iconic scales in ASL. MS, Institut Jean Nicod, CNRS.

Kuhn, Thomas. 1962. *The structure of scientific revolutions*. Chicago: University of Chicago Press.

Kuipers, Aert H. 1960. *Phoneme and morpheme in Kabardian*. The Hague: Mouton.

Kuryłowicz, Jerzy. 1947. Contribution à la théorie de la syllabe. *Biuletyn Polskiego Towarzystwa Językoznawczego* 8, 80–113.

Labrune, Laurence. 2012. *The phonology of Japanese*. Oxford: Oxford University Press.

LaCharité, Darlene & Carole Paradis. 1993. Introduction: The emergence of constraints in Generative Phonology and a comparison of three current constraint-based models. *Canadian Journal of Linguistics* 38.2, 127–53.

Ladd, D. Robert. 2008. *Intonational Phonology*, 2nd edn. Cambridge: Cambridge University Press.

Ladd, D. Robert. to appear. Mid-century American phonology: The post-Bloomfieldians. In B. Elan Dresher & Harry van der Hulst (eds.), *The handbook of the (early) history of phonology*. Oxford: Oxford University Press.

Ladefoged, Peter. 1968. *A phonetic study of West African languages: An auditory-instrumental survey*. Cambridge: Cambridge University Press.

Ladefoged, Peter. 1971. *Preliminaries to linguistic phonetics*. Chicago: University of Chicago Press.

Ladefoged, Peter. 1973. The features of the larynx. *Journal of Phonetics* 1.1, 73–83.

Ladefoged, Peter. 2001. *Vowels and consonants: An introduction to the sounds of languages*. Malden, MA, and Oxford: Blackwell.

Ladefoged, Peter, A. Cochran & S. Disner. 1977. Laterals and trills. *Journal of the International Phonetic Association* 7.2, 46–54.

Ladefoged, Peter & Ian Maddieson. 1996. *The sounds of the world's languages*. Oxford: Blackwell.

Ladefoged, Peter & Anthony Traill. 1984. Linguistic phonetic descriptions of clicks. *Language* 60.1, 1–20.

Ladefoged, Peter & Anthony Traill. 1994. Clicks and their accompaniments. *Journal of Phonetics* 22, 33–64.

Lahiri, Aditi & Sheila E. Blumstein. 1984. A re-evaluation of the feature coronal. *Journal of Phonetics* 12.2, 133–46.

Lambert, Dakotah & James Rogers. 2019. A logical and computational methodology for exploring systems of phonotactic constraints. *Proceedings of the Society for Computation in Linguistics (SCiL)* 2019, 247–56.

Lass, Roger. 1975. How intrinsic is content? Markedness, sound change, and 'family universals'. In D. L. Goyvaerts & Geoffrey K. Pullum (eds.), *Essays on the sound pattern of English*, 475–504. Ghent: Story-Scientia.

Lass, Roger. 1976. *English phonology and phonological theory: Synchronic and diachronic studies*. Cambridge: Cambridge University Press.

Lass, Roger. 1984. *Phonology: An introduction to basic concepts*. Cambridge: Cambridge University Press.

Lass, Roger & John M. Anderson. 1975. *Old English phonology*. Cambridge: Cambridge University Press.

Laver, John. 1994. *Principles of phonetics*. Cambridge: Cambridge University Press.

Laver, John. 2009. *The phonetic description of voice quality*. Cambridge: Cambridge University Press.

Leben, William R. 1973. *Suprasegmental phonology*. PhD dissertation, MIT.

Lee-Kim, Sang-Im. 2014. Revisiting Mandarin 'apical vowels': An articulatory and acoustic study. *Journal of the International Phonetic Association* 44.3, 261–82. doi:10.1017/S0025100314000267

Lee, Seunghun Julio. 2008. *Consonant–tone interaction in Optimality Theory*. PhD dissertation, Rutgers University.
Lehiste, Ilse. 1970. *Suprasegmentals*. Cambridge, MA: MIT Press.
Leitch, Myles F. 1996. *Vowel harmonies of the Congo Basin: An Optimality Theory analysis of variation in the Bantu zone C*. PhD dissertation, University of British Columbia.
Levin, Juliette. 1985. *A metrical theory of syllabicity*. PhD dissertation, MIT.
Li, Bing. 1996. *Tungusic vowel harmony: Description and analysis*. PhD dissertation, University of Amsterdam.
Liberman, Alvin M. & Ignatius G. Mattingly. 1985. The motor theory of speech perception revised. *Cognition* 21.1, 1–36.
Liberman, Mark. 1975. *The intonational system of English*. PhD dissertation, MIT.
Liberman, Mark. 2017. Towards progress in theories of language sound structure. In Diane Brentari & Jackson L. Lee (eds.), *Shaping phonology*, 201–22. Chicago: University of Chicago Press.
Liberman, Mark & Janet Pierrehumbert. 1984. Intonational invariance under changes in pitch range and length. In Mark Aronoff & Richard Oehrle (eds.), *Language sound structure*, 157–233. Cambridge, MA: MIT Press.
Liberman, Mark & Alan Prince. 1977. On stress and linguistic rhythm. *Linguistic Inquiry* 8.2, 249–336.
Liddell, Scott K. 1980. *American Sign Language Syntax* (Approaches to Semiotics 52). The Hague: Mouton.
Liddell, Scott K. 1990. Structures for representing handshape and local movement at the phonemic level. In Susan D. Fischer & Patricia Siple (eds.), *Theoretical issues in sign language research*, vol. 1, 37–65. Chicago: University of Chicago Press.
Liddell, Scott K. & Robert E. Johnson. 1984. Structural diversity in the ASL lexicon. *Chicago Linguistic Society (CLS)* 20, 173–87.
Liddell, Scott K. & Robert E. Johnson. 1989. American Sign Language: The phonological base. *Sign Language Studies* 64, 197–277.
Lightner, Theodore M. 1968. On the use of minor rules in Russian phonology. *Journal of Linguistics* 4.1, 69–72.
Liljencrants, Johan & Bjorn Lindblom. 1972. Numerical simulation of vowel quality systems: The role of perceptual contrast. *Language* 48.4, 839–62.
Lin, Yen-Hwei. 2011. Affricates. In Marc van Oostendorp, Colin J. Ewen, Elizabeth Hume & Keren Rice (eds.), *The Blackwell companion to phonology*, vol. 1, 367–90. Oxford: Wiley-Blackwell.
Lindau, Mona. 1975. A phonetic explanation to reduced vowel harmony systems. *UCLA Working Papers in Phonetics* 11, 43–54.
Lindau, Mona. 1976. Larynx height in Kwa. *UCLA Working Papers in Linguistics* 31, 53–61.
Lindau, Mona. 1979. The feature [Expanded]. *Journal of Phonetics* 7, 163–76.

Lindblom, Bjorn. 1986. Phonetic universals in vowel systems. In John J. Ohala & Jeri Jaeger (eds.), *Experimental phonology*, 13–44. Orlando, FL: Academic Press.

Lindblom, Björn. 1990. Explaining phonetic variation: A sketch of the H&H theory. In William J. Hardcastle & Alain Marchal (eds.), *Speech production and speech modelling*, 403–39. Dordrecht: Kluwer.

Lindblom, Björn & Olle Engstrand. 1989. In what sense is speech quantal? *Journal of Phonetics* 17, 107–21.

Linnell, Per. 1979. *The psychological reality of Generative Phonology* (Cambridge Studies in Linguistics 25). Cambridge: Cambridge University Press.

Lisker, Leigh & Arthur S. Abramson. 1964. A cross-language study of voicing in initial stops: Acoustical measurements. *Word* 20.3, 384–422.

Lombardi, Linda. 1991. *Laryngeal features and laryngeal neutralization*. PhD dissertation, University of Massachusetts, Amherst. Published 1994, New York: Garland.

Lombardi, Linda. 1995a. Laryngeal features and privativity. *The Linguistic Review* 12, 35–59.

Lombardi, Linda. 1995b. Laryngeal neutralization and syllable wellformedness. *Natural Language & Linguistic Theory* 13.1, 39–74.

Lombardi, Linda. 2001. Why place and voice are different: Constraint-specific alternations in Optimality Theory. In Linda Lombardi (ed.), *Segmental phonology in Optimality Theory: Constraints and representations*, 13–45. Cambridge: Cambridge University Press.

Louwrens, Louis J., Ingeborg M. Kosch & Albert E. Kotzé. 1995. *Northern Sotho*. Munich: LINCOM.

Lowenstamm, Jean. 1996. CV as the only syllable type. In Jacques Durand & Bernard Laks (eds.), *Current trends in phonology: Models and methods*, 419–42. Salford: European Studies Research Institute.

McCarthy, J. 1979. *Formal problems in Semitic phonology and morphology*. PhD dissertation, MIT.

McCarthy, John J. 1988. Feature Geometry and dependency: A review. *Phonetica* 43, 84–108.

McCarthy, John J. 1990. Guttural phonology. MS, University of Massachusetts, Amherst.

McCarthy, John J. 1991. Semitic gutturals and distinctive feature theory. In Bernard Comrie & Mushira Eid (eds.), *Perspectives on Arabic linguistics*, 63–91. Amsterdam and Philadelphia: John Benjamins.

McCarthy, John J. 1994. The phonetics and phonology of Semitic pharyngeals. In Patricia A. Keating (ed.), *Papers in Laboratory Phonology III: Phonological Structure and Phonetic Form*, 191–233. Cambridge: Cambridge University Press.

McCarthy, John J. 2010. An introduction to harmonic serialism. *Language and Linguistics Compass* 4.10, 1001–18.

McCawley, John J. 1967. Le rôle d'un système de traits phonologiques dans une théorie du langage. *Langages* 8: 112–123. Published 1972, in the original English, as 'The role of a phonological feature system in a theory of language' in Valerie B. Makkai (ed.), *Phonological theory: Evolution and current practice*, 522–528. New York: Holt, Rinehart and Winston.

McGurk, Harry & John MacDonald. 1976. Hearing lips and seeing voices. *Nature* 264, 746–8.

McLeod, Sharynne & Kathryn Crowe. 2018. Children's consonant acquisition in 27 languages: A cross-linguistic review. *American Journal of Speech-Language Pathology* 27.4, 1546–71.

McMurray, Bob, Richard N. Aslin & Joseph C. Toscano. 2009. Statistical learning of phonetic categories: Insights from a computational approach. *Developmental Science* 12.3, 369–78.

MacNeilage, Peter F. 2008. *The origin of speech*. Oxford: Oxford University Press.

Maddieson, Ian. 1984. *Patterns of sounds*. Cambridge: Cambridge University Press.

Maddieson, Ian. 1989a. Aerodynamic constraints on sound change: The case of bilabial trills. *UCLA Working Papers in Phonetics* 72, 91–115.

Maddieson, Ian. 1989b. Linguo-labials. In R. Harlow & R. Cooper (eds.), *VICAL 1: Oceanic languages, part 2*, 349–76. Auckland: Linguistic Society of New Zealand.

Maddieson, Ian. 2006a. Bilabial and labio-dental fricatives in Ewe. *Studies in African Linguistics* 35 (Suppl. 11), 159–75.

Maddieson, Ian. 2006b. Correlating phonological complexity: Data and validation. *Linguistic Typology* 10.1, 106–23.

Maddieson, Ian. 2007. Issues of phonological complexity: Statistical analysis of the relationship between syllable structures, segment inventories and tone contrasts. In M-J. Solé, P. Beddor & M. Ohala (eds.), *Experimental Approaches to Phonology*, 93–103. New York: Oxford University Press.

Maddieson, Ian. 2009a. Calculating phonological complexity. In François Pellegrino, Egidio Marsico, Ioana Chitoran & Christophe Coupé (eds.), *Approaches to phonological complexity*, 83–110. Berlin and New York: Mouton de Gruyter.

Maddieson, Ian. 2009b. Prenasalized stops and speech timing. *Journal of the International Phonetic Association* 19.2, 57–66.

Maddieson, Ian. 2010. Correlating syllable complexity with other measures of phonological complexity. *Phonological Studies* 13, 105–16.

Maddieson, Ian & Peter Ladefoged. 1993. Phonetics of partially nasal consonants. In Marie K. Huffman & Rena A. Krakow (eds.), *Phonetics and phonology* (Phonetics and Phonology 5), 251–301. San Diego, CA: Academic Press.

Maddieson, Ian & Kristin Precoda. 1992. Syllable structure and phonetic models. *Phonology* 9.1, 45–60.

Mandel, Mark A. 1981. *Phonotactics and morphophonology in American Sign Language*. PhD dissertation, University of California, Berkeley.

Maran, La Raw. 1971. *Burmese and Jingpho: A study of tonal linguistic processes* (Occasional Papers of the Wolfenden Society on Tibeto-Burman Linguistics 4). Urbana: Center for Asian Studies, University of illinois.

Marcus, Solomon. 1967. *Algebraic linguistics; Analytical models*. New York: Academic Press.

Markó, Alexandra, Tekla Etelka Fráczi & Judit Bóna. 2010. The realization of voicing assimilation rules in Hungarian spontaneous and read speech: Case studies. *Acta Linguistica Hungarica* 57.2–3, 210–38.

Marlett, S. A. & Joseph P. Stemberger. 1983. Empty consonants in Seri. *Linguistic Inquiry* 14.4, 617–39.

Martinet, André. 1948. Phonologie. *École Pratique des Hautes Études, Section des Sciences Historiques et Philologiques* 80.1, 54–5.

Martinet, André. 1949. La double articulation linguistique. *Travaux du Cercle Linguistique de Copenhague* 5, 30–7.

Mascaró, Joan. 1984. Continuant spreading in Basque, Catalan and Spanish. In Mark Aronoff & Richard T. Oehrle (eds.), *Language sound structure*, 287–98. Cambridge, MA: MIT Press.

Mascaró, Joan. 1986. Compensatory diphthongization in Majorcan Catalan. In W. Leo Wetzels & Engin Sezer (eds.), *Studies in compensatory lengthening*, 133–46. Dordrecht: Foris.

Maye, Jessica & LouAnn Gerken. 2000. Learning phonemes without minimal pairs. In S. Catherine Howell, Sarah A. Fish & Thea Keith-Lucas (eds.), *Proceedings of the 24th Boston Conference on Language Development*, 522–33. Somerville, MA: Cascadilla.

Melis, Ed. 1976. Fonologische verschijnselen in onderlinge samenhang: Een hypothese. In Geert Koefoed & Arnold Evers (eds.), *Lijnen van taaltheoretisch onderzoek*, 367–80. Groningen: H. D. Tjeenk Willink.

Mester, R. Armin. 1988. *Studies in tier structure*. PhD dissertation, University of Massachusetts, Amherst.

Mielke, Jeff. 2005. Ambivalence and ambiguity in laterals and nasals. *Phonology* 22.2, 169–203.

Mielke, Jeff. 2008. *The emergence of distinctive features*. Oxford: Oxford University Press.

Miller, Amanda. 2011. The representation of clicks. In Marc van Oostendorp, Colin J. Ewen, Elizabeth Hume & Keren Rice (eds.), *The Blackwell companion to phonology*, vol. 1, 416–39. Oxford: Wiley-Blackwell.

Miller, Amanda L. 2017. Palatal click allophony in Mangetti Dune !Xung: Implications for sound change. *Journal of the International Phonetic Association* 47.3, 1–29.

Miller, Amanda L., Levi Namaseb & Khalil Iskarous. 2007. Tongue body constriction differences in click types. *Laboratory Phonology* 9, 643–56.

Miller, Brett. 2012. *Feature patterns: Their sources and status in grammar and reconstruction*. PhD dissertation, Trinity College, University of Cambridge.

Milner, George B. 1956. *Fijian grammar*. Suva: Fiji Government Printer.

Mohanan, K. P. 1983. The structure of the melody. MS, MIT and National University of Singapore.

Moisik, Scott R. 2013. *The epilarynx in speech*. PhD dissertation, University of Victoria.

Moisik, Scott R., Ewa Czaykowska-Higgins & John H. Esling. 2011. The epilaryngeal articulator: A new conceptual tool for understanding lingual–laryngeal contrasts. In Jenny Loughran & Alanah McKillen (eds.), *Proceedings from Phonology in the 21st Century: In Honour of Glyne Piggott. McGill Working Papers in Linguistics* 22.1, 210–24. Toronto: McGill University.

Morelli, Frida. 1999. *The phonotactics and phonology of obstruent clusters in Optimality Theory*. PhD dissertation, University of Maryland at College Park.

Morén, Bruce. 2003. The parallel structures model of Feature Geometry. *Working Papers of Cornell Phonetics Laboratory* 15, 194–270.

Morén, Bruce. 2007. Minimalist/substance-free feature theory: Case studies and implications. MS/handout at the Eastern European Generative Grammar Summer School (Brno, August 6–10).

Morton, Deborah. 2012. [ATR] harmony in an eleven vowel language: The case of Anii. In Michael R. Marlo, Nikki B. Adams, Christopher R. Green, Michelle Morrison and Tristan M. Purvis (eds.), *Selected Proceedings of the 42nd Annual Conference on African Linguistics*, 70–8. Somerville, MA: Cascadilla.

Mous, Maarten & Harry van der Hulst. 1992. Transparent consonants. In Roeland van Hout & Reineke Bok-Bennema (eds.), *Linguistics in the Netherlands*, 101–12. Amsterdam and Philadelphia: John Benjamins.

Murray, R. W. & Theo Vennemann. 1983. Sound change and syllable structure in Germanic phonology. *Language* 59.3, 514–28.

Mutlu, Filiz. 2020. Embedding of the same type in phonology. In Phillip Backley & Kuniya Nasukawa (eds.), *Morpheme-internal recursion in phonology*, 177–200. Berlin and New York: Mouton de Gruyter.

Nasukawa, Kuniya. 2005. *A unified approach to nasality and voicing*. Berlin and New York: Walter de Gruyter.

Nasukawa, Kuniya. 2015. Features and recursive structure. *Nordlyd* 41.1, 1–19.

Nasukawa, Kuniya. 2016. A precedence-free approach to (de-)palatalisation in Japanese. *Glossa: A Journal of General Linguistics* 1.1, 9. doi:10.5334/gjgl.26

Nasukawa, Kuniya. 2017. The phonetic salience of phonological head-dependent structure in a modulated-carrier model of speech. In Bridget Samuels (ed.), *Beyond markedness in formal phonology* (Linguistik Aktuell), 121–52. Amsterdam and Philadelphia: John Benjamins.

Nasukawa, Kuniya & Philip Backley. 2005. Dependency relations in Element Theory. In Nancy C. Kula & Jeroen van de Weijer (eds.), *Proceedings of the Government Phonology Workshop (Leiden, 3 December 2004)*, vol. 2, 77–93. Special issue of *Leiden Papers in Linguistics*.

Nasukawa, Kuniya & Phillip Backley. 2015. Heads and complements in phonology: A case of role reversal? *Phonological Studies* 18, 67–74.

Nathan, Geoffrey S. 2009. Is the phoneme usage-based? Some issues. *International Journal of English Studies* 6.2, 141–72.

Navarro, Sylvain. 2018. Rhotics and the derhoticization of English: A Dependency Phonology analysis. In Roger Böhm & Harry van der Hulst (eds.), *Substance-based grammar: The (ongoing) work of John Anderson* (Studies in Language Companion Series 204), 339–64. Amsterdam and Philadelphia: John Benjamins.

Nazarov, Aleksei. 2014. A radically emergentist approach to phonological features: Implications for grammars. *Nordlyd* 41.1, 21–58.

Neeleman, Ad & Hans van de Koot. 2006. On syntactic and phonological representations. *Lingua* 116.10, 1524–52.

Nepveu, Denis. 1994. *Georgian and Bella Coola: Headless syllables and syllabic obstruents*. MA dissertation, University of California, Santa Cruz.

Newkirk, Donald. 1981. On the temporal segmentation of movement in American Sign Language. MS, Salk Institute of Biological Studies, La Jolla, California. Published 1988, *Sign Language & Linguistics* 8/1–2: 173–211.

Newman, Paul. 1986. Contour tones as phonemic primes in Grebo. In Koen Bogers, Harry van der Hulst & Norval Smith (eds.), *The phonological representation of suprasegmentals*, 175–94. Dordrecht: Foris.

Newman, Stanley. 1947. Bella Coola I: Phonology. *International Journal of American Linguistics* 13.3, 129–34.

Newman, Stanley. 1971. Bella Coola reduplication. *International Journal of American Linguistics* 37.1, 34–8. doi:10.1086/465133

Novikova, Klara A. 1960. *Ocherki dialektov Evenskogo jazyka: Ol'skij govor*, vol. 1. Leningrad: Nauka.

Odden, David. 1991. Vowel geometry. *Phonology* 8.2, 261–89.

Odden, David. 2013. *Introducing phonology*, 2nd edn (Cambridge Introductions to Language and Linguistics). Cambridge: Cambridge University Press.

Odden, David. to appear. Tone in African languages. In Rainer Vossen & Gerrit J. Dimmendaal (eds.), *Handbook of African languages*. Oxford: Oxford University Press.

Ohala, John J. 1975. Phonetic explanations for nasal sound patterns. In Charles A. Ferguson, Larry M. Hyman & John J. Ohala (eds.), *Nasalfest: Papers from a symposium on nasals and nasalization*, 289–316. Stanford: Stanford University.

Olson, Kenneth S. & John Hajek. 2003. Crosslinguistic insights on the labial flap. *Linguistic Typology* 7.2, 157–86.

Olson, Kenneth S. & John Hajek. 2004. A crosslinguistic lexicon of the labial flap. *Linguistic Discovery* 2.2, 21–57.

Olson, Kenneth S. & David Mbiri Koogibho. 2013. Labial vibrants in Mangbetu. *Afrikanistik Aegyptologie Online*, <http://www.afrikanistik-online.de/archiv/2013/3851> (last accessed 21 January 2020).

Olson, Kenneth S., D. William Reiman, Fernando Sabio & Filipe Alberto da Silva. 2009. The voiced linguolabial plosive in Kajoko. *Chicago Linguistic Society (CLS)* 45.1, 519–30.

Otelemate, Harry. 2004. *Aspects of the tonal system of Kalabari-Ijo*. Stanford: CSLI.

Paradis, Carole & Jean-François Prunet. 1991. *The special status of coronals: Internal and external evidence*. San Diego, CA: Academic Press.

Parker, Stephen G. 2012a. *The sonority controversy*. Boston: Mouton de Gruyter.

Parker, Stephen G. 2012b. Sonority distance vs. sonority dispersion: A typological survey. In Steve Parker (ed.), *The sonority controversy* (Phonology and Phonetics 18), 101–65. Berlin and New York: Mouton de Gruyter.

Parker, Stephen G. 2016. Reconsidering sonority dispersion and liquid vs. glide offsets: What do the typological facts indicate? *WINAK: Revista de Estudios Interculturales* 26, 11–42.

Paulian, Christiane. 1975. *Le Kukuya: Langue Teke du Congo (Phonologie; Classes nominales)* (Bibliothèque de la SELAF 49–50). Paris: SELAF.

Percival, W. Keith. 1990. Reflections on the history of dependency notions in linguistics. *Historiographia linguistica* 17.1–2, 29–47.

Perlmutter, David M. 1992. Sonority and syllable structure in American Sign Language. *Linguistic Inquiry* 23.3, 407–42.

Perniss, Pamela, Robin L. Thompson & Gabriella Vigliocco. 2007. Iconicity as a general property of language: Evidence from spoken and signed languages. *Frontiers in Psychology* 1, 1–15. doi:10.3389/fpsyg.2010.00227

Phillips, Colin. 1994. Are feature hierarchies autosegmental hierarchies? *MIT Working Papers in Linguistics* 21, 173–226.

Pierrehumbert, Janet B. 1980. *The phonology and phonetics of English intonation*. PhD dissertation, MIT.

Piggott, Glyne L. 1988. Prenasalization and Feature Geometry. *Proceedings of the North East Linguistic Society (NELS)* 19, 345–52.

Piggott, Glyne L. 1992. Variability in feature dependency: The case of nasality. *Natural Language & Linguistic Theory* 10.1, 33–77.

Pike, Kenneth L. 1947. *Phonemics: A technique for reducing languages to writing*. Ann Arbor, MI: University of Michigan Press.

Pike, Kenneth L. & E. V. Pike. 1947. Immediate constituents of Mazateco syllables. *International Journal of American Linguistics* 13.2, 78–91.

Pinker, Steven & Ray Jackendoff. 2005. The faculty of language: What's special about it? *Cognition* 95, 201–36.

Piriyawiboon, Nattaya. 2007. Coda restrictions in Italian and Menominee. Paper presented at Coronals Workshop, University of Toronto.

Pöchtrager, Markus A. 2006. *The structure of length*. PhD dissertation, University of Vienna.

Pöchtrager, Markus A. 2015. Binding in phonology. In Marc van Oostendorp & Henk van Riemsdijk (eds.), *Representing structure in phonology and syntax*, 255–75. Berlin and New York: Mouton de Gruyter.

Pöchtrager, Markus A. 2018. Sawing off the branch you are sitting on. *Acta Linguistica Academica* 65.1, 47–68. doi:10.1556/2062.2018.65.1.3

Pöchtrager, Markus A. 2020. Recursion and GP 2.0. In Phillip Backley & Kuniya Nasukawa (eds.), *Morpheme-internal recursion in phonology*, 231–58. Berlin and New York: Mouton de Gruyter.

Pöchtrager, Markus A. & Jonathan Kaye. 2013. GP 2.0. *SOAS Working Papers in Linguistics and Phonetics* 16, 51–64.

Polgárdi, Krisztina. 1998. *Vowel harmony: An account in terms of government and optimality*. PhD dissertation, Leiden University.

Poppe, Clemens. 2020. Head, dependent, or both: Structural dependency between elements in vowels. In Kuniya Nasukawa (ed.), *Morpheme-internal recursion in phonology*. Berlin and New York: Mouton de Gruyter.

Poser, William J. 1979. *Nasal contour consonants and the concept of segment in phonological theory*. BA dissertation, Harvard University.

Prince, Alan. 1975. *The phonology and morphology of Tiberian Hebrew*. PhD dissertation, MIT.

Prince, A. and P. Smolensky. 1993. *Optimality Theory & Constraint Interaction in Generative Grammar*. Technical Report no. 2 of the Rutgers Center for Cognitive Pulleyblank, Douglas. 1986. *Tone in Lexical Phonology*. Dordrecht: Reidel.

Pullum, Geoffrey K. & William A. Ladusaw. 1996. *Phonetic symbol guide*. Chicago: University of Chicago Press.

Reiss, Charles. 2018. Substance-free phonology. In S. J. Hannahs & Anna R. K. Bosch (eds.), *The Routledge handbook of phonological theory* (Routledge Handbooks in Linguistics), 425–52. London: Routledge.

Rennison, John R. 1984. On tridirectional feature systems for vowels. *Wiener Linguistische Gazette* 33–4, 69–94.

Rennison, John R. 1986. On tridirectional feature systems for vowels. In Jacques Durand (ed.), *Dependency and non-linear phonology*, 281–303. London: Croom Helm.

Rennison, John R. 1987. Vowel harmony and tridirectional vowel features. *Folia Linguistica* 21.2–4, 337–54.

Rennison, John R. 1990. On the elements of phonological representations: The evidence from vowel systems and vowel processes. *Folia Linguistica* 24, 175–244.

Repetti, Lori (ed.) 2000. *Phonological theory and the dialects of Italy* (Current Issues in Linguistic Theory 212). Amsterdam and Philadelphia: John Benjamins.

Riad, Tomas. 2014. *The phonology of Swedish* (Phonology of the World's Languages). Oxford: Oxford University Press.

Rice, Keren. 1992. On deriving sonority: A structural account of sonority relationships. *Phonology* 9.1, 61–99.

Rice, Keren. 1993. A reexamination of the feature [sonorant]: The status of sonorant obstruents. *Language* 69.2, 308–44.

Rice, Keren. 1995. On vowel place features. *Toronto Working Papers in Linguistics* 14, 73–116.
Rice, Keren. 2007. Markedness in phonology. In Paul de Lacy (ed.), *The Cambridge Handbook of Phonology*, 79–97. Cambridge: Cambridge University Press.
Rice, Keren & Peter Avery. 1989. On the interaction between sonorancy and voicing. *Toronto Working Papers in Linguistics* 10, 65–82.
Rice, Keren & Peter Avery. 1990. On the interaction between sonorancy and voicing. *Proceedings of the North East Linguistic Society (NELS)* 20, 428–42.
Rice, Keren & Peter Avery. 1991. On the relationship between laterality and coronality. In Carole Paradis & Jean-François Prunet (eds.), *The special status of coronals: Internal and external evidence*, 101–24. San Diego, CA: Academic Press.
Ridouane, Rachid & Pierre A. Hallé. 2017. Word-initial geminates: From production to perception. In Haruo Kubozono (ed.), *The phonetics and phonology of geminate consonants* (Oxford Studies in Phonology and Phonetics), 66–84. Oxford: Oxford University Press.
Riehl, Anastasia K. & Abigail C. Cohn. 2011. Partially nasal segments. In Marc van Oostendorp, Colin J. Ewen, Elizabeth Hume & Keren Rice (eds.), *The Blackwell companion to phonology*, vol. 1, 550–77. Oxford: Wiley-Blackwell.
Ringen, Catherine O. 1975. *Vowel harmony: Theoretical implications*. PhD dissertation, Indiana University. Published 1988, New York: Garland.
Ringen, Catherine O. 1978. Another view of the theoretical implications of Hungarian vowel harmony. *Linguistic Inquiry* 9.1, 105–15.
Ritter, Nancy A. 1995. *The role of Universal Grammar in phonology: A Government Phonology approach to Hungarian*. PhD dissertation, New York University.
Ritter, Nancy A. 1997. Headedness as a means of encoding stricture. In Geert E. Booij & Jeroen van de Weijer (eds.), *Phonology in progress: Progress in phonology* (HIL Phonology Papers II), 333–65. The Hague: Holland Academic Graphics.
Ritter, Nancy A. 2000. Hungarian voicing assimilation revisited in Head-Driven Phonology. In Gábor Alberti & István Kenesei (eds.), *Approaches to Hungarian 7 (Papers from the Pécs conference)*, 23–50. Szeged: JATE Press.
Ritter, Nancy A. 2005. On the status of linguistics as a cognitive science. *The Linguistic Review* (special issue) 22.2–4, 117–33.
Ritter, Nancy A. 2006. Georgian consonant clusters: The complexity is in the structure, not the melody. *The Linguistic Review* 23.4, 429–64.
Ritter, Nancy A. to appear. Government Phonology. In B. Elan Dresher & Harry van der Hulst (eds.), *The handbook of the (early) history of phonology*. Oxford: Oxford University Press.
Robinson, Jane J. 1970. Dependency structures and transformational rules. *Language* 46.2, 259–85. doi:10.2307/412278
Rood, David S. 1975. The implications of Wichita phonology. *Language* 51.2, 315–37.

Rose, Sharon. 1996. Variable laryngeals and vowel lowering. *Phonology* 13, 73–117.
Rosenthall, Sam. 1992. Prenasalized stops and Feature Geometry. In Wolfgang U. Dressler, Hans C. Luschützky, Oskar E. Pfeiffer & John R. Rennison (eds.), *Phonologica 1988: Proceedings of the Sixth International Phonology Meeting*, 249–58. Cambridge: Cambridge University Press.
Round, Erich R. 2011. Word final phonology in Lardil: Implications of an expanded data set. *Australian Journal of Linguistics* 31.3, 327–50.
Rowicka, Grażyna J. 1999a. *Ghost vowels: A strict CV approach*. PhD dissertation, Leiden University.
Rowicka, Grażyna J. 1999b. On trochaic proper government. In John R. Rennison & Klaus Kühnhammer (eds.), *Phonologica 1996: Syllables!?*, 273–88. The Hague: Thesus.
Rowicka, Grażyna J. & Jeroen van de Weijer. 1992. Nasal vowels in Polish. In Sjef Barbiers, Marcel den Dikken & Clara Levelt (eds.), *Leiden Conference for Junior Linguists*, vol. 3, 219–31. Leiden: HIL.
Rubach, Jerzy & Geert E. Booij. 1990. Edge of constituent effects in Polish. *Natural Language & Linguistic Theory* 8.3, 427–63.
Ruhlen, M. 1991. *A guide to the world's languages: Classification*. Stanford: Stanford University Press.
Saffran, Jenny R., E. Newport & R. Aslin. 1996. Statistical learning by eight-month-old infants. *Science* 274, 1926–8.
Sagey, Elizabeth C. 1986. *The representation of features and relations in non-linear phonology*. PhD dissertation, MIT.
Sagey, Elizabeth C. 1988. Degree of closure in complex segments. In Harry van der Hulst & Norval Smith (eds.), *Features, segmental structure and harmony processes*, vol. 1, 170–208. Dordrecht: Foris.
Sagey, Elizabeth C. 1990. *The representation of features in non-linear phonology: The articulator node hierarchy*. New York: Garland.
Salting, Don. 1998. *The nested subregister model of vowel height*. PhD dissertation, Indiana University.
Salting, Don. 2004. Feature diagrams in phonology. In Alan Blackwell, Kim Marriott & Atsushi Shimojima (eds.), *Diagrammatic representation and inference* (Lecture Notes in Computer Science 2980), 398–401. Berlin and Heidelberg: Springer.
Salting, Don. 2005. The geometry of harmony. In Marc van Oostendorp & Jeroen van de Weijer (eds.), *The internal organization of phonological segments*, 93–120. Berlin: Mouton de Gruyter.
Samarin, William J. 1966. *The Gbeya language: Grammar, texts, and vocabularies*. Berkeley and Los Angeles: University of California Press.
Sanders, Gerald. 1972. *The simplex feature hypothesis*. Bloomington: Indiana University Linguistics Club.
Sandler, Wendy. 1986. The spreading hand autosegment of American Sign Language. *Sign Language Studies* 50.1, 1–28.

Sandler, Wendy. 1989. *Phonological representation of the sign: Linearity and nonlinearity in American Sign Language*. Dordrecht: Foris.

Sandler, Wendy. 1993. A sonority cycle in American Sign Language. *Phonology* 10.2, 243–79.

Sandler, Wendy. 1995. Markedness in the handshapes of sign language: A componential analysis. In Harry van der Hulst & Jeroen van de Weijer (eds.), *Leiden in last* (HIL Phonology Papers I), 369–99. The Hague: Holland Academic Graphics.

Sandler, Wendy. 2008. The syllable in sign language: Considering the other natural modality. In Barbara L. Davis & Krisztina Zajdo (eds.), *The syllable in speech production*, 379–408. New York: Taylor & Francis.

Sandler, Wendy. 2011. The phonology of movement in sign language. In Marc van Oostendorp, Colin J. Ewen, Keren Rice & Elizabeth Hume (eds.), *The Blackwell companion to phonology*, vol. 5, 577–603. Oxford: Wiley-Blackwell.

Sandler, Wendy. 2012. The phonological organization of sign languages. *Language and Linguistics Compass* 6.3, 162–82.

Sandler, Wendy. 2014. The emergence of phonetic and phonological features in sign language. *Nordlyd* 41.1, 183–212.

Sands, Bonny E. & Tom Güldemann. 2009. What click languages can and can't tell us about language origins. In Rudolf Botha & Chris Knight (eds.), *The cradle of language*, 204–18. Oxford: Oxford University Press.

Sawashima, M. & Hajime Hirose. 1983. Laryngeal gestures in speech production. In Peter F. MacNeilage (ed.), *The production of speech*, 11–38. New York: Springer.

Schadeberg, T. C. 1982. Nasalization in UMbundu. *Journal of African Languages and Linguistics* 4, 109–32.

Schane, Sanford A. 1971. The phoneme revisited. *Language* 47.3, 503–21.

Schane, Sanford A. 1973. [back] and [round]. In Stephen R. Anderson & Paul Kiparsky (eds.), *A Festschrift for Morris Halle*, 174–84. New York: Holt, Rinehart and Winston.

Schane, Sanford A. 1984. The fundamentals of Particle Phonology. *Phonology Yearbook* 1, 129–55.

Schane, Sanford A. 1985. An introduction to Particle Phonology. *Linguistic Notes from La Jolla* 12, 1–17.

Schane, Sanford A. 1990. Lowered height, laxness, and retracted tongue root: Different manifestations of phonological aperture. *Word* 41.1, 1–16.

Schane, Sanford A. 1995. Diphthongization in Particle Phonology. In John Goldsmith (ed.), *The handbook of phonological theory*, 586–605. Oxford: Blackwell.

Schane, Sanford A. 2005. The aperture particle |a|: Its role and functions. In Philip Carr, Jacques Durand & Colin J. Ewen (eds.), *Headhood, elements, specification and contrastivity*, 313–38. Amsterdam and Philadelphia: John Benjamins.

Scheer, Tobias. 1998. A unified model of Proper Government. *The Linguistic Review* 15.1, 41–68.

Scheer, Tobias. 2004. *A lateral theory of phonology: What is CVCV, and why should it be?* Berlin: Mouton de Gruyter.

Scheer, Tobias. 2008. Syllabic and trapped consonants in (Western) Slavic: Different but still the same. MS, Université de Nice.

Scheer, Tobias. 2010. Why Russian vowel–zero alternations are not different, and why Lower is correct. *Journal of Language and Verbal Behaviour (St Petersburg)* 9, 77–112.

Scheer, Tobias. 2011. *A guide to morphosyntax–phonology interface theories.* Berlin and New York: Walter de Gruyter.

Scheer, Tobias. 2013. Why phonology is flat: The role of concatenation and linearity. Paper presented at the 11th Rencontres du Réseau Phonologique Français, Nantes.

Scheer, Tobias & Eugeniusz Cyran. 2018a. Interfaces in Government Phonology. In S. J. Hannahs & Anna R. K. Bosch (eds.), *The Routledge handbook of phonological theory* (Routledge Handbooks in Linguistics), 293–324. London: Routledge.

Scheer, Tobias & Eugeniusz Cyran. 2018b. Syllable structure in Government Phonology. In S. J. Hannahs & Anna R. K. Bosch (eds.), *The Routledge handbook of phonological theory* (Routledge Handbooks in Linguistics), 262–92. London: Routledge.

Scheer, Tobias & Nancy C. Kula. 2018. Government Phonology: Element Theory, conceptual issues and introduction. In S. J. Hannahs & Anna R. K. Bosch (eds.), *The Routledge handbook of phonological theory* (Routledge Handbooks in Linguistics), 226–61. London: Routledge.

Schein, Barry & Donca Steriade. 1986. On geminates. *Linguistic Inquiry* 17.4, 691–744.

Schütz, Albert J. 1994. *The voices of Eden: A history of Hawaiian language studies.* Honolulu: University of Hawai'i Press.

Schwartz, Geoffrey. 2020. Defining recursive entities in phonology: The Onset Prominence framework. In Phillip Backley & Kuniya Nasukawa (eds.), *Morpheme-internal recursion in phonology*, 297–316. Berlin and New York: Mouton de Gruyter.

Schwartz, Jean-Luc, Louis-Jean Boë, Nathalie Vallee & Christian Abry. 1997. Major trends in vowel system inventories. *Journal of Phonetics* 25, 233–53.

Scobbie, James M. 1991. *Attribute-value phonology.* PhD dissertation, University of Edinburgh.

Scobbie, James M. 1992. Towards declarative phonology. In Steven Bird (ed.), *Declarative perspectives on phonology*, 1–26. Edinburgh: University of Edinburgh.

Sedlak, Philip. 1969. Typological considerations of vowel quality systems. *Working Papers on Language Universals (Stanford)* 1, 1–40.

Selkirk, Elisabeth O. 1980. *On prosodic structure and its relation to syntactic structure.* Bloomington: Indiana University Linguistics Club.

Selkirk, Elisabeth O. 1984. On the major class features and syllable theory. In Mark Aronoff & Richard T. Oehrle (eds.), *Language sound structure*, 107–36. Cambridge, MA: MIT Press.

Selkirk, Elisabeth O. 2011. The syntax–phonology interface. In John A. Goldsmith, Jason Riggle & Alan Yu (eds.), *The handbook of phonological theory*, 2nd edn, 435–84. Oxford: Wiley-Blackwell.

Seo, Misun. 2011. The syllable contact law. In Marc van Oostendorp, Colin J. Ewen, Elizabeth V. Hume & Keren Rice (eds.), *The Blackwell companion to phonology*, vol. 2, 1245–62. Oxford: Wiley-Blackwell.

Shaw, Patricia A. 1991. Consonant harmony systems: The special status of coronal harmony. In Carole Paradis & Jean-François Prunet (eds.), *The special status of coronals: Internal and external evidence*, 125–57. San Diego, CA: Academic Press.

Sheehan, Michelle & Jenneke van der Wal. 2018. Nominal licensing in caseless languages. *Journal of Linguistics* 54.3, 527–89. doi:10.1017/s0022226718000178

Sherrington, Charles. 1947. *The integrative action of the nervous system*, 2nd edn. New Haven: Yale University Press.

Shih, Stephanie S. & Sharon Inkelas. 2014. A subsegmental correspondence approach to contour tone (dis)harmony patterns. In John Kingston, Claire Moore-Cantwell, Joe Pater & Amanda Rysling (eds.), *Proceedings of the 2013 Meeting on Phonology*. Washington, DC: Linguistic Society of America.

Shih, Stephanie S. & Sharon Inkelas. 2019a. Autosegmental aims in surface optimizing phonology. *Linguistic Inquiry* 50.1, 137–96.

Shih, Stephanie S. & Sharon Inkelas. 2019b. Q-Theory representations are logically equivalent to autosegmental representations. In Nick Danis & Adam Jardine (eds.), *Proceedings of the Society for Computation in Linguistics (SCiL) 2019*, 29–38.

Siegel, Dorothy C. 1974. *Topics in English morphology*. PhD dissertation, MIT.

Silverman, Daniel. 1997. *Phasing and recoverability*. London: Routledge.

Silverman, Daniel. 2012. *Neutralization*. Cambridge: Cambridge University Press.

Silverman, Daniel. 2017. *A critical introduction to phonology: Functional and usage-based perspectives* (Bloomsbury Critical Introductions to Linguistics). London and New York: Bloomsbury.

Singler, John V. 2008. The restructuring of the Klao vowel system and its morphophonemic consequences. Handout of paper presented at the Association of Contemporary African Linguistics 39, 18 April 2008.

Siple, Patricia. 1978. Visual constraints for sign language communication. *Sign Language Studies* 19, 97–112.

Siptár, Péter. 1996. A Janus-faced Hungarian consonant. *The Even Yearbook* 2, 83–96.

Skousen, Royal. 1975. *Substantive evidence in phonology: The evidence from Finnish and French*. The Hague: Mouton.

Slis, I. H. 1986. Assimilation of voice in Dutch as a function of stress, word boundaries, and sex of speaker and listener. *Journal of Phonetics* 14, 311–26.

Sloos, Marjoleine, Yunyun Ran & Jeroen van de Weijer. 2018. Register, tone, and consonant–vowel coarticulation. In Katarzyna Klessa, Jolanta Bachan, Agnieszka Wagner, Maciej Karpiński & Daniel Śledziński (eds.), *Proceedings of the 9th International Conference on Speech Prosody, Poznań*, 15–9. Poznań: International Speech Communication Association.

Smeets, Ineke. 2008. *A grammar of Mapuche* (Mouton Grammar Library 41). Berlin and New York: Mouton de Gruyter.

Smith, Jennifer L. 2002. *Phonological augmentation in prominent positions*. PhD dissertation, University of Massachusetts, Amherst.

Smith, Jennifer L. 2003. Onset sonority constraints and subsyllabic structure. *Rutgers Optimality Archive* 608, <http://roa.rutgers.edu/article/view/618> (last accessed 22 January 2020).

Smith, Jennifer L. 2007. Representational complexity in syllable structure and its consequences for Gen and Con. In Sylvia Blaho, Patrik Bye & Martin Krämer (eds.), *Freedom of analysis?*, 257–80. Berlin and New York: Mouton de Gruyter.

Smith, Jennifer L. 2008. Phonological constraints are not directly phonetic. *Chicago Linguistic Society (CLS)* 41.1, 457–71.

Smith, Norval. 1988. Consonant place features. In Harry van der Hulst & Norval Smith (eds.), *Features, segmental structure and harmony processes*, vol. 1, 209–35. Dordrecht: Foris.

Smith, Norval. 1999. A preliminary account of some aspects of Leurbost Gaelic syllable structure. In Harry van der Hulst & Nancy A. Ritter (eds.), *The syllable: Views and facts*, 557–630. Berlin and New York: Mouton de Gruyter.

Smith, Norval. 2000. Dependency theory meets OT: A proposal for a new approach to segmental structure. In Joost Dekkers, Frank van der Leeuw & Jeroen van de Weijer (eds.), *Optimality Theory: Phonology, syntax, and acquisition*, 234–76. Oxford: Oxford University Press.

Smith, Norval. 2003. Evidence for recursive syllable structures in Aluku and Sranan. In Dany Adone (ed.), *Recent developments in creole studies* (Linguistische Arbeiten 472), 31–52. Berlin and New York: Mouton de Gruyter.

Smith, Norval & Bert Botma. 2007. A dependency-based typology of nasalisation and voicing phenomena. In Bettelou Los & Marjo van Koppen (eds.), *Linguistics in the Netherlands 2007*, 36–48. Amsterdam and Philadelphia: John Benjamins.

Smith, Norval, Heleen de Wit & Roland Noske. 1988. Yurok retroflex harmony. MS, University of Amsterdam.

Snider, Keith L. 1984. Vowel harmony and the consonant /l/ in Chumburung. *Studies in African Linguistics* 15.1, 47–57.

Snider, Keith L. 1988. Towards the representation of tone: A three-dimensional approach. In Harry van der Hulst & Norval Smith (eds.), *Features, segmental structure and harmony processes*, vol. 1, 237–69.

Snider, Keith L. 1990a. *Studies in Guang phonology*. PhD dissertation, Leiden University.

Snider, Keith L. 1990b. Tonal upstep in Krachi: Evidence for a register tier. *Language* 66.3, 453–74.

Snider, Keith L. 1999. *The geometry and features of tone.* Dallas: Summer Institute of Linguistics and the University of Texas at Arlington.

Snider, Keith and Harry van der Hulst. 1993. Issues in the representation of tonal register. In Harry van der Hulst and Keith Snider (eds.), *The representation of tonal register*, 1–27. Berlin and New York: Mouton de Gruyter.

Snoeren, Natalie D. & Juan Segui. 2003. A voice for the voiceless: Voice assimilation in French. In Maria-Josep Soleĭ, Recasens Daniel & Joaquin Romero (eds.), *Proceedings of the 15th International Congress of Phonetic Sciences*, 2325–8.

Snyman, J. W. 1978. The clicks of Zul'hõasi. In E. J. M. Baumbach (ed.), *Second Africa Languages Congress of UNISA*, 144–68. Pretoria: University of South Africa.

Sproat, Richard. to appear. Writing systems. In B. Elan Dresher & Harry van der Hulst (eds.), *The handbook of the (early) history of phonology.* Oxford: Oxford University Press.

Stack, Kelly M. 1988. *Tiers and syllable structure in American Sign Language: Evidence from phonotactics.* MA dissertation, University of California, Los Angeles.

Stampe, David. 1973. *A dissertation on Natural Phonology.* PhD dissertation, University of Chicago.

Stanley, Richard. 1967. Redundancy rules in phonology. *Language* 43.2, 393–436.

Staun, Jørgen. 1996a. On structural analogy. *Word* 47.2, 193–205.

Staun, Jørgen. 1996b. On the location description of consonants. *Travaux du cercle linguistique de Copenhague* 29, 1–137.

Staun, Jørgen. 2013. Fission in component-based phonology. *Language Sciences* 40, 123–47.

Stefanuto, Muriel & Nathalie Vallée. 1999. Consonant systems: From universal trends to ontogenesis. *Proceedings of the 14th International Congress of Phonetic Sciences*, 1973–6.

Stemberger, Joseph P. 1993. Glottal transparency. *Phonology* 10.1, 107–38.

Stephenson, Edward A. 1978. In defense of the phoneme. *Word* 29.2, 161–85.

Steriade, Donca. 1982. *Greek prosodies and the nature of syllabification.* PhD dissertation, MIT.

Steriade, Donca. 1987a. Locality conditions and Feature Geometry. *Proceedings of the North East Linguistic Society (NELS)* 17, 339–62.

Steriade, Donca. 1987b. On class nodes. MS, MIT.

Steriade, Donca. 1987c. Redundant values. *Chicago Linguistic Society (CLS)* 23, 339–62.

Steriade, Donca. 1993a. Closure, release, and nasal contours. In Marie K. Huffman & Rena A. Krakow (eds.), *Nasals, nasalization, and the velum* (Phonetics and Phonology 5), 401–70. San Diego, CA: Academic Press.

Steriade, Donca. 1993b. Segments, contours and clusters. In André Crochetière, Jean-Claude Boulanger & Conrad Ouellen (eds.), *Actes du 15ème Congrès International des Linguistes*, 71–82. Sainte Foy: Presses universitaires Laval.

Steriade, Donca. 1994. Complex onsets as single segments: The Mazateco pattern. *Perspectives in Phonology*, 203–91.

Steriade, Donca. 1995. Underspecification and markedness. In John Goldsmith (ed.), *The handbook of phonological theory*, 114–74. Oxford: Blackwell.

Steriade, Donca. 1999. Alternatives to the syllabic interpretation of consonantal phonotactics. In Osamu Fujimura, Brian Joseph & Bohumil Palek (eds.), *Item order in language and speech*, 205–42. Prague: Karolinum Press.

Steriade, Donca. 2003. The syllable. In William J. Frawley (ed.), *International Encyclopedia of Linguistics*, 2nd edn, vol. 4, 189–95. Oxford: Oxford University Press.

Stevens, Kenneth N. 1972. The quantal nature of speech: Evidence from articulatory-acoustic data. In Edward E. David & Peter B. Denes (eds.), *Human communication: A unified view*, 51–66. New York: McGraw-Hill.

Stevens, Kenneth N. 1989. On the quantal nature of speech. *Journal of Phonetics* 17.1, 3–45.

Stevens, Kenneth N. & Samuel J. Keyser. 1989. Primary features and their enhancement in consonants. *Language* 65.1, 81–106.

Stevens, Kenneth N., Samuel J. Keyser & Haruko Kawasaki. 1986. Toward a phonetic and phonological theory of redundant features. In Joseph Perkell & Dennis Klatt (eds.), *Invariance and variability in speech processes*, 426–49. Hillsdale NJ: Lawrence Erlbaum.

Stokoe, William C. 1960. *Sign language structure: An outline of the visual communication systems of the American deaf* (Studies in Linguistics: Occasional Paper 8). Buffalo, NY: Department of Anthropology and Linguistics, University of Buffalo.

Stokoe, William C. 1991. Semantic phonology. *Sign Language Studies* 71, 107–14.

Strazny, P. 2003. Depression in Zulu. In Jeroen van de Weijer, Harry van der Hulst & Vincent J. van Heuven (eds.), *The phonological spectrum*, vol. 1, 223–39. Amsterdam and Philadelphia: John Benjamins.

Supalla, Ted & Elissa L. Newport. 1978. How many seats in a chair? The derivation of nouns and verbs in American Sign Language. In Patricia Siple (ed.), *Understanding language through sign language research*, 91–132. New York: Academic Press.

Sutton-Spence, Rachel & Penny Boyes Braem. 2013. Comparing the products and the processes of creating sign language poetry and pantomimic improvisations. *Journal of Nonverbal Behavior* 37.4, 245–80.

Svantesson, Jan-Olof. 1985. Vowel harmony shift in Mongolian. *Lingua* 67.4, 283–327.

Szigetvári, Péter. 1998. Voice assimilation in Hungarian: The hitches. *The Even Yearbook* 3, 223–36.

Tak, Jin-young. 2011. Universals of prenasalized consonants: Phonemic or derived, single or complex? *Journal of Universal Language* 12.2, 127–58.

Tang, Elizabeth Katrina. 2008. *The phonology and phonetics of consonant–tone interaction*. PhD dissertation, University of California, Los Angeles.

Taylor, John R. 2006. Where do phonemes come from? A view from the bottom. *International Journal of English Linguistics* 6.2, 19–54.

Tesnière, Lucien. 1959. *Éléments de syntaxe structurale*. Paris: Klincksieck.

Thráinsson, Hoskuldur. 1978. On the phonology of Icelandic pre-aspiration. *Nordic Journal of Linguistics* 1.1, 3–54.

Tingsabadh, Kalaya & Arthur S. Abramson. 1993. Thai. *Journal of the International Phonetic Association* 23.1, 24–8.

Toft, Zoë. 2002. The phonetics and phonology of some syllabic consonants in Southern British English. *ZAS Papers in Linguistics* 28, 111–44.

Topintzi, Nina. 2008. On the existence of moraic onset geminates. *Natural Language & Linguistic Theory* 26.1, 147–84.

Törkenczy, Miklós & Péter Siptár. 1999. Hungarian syllable structure: Arguments for/against complex constituents. In Harry van der Hulst & Nancy A. Ritter (eds.), *The syllable: Views and facts*, 249–84. Berlin: Mouton de Gruyter.

Traill, Anthony. 1985. *Phonetic and phonological studies of !Xóõ Bushman*. Amsterdam and Philadelphia: John Benjamins.

Traill, Anthony. 1986. The laryngeal sphincter as a phonatory mechanism in !Xóõ. In R. Singer & J. K. Lundy (eds.), *Variation, culture and evolution*, 123–31. Johannesburg: Witwatersrand University Press.

Traill, Anthony. 1993. The Feature Geometry of clicks. In Paul M. von Staden (ed.), *Linguistica: Festschrift E. B. van Wijk*, 134–40. Pretoria: J. L. van Schaik.

Traill, Anthony. 1994. *A !Xóõ dictionary*. Cologne: Rudiger Köppe.

Traill, Anthony. 1995. Place of articulation features for clicks: Anomalies for universals. In Jack Windsor Lewis (ed.), *Studies in general and English phonetics: Essays in honour of Professor J. D. O'Connor*, 121–9. London and New York: Routledge.

Trask, R. L. 1996. *A dictionary of phonetics and phonology*. Abingdon and New York: Routledge.

Traunmüller, Hartmut. 1983. *On vowels: Perception of spectral features, related aspects of production and sociophonetic dimensions*. PhD dissertation, University of Stockholm.

Trigo, Loren. 1991. On pharynx–larynx interactions. *Phonology* 8.1, 113–36.

Trommelen, Mieke. 1983. *The syllable in Dutch: With special reference to diminutive formation*. Dordrecht: Foris.

Trubetzkoy, Nikolai S. 1929. Zur allgemeinen Theorie der phonologischen Vokalsysteme. *Travaux du cercle linguistique de Prague* 1, 39–67.

Trubetzkoy, Nikolai S. 1939. *Grundzüge der Phonologie*. Prague: Travaux du cercle linguistique de Prague.

Trubetzkoy, Nikolai S. 1939 [1960]. *Grundzüge der Phonologie [Principles of Phonology]*, trans. Christine A. M. Baltaxe. Berkeley and Los Angeles: University of California Press.

Trubetzkoy, Nikolai S. 1939 [1977]. *Grundzüge der Phonologie*, 6th edn. Göttingen: Vandenhoeck and Ruprecht.

Twaddell, W. Freeman. 1935. On defining the phoneme. *Language Monograph* 16.

van de Weijer, Jeroen. 1991. Towards a theory of phonological complexity. In Frank Drijkoningen & Ans van Kemenade (eds.), *Linguistics in the Netherlands 1991*, 141–50. Amsterdam and Philadelphia: John Benjamins.

van de Weijer, Jeroen. 1992. Basque affricates and the manner–place dependency. *Lingua* 88.2, 129–47.

van de Weijer, Jeroen. 1993. The manner–place dependency in complex segments. *Linguistics* 31.1, 87–110.

van de Weijer, Jeroen. 1996. *Segmental structure and complex segments* (Linguistische Arbeiten 350). Tübingen: Niemeyer.

van de Weijer, Jeroen. 2014. The origin of OT constraints. *Lingua* 142, 66–75. doi:10.1016/j.lingua.2014.01.007

van de Weijer, Jeroen. 2019. Where now with Optimality Theory? *Acta Linguistica Academica* 66.1, 115–35. doi:10.1556/2062.2019.66.1.5

van de Weijer, Jeroen, Kensuke Nanjo & Tetsuo Nishihara (eds.). 2005. *Voicing in Japanese* (Studies in Generative Grammar 84). Berlin and New York: Mouton de Gruyter.

van de Weijer, Jeroen & Jason Zhang. 2008. An X-bar approach to the syllable structure of Mandarin. *Lingua* 118, 1416–28.

van der Hulst, Harry. 1977. Towards a lexical theory of phonological change. *Linguistics in the Netherlands 1977–9*, 170–82.

van der Hulst, Harry. 1984. *Syllable structure and stress in Dutch*. Dordrecht: Foris.

van der Hulst, Harry. 1985. Ambisyllabicity in Dutch. *Linguistics in the Netherlands 1985*, 57–66.

van der Hulst, Harry. 1988a. The dual interpretation of |i|, |u| and |a|. *Proceedings of the North East Linguistic Society (NELS)* 18, 208–22.

van der Hulst, Harry. 1988b. The geometry of vocalic features. In Harry van der Hulst & Norval Smith (eds.), *Features, segmental structure and harmony processes*, vol. 2, 77–125. Dordrecht: Foris.

van der Hulst, Harry. 1989. Atoms of segmental structure: Components, gestures and dependency. *Phonology* 6.2, 253–84. doi:10.1017/S0952675700001020

van der Hulst, Harry. 1990a. The book of segments. MS, Leiden University.

van der Hulst, Harry. 1990b. The segmental spine and the non-existence of [±ATR]. In Joan Mascaró & Marina Nespor (eds.), *Grammar in progress: A Festschrift for Henk van Riemsdijk*, 247–57. Dordrecht: Foris.

van der Hulst, Harry. 1993a. Les atomes de la structure segmentale: Composants, gestes, et dépendances. In Bernard Laks & Annie Rialland (eds.), *L'Architecture des représentations phonologiques*, 255–90. Paris: CNRS.

van der Hulst, Harry. 1993b. Units in the analysis of signs. *Phonology* 10.2, 209-41.

van der Hulst, Harry. 1994. Radical CV Phonology: The locational gesture. *UCL Working Papers in Linguistics* 6, 439-77.

van der Hulst, Harry. 1995a. The composition of handshapes. *Trondheim Working Papers* 23, 1-17.

van der Hulst, Harry. 1995b. Head-dependency relations in the representation of signs. In Heleen F. Bos & Gertrude M. Schermer (eds.), *Sign language research 1994: Proceedings of the Fourth European Congress on Sign Language Research*, 11-38. Hamburg: Signum.

van der Hulst, Harry. 1995c. Radical CV Phonology: The categorial gesture. In Jacques Durand & Francis Katamba (eds.), *Frontiers of phonology: Atoms, structures, derivations*, 80-116. London: Longman.

van der Hulst, Harry. 1996a. Acquisitional evidence for the phonological composition of handshape. *Proceedings of GALA 1985*, 39-56.

van der Hulst, Harry. 1996b. On the other hand. *Lingua* 98, 121-44.

van der Hulst, Harry. 1996c. Radical CV Phonology: The segment-syllable connection. In Jacques Durand & Bernard Laks (eds.), *Current trends in phonology: Models and methods*, vol. 1, 333-63. Paris: CNRS/ESRI.

van der Hulst, Harry. 1999a. Cellese: The language of the cell. MS, Skidmore College.

van der Hulst, Harry. 1999b. Issues in foot typology. In S. J. Hannahs & Mike Davenport (eds.), *Issues in phonological structure*, 95-127. Amsterdam and Philadelphia: John Benjamins.

van der Hulst, Harry. 1999c. Word accent. In Harry van der Hulst (ed.), *Word prosodic systems in the languages of Europe*, 3-116. Berlin and New York: Mouton de Gruyter.

van der Hulst, Harry. 2000a. Features, segments and syllables in Radical CV Phonology. In John R. Rennison & Klaus Kühnhammer (eds.), *Phonologica*, 89-111. The Hague: Thesus.

van der Hulst, Harry. 2000b. Modularity and modality in phonology. In Noel Burton-Roberts, Philip Carr & Gerard J. Docherty (eds.), *Phonological knowledge: Conceptual and empirical issues*, 207-43. Oxford: Oxford University Press.

van der Hulst, Harry. 2003. Dutch syllable structure meets Government Phonology. In Takeru Honma, Masao Okazaki, Toshiyuki Tabata & Shin-ichi Tanaka (eds.), *A new century of phonology and phonological theory: A Festschrift for Professor Shosuke Haraguchi on the occasion of his sixtieth birthday*, 313-43. Tokyo: Kaitakusha.

van der Hulst, Harry. 2004. Phonological dialectics: A short history of Generative Phonology. In Piet G. J. van Sterkenburg (ed.), *Linguistics today: Facing a greater challenge*, 217-42. Amsterdam and Philadelphia: John Benjamins.

van der Hulst, Harry. 2005a. The molecular structure of phonological segments. In Phil Carr, Jacques Durand & Colin J. Ewen (eds.), *Headhood, elements, specification and contrastivity*, 193–234. Amsterdam and Philadelphia: John Benjamins.

van der Hulst, Harry. 2005b. Why phonology is the same. In Hans Broekhuis, Norbert Corver, Riny Huijbregts, Ursula Kleinhenz and Jan Koster (eds.), *Organizing grammar: Studies in honor of Henk van Riemsdijk*, 252–62. Berlin and New York: Mouton de Gruyter.

van der Hulst, Harry. 2006a. Dependency Phonology. In Keith Brown (ed.), *The encyclopedia of language and linguistics*, 2nd edn, vol. III, 220–33. Oxford: Elsevier.

van der Hulst, Harry. 2006b. Licensing in phonology. *The Linguistic Review* 23.4, 383–428.

van der Hulst, Harry. 2006c. On the parallel organization of linguistic components. In Ricardo Bermudez-Otero & Patrick Honeybone (eds.), *Phonology and syntax: The same or different?* Special issue of *Lingua 116.5*, 657–88.

van der Hulst, Harry. 2008. The Dutch diminutive. *Lingua* 118.9, 1288–306.

van der Hulst, Harry. 2009. Two phonologies. In Janet Grijzenhout & Barış Kabak (eds.), *Phonological domains: Universals and deviations*, 315–52. Berlin: Mouton de Gruyter.

van der Hulst, Harry. 2010. A note on recursion in phonology. In Harry van der Hulst (ed.), *Recursion in human language*, 301–42. Berlin: Mouton de Gruyter.

van der Hulst, Harry. 2011a. Constraint-based phonologies. In Nilufer Sener, Carlos Buesa García & Tsuyoshi Sawada (eds.), *Mirror Lake Paper: University of Connecticut Working Papers*, vol. 15.

van der Hulst, Harry. 2011b. Dependency-based phonologies. In John Goldsmith, Jason Riggle & Alan C. L. Yu (eds.), *The handbook of phonological theory*, 2nd edn, 533–70. Malden, MA: Blackwell.

van der Hulst, Harry. 2011c. Pitch accent systems. In Marc van Oostendorp, Colin J. Ewen, Elizabeth V. Hume & Keren Rice (eds.), *The Blackwell companion to phonology*, vol. 2, 1003–26. Oxford: Wiley-Blackwell.

van der Hulst, Harry. 2013. The discoverers of the phoneme. In Keith Allan (ed.), *The Oxford handbook of the history of linguistics* (Oxford Handbooks in Linguistics), 167–91. Oxford: Oxford University Press.

van der Hulst, Harry. 2015a. The laryngeal class in RcvP and voice phenomena in Dutch. In Johanneke Caspers, Yiya Chen, Willemijn Heeren, Jos Pacilly, Niels O. Schiller and Ellen van Zanten (eds.), *Above and beyond the segments*, 323–49. Amsterdam and Philadelphia: John Benjamins.

van der Hulst, Harry. 2015b. The opponent principle in RcvP: Binarity in a unary system. In Eric Raimy & Charles Cairns (eds.), *The segment in phonetics and phonology*, 149–79. Oxford: Wiley-Blackwell.

van der Hulst, Harry. 2016a. Monovalent 'features' in phonology. *Language and Linguistics Compass* 10.2, 83–102.

van der Hulst, Harry. 2016b. Phonology. In Keith Allan (ed.), *The Routledge handbook of linguistics*, 83–103. Abingdon and New York: Routledge.

van der Hulst, Harry. 2018. *Asymmetries in vowel harmony: A representational account.* Oxford: Oxford University Press.

van der Hulst, Harry. in prep. Accent and rhythm. MS, University of Connecticut.

van der Hulst, Harry. to appear-a. The history of sign language phonology. In B. Elan Dresher & Harry van der Hulst (eds.), *The handbook of the (early) history of phonology.* Oxford: Oxford University Press.

van der Hulst, Harry. to appear-b. A Guide to Radical CV Phonology, with special reference to tongue root and tongue body harmony. In Laurence Voeltzel (ed.), *Perspectives on Element Theory.* Berlin and New York: Mouton de Gruyter.

van der Hulst, Harry & Marian Klamer. 1996. Reduplication in Leti. In Crit Cremers & Marcel den Dikken (eds.), *Linguistics in the Netherlands 1996,* 109–20. Amsterdam and Philadelphia: John Benjamins. Repr. 1998, in Matthew Pearson (ed.), Recent papers in Austronesian linguistics. UCLA Occasional Papers in Linguistics 21, 147–58.

van der Hulst, Harry & Nancy A. Ritter. 1998. Kammu minor syllables in Head-Driven Phonology. In Eugeniusz Cyran (ed.), *Structure and interpretation: Studies in phonology,* 163–82. Lublin: Folium.

van der Hulst, Harry & Norval Smith. 1982a. An overview of Autosegmental and Metrical Phonology. In Harry van der Hulst & Norval Smith (eds.), *The structure of phonological representations,* vol. 1, 1–45. Dordrecht: Foris.

van der Hulst, Harry & Norval Smith (eds.). 1982b. *The structure of phonological representations,* 2 vols. Dordrecht: Foris.

van der Hulst, Harry & Norval Smith. 1987. Vowel harmony in Khalkha and Buriat (East Mongolian). In Frits Beukema & Peter Coopmans (eds.), *Linguistics in the Netherlands 1987,* 81–91. Dordrecht: Foris.

van der Hulst, Harry & Norval Smith. 1988a. *Autosegmental studies on pitch accent.* Dordrecht: Foris.

van der Hulst, Harry & Norval Smith. 1988b. *Features, segmental structure and harmony processes,* 2 vols. Dordrecht: Foris.

van der Hulst, Harry & Norval Smith. 1988c. Tungusic and Mongolian vowel harmony: A minimal pair. In Peter Coopmans & Aafke Hulk (eds.), *Linguistics in the Netherlands 1988,* 79–88. Dordrecht: Foris.

van der Hulst, Harry & Norval Smith. 1990. Zurichtuutsch umlaut and the non-existence of [+/- tense]. In Joan Mascaró & Marina Nespor (eds.), *Grammar in progress: A Festschrift for Henk van Riemsdijk,* 397–409. Dordrecht: Foris.

van der Hulst, Harry & Keith L. Snider. 1993. Issues in the representation of tonal register. In Harry van der Hulst & Keith L. Snider (eds.), *The phonology of tone: The representation of tonal register,* 1–27. Berlin and New York: Mouton de Gruyter.

van der Hulst, Harry & Jeroen van de Weijer. 1991. Topics in Turkish phonology. In Hendrik E. Boeschoten & Ludo T. Verhoeven (eds.), *Turkish linguistics today,* 11–59. Leiden: Brill.

van der Hulst, Harry & Jeroen van de Weijer. 2018a. Degrees of complexity in phonological segments. In Roger Böhm & Harry van der Hulst (eds.), *Substance-based grammar: The (ongoing) work of John Anderson* (Studies in Language Companion Series 204), 385–429. Amsterdam and Philadelphia: John Benjamins.

van der Hulst, Harry & Jeroen van de Weijer. 2018b. Dependency Phonology. In S. J. Hannahs & Anna R. K. Bosch (eds.), *The Routledge handbook of phonological theory* (Routledge Handbooks in Linguistics), 325–59. London: Routledge.

van der Hulst, Harry & Els van der Kooij. 2006. Phonetic implementation and phonetic pre-specification in sign language phonology. In Louis Goldstein, Douglas H. Whalen & Catherine T. Best (eds.), *Papers in Laboratory Phonology 8*, 265–86. Berlin and New York: Mouton de Gruyter.

van der Hulst, Harry & Els van der Kooij. to appear. Phonological structure of signs: Theoretical perspectives. In Josep Quer, Roland Pfau & Annika Herrmann (eds.), *The Routledge handbook of theoretical and experimental sign language research*. London: Routledge.

van der Hulst, Harry & Aone van Engelenhoven. 1995. Metathesis effects in Tutukeian-Letinese. In Harry van der Hulst & Jeroen van de Weijer (eds.), *Leiden in last* (HIL Phonology Papers 1), 243–67. The Hague: Holland Academic Graphics.

van der Kooij, Els. 2002. *Phonological categories in Sign Language of the Netherlands: Phonetic implementation and iconicity*. PhD dissertation, Leiden University.

van der Kooij, Els & Harry van der Hulst. 2005. On the internal and external organization of sign segments: Some modality specific property of sign segments in NGT. In Marc van Oostendorp & Jeroen van de Weijer (eds.), *The internal organization of phonological segments* (Studies in Generative Grammar 77), 153–80. Berlin and New York: Mouton de Gruyter.

van der Torre, Erik Jan. 2003. *Dutch sonorants: The role of place of articulation in phonotactics*. PhD dissertation, Leiden University.

van Lessen Kloeke, W. U. S. 1982. *Deutsche Phonologie und Morphologie: Merkmale und Markiertheit*. Tübingen: Niemeyer.

van Nice, Kathy. 1991. Hierarchical Particle Phonology. In John van Lit, René H. Mulder & Rint Sybesma (eds.), *Proceedings of LCJL 2*, 233–44. Leiden: Holland Institute of Generative Linguistics.

VanDam, Mark. 2004. Word final coda typology. *Journal of Universal Language* 5.1, 119–48.

Vaux, Bert. 1998. The laryngeal specifications of fricatives. *Linguistic Inquiry* 29.3, 497–511.

Vaux, Bert & Bridget Samuels. 2005. Laryngeal markedness and aspiration. *Phonology* 22.3, 395–436. doi:10.1017/S0952675705000667

Vaux, Bert & Bridget Samuels. 2015. Explaining vowel systems: Dispersion theory vs. natural selection. *The Linguistic Review* 32.3, 573–99.

Vennemann, Theo. 1971. Natural Generative Phonology. Paper presented at the LSA meeting, St Louis, Missouri.

Vennemann, Theo. 1972. Phonological uniqueness in natural Generative Grammar. *Glossa* 6, 105–16.

Vennemann, Theo. 1974. Words and syllables in Natural Generative Grammar. In Anthony Bruck, Robert A. Fox & Michael W. La Galy (eds.), *Chicago Linguistic Society: Parasession on Natural Phonology*, 346–74. Chicago: Chicago Linguistic Society.

Vennemann, Theo. 1979. Vowel alternations in English, German, and Gothic: Remarks on realism in phonology. In Mohammad Ali Jazayery, Edgar C. Polomé & Werner Winter (eds.), *Linguistic and literary studies in honor of Archibald A. Hill. Vol. 1: General and theoretical linguistics*, 337–60. Berlin and New York: Mouton de Gruyter.

Vennemann, Theo. 1988. *Preference laws for syllable structure and the explanation of sound change: With special reference to German, Germanic, Italian, and Latin*. Berlin: Mouton de Gruyter.

Vihman, Marilyn May. 1996. *Phonological development: The origins of language in the child*. Oxford: Blackwell.

Vihman, Marilyn May. 2013. *Phonological development: The first two years*. Malden, MA, and Oxford: Wiley-Blackwell.

Vogt, Hans. 1958. Structure phonémique du géorgien. *Norsk Tidsskrift for Sprogvidenskap* 18, 5–90.

Volenec, Veno & Charles Reiss. 2017. Cognitive phonetics: The transduction of distinctive features at the phonology–phonetics interface. *Biolinguistics* 11, 251–94.

Völtz, Michael. 1999. The syntax of syllables: Why syllables are not different. In John R. Rennison & Klaus Kühnhammer (eds.), *Phonologica 1996*, 315–21. The Hague: Holland Academic Graphics.

Wagner, Michael. 2005. *Prosody and recursion*. PhD dissertation, MIT.

Walker, Rachel. 1996. Prominence-driven stress. MS, University of California, Santa Cruz.

Walker, Rachel & Sharon Rose. 2015. Guttural semi-transparency. Paper presented at AMP 2015, 10 October, Vancouver+.

Wang, William S. Y. 1969. Competing changes as a cause of residue. *Language* 45.1, 9–25.

Watson, James D. & Francis H. C. Crick. 1993. Molecular structure of nucleic acids: A structure for deoxyribose nucleic acid. *Nature* 171, 737–8.

Weidert, Alfons. 1981. *Tonologie*. Tübingen: Niemeyer.

Wetzels, W. Leo & Joan Mascaró. 2001. The typology of voicing and devoicing. *Language* 77, 207–44.

Whalen, Douglas H. & Andrea G. Levitt. 1995. The universality of intrinsic Fo of vowels. *Journal of Phonetics* 23.3, 349–66.

White, David L. 2016. Old English without short diphthongs: An alternative historical phonology. *Anglica: International Journal of English Studies* 25.2, 5–29.

Wiese, Richard. 2000. *The phonology of German.* New York: Oxford University Press.
Wiesemann, Ursula. 1972. *Die Phonologische und Grammatische Struktur der KaingangSprache.* The Hague: Mouton.
Wilbur, Ronnie B. 1987. *American Sign Language: Linguistic and applied dimensions*, 2nd edn. Boston: Little, Brown.
Wilbur, Ronnie B. 1990. An experimental investigation of stressed sign production. *International Journal of Sign Language* 1, 41–60.
Wilbur, Ronnie B. 1993. Syllables and segments: Hold the movement and move the holds! In Geoffrey R. Coulter (ed.), *Current issues in ASL phonology*, 135–68. New York: Academic Press.
Wilbur, Ronnie B. 2003. Representations of telicity in ASL. *Chicago Linguistic Society (CLS)* 39, 354–68.
Wilbur, Ronnie B. 2010. The role of contact in the phonology of ASL. *Sign Language & Linguistics* 13.2, 203–16.
Wilkinson, Karina. 1988. Prosodic structure and Lardil phonology. *Linguistic Inquiry* 19.2, 325–34.
Williamson, Kay. 1977. Multivalued features for consonants. *Language* 53.4, 843–71.
Wiltshire, Caroline. 1992. Syllabification and rule application in harmonic phonology. PhD dissertation, University of Chicago.
Woll, Bencie. 2001. The sign that dares to speak its name: Echo phonology in British Sign Language. In Penny Boyes-Braem & Rachel Sutton-Spence (eds.), *The hands are the head of the mouth: The mouth as articulator in sign languages*, 87–98. Hamburg: Signum.
Wood, Sidney A. J. 1975. Tense and lax vowels: Degree of constriction or pharyngeal volume? *Working Papers of the Phonetics Laboratory, Department of General Linguistics, Lund University* 11, 109–33.
Wood, Sidney A. J. 1979. A radiographic analysis of constriction locations for vowels. *Journal of Phonetics* 7.1, 25–43.
Wood, Sidney A. J. 1982. X-ray and model studies of vowel articulation. *Working Papers of the Phonetics Laboratory, Department of General Linguistics, Lund University* 23, 1–49.
Wood, Sidney A. J. 1991. Vertical, monovocalic and other 'impossible' vowel systems: A review of the articulation of the Kabardian vowels. *Studia Linguistica* 45.1–2, 49–70.
Wright, Richard, Ian Maddieson, Peter Ladefoged & Bonny Sands. 1995. A phonetic study of Sandawe clicks. *UCLA Working Papers in Phonetics*, 1–24.
Yip, Moira. 1980. *The tonal phonology of Chinese.* PhD dissertation, MIT.
Yip, Moira. 1989. Contour tones. *Phonology* 6.1, 149–74. doi:10.1017/S095267570000097X
Yip, Moira. 1999. Tone register in East Asian languages. In Harry van der Hulst & Keith L. Snider (eds.), *The phonology of tone: The representation of tonal register*, 245–68. Dordrecht: Foris.

Yip, Moira. 2001. Tonal features, tonal inventories and phonetic targets. *UCL Working Papers in Linguistics* 13, 161–88.

Yip, Moira. 2002. *Tone*. Cambridge: Cambridge University Press.

Yu, A. C. L. 2004. Explaining final obstruent voicing in Lezgian: Phonetics and history. *Language* 80.1, 73–97.

Zhang, Jisheng. 2006. *The phonology of Shaoxing Chinese*. PhD dissertation, Leiden University.

Zonneveld, Wim. 1978. *A formal theory of exceptions in Generative Phonology*. Lisse: Peter de Ridder Press.

Zsiga, Elizabeth C. 2013. *The sounds of language: An introduction to phonetics and phonology* (Linguistics in the World). Oxford: Wiley-Blackwell.

Zukoff, Sam. 2017. *Indo-European reduplication: Synchrony, diachrony, and theory*. PhD dissertation, MIT.

Zúñiga, Fernando. 2000. *Mapudungun* (Languages of the World/Materials 74). Munich: Lincom Europa.

Subject index

absolute orientation, 367–8
abstractness, 4, 29, 119, 207, 258
accent, 12, 100, 108, 217, 424
accidental gaps, 21
acoustics, 12, 18, 40–1, 47, 52, 65, 67, 69, 81–4, 88, 160–3, 185–6, 353, 381, 401, 409, 412–13
   acoustic affinity, 185
acquisition, 5, 13, 15, 20, 48, 137, 169, 172, 183, 301, 317, 335, 353
acuity, 368–9
acuteness, 41, 50
adjunction, 92, 95, 120, 138, 167, 173, 251, 254–5, 257, 265, 281, 305, 418
Advanced Tongue Root (ATR), 39, 45, 50, 61–5, 69–70, 84–5, 153, 156–61, 201–2, 205, 235, 239, 294–6, 326, 329–33, 338, 343, 346, 382–3, 391, 404, 417, 420–1, 423, 428
affricates, 40, 66, 78, 93, 112–18, 123–4, 128–9, 137, 182, 189–90, 263–5, 272–3, 277–8, 284–5, 291, 302, 304, 344, 356, 383, 404, 407
affrication, 115–16, 124, 190
Agreement-By-Correspondence (ABC), 408
airstream, 46, 49–50, 56–7, 267–8, 276
Aitken's Law, 54, 142

allomorphy, 8, 23–4, 31–2, 285
allophone, 22, 24, 117, 190, 420
alphabetic writing, 9, 22, 59
alphabets, 12, 27, 85
alternations, 1, 8, 13, 25, 28, 31, 33, 132, 243–4, 246–7, 249, 258, 260, 285, 325, 336, 406, 414, 424
   consonant–zero alternations, 244, 258–9
   vowel–zero alternations, 13, 243–4, 246–7, 249, 260
ambiguity, 8, 125, 156, 158, 159, 201, 329, 386, 387
American structuralism, 24, 81
antagonistic pair, 37, 67, 74, 417
anterior, 113, 179–81, 189, 205, 313–14, 358, 363
aperture change, 364, 367, 371, 375
approximant, 49, 59, 112, 123–4, 128, 132, 141, 144, 194, 198, 382, 404
articulator, 129, 358–64, 367–8, 372–3, 376, 381, 395, 399–400, 402, 404, 415, 430
articulator node, 358–9, 367, 373, 381, 415
articulatory gesture, 46, 52, 56–7, 379
Articulatory Phonology, 20, 21, 45, 395, 398, 407–8
arytenoid cartilages, 213
aspiration, 22–3, 49, 57, 114, 122, 126, 134, 139, 207, 209–10, 212,

479

480 Subject index

aspiration (cont.)
    214–16, 227–8, 230–4, 271–5,
    294, 296–7, 315, 326, 333, 338,
    346
assimilation, 107, 140–1, 155, 169,
    204, 214, 234, 367, 379
association, 27, 75, 90, 96, 376, 383,
    385, 387
  association lines, 75, 385
asymmetries, 37–8, 43, 44, 48, 80,
    87–8, 99, 149, 172, 178, 188,
    203, 216, 351, 377, 381, 390,
    403, 413
augment, 409
automatic processes, 8, 31, 75
autosegmental phonology, 16, 45,
    219, 224, 385, 407–8, 424

beat, 187
binarity, 37, 83, 85, 262, 353, 355,
    384, 410, 416
Binarity Principle, 353
binary features, 13, 20, 36–7, 40, 48,
    69, 83, 209, 238, 325, 330, 355,
    380, 382, 403
biuniqueness, 24, 26
boundary, 29, 146, 250, 355
boundary tones, 355
branching, 89, 96, 113, 131, 133–4,
    144, 165, 169, 184, 240, 250–1,
    264, 279, 281–2, 298, 367, 371,
    415
breathy voice, 161, 208–9, 211–12,
    215–16, 227–8, 235–6, 239, 263,
    271, 275–6, 280, 430
bridge, 93, 99–100, 108, 114, 119,
    121, 130–6, 138, 141, 149,
    155, 164–7, 171–3, 177, 179,
    204, 207, 240, 286, 288, 298–9,
    306–13, 316, 322, 425, 427
Broca, 184

categorial gesture, 46, 49, 52, 379
categorisation, 19, 22, 78, 81, 110,
    153, 178, 184, 190, 199, 353,
    355, 396, 410, 413
centrality, 44–5, 50, 61, 415
charm, 62–6, 71, 168
clicks, 4, 50, 57, 123, 191, 242, 264,
    266–76, 278–9, 281–2, 377, 408,
    419, 429–30
clitic, 255, 257
clusters, 49, 59, 93, 97–8, 118–20,
    133–4, 136–8, 140, 167, 223,
    238, 240, 244, 247–9, 250–4,
    256, 265, 267–8, 280–1, 300,
    307–8, 413, 418
co-articulation, 324
coda conditions, 165–8, 170, 204, 301
codas, 96–7, 135, 141, 150, 155,
    165–8, 170, 173, 203–4, 240,
    244, 250, 253–5, 269, 298–9,
    310, 317, 406, 417
cognitive phonetics, 31
cognitive phonology, 9, 412
cold vowel, 61–2, 64–6, 153, 423
colour, 27, 40, 43–5, 67–8, 87, 151–2,
    175, 179, 289–90, 292, 320–1,
    328, 333, 340, 342–3, 347–8,
    351, 388, 422–3
Combinatorial Principle, 81, 178, 353
complement, 102–3, 328–30, 334, 406
complementarity, 234, 388
complementary distribution, 24, 59,
    61, 84, 224, 235, 241, 279, 309,
    387
complex consonants, 58, 144, 253–4,
    263
complex segments, 2, 4, 50, 57, 105,
    134, 136–7, 242, 254, 263–4,
    266, 281, 384, 390, 419
complexity, 21–2, 38, 45, 48, 55, 80,
    87, 92, 96, 112, 119, 123–4,
    128–9, 142, 149, 168, 184, 196,
    203, 216, 254, 264–5, 279–80,
    282, 287, 293, 300, 303, 316,
    318–23, 325, 339–40, 343, 352,
    366, 377, 412, 418

Subject index 481

component, 26, 30–1, 36, 47, 52, 55–6, 74, 79, 105, 230, 268, 361, 419
compound structure, 191, 224, 266, 267, 277–8, 281–2
compression, 213
concatenative morphology, 374
concept, 22, 42, 49, 59, 64, 67, 407, 410
consonant clusters, 97, 133, 244, 249, 250, 253, 254, 256, 267, 307, 386
consonantal, 45, 47–8, 51, 54, 59, 90, 93, 150, 152, 184–5, 192, 197–8, 202, 205, 217, 225, 254, 256, 260, 280, 292, 298, 319, 322, 328, 345–6, 354, 380–1, 383, 389, 405, 423–4
constituency, 13, 28, 100, 102
constituent structure, 12, 28, 76–7, 90, 409
constraint-and-repair, 17
constraints, 5, 10, 12, 17, 29, 120, 134, 138, 146, 168, 170, 178, 253–4, 256–7, 299, 301, 318, 325, 332, 346–52, 363, 408, 418
  constraint ranking, 17
constricted glottis, 49, 147, 208, 214, 238–9, 257, 267, 417
constriction, 57, 65, 69, 93, 122, 155, 172, 192, 208, 239
continuant, 48, 54, 65, 84, 110, 113, 123–4, 132, 150, 211, 264, 286, 327, 333, 363, 417
contour segments, 264, 281, 407
contour tones, 165, 217–24, 264, 278–80, 347, 356, 407
  unitary contour tones, 223–4, 279–80, 347
contrast, 1, 2, 5, 8, 19–24, 33, 37–9, 41, 44–5, 49–51, 54–6, 59–61, 67, 70, 73, 78, 80–3, 87–8, 105–6, 109, 111–12, 115–18, 123–8, 131, 136, 142–4, 148, 151, 154, 156–9, 161, 163, 166–8, 177–8, 180, 183, 185, 187, 190–2, 196, 201, 206, 208, 210–15, 217–18, 220–1, 223–34, 236–8, 240, 258, 262–3, 269, 272, 274, 279–80, 284–5, 288, 290, 301–4, 307, 315, 318, 322, 324, 327–8, 331, 334–9, 338–9, 341–2, 344, 346–50, 363, 366, 383, 394, 403–4, 406–7, 409, 411–13, 416, 420–1, 423
contrastive specification theory, 38
contrastivity, 35, 110, 128
creaky voice, 122, 194, 208–9, 211–12, 215–16, 227–8, 235, 239, 263, 267, 272, 276, 280, 430
cross-class harmony, 284, 288, 291, 292, 293, 297
cyclicity, 10, 31, 33

Declarative Phonology, 16
default, 5, 38–9, 70, 79, 88, 143, 166, 191, 262–3, 267, 307, 324, 328–30, 334, 341, 365, 372
delayed release, 113
deletion, 147, 247, 384, 387, 412
Dependency Grammar, 14, 26–8
Dependency Phonology, 1, 15, 35ff, 45, 56, 60
dependency, 1, 3, 11–16, 18, 268, 33, 35ff, 95, 100–2, 108, 121, 149–50, 205, 244, 284, 323, 347, 351, 361, 377, 381, 384, 389–90, 392, 396, 409
  mutual/bilateral dependency, 43
derivation, 10–11, 15, 17, 29, 38, 328
devoicing, 23–4, 49, 140–1, 166, 234, 327
diachronic, 8, 147
diphthongisation, 37, 386–9
diphthongs, 56, 98, 165, 169, 171, 174–5, 242, 277–9, 343
  short diphthongs, 174, 242, 277–9
disharmony, 137, 300

482   Subject index

dispersion, 10, 184, 301, 303–21, 323, 337, 340
  paradigmatic dispersion, 309, 311–13
distinctive features, 31, 47, 82, 184, 330, 363
distributed, 51, 70, 113, 180–1, 358, 389, 415
distributional constraints, 301, 318
domains, 12, 21, 27, 33, 238, 401–3, 412
dominant, 33, 43, 51, 156, 158–9, 184, 294, 367, 373
downdrift, 220, 279
downstep, 217, 220, 279, 324
Duanmu's syllable model, 103
duration, 123

edge, 91–3, 108–11, 114, 119–22, 130–1, 133–5, 138–9, 144–5, 149, 155, 160, 162, 177, 179–81, 187–8, 197, 199, 202, 204–5, 207, 240, 250, 253–7, 269, 278, 283, 286, 288–9, 292, 295, 298, 302–4, 310, 312–13, 315, 326, 367, 417, 426–7
effort reduction, 185
egressive airflow, 56
ejective, 122, 208, 212, 215–16, 271, 273, 275
E-language, 24–5
element, 1, 2, 4–6, 11, 19–20, 36–8, 40, 42–7, 49–53, 55–8, 60–72, 74–82, 84–6, 88, 92, 106–11, 113–15, 119, 122–3, 129, 132–3, 139, 145, 151–3, 155–9, 161–2, 176, 182, 185–6, 191–4, 198–201, 207, 214, 216, 222, 224, 226–32, 234, 236, 242, 246–7, 258, 261–3, 266–8, 272–3, 279, 281, 283–91, 293–7, 299, 301–3, 319–21, 323, 328, 331–43, 346, 348–9, 352, 378, 389–91, 393, 404–6, 414–16, 420–3

embedding, 100, 102, 104
emphasis, 16
empty nuclei, 12, 20, 79, 92, 120, 126, 138, 167, 170, 173, 243–5, 248–9, 251–61, 281, 418
empty segments, 107, 282
enhancement, 20, 159, 230–1, 233–4, 346
epenthesis, 123, 204, 246–9, 256, 292, 361, 386–7
epenthetic vowels, 256, 292
epiglottis, 84, 192, 358
exceptions, 23, 31, 33, 107, 165, 245, 251, 259, 288, 322, 384
exemplar-based approaches, 21
exhaustivity operator, 41, 76
extrinsic ordering, 13, 29

faithfulness, 166, 170
falling tones, 224, 279, 356
feature economy, 320
feature geometry, 1, 378, 394, 398
feet, 10, 105, 374
final devoicing, 23–4, 140–1, 166, 327
final licensing, 245
FingerConfiguration, 363–4, 366, 370
FingerSelection, 363–6
fission, 86, 387
flap, 143–4, 198
foot, 12, 84, 95, 100, 102–5, 146–7, 405, 424
  foot typology, 105
fortis, 213–14, 257
fricative vowels, 162–3
fricatives, 47–8, 51, 54, 66, 77, 109–20, 122–4, 127–9, 140, 141–9, 169, 177, 182, 189, 191, 193–5, 203, 215, 232–4, 262, 264–5, 277, 284–5, 289, 291–7, 301–4, 314, 327, 333–4, 336–7, 344–6, 362, 404, 406
  mellow fricatives, 110, 118, 122–3, 291, 337

frontness, 41, 44, 152
functional explanations, 190
fundamental frequency, 69
fusion, 60–3

geminates, 98, 166, 168, 174, 176, 244, 257, 384, 386–7
  initial geminates, 244, 257
gemination, 259–60
generative phonology, 14–17, 28, 31–2, 39, 238, 348, 379, 411
generative syntax, 15
gesture, 45–7, 49, 51–3, 55–7, 112, 160, 191, 215, 269, 379, 400
ghost consonants, 244, 259
glides, 98, 132–5, 138–9, 143–6, 165, 169, 171–3, 179, 198, 204, 228, 298–9, 307–12, 322
glossematics, 20, 27
glottal stop, 114, 147–8, 193–4, 196, 203, 261–2, 419, 429
glottal width, 208–9, 213–14, 240
glottalic, 49, 57, 122, 209, 212, 267
glottalisation, 68, 208, 228, 294–6, 315
glottis, 49–50, 147, 207–8, 210, 213–15, 226, 238–9, 257, 267, 404, 417, 422–3
government, 1, 3, 13, 16, 35ff, 170, 244, 246, 248, 252, 404
Government Phonology, 1, 3, 35ff, 404
  Government Phonology 2.0, 60, 404
governor, 244
grave, 180, 185–6
grid, 341
grounding, 153, 323, 402–3

handshape, 355–6, 360–1, 364–7, 369, 372–3, 377
harmony, 2, 31–3, 37, 44, 51, 65, 68, 85, 88, 107, 125, 136, 149, 152–3, 156–62, 182, 186, 198, 201, 202, 246–8, 283–319, 323, 330, 336, 346, 381, 390, 392, 408, 414, 418, 420–1, 424
h-aspiré, 259
head, 1, 3, 4, 5, 11–12, 18, 28, 42–3, 47, 53, 60–6, 69–70, 74–80, 82–8, 91–4, 96, 98, 99, 104, 107–10, 113–14, 119–21, 125, 130–2, 135–7, 141–3, 145, 147–54, 159, 165–6, 172–3, 177–80, 182, 185, 187, 189–90, 193, 198–9, 201–2, 207, 214–17, 220–1, 224, 228–9, 231–2, 234–5, 239–40, 242, 261, 264–6, 272, 278–9, 284–303, 306–8, 310–17, 319–20, 322, 331, 334, 337–9, 341–2, 345, 348, 352, 361, 364–8, 370, 377–8, 381, 390, 396–8, 404, 406, 414–17, 420–3, 425
  head-dependency principle, 178, 353, 389, 410
  head-dependent asymmetries, 80, 149, 178, 377, 390
headedness, 12, 28, 42, 65–6, 68, 69, 77, 88, 98, 153, 159, 222–3, 242, 266, 290, 355, 390, 410, 412
heterosyllabic, 134, 253
high tone, 65, 83, 152, 218–19, 221, 237–8, 241, 286, 289–91, 296, 315–16, 417
historical change, 48
homorganic, 112, 116, 136–7, 165, 168, 170

iconic, 365, 400–1
identity rule, 288
I-language, 24–5
implosive, 122, 208–9, 212, 215–16, 239, 276
inalterability, 386–7
independently pronounceable, 68
ingressive airstream, 267
initiatory gesture, 46, 49

484 *Subject index*

innate, 5, 13, 18–19, 27, 190, 349–50, 352–3, 363, 393, 409–10
input, 8, 17, 24, 27–9, 31, 55, 376, 387, 413
inrounded, 201, 205, 293
integrity, 99, 386–7
interlude, 167–9
intermediate level, 29, 217, 223, 224, 279
International Phonetic Alphabet (IPA), 41, 44, 110, 114, 189, 192, 196–7, 200–1, 208, 217–18, 231, 262, 349, 429
interpretation functions, 3, 73, 76, 83, 90
intervocalically, 134, 210, 250, 329, 387
intonation, 30

juncture, 115

labialisation, 112, 122, 129, 136, 147, 152, 187–8, 198, 202, 205, 264–5, 294, 296, 417, 419, 421
labiality, 44, 50, 133
labiodental fricative, 112, 118
laryngeal consonants, 115, 143, 146–8, 169, 172–3, 193–6, 242, 261, 419
laryngeal features, 45, 57, 257, 380, 391, 394, 400, 409
laryngeal realism, 4, 207, 225, 230, 231
laryngealisation, 208–9, 211, 228, 236, 238, 276
larynx, 84, 161, 192, 209, 211–12, 226, 239, 267, 270, 358, 404
laterals, 13, 47, 51–4, 58, 88, 90, 115, 121, 127–30, 133, 135, 143–6, 155, 160, 164, 171, 173, 178, 197, 213, 270, 273, 276, 299, 311–12, 358, 363, 380, 383, 392, 404, 427–8, 430
lateralisation, 52, 127, 142, 419

laxness, 153, 391
learnability, 346
learning path, 335, 341–2
length, 4, 152, 219, 258, 280
lengthening, 406
lenis, 212
lenition, 48, 185
level tones, 217–24, 279, 315
levels, 1, 6, 10, 12, 24, 28–30, 34, 54, 74, 95, 98, 146, 218, 223, 333, 337–8, 341, 377, 390, 409, 412, 414, 424
lexical, 4, 9, 17, 20, 22–3, 28, 30–3, 80, 95, 141, 172, 183–4, 220–1, 224, 232, 247–9, 259–61, 279, 283, 301–2, 314, 327, 340, 346, 355, 361, 370, 374, 414, 418, 423
lexical diffusion, 30
lexical entries, 22, 32, 261
lexical level, 220–1, 232, 327, 355
Lexical Phonology, 30
lexicon, 26, 48, 95–6, 202, 217, 323, 350, 413
licensing, 13, 32, 75, 88, 90, 119, 166, 168, 245–7, 252–3, 259, 348–9
linear order, 59, 74, 94–5, 366–7
linearisation, 89, 116, 300, 375–6, 388
liquids, 51, 54, 92–3, 98, 133–6, 138, 143, 149, 166–7, 169–72, 179, 202–3, 250, 252, 298–9, 301, 307–10, 313, 316, 322, 326–7, 333
LML skeleton, 357
loanwords, 128, 138, 317
local movement, 371
locality, 88, 247
location, 3, 86, 110, 115, 137, 174, 179, 182, 186, 190, 192, 197, 199–200, 202, 204–5, 214, 244, 261, 265–6, 289, 297, 313, 321, 355–62, 367–73, 375, 383, 390–1, 398–400, 402

Subject index   485

logographic writing, 22
lowered velum, 123

macrophoneme, 21
macrostructure of signs, 357
major articulators, 410
major class, 3, 46–9, 56, 75, 77, 90–1,
    96–8, 108, 115, 120, 171, 287,
    380, 383, 394, 418, 425
manner, 1–4, 39, 46–9, 54–8, 65–6,
    68, 71, 73–5, 77, 79–80, 82–5,
    87, 96, 98–9, 105, 107–15,
    117–25, 127–31, 133–45,
    147–55, 157, 159–69, 171–3,
    175–9, 181–3, 186–91, 193–200,
    202, 204–5, 207, 209, 213–14,
    216, 227, 229–31, 235, 242,
    258, 261–5, 270, 272–3, 276–7,
    279–80, 283–93, 295–9, 301,
    303, 305–6, 309, 314, 317,
    319–21, 323, 327, 33–45, 347,
    351–2, 356, 358–9, 361–2,
    369–74, 379–80, 382–4, 389–90,
    392–4, 396–7, 400, 403–4,
    409–10, 415, 417–23, 426–9
  manner of articulation, 190, 279,
    358
  manner-only, 261, 277, 319
manual, 355, 402
markedness, 5, 37–9, 44–5, 48, 62, 70,
    106, 145, 148, 182–4, 186, 287,
    293, 307, 325, 339–40, 352
Massachusetts Institute of Technology
    (MIT), 11, 14, 16, 57–8
maximal binarity, 85
M-command, 406
medionasal, 124
meiosis, 387–9
melody, 223, 405
merge, 261, 412
metaphony, 152
metatheory, 1, 83, 106, 323, 352
Metrical Phonology, 15
metrical theory, 16, 105

metrical tree, 341
microphonemes, 21
microstructure of signs, 363
minimal pairs, 125, 249, 349–50, 407
minimal specification, 2, 5, 20–2, 36,
    58, 262, 324ff
minimalist programme, 66, 415
mono-bisegmental controversy, 126
monovalency, 35–6, 353
mora, 90, 257, 357
morpheme boundary, 250
morphemes, 9, 23, 25, 29, 32–3, 101,
    167, 202–3, 217, 245–8, 250,
    257, 259–61, 361–3
morphological contexts, 32, 327
morphological processes, 32
morphological structure, 31–3, 256
morphology, 11–12, 24, 26, 32, 95,
    374–5
morphophonemic level, 24–5
movement, 18, 213, 355–7, 359–62,
    364, 366–7, 370–2, 375, 377,
    397, 401–2
multiply-articulated consonants, 4
multivalued, 409
murmur, 208–9, 239

nasal, 38, 46, 52–3, 56, 58, 63, 65,
    91, 109, 112, 121–7, 130, 134–5,
    138–40, 144, 146, 148, 154–5,
    160, 164, 166, 168–73, 178, 183,
    190–1, 196–7, 202–3, 229–30,
    235–6, 261–2, 264, 269, 271–2,
    274–6, 281, 286, 295, 299, 307,
    309, 311, 312, 313, 317, 320,
    322, 326, 333, 338, 380, 392,
    404, 408, 417, 427, 430
nasalisation, 56, 63, 123–4, 139, 142,
    155, 196, 203, 237, 281, 294,
    296, 313, 327, 417, 421
nasality, 45, 51–2, 56, 58, 122–3, 125,
    127, 139, 150, 152, 155, 157,
    213, 229–30, 235–6, 261–2, 272,
    343, 390, 409, 419

486 Subject index

Natural Generative Phonology, 16, 31
Natural Phonology, 40, 349
nested subregister model, 86, 391–2
neutral space, 359, 361, 368–70, 374
neutral vowels, 37, 159–61, 336, 341
neutralisation, 8, 22–3, 25–6, 30–1,
    37, 41, 151, 166, 183, 185,
    326–7, 332–3
non-automatic allomorphy, 32
non-manual, 355, 360, 396–7
nuclei, 12, 20, 88, 92, 96, 120, 133,
    138, 166–7, 173, 176, 203,
    244–5, 249, 251–9, 261, 406, 418
nucleus, 79, 82–5, 88, 89, 91, 93,
    97–8, 108, 120, 126, 133, 144–5,
    149–50, 154–5, 164–5, 170–1,
    173, 177, 198–9, 201–2, 204–5,
    217, 225, 235, 241, 243–5,
    248–9, 251–3, 258, 260–1, 281,
    286, 288–9, 292–3, 295, 300,
    305, 308, 312, 314–16, 339, 341,
    405–6, 423–4, 426–8

obstruents, 22, 37–9, 48, 77, 91, 93,
    96–7, 108–10, 112, 114–15,
    117–19, 121–2, 125, 128, 130–1,
    134, 139, 141–2, 145, 148–50,
    155, 165–70, 172–4, 176, 179,
    182–3, 185, 188, 192, 196–9,
    202–3, 206, 212–13, 225–9,
    230–4, 237, 240, 253, 256, 263,
    269, 277–8, 284–5, 289, 290–4,
    296, 298, 303–4, 307, 312, 315,
    317, 319, 326–7, 329, 331–6,
    362, 392, 394, 406–8, 417–18
onsets, 89, 93, 96–7, 103, 119–20,
    125–7, 133–4, 136–8, 145–6,
    149, 166–8, 170, 243, 245–6,
    250–4, 256–7, 259, 261, 264–5,
    267, 269, 281, 302, 308–9, 314,
    317, 329, 335, 349, 406, 417–18
  branching onset, 131, 133, 240,
    251, 298
  obligatory onset, 349

onset dependent, 3, 93–4, 97, 99,
    107, 121, 131, 148, 307, 327
onset head, 3, 76–7, 83–4, 91, 93–4,
    98–9, 109–10, 119–20, 125, 131,
    135–6, 141–2, 145, 148–9, 166,
    172, 178–80, 182, 185, 187, 190,
    202, 207, 224, 232, 235, 279,
    289, 291–2, 294–6, 299, 301–3,
    306–8, 310–11, 313, 315–17,
    319, 322, 334, 345
ontogenetic development, 19, 78
opacity, 17
Opponent Principle, 19, 78, 81, 153,
    178, 284, 353, 403, 410, 413
oppositions, 21, 43, 59, 91, 166, 225,
    370
Optimality Theory (OT), 15–17, 138,
    146, 166, 168, 170, 349, 418
oral closure, 109, 139
orientation (sign language), 355, 362,
    366–8, 371, 375
output, 8–9, 17, 28, 29, 31, 328
outrounded, 201, 205, 293

palatalisation, 122, 142, 147, 152,
    187–9, 198, 202, 204–5, 264–5,
    294–6, 417, 421
paradigmatic, 10, 59, 92, 106, 136,
    182, 283–4, 287–8, 291–3, 298,
    303, 308–9, 311–14, 316–17,
    323, 326–7, 329, 332, 335, 348,
    377
  paradigmatic contextual
    neutralisation, 326, 332
  paradigmatic harmony, 182, 283,
    287–8, 291–3, 303, 308–9, 314,
    316
paradox, 44, 278, 309
parallel structure model, 393, 410
parametric variation, 244
parsing, 133, 342–5, 350–1, 403
Particle Phonology (PP), 42, 51, 56,
    58, 60, 111, 115, 118, 128, 139,
    142–4, 154, 162, 189–91, 198,

211–12, 228, 236, 268, 271, 274, 379, 384–5, 389, 393, 410
passive voicing, 229, 231–2, 234
path movement, 370–2, 397
peak, 95, 203, 256, 278
percept, 81
perceptible form, 7, 9
perception, 18–19, 27, 78, 184, 186, 376–7, 401, 413
  perceptual acuity, 368
  perceptual ease, 321
peripheral, 57, 138, 143, 180, 182–3, 186, 191, 203, 225, 268, 286, 289, 296, 318, 369, 392, 421–2
phonation, 4, 46–7, 49–54, 56–7, 65, 75, 80, 84, 139, 161, 166, 206–17, 219, 221, 223–41, 267, 269, 272, 276, 279–80, 294, 315, 321, 333, 344–6, 379, 383
phonemes, 2, 4, 7–9, 12–13, 21–6, 30, 41, 59, 61, 84, 106, 111, 138, 141, 162, 174, 187, 218, 283, 301, 330, 349–51, 356, 361–2
  phonemic overlap, 23
phonetic allomorphy, 23, 32
phonetic implementation, 2, 3, 7–10, 19–21, 23, 26, 30–2, 48, 75, 82, 93, 118–19, 124, 142, 172, 219, 227, 230–2, 234, 243–5, 256, 258, 262, 285, 324–5, 327–8, 332–5, 345–6, 354, 413–14, 419
phonetic interpretation, 53, 69, 78, 83–4, 132, 201, 209, 223–4, 227, 230, 244, 263, 267, 278, 285, 335–6, 365
phonetic similarity, 22, 59
phonetic spaces, 77, 81, 106, 284, 353, 363, 391, 398, 400, 423
phonetic split, 157
phonological word, 256
phonotactics, 168, 307, 418
  phonotactic constraints, 256–7, 351, 418

phonotactic restrictions, 138, 174
pitch, 217, 219–21, 226, 235, 239, 241, 289, 328, 333, 355, 377
pitch accent, 217
place of articulation, 50, 116–17, 123–4, 133, 136, 147, 166, 182, 186, 190–1, 196–7, 280, 302, 344, 355, 358–60, 395–6, 399
  alveolar, 50–1, 116–17, 128, 140, 162–3, 169, 180–1, 185–7, 189, 191, 198, 268–70, 276, 359, 430
  alveo-palatal, 189, 264
  apical, 50–1, 127–30, 140, 163, 181, 187–8, 395
  apical alveolars, 187
  bilabial, 111–12, 116–18, 139, 187, 191, 267–70, 273
  coronal, 57, 59, 65, 109–12, 115, 117, 124, 128, 130, 136, 139, 143, 166, 170, 179–91, 198, 205, 225, 266–9, 278, 282, 286, 289–91, 293, 295–6, 299, 302, 308, 314, 317, 335, 338, 358, 380–1, 392–3, 399, 421
  dental, 32, 50–1, 112, 117, 180, 185–7, 189, 191, 198, 268–70, 276, 286, 399, 430
  denti-alveolar, 180, 187, 200
  dorsal, 57, 59, 110–11, 129, 179–80, 182, 185, 188–9, 191, 194, 197, 199, 205, 215, 225, 239, 266, 268–9, 276, 278, 289, 296, 304, 314, 317, 358, 360, 380–1, 392–3, 399, 422, 430
  epiglottal, 111, 142, 193–6, 262, 429
  epiglotto-pharyngeal, 193
  glottal, 45–6, 49, 56, 114, 147–8, 194, 196, 203, 208–9, 211–14, 227, 239–40, 261, 275, 295, 297, 338, 380, 383, 417, 419
  guttural, 149
  interdental, 117, 180

488 Subject index

place of articulation (*cont.*)
  labial, 50, 57, 59, 83, 110, 112, 116–17, 121, 124–5, 127, 134, 139, 141, 152, 166, 179–80, 182–3, 185, 187–91, 197, 199, 201–2, 205, 215, 225, 266, 268–9, 276, 286, 289, 291, 295–6, 313–14, 335, 338, 358–9, 380–1, 392–3, 399, 417, 422, 428, 430
  labial-velar, 267–8
  labiodental, 111–12, 116–18, 190, 291
  laminal, 50–1, 129–30, 180–1, 187–8, 192, 395
  laminal post-alveolar, 190, 192
  lamino-domal, 190
  lingual, 50, 182, 191, 269, 393
  linguo-labial, 191, 268–9, 278
  palatal, 69, 83, 115, 124, 139, 141–2, 152, 158–9, 163, 180, 189–92, 196, 198, 201, 264, 270, 276–7, 295, 358, 399, 417, 426, 428, 430
  palato-alveolar, 115–16, 180, 189–90, 192, 291
  palato-velar, 196
  post-alveolar, 142, 163, 180, 186, 192, 200
  posterior, 179, 189, 205, 291, 313–14, 396
  post-velar, 192, 196, 421
  radico-pharyngeal, 193
  velar, 69, 111, 115–16, 128, 137, 139, 146, 166, 169, 187, 189–92, 197–8, 267, 269, 271–6, 322, 358
plane, 12, 26–7, 33, 79, 95, 318, 425
  content plane, 26–7
  expression plane, 26–7
polysyllabic, 302
polysystematicity, 3, 21–2, 36, 58, 108, 138, 253, 284, 322
post-lexical, 30, 221, 355

post-tonic, 322
preaspiration, 45, 210, 384
predictability, 2, 4, 283ff
preference, 4, 82, 85, 91, 97–8, 108–10, 117, 119–20, 135, 149, 165, 167–72, 183, 186–7, 203–4, 283ff
  preference ranking, 97–8, 120, 169–70, 204, 283, 293, 299–303, 311, 315, 323
preferred segmental systems, 4, 283, 301, 318
prefix, 137
preglottalisation, 208
prenasalisation, 121–9, 139, 196, 263–5, 275, 294, 318, 356, 407
pre-stopped nasal, 126–7
pretonic, 322
primary specifications, 75, 149, 196, 295, 296
primary structures, 79, 92, 265
privative, 37
projection, 10, 96, 152, 381
prominence, 17, 42, 47, 152, 341, 374
  prominence systems, 152
prominent positions, 138, 146
proper government, 244, 246, 248, 252
proprioceptions, 18, 20
prosody, 6, 10, 12, 16, 21, 33, 95, 101, 104, 146, 322, 405
psychologically realistic, 25

Q-theory, 356, 383, 407–9

radical underspecification, 38, 227, 262, 324–5, 328–9, 331, 334
  radical underspecification theory, 38
raising, 33, 140, 152–3, 155, 158, 161, 211–12, 239, 267, 424
recursion, recursivity, 19–20, 27, 55, 78, 85–7, 95, 100–5, 310, 330, 394, 400, 405–6
  recursive splitting, 5, 19–20, 44, 46,

57, 77–8, 86, 86, 89, 150, 284, 330, 353, 400
recursive syllables, 105
redundancy, 5, 20–1, 33, 38, 49–50, 54, 59, 85, 139, 213, 230, 233, 262, 285, 324–30, 332, 346, 348, 358, 360, 362, 421
redundant properties, 325–6, 332
reduplication, 137
register, 4, 80, 217–24, 235–41, 279–80, 294–6, 334, 338–9, 347, 383
relative clause, 100
relative orientation, 367
repair strategies, 17
resolution, 263
retracted tongue root (RTR), 39, 50–1, 69, 155–9, 162, 239, 294–6, 338, 347, 417
retraction, 157, 159–60, 162, 192, 239, 269
retroflex, 128–30, 139–40, 142–5, 162, 163, 169, 181, 198, 265, 280, 358, 419, 427
reversal, 39, 64, 310
rhotic, 58, 83, 121, 127–8, 130, 135, 140, 143–4, 146, 155, 160, 162–4, 171, 173, 177–8, 181, 197–8, 299, 311–12, 427–8
rhoticisation, 128
rhyme, 3, 10, 13, 89–96, 98–9, 103, 108, 121, 131, 136, 145, 149–51, 154, 160, 164–5, 167–8, 171, 198–9, 201, 217, 241, 243, 250–1, 253–6, 259, 279, 281, 294–6, 307, 310, 312, 314, 319, 335, 343, 357, 405, 411, 415, 423, 425
rhyming, 103
rhythm, 12, 100, 374
rising tone, 219, 221, 237
root node, 96, 174, 223, 281, 380, 383–5, 387, 424
root-and-pattern morphology, 260

roots, 1, 15, 27, 160, 259, 322
round, 36–9, 44, 60–1, 83, 152, 154, 166, 199–200, 225, 286, 289, 291–20, 326–7, 330–5, 363, 383, 404
rounding, 37, 40, 69, 152, 248, 289–90, 293, 321, 326, 332, 335, 343
roundness, 37–8, 41, 44, 50, 329
rules, 2, 8, 13, 15, 17, 20, 22–3, 25–6, 29–33, 38–9, 48–9, 79, 125, 204, 230, 234, 249, 286, 295, 297, 325, 327–8, 339, 348, 354, 356, 379, 386

salience, 12, 45, 47, 69, 75–7, 82, 104, 107–8, 111, 148, 152, 185–6, 187, 318, 321, 339–40, 352, 361, 364, 367, 369, 377, 403, 412
sandhi, 218
schwa, 44, 176, 225, 244, 258, 261, 322, 389
secondary manner, 110, 120–4, 127–32, 136, 139–40, 142, 144–5, 147–9, 154–5, 160–2, 164–5, 173, 178, 181, 187–9, 191, 194–6, 198, 202, 262, 264–5, 272, 276, 280, 300, 419, 421
secondary movements, 372
secondary place, 122, 129, 133, 136, 142, 181, 189, 196, 202, 204, 264–5, 294, 297, 419–21, 423
secondary specifications, 75, 127, 136, 149, 177, 196, 201, 205, 241–2, 293–5, 300, 315–16, 419
secondary structures, 54, 87, 188
segment inventory, 2, 21, 105, 283–4, 424
segment structure rules, 348
segmental integrity, 99
segmental system, 4, 62, 79, 112, 183, 227, 283, 301, 303–4, 318–19, 322–3, 343, 403

segmentation assumption, 9
segment-internal grouping, 15, 36
segment–syllable connection, 98, 412
Semantic Phonology, 401
semivowel, 132
sentence phonology, 31
sibilants, 54, 111, 115
sign phonology, 5, 353ff, 385, 390
silencing, 246–9
simplex words, 101
simplification, 15, 363, 387
singleton, 93
skeleton, 90, 244, 356–7, 375–6, 386
slack, 65, 208–9, 212–14, 238, 239
sonorant, 48–9, 52–4, 83, 85, 90–1, 93–9, 108–11, 115, 119–22, 125, 128, 130–2, 136, 138–46, 148–9, 155, 164–6, 169–73, 178, 197–8, 202, 204, 209, 213, 227–9, 234, 250, 254, 298–9, 310–12, 322, 326, 333, 345, 380, 382, 390, 392, 417, 425–7
Sonorant Voice, 392
sonority, 40–1, 47–50, 52, 64, 75, 89, 91, 95, 97–8, 107–8, 110–11, 119, 125–6, 132, 134, 138, 146, 166–9, 171–2, 182, 186, 203, 252–4, 299, 307–9, 371, 382, 391, 394, 417–18
  Minimum Sonority Distance, 307
  Sonority Dispersion Principle, 307
  sonority hierarchy, 126
  sonority peak, 95
  sonority scale, 132, 307, 371, 418
  Sonority Sequencing Generalisation, 89, 91, 95, 97
  sonority threshold, 254
specifiers, 28, 77, 415
speech errors, 95, 301
spelling, 22, 59, 345
spread glottis, 50, 147, 207–8, 210, 213, 238–9, 417, 422–3
spreading, 75, 107, 152, 202, 207, 214, 259, 359, 374, 388, 412

square brackets, 26, 41, 60, 230
stability, 45, 75, 107–8
stem, 24
stiff, 65, 208–9, 212–14, 236, 238–9, 404
stops, 25, 47–9, 54, 59, 66, 77–8, 109–10, 112–20, 122–4, 126–9, 147, 169, 187, 189–95, 203, 210–11, 215, 226, 231–4, 262, 265, 267–8, 272, 284, 289, 294, 296–7, 299, 301–3, 305, 318–19, 326, 333–7, 344–6, 362, 383–4, 400, 404, 406
  unreleased stops, 66, 114
strength, 18, 48, 107, 172, 182, 210, 351
stress, 16, 81, 90, 104, 108, 138, 146, 152, 203, 234, 289, 293, 322, 326, 343, 355, 424
  primary stress, 234
  secondary stress, 146, 234
strict CV, 13, 73, 136, 250–1, 281
strict locality, 88
stridency, 111–18, 142, 193, 277, 285, 304
strident, 47, 110–11, 113–14, 116–18, 122, 160–1, 164, 177, 182, 190, 193, 199, 277, 280, 285–7, 302, 337, 380
strong hand, 373
structural analogies, 101, 106, 397
structural analogy, 2, 7, 14, 16, 26–7, 55, 77, 85, 277, 382, 384, 391, 393, 416–17, 419, 422
  structural analogy assumption, 26
structuralist, 11, 24, 31
structure-preserving, 31
subclass, 74, 75, 77, 79, 81, 83–4, 86–7, 109, 114, 207, 214–15, 226, 265, 316, 414
subjunction, 28, 74, 91, 95
subordinate, 381–2
substance-based, 12–13, 20, 82, 412
substance-free phonology, 403

Subject index   491

Successive Division Algorithm, 19, 330
superclass, 74
superfoot, 102
suppletive, 32
supralaryngeal, 68, 74, 80, 87, 216, 225, 343, 380
surface constraints, 17
  surface level, 30
syllabic consonant, 93, 96, 145, 172–3, 183, 202–3, 244, 250–1, 253, 255, 312–13
  syllabic liquid, 203
  syllabic nasal, 173, 202–3, 313
syllabic nuclei, 203
syllabification, 138, 203, 246, 249, 253
syllable structure, 1, 3–4, 10, 59, 73, 76, 82, 89–90, 92, 95–6, 98, 100–2, 105, 136–8, 165, 170, 174, 243–4, 246, 250, 256, 260, 278, 281, 349, 374–7, 381, 390, 418, 424
  appendix, 6, 92, 170, 183, 187, 241, 255, 257, 425–30
  closed syllable, 103, 165, 243
  complex onsets, 119–20, 125, 127, 133–4, 136–8, 141, 149, 245–6, 252, 302, 307–8, 317, 326–7, 333, 417–18
  extra-syllabic, 183, 254, 255
  syllabicity, 203
  syllable contact law, 167
  syllable division, 137
  syllable node, 253
  syllable weight, 90
syllables, 9–10, 12, 92, 95–6, 100–3, 105, 133, 138, 147, 165–6, 173, 223, 230, 255–6, 258, 278, 298, 322, 346, 349, 374, 381, 411
symmetry condition, 372
synchronic phonology, 13
syntagmatic, 10, 13, 65, 90, 92, 106, 136, 299–300, 308–10, 316–17, 323, 326–7, 329, 332–3, 335, 344, 377

tap, 143–4, 169, 393, 427
tautosyllabic, 96
templates, 97, 103, 125, 171, 244, 260–1, 349, 383
  morphological templates, 244, 260
  syllable template, 125
tenseness, 80, 153, 371
ternary foot, 102
thumb, 360, 363–6, 396
tier, 62, 64, 90, 96, 224, 382, 408, 410
timing, 126, 210, 407
tonal root node, 223, 424
tone, 4, 52, 57, 65, 75, 80, 82–4, 148, 150, 152, 155, 165, 207–9, 211, 213, 215, 217–25, 227, 229, 231, 233, 235–41, 261, 279–80, 286, 289–91, 293, 296, 315–16, 321, 327, 333, 335, 340, 343, 383, 409, 417, 423–4
  tonal genesis, 238
  tonal melody, 223
  tone-bearing unit, 165, 219, 223, 280, 408
tongue body, 50, 140, 142, 153, 158, 162–3
Toronto model, 392
transparency, 125, 149, 160
tree, 270, 341, 344, 384–6
triangular, 36, 40–1, 45, 153, 156, 319, 340
trill, 53, 127–9, 139–40, 142
two-handed signs, 359, 372–3
two-root structure, 281
typology, 4, 32, 105, 283, 301, 325–6, 332, 371, 414

ultimate head, 341, 423
underlying forms, 29–30, 210
underspecification, 5, 20, 29, 38, 58–9, 79, 227, 262, 324–5, 328–9, 331, 334, 339–40, 342, 373, 409, 414
Universal Grammar, 27

492 Subject index

Universal Harmony Rule, 286
unstressable vowels, 258
utterance phonology, 7–9, 20, 31, 33, 256, 354, 371, 413
uvula, 111, 128

variability, 11, 16, 26, 162–3, 325, 335–6, 343, 361
variable vowel, 246, 248–9
velaric suction, 49, 56, 267
velarisation, 129, 132, 265
velarity, 44
vertical vowel system, 79, 292, 327–8, 333
via-rules, 32
visual system, 27
vocoid, 198, 382
voice, 36, 38–9, 48–9, 53, 65, 85, 122, 140, 148, 166, 183, 185, 194, 207–9, 211–16, 219, 221, 224–5, 228–36, 239–41, 262–3, 276, 280, 326–7, 329, 331–3, 392, 417, 429
voice assimilation, 140, 234
voiced, 22, 25, 36–8, 47–9, 53–4, 58, 83, 112, 116–18, 124, 126–9, 136, 140, 142, 148, 161, 185, 192–4, 207–16, 225, 227, 229, 230–4, 238, 240, 261–3, 271–6, 278, 280, 286, 289, 291, 295–6, 315, 318, 327, 333–5, 344, 406, 417, 426, 429
  strong voicing, 232–4
voiceless, 22–3, 25, 37–8, 47–9, 59, 109–10, 116–18, 126–9, 136–7, 139–40, 181, 185, 192–4, 207, 209–12, 214–16, 225–9, 232–4, 238, 261, 263, 271–5, 280, 289–91, 293, 296, 315, 326, 329, 331, 333, 344, 346, 423
voicelessness, 65, 109, 122, 127, 210, 212, 280, 331
Voice Onset Time (VOT), 207, 210
vowel harmony, 2, 31–2, 37, 44, 68, 88, 149, 152–3, 156, 158–60, 198, 201, 246, 248, 330, 336, 381, 390, 392, 408, 414, 418, 420, 424
  height harmony, 152
  labial harmony, 152, 201–2
  palatal harmony, 152, 158, 201
vowel height, 86, 152, 154–5, 209, 218, 289–92, 296, 382, 391, 404
vowel length, 219
vowel reduction, 258
vowel sequence, 260
vowels, 4, 18, 21, 33, 35–45, 49–52, 56–7, 60–3, 65, 68, 70–1, 74, 76, 79–80, 84, 87–8, 91, 95–6, 98, 108, 110, 112, 124, 127, 132, 142, 148–52, 154–67, 173–4, 186, 198–203, 205–7, 211, 214, 217, 223–4, 226, 228–9, 235–6, 238–42, 249–50, 254, 256, 258, 260, 262, 264, 277–81, 289–96, 298, 300, 306–7, 312–15, 317–18, 320–2, 326–9, 332–6, 338, 340–8, 356, 362, 368, 374, 381–5, 389, 391–2, 394, 408–10, 417–18, 420–4
  ATR vowels, 157, 159, 329, 348
  high vowels, 248, 289, 291–2, 321, 400, 420
  lax vowels, 96, 133, 250
  long vowels, 95, 98, 165–6, 174, 254, 280, 343, 384–5
  nasal vowels, 262, 281, 408
  tense vowels, 92, 133
  voiceless vowels, 280
vowel/zero alternations, 13, 243–9, 260

weak hand, 373
weak voicing, 232–3
window, 1
word accent, 12
word edges, 92, 120, 254

word level, 21, 33, 108, 230, 285, 346
word phonology, 31

X-bar (theory), 1, 28, 77, 81, 101, 141, 380, 398, 406, 412, 414–16

yers, 248

zero, 82, 213, 227, 234, 243–4, 246–7, 249, 258–60, 291, 328, 334, 336, 340

Language index

Abkhaz, 151, 292
Acoma, 143
Adyghe, 79, 151
African languages, 156–60, 218, 220–1, 223, 267–8, 279–80
Afro-Asiatic, 215
Agul, 193
Akan, 160, 203
Al-Sayyid Bedouin Sign Language, 361
Alabama, 118
Alawa, 124, 129
Amahuaca, 143
American Sign Language / ASL 355, 366–8
Amharic, 147, 419
Andamanese, 118, 124
Anii, 420–1
Apache, 116
   Chiricahua Apache, 116
Apinaye, 125
Arabic, 260, 315
Aranda, 129
Araucanian, 118
Armenian, 210
   Eastern Armenian, 210
Asian languages, 79, 158–9, 219–21, 239
Austronesian, 118
Axininca, 167
   Axininca Campa, 167

Badaga, 162

Baka, 421
Bambara, 143
Bandjalang, 226
Bantu languages, 126, 156, 322
Basque, 143
Benchnon, 218
Berber, 97, 138, 174, 255–7
   Imdlawn Tashlhiyt Berber, 255
   Tashlhiyt, 97, 138, 174, 255–7
Berta, 124
Boni, 421
Breton, 140
Burmese, 209, 232

Cantonese, 221
Caucasian languages, 79
Cayapa, 118
Chacobo, 143
Chadic language, 198
child language, 109, 137
Chinantec, 56
Chinese, 22, 115, 147, 151, 162, 321
   Mandarin, 151, 162
Chipewyan, 113, 183
Chori, 218
Chumburung, 420
Czech, 128, 140–5, 202, 246, 248–9

Dahalo, 192
Dan, 218
Daribi, 143
Dedua, 267
Dinka, 118, 236

Diola Fogny, 167–8
Diyari, 127
Dravidian languages, 180
Dschang, 223
Dutch, 21–5, 92–3, 97, 102–3, 133–4,
    136, 138, 142, 165, 170, 172–3,
    176, 183, 214, 231–4, 250–4,
    256–7, 265, 281, 309, 315, 346

English, 12, 21–22, 30, 32, 49–50, 59,
    92–3, 97, 102–3, 114–15, 117,
    128, 132, 136, 147, 162, 170,
    172–3, 176, 183–4, 187, 189,
    202, 211, 230–4, 250, 253–4,
    258, 261, 265, 279, 281, 285,
    300, 302, 304–5, 312, 317, 322,
    327, 346, 356, 366
  American English, 132, 184
  Old English, 261, 279
Enindhilyagwa~Anindilyakwa, 292
European languages, 198
Even, 160
Ewe, 116–18, 143

Faroese, 210
Fasu, 118
Fijian, 126, 279
Franconian dialects, 289
French, 32, 63, 187, 211, 225, 230–4,
    258–9
Fula, 125–6, 211
Fwe, 266

Gaelic, 210
Gbeya, 124, 126
Georgian, 138, 254
German, 112, 116, 225
  Swiss German, 116
Germanic languages, 4, 96, 146, 166,
    183, 207, 211, 231–2, 250, 300
Gimi, 194
Gothic, 137
Guarani, 143
Gwandara, 267

Hakka, 125
Hausa, 118
Hawaiian, 118, 138, 190, 211
Hindi, 212
Hungarian, 141–2, 254, 336, 418
Hupa, 147, 419

Iai, 116, 118
Icelandic, 45, 210, 279, 384, 389
Idoma, 267
Igbo, 124, 147, 212, 419
  Owerri Igbo, 212
Indo-Aryan languages, 212
Indonesian, 257
Inupiaq, 169
Irish, 151
Israeli Sign Language, 367
Italian, 63, 117, 166–70
  Venetian Italian, 117

Japanese, 22, 117, 166–70, 280
Jaqaru, 115, 192
Jingpho, 194

Kaingang, 124
Kalabari, 236
Kaliai, 125
Kan, 118
Kanembu, 421
Kanite, 198
Kanuari, 116
Karok, 143
Kate, 267
Kaytetye~Kaititj, 292
Kele, 127–8
Kesukuma, 126
Kewa, 118, 125
Khalaj, 143
Kharia, 140
Khoisan, 160–1
Kikuyu, 156
Kiribati, 118
Komi, 115
Korean, 133, 166, 212, 257

Koryak, 203
Kota, 143
Kotoko, 198
Kpokolo, 61–3, 420–1
Kru languages, 157
Kunimaipa, 143
Kurdish, 142
K'ekchi, 228, 423

Lama, 421
Lango, 118
Lardil, 166–7, 183
Lendu, 203, 212
Leti, 257
Lezgian, 37
Lithuanian, 198
Logbara, 267
Luo, 143
Luvale, 124

Malagasy, 129
Malayalam, 143
Mangbetu, 139, 143
Maori, 211
Mape, 267
Mapuche, 128
Mapudungun, 128
Marathi, 212
Margi, 292
Marshallese, 151–2, 257, 292
Mayan languages, 228
Mazatec, 124, 235, 236
    Jalapa Mazatec, 235–6
Melpa, 198
Miao, 218
    Black Miao, 218
Mid-Waghi, 198
Mixtec, 183
Moloko, 151
Mongolian, 158–9
Moro, 143
Mpi, 236–8
Muinane, 118

Nama, 274–5
Nama-Hottentot, 169
Nambakaengo, 124
Nambiquara, 143, 183
Native American languages, 128
Navajo, 116
Ndau, 269
Nenets, 196
New Guinea languages, 215, 267
Nez Perce, 330
Ngizim, 124, 142
Nilo-Saharan, 215
Nootka, 147, 196
Nuxalk, 138, 174, 255–6

Ocaina, 118
Olgolo, 127
Ono, 267
Otomi, 118

Paez, 124, 198
Papago, 143
Pawaian, 143
Phuthi, 116
Polish, 115, 202, 252, 254, 281
Ponapean, 168
Portuguese, 41, 322
    Brazilian Portuguese, 41, 322

Romance, 152, 231
Romance languages, 152, 231
Rotokas, 143
Russian, 126, 247–8

Sami, 279
Sanskrit, 137, 203
Sara, 124
Scots, 45, 54, 142
Sedang *see* Andamanese
Selepet, 125, 143
Semitic languages, 260
Serer, 211
Seri, 260
Sesotho, 116

Shilha, 139
Sinhala, 125–6
Sinhalese, 143
Sino-Tibetan language, 236
Siona, 147, 419
Siriono, 124, 143
Slavic languages, 138, 202, 247–8
Slovak, 248
Somali, 142
Spanish, 147, 187, 305, 321
Sui, 118
Swedish, 43, 128, 201, 233–4

Tamil, 204
Taoripi, 183
Tarascan, 162
Teke, 112
Telugu, 143
Temne, 187
Thai, 155, 211, 223, 279
Tlingit, 128, 183
Tongan, 211
Trique, 218, 257
　Copala Trique, 218
Tsonga, 112, 116
　Xinkuna dialect, 116

Tungusic languages, 160
Turkana, 280
Turkish, 44, 248, 249, 314, 320–1
Tuscan, 117

Ubykh, 292
UMbundu, 124

Wantoat, 124
Washkuk, 118, 124–5, 143
Welsh, 128
Western Desert, 143
Wichita, 151–2, 183, 292
Wolof, 128
Wubuy, 180

Xhosa, 274

Yagaria, 198
Yakut, 140
Yareba, 118
Yeletnye, 267
Yeyi, 266
Yowlumne, 244–5, 248–9

EU representative:
Easy Access System Europe
Mustamäe tee 50, 10621 Tallinn, Estonia
Gpsr.requests@easproject.com

www.ingramcontent.com/pod-product-compliance
Lightning Source LLC
Chambersburg PA
CBHW051802230426
43672CB00012B/2598